MANAGERIAL
ECONOMICS

MANAGERIAL ECONOMICS

Steven T. Call
Metropolitan State College
and University of Colorado, Denver

William L. Holahan
University of Wisconsin, Milwaukee

Wadsworth Publishing Company
Belmont, California
A Division of Wadsworth, Inc.

Economics Editor: Stephanie Surfus

Production: Del Mar Associates

Designer: John Odam

Manuscript Editor: Rebecca Smith

Technical Illustrators: Richard Carter, Kim Fraley, Pam Posey

Printed in the United States of America

1 2 3 4 5 6 7 8 9 10 — 88 87 86 85 84

ISBN 0-534-02685-0

Library of Congress Cataloging in Publication Data

Call, Steven T.
    Managerial economics.

    Bibliography: p.
    Includes index.
    1. Managerial economics.   I. Holahan, William L.
II. Title.
HD30.22.C34   1984   338.5   83–6602
ISBN 0-534-02685-0

PREFACE

We have written *Managerial Economics* in the conviction that management skills can be greatly improved by exposure to carefully selected business topics in microeconomics. Our book has a three-part objective: (1) to provide a conceptual framework for thinking about the decision-making process; (2) to build and reinforce the economic intuition of managerial economists; and (3) to help people see how their firms fit into the overall market system and thereby avoid the errors in decision making that may arise when businesses act as if they are isolated from broad market forces and external constraints. Managerial economics is a unifying system of analysis that provides a deep awareness of the market system of which each firm is a small component.

A number of teachers and reviewers familiar with our *Microeconomics, Second Edition* urged us to apply our nonmathematical approach to the study of managerial economics. This managerial book draws on our previous approach to problem solving and, through abundant real-world examples, shows how microeconomic theory may be applied to business problems. We do try, however, to avoid topics that are primarily of interest to social scientists. For example, *Managerial Economics* contains chapters on antitrust matters and special topics in pricing but no chapters on general equilibrium, indifference analysis, or neoclassical labor theory.

In an attempt to keep this book within the reach of undergraduate students who are not necessarily well trained in quantitative subjects, we have employed both verbal and graphic exposition, supplemented occasionally by elementary algebra. Complex ideas are frequently explained simply and intuitively. Therefore, although the book maintains a high standard of rigor throughout, it does not use difficult mathematical expositions.

Choosing to take a nonmathematical approach to the subject does not mean that we deny the importance of such mathematical modeling techniques as forecasting and linear programming. However, most managers are not involved in making decisions that require the use of such techniques. Those who are require far more than a one-semester exposure to calculus, regression analysis, and operations research. And even those who are involved in more technical analyses may find it useful to confront such complex ideas intuitively before seeing them in mathematical form.

To the Instructor

For any subject, student interest must be engaged before any real learning can take place. In an attempt to do this, we have presented a variety of stimulating applications of managerial economic theory. A complete list of applications follows the table of contents.

Of course theory is just as important. Thus we have taken care to include these central topics in our book:

Perfect versus pure competition: Business students have little patience with theory that does not have direct applicability. The distinction in this book between pure and perfect competition makes it possible for students to analyze competitive industries that are not composed of identical firms but are still governed by price-taking behavior.

Multiplant firms: Although firms commonly operate numerous plants, the usual graphic analysis considers firms consisting of just one plant. Multiplant analysis draws students closer to the world they see outside the classroom.

Multiproduct firms: Firms commonly produce a product mix, not the single product typically analyzed in managerial economics textbooks. In addition, most treatments of the multiproduct firm are highly mathematical. We present a simple verbal and graphic approach to the subject.

Multidivision firms: Firms commonly operate several divisions. We present the theory of transfer pricing in detail—to show how prices internal to the firm can coordinate firm activities in the same way that prices external to the firm coordinate economic activity outside the firm.

Cartel analysis: This topic forms a natural bridge between treatments of competition and monopoly, permitting the analysis of collusion among firms.

Dominant-firm analysis: This model describes the incentives of firms operating in an industry that is dominated by a large firm or a cartel. It is fundamental to the understanding of antitrust matters.

Antitrust analysis: We devote an entire chapter to the economic effects of many of the business acts and practices that are illegal under the antitrust laws. We do not merely list the statutes themselves.

Joint products and externalities: Joint product theory, the core of externality theory, aids in the analysis of modern approaches to environmental protection.

Design and Format for Learning

In *Managerial Economics,* we have tried to engage the reader's interest right from the start. Part of this effort shows in the analytical content of the book. Another part shows in the design and format of the book, which include these features:

An imaginative and pleasing design meant to enhance learning

Crystal-clear artwork

Extensive explanatory figure captions

A total of eighty-four Applications

An average of over twenty-five end-of-chapter problems

An instructor's manual that includes answer sketches to all end-of-chapter problems and provides additional problems

An end-of-book glossary defining all terms highlighted in the book

Acknowledgments

The preparation of this book has given us another marvelous opportunity to work with the fine people at Wadsworth Publishing Company and Del Mar Associates. We thank Bill Oliver and the staff at Wadsworth for their excellent assistance along the way. Among other things, they arranged for an extensive and detailed review of the manuscript by teachers of managerial economics; we are grateful to the following for their suggestions: M. Neil Browne, Bowling Green State University; Ralph Byrns, Metropolitan State College; Joseph M. Jadlow, Oklahoma State University; John Morris, University of Colorado, Denver; Petrea Payne, Metropolitan State College; John Pisciotta, Baylor University; Gerald Stone, Metropolitan State College; and Philip R. Swensen, Utah State University.

Joyce Miezen has once again provided unexcelled typing of our manuscript. Production of this book was an effort by a great team. Sandra Craig of Wadsworth and Nancy Sjoberg of Del Mar Associates supervised the editing and production, and Rebecca Smith, our tireless editor, translated our manuscript into English. John Odam designed the book and its cover; Richard Carter supervised the team of artists. The attention to detail lavished on this book by the production team enhanced it greatly.

Finally, we extend sincere thanks to the many teachers who have helped us appreciate economic theory and its application. Steve Call's greatest debt is to Richard Wirthin and Dean Rickenbach, who sparked his interest in economics, and to James Witte and Elmus Wicker, whose example of superior scholarship and masterful teaching convinced him that economics was his life's work. Bill Holahan is especially grateful to John Prather Brown for demonstrating the wide applicability of economic theory as a device for organizing thoughts and to Martin Beckmann for teaching elegant sneak-attack problem solving. We both gratefully acknowledge the many teachers, colleagues, students, and historical and contemporary scholars who have influenced our thinking and deepened our commitment to teaching and research in economic science.

CONTENTS

APPLICATIONS

MANAGERIAL
ECONOMICS

1

STUDYING MAN- AGERIAL ECONOMICS

Your primary responsibility as a business manager will be to make decisions that promote the objectives of your firm. This is no easy task. The objectives themselves may be contradictory and inconsistent. At every decision point, the alternative courses of action will be complex and lead to uncertain outcomes. And the information you need to make your decisions will nearly always be incomplete and expensive to obtain. To cope with these difficulties, you need a conceptual framework for organizing your thoughts, stimulating ideas, and untangling the web of business problems soon to be faced.

Effective business management requires diverse skills. Successful managers learn to benefit from knowledge drawn from many fields. That's why such core business courses as accounting, finance, personnel, marketing, and production are so important. In addition, the well-rounded manager has been exposed to such quantitative tools as statistics and operations research and to many principles of human behavior borrowed from psychology and sociology. Decision-making expertise is truly interdisciplinary.

One science—economics—is especially useful to managers. Specifically, managerial economics, the subject of this book, is the application of economic science to decision making. It emphasizes business decisions but also encompasses the management of public enterprises and nonprofit organizations.

The study of economics is peculiarly well suited in developing managers' decision-making skills—for at least three reasons. First, economics is the science of choices. Economists study decisions about limited resources made with limited information, which is precisely the nature of business decisions. Second, economics encompasses a well-established "theory of the firm," which explains many useful principles of business behavior. The theory of the firm is a powerful organizer of thoughts about business problems.

Finally, economics can help managers understand and respond to an often hostile environment. The business firm, one small component of a larger economic system, operates within an industry or a network of industries. Profitability is affected by such industry-wide factors as degree of competition, prices of outputs and inputs, and speed of entry of new competitors and such economywide factors as inflation and unemployment rates, credit availability, and income levels. Firms also interact with various institutions, including banks, labor unions, government agencies, consumer advocacy groups, and marketplaces. But these economic forces and institutions are economists' turf, and so managers can improve their firms' chances of survival by taking advantage of economists' accumulated knowledge.

Defining Managerial Economics

The interests shared by managers and economists fall into a category known as managerial economics. The value of training managers to think like economists—logically and factually—is so widely accepted that a course in managerial economics is now required or strongly suggested in most business schools. However, economics is a far-reaching science, and there is little agreement in the profession about which of its many components are most useful to managers and at what level these topics should be presented. This controversy arises in large part because managerial economics is a relatively new field of applied economic theory and has not yet been distilled into a uniform subject. In the face of such ambiguity, we have a responsibility to tell you about our philosophy of managerial economics and, in doing so, to set the tone for the remainder of the book.

A Professional Job Description

The term *managerial economics* can be misleading, because it means different things. Let's dispose first of the least relevant meaning as far as this book is concerned. Managerial economics could be defined as what managerial economists do. Many large corporations presently employ highly trained professionals called managerial economists whose job it is to gather and analyze data and to aid management in making decisions. A top-flight managerial economist must be well trained in such analytical fields as economic theory, mathematics, computer science, operations research, statistics, econometrics, and decision theory. Graduate study in many of these fields is a prerequisite in most cases. We hasten to say that our book is only an initiation in this training.

An Undergraduate Business Course

In another sense, managerial economics is the material covered in the undergraduate business course for which we have prepared this book. But the managerial economics course is not intended solely for those few students intending to become highly technical business economists. Instead, it is designed to expose business students to economic reasoning for the purpose of strengthening their management craft and decision-making skills.

Model Building and Managerial Economics

Economics is a social science that employs the scientific method to study people's economic choices. Managerial economics is the application of economic principles to the choices of business managers. However, these choices are so utterly complex that they cannot be understood without a systematic method of simplification. Thus economists have produced a variety of **theories** or **models,** which are hypotheses about economic relationships based on simplifying assumptions. A road map is a model of the terrain between cities; it is not a complete description of the actual terrain. The map is a greatly oversimplified representation of the facts, yet it contains enough information for the problem at hand—helping drivers reach their destinations. Likewise, economists build models for the purpose of paring complex problems down to size. Some of these models have become household words, *supply and demand* and *diminishing returns* no doubt leading the list in name recognition.

Model building in managerial economics guides our thinking as we grope, often by trial and error, toward beneficial solutions to business problems. The following chapters present many applications, some of which are theories that have been thoroughly tested and confirmed empirically and others that merely suggest ways of tackling particular problems, even where the data to accompany the models do not exist or are too expensive for the firm to obtain. The point is that we should not limit ourselves to studying only data-oriented models; they are a very small subset of the useful models of business behavior that economists have produced. Even when data are unavailable, theory can inform or instruct.

Scarcity and Choice

Two elementary facts that face the world and every individual in it are at the heart of all economic models: limited resources and relatively unlimited wants. The combination of these two facts creates scarcity and the need for individuals, firms, and society to make choices among the virtually limitless possible activities that can be undertaken and goods that can be enjoyed. Robert Frost's poem "The Road Not Taken" portrays the inherent need to choose; the horseman could not travel both roads. Similarly, a football player who also plays trumpet cannot play both football and trumpet in the pep band; he must choose. Nor can individual consumers and entire societies produce and consume all they would like. Resource limitations simply do not permit fulfillment of all wants. Thus a community may spend money on rat control or wastewater treatment or some combination of the two, but no community has sufficient resources to kill every rat and return all its wastewater to pristine condition. Likewise, a firm must choose an effective advertising balance, because its budget cannot provide for full advertising of its entire product line. Choice among alternatives is a fact of daily life imposed on us by scarcity.

This need to choose gives rise to the key word in economics— *substitutes* (see Chapter 2 for a fuller discussion). Consumers, business firms, and governments must constantly evaluate substitute activities, determining what they must give up in order to purchase a good or engage in an activity. The two fundamental constraints on their activities are income and time. Both are limited.

The fact that all activities require some income and/or some time leads to a second key concept in economics—*opportunity cost,* or alternative cost. When you select one among many substitute ways of spending your limited income and time, you presumably choose the most valuable option and leave a rather long list of alternative wants unfulfilled. Suppose you choose to go to a movie, spending $3 for a ticket and 2 hours in time. You have many other uses for that income and time, but you choose the movie. The most sensible and complete way of describing the cost of the movie is to measure **opportunity cost,** the value of the best forgone option. Your money and time have alternative uses that you forgo by going to the movie. The value of your time and money in their next most valuable and forgone use is the opportunity cost of the movie. Even if your best friend is the ticket taker and lets you in free, the opportunity cost is not zero, because your time could have been spent in other valuable ways. The money price of an activity may be zero, but the opportunity cost is never zero as long as alternatives exist.

Resources have not only alternative uses in the current period but also alternative time periods of use. Consumers decide what proportion of their incomes to spend on goods and services in the current period and what proportion to save for future consumption. Sellers decide whether to sell all their available inventories in the current period or to hold some back for future sale. Decisions like these cannot be made effectively without evaluating the benefits and opportunity costs of particular choices. But the opportunity cost is

1.1

Price versus Cost

Learning about managerial economics often requires one to distinguish between the ordinary meanings of words in everyday English and the specific, scientific meanings of those words when used formally by economists. For example, the words *price* and *cost* are often used interchangeably in ordinary English. But they mean different things to economists, as Chapter 2 explains.

Price, the amount of money (or goods in a barter economy) that a buyer gives to a seller in exchange for a good or service, is quite different from cost, the forgone value in other uses of the resources devoted to the production of a good or service. Price represents a money payment, whereas cost measures the value of opportunities forgone. Under some circumstances, product price equals the opportunity cost of production. In many circumstances, however, price and cost are not the same. Consider the following examples, which are described in more detail throughout the book.

Electricity Pricing
The cost of producing electric power is low during periods of slack demand (for example, 3:00 a.m.) and higher during periods of peak demand (11:00 a.m. on weekdays). When electricity is priced at a fixed rate, without regard to the actual cost of generation at time of use, price does not reflect cost.

Price Controls
Price ceilings hold down money prices but produce shortages, which in turn raise customers' costs. Consider the time wasted standing in line, the incon-

venience of not knowing whether a product will be available, higher search costs, the need to buy less-preferred products in order to reduce waiting time and aggravation, reductions in product quality, and discrimination against surplus buyers because of race, age, or sex.

Monopoly Pricing
Firms with monopoly power often set prices far above costs. Hence monopoly and cartel prices do not reflect the value of the resources devoted to producing their product.

Pollution
Many firms dump their waste materials into the air and water without paying any fee. The price of such pollution to these firms is zero, even though the cost of pollution to society, measured in terms of environmental damages and forgone opportunities, may be immense.

the same as before: Using a resource in one time period forecloses the option of using the resource in the next most valuable time period. Opportunity costs are always measured by the value of forgone options.

The opportunity costs of goods are usually measured in terms of their money prices. But even under ideal market circumstances, prices reflect full opportunity costs only if time costs of consumption are negligible and if the price accurately reflects the costs of the goods. Exceptions abound: Monopolists charge prices in excess of money costs; bus fares alone underrepresent passenger costs, because they do not include time costs; the price of an energy source may fail to reflect the costs of environmental damage and the consequent use of resources that become unavailable for alternative uses. Thus prices are only a rough guide to opportunity costs; there are occasions when money prices need to be adjusted in order to evaluate the full opportunity cost of certain activities. We deal with this subject in greater detail in later chapters.

Profit Maximization
Nearly all economic models of business behavior rest on the assumption that firms' actions are forever motivated by a search for

Key Terms
models 3
opportunity cost 4
scarcity 4
theories 3

maximum profit. This assumption ignores many additional goals that firms may hold. Still, it is a useful simplification for several reasons. First, profit maximization is a reasonable first approximation of business motivation. If satisfactory profit levels are not maintained, stockholders will withdraw their financial support from the firm. Next, models built on the profit-maximization axiom have generated verifiable predictions about business behavior. Finally, no alternative business objectives have been proposed that have the explanatory power of profit maximization. The assumption is, in short, the best we have.

No aspect of American business structure has come under stronger attack in recent years than what some critics refer to as "obscene" profits. Even businesspeople object to having their behavior linked to such greedy motivations. This attitude is unfortunate, because it reveals ignorance about the true economic role of profit in a market economy. As authors, we aspire to give you a fuller appreciation of the profit motive, from the viewpoint of managerial decision making and as a means of social control.

Economists' model building has produced several well-worn, sensible ideas that are reapplied daily by economists and businesspeople. A first principle of economic analysis is that people follow their incentives. Economics studies the implications that result from assuming that people act in their own self-interest. We hope to teach you to appreciate the usefulness of economic models based on the assumption of profit maximization.

A Hint and a Hope

Every introductory chapter should contain one solid piece of advice to students. Here is ours: We have learned not only to love economics but also to appreciate the difficulty in learning it. Economics is a deeply logical subject; short-term memory for facts does virtually no good. So study it regularly, in small doses and in a hard wooden chair, not in marathon sessions just prior to exams. With this counsel, we invite you to begin your study of the fascinating and multifaceted subject of managerial economics. We hope you will find it rewarding.

Suggested Readings

Friedman, Milton. "The Methodology of Positive Economics." In *Essays in Positive Economics*, pp. 3–46. Edited by Milton Friedman. Chicago: University of Chicago Press, 1953.

Lange, Oscar. "The Scope and Method of Economics." *Review of Economic Studies* 8 (1945/1946): 12–32.

Wicksteed, Philip H. "The Scope and Method of Political Economy." *Economic Journal* 24 (1914): 1–23.

2

SUPPLY AND DEMAND

Your first duty as a manager is to make decisions that allow the firm to achieve its objectives. Thus it is quite unlikely that you can succeed as a manager without a solid understanding of market forces. This is so because your firm cannot isolate itself completely from these forces.

The firm is one small element in a larger network called the market system. The market system in general and many of its component business firms in particular, especially those reporting high profit rates, are the frequent target of harsh criticism. But the market system is often poorly defended by businesspeople, because they see only their own part in it. This tunnel vision is especially unfortunate in light of the many valuable functions the market performs.

Your firm's success will depend in part on its ability to adapt to varying economic conditions and to a changing regulatory environment. Throughout your career, your management and decision-making abilities will be tested constantly by changing conditions. As your skills mature, you will be called on to deliver speeches or to prepare position papers detailing the impact on your firm of government regulations, current events, natural disasters, changing consumer preferences, long-term trends, and so forth. You may even become an industry speaker. But you simply cannot function responsibly as a firm manager or industry representative without a working knowledge of supply, demand, and market forces. Indeed, the concepts embodied in the supply and demand model are among the most profitable and rewarding ideas you will encounter in your professional management training.

The importance of obtaining a solid grasp of supply and demand is magnified when you consider that almost every aspect of our lives has an economic component—birth, education, marriage, family rearing, career choices, residential decisions, divorce, insurance, taxes, religion, retirement, death.

This chapter presents the bare bones of the supply and demand model on an intuitive basis, leaving measurement problems, implications for firm behavior, and more sophisticated applications to later chapters. This chapter gives you an opportunity to review the form, language, and logic of supply and demand in a relatively nontechnical setting.

Demand

Consider a familiar product, McDonald's Big Mac. Someone who was thinking of buying a Big Mac would have some alternatives, including other fast foods (the Colonel's fried chicken for example), medium-speed food (restaurants with tablecloths and waitresses), slow food (home cooking), or no food (dieting or fasting). Even the most ardent Big Mac devotee would rely more heavily on the substitutes if the money or time cost of the Big Mac rose while the costs of the substitutes stayed the same. Consumers buy fewer Big Macs at high prices than at low prices. This inverse relationship between product price and the amount consumers purchase is observed so regularly that it is called the **law of demand**.

Let's consider another example, natural gas. Table 2.1 lists the uses of natural gas and substitutes in the event that the price of natural gas rises. Although there may be no substitutes for using natural gas in an existing furnace, hot water heater, stove, or appliance, there are substitute ways to heat and cook. It is also possible to reduce or eliminate some uses. In time, the existing furnace or stove may even be replaced by one that uses less gas or a different fuel.

People become interested in substitutes for natural gas because the law of demand is at work in the natural gas market. When natural gas prices rise, consumers seek relatively less costly substitutes; when prices drop, buyers shift away from gas substitutes and toward natural gas. Note the central role of substitutes in deriving the law of demand—and the inverse relationship between price and quantity purchased.

Table 2.1
Uses and Substitutes for Natural Gas

Use	Possible Substitutes
Home heating	Reduce heat in some rooms Lower thermostat and wear sweater Insulate house Use oil heat Use coal heat Use solar heat Move to the Sun Belt
Heating domestic hot water	Reduce water temperature Turn off water heater at night Use electric razor for shaving Take showers instead of tub baths Take fewer showers (when cleanliness is costly, some filth is optimal)
Running clothes dryer	Use clothes line Use electric dryer Buy drip-dry clothes Wash clothes less frequently
Cooking	Cook more stove-top meals Buy new, smaller oven Cook in microwave oven Use electric stove Use wood stove Eat cold food Cook meals that use less energy (eggs instead of turkey) Cook in bulk and save leftovers for cold meals
Lighting decorative gas lamps	Switch to electric lamps Use decorative lamps less often

The Big Mac and natural gas examples emphasize the importance of **price**—the amount of money paid for a unit of output—in consumers' buying decisions. Yet there are other factors that influence these decisions as well. We need a definition of demand that takes into account all the factors that influence consumer buying. Equation 2.1 is a useful beginning point:

$$Q_d = f(P, P^s, P^c, I, N, \ldots) \qquad (2.1)$$

where

Q_d = quantity demanded of the good
P = product price
P^s = price of substitutes
P^c = price of complements
I = consumer income
N = number of consumers
$\ldots$ = all other factors not mentioned explicitly

This demand equation indicates that the quantity of a good consumers wish to buy depends on many factors, including the price of the good, the prices of substitutes and complements, consumer income, the number of consumers demanding the good, and a variety of other factors. The ellipsis dots in Equation 2.1 emphasize that demand is ordinarily affected by many more factors than the few listed explicitly in the equation, including fads, time to adjust, expectations of price changes, laws, regulations, and customs. The demand equation stresses an important fact: **Demand** is the multidimensional relationship between the quantity consumed and the factors that determine how much is consumed.

The visual representation of the demand equation is the **demand curve**. And here we face a problem common to nearly every aspect of economics: How can a multidimensional relationship be illustrated in two dimensions? Equation 2.1 can be used to illustrate the analytic technique involved:

$$Q_d = f(\underset{\substack{\uparrow \\ \text{movement} \\ \text{parameter}}}{P}, \underbrace{P^s, P^c, I, N, \ldots}_{\substack{\text{shift} \\ \text{parameters}}})$$

The determinants of demand are divided into two groups: a **movement parameter** (price) and **shift parameters** (all demand determinants except price). Holding the values of all shift parameters constant, we can trace out a two-dimensional relationship between the movement parameter (P) and quantity demanded (Q_d). The visual result is the demand curve, illustrated in Figure 2.1. Price is measured on the vertical axis and quantity demanded on the horizontal axis.

Note that the demand curve in Figure 2.1 is negatively sloped. This slope is the graphic expression of the law of demand: Consumers buy less at higher prices. The demand curves for Big Macs and natural gas are also negatively sloped. Holding all shift parameters constant, price and quantity demanded are inversely related.

We now have a precise definition of the demand curve: the relationship between the quantities of a good that consumers are willing to buy and all possible prices, in a specified time period, *ceteris paribus*. The phrase *in a specified time period* emphasizes that demand is a flow of purchases over time; thus demand for one week will differ from demand for one month. The Latin phrase *ceteris paribus* means "other things constant." Holding the shift parameters constant allows us to focus on the relationship between price and quantity and to draw a demand curve in two dimensions.

Table 2.2 shows that the information contained in a demand

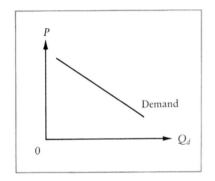

Figure 2.1
Demand Curve

The demand curve is negatively sloped because consumers seek out less costly substitutes when price rises, *ceteris paribus*.

curve can be summarized in a table, although only a few data points can be shown. The demand curve and its tabular equivalent remind us that demand is not a single number (say 2,000 cubic feet of natural gas); rather, it encompasses the number of units desired at each price, *ceteris paribus*.

Now consider the black demand curve, D_0, in Figure 2.2. If the price rises from P_0 to P_1, consumers will cut purchases from Q_0 to Q_1. The price increase thus causes a movement from point A to point B along the demand curve D_0. This movement is not a change in demand, however, because consumers have cut their purchases only as a result of the increased price. If price remained the same, the original amount would be purchased. The higher price reduces the quantity demanded from Q_0 to Q_1, but points A and B are still two of many points on the same demand curve. Thus movement along a stationary demand curve is a change in **quantity demanded,** not a change in demand.

Demand changes only when the entire demand curve shifts, as illustrated by the shift from demand curve D_0 to D_1. And the demand curve shifts only when the values of the shift parameters (all factors except price) change. We will study the specific causes of demand shifts later. For now, recognize that a change in demand means only one thing: Consumers want to purchase a different amount of output than before *at each price*. At point C on demand curve D_1, consumers have reduced the quantity demanded from Q_0 to Q_1 at the same price P_0. Point A and point C lie on different demand curves at the same price (P_0) and therefore the move from A to C indicates a change in demand. In essence, the original demand curve, D_0, disappears and is replaced with a new price-quantity relationship, D_1. This happens only if one or more of the shift parameters change.

This discussion about demand has made a distinction that is of incalculable significance: Movement along a stationary demand curve is caused *only* by a change in price (the movement parameter), holding all shift parameters constant. Price is the movement parameter because only changes in price cause movements along the demand curve. It is conventional to call movement along a stationary demand curve a **change in quantity demanded.** A shift of the demand curve, on the other hand, is caused *only* by a change in one or more of the shift parameters and appears as a shift of the entire demand curve. The shift parameters are so named because changes in their values shift the demand curve. It is conventional to call a shift of a demand curve a **change in demand.**

Demand has now been described in four ways: verbally, graphically (Figure 2.1), as a schedule (Table 2.2), and as a function (Equation 2.1). You must learn to recognize the demand concept in all of its many disguises.

Table 2.2
Quantity Demanded for Natural Gas

Price of Natural Gas per 1,000 Cubic Feet	Quantity of Natural Gas Demanded per Specified Time Period
70¢	1,200 cu. ft.
60	1,600
50	2,000
40	2,400
30	2,800

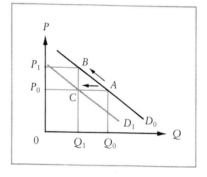

Figure 2.2
Demand Curve: Movements versus Shifts

The movement from A to B along demand curve D_0 is a reduction in quantity demanded due to a price increase. The shift from demand curve D_0 to D_1 is a reduction in demand, because consumers want to purchase less at each price.

Supply

We can now approach the subject of supply intuitively by returning to the Big Mac example. What is McDonald's supply response to higher prices for fast food? The central concept is again substitution—in this case, alternative methods of producing more Big Macs. Some of the possibilities are:

More grill and storage space for Big Macs.

More restaurant locations.

More-expensive equipment.

More-expensive and better-trained workers.

More workers per Big Mac.

Faster service.

When Big Mac prices are low compared to costs and to the prices of other menu items, McDonald's has little profit incentive to sell many Big Macs or to engage in high-cost production techniques. However, at higher prices the firm has the incentive to produce more Big Macs by adopting some higher-cost production methods. Like McDonald's, firms reevaluate alternative production and sales techniques and increase the quantities supplied when product price rises, *ceteris paribus*. But output usually cannot be increased without increasing average production costs. Thus firms are usually unwilling to increase costs by expanding production unless they have reasonable expectations of higher prices.

On the supply side of the natural gas market, the following production substitutes may be induced by higher prices:

1. Sell to different markets
   a. Home
   b. Industry
   c. Agriculture

2. Explore more
   a. Offshore
   b. In Alaska
   c. Off New York coast
   d. Near known sources

3. Extract more from existing wells
   a. Dig deeper
   b. Explode rock formations

4. Transfer natural gas being saved for future sales to the current market

5. Import more from Russia and Malaysia

As the price rises, natural gas suppliers get the message, communicated by profit impulses, to increase the quantity of gas supplied by engaging in production methods that would not be profitable at lower gas prices.

Now a formal definition of the **supply curve**: the relationship between the quantities of a good that suppliers are willing to sell at all possible prices, in a specified time period, *ceteris paribus*.

The definition of supply, the depiction of the supply curve, the distinction between movement along a stationary supply curve and a shift in the supply curve, and the problem of illustrating a multidimensional supply concept in two dimensions closely parallel the demand discussion. In functional notation, supply may be represented as

$$Q_s = f(\underset{\uparrow}{P}, \underbrace{w, r, T, \ldots}) \qquad (2.2)$$

$$\underset{\substack{\text{movement} \\ \text{parameter}}}{} \quad \underset{\text{shift parameters}}{}$$

where

Q_s = quantity supplied
P = product price
w = price of labor
r = price of capital
T = level of technology

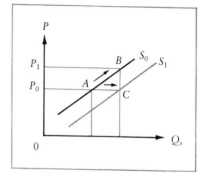

Figure 2.3
Supply Curve: Movements versus Shifts

The movement from *A* to *B* along supply curve S_0 is an increase in quantity supplied due to a price increase. The shift from supply curve S_0 to S_1 is an increase in supply, because firms wish to sell more at each price.

As with demand, **supply** is the multidimensional relationship between the **quantity supplied** and all of its determinants. Such an unwieldy concept is made tractable by breaking it into its component parts—the movement parameter and shift parameters. Like demand, the movement parameter for supply is price. However, the supply shift parameters usually differ from the demand shift parameters. Equation 2.2 includes three specific shift parameters important to supply: the price of labor, the price of capital, and the level of technology. The three ellipsis dots allow for the inclusion of other relevant supply determinants, such as weather, transportation costs, government regulation, taxes, producer expectations, and so forth.

The supply curve is the two-dimensional relationship between the movement parameter (P) and the quantity supplied (Q_s), holding all shift parameters constant. Supply curve S_0 in Figure 2.3 is drawn with a positive slope; the supply increases with the price. The movement from point A to point B is movement along a stationary supply curve or, alternatively, a **change in quantity supplied** (in this case, an increase). It results from an increase in the movement parameter, which is price. On the other hand, the shift from supply curve S_0 to S_1 is a **change in supply** (also an increase) resulting from improvements in technology, reductions in price of the factors of production, or similar cost-reducing changes in other shift parameters. When production costs fall, the firm has a profit incentive to sell more output *at each price*. This is the meaning of an increase in supply. Movement from point A to point C results from an increase in supply; more is offered for sale at the same price. But remember: For supply to increase at a given price, one or more of the shift parameters must change.

As with demand, supply may be expressed verbally, graphically, as a schedule, and in functional form. One pleasing feature of economics is that analytic methods learned in one context often carry over into others. If you understand demand, supply should be child's play.

Market Equilibrium, Shortages, and Surpluses

Thus far we have encountered two market forces, supply and demand. Although each is influenced by price, neither supply nor demand by itself can determine price. Actual market prices are determined by the balance of these two market forces.

Figure 2.4 combines supply and demand curves. Is there one price toward which the market will move, or is the actual price random? As a matter of fact, price tends to approach P_e, the **equilibrium price**. In general, **equilibrium** describes a state of balance, a position of rest, or a position that can be maintained if achieved. Why is the price P_e the only possible price "at rest," or the only price that can last?

Consider price P_1, a price below the equilibrium price. At price P_1 the quantity demanded, Q_2, exceeds the quantity supplied, Q_1. This difference is an excess demand, or **shortage**. At price P_1 firms have little profit incentive to produce, even though consumers wish to purchase in large quantities because they regard this good favorably in comparison to its relatively more expensive substitutes. But only Q_1 units will be available at P_1, because the supply decisions of firms limit availability. The disappointed buyers will begin to bid for the limited supplies by offering higher prices, and so price P_1 cannot be maintained. Shortages tend to disappear in uncontrolled markets by the upward price haggling of disappointed consumers. As price rises, there are movements along both curves: Price increases encourage firms to sell more and consumers to buy less. In this way the shortage is eliminated. The price P_e is the limit of this price increase because at price P_e the quantity demanded equals the quantity supplied, both Q_e. At price P_e there are no disappointed consumers (or sellers); and the previous forces urging price increases have run their course. With all market participants satisfied, the price P_e is sustainable; the market is in equilibrium.

Suppose the price is temporarily above P_e, at P_2. Now there is an excess supply, or **surplus.** At price P_2, firms wish to sell many units in order to increase profits, whereas the high price discourages buyers and pushes them toward more attractive substitutes. Thus the firms will be unable to sell their desired quantities, and unwanted inventories will accumulate. But the surplus will be eliminated as firms lower their prices in order to reduce unwanted inventories. These price reductions eliminate the surplus partly by inducing firms to produce less but also by increasing the quantities demanded by consumers. As before, the price will stop falling once a price is achieved that balances the desires of both buyers and sellers. This occurs only at price P_e.

The process by which prices are bid up and down can be simple or complex. The simplest bidding process is an auction, where buyers and sellers bid personally in response to shortages and surpluses. In the stock market, buyers and sellers make bids through an agent—the stockbroker. In most other markets, such as food, drugs, clothing, and hardware, long strings of intermediaries between the original manufacturer and the final consumer make personal bidding impossible. Still, a shortage is evidence to sellers of

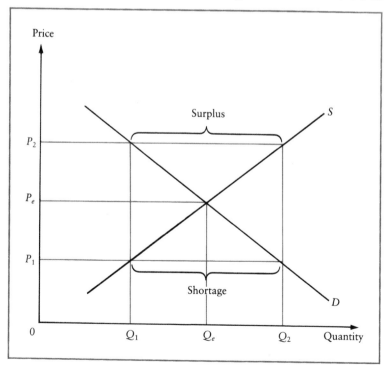

Figure 2.4
Market Equilibrium

Equilibrium price is P_e, and equilibrium quantity is Q_e. All shortages and surpluses are eliminated in equilibrium.

APPLICATION

2.1

Business Risk and Supply and Demand

One of the more important shift parameters in the supply curve of any product is the uncertainty of future business costs. Chapter 8 shows in detail how firms react to risk, but elementary supply and demand analysis at this point can introduce you to the complex problem of risk and the way in which the market allocates its effects.

In the interest of simplicity, assume that the only element of risk in a particular market is the fluctuating level of the interest rate. Interest rates that fluctuate around a particular average, say 10 percent, are more risky than rates that are steady at that level. Firms cannot tell precisely when they will want to borrow, and hence they run the risk of needing cash when rates have risen above 10 percent.

Because firms view risk as a cost, the effect of higher business risk is to shift the supply curve to the left and to raise the price to consumers. In other words, part of the risk is shifted to consumers, as is any cost increase.

buyers' willingness to pay higher prices rather than go without some units of the good. Thus shortages send signals to sellers, all the way from retail stores to the manufacturer, to raise prices, even though buyers are not personally offering higher prices. And as prices rise, shortages are eliminated.

Let's study the bidding process further by taking a concrete example—natural gas. Suppose that natural gas prices are not controlled by the government and that the market price is temporarily below equilibrium. A natural gas shortage will ensue. But it is unlikely that all natural gas users will feel the shortage simultaneously. Some users will be able to buy all the natural gas they want at the lower price, even though a shortage exists. However, the customers who cannot buy the quantities they want will offer higher prices to assure delivery of natural gas. Thus natural gas suppliers will divert sales to the customers offering the top prices. As the shortage is shifted from one market segment to others, a new group of customers will bid higher prices. Inevitably, prices rise and the gas shortage is eliminated, in part by reductions in the quantity demanded by buyers and in part by an increase in the quantity of natural gas supplied. Such movements along supply and demand curves take place over time. An equilibrium price is achieved when all buyers are able to purchase the quantities they want and all suppliers can sell the quantities they want at the price established by the market. Equilibrium is the absence of price-changing forces.

Equilibrium price is usually not achieved and maintained immediately after a market disturbance, as in the movement of an arrow to its target; rather, equilibrium is a central tendency, a price toward which the market moves. Just as a marble dropped into a fruit bowl will roll around before it reaches a resting position (equilibrium), so may market prices tend to overshoot or undershoot as they move ever closer to an equilibrium position.

Demand and supply are written in functional form as follows:

$$\text{Demand} = Q_d = f(P, P^s, P^c, I, N, \ldots)$$

$$\text{Supply} = Q_s = f(P, w, v, T, \ldots)$$

Holding all shift (nonprice) parameters constant, these two equations are the algebraic equivalents of the demand and supply curves. Equilibrium is achieved by finding the price that equates the quantity supplied and the quantity demanded. Equilibrium price is found by setting the demand and supply equations equal and solving for price:

$$Q_s = Q_d \qquad\qquad (2.3)$$

equilibrium condition

The price that satisfies Equation 2.3 eliminates shortages and surpluses; Equation 2.3 is therefore the algebraic equivalent of the intersection of supply and demand curves. It is the solution to the system of simultaneous equations contained in the demand and supply equations.

To summarize, undesired inventories force prices down whenever price exceeds equilibrium, whereas unsatisfied consumer demand forces price up when price is less than equilibrium. In a free market surpluses and shortages tend to be self-eliminating as the market pushes toward equilibrium. Price—the movement parameter—plays the dominant role in market analysis because it is the only economic variable that always influences both the supply and demand sides of the market.

Demand and Supply Curve Shifts

Consider the following demand function for natural gas:

$$Q_d = f(P, P^s, P^c, I, \text{weather}, \ldots)$$

For initial values of the shift parameters P^s (prices of substitutes), P^c (prices of complements), I (income), weather, and all other factors, there is a two-dimensional relationship between price and quantity demanded. This is the demand curve for natural gas, labeled D_0 in Figure 2.5a. Let's see how the demand curve shifts when the values of these shift parameters change.

Suppose that the price of No. 2 heating oil, a **substitute** for (or

Figure 2.5
Shift of the Demand Curve: Substitutes

(a) The demand for natural gas increases (shifts) when the price rises for No. 2 heating oil, a substitute.
(b) A price increase results in a reduction in the quantity demanded of No. 2 heating oil.

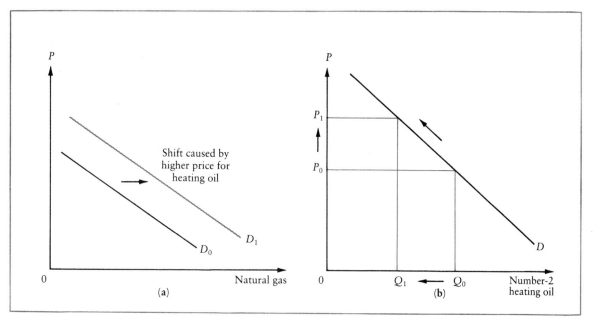

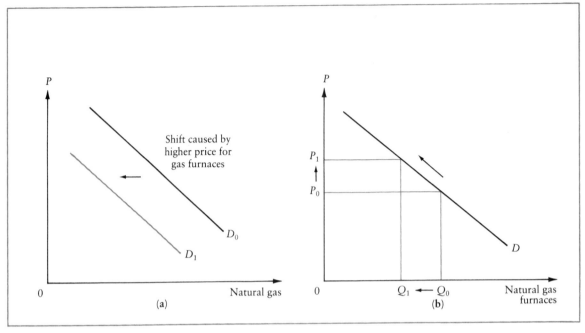

(a)   (b)

**Figure 2.6
Shift of the Demand Curve:
Complements**

(a) The demand for natural gas falls
(shifts) when the price rises for gas
furnaces, a complement.
(b) When prices increase, there is a
reduction in the quantity demanded
of gas furnaces.

**Figure 2.7
Shift of the Demand Curve:
Other Factors**

The demand for natural gas is
greater during a cold winter than a
warm winter.

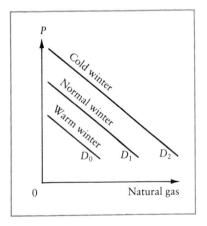

alternative to) natural gas, rises from P_0 to P_1 in Figure 2.5b. Consumers will purchase less heating oil than before and, as a result, will want more natural gas at each price of natural gas. The higher price of the substitute shifts the natural gas demand curve from D_0 to D_1 (to the right in Figure 2.5a).

If the price rises for a **complement** (a good required for, or at least enhancing, use of the good in question), the demand curve shifts to the left. Thus an increase in the price of gas furnaces from P_0 to P_1 reduces consumers' desire to buy natural gas at each price as illustrated in Figure 2.6.

Finally, nothing alters one's appreciation for natural gas as a home-heating fuel so much as changes in the weather. In Figure 2.7, the natural gas demand curve for a warm winter, D_0, shifts to D_1 for a normal winter and to D_2 for a cold winter.

A full discussion of the income shift parameter will be postponed until Chapter 4 because of its special role in managerial analysis. Suffice it to say that an increase in income may shift the demand curves for chicken necks and caviar differently. People may reduce their consumption of chicken necks when their incomes rise because they can afford higher-quality and more-expensive foods. If so, chicken necks are "inferior goods." On the other hand, higher incomes may induce greater consumption of caviar, a "normal good." (See Chapter 4 for a more complete discussion of normal and inferior goods.)

Now let's turn to supply shifts. Consider the following supply function for natural gas:

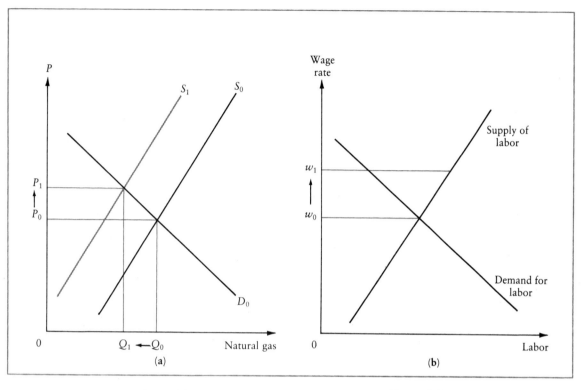

$$Q_s = f(P, w, \ldots)$$

The supply curve S_0 in Figure 2.8a is the two-dimensional relationship between price and quantity supplied, holding the wage rate (w) and all other nonprice supply factors constant at their initial values. Figure 2.8b contains the supply and demand curves for workers employed in the natural gas industry. The equilibrium wage, w_0, establishes the position of the original supply curve for natural gas, S_0. If the labor union succeeds in establishing a wage floor of w_1, the higher labor costs shift the natural gas supply curve to S_1. The equilibrium price of natural gas increases from P_0 to P_1, and the equilibrium quantity falls from Q_0 to Q_1.

Caution: In Figure 2.8 the supply of natural gas has fallen. Suppliers sell less at each price because of higher labor costs, a shift parameter. Meanwhile, the demand for natural gas has not fallen, because all demand shift parameters are unchanged. The higher price causes a movement along the stationary demand curve, D_0. Thus quantity demanded has fallen; demand has not.

These are only a few examples of the forces that cause supply and demand curves to shift. Remember that a change in the value of any nonprice determinant of supply and/or demand will shift the curves. When the curves shift, the bidding process leads the market toward its new equilibrium.

Figure 2.8
Shift of the Supply Curve

(a) The supply of natural gas falls (shifts) when wage costs rise, resulting in a rise in price. Demand does not change, however. **(b)** The wage rises artificially from w_0 to w_1 through union bargaining.

A P P L I C A T I O N

2.2

Fallacy of Composition

One fallacy of logic that must be recognized and avoided in formulating managerial decisions is the **fallacy of composition.** This fallacy comes into play when someone argues that what is true of the part must also be true of the whole. For example: "Any one individual can exit the theater in less than 30 seconds, therefore all can leave in 30 seconds." To argue that what is true of one individual (the part) acting alone is necessarily true of all individuals (the whole) acting together is to fall prey to the fallacy of composition.

Say that Farmer Brown tries to increase his income by planting an additional field of corn. Assuming constant weather, rain, and other growing conditions, he may well be able to increase his income.

But it is foolish to extend the argument and say that all farmers can increase their incomes by increasing corn acreage. Farmer Brown is such a small component of the corn market that his deci-sion cannot affect market price. Thus he may be able to sell more corn at a constant price and thereby increase his income. But if all farmers simultaneously increase corn acreage, the effect will be to shift the corn supply curve to the right, reduce the market price of corn, and increase the quantity of corn sold. The possibility exists that more corn sold at a lower price could actually reduce total farm income.

Business analysis is replete with similar situations. We must be careful not to allow the fallacy of composition to interfere with clear thinking.

A P P L I C A T I O N

2.3

Comparative Statics

Comparative statics, a term used frequently in this book and in other books on managerial economics, is a method of comparing different equilibrium positions. For example, if the original demand and supply curves in the accompanying figure are D_0 and S_0, the initial equilibrium price and equilibrium quantity sold are P_0 and Q_0.

Now suppose that the demand curve shifts to the right, to D_1. The increase in demand increases both price and quantity sold, to P_1 and Q_1. By changing one shift parameter at a time, we can compare the initial equilibrium with the new equilibrium. This comparison is called comparative statics.

Use of the word *statics* emphasizes that we are interested in only the beginning and ending equilibrium values and not in the dynamic processes of adjustment. The dynamics of change, such as the timing of the adjustment, are important but not relevant in static analysis.

Comparative static analysis is also applicable with multiple changes in shift parameters, although qualitative predictions may become clouded. For exam-ple, if supply falls to S_1 at the same time that demand increases to D_1, the equilibrium price could increase to P_2. But these shifts would have an ambiguous effect on equilibrium quantity. Under these conditions, information about the relative magnitude of the demand and supply shifts is necessary in order to determine the comparative static effect on quantity sold.

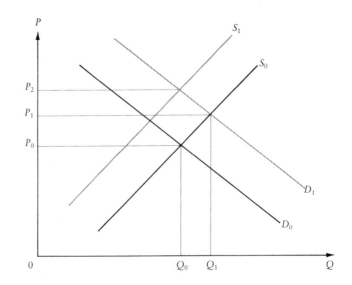

Curve Shifts and Market Equilibrium
Comparative statics is the comparison of market equilibria before and after a market disturbance.

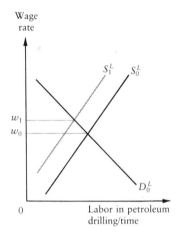

A P P L I C A T I O N

2.4

Comparative Statics in Related Markets

Changes in the static equilibrium of one market may set off a chain reaction in closely related markets. Suppose that the supply of labor available for drilling petroleum falls from S_0^L to S_1^L, as shown in Figure A. The market equilibrium readjusts to a higher wage rate and lower quantity of labor. However, the wage rate is a shift parameter in the supply curve of petroleum, as shown in Figure B. When wages rise, the supply of petroleum falls from S_0^P to S_1^P, and the equilibrium price rises from P_0^P to P_1^P. In turn, the supply of antifreeze is affected by all input prices, one of which is the price of petroleum. Thus when the wages of petroleum drillers rise, antifreeze supply falls and its equilibrium price rises, as seen in Figure C.

In short, when equilibrium values are shift parameters in other markets, a change in one market rattles around the system and disturbs all equilibrium values in a chain reaction. Since most firms operate in several important markets simultaneously, managers should be able to use comparative statics to see how their markets fit together and interact.

Figure A
Labor Market Equilibrium
A reduction in labor supply increases wages.

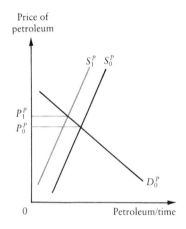

Figure B
Petroleum Market Equilibrium
Higher wages reduce the supply of petroleum and increase the price of petroleum.

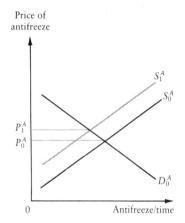

Figure C
Antifreeze Market Equilibrium
Higher petroleum prices reduce the supply of antifreeze and increase antifreeze prices.

Functions of the Market

Now that we have seen how market forces determine prices, let's study the social significance of prices. In the process of determining prices and output, a market system provides guidance, rationing, information, impersonality, and allocation of tasks.

Guidance

To understand the guidance function of the market, suppose that the supply and demand for honey (see Figure 2.9) determine the initial equilibrium price P_0 and quantity Q_0 (point A). Now assume that the demand for honey rises from D_0 to D_1. The initial shortage AB is eliminated by price adjustments as the new price P_1 and

Figure 2.9
Guidance Function of the Market

An increase in demand raises price
and attracts resources into the
market.

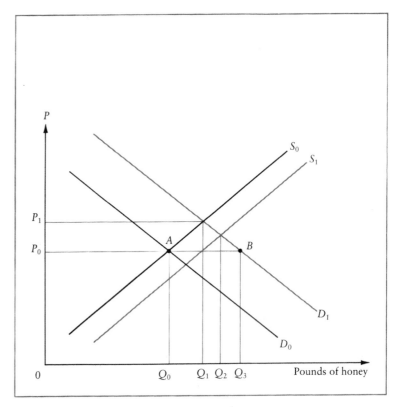

output Q_1 are approached. Higher honey prices encourage profit-motivated producers to increase their production and sales of honey. Thus the increased consumer demand for honey is communicated to suppliers via price adjustments, and these price adjustments encourage firms to produce the additional honey that consumers demand.

In this way society's scarce resources are channeled toward uses that consumers prefer. Resources are guided by the pricing mechanism; price adjustments signal firms to increase production when increases in demand raise prices and to decrease production when reductions in demand reduce prices. Prices coordinate the communication between buyers and sellers, communication that must take other forms in nonmarket economies.

In the honey example, the output of existing firms will tend to rise in the short run from Q_0 to Q_1. In the longer run, higher prices may even attract new firms from other industries if expected profits in the honey industry exceed the profits in their present occupations. If new firms are attracted into the industry, the output of honey will increase to Q_2 and prices will fall.

In summary, increases in consumer demand increase prices, which gives the established honey-producing firms the incentive to increase production in the short run and also attracts new honey producers in the longer run. Resources are directed toward honey production and away from alternative uses, and the guiding mechanism is price.

Rationing

In Figure 2.9 the initial increase in the demand for honey from D_0 to D_1 causes a shortage $\overline{AB}$. The sellers' quantity supplied of Q_0 units places a limit on the amount of honey that consumers can buy at price P_0, even though they want to purchase the larger quantity Q_3 at that price. How is it decided which customers to disappoint and which uses of honey to forgo? This is clearly a rationing problem.

The most straightforward rationing device is **price rationing,** under which prices would rise. At higher prices, honey producers would increase their quantities of honey supplied, whereas consumers would reduce their quantities demanded by switching to honey substitutes and by eliminating less important uses of honey. In Figure 2.9, when the price rises to P_1, the initial shortage $\overline{AB}$ is rationed among buyers by price adjustments and, in the process, is eliminated. In nonmarket or controlled-market economies, other means must be used to allocate such shortages among consumers.

Information

The price system provides information to market participants at low cost. Producers use market prices to determine consumer interest in their products. Consumers decide on the quantity and variety of goods to buy by checking their relative prices. In addition, the market provides information about the location and availability of goods. If you know the location of a gas station, you usually know the location of gas. However, this was not true in 1979, when gas shortages induced by price controls and the associated waiting lines, quotas, and unexpected closings of gas stations made it very difficult to know where to buy gasoline. The search and information costs for determining the location, availability, and quality of goods rise whenever nonprice rationing systems are substituted for price rationing.

Impersonality

The price system operates on money transactions. Any buyer who can pay the asking price can buy the good. This impersonal nature of market transactions has two important implications. First, the market satisfies demands, not needs. Goods and services are obtained by those who can pay for them, even though legitimate needs and wants of other consumers remain unfulfilled because of their inability to pay market prices. The market responds strictly to purchasing power and, in this sense, has no conscience.

The second aspect of impersonal markets is the anonymity with which goods are bought and sold. At the equilibrium price, the quantity supplied equals the quantity demanded, so there are no extra customers in the market, as there are during shortages. Thus sellers cannot refuse to serve customers without sacrificing profits, because customers who are turned away can go elsewhere to purchase their goods. During shortages, sellers typically refuse to sell to some customers for two reasons: (1) discrimination against the customer based on personal characteristics (such as race, religion, or sex) and (2) discrimination against the customer based on "worthiness" (which customers are the most important?). Under price controls, waiting lines of unsatisfied customers make it possible for sellers to pick and choose among customers without loss in profits. Thus the impersonality of the market system, where goods must be sold to anyone with enough money, serves as an imperfect but important check on discriminatory behavior and, in general, protects against the abuse of power.

Allocation of Tasks

When buyers and sellers can use prices as signals, they can readily calculate and compare benefits and costs arising from their choices. All consumers and firms must decide whether to rely on the market to provide goods, services, training, and opportunities or whether to seek a degree of **vertical integration** by owning goods outright and providing services themselves. For example, consumers can hire all their typing services in the marketplace, or they can buy a typewriter and learn to type. Firms can rely on markets to provide the resources needed for production, or they can vertically integrate by producing and storing the necessary resources themselves. An efficient balance between vertical integration and market reliance depends on the benefits and costs of the alternatives. The benefits and costs are conveyed by market prices.

How is the allocation of tasks altered when market forces are frustrated? Price controls often lead to **hoarding,** which means that buyers partially take on the task of holding inventories instead of relying on the market. Imagine the inefficiency of an economic system in which market disruptions lead consumers to store clothing, toothpaste, soap, refrigerators, and automobiles for future use. In addition, market controls that distort price signals can skew the decision whether to rent or own. Ownership, a form of vertical integration, is encouraged by market controls. Hence the regulation of markets thwarts the market function of providing an efficient allocation of tasks.

2.5

Subsidies: A Free Lunch?

The verity "There is no such thing as a free lunch" expresses succinctly the idea that you can't get something for nothing. Every choice requires sacrifice of one opportunity for another. This sacrifice of alternatives is called the "opportunity cost" (a concept discussed in more detail in Chapter 6).

Nevertheless, governments often attempt to give us a "free lunch" by subsidizing the production or consumption of various goods. A **subsidy** is the difference between the price that buyers pay and the price that sellers receive. Thus supply and demand concepts help us investigate the effects of subsidies.

In the adjacent figure, the pre-subsidy supply and demand curves, S_0 and D_0, establish the initial equilibrium values for price and quantity, P_0 and Q_0. Whether the government chooses to subsidize the producers or the consumers, the results will be the same.

Let's begin with a subsidy paid to suppliers. Say that the seller receives a total payment equal to the price the consumer pays augmented by the per-unit subsidy. This subsidy raises the supply curve from S_0 to S_1. As a result, a larger quantity of output than before will be supplied at each consumer price. The new supply curve lies below the old one by exactly the amount of the per-unit subsidy. The subsidy therefore reduces the consumer price to P_1 and raises output to Q_1.

Direct consumer expenditure on the good is now $0P_1 \cdot 0Q_1$, or the area $0P_1LQ_1$. The total subsidy is the per-unit subsidy times units sold, $P_1P_2 \cdot 0Q_1$, or the area P_1P_2RL. But the subsidy must be paid from taxes, an indirect consumer payment. Thus the total consumer expenditure for the good—the direct payment plus the taxes to cover the subsidy— equals the area $0P_2RQ_1$. This

amount is larger than the pre-subsidy expenditure, $0P_0NQ_0$, as you can easily see in the figure.

Subsidies, by encouraging expenditures in selected markets, transfer resources from other markets. Thus they do not provide a free lunch. The fact that the direct price the consumer pays is lower than before should not blind us to the true opportunity costs of expanding output in subsidized markets.

The results are the same when the government subsidizes consumers instead of producers. The subsidy shifts the demand sched-

ule from D_0 to D_1, the vertical distance between D_0 and D_1 being the per-unit subsidy to buyers. The new demand curve must pass through point R, because R lies vertically above L by the amount of the subsidy. In equilibrium, price and quantity increase to P_2 and Q_1. But these equilibrium results are the same as when the subsidy is given to the producer.

Now is the perfect time to distinguish between price and cost: Price is the money value put on a product; **cost** includes price and the value of all other factors involved in buying or selling a product. Thus subsidies cannot provide a free lunch in the sense of giving us more output at a lower cost. All they can do is provide a low-priced lunch that costs a lot.

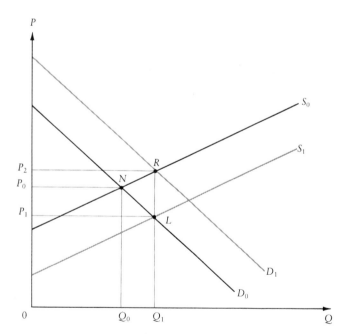

Subsidizing Producers and Consumers
Per-unit subsidies achieve the same results, whether given to buyers or sellers. Consumer subsidies shift the demand curve, and producer subsidies shift the supply curve.

Buyer and Seller Response to Nonprice Rationing

To further emphasize the services that the market provides, let's examine consumers' and sellers' responses to shortages caused by **nonprice rationing**—that is, allocating shortages by means other than price increases.

General Response of Consumers to Shortages

Suppose that the initial equilibrium price of gasoline is P_0 in Figure 2.10 and that the quantity sold is Q_0. Assume further that demand increases from D_0 to D_1. Finally, suppose that the government imposes a **price ceiling** at P_0 to assure that the price of gasoline does not rise. How do customers respond to such price controls?

At price P_0, there is an initial shortage of $\overline{AB}$. Where possible, consumers respond to shortages by hoarding, which is an effort to lower the risk of not finding future supplies. For example, during the 1973–1974 gas shortages and price controls, it was estimated that the average gas tank was kept three-quarters full (it was kept one-quarter full before the price controls). If the average tank holds 20 gallons, there was an average increase in gasoline storage of 10 gallons. With about 100 million cars in the United States, the increase in hoarding in gas tanks alone was 1 billion gallons in the first two weeks of the price controls. The sudden increase in demand caused by hoarding exacerbated the shortage.

Figure 2.10
Buyer and Seller Response to Price Ceilings

Buyers respond to shortages induced by price controls by hoarding, making illegal payments, wasting time in queues, and increasing information costs. Sellers shift production to unregulated markets, eliminate low-price products, reduce product quality, and increase discrimination.

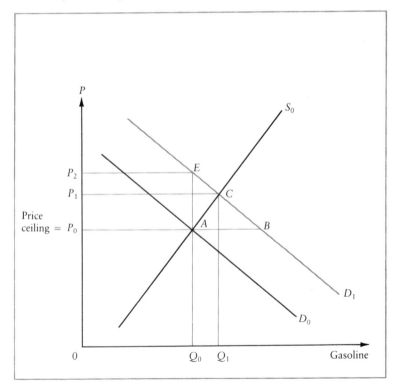

2.6

Toilet Paper Shortages: Not Funny

Economists use the term *shortage* in a special way. It refers to the excess of quantity demanded over quantity supplied *at a given price*. Therefore, both the supply and demand sides of the market contribute to the shortage. When the price is below equilibrium, sellers reduce their quantities supplied and buyers increase their quantities demanded by comparison to equilibrium values. Thus suppliers and consumers both contributed to the toilet paper shortage of 1973.

During the summer and fall of 1973, many markets, including the market for paper pulp, experienced shortages created by price controls. Shortages of newsprint caused some newspaper publishers to adopt smaller print to conserve paper. Toilet paper producers, unable to buy the amounts of paper needed to satisfy all their customers, needed to decide which of their customers to disappoint. They decided to disappoint the buyers of the lowest-grade toilet paper because prices and profits were higher for the perfumed and decorated product.

When production shifted to the higher-grade lines, the toilet paper industry did indeed contribute to a shortage of low-grade toilet paper by the economist's definition: At the controlled price, quantity demanded exceeded quantity supplied. Buyers

of low-grade toilet paper were left with a considerable problem.

One of the major purchasers of low-grade toilet paper is the military, which was experiencing difficulty buying its usual brand. What was a garden-variety shortage (with the potential of upgrading military toilet paper) became an all-out crisis when Johnny Carson, extrapolating the military's problem to the entire country, said it looked like the United States faced a toilet paper shortage. The "Tonight Show" audience was silent, and Carson changed the subject. But the next morning, toilet paper shelves were gutted by consumer hoarding. Attempts to ration supplies with one-to-a-customer limits merely prompted people to bring their spouse, parents, children, and neighbors' children, each counting as one customer.

Sources close to the toilet paper industry claimed there was no shortage, but the empty shelves put the lie to such claims. Many people presumed that the shortage was artificially induced by the industry in order to justify higher prices. But for whatever cause, people were now going to

the neighbors to borrow toilet paper. The shortage of low-grade paper, affecting the military primarily, was extended to all users of toilet paper by consumer hoarding.

It is probable that Carson could have cleared up the confusion right when it began if his audience had laughed at the first line and encouraged more on the subject. But toilet paper shortages are not funny; they represent disappointed customers. Thus the 1973 toilet paper shortage began in the government's decision to control prices, was helped along by suppliers' decisions to put limited paper supplies into the higher-grade products, and was further accelerated by consumer hoarding in response to Carson's monologue. Buyers *and* sellers contributed to the shortage.

This example illustrates another effect of price controls. Price controls are often advanced as a means to aid the poor. But as we have seen, price controls on paper products forced the low-grade toilet paper off the market. Similarly, low-grade wieners were forced off the market because meat packers, faced with short supplies, used scarce meat in the more expensive preparations, including bratwurst and Polish sausages. Thus price controls often discourage the production of the low-grade commodities that the poor rely on.

In Figure 2.10, quantity Q_0 sets the limit on the gas that consumers can buy at the controlled price, P_0. But consumers are willing to pay price P_2 for quantity Q_0. This fact, and the prevailing shortage $\overline{AB}$ at price P_0, suggests that the real price of buying gasoline will rise even if the money price is constant.

Suppose that the shortage $\overline{AB}$ is rationed by queue pricing— that is, first come, first served. In order for a quasi equilibrium to be achieved, the quantity supplied must equal the quantity demanded. Ignoring illegal (black market) payments for now, we would find that consumers would be willing to pay as much as P_2 for quantity Q_0. Because consumers could legally pay only P_0, they would have to pay the difference in nonmoney terms (such as waiting time). Thus the market would achieve a kind of equilibrium: Quantity demanded equals quantity supplied when buyers pay a total price of P_2 per unit of gas purchased. P_0 is money price, and $\overline{P_0P_2}$ is the value of waiting time spent per unit of gasoline.

Two observations are now appropriate. First, the total real price paid, P_2 (money price plus waiting time), is higher than the equilibrium price that would be reached if prices were free to fluctuate, P_1. Second, the dollars that consumers transfer to oil companies during periods of high prices can be reinvested, either in the discovery of additional oil supplies or some alternative economic investment. In contrast, the time that customers waste waiting in lines cannot be transferred; it is a "dead-weight loss" of a valuable resource.

Another consumer response to shortages is to offer illegal side payments. In Figure 2.10, the distance $\overline{P_0P_2}$ may represent, instead of waiting time, the incentive to make illegal black market payments. These payments can take subtle forms. For instance, when rent controls create shortages on rental housing, prospective renters, who cannot legally make a rent offer above the controlled level, may offer to purchase an extra set of keys for $200. Such an offer gives the renter an advantage in obtaining scarce housing space. Customers who make such offers are said to belong to the "key club." During gasoline shortages, customers who join the "rabbit's foot club" (buy a rabbit's foot for $50) or the "battery club" (buy a worn-out battery for $50) can obtain special treatment from the station owner and assure themselves of gas supplies. In similar fashion, financial institutions with names like Murder, Inc. loan money to borrowers at interest rates far in excess of the maximum legal rates set by usury laws.

To summarize: The basic consumer responses to shortages are hoarding, illegal side payments, increased efforts to seek information, and time wasted both on waiting in line and in figuring out which lines to wait in.

General Response of Sellers to Shortages

Again, Figure 2.10 indicates that firms would sell Q_1 units if the price could rise to P_1 but would sell the smaller quantity, Q_0, if prices were controlled at P_0. In other words, the firm's initial response to price controls is to reduce its output by comparison with its uncontrolled output. A related response may be to use the price-controlled inputs to increase the quality of goods not subject to regulation. For example, price-controlled petroleum products may be used to increase the quality of clothing or of antifreeze, whose prices may not be controlled, instead of gasoline. Also, when firms produce several lines of a product, they may eliminate their low-priced lines and produce the high-priced lines, whose prices are controlled at higher levels.

Shortages tend to reduce the quality of the good whose price is controlled. In the case of gasoline, the ancillary filling station services, such as tire pressure checks, free maps, and restroom stops, were curtailed during the 1979 gas shortages. The equivalent response in rent-controlled housing markets is to reduce repairs, upkeep, and renovation. Profit-motivated firms, when restricted from increasing their revenues by price adjustments, tend to reduce costs by quality reductions. And because of the waiting list of customers, the firm can get away with such actions.

Firms facing long lines of customers who cannot all be served are put in the position of deciding which customers are important. In the case of gas shortages, the decision to sell only to commuters or only to familiar faces allows the seller of gas to make arbitrary decisions concerning who will be served. In short, the gasoline station manager becomes the local "maharaja of petroleum." In a closely related point, prejudices are exercised during shortages because of the power that circumstances give to sellers. Such prejudices can be exercised without loss of profits during shortages.

These responses to shortages on the supply and demand side of the market make it doubtful that price controls can achieve even their primary purpose—holding prices down. True prices, which include opportunity costs as well as money prices, usually rise when a good becomes more scarce.

A P P L I C A T I O N

2.7

Vertical Integration, Price Controls, and the Little Guy

Vertical integration occurs when a firm or individual owns the means of production in two or more successive stages of production. If the Continental Baking Corporation owns a fleet of trucks used to deliver its baked bread to wholesale outlets, it is vertically integrated to a degree. If it grows its own wheat, it is even more integrated vertically.

Vertical integration allows a firm to substitute permanent or partial ownership for market exchange. Its purpose is to reduce risk, but the reduction of risk comes at a cost. For example, many people own rather than rent cars because of the greater convenience, the certainty of supply, and the greater control over repairs and safety. Many others rent instead of own because they

need automobile transportation infrequently or because they fly to distant cities and then rent cars on arrival.

In the taxi industry, drivers for large fleets typically get gasoline at the fleet tank; independent cabbies use the market and buy gas at retail filling stations. The taxi fleet therefore achieves greater vertical integration than the independent driver.

Suppose the government establishes price controls on gasoline,

and gas shortages appear. The fleet driver is partially insured against shortages by vertical integration. In contrast, independent drivers experience difficulty in obtaining gasoline because their supply depends on an orderly market. In this situation, fleet drivers may gain customers from the independents. Similarly, bread distributors who own their own gasoline tanks will get their bread to market quicker and at lower cost than the small bakers who rely on the market for gasoline.

The proposition that price controls protect the little guy is highly questionable. Larger firms that can afford vertical integration are more likely to avoid the higher costs imposed by price controls.

2.8

Impact of Usury Laws on Business Firms

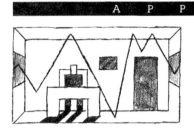

It is part of a manager's job to know how his or her firm fits into the economy. This task requires more than passing familiarity with both the markets in which the firm purchases inputs and the markets for the firm's products. In our mixed economy, public policy has a significant impact on these markets. Hence, business-people have a justifiable interest in influencing public policy.

One of the policies that should interest businesspeople is the **usury law,** which puts a ceiling on interest rates. It would appear that businesses would favor usury laws. After all, don't lower interest rates permit higher profits? The adjacent diagram will help us answer this question.

The figure depicts the supply and demand curves of loanable funds, along with a ceiling interest rate. The ceiling keeps interest rates from rising to equilibrium,

and so a shortage of loanable funds equal to distance $\overline{AB}$ exists. How does this shortage manifest itself?

1. Since usury ceilings are state laws, businesses in states with lower ceilings have a tougher time borrowing than those in states with higher ceilings or no ceilings at all.
2. Since businesses vary in their riskiness, banks must charge different loan rates to reflect that variation. Interest rate ceilings force banks to avoid making loans to high-risk businesses, because the equilibrium interest rate for a high-risk business is more likely to be above the ceiling than the equilibrium rate for a less risky business is.

Therefore, usury laws tend to make it harder for newer and smaller businesses to get credit; larger, more diversified firms will find credit more readily.

So before you twist your state legislator's arm to urge interest ceilings, remember how the inexorable forces of the market will react. Will the interest ceiling make it harder for your firm to find credit sources? Even if your firm is well-diversified, a good credit risk, and able to borrow despite the shortage of funds, a ceiling may make it harder for your customers to obtain credit and thereby affect your sales.

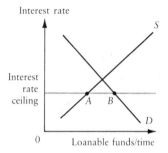

Effect of Interest Rate Controls

An interest rate ceiling results in credit shortages in the market for loanable funds. Small, high-risk firms are shut out of loans because the controlled interest rate makes low-risk firms more profitable for banks.

Summary

"Supply and demand" is a model that allows us to study the results of interactions among many buyers and sellers in the production and sale of a given product. Substitution by buyers and sellers is the key concept in an intuitive development of supply and demand curves. When shortages or surpluses occur at a given price, they are eliminated and equilibrium achieved by suitable price adjustments.

Product price is important to both buyers and sellers. For this reason, price is treated as the movement parameter for both supply and demand curves. Price controls interfere with the self-adjustment of market price and distort the adjustment of the only parameter that is always of key importance to both sellers and buyers—price. Thus price controls limit the ability of price to (1) guide scarce resources to their most valuable uses, (2) ration supplies among consumers, (3) provide low-cost information to market participants, (4) maintain market transactions on an impersonal basis, and (5) achieve an efficient allocation of tasks.

Problems

1. Consider the market for wheat in the United States.
   a. List five substitutes for wheat.
   b. Write the demand equation for wheat, identifying the movement parameter and the shift parameters.
   c. List the factors that affect the supply of wheat. (If you are not a farmer, use your imagination. Your ability to manipulate the curves is what is important.)
   d. Write the supply equation for wheat that corresponds to your list in part c. Identify the movement parameter and shift parameters.
   e. Put the supply and demand curves together and identify the equilibrium price and quantity for wheat.
2. Assume that there is a crop failure in the U.S. wheat market due to bad weather. Show the impact of the bad weather on the wheat market by describing its effect on shift parameters and on the equilibrium values of price and quantity.
3. Show the effect of a crop failure due to bad weather in the Soviet Union. How does this case differ from a U.S. crop failure?
4. Corn is a substitute for wheat. Analyze the effects in the corn market that would result from the crop failures described in questions 2 and 3.
5. Assume that the price of gasoline in Saudi Arabia is 10 cents per gallon and that the price in the United States is 60 cents. Assume that the transport cost from Saudi Arabia to the United States is 1 cent per gallon. Now distinguish between the price and cost of gasoline in Saudi Arabia.
6. Assume that, due to price controls, gasoline is selling for $1.00 a gallon and that long waiting lines form at the gas stations. In periods of shortages like this, managers often limit purchases to, say, 10 gallons per customer.
   a. What is the price of gas? What is the cost of gas?
   b. How does the 10-gallon limit affect costs? Does it affect all people the same way?
7. Many freeway projects are designed to save time for shippers and commuters. Does an hour saved have the same value if it comes all at once as if it comes in 120 segments 30 seconds long? (Hint: What can you do with the time?)
8. Northwestern Mutual Life Insurance Company provides a free lunch for its approximately 2,000 employees who work in the home office in Milwaukee, Wisconsin. In what sense is this a free lunch? Distinguish clearly between price and cost.
9. Dental care can usually be obtained at university dental clinics for about half the price of going to a dentist in private practice. Most of the patients at such dental clinics are children, women, or elderly

persons. Can you develop an explanation for this observation using the concept of opportunity cost?

10. Board chairpersons of large corporations occasionally proclaim their support for wage and price guideposts and controls. Can you explain why such captains of industry would approve of government interference in the marketplace?

11. Say that your boss asks you to prepare a speech extolling the virtues of price controls as "protector of the little guy." Your boss will deliver the speech at the annual meeting of the National Independent Meatcutters Trade Association. After telling her you're not sure that small butchers fared very well during the 1972–1973 controls on meat prices, your boss says, "Well, then just write a speech about price controls that makes me look good." What theoretical arguments would be useful? What data would you look for? Suppose your boss gave you a $200 budget for telephone calls. Whom would you call? What questions would you ask?

12. Draw a demand curve for attendance at a private college. Analyze separately the impact of a tuition increase, a tuition subsidy at the nearby state college, and the discovery that the private college's graduates seldom get jobs.

13. List some of the factors underlying the demand for coffee. Divide the list into movement parameters and shift parameters. What is the impact of a frost in Brazil?

14. List some of the factors that determine the supply of rental apartments. Divide the list into movement parameters and shift parameters. What is the impact of a fire that destroys 10 percent of the apartments?

15. Is owning an iron a form of vertical integration? Is learning how to iron a form of vertical integration? Are gardening and snow shoveling forms of vertical integration?

16. Let's say that the government decides to promote jobs for teenagers.
    a. Use supply and demand curves to develop a list of effects resulting from the establishment of minimum wages above the market wage. Do you think minimum wages help teenage workers?
    b. Use supply and demand curves to analyze the impact of a job tax credit, under which the government pays employers 50 percent of the cost of hiring unskilled teenage workers.

17. Suppose you own a complex of apartment buildings in Texas. Your property tax liability is slashed by the passage of Question 7 in a general referendum vote. Your management team advises you to reduce rents in order to allow your tenants to share in the tax reduction. They claim that lowering rents will benefit the public and thereby build goodwill toward your firm. Do you agree with your management team? (Hint: What will happen if rents are lowered? Are you sure goodwill is enhanced? What badwill could be engendered? What extra decisions will you face after rents are lowered?)

18. Who rents a dwelling instead of owns? Why? What are the predictable effects of rent controls? Do rent controls protect the little guy?

19. You are given the assignment of pricing tickets for the New York Yankees. What are the likely effects of setting prices so low that there is excess demand for tickets? Would you expect your fans to appreciate the low prices? Do scalpers serve any economic purpose?

20. a. Suppose that the demand curve for a good corresponds to the following formula:

$$q = 400 - 5P$$

where

    q = quantity demanded
    P = product price

Compute a table of quantities for the good and their corresponding prices.

b. Now suppose that the supply curve for the good can be represented by the following formula:

$$q = 30 + 4P$$

Compute a table of the quantities supplied and their corresponding prices.

c. Find the equilibrium price and quantity for the good.

21. Suppose that the position of the supply curve in question 20 shifts upward, to twice its original height. Rewrite the supply equation, and then redo parts b and c of question 20.

22. a. Consider the information in question 20 again. Suppose that a price ceiling of $10 is placed on the product. Calculate the shortage or surplus that will resiult.

b. Using the information in question 21, calculate the shortage or surplus that will result from a price ceiling of $10.

c. Recalculate the shortage or surplus for the information in question 20 using a price ceiling of $40.

d. Using the $40 price ceiling and the information in question 21, what is the shortage or surplus.

23. Suppose that the position of the demand curve for a good is represented by the formula

$$q = 500 - 6P + 2W$$

where

    W = weather
    q = quantity demanded
    P = product price

a. Construct a table of quantities and prices when the weather variable equals 5.

b. Construct a table of quantities and prices when the weather variable equals 10.

c. Which way does the weather variable shift the demand curve?

d. Suppose that there is a shortage of 100 units when the weather variable equals 5. What is the shortage when the weather variable is 10? (Explain what you need to assume about the price in order to make your calculation.)

24. Draw supply and demand curves and note the equilibrium price and quantity in the market. Now assume that the curves both shift up to twice their original height. Draw in the new equilibrium and the new price and quantity traded.

25. Draw supply and demand curves and note the equilibrium price and quantity traded. Now assume that the supply curve slopes upward at twice the original slope. What must be true about the price and quantity? Can you place numerical limits on the resulting price and quantity? (Hint: Can the price be more than twice the original price?)

26. Draw supply and demand curves that intersect at a price of $10 and a quantity of 100 units. If a shift in the demand curve produces proportional changes in the price and quantity, what do we know about the supply curve?

27. Draw supply and demand curves that intersect at a price of $100 and a quantity of 100 units. Now suppose that a price ceiling is imposed that creates a shortage of 50 units but only a 10-percent change in the quantity supplied. How much did quantity demanded change?

28. Draw supply and demand curves that intersect at a price of $100 and a quantity demanded of 1,000 units. Suppose that a price *floor* of $200 is imposed and that the resulting surplus is 1,000 units.

a. If the quantity supplied rose by 400 units and the quantity demanded fell by 600 units due to the price floor (and the curves are straight lines), what would be the surplus if the floor were placed at $150?

b. What would be the shortage if the price floor were limited to $50?

Suggested Readings

Bain, Joe S. *Industrial Organization.* New York: Wiley, 1965.

Clarkson, Geoffrey P. *The Theory of Consumer Demand: A Critical Appraisal.* Englewood Cliffs, N.J.: Prentice-Hall, 1975.

Lipsey, R. G., and Steiner, P. O. *Economics.* 6th ed. New York: Harper & Row, 1981, chap. 5.

Marshall, Alfred. *Principles of Economics,* book 5. 8th ed. New York: Macmillan, 1961, chap. 3.

Spencer, Milton, *et al. Managerial Economics.* 4th ed. Homewood, Ill.: Irwin, 1975.

3

REASONING ON THE MARGIN

Chapter 2, which emphasizes market-wide forces, is the overture to this book. It sets the stage and gets us on common ground regarding an important foundation of economic analysis—supply and demand. Now we can ring up the curtain on a fundamental element of economic and business reasoning: thinking on the margin. Our focus now is the microeconomics of decision making.

Every course of action evokes benefits and costs arising directly from the decision itself; these benefits and costs are added to and subtracted from satisfaction, profit, or some other goal. Some examples of balancing benefits and costs:

Raising advertising outlays in the anticipation of increasing revenues even more.

Pulling the goalie late in the last period of hockey when the team is one point behind. Nothing is lost if the opposition scores another point; the potential gain lies in the greater probability of tying the score.

Lowering the air fare for customers willing to take one- or two-stop flights. Such pricing allows the airline to fill up planes, run fewer partially filled nonstop flights, and thereby enjoy a cost saving greater than the lost revenue per passenger.

Pricing off-peak electricity below peak-load electricity. Some consumers will switch part of their optional use to the off-peak period, thereby lowering the system's capacity requirements and overall system costs.

Jogging an extra half hour. Extra costs are incurred, such as time costs and wear and tear on shoe leather and hip joints, but extra benefits include additional cardiovascular exercise, use of additional calories, and exposure to a different environment. But some costs are not compounded by jogging for an extra half hour; changing clothes, showering, and traveling to the gym or trail must take place regardless of the time spent jogging. Only the extra costs count in deciding to run the extra time.

Decisions like these enter into every aspect of life.

The key to decision making is a proper comparison of the extra benefits and the extra costs of a decision. Managers use the word *marginal* as a synonym for *extra* or *additional*. Thus **marginal cost** is the extra cost arising from a decision, and **marginal benefit** is the extra benefit. Logically, an activity is worthwhile if it evokes more marginal benefits than marginal costs. Thus we take a giant step forward in decision making if we can school ourselves to think on the margin—that is, to take into account only those benefits and costs that vary with our decisions.

Marginalist reasoning (or marginalism) requires a disciplined mind. Managers must steadfastly ignore factors that do not change when a decision is made. The decision to shut down a plant must ignore the bank loan that must be paid whether or not the plant produces. The bank loan is a cost, to be sure, but it is not on the margin because it is not affected by the decision to shut down. Similarly, the decision to repair broken equipment must ignore the repair costs incurred on the same machines last month. Unless the repair decision is based solely on a comparison of the marginal costs and marginal benefits of the present decision, we may easily throw good money after bad. Last month's repair bill is a "sunk" cost; it is not a cost on the margin and therefore must be ignored in current-period decisions.

The term **incremental cost** is often used in place of *marginal cost* when lumpy, discrete decisions are involved. Hence the extra cost of a modest expansion of output (a small decision) is a marginal cost; the extra cost of adding a wing to the production plant or of taking out a $50 million loan (larger decisions) is referred to as an incremental cost. This book does not distinguish between these terms because they differ only in degree and because they both convey the critical idea in analysis—measuring extra costs. Moreover, a $50 million loan may be small to Chase Manhattan Bank but vital and quite lumpy to a brand-new export business in

Tecusa, Oklahoma. Thus *marginal* and *incremental* are used synonymously in this book.

Marginal Productivity: The Basis for Marginal Cost

A firm is a business organization that hires factors of production, combines the factors in a production process to create output, and sells the resulting output. We may assume that the firm organizes its production and sales activities in order to achieve maximum total profit.

Selecting the rate of production that will maximize profit requires knowledge about the extra cost incurred (our concern here) and extra revenue obtained when output is expanded. Suppose a firm expands output from 2,000 units per week to 2,001 per week. To produce the extra or marginal output, the firm must hire extra workers and other inputs. The marginal cost of producing the 2,001st unit therefore depends on how many more factors of production are needed and the prices of those factors. Let's assume that the individual firm cannot influence such factor prices as wage rates, interest rates, and prices of raw materials. Hence marginal cost depends on the technical relationship between changes in output and changes in inputs.

The **production function** represents our knowledge of the amount of final output that can be produced from specific combinations of inputs:

$$Q = f(a_1, a_2, a_3, \ldots, a_n) \tag{3.1}$$

where

$$Q = \text{physical units of final output produced}$$
$$a_i, \ldots, a_n = \text{the firm's productive inputs}$$

The simplest production function imaginable would involve one input and one output, such as a singer performing *a capella*. The input is the singer, and the output is the song. At the other extreme are firms that use many inputs in the production of multiple outputs, such as a farmer employing land, capital equipment, labor, fertilizer, and advanced technology to produce a wide variety of agricultural and dairy products. The middle ground between these extremes defines a production function in which the firm uses only two inputs to produce a single output. This compromise allows the main ideas of production theory to be expressed graphically within the limits imposed by two-dimensional paper. It also permits us to derive the important concepts inherent in all production analysis, which can then be extended conceptually (although not always geometrically) to the more complex cases of multiple input and output.

The simplified production function is written as follows:

$$Q = f(L, K) \tag{3.2}$$

where

Q = physical units of final output produced
L = units of labor
K = units of capital equipment

This apparent oversimplification of the two-input, one-output production function may be rationalized somewhat by regarding **labor** and **capital inputs** as broad surrogate groupings into which all inputs may be categorized. Thus labor represents all **variable inputs** of production: those factors that, like labor, can be easily added to or deleted from a production process in a relatively short period of time. Capital represents all **fixed inputs** not so easily varied, such as land, buildings, accesses, improvements, machinery, and equipment. Of course, labor is sometimes less variable than capital; tenured professors last longer than some buildings. Still, the labor/capital division allows us to study general propositions of production theory when some inputs are variable and others are not.

To get a better understanding of marginal productivity, let's travel again through the golden arches of a McDonald's hamburger emporium. You have seen McDonald's incredibly clean capital equipment (K)—the griddles, counter space, cash registers, tables and chairs, floor space, and refrigerators. You have also seen the workers (L), impeccably dressed and trained to a peak of cheerfulness and efficiency. And you have no doubt enjoyed McDonald's final output (Q)—a sandwich served in record time.

Suppose a particular McDonald's franchise hires only one worker. This worker would be required to perform all the tasks involved in the business, such as cleaning, unwrapping raw food, ordering from wholesalers, cooking, wrapping cooked food in paper, taking orders, serving, making change, and filling out the bank deposit forms. Let's say the worker can produce 10 hamburgers per hour under these conditions. If a second worker is hired, the manager presumably could assign the new worker to exactly the same set of tasks and thereby double the output to 20 hamburgers per hour. Instead, the manager will most likely divide the tasks so that each worker can specialize—perhaps one doing all of the cooking while the other waits on customers. Such a **division of labor** will result in the production of more than 20 hamburgers per hour, perhaps 30 hamburgers per hour.

This example illustrates a basic point in production theory: The division of tasks will raise workers' productivity. In the McDonald's example, an employee working alone produces 10 hamburgers;

adding a second worker yields 20 extra hamburgers, because of the economies of dividing up the tasks and allowing the workers to specialize their efforts.

The **marginal product of labor** (MP_L) is the change in output resulting from a one-unit change in the variable labor input, holding capital fixed:[1]

$$MP_L = \frac{\Delta Q}{\Delta L}\bigg|_K \qquad (3.3)$$

In the McDonald's example, the marginal product of the first worker is 10, and the marginal product of the second worker is 20; thus the division of tasks increased the labor force's marginal productivity.

The marginal product of labor cannot rise indefinitely by hiring additional workers and specializing their tasks, however, because of the fixed amount of capital. Eventually, the increases in marginal productivity resulting from specialization will be limited by the amount of capital each worker has to work with. As the McDonald's franchise hires more workers, it becomes increasingly difficult to find counter space to wrap sandwiches, walking space to fill orders, and punching space to operate the cash registers. In the extreme, the labor force could become immobilized by the presence of too many workers in a limited work space. Hence there are two important countervailing forces in production: efficiencies resulting from the division of tasks versus inefficiencies ultimately arising from congestion of the capital stock.

The marginal product curve for labor is illustrated in Figure 3.1, a graphical depiction of the empirically observed relationship between productive effort and results. Units of labor are measured on the horizontal axis, and the *extra* output generated by hiring one more worker—the marginal product of labor—is measured on the vertical axis. Whether marginal product rises or falls when the labor force is expanded depends on whether the efficiencies of task division are more or less important than the inefficiencies imposed by a fixed capital stock. As the labor force is expanded up to worker L_1 in Figure 3.1, the marginal product rises, because the division of labor is most important to productivity. But beginning with that worker and beyond, the marginal product of labor falls, because the capital constraint begins to assert itself.

One of the most widely publicized "laws" in economics—and perhaps the least understood—is the **law of diminishing returns** (or law of diminishing marginal product): When additional units of a variable factor are used in combination with a fixed factor, the increases in output that result must eventually become smaller and

---

1. The general notation $A|_{(x, y, z, \ldots)}$ is shorthand meaning that the calculation of A takes place holding the terms $(x, y, z, \ldots)$ fixed.

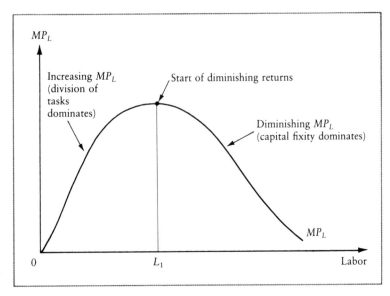

smaller. In Figure 3.1, diminishing returns begin with worker L_1.

Now that you have seen how McDonald's illustrates the marginal productivity principle, you may be able to apply it to many other production processes. Try these examples: bank services, libraries, dairies, homework, meetings, airport ticket counters, assembly lines, wheat farming, garbage collection. The key is to identify the variable and fixed factors of production. You should develop confidence in the general proposition that, whenever there are fixed inputs, the marginal product of the variable input will eventually diminish. This is an important point to remember when using the marginal product curve to derive the firm's marginal cost curve.

Marginal Cost

Marginal cost (MC) is the change in total cost (TC) resulting from a one-unit expansion in output:

$$MC = \frac{\Delta TC}{\Delta Q} \tag{3.4}$$

Marginal cost is the relevant cost concept in selecting the firm's correct rate of output, as we are soon to see. Thus if marginal cost can be determined with precision, or even only approximately, the manager can make output decisions by limiting cost considerations solely to those that vary with production.

The marginal cost curve is exhibited in Figure 3.2. Output is measured on the horizontal axis, and the extra cost of producing each additional unit—the marginal cost—is measured on the verti-

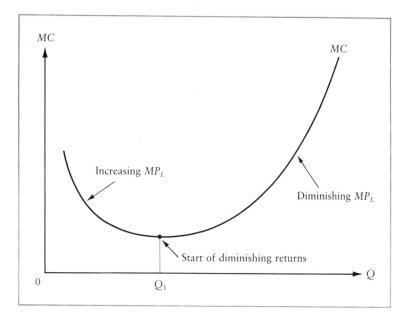

Figure 3.2
Marginal Cost Curve and Marginal Product of Labor
Marginal cost declines when MP_L rises. When labor's marginal product diminishes, marginal cost rises. Hence MC and MP_L are inversely related.

cal axis. Note that the additional cost of output expansion falls until unit Q_1 is produced, after which it is increasingly expensive to produce extra units of output. The reason that marginal cost gets lower at first and then starts to rise has to do with how effective the variable inputs are in producing output. In other words, marginal cost is tied directly to marginal productivity.

Let's assume that the firm can hire any number of workers at the same wage. Expanding the work force is the only way for the firm to increase output in a short-run period in which capital is fixed. If each new worker hired earns the same wage as all other workers but gives the firm larger and larger additions to its output, the new units of output are being produced at lower and lower marginal cost. When the marginal productivity of labor starts to diminish, marginal cost inevitably rises. Hence the marginal cost curve is just another reflection of marginal productivity. Marginal cost measures the financial consequences of the extra labor effort needed to produce extra output.

In Figure 3.2, each unit of output up to Q_1 is produced under conditions of increasing marginal productivity and (what is the same thing) decreasing marginal cost. Beyond output Q_1, capital fixity forces the marginal product to decline and the marginal cost therefore to rise. The previous conclusion—that the marginal product of labor must eventually fall—has its marginal cost analogue: Marginal cost must eventually rise.

The shapes of the marginal product and marginal cost curves are important in deriving some general principles of profit-maximizing behavior. The importance of marginal cost considerations in rational decision making will become clear as our analysis progresses.

Marginal Revenue

Now that we know how to think about the marginal cost of output expansion, we are ready to study marginal revenue. **Marginal revenue** (*MR*) is the change in total revenue (*TR*) that results from a one-unit expansion in output sold per time period:

$$MR = \frac{\Delta TR}{\Delta Q} \qquad (3.5)$$

Output expansion increases profit only if the marginal revenue exceeds the marginal cost of the decision.

Suppose your firm decides to increase its rate of output and sales by one unit per time period. What is the marginal revenue of this decision? The answer depends on the degree of monopoly power your firm enjoys. Marginalist reasoning helps us sort out these differences and come to a clear understanding of how revenue changes when output changes.

The most general way to think about marginal revenue is to see it as the algebraic difference of two terms:

$$MR = \begin{bmatrix} \text{price charged} \\ \text{for the} \\ \text{marginal unit} \end{bmatrix} - \begin{bmatrix} \text{revenue foregone on units} \\ \text{that could have sold} \\ \text{at higher prices} \end{bmatrix} \qquad (3.6)$$

One component of marginal revenue is the price received on the last unit sold. This is the first term in Equation 3.6. Every firm, regardless of its monopoly power or lack thereof, can count the price of the new output sold as part of its marginal revenue. Our real interest, however, lies in the second term in Equation 3.6. Will the firm have to lower its price on *all* units sold in order to induce consumers to buy a large quantity of output? If so, the marginal revenue will be the difference between the price of the last unit sold and the loss of revenue due to the price reductions on units that, save for the firm's desire to sell more output, could have yielded higher prices. Thus marginal revenue depends on the extent to which the firm has to lower prices on all units to capture new sales on the margin.

Let's examine two separate cases. Consider the competitive firm first. The main idea underlying **competition** is that each firm's output is so miniscule relative to industry output that the firm cannot influence industry price by expansion or contraction of its own production. For example, if there are 1,000 identical firms in a competitive industry and each firm produces 1,000 units of output per time period, then each firm holds a 1/1000 or 0.001 share of the market. If one firm expands its output by 10 percent to 1,100 units, its market share rises only to 0.00109. Such a tiny increase in output will not noticeably change the intersection of the industry supply and demand curves. Accordingly, the competitive firm cannot influence industry price and is merely a **price taker.** It is common to refer to this characteristic of competitive markets as **parametric pricing:** All firms accept the industry price as a parameter because they cannot influence it.

A competitive, price-taking firm can expand its rate of sales without changing price, and so the marginal revenue of an extra unit of sales is equal to product price. Thus the second term of Equation 3.6 is irrelevant and reduces to

$$MR = P \qquad (3.7)$$

marginal revenue for competitive firm

Figure 3.3 clarifies this result. Panel b shows the industry supply and demand curves for a competitively produced good. Each firm takes the equilibrium price, P, as a given. Panel a shows the demand curve facing any one of the industry's firms. The horizontal price line in panel a is the firm's demand curve; it expresses the chief implication of competition: The firm can sell various amounts of output without changing price.

Note that the downward-sloping demand curve in panel b is relevant for determining industry price but that the demand curve relevant to firm decision making is the horizontal line in panel a. A relatively small firm whose pricing policy is to charge the industry price can calculate the marginal revenue of its output expansion easily: Marginal revenue equals the price of each unit sold.

Now let's consider the marginal revenue of firms that have monopoly power. The essential distinction between a competitive

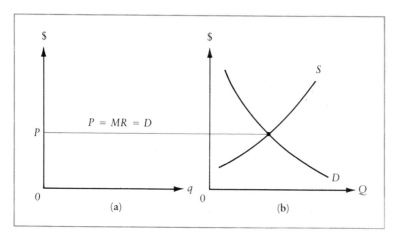

Figure 3.3
Marginal Revenue Curve for a Competitive Firm

(a) Marginal revenue for a competitive firm is constant and equals product price: $MR = P$.
(b) Industry supply and demand forces determine market price and hence the competitive marginal revenue.

firm and a monopoly firm lies in the demand curves and marginal revenue curves that the two firms face. The competitive firm faces a horizontal demand curve, and price equals marginal revenue. In contrast, the **monopolist** is the only firm in the industry and thus faces the industry demand curve. The monopolist must tie its price and output decisions directly to the demands of consumers. Therefore, marginal revenue no longer equals price, and the second term in Equation 3.6 becomes important.

Note, however, that this discussion pertains only to **simple monopoly**, in which the monopolist must sell its output to all customers at a uniform price. A monopolist may be tempted to charge higher prices for its product in areas exhibiting stronger demand. But if the monopolist's product is subject to arbitrage, differential pricing will break down. **Arbitrage** occurs when someone buys the monopolist's product at low prices and resells it in the high-priced market at prices that undercut the monopolist's prices. Arbitrage tends to equalize prices in all of the monopolist's markets. Thus a simple monopolist, being subject to arbitrage, charges uniform prices to all customers. Chapter 12 deals with price discrimination in monopoly pricing, in which the monopolist can separate markets, avoid arbitrage, and thereby charge different prices in different markets. In fact, some monopolists can charge the same customer different prices for different units of sales. Figure 3.4 shows the demand curve of a simple monopolist. (Ignore the curve labeled *MR* for now.) When the monopolist sets the price at $10, consumers buy 3 units per time period, and total revenue is $30. If the monopolist wants to sell 4 units per time period, it must lower price from $10 to $9. But bear in mind that pricing must be uniform; the price is $9 for unit 4 as well as for units 1 through 3, which could have been sold for $10 each. Thus total revenue is $36 when the price is $9.

Now we have two ways to think about marginal revenue. Using Equation 3.5, it is

$$MR = \frac{\Delta TR}{\Delta Q} = \frac{\$36 - \$30}{4 - 3} = \frac{\$6}{1} = \$6$$

Using Equation 3.6, it is

$$MR = \text{price of unit } 4 - \$1 \text{ loss each on units 1 through 3}$$

$$= \$9 - \$3$$

$$= \$6$$

Either way, $MR = \$6$. But the price of the fourth unit is $9. Hence we can derive a general principle for monopoly: $MR < P$.

Marginalist reasoning helps interpret this conclusion. Marginal

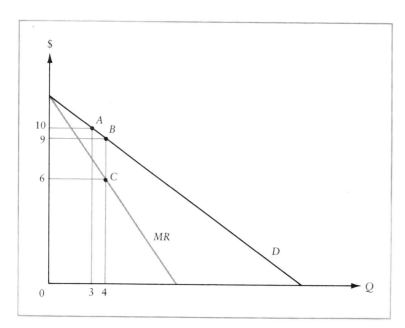

Figure 3.4
Marginal Revenue Curve for a
Monopolist

MR < *P* for the monopolist, because gaining extra sales requires a price reduction on all units sold per time period, not merely on the last unit sold.

revenue must be less than price in monopoly because the price must fall on all units in order to increase the flow of goods sold. Although revenue will be gained by selling the marginal unit (the first term in Equation 3.6), revenue will also be lost on the units that could have been sold at higher prices if the marginal unit of sales had not been desired (the second term in Equation 3.6). Marginal revenue is the balance of these two effects.

Clearly, marginal revenue can even be negative if the second term is greater than the first. In selecting price and output levels, the monopolist should avoid expanding output if such expansion will result in a negative marginal revenue.

The graphic equivalent of *MR* < *P* is shown in Figure 3.4. For every rate of output, the marginal revenue curve is lower than the demand curve. This wedge that monopoly drives between marginal revenue and price is a key factor in the social waste attributed to monopoly. We will return time and again to these issues throughout the book.

Marginal Rules for Profit Maximization

A man brings his Rolls Royce to a screeching halt in front of Chicago's O'Hare airport, runs to concourse B, gate 13, boards WTA flight 263 for Trinidad, and never sees his car again. How can we explain this behavior? Simple. The expected marginal benefit of the decision to abandon the automobile is greater than the expected marginal cost. Maybe the police are after him. Perhaps he is rushing to a tryst in Trinidad with a movie queen. Whatever the facts may

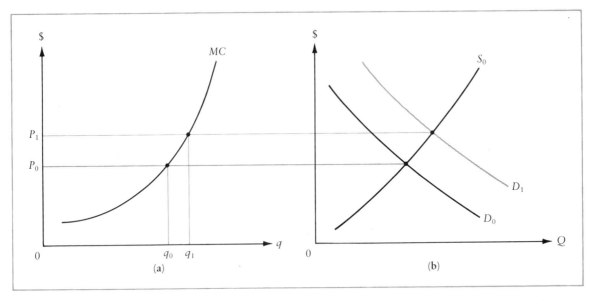

Figure 3.5
Profit Maximization for a
Competitive Firm

(a) $P = MC$ is the competitor's profit-maximizing condition. When the industry price is P_0, the firm produces q_0. **(b)** If the industry price rises to P_1 because of increased demand, the firm increases its quantity supplied to q_1. Since the marginal cost curve identifies the profit-maximizing quantity supplied at each price, it is the firm's supply curve.

be, the decision is rational if the marginal benefit of the decision exceeds its marginal cost. Most of us decide against abandoning our cars at airports for the opposite reason—marginal cost is greater than marginal benefit. Comparing these marginal values can tell us whether certain courses of action are prudent or foolish. Even when marginal benefits and costs cannot be measured precisely, we can still improve our decision making by using these marginalist ideas to get a feel for the choice at hand.

To devise a model of the competitive firm's rate-of-output decision, we may assume that the firm will make choices that maximize profit. Figure 3.5 depicts the rudiments of the competitive model. The industry supply and demand curves, S_0 and D_0 in panel b, determine the market price P_0; the competitive firm, depicted in panel a, faces a horizontal demand curve. Recall that price, demand, and marginal revenue are all the same for the competitive firm, a fact that follows from the competitive price-taking assumption. The marginal cost curve in Figure 3.5 is repeated from Figure 3.2. Its rise reflects the fixed capital stock that eventually causes each unit of output to be produced at a higher marginal cost.

Now we have the firm's marginal revenue and marginal cost of production together in the same diagram. How much output should the firm produce in order to maximize profit? The logic (if not the measurement) of the decision is simple. Profits rise whenever an extra unit of production adds more to revenues than to costs. Conversely, profits fall if an extra unit of output adds more to costs than to revenues. Because profits rise when $MR > MC$ and begin to fall as soon as $MC > MR$, it follows that profits are at a maximum when production is driven to the point where marginal revenue equals marginal cost. Since marginal revenue is price in competition, the rule for **profit maximization** is[2]

$$P \equiv MR = MC \qquad (3.8)$$

profit-maximizing rule for competition

When the price is P_0, the profit-maximizing rule is achieved at output q_0 in Figure 3.5. Profit will fall if output is either expanded or contracted from q_0. If output falls, the extra cost savings (MC) is less than the extra revenue forgone (MR, which equals P_0). If output rises above q_0, the extra costs incurred (MC) exceed the additional revenue obtained (MR, which still equals P_0). Hence, output q_0 is the best available to the firm because it is the only output for which marginal revenue equals marginal cost.

Now suppose the industry demand curve in Figure 3.5 rises to D_1. Product price rises to P_1, and the firm must change its rate of output in light of this new information. Output should be expanded to q_1, where $P_1 = MR = MC$. Now we can see the importance of the marginal cost concept. The competitive firm cannot influence the price of its product or the price it pays for its inputs. Its only control over profit is to adjust output and thereby make marginal cost equal to price.

Price changes force the competitive firm to slide along the marginal cost curve as it seeks the best output for a given price. Rising prices provide the profit incentive for the firm to move up the marginal cost curve by expanding output. When prices fall, the firm slides down its marginal cost curve and reduces output. Since the marginal cost curve identifies the quantities of output that the competitive firm desires to sell at all prices, it is in fact the firm's supply curve. (This generalization is qualified in Chapter 7.) For this reason, it is common for managerial economists to use the terms *marginal cost* and *competitive supply* synonymously.

The logic of profit maximization is the same for monopolists as for competitive firms, even though the diagram looks different. The monopolist's marginal revenue and marginal cost curves are drawn in Figure 3.6. Marginal revenue diminishes for the monopolist because the firm must lower prices on all units in order to expand sales. Marginal cost rises eventually due to diminishing marginal productivity. All units of output up to $\hat{Q}$ add to profits, because $MR > MC$. Any units sold in excess of $\hat{Q}$ worsen profit, because $MR < MC$. Thus profit is maximized by producing $\hat{Q}$, the only rate of output for which marginal revenue and marginal cost are equal.

$$MR = MC \qquad (3.9)$$

profit-maximizing rule for monopoly

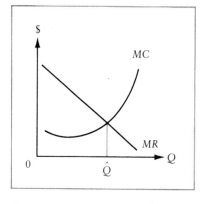

Figure 3.6
Profit Maximization for a Monopolist

$MR = MC$ is the monopolist's profit-maximizing condition. The monopolist can equate MR and MC by producing Q units per time period. Any other production rate would involve a loss of profit.

2. The first part of Equation 3.8 is read as "P is equal by definition to MR"; the $\equiv$ symbol denotes identity.

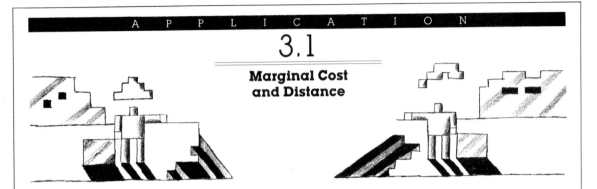

3.1

Marginal Cost and Distance

The usual economic model of firm behavior presented to students does not treat the element of distance. Yet in reality, the shipment of goods from one geographic area to another is important to profit maximization. Distance is costly; it imposes an additional marginal cost consideration that helps the firm determine what to produce and which customers to sell to. The management-science field known as "location theory" adds the question of where to produce to the time-honored trio—what to produce, how to produce, and for whom to produce.

The marginal cost of transportation is shown in Figure A as MC_{ship}, where d = distance from the firm. MC_{ship} rises with distance from the firm. Assume for ease that the marginal cost of production, MC_{prod}, is constant. Then the full marginal cost is $MC_{ship} + MC_{prod}$, derived by adding the two marginal cost components vertically. If the firm is competitive and faces price P, then the firm maximizes profit by shipping goods as far as distance d, which is the market boundary. The market boundary is set by the profit-maximizing condition $P = MC_{ship} + MC_{prod}$.

Now consider a firm producing two products with different marginal costs of shipping—corrugated paper board and glassine paper. The differences in shipping costs give these two paper products considerably different market structures.

Corrugated paper board consists of fluted paper lined on one or two sides with a flat sheet of paper, as illustrated in Figure B. Doubtless you have used such board formed into boxes to ship goods. Corrugated boxes are relatively lightweight and durable. But because of the fluting, corrugated paper itself is over 50 percent air. Rather than ship empty corrugated boxes (with even more air) long distances at high marginal cost, box manufacturers usually make them near their end use. Hence a firm that

needs corrugated boxes usually has only a few local container manufacturers to buy from; the market is regional and not national. The nature of the product and the marginal cost of shipping create a relatively small market boundary.

Glassine paper is a specialty paper used to wrap, among other things, the three most important food groups: junk food, ice cream, and sugar-coated cereals and crackers. It is sold in huge, tightly wrapped rolls (no air, as in corrugated paper

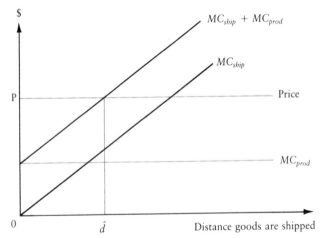

Figure A
Market Boundary and Marginal Cost of Shipping

MC_{ship} is the marginal cost of shipping goods; MC_{prod} is the marginal cost of producing goods. Since each cost component is incurred for shipped goods, the correct MC curve for decisions is their vertical sum, MC_{ship} $+ MC_{prod}$—given the price $P = MC$ at distance d, which defines the market boundary. Goods will not be shipped past distance d unless the price rises or the MC components fall.

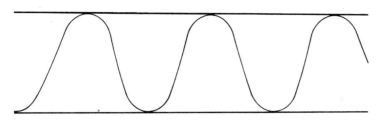

Figure B
Side View of Corrugated Paper
A layer of fluted paper is sandwiched between two flat pieces of paper.

board) and therefore has very low shipping costs per square foot. For this reason, suppliers sell glassine paper much farther from the point of production. As a result, the regional monopoly effect is less for glassine paper than for corrugated paper. It pays to ship glassine paper greater distances.

The basic principle, then, is as follows: The higher the marginal cost of shipping, the shorter shipping distances are. This is an intuitive conclusion. But we can go

farther and note that marginal costs of shipping also help determine a firm's product mix. Glassine paper is often coated with wax to make the shiny white waxed paper used for wrapping candy bars. But wax adds weight, which in turn affects shipping costs. So a paper company will often wax glassine paper for a nearby end user but sell the unwaxed paper to a distant firm (called a converter) that will wax the paper for a distant end user. Hence the marginal cost of shipping helps determine what the firm will sell, how products are produced, where they will be finished, and where they will be sold.

A Note on Terminology: Marginal, Inframarginal, and Extramarginal Units

At this point, it is appropriate to become acquainted with some language that will be used to clarify many aspects of economic analysis throughout the book. Refer to Figure 3.7. When price is P_0, unit Q_0 may be called the **marginal unit;** the marginal cost of unit Q_0 equals price. All units up to but not including unit Q_0 are **inframarginal units,** because for each of these units the marginal cost is less than price. Each inframarginal unit provides the firm a surplus and is therefore profitably produced. But all units in excess of the unit Q_0 are **extramarginal units** and will not be produced, because marginal cost exceeds price.

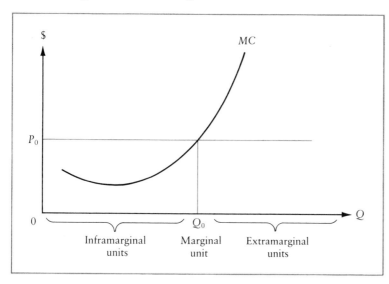

Figure 3.7
Marginal, Inframarginal, and Extramarginal Units

When price is P_0, the firm produces all units up to Q_0. The Q_0th unit is the marginal unit, because the price received for it equals the marginal cost of producing it. Units between 0 and Q_0 are inframarginal. The firm earns a surplus on these because $P > MC$. Units in excess of Q_0 are extramarginal and will not be produced, because $P < MC$.

Thus at a given price, units of output are either marginal, inframarginal, or extramarginal. The marginal unit is just worthwhile; the inframarginal units provide a surplus to the firm; and the extramarginal units are not produced. Note carefully that these concepts are defined in relation to "a given price."

Using Marginal Curves to Measure Total Magnitudes

Suppose your firm's output responds to changes in its labor force in the manner depicted in Table 3.1. As the work force expands, output can be recorded in two ways: as either the additional output that each worker contributes to the firm (marginal product) or the total units produced by each work force. The two measures are related, of course, because the total output must equal the sum of the individual marginal products for each worker. For example, the total output from four workers is[3]

$$Q(4) = \sum_{i=1}^{4} MP_i = 30 + 10 + 5 + 3 = 48$$

Given the marginal product data like those in Table 3.1, total output can be computed by summing the marginal products.

This fact establishes a convenient graphic rule: The area beneath a marginal curve measures the related total magnitude. For example, Figure 3.8a shows the marginal revenue of a competitive firm. If the firm sells Q_0 units of output at a price of P each, the total revenue equals the area beneath the marginal revenue curve up to Q_0 units, or area $0PAQ_0$. Similarly, a monopolist facing the negatively sloped marginal revenue curve in Figure 3.8b and selling Q_1 units earns a total revenue equal to the area beneath the curve, or area $0ABQ_1$.

Table 3.1

Marginal Product of Labor and Total Output

Workers (L)	Marginal Product (MP)	Total Output (Q)
1	30	30
2	10	40
3	5	45
4	3	48
5	0	48

Figure 3.8
Using Marginal Curves to Measure Total Magnitudes

(a) A competitive firm selling Q_0 units at price P earns a total revenue of $0PAQ_0$, which is the area beneath the marginal revenue curve. **(b)** A monopolist faces a negatively sloped marginal revenue curve. When Q_1 units are sold, total revenue is $0ABQ_1$, the area beneath the marginal revenue curve.

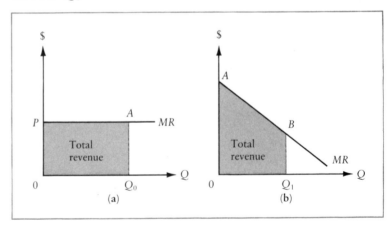

3. The symbol Σ, the Greek letter sigma, means "addemallup." The subscript $i = 1$ combined with the superscript 4 means that summation covers the marginal product of the first through fourth workers. The i used here is a code, called an index, that helps identify marginal products.

3.2

Marginal Principles and the Coordination of Activities within Firms

We have studied the marginal rules for profit maximization using the simple assumption that marginal cost includes only the extra cost of getting new goods produced. However, the typical firm must coordinate many activities, all of which may add to costs when output is expanded. The firm must coordinate its production of goods with its sales staff, advertising department, personnel office, and so forth. When output expansion changes the cost in other divisions of the firm, the marginalist principle of profit maximization becomes more complicated, although the essence remains the same.

Suppose a firm seeking the profit-maximizing rate of output has two distinct cost components—the costs of production and the cost of selling the goods once they are produced. Figure A diagrams the logic of profit maximization. The marginal cost curve of production, MC_{prod}, and the marginal cost curve for selling, MC_{sell}, are depicted separately. They both slope upward because of the increased effort needed to produce and sell additional units of output.

The marginal cost curve relevant to decision making is the curve labeled $MC = \Sigma_v(MC_{prod} + MC_{sell})$. It is derived by **vertical summation.**[*] For each rate of output, the firm's marginal cost is the vertical sum of the extra costs incurred in both departments. Vertical summation is appropriate because both departments incur extra costs in placing the *same* unit on the market. Production and sales are complementary activities.

The firm's marginal revenue curve is labeled MR. The profit-maximizing rate of output is Q_1, where $MR = MC$. But bear in mind that there is no reason why

[*]The symbol Σ_v denotes vertical summation; Σ_h denotes horizontal summation.

MC_{prod} must equal MC_{sell} at Q_1. For example, at Q_1, $\overline{Q_1A} < \overline{Q_1B}$. This fact is not a departure from the equal marginal cost principle; it merely indicates that neither component by itself is a proper measure of marginal cost. This example illustrates how managers must add structural realism to simple economic models in order to make them useful for decision making.

Vertical summation is needed to derive the marginal cost curve

Figure A
Marginal Cost When Cost Components Are Complements
Producing and selling goods are complementary activities. Hence, full marginal cost is the vertical summation of the marginal costs of selling and production.

in problems like this one because selling and production costs are incurred on each unit of output. Now let's extend the example to see how the equal marginal cost principle and the profit-maximizing marginal rules combine to determine the firm's best rate of production when its output is produced in one location but can be sold in two separate market areas. Selling a unit of output in one market is a substitute for selling the same unit in the second market.

Figure B illustrates how the correct marginal cost curve is derived to organize decision making. The left-hand panel and the center panel contain the marginal cost curves for selling in markets 1 and 2, labeled $MC_{sell\,1}$ and $MC_{sell\,2}$, respectively. (There is no reason why these curves should have the same slopes.) The firm will seek to satisfy the equal marginal cost principle for each rate of output, because selling at different marginal costs

Continued on page 52

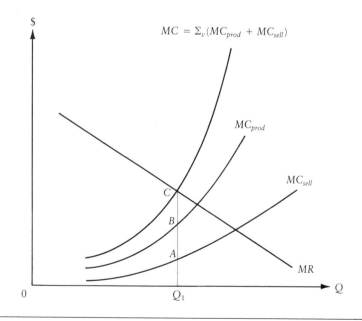

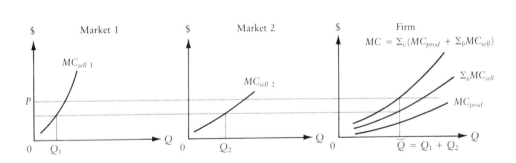

Figure B
Marginal Cost When Sales Occur in Two Markets

The $MC_{sell\,1}$ and $MC_{sell\,2}$ curves are summed horizontally to obtain $\Sigma_h MC_{sell}$. The MC_{prod} and $\Sigma_h MC_{sell}$ curves are summed vertically to obtain $MC = \Sigma_v(MC_{prod} + \Sigma_h MC_{sell})$. $P = MC$ yields the profit-maximizing output Q. The output sales components Q_1 and Q_2 are determined by equating $MC_{sell\,1}$ and $MC_{sell\,2}$ and $Q_1 + Q_2 = Q$.

fails to minimize total cost for a given rate of sales. Thus we can derive the firm's marginal cost curve of selling by **horizontal summation.** The curve labeled $\Sigma_h MC_{sell}$ in the right-hand panel is

the horizontal sum of $MC_{sell\,1}$ and $MC_{sell\,2}$. Each point on the $\Sigma_h MC_{sell}$ curve is the sum of the units of output the firm will sell in both markets at each marginal cost, under the assumption that the equal marginal cost principle is satisfied at all times.

Now consider the right-hand panel of Figure B more carefully. To obtain the correct marginal cost curve for decision making, the manager must add the production costs to the selling costs. This requires vertically summing MC_{prod} and $\Sigma_h MC_{sell}$ to obtain the full marginal cost, labeled $MC = \Sigma_v(MC_{prod} + \Sigma_h MC_{sell})$.

With the curves in place, we can discuss the firm's decisions.

Suppose the firm receives the same price for goods sold in both markets, depicted in Figure B by the horizontal price line P. Profit-maximizing output is $\overline{Q}$ in the right-hand panel, where $P = MC$. Of the total output $\overline{Q}$, Q_1 is sold in market 1 and Q_2 is sold in market 2. This division of sales is determined by equating $MC_{sell\,1}$ and $MC_{sell\,2}$. Thus, $\overline{Q} = Q_1 + Q_2$.

Marginal rules help identify both the best rate of production and the best allocation of sales effort. Note that the equal marginal cost principle is intact for a multimarket selling effort. However, as in Figure A, it does not hold for production and selling, which are complements.

Equal Marginal Cost Principle

Any given rate of industry output will be produced at the lowest possible total cost when all firms or plants produce at the same marginal cost (the **equal marginal cost principle**). This is true whether we consider many privately owned competitive firms or a single firm using several plants to produce goods. Total production costs are minimized for a given output when marginal cost is equal in all firms or plants:

$$MC_1 = MC_2 = \ldots = MC_n \qquad (3.10)$$

To see why cost minimization requires equal marginal costs at all points of production, assume that marginal costs are not equal in two of a firm's n plants. Figure 3.9 depicts the marginal cost curves of plant 1 and plant 2. Plant 1 (panel a) produces 50 units of output at a marginal cost of $5, and plant 2 (panel b) produces 100 units

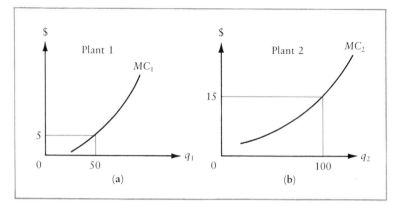

Figure 3.9
Equal Marginal Cost Principle
If a firm produces in multiple plants, each rate of output is produced at least cost when the marginal cost is equal in all plants. The rule is violated here, so costs can be reduced by transferring some production from plant 2 **(b)** to plant 1 **(a)**.

at a marginal cost of $15. If a unit of output could be shifted from plant 2 to plant 1, the combined output would remain the same but the total cost of production would fall by $10. This is because the total cost in plant 1 rises by $5 and the total cost in plant 2 falls by $15.

Whenever marginal costs in all plants are not equal, total cost reductions can be achieved by transferring output from plants with high marginal costs to plants with lower marginal costs. When marginal costs in all plants are equal, the firm's total costs are minimized for that level of output.

Equal Marginal Revenue Principle

We know that equating the marginal costs of production for all firms or plants minimizes the total cost of production. We may now consider the companion revenue concept, the **equal marginal revenue principle.** Suppose a firm is able to sell its output in various markets around the world. The total revenue from the sale of a given quantity of output will be maximized when the marginal revenues are equal in all markets, or when

$$MR_1 = MR_2 = \ldots = MR_n \qquad (3.11)$$

To prove the assertion, consider a counterexample in which marginal revenues are not the same. Figure 3.10 shows a firm's marginal revenue curves for output sold in two separate markets. The firm sells 25 units of output in market 1 and receives a marginal revenue of $30 for the last unit sold. In market 2, 100 units are sold at a marginal revenue of $20. If the firm could transfer a unit of sales from market 2 to market 1, total revenue would rise on balance, because marginal revenue is highest in market 1. Specifically, total revenue would rise by $10: The firm would give up the marginal

3.3

Grocers and the Equal Marginal Revenue Principle

The grocery store can be viewed as a multiproduct firm selling thousands of items or as a single-product firm selling space. The manager of a grocery store selling space can use the equal marginal revenue principle not only to determine how much space to supply but also how to allocate space to each item.

To start simply, suppose the grocer has a store of a given size, stocks only two products (Cheerios and Wheaties), and devotes the same shelf space to each product. The marginal revenue of Cheerios is best interpreted as the change in total revenue due to a change in the shelf space devoted to Cheerios. The same is true for Wheaties. The marginal revenue of shelf space for each cereal is a function of the difference between wholesale and retail prices and the length of time each box sits on the shelf. Assuming the markup to be identical for both products, the marginal revenue of space is solely a function of sales per foot of shelf space per unit of time.

The grocer cannot violate the equal marginal revenue principle without sacrificing profit. If Cheerios sales are brisker than Wheaties sales, the marginal revenue of space devoted to Cheerios exceeds that devoted to Wheaties. The manager should devote more space to Cheerios than to Wheaties until the marginal revenues are equal. Only then is the shelf space being used efficiently.

The principle extends quite readily to more goods. Suppose a sales representative for a dog food company convinces the grocery store manager that the marginal revenue of dog food is higher than the equalized marginal revenues of Cheerios and Wheaties. Then dog food should be added to the product line and space reshuffled between dog food and the two cereals until their marginal revenues are equal. Items with lower marginal revenues are not added to the store's product line. In the same way, the marginal revenues of shelf space can be equated for all products carried by the store.

The limit on total shelf space is itself artificial. By building shelves higher or longer or by knocking out walls for expansion, more shelving can be provided. Such expansion is profitable if the equalized marginal revenues for all products exceeds the marginal cost of expansion. Once the store has been expanded, shelf space once again should be allocated until marginal revenues are equal.

But how would the grocer discover these principles without reading this page? Merely by observation! The rate at which customers remove products from the shelves determines the marginal revenue of shelf space. If one item runs out faster than the others, the grocer quickly learns that more shelf space must be devoted to the faster-selling good and less to the others. The grocer, through step-by-step comparisons of the flow of revenue from adjacent products, approaches the profit-maximizing space allocation without even formally trying to.

Just as the billiard player learns through practice how balls bounce and carom, the grocer learns to maximize profits. The billiard player learns an element of physics; the grocer learns the equal marginal revenue principle. Their individual success depends on how quickly they learn these lessons and how comprehensively they can apply them. But both would benefit from a systematic introduction to the principles governing their business; this is why you are taking a course on managerial economics and why billiard players take advice from better players.

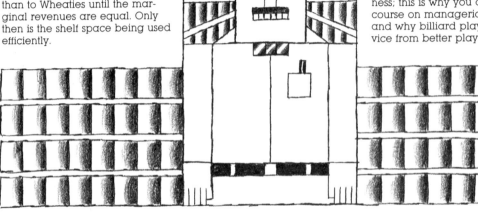

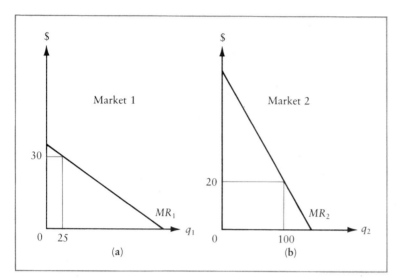

Figure 3.10
Equal Marginal Revenue Principle

A firm's total revenue is maximized for a given output when the marginal revenue is equal in all markets. Output sales should be switched from market 1 **(a)** to market 2 **(b)** until $MR_1 = MR_2$.

revenue of $20 in market 1 but would gain marginal revenue of $30 in market 1. The total revenue increases each time the firm transfers sales from a market with lower marginal revenue to one with higher marginal revenue. All such gains in total revenue are exhausted when the marginal revenue is the same in all markets.

Summary

Marginalist reasoning is at center stage in managerial economics, and that's why marginal analysis has been introduced at the earliest possible place in this book. The central theme of marginalist reasoning is the comparison of the extra benefits and costs of each decision. Part of decision making is deciding which costs and benefits will change with the decision and which ones will not. Developing an instinct that quickly identifies the costs and benefits of a course of action that are truly marginal will advance your management skills as much as the application of any other economic principle.

This chapter starts the development of marginalist reasoning. Look for this theme in every following chapter as well, for its importance can scarcely be overstated.

Problems

1. Fast Foods, Inc. offers birthday parties for children under ten years of age. The food is purchased at regular prices, but a free cake and free table service is provided, along with assorted party favors. Yet the parties are very profitable. Use marginalist reasoning to explain.

2. The student body of an urban university includes an increasingly higher percentage of older students. The school decides that it can serve them at greater profit by holding Saturday classes. But traditional students, ages eighteen to twenty-one, avoid Saturday classes

Key Terms

arbitrage 44
capital inputs 38
competition 42
division of labor 38
equal marginal cost principle 52
equal marginal revenue principle 53
extramarginal units 49
fixed inputs 38
horizontal summation 52
incremental cost 36
inframarginal units 49
labor 38
law of diminishing returns 39
·marginal benefit 36
marginal cost 36
marginalist reasoning 36
marginal product of labor 39
marginal revenue 42
marginal unit 49
monopolist 44
parametric pricing 43
price taker 43
production function 37
profit maximization 47
simple monopoly 44
variable inputs 38
vertical summation 51

like the plague. Use marginalist reasoning to demonstrate that older students are cheaper to educate.

3. List the fixed and variable factors of production in wheat farming; at airport ticket counters. Use your lists to illustrate the law of diminishing returns.

4. To draw a marginal cost curve sensibly, your axes must be carefully chosen. Draw marginal cost curves for the following, and state clearly your reasons for choosing the output measure on the horizontal axes of these curves:
   a. Library services
   b. Garbage collection
   c. Textbook writing

5. Is your fifty-year-old brilliant, aging, energetic, breathless, experienced, out-of-date professor a marginal, inframarginal, or extramarginal member of the faculty? Explain your answer.

6. Raw lumber undergoes considerable weight reduction in the early stages of its transformation into finished lumber. Would you expect to find lumber milling near the trees or near the end use? (Refer to the glassine/corrugated paper example in the chapter.)

7. Bulk milk is shipped long distances before being packaged for the resale market. Why not package it right at the dairy farm?

8. Explain why the marginal cost of two plants should be equal whereas the marginal cost of successive stages of production must be added to measure total marginal cost.

9. Department stores have both permanent and portable display cases. During the 1982 recession, there was noticeably more room in department stores. Why would they reduce their sales effort when sales fell off?

10. The coal and ore used in iron and steel fabrication weighs much less than the final product. Use this fact to explain the location of steel factories.

11. Use the location of steel factories to explain the location of automobile parts plants.

12. Automobiles are assembled close to the point of sale, but parts are not. Why aren't cars assembled where the parts are made?

13. Suppose the grocer in Application 3.3 discovers that the marginal revenue of the first foot of shelf space devoted to canned soup is less than the marginal revenue of the tenth foot devoted to Captain Crunch. What should happen according to the principle of equal marginal revenue?

14. Suppose that a firm operates two plants that produce pulp paper and that the firm hires an outside firm to market its product for a fee of $10 per ton. Draw the firm's marginal cost curves and derive the equilibrium value for the firm if the market price is $20 per ton.

15. Draw the individual marginal cost curves and their sum for a firm that produces a product, exerts sales efforts, and pays a tax per unit sold.

16. Draw a marginal cost curve and a price line at the $5 level that intersects the MC curve at the quantity of 500 units. Now suppose that the curve rises to twice its original height. What limits can you

place on the shift in the quantity produced? (Hint: Will the quantity produced fall by 50 percent?)

17. Draw a marginal cost curve and a price line at the $10 level that intersects the *MC* curve at the quantity of 100 units. Suppose that the price rises by $1 and that the quantity produced rises by 10 units. What will happen if the price rises by another dollar?

18. Draw two horizontally aligned marginal cost curves for two breweries operated by a beer producer. Suppose that the marginal cost curve for one of the plants falls by half its original height following the replacement of obsolete equipment.
    a. What will happen to the amount of beer produced in each plant?
    b. What will happen to the total amount of beer produced by the firm?
    c. What numerical limits can you place on the answers to parts a and b?

19. Suppose that the demand curve facing a firm is represented by the formula $P = 200 - Q$ and that the marginal cost curve is represented by the formula $MC = 30 + 5Q$. Derive a table of the firm's total revenue, marginal revenue, and marginal cost and indicate which level of output maximizes profit.

20. Suppose that the demand curve for a firm's product is horizontal at $5. What is the area under the marginal revenue curve when 50 units are sold?

21. Suppose that the demand curve facing a firm is represented by the formula $P = 500 - Q$. What is the area under the marginal revenue curve when 400 units are sold?

22. Suppose that the marginal cost in one plant is $5 and that the marginal cost in another is $10. How much money can be saved by reallocating one unit of production?

23. Suppose a firm faces a demand curve represented by the formula $P = 600 - 2Q$, a marginal cost of selling represented by the formula $MC_{sell} = 10 + 5Q$, and a marginal cost of production represented by the formula $MC_{prod} = 20 + 6Q$. Draw a table that can be used to calculate the profit-maximizing level of price and output.

24. Suppose the marginal revenue in one market is $10 and $40 in another.
    a. If the product is subject to instantaneous resale, how much additional revenue can be earned by rearranging the sales in the two markets?
    b. What if there is no possibility of resale?

25. Redraw Figure B from Application 3.2. Suppose the marginal cost of selling in market 2 rises to twice its original height. Make all of the associated shifts on your diagram and derive the new equilibrium output levels.

26. Redraw Figure B from Application 3.2. Suppose that the price of the product rises to twice its original height. Make all of the associated shifts on your diagram and derive the new equilibrium output levels.
    a. Will the output be more or less than twice the previous amount?

b. What property of marginal cost curves allows you to answer part a?

27. Redraw Figure A from Application 3.1. Suppose that the product price rises to twice its original height.
    a. What will happen to the distance that goods are shipped?
    b. Will that distance be more or less than twice the original distance?
    c. What properties of economics allow you to answer part b?

28. Redraw Figure 3.6. Suppose that the demand curve associated with the marginal revenue curve in Figure 3.6 rises to twice its original height. Redraw the marginal revenue curve to correspond to the change in the demand curve.

29. Redraw Figure 3.2 and add a price line that intersects the marginal cost curve twice—once in the downward-sloping portion and again in the upward-sloping portion. Why will the firm operate at only one of the intersections?

30. Redraw Figure 3.2. Suppose that the marginal cost of production falls to half its original height. Make all of the associated shifts on your diagram and derive the new equilibrium output.

Suggested Readings

Baumol, William. *Economic Theory and Operations Analysis*. 4th ed. Englewood Cliffs, N.J.: Prentice-Hall, 1977.

Hirschleifer, Jack. "The Firm's Cost Function: A Successful Reconstruction." *Journal of Business*, July 1962, pp. 235–255.

Naylor, Thomas H., and Vernon, John M. *Microeconomics and Decision Models of the Firm*. New York: Harcourt Brace Jovanovich, 1969.

Sherman, Roger. *The Economics of Industry*. Boston: Little, Brown, 1974.

4

DEMAND FUNCTIONS AND ELASTICITIES

Chapters 2 and 3 presented a broad overview of managerial microeconomic analysis, focusing on two powerful ideas: market forces (Chapter 2) and marginalist reasoning (Chapter 3). The topic of market demand is prominent in these chapters. With the rudiments of demand analysis already in place, we may now deepen our understanding of the concept and apply it to many areas of vital interest to managers.

Successful, profitable business enterprise requires firms to identify product lines that are valued by consumers. Even with expert management, well-trained sales forces, and efficient production lines, firms cannot earn a profit unless buyers are willing to purchase the firm's products. Demand and the associated generation of revenue are key components of business profit. Thus the relationship between demand curves and sales revenue is of central concern in this chapter.

Identifying the Appropriate Demand Curve

Managers must have a firm grasp of the concept of demand and how it applies to their decision making. But there are several kinds of demand curves, and the key to understanding and applying demand analysis is the identification of the appropriate demand curve for the problem at hand. Three demand curves concern us here: the individual consumer demand curve, the industry demand curve, and the firm-relevant demand curve.

Individual Consumer Demand Curve

The basic building block in the theory of demand is the demand curve of an individual consumer. This concept is presented on an intuitive basis in Chapter 2. Economists have left few stones unturned in developing rigorous theoretical models of consumer behavior.[1] These theories are beyond the scope of this book and largely unnecessary for managerial decisions. However, their major conclusions about the slope of the individual demand curve are useful. Specifically, these theories state that demand curves are always negatively sloped.

When the price of good X rises, *ceteris paribus*, the consumer is affected in two principal ways. First, the price increase makes good X a relatively poorer bargain compared with its substitutes, so the consumer substitutes other goods for X. This is the **substitution effect of a price change.** Also, the consumer's real income (purchasing power) is reduced, because the higher price uses up money resources that the consumer could use to purchase other commodities. This is the **income effect of a price change.** Thus when the price of X changes, *ceteris paribus*, the ultimate effect on the consumer's quantity demanded is the sum of these two effects. Let's examine each in more detail.

SUBSTITUTION EFFECT   The substitution effect owes its existence to the fact that most human wants can be met in various ways. If the price of Coca-Cola falls, *ceteris paribus*, the consumer buys more of it and less of the alternatives, because Coca-Cola has become a relatively less costly method of slaking thirst.

The substitution effect always moves in the direction opposite to the price change. If the price of X falls, the consumer's quantity of X demanded rises. If the price of X rises, the substitution effect reduces the quantity of X demanded.

INCOME EFFECT   If the price of X rises, *ceteris paribus*, the consumer's real purchasing power is cut, because the buyer would not have enough income to buy the same combination of goods as before. Hence a price change, in effect, alters the real purchasing power of the consumer. How will a consumer respond when a price change for good X modifies purchasing power?

---

1. See Chapter 3 in Steven T. Call and William L. Holahan, *Intermediate Microeconomics*, 2nd ed. (Belmont, Calif.: Wadsworth, 1983) for a rigorous treatment of cardinal and ordinal utility theory.

For purposes of understanding the income effect, it is useful to categorize products as either **normal goods** or **inferior goods.** A good is normal if an *increase* in income leads the consumer to *increase* the quantity of the good purchased. Consider solid oak chairs, no doubt a normal good for most families. If the price of oak chairs falls, quantity demanded rises, because the substitution effect and the income effect are reinforcing. The substitution effect causes oak chairs to be substituted for wicker, rattan, vinyl, and beanbag chairs. In addition, the higher real income caused by the price reduction encourages an increase in the quantity of oak chairs demanded. Thus the demand curve for a normal good is negatively sloped; the income and substitution effects of a price cut both work to increase quantity demanded.

A good is inferior if an increase in income reduces the consumer's quantity demanded (and vice versa). For example, generic canned goods and chicken necks are goods that consumers are less likely to buy when their income increases. Theoretically, demand curves for inferior goods could be positively sloped, although empirically they never are. Suppose the price of chicken necks falls, *ceteris paribus*. Now the substitution and income effects are at cross-purposes. The consumer increases the quantity demanded by substituting chicken necks for other food items. If the income effect were ignored, the demand curve would be negatively sloped solely because of the substitution effect. However, the price reduction increases real purchasing power, and because of the income effect for an inferior good, the quantity of chicken necks demanded is reduced.

Whether or not the demand curve for an inferior good exhibits the standard negative slope depends on which of these two effects is greater. If the substitution effect of an inferior good is larger than the income effect, the demand curve slopes downward and the law of demand is intact. Only a very powerful income effect, large enough to more than offset the substitution effect, could produce a positively sloped demand curve.

Consumer theory is unable to rule out the possibility of upward-sloping demand curves because theoretically the income effect of an inferior good could exceed the substitution effect. Goods that fall into this category are called **Giffen goods.** However, such demand curves are seldom, if ever, observed. Thus the law of demand is not deduced from any theory of consumer behavior but is generalized from the complete lack of empirical evidence of positively sloped demand curves. (The famous Giffen good, a supposed exception to the law of demand, has created far more interest among economic historians trying to identify Mr. Giffen, the unverified discoverer of the phenomenon, than among research economists looking for an upward-sloping demand curve.)

Industry Demand Curve

Individual demand curves are merely the starting point in demand analysis. One person's demand for Mary Washington asparagus, the queen of the vegetables, is thoroughly unimportant to business managers and managerial economists except as a point of departure. In contrast, the total demand of all asparagus buyers is important. We may gain insight into consumer behavior by studying individual demand curves, but we must realize that demand has more rewarding implications for decisions when individual demand curves are summed to produce the **industry demand curve.**

The industry demand curve is derived by horizontally summing individual demand curves. In Figure 4.1, the demand curves d_1 and d_2 represent the only two consumers in a particular market. Each point on the demand curve, D, is the horizontal sum of individual quantities demanded at a given price. Thus, adding horizontally, $A = a_1 + a_2$ at price P_1, and $B = b_1 + b_2$ at price P_2. The collection of all points like A and B defines the industry demand curve, labeled $D = \Sigma_h(d_1 + d_2)$. The industry demand curve slopes downward because both individual components do.

The industry demand curve incorporates those demand forces that intermingle with opposing industry supply forces to determine equilibrium price in a competitive market. The industry demand curve is also helpful to a monopoly firm. Since the monopolist does not have to divide the market among rival companies, it can employ

**Figure 4.1
Deriving the Market Demand
Curve from Individual Demand
Curves**

At each price, the horizontal positions of each demand curve are added to derive the aggregate curve.

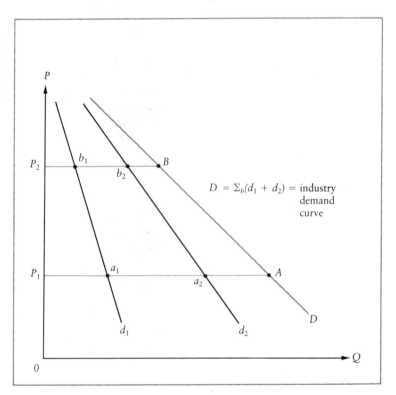

the industry demand curve to make pricing decisions. And government regulatory commissions use the industry demand curve in deciding on the correct means for regulating such public monopolies as electric, natural gas, and telephone companies. In addition, most studies of the elasticity of demand—a topic of this chapter— are related to industrywide demand functions.

Firm-Relevant Demand Curve

It is of paramount importance to decision making that managers have sufficient intuition and understanding to distinguish between the total industry demand curve and the demand curve facing their individual firms. Sometimes these demand curves are the same. Most often they are not.

If a firm has complete monopoly power, it does face the industry demand curve. But as Chapter 3 explains, a competitive, price-taking firm faces a horizontal demand curve even when the industry demand curve has the customary negative slope. This fact reflects the numerous substitutes available to customers buying a product in a competitive market.

Between competition and monopoly lie many other forms of market structure, which will occupy our attention in following chapters. For now, however, heed this general warning: Do not make *firm-level* decisions based on *industrywide* demand studies. Surely the demand for cigarettes in general is different from the demand for Camel cigarettes, since there are few substitutes for cigarettes per se but many substitutes for a particular brand.

4.1

Upward-Sloping Demand Curves?

Perhaps the most significant fact about demand is this intuitively obvious proposition: Consumers buy more at lower prices, *ceteris paribus*. Virtually all empirical demand studies verify this conclusion. Demand curves are negatively sloped.

Theoretically, of course, upward-sloping demand curves are a possibility. We have now encountered the Giffen good, an inferior good whose income effect exceeds its substitution effect.

There are other cases. For the good with "snob appeal," a higher price may be considered a positive attribute and itself a reason to buy more. Expensive wines, opulent automobiles, and designer jeans are examples. But the presence of buyers who are not motivated by snob appeal should be expected to offset the

demand by those who are. Some individuals who are susceptible to a good's snob appeal may have upward-sloping demand curves over a range of prices, but industry demand curves for these products will most likely be negatively sloped. There are usually buyers—not the least concerned about appearances—who would love to buy, say, a particular brand of high-society wine if only the price would fall sufficiently.

Another possible explanation of upward-sloping demand curves arises when consumers use price as an index of product quality. Since everyone knows that the

recipe and the average quality of the Big Mac are unchanging as a business practice, changes in price do not influence our expectations about quality. But consider another example—brain surgery. At $10 per operation, we are not interested in buying, because the low price affects our perceptions of the quality of the surgery. But for $5,000 per operation, we are more inclined to accept the operation. The demand curve for brain surgery— over some prices—may therefore be positive sloped, because price itself is a proxy for quality.

These exceptions to the law of demand are toy examples: fun to think about but never verified empirically. Managers may be confident that the demand curves for any products they are likely to produce will be negatively sloped.

4.2

Shifting the Industry Demand Curves for Electricity

The demand for any good depends in part on the price of its substitutes. Let's use this principle to see how demands for a product in different time periods influence each other.

Consider the demand for electricity. Consumption of electricity at 11 a.m. is a substitute for consumption at 8 p.m. The industry demand curves for electricity in the accompanying figure are the horizontal sums of individual electricity demand curves. Electricity is measured in kilowatt-hours (kwh). The initial demand curves are labeled D_0 in each panel. If a uniform price of P_0 is charged, regardless of the time of day, $\overline{P_0A}$ units are demanded at 11 a.m. and $\overline{P_0B}$ units are demanded at 8 p.m. Typically, more electricity is consumed during the peak-demand, daytime hours than during the evening, off-peak hours.

Suppose it is considered desirable to cut the daytime use of electricity and shift it to evening use. One way to accomplish this would be to raise the price for daytime use and lower the price on electricity consumed in the evening. We may do so in two steps:

1. Raise the 11 a.m. price to P_1. Daytime users will cut their quantities demanded to $\overline{P_1C}$ by moving from A to C along demand curve D_0. In addition, the 8 p.m. demand curve will shift to the

right, to the curve labeled D_1. The 11 a.m. price is a shift parameter in the 8 p.m. demand curve, because electricity uses at different times of the day are substitutes. As long as the 8 p.m. price remains at P_0, consumers will purchase $\overline{P_0E}$ kilowatts of electricity at 8 p.m.

2. Reduce the 8 p.m. price to P_2. This change causes the 8 p.m.

Peak-Load Pricing of Electricity

Peak-load pricing of electricity cuts down on its use during peak periods (like 11 a.m.) and shifts it to off-peak periods (like 8 p.m.).

quantity demanded to rise to $\overline{P_2F}$ along curve D_1. Also, the 11 a.m. demand curve shifts leftward, to the curve D_1, since there has been a reduction in the price of a substitute. Consumers buy $\overline{P_1G}$ kilowatts at 11 a.m.

The effect of pricing policies is to rearrange electricity purchases by time of day. But note that the increase in 8 p.m. purchases and the reduction in 11 a.m. purchases takes two forms: (1) movements *along* stationary demand curves, which take into account only the price change in each separate time period, and (2) shifts of both demand curves, which occur because each price is a shift parameter in the other demand curve. This is how time-of-day electricity pricing can rearrange some electricity usage from peak to off-peak periods.

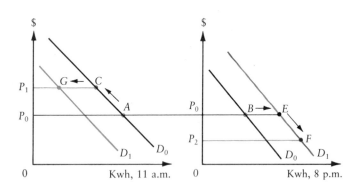

Demand Elasticities

Business managers need to have a feel for how consumer purchases are influenced by changing economic circumstances. Both the direction and the magnitude of the effects are important. If a sporting goods shop lowers the price of racquetballs, *ceteris paribus,* will it sell just a few more balls or attract an avalanche of new customers? Will higher relative prices for hospital rooms discourage just a few patients or many? And how will hospital revenues be affected? Will a recession that reduces consumers' incomes reduce or increase their demand for your product? And by how much? How many sales will your glue company lose if there is a reduction in the price of cellophane tape? Answers to such questions require more information about demand relationships than knowing merely the slopes of demand curves. We need a new concept—elasticity.

Elasticity is a fancy term for a simple idea: the responsiveness of a dependent variable to changes in an independent variable. Indeed, each time the meaning of the word *elasticity* begins to get away from you, an easy way to reel it back in is to substitute the word *responsiveness*.

The most general definition of elasticity (ε) is

$$\varepsilon = \frac{\% \, \Delta \text{ dependent variable}}{\% \, \Delta \text{ independent variable}} \bigg|_{(x, \, y, \, z, \, \ldots)} \tag{4.1}$$

Remember that the notation $A|_{(x, \, y, \, z, \, \ldots)}$ means that the calculation of A takes place holding the terms $(x, \, y, \, z, \, \ldots)$ fixed. Hence, elasticity focuses solely on the percentage changes in the dependent variable arising from a percentage change in one independent variable, *ceteris paribus,* that is, holding all other possible influences fixed.

Now let's turn to specific demand elasticities. Consider the following demand equation for good X:

$$X = f(P, I, P_Y, \ldots) \tag{4.2}$$

The dependent variable, X, is influenced by many independent variables. An elasticity can be calculated for each separate factor, *ceteris paribus.* Hence:

$$\text{Price elasticity} = \varepsilon_{XP} = \frac{\% \, \Delta X}{\% \, \Delta P} \bigg|_{(I, \, P_Y, \, \ldots)} \tag{4.3}$$

$$\text{Income elasticity} = \varepsilon_{XI} = \frac{\% \, \Delta X}{\% \, \Delta I} \bigg|_{(P, \, P_Y, \, \ldots)} \tag{4.4}$$

$$\text{Cross-price elasticity} = \varepsilon_{XP_Y} = \frac{\% \, \Delta X}{\% \, \Delta P_Y} \bigg|_{(P, \, I, \, \ldots)} \tag{4.5}$$

Any other demand elasticity, such as advertising, uses a similar formula.

Four points regarding elasticity require clarification. First, every elasticity is the ratio of percentage changes, with the dependent variable in the numerator and the independent variable in the denominator. A percentage change is the absolute change in a variable's value divided by the base value; hence, elasticity can be expressed as follows, using price elasticity of demand as a specific example:

$$\varepsilon_{XP} = \frac{\% \, \Delta X}{\% \, P} = \frac{\dfrac{\Delta X}{X}}{\dfrac{\Delta P}{P}} = \frac{\Delta X}{\Delta P} \cdot \frac{P}{X} \tag{4.6}$$

In the last part of Equation 4.6, elasticity is the product of two term: $\Delta X / \Delta P$, the inverse of the slope of the demand curve, and P/X, the ratio of bases. This formulation will prove useful as we proceed. All other elasticities take the same general form—the product of a slope term and a ratio of bases.

The second point about elasticity is that slope alone cannot be used to estimate responsiveness. For example, the most straight-forward expression of responsiveness of quantity demanded to price changes would appear to be the slope of the demand curve, $\Delta P / \Delta X$, or its inverse, $\Delta X / \Delta P$. However, slope has a major defect as an estimate of responsiveness: Its value depends on the units by which X and P are measured. Thus if price is measured in dollars in Figure 4.2, the slope of the demand curve between points A and B is -0.1; but if price is measured in cents, the slope is -10. Slope varies in cases like this because of arbitrary measurement choices; actual responsiveness does not change. Slope is a confusing measure, and so we use elasticity in its place, which eliminates the problem by measuring percentage changes rather than absolute changes.

Equation 4.6 demonstrates that elasticity and slope are not equivalent, although they are related. The term $\Delta X / \Delta P$, the inverse of slope, is one component of the elasticity formula. Multiplying the inverse of the slope by P/X produces a measure of responsiveness that is unaffected by arbitrary unit choices. Because elasticity compares percentage changes of X and P, it does not matter which units are selected. You can use Figure 4.2 to verify the previous sentence by computing the price elasticity of demand between A and B for both price measures. The slopes differ; the elasticities do not.

The third point to understand about elasticity is that the signs of the various elasticity coefficients are important. The price elasticity coefficient, ε_{XP}, is negative, because price changes cause changes in quantity demanded of the opposite direction. Even so, absolute values of price elasticities are frequently used for convenience, a convention adopted in this book. However, the income elasticity coefficient, ε_{XI}, is positive for normal goods and negative for inferior goods. The cross-price elasticity coefficient, ε_{XP_Y}, is positive when Y is a substitute for X and negative when Y is a complement.

The fourth point is that we can, at least conceptually, define an elasticity between any dependent and independent variables, such as the elasticity of housing starts with respect to increases in mortgage interest rates, the elasticity of car accidents with respect to higher travel speeds, or the elasticity of the waistline with respect to addi-

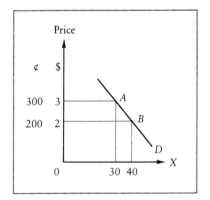

Figure 4.2
Measurement of Elasticity

It is essential to measure elasticity not as the slope of the demand curve but as the ratio of percentage changes in quantities divided by the percentage change in price. Otherwise, arbitrary measurement choices will distort the results.

tional consumption of chocolate bars. Our current topic is product demand, so the various demand elasticities—price, cross-price, and income—have been emphasized. The same concept is used later to estimate supply relationships, degrees of input substitutability, factor supply and demand responses, and so forth.

Study Equation 4.6, the formula for price elasticity of demand, to make sure you understand that it is a ratio of percentage changes. Then write out the cross-price and income demand elasticities using the form in Equation 4.6, as well as the elasticity formulas for housing starts, car accidents, and inches around the waist. Then you will be ready to proceed.

Price Elasticity of Demand and Total Revenue

Firms' **total revenue** (TR) is identical to consumers' **total expenditures** (TE). Both equal the number of units purchased times the price per unit and are opposite sides of the same transactions.

$$TR = TE = P \cdot X \tag{4.7}$$

How is total revenue influenced by a price reduction? If X, the quantity purchased, were to remain constant, a lower price would reduce total revenue. But the law of demand teaches us that a lower price will raise X, tending to raise total revenue. Every price change moves the quantity sold in the opposite direction. Whether total revenue rises, falls, or stays the same when price changes depends on how responsive X is to P. Thus, we must know the price elasticity of demand in order to estimate the effect of a price change on total revenue.

The absolute value of the price elasticity of demand is

$$|\varepsilon_{XP}| = \frac{\% \, \Delta X}{\% \, \Delta P} \tag{4.8}$$

Suppose a 1-percent price reduction causes a 20-percent increase in quantity sold. In this case, $|\varepsilon_{XP}| > 1$, because the numerator exceeds the denominator. Total revenue rises, because the upward pull on revenue due to sales expansion outweighs the downward pull due to the lower price. Quantity sold is thus quite responsive to price changes. In general, demand is **price elastic** if a price change leads to a change in total revenue of the opposite direction. $|\varepsilon_{XP}| > 1$ because the price change causes a greater-than-proportional change in quantity demanded.

If a 20-percent reduction in price generates only a 1-percent increase in units sold, total revenue falls, because the downward pull on revenue due to the lower price per unit is now relatively stronger than the upward pull from selling more X. In this case, $|\varepsilon_{XP}| < 1$, and the quantity sold is not very responsive to price changes. Demand is **price inelastic** if a price change leads to a change in total revenue of the same direction. $|\varepsilon_{XP}| < 1$ because the price change causes a less-than-proportional change in quantity demanded.

Finally, suppose a 1-percent reduction in price causes a 1-percent increase in quantity sold. Total revenue remains the same, and $|\varepsilon_{XP}| = 1$. Demand is **unit elastic** if a price change leaves total revenue unchanged. $|\varepsilon_{XP}| = 1$ because the price change and the resulting change in quantity demanded are proportional.

Table 4.1 summarizes these relationships between price elasticity of demand and total revenue.

Table 4.1
Total Revenue and Price Elasticity of Demand

If $|\varepsilon_{XP}|$	Demand Is	A Percentage Change in P	A Change in P
> 1	Price elastic	Causes a greater-than-proportional change in X	Causes TR in the opposite direction
< 1	Price inelastic	Causes a less-than-proportional change in X	Changes TR in the same direction
$= 1$	Unit elastic	Causes a proportional change in X	Does not change TR

Price Elasticity of Demand and Marginal Revenue

We have just learned intuitively about the relationships among price changes, total revenue changes, and price elasticity of demand. Here these relationships are formalized in a simple but useful formula, with special attention paid to the interpretation of revenue changes. The analysis proceeds systematically through four steps.

STEP 1.   Consider the move from A to B along the demand curve in Figure 4.3. Price must be lowered in order to sell more output. The total revenue at each point is price times quantity:

$$\text{Total revenue at } A = P \cdot X$$

$$\text{Total revenue at } B = (P + \Delta P)(X + \Delta X)$$

where
$$\Delta P < 0$$
$$\Delta X > 0$$

The change in total revenue from A to B is

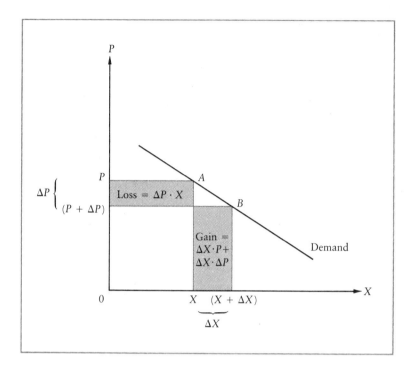

Figure 4.3
Price Elasticity and Marginal Revenue

Marginal revenue must be calculated as the gain in revenue resulting from increased sales due to a price decrease minus the loss in revenue resulting from a cut in price on units that could have been sold at higher prices.

$$\Delta R = \underbrace{(P + \Delta P)(X + \Delta X)}_{\substack{\text{revenue} \\ \text{at } B}} - \underbrace{P \cdot X}_{\substack{\text{revenue} \\ \text{at } A}}$$

Expanding and simplifying the previous equation yields

$$\Delta R = \Delta P \cdot X + \Delta X \cdot P + \Delta X \cdot \Delta P$$
$$= \Delta X(P + \Delta P) + \Delta P \cdot X \qquad (4.9)$$

The change in total revenue, ΔR, is the result of two forces, illustrated by the shaded rectangles in Figure 4.3: The term $\Delta X(P + \Delta P)$ is the gain in revenue from selling ΔX new units of output at the lower price $(P + \Delta P)$; the term $\Delta P \cdot X$ is the loss in revenue from lowering the price by ΔP on X units that previously sold at the higher price. Whether ΔR is positive, negative, or zero depends on the relative sizes of the gain and loss terms. For example:

$$P = \$30, (P + \Delta P) = \$25, \Delta P = -\$5$$

$$X = 20 \text{ units}, (X + \Delta X) = 30 \text{ units}, \Delta X = 10 \text{ units}$$

$$\Delta R = \underbrace{(\$25 \cdot 30)}_{\substack{\text{total revenue} \\ \text{at lower} \\ \text{price}}} - \underbrace{(\$30 \cdot 20)}_{\substack{\text{total revenue} \\ \text{at higher} \\ \text{price}}} = \$150$$

The change in revenue, $\Delta R = \$150$, breaks down as follows:

$$\Delta R = \Delta X (P + \Delta P) + \Delta P \cdot X$$

$$\Delta R = \underset{\substack{\text{gain in} \\ \text{revenue} \\ \text{from selling} \\ \text{extra units}}}{10(\$25)} + \underset{\substack{\text{loss in revenue} \\ \text{from lowering} \\ \text{price on units} \\ \text{that could have} \\ \text{been sold at} \\ \text{higher prices}}}{-\$5 \cdot 20} = \$150 > 0$$

Since a price cut increases total revenue by \$150, demand is price elastic: gains > losses.

STEP 2.   We can simplify terms somewhat by selecting a small enough move along the demand curve so that the term $\Delta X \cdot \Delta P$ in Equation 4.9, the product of two arbitrarily small numbers, can be ignored. Thus,

$$\Delta R = \underset{\text{gain}}{\Delta X \cdot P} + \underset{\text{loss}}{\Delta P \cdot X} \qquad (4.10)$$

This equation for ΔR has the same interpretation as before, except it is simplified to take into account small, continuous movements in price and quantity. The rectangles in Figure 4.3 that indicate revenue gain and loss have the same interpretation. Revenue rises by $\Delta X \cdot P$ because ΔX new units of X are sold when price falls to P; but revenue falls by $\Delta P \cdot X$ because the price reduction—which is necessary to capture extra sales—involves a price cut ΔP on X units previously selling at higher prices. For example,

$$P = \$100 = \text{lower price needed to increase sales}$$

$$X = 500 \text{ units} = \text{initial units sold per time period}$$
$$\text{at higher price}$$

$$\Delta P = -\$1 = \text{price reduction}$$

$$\Delta X = 3 \text{ units} = \text{extra units sold when price falls}$$

$$\Delta R = \underset{\text{gain}}{\Delta X \cdot P} + \underset{\text{loss}}{\Delta P \cdot X}$$

$$\Delta R = 3 \cdot \$100 + -\$1 \cdot 500 = -\$200 < 0$$

Since a price cut reduces total revenue by \$200, demand is price inelastic: losses > gains.

STEP 3.   The term ΔR is the total change in total revenues. If we divide Equation 4.10 by ΔX, we obtain

$$\frac{\Delta R}{\Delta X} = P + X\frac{\Delta P}{\Delta X} \qquad (4.11)$$

$$\underset{\text{gain}}{} \quad \underset{\text{loss}}{}$$

The term $\Delta R/\Delta X$ is marginal revenue, which is defined as the change in total revenue, ΔR, resulting from a change in the units of X sold, ΔX. In other words, marginal revenue is the change in total revenue per unit increase in X. Equation 4.11 expresses marginal revenue as the net result of a gain and a loss, as before, but now on a per-unit-of-X basis: P is the gain in revenue from selling one more unit; $X(\Delta P/\Delta X)$ is the loss in revenue from selling X units per time period at lower prices than before. For example,

$$P = \$40 = \text{new, lower price needed to expand sales}$$

$$X = 70 \text{ units} = \text{units previously sold at higher price}$$

$$\Delta P = -\$2 = \text{price reduction}$$

$$\Delta X = 1$$

$$MR = \frac{\Delta R}{\Delta X} = P + X\frac{\Delta P}{\Delta X}$$

$$\underset{\text{gain}}{} \quad \underset{\text{loss}}{}$$

$$MR = \$40 + 70\left(\frac{-\$2}{1}\right) = -\$100 < 0$$

Since MR is negative, the price cut reduces total revenue: demand is price inelastic.

STEP 4. With a definition of marginal revenue in place, we can relate it rigorously to price elasticity of demand. Dividing Equation 4.11 by price gives us

$$\frac{MR}{P} = \frac{P}{P} + \frac{X}{P} \cdot \frac{\Delta P}{\Delta X} = \left(1 + \frac{1}{\varepsilon}\right) \qquad (4.12)$$

because $X/P \cdot \Delta P/\Delta X$ is the inverse of the price elasticity of demand, ε. Now multiply each side by P:

$$MR = P\left(1 + \frac{1}{\varepsilon}\right) \qquad (4.13)$$

The elasticity term ε is a negative number. Since we are following the convention of using the absolute value of ε, or $|\varepsilon|$, Equation 4.13 can be rewritten as

$$MR = P\left(1 - \frac{1}{|\varepsilon|}\right) \tag{4.14}$$

Marginal revenue depends on the price elasticity of demand. Marginal revenue is zero when $|\varepsilon| = 1$, positive when $|\varepsilon| > 1$, and negative when $|\varepsilon| < 1$. Table 4.2 summarizes.

Table 4.2
Marginal Revenue and Price Elasticity of Demand

Demand Is	When $|\varepsilon|$	Implying $MR = \Delta TR/\Delta X$
Perfectly elastic	$= \infty$	> 0
Elastic	> 1	> 0
Unit elastic	$= 1$	$= 0$
Inelastic	< 1	< 0
Perfectly inelastic	$= 0$	$= -\infty$

Computations: Arc versus Point Elasticity

We may now turn to the specifics of elasticity computations. Consider the demand curve in Figure 4.4. It is usually meaningless to talk about the elasticity of the entire demand curve.[2] Rather, we may measure elasticity along a small "arc" of the curve—between points A and B, for instance. This technique is called an **arc elasticity** determination. We can make the arc as small as we please. When the arc shrinks to a single point, we measure **point elasticity**. Arc elasticity estimates responsiveness between two points; point elasticity refers to responsiveness suitably close to a single point.

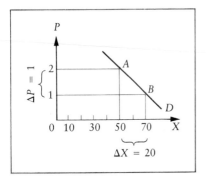

Figure 4.4
Arc Elasticity versus Point Elasticity

The elasticity formula requires the measurement of percentage changes for both the denominator and the numerator. The most accurate method is to use the arc elasticity formula: $|\varepsilon| = \Delta X/\Delta P \cdot P/X$.

ARC ELASTICITY.   Let's begin by computing arc elasticity between points A and B in Figure 4.4. The formula, using absolute values for convenience, is

$$|\varepsilon| = \frac{\dfrac{\Delta X}{X}}{\dfrac{\Delta P}{P}} = \frac{\Delta X}{\Delta P} \cdot \frac{P}{X} \tag{4.15}$$

The percentage change of price is the absolute price change, ΔP, divided by the base price, P. Using the beginning base $P = 2$ and moving from A to B, the percentage change in price is $\Delta P/P = 1/2$. Similarly, $\Delta X/X = 20/50$. Thus $|\varepsilon| = (2/5)/(1/2) = 4/5$.

However, if we move from B to A, using the original values as

2. Exceptions would include the special cases of empirical demand data that are "fitted" statistically to an exponential demand curve and demand curves that are unit elastic throughout their full range.

bases, $|\varepsilon| = (20/70)/(1/1) = 2/7$. The responsiveness of X to price increases and decreases is the same between A and B. But the elasticity coefficients differ because different bases are used in computing percentage changes.

This problem is solved by selecting a base that is neither the beginning nor ending base but the average of the two. This average base, called the **midpoint base,** is calculated for X and P, respectively, as $(X_1 + X_2)/2$ and $(P_1 + P_2)/2$. Thus arc elasticity may be expressed, using the midpoint base, as

$$|\varepsilon| = \frac{\Delta X}{\Delta P} \cdot \frac{(P_1 + P_2)/2}{(X_1 + X_2)/2} \qquad (4.16)$$

Accordingly, arc elasticity between A and B in Figure 4.4 is

$$|\varepsilon| = \frac{(20)}{1} \cdot \frac{(2 + 1)/2}{(50 + 70)/2} = \frac{1}{2}$$

Demand is price inelastic between A and B.

Several points regarding Equation 4.16 are worth noting:

Using this formula, price elasticity is the same regardless of the direction of movement on the demand curve. Arc elasticity measures the average elasticity between two points.

If the numbers are easy, as in the example above, the midpoint bases can be determined readily by finding the number halfway between the points without resorting to the amount of arithmetic that Equation 4.16 calls for. However, if $P_1 = 13.64$ and $P_2 = 17.03$, the midpoint base is best calculated by changing one of the numbers so that the sum is evenly divisible by 2: $(13.65 + 17.03)/2 = 15.34$.

Since both the price and quantity midpoint bases have a 2 in their denominators, the 2s cancel. Thus, for calculation, $|\varepsilon|$ may be written as follows:

$$|\varepsilon| = \frac{\Delta X}{\Delta P} \cdot \frac{(P_1 + P_2)}{(X_1 + X_2)} \qquad (4.17)$$

POINT ELASTICITY. What is the point elasticity of demand at point A on the linear demand curve in Figure 4.5? There is no need to calculate average bases now, because we are not moving along the demand curve as when measuring elasticity. Thus the elasticity formula can be applied directly. Recall that $|\varepsilon| = \Delta X/\Delta P \cdot P/X$ has two terms: the inverse of the slope of the demand curve, $\Delta X/\Delta P$, and the ratio of bases, P/X. In Figure 4.5, the inverse of the slope, in absolute value, is $6/60 = 10$. The ratio of bases at point A, P/X, is $4/20$.

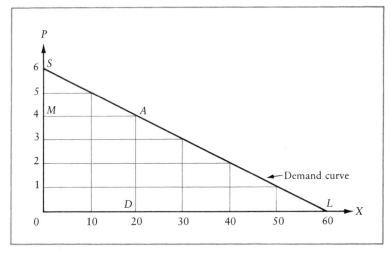

Thus $|\varepsilon| = 10 \cdot 4/20 = 2$. Demand is therefore price elastic at A.

A simple visual test can be applied to check point elasticity. The inverse of the slope of the demand curve in Figure 4.5 is $\overline{DL}/\overline{AD}$, and the ratio of bases is $\overline{AD}/\overline{OD}$. Hence elasticity in Figure 4.5, in absolute terms, is

$$|\varepsilon| = \frac{\Delta X}{\Delta P} \cdot \frac{P}{X} = \frac{\overline{DL}}{\overline{AD}} \cdot \frac{\overline{AD}}{\overline{OD}} = \frac{\overline{DL}}{\overline{OD}}$$

The term $\overline{DL}/\overline{OD}$ is a ratio of line segments. It is greater than unity because $\overline{DL} > \overline{OD}$. Thus demand is elastic at point A.

Through the geometric properties of similar right triangles, the test just described can also be applied to line segments on the vertical axis—or on the demand curve itself. Thus at point A,

$$|\varepsilon| = \underset{\substack{\text{using} \\ \text{horizontal} \\ \text{axis}}}{\frac{\overline{DL}}{\overline{OD}}} = \underset{\substack{\text{using} \\ \text{vertical} \\ \text{axis}}}{\frac{\overline{OM}}{\overline{MS}}} = \underset{\substack{\text{using} \\ \text{demand} \\ \text{curve}}}{\frac{\overline{AL}}{\overline{SA}}}$$

If the demand curve is nonlinear, as in Figure 4.6, the procedure needs only one modification. The slope at point A is determined by drawing a tangent to the demand curve at point A and computing the slope of the tangent. The slope at A is $\overline{AD}/\overline{DL}$, hence its inverse is $\overline{DL}/\overline{AD}$. Now we may proceed as before:

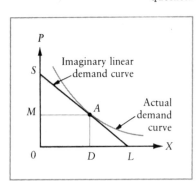

$$|\varepsilon| = \frac{\Delta X}{\Delta P} \cdot \frac{P}{X} = \frac{\overline{DL}}{\overline{AD}} \cdot \frac{\overline{AD}}{\overline{OD}} = \underset{\substack{\text{using} \\ \text{horizontal} \\ \text{axis}}}{\frac{\overline{DL}}{\overline{OD}}} = \underset{\substack{\text{using} \\ \text{vertical} \\ \text{axis}}}{\frac{\overline{OM}}{\overline{MS}}} = \underset{\substack{\text{using} \\ \text{demand} \\ \text{curve}}}{\frac{\overline{AL}}{\overline{SA}}}$$

These ratios are less than 1. Demand at point A is therefore price inelastic.

Now consider the straight-line demand curve in Figure 4.7. Using the technique just described, we can determine that unit elasticity occurs only at the midpoint, B. Only there is the ratio $\overline{BC}/\overline{AB}$ equal to 1. Any point between A and B is price elastic, and any point between B and C is price inelastic.

Furthermore, demand is most price elastic at the top of the demand curve and becomes relatively less elastic as price is lowered. Recall that $|\varepsilon| = \Delta X/\Delta P \cdot P/X$. The term for the inverse of slope is constant, because the demand curve is linear. Elasticity differs at different points on the demand curve only because the bases used to calculate percentage changes vary. A movement down the demand curve lowers P and raises X, thereby reducing P/X and $|\varepsilon|$. Price elasticity falls in absolute value as price falls along a linear demand curve.

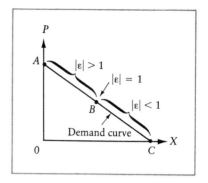

Figure 4.7
Elasticities along a Linear Demand Curve

Linear demand curves are always unit elastic at the midpoint. The elastic range lies above and to the left and the inelastic range lies below and to the right, regardless of the slope of the curve.

Graphing Total Revenue and Marginal Revenue

We know that marginal revenue is related to price elasticity of demand according to Equation 4.14:

$$MR = P\left(1 - \frac{1}{|\varepsilon|}\right)$$

We may now use this fact along with the graphic rules of point elasticity that we have just studied to derive total revenue and marginal revenue curves.

Consider the linear demand curve in Figure 4.8a. Demand is price elastic along range $\overline{AB}$ of the demand curve. Suppose the firm starts at A and gradually lowers price to B. Since $|\varepsilon| > 1$ in this range, total revenue must rise each time the price falls and the output sold increases. But total revenue cannot rise when the firm expands output without marginal revenue being positive. Equation 4.14 verifies that $MR > 0$ when $|\varepsilon| > 1$. Hence, the darkened segments of the three curves in Figure 4.8 all reflect the elastic portion of the demand curve. Lowering price when demand is price elastic results in a higher total revenue, or what amounts to the same thing, a positive marginal revenue.

Next, suppose the firm makes a miniscule price reduction in the neighborhood of B. Since $|\varepsilon| = 1$ at B, it follows that the total revenue is unchanged, which in turn implies that marginal revenue equals zero. Hence, the three points labeled B, D, and E are different ways of expressing the same idea: A price change when $|\varepsilon| = 1$ does not affect revenues. Maximum TR, zero MR, and $|\varepsilon| = 1$ all occur at the same rate of output.

Finally, consider the demand curve range $\overline{BC}$, where demand is price inelastic. If the firm gradually drops price from B to C, its total

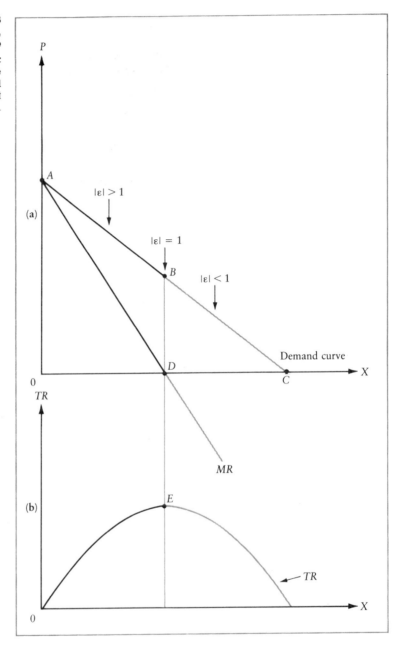

Figure 4.8
Total Revenue, Marginal Revenue,
and the Demand Curve

(a) Marginal revenue is unit elastic
where the *MR* curve crosses the
horizontal axis (*MR* = 0). **(b)** Total
revenue peaks at the same output
where marginal revenue is zero.

revenue will fall with each price reduction, because $|\varepsilon| < 1$. But a declining *TR* implies a negative *MR*. Thus the light segments of all three curves are alternative ways to exhibit the effect of price inelasticity.

Figure 4.8 is a compact graphic method of interrelating the firm's revenue curves and demand curve. We will use it often as we delve into models of firm behavior in other chapters.

Table 4.3

Relationship among $|\varepsilon|$, Total Revenue, and Marginal Revenue

When $|\varepsilon|$	MR	TR
> 1 (elastic)	> 0	Is rising
$= 1$ (unit elastic)	$= 0$	Attains its maximum
< 1 (inelastic)	< 0	Is falling

Table 4.3 summarizes the relationships between $|\varepsilon|$, MR, and TR. Knowing $|\varepsilon|$ allows us to deduce the other values.

Determinants of Price Elasticity of Demand

Empirical demand studies are somewhat rare, because they are expensive to produce and are produced too late to be useful in decision making. Thus managers and public officials must develop a feel for the price elasticities of goods and services that will enable them to make decisions in the absence of econometric studies. Here is a rough guide to the major determinants of price elasticity of demand:

Availability of substitute goods: Demand tends to be more price elastic the greater the presence of alternative goods that consumers can select when a product's relative price rises. *Substitution* is a key word in economics and is perhaps the most important determinant of price elasticity.

Time consumers have to adjust to price changes: Demand is less elastic in the short run than in the long run, because consumers need time to seek out substitutes when relative prices change. If heating prices rise, turning down the thermostat may be the only short-run adjustment possible, whereas moving to Ecuador may be considered in the long run.

Price proximity of substitutes: Price elasticity tends to be higher the closer available substitutes are in price. Physical substitutes may exist, but substitution is not feasible if their prices are too high. Jogging and a vacation in Hawaii may be alternative means of relaxing, but they are not economic substitutes for most people because of the disparity in prices.

Importance of product: Necessities tend to exhibit lower elasticity than luxuries. Potatoes are less price elastic than women's hats. Heart bypass surgery is less elastic than nose jobs.

Price of good in relation to consumer's budget: Salt, straight pins, and shaving cream take a trivial amount of the typical consumer's budget. Theoretically, price increases for such products should not discourage much consumption. However, pickled kumquats are probably relatively elastic despite their low burden on budgets. Thus little confidence should be attached to this rule of thumb.

4.3

Price Elasticity of Gas and Oil Demand over Time

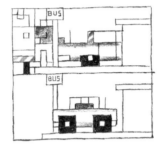

The oil crisis of the mid-1970s provides an example of the usefulness of elasticity in economic analysis. As fuel supplies shrank, the upward pressure on gasoline prices was immense. However, many people in responsible places argued against permitting gasoline prices to rise in response to market forces for two reasons: First, there is virtually no substitute for gasoline in our present automobiles. Thus people cannot cut back their consumption of gasoline in response to higher prices. Second, higher gasoline prices can only increase consumer expenditures on gasoline.

Let's investigate the logic of these two assertions by referring to the accompanying figure, which exhibits three demand curves. Consumers buy G_0 gallons of gas at the initial price P_0. Now suppose the market price of gas increases to P_1. In the very shortest of runs, before the consumer has time to seek out any substitutes for the higher-priced gas, the same G_0 gallons of gas are purchased at the higher price. The corresponding immediate short-run demand curve is labeled D_{IS}. It is totally inelastic because of the complete absence of substitution during the limited time period.

Substitution increases in the long run as the consumer consolidates shopping trips, uses mass transit, forms car pools, replaces worn-out large-engine cars with gas-efficient compacts, and even changes place of residence to be closer to bus and rail terminals or closer to work. The full long-run demand adjustment to gas price P_1 reduces consumption to G_2; the long-run demand curve is D_L.

However, the move from G_0 to G_2 is gradual. Consumers may make intermediate adjustments by selecting G_1 on the way to long-run equilibrium. Curve D_S is a short-run demand curve that lies between the two extremes of making no substitutions (curve

D_{IS}) and completing all adjustments (curve D_L). Demand elasticity increases in the long run·as greater substitutability comes into play.

The actual elasticity coefficients of short-run versus long-run demand are empirical questions, the computations of which should play a central role in the current debate concerning gasoline price controls. Theoretically at least, it is possible for gas price increases to reduce consumers' total expenditures on gasoline if the price increases generate suf-

ficient long-run alternatives.* The usual arguments in favor of gas price controls ignore the role of substitution in consumer decision making (as well as the other side effects of price controls suffered by consumers, which are discussed in Chapter 2).

*Professor Louis Philips has estimated long- and short-run consumer demand price elasticities for gasoline and oil. He reports a short-run price elasticity of -0.11 and a long-run price elasticity of -0.68; demand is price inelastic in both the short and long run but much less inelastic in the long run. According to these figures, total consumer expenditures on gasoline and oil will increase in both the short run and long run. See Louis Philips, "A Dynamic Version of the Linear Expenditure Model," *Review of Economics and Statistics* 54 (1972): 450–488.

Changes in Demand Elasticity over Time

The price elasticity of demand depends on the amount of time that people have to respond. The immediate response to increased gasoline prices is simply to pay the higher price. The short-run response is more elastic, and the long-run response is greater still.

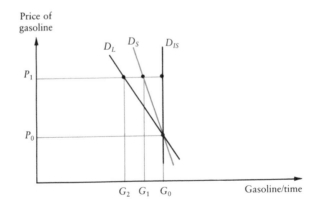

A P P L I C A T I O N

4.4

Elasticity of Public Transportation: Transit Fares and Frequency

The demand for transit rides is a function of the money price (the fare) and the "time price." Riders are sensitive to increases in both of these prices. In the case of buses, the time price is a function of bus frequency; it enters people's decisions in two ways:

1. *Frequency delay:* Many people are only vaguely aware of bus schedules. Riders will find that waiting time is a function of how frequently a bus arrives at their stop (the more buses, the smaller the delay). Still, many buses do not adhere to schedules because of traffic congestion or the incompetence of schedulers and drivers.
2. *Schedule delay:* When buses do adhere strictly to a schedule, bus frequency is still important, even though there is very little

waiting at the stop. People must adjust their work, leisure, and shopping trips to the transit schedule, so the greater the bus frequency, the smaller the interference with their daily schedule and the lower their opportunity cost of taking the bus.

For these reasons, $R = f(P, B)$. That is, ridership (R) is a function of bus fare (P) and the number of buses (B), which is a proxy for bus frequency.

Professor James P. Moody, in a study of the Milwaukee County

Transit System, discovered that ridership is inelastic ($|\varepsilon_p| = +0.558$) with respect to money price (fare); ridership is roughly unit elastic with respect to bus frequency ($|\varepsilon_B| = +1.04$).[*] This means that the reduction in fares favored by many ardent proponents of public transit would reduce revenue and perhaps, in this age of taxpayer revolt, cause the bus system to reduce frequency, which is far more important in retaining riders.

[*]James P. Moody, "Supply and Demand for Urban Bus Travel: Theoretical Revision and Empirical Estimation" (Department of Economics, University of Wisconsin, Milwaukee, 1974, Mimeographed). Professor Moody is currently the U.S. Congressman from the 5th congressional district of Wisconsin.

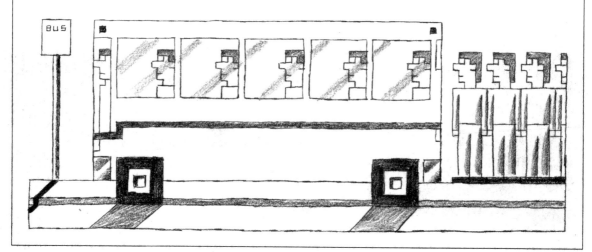

Income, Cross-Price, and Other Demand Elasticities

The demand function relates the quantity demanded of a good to all independent variables that exert an influence on consumer decisions. Graphing the demand function in two dimensions is made possible by the *ceteris paribus* technique: The demand curve relates price and quantity demanded, *ceteris paribus*. We have used the demand curve to study price elasticity of demand and the implications for the firm's revenue.

Emphasis on the ordinary demand curve should not blind us to the fact that it is frequently important to focus attention on some independent variable besides price. An **Engel curve** relates the quantities demanded of a good and various levels of income, *ceteris paribus*. Thus income is the movement parameter for an Engel curve, and all other demand determinants are held constant, including price.

Two Engel curves of different slope are shown in Figure 4.9. Just as price elasticity of demand differs from the slope of the demand curve, so income elasticity differs from the slope of the Engel curve. Income elasticity of demand, ε_{XI}, measures the percentage change in purchases of X due to a percentage change in consumers' income, *ceteris paribus*:

$$\varepsilon_{XI} = \frac{\% \; \Delta X}{\% \; \Delta I} = \frac{\Delta X}{\Delta I} \cdot \frac{I}{X} \qquad (4.18)$$

Since income elasticity is the product of a slope term, $\Delta X / \Delta I$, and a ratio of bases, I/X, the income elasticity coefficients of the two Engel curves have different signs (because they have different slopes). Specifically, $\varepsilon_{XI} < 0$ for chicken necks, an inferior good, and $\varepsilon_{XI} > 0$ for color television sets. For either case, the larger the elasticity coefficient in absolute value, the more responsive purchasers are to changes in income. Generally, the income elasticity value will be different at various points on the Engel curve.

Income elasticities are important to businesses in estimating sales for their products at various stages in the economic cycle. Firms expecting recession and falling consumer incomes may add product lines regarded as income inferior in order to protect their

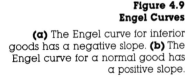

**Figure 4.9
Engel Curves**

(a) The Engel curve for inferior goods has a negative slope. **(b)** The Engel curve for a normal good has a positive slope.

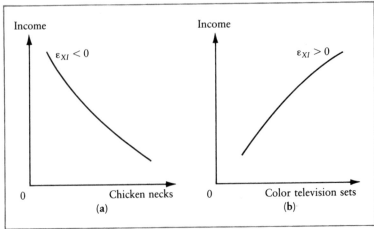

revenues during downturns; reductions in income increase sales of inferior goods. Income elasticities are important in business planning. They also have public policy implications.

Cross-price elasticity of demand, ε_{XP_Y}, measures how responsive sales of X are to changes in the price of good Y:

$$\varepsilon_{XP_Y} = \frac{\% \, \Delta X}{\% \, \Delta P_Y} = \frac{\Delta X}{\Delta P_Y} \cdot \frac{P_Y}{X} \qquad (4.19)$$

Figure 4.10 shows two possible relationships between good X (television sets) and the prices of other products. If good Y represents home video games, which are played on a separately purchased TV set, a higher price for such games would reduce TV sales, as shown in the negatively sloped curve in panel a. If, on the other hand, good Y is movies shown exclusively in theaters, the number of TV sets purchased should increase when movie prices go up, *ceteris paribus* (see panel b). Hence, cross-price elasticity between movies and TV should be positive. Note that negative cross-price elasticities identify goods that are complements, whereas positive elasticities reveal that goods are substitutes. As always, the greater the absolute values of the coefficient, the higher the elasticity.

Note that cross-price elasticity is an asymmetrical measure of substitutability and complementarity between goods, because it deals only with good X and the price of Y. There is no reason to expect sales of good Y to respond equally to a change in the price of X. A change in the price of home video games may influence TV sales more (or less) than a change in the price of TV sets influences sales of video games. Of course, cross-price elasticities would be near zero for products only remotely related to each other, such as dog licenses and creamed spinach.

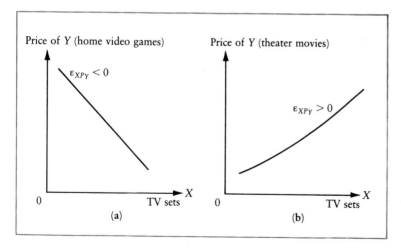

Figure 4.10
Cross-Price Elasticity versus Consumption

(a) As the price of a complement rises, the quantity demanded falls.
(b) As the price of a substitute rises, the quantity demanded rises.

4.5

Job Training and Wage Elasticity of Labor Demand

Wage elasticity of labor demand is important in selecting suitable industries for government job-training programs. It is crucial that job training be applied to jobs with relatively high wage elasticities of demand.

Job training increases the labor supply, as illustrated by the shift from supply curve S_0 to S_1 in the figure. At each wage, the horizontal distance between S_0 and S_1 represents the newly trained workers. Institution of a job training program reduces the wage for all workers from w_0 to w_1 and increases the number of jobs from L_0 to L_1.

If wage elasticity of demand is relatively low, as illustrated in the figure, few new jobs are produced, but the wages of existing employees are cut substantially. New workers $\overline{L_1L_2}$ are hired, but only $\overline{L_1L_0}$ new jobs are created. Thus, $\overline{L_0L_2}$ represents the significant number of workers who voluntarily leave the industry because of the lower wage.

The higher the wage elasticity of labor demand, the less the wage reduction of a given job-training program, the greater the creation of new jobs, and the less the wage-induced voluntary exit of existing workers.

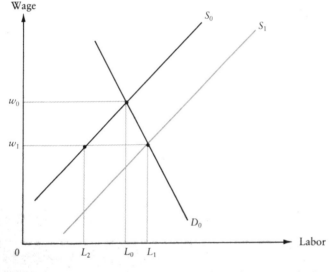

Wages and Labor Demand

The greater the wage elasticity of labor demand, the smaller the displacement of existing workers as a result of a job-training program. Greater elasticity means more jobs created per trainee, because some workers will be eased out by the trainees when wages are held down.

4.6

Using Industry Demand Elasticities at the Firm Level

Say that, as the owner of a firm producing electronic components, you receive a steady stream of market reports containing demand elasticities with respect to price, income, population, and so forth. The latest report includes these elasticities:

$|\varepsilon_{XP}|$ = price elasticity of demand = 0.1

$\varepsilon_{X, POP}$ = population elasticity of demand = 1.0

How can you use these figures in the internal management decisions of your firm?

Demand theory helps you proceed cautiously and intelligently by alerting you to a simple truth: Industry statistics cannot be used directly at the firm level. Even though industry price elasticity of demand is +0.1, your firm cannot increase price 10 percent and experience a mere 1 percent reduction in units sold. If all firms in the industry raised price 10 percent, units sold would fall collectively by 1 percent. But if your industry is extremely competitive, your firm's price elasticity of demand will be vastly more elastic than the overall industry's because of the abundant substitutes your customers have to choose from. A price increase may well lower your firm's revenue, the industry price elasticity of +0.1 notwithstanding. So industry elasticity figures must be used with extreme caution by individual firms.

Next consider the unit-elastic population elasticity. An increase in population of 10 percent increases the quantity demanded of computer components by 10 percent at each price. The population increase thus shifts the demand curve to the right by 10 percent. How much does product price rise? Because of the +0.1 price elasticity, we can write $\varepsilon = \%\Delta X/\%\Delta P = 0.1$. It follows that $\%\Delta P = 10$ percent/$0.1 = 100$ percent—or a doubling of price. However, this result would occur only if the supply curve had zero price elasticity of supply.

The shortage of electronic components arising from the increased population must be eliminated solely by price adjust-

ments if the supply curve is vertical and stationary. But we cannot depend on this. If the higher prices attract new competition and also a higher rate of sales from firms already in the industry, supply will adjust and price rises will be moderated. Depending on the speed of supply adjustments, there may be very little price rise at all.

This discussion should forewarn

against the careless and indiscriminate use of industrywide demand studies by single firms. The degree of industry competition and the size of the firm relative to the industry must be taken into account in employing market elasticity figures. This fact is why informed judgment, not mere technical skill, is considered so important in managerial decision making.

Methods of Measuring Empirical Demand Functions

Numerous demand studies have been undertaken over the years to quantify the elasticity coefficients that we have studied in this chapter. The modest purpose of this section is to provide an overview of the methods employed, to point up some major difficulties, and to counsel caution in using empirical demand curves.

Laboratory Experiments

One method of estimating demand elasticities is to conduct laboratory experiments. Participants start out with spendable income and are presented with a list of products to buy. (Consumers are frequently allowed to keep the goods they "purchase" as an inducement to participate in the experiment.) By varying the subjects' income and the prices of the products and observing the participants' buying patterns, data can be gathered on price, income, and cross-price elasticities.

Laboratory experimentation is a relatively unreliable method for estimating demand relationships. The sheer expense of running such consumer clinics results in very small sample sizes—in both the number of consumers and the product choices. Subjects might respond to a price increase for Tide detergent far differently in the lab, where substitutes are limited to (say) Oxydol and Fels Naphtha, than in "real life," where consumers choose from the standard floor-to-ceiling shelves of alternative detergents. Also, it is virtually impossible to obtain long-run data in this fashion. Finally, the data are suspect because participants who know their every move is being recorded cannot be depended on to reveal their true preferences for goods.

Interviews

Rather than go to the expense of setting up laboratory clinics, researchers often merely interview a representative sample of consumers about their preferences. How many bottles of Scope mouthwash would you buy per year if the price were $1.39? If your income increased by 25 percent, would you buy more or less Scope per year? How much more or less?

Consumer interviews share many of the limitations of the laboratory method. Consumers are asked to make snap judgments about many hypothetical questions that have no counterpart in their experience. Consumers cannot be relied on to reveal true preferences under the inquisitive prodding of an interviewer. The interview method also focuses solely on short-run behavior.

Market Experimentation

Industry demand curves can be estimated by changing product prices in the marketplace and measuring the effect on consumer purchases. Perhaps the most famous market experiment involved oranges.[3] Researchers at the University of Florida selected Grand Rapids, Michigan as a test market in which to study the demand for three varieties of oranges—two Florida oranges and a California orange. Several area supermarkets took part in the study. Price changes in all stores were coordinated over 31 days in order to estimate price elasticities for each orange variety and the relevant cross-price elasticities.

The results of this experiment were interesting. Each orange variety had a price elasticity coefficient of about 3 in absolute value, indicating that consumers cut orange purchases considerably as prices rose. The cross-price elasticities were also interesting. All coefficients had positive signs, suggesting that all orange varieties were substitutes. But the coefficients were much larger between the two Florida varieties than between either Florida variety and the California orange. In effect, Michigan consumers did not consider California and Florida oranges to be close substitutes.

Industry demand studies like this one require the cooperation of many groups and institutions, including the participating firms—which must be willing to run the risk of lower profits during the experimental period. Because the experiments are so expensive, they are usually short-run projects. Long-run adjustments to price changes therefore cannot be deduced with this method. Perhaps the greatest limitation of such studies is that virtually none of them are firm-specific. For example, the data in the orange study was gathered by having all participating supermarkets change prices simultaneously. But unless firms form a cartel and make joint pricing decisions (which is both difficult and illegal), they cannot act on the information. Surely a single firm raising its orange prices, *ceteris paribus* (all other firms keeping prices constant), would find greater elasticity of demand than in the industry study, in which the prices

3. Marshall B. Godwin, W. Fred Chapman Jr., and William T. Hanley, *Competition between Florida and California: Valencia Oranges in the Fruit Market*, bulletin 704 (Gainesville, Fla.: Agricultural Experiment Stations, Institute of Food and Agricultural Services, University of Florida in cooperation with the U.S. Department of Agriculture and the Florida Citrus Commission, December 1965).

of oranges were increased simultaneously all over town. This phenomenon is another warning against using industry demand data at the firm level.

Another difficulty is the rate of obsolescence of the data. The various orange elasticities, reported in 1965, are sure to be influenced by events. The expansion of the interstate highway system, improved refrigeration facilities, deregulation of trucking, the introduction of cranberry juice, and similar structural changes have changed the relevant elasticities, perhaps dramatically.

Statistical Demand Estimates

Rather than pull demand data from consumers via interviews, clinics, or market experiments, researchers often employ statistical and econometric techniques to make deductions from data already in existence. These studies take two principal forms. **Time-series studies** involve plotting price and quantity points for a series of months or years and then fitting a curve through the plots, using least squares or any of several other statistical methods. **Cross-section studies** evaluate the performance in a given time period of a cross-section of consumers in different income groups, geographical areas, age brackets, and so forth.

Many technical and logical barriers must be overcome in turning the economist's theory of demand into a specified function with parameters that reflect consumer behavior. Utmost care and a sensitive use of rigorous statistical and econometric techniques are needed to produce reliable elasticity coefficients. We cannot study statistical estimating techniques here without vastly exceeding the scope of this book. However, be advised that statistical studies should be carried out by highly skilled professional econometricians and should be evaluated by management with caution.

Summary

This chapter provides an introduction to demand analysis, which is an essential part of the managerial economist's tool kit. At the qualitative level, the managerial economist must understand what a demand curve is: a diagram of consumers' reactions to price changes. At the quantitative level, the demand curve is a two-dimensional relationship between price and quantity demanded, holding all other relevant variables fixed. The demand curve slopes downward, because an increase in price induces substitutions of other goods and because higher prices affect the spending power of consumer income.

Managers must also understand numerical representations of the effect of price on quantity demanded. Price elasticity of demand, the ratio of the percentage changes in the quantity demanded of a good divided by the percentage changes in the price of the good, measures demand responsiveness without reliance on units of measurement. Income elasticity differs in that the denominator is the percentage change in income. Similarly, cross-price elasticity is the percentage change of

Key Terms

the quantity demanded divided by the percentage change in the price of some other related good; cross-price elasticity is used to measure the effect of price on the quantity demanded of more than one good.

The price elasticity of gas and oil demand and of the demand for labor services illustrate the wide applicability of the elasticity concept. Even unusual elasticities have their significance—for example, the elasticity of bus ridership with respect to the frequency of buses. But one must use elasticities cautiously. Since industry elasticities may have been unreliably determined and generally do not apply to any particular firm, they may be poor bases for firm decision making. Nevertheless, the concept of elasticity is indispensable in organizing thoughts about the demand for goods and services.

Problems

1. "I don't care how much you charge for water. I will never reduce my consumption below X gallons per day."
   a. Draw the demand curve corresponding to this statement.
   b. Are you skeptical about the statement? Why or why not?
2. "My car needs four tires and a spare. Therefore, my demand curve for tires is vertical." Criticize this statement.
3. In this chapter, the following expression was derived: $\Delta R/\Delta X = MR = P(1 + 1/\varepsilon)$. Using similar algebra, show that $\Delta R/\Delta P = X(1 + \varepsilon)$. Draw up a table similar to Table 4.1 to demonstrate the relationship between price elasticity of demand and the total revenue changes caused by price changes.
4. Use the formula for price elasticity of demand to prove these statements:
   a. A linear demand curve cannot have constant elasticity.
   b. A demand curve with unit elasticity over its entire range cannot be linear.
5. Suppose that marginal revenue, $\Delta R/\Delta X$, is $6, income elasticity is 0.8, point price elasticity is -2, cross-price elasticity is 3, and arc price elasticity is -1.8. Find the product price.
6. Why is price elasticity of demand considered a more useful measure than the slope of the demand curve?
7. If the price elasticity of demand for houses in Denver is 0.8 and the price of houses has decreased by 10 percent, by how much has the quantity of houses sold increased?
8. Suppose that a particular gas station raises the price of gasoline from $1.36 per gallon to $1.40 per gallon. The quantity of gasoline sold falls from 1,000 gallons per day to 900 gallons per day. What is the price elasticity of demand for gasoline in this range of consumption? Why specify "in this range of consumption"?
9. Suppose a beer drinker likes each successive beer more than the last until he is comatose. Draw the demand curve representing this behavior. Label your graph carefully.
10. "The price of gasoline has nothing to do with peoples' driving habits. The American people simply have to drive." Comment on this statement, using demand curves.

11. Given the hypothetical data in Table 4.4 for price, income, and quantity demanded, calculate price elasticities and income elasticities of demand. Are your calculations arc or point elasticities? What demand curves can you sketch?

12. The average age of the American car has risen by over 15 months, to 7.2 years. Would you expect the elasticity of demand with respect to monthly car loan payments to be greater or smaller as the average car age rises?

13. Suppose that the tax code is changed to eliminate the deduction of home mortgage interest.
    a. If income elasticity is 1.0, how would this change affect the demand for housing?
    b. How would the change affect the availability of housing in different price ranges?

14. Suppose that the price of both natural gas and home heating oil are completely deregulated. What would you predict about their cross-price elasticities?

15. Would you expect the following cross-price elasticities to be positive or negative? Explain your answers.
    a. Between pizza and cola beverages
    b. Between oil and natural gas
    c. Between rental housing and bus fares
    d. Between cat food and dog food
    e. Between skilled and unskilled labor

16. Suppose that the price of a good rises by 40 percent and that the revenue from selling it rises by 10 percent. What can you say about the elasticity of demand for the good?

17. Your city council raises the bus fare from 75 cents to $1, and ridership subsequently falls by 40 percent.
    a. Calculate the elasticity of demand for bus rides.
    b. Say that the bus schedule is changed so that buses are 10 percent more frequent and that ridership subsequently rises to the level that existed before the fare increase. What is the frequency elasticity?

18. Suppose that the elasticity of demand during the peak hours of electricity use is 0.1 and that elasticity during the off-peak hours is 0.9. How much can price be reduced for off-peak use to offset a 50-percent increase in price for peak use?

19. Suppose that the wage elasticity of labor demand for a certain kind of semiskilled worker is 0.5 and that the minimum wage is raised 15 percent. How many workers are displaced?

20. If the cross-price elasticity of demand for Florida oranges with respect to the price of California oranges is 0.5, what can we say about the perceived quality of the two oranges? Would either grower's association advertise? If so, which one?

21. Suppose that a market is composed of 300 clones who have individual price elasticities for pizza of 0.6. What is the market price elasticity?

22. If the price elasticity of demand for gasoline is 0.5 for a 4-month period of adjustment and 0.6 for an 8-month period of adjustment, what will it be for a 12-month period of adjustment?

Table 4.4

Quantity Demanded Given Hypothetical Prices and Incomes

Price	$10,000 per Year	$20,000 per Year
$0.50	1,000 units	1,500 units
1.00	900	1,100
1.50	800	900

23. Suppose that the short-run elasticity of demand for a product is 0.5. A perfect substitute for the product sells at twice the current price. What would you expect to happen to the elasticity of the first product as the prices of the two goods came closer together?

24. a. If the price elasticity of demand is 0.5 and the product price is $10, what is the marginal revenue?
    b. If the demand curve were to shift up by 10 percent, what would happen to marginal revenue?

25. a. If the elasticity of demand for glassine paper is 0.5, what can a firm selling the paper conclude about its ability to raise the price over the original market price?
    b. What would you expect to happen to the elasticity of demand if the price of cellophane, a substitute for glassine, were to rise?

26. Suppose that the transportation cost of steel is a significant component of the cost of its production and distribution. What would you expect to happen to the elasticity of demand as a function of distance from the plant?

27. Suppose that the elasticity of demand for in-theater movies is 0.7 and that the elasticity of demand for cable TV hookups is 2.0. What pricing strategy should cable companies pursue as they attempt to enter the market for the first time?

28. Suppose that a firm has 25 percent of the market and that the industry demand elasticity is 4.3. What can you conclude about demand elasticity for the firm?

29. Why would you expect the cross-price elasticity between two brands of Florida oranges to be large and that between Florida oranges and California oranges also to be large?

30. Suppose a survey leads to an estimate that the demand elasticity for kumquats is 0.5. Later, an analysis of actual response to prices shows that the demand elasticity is 1.5. What might account for the difference?

Suggested Readings

Elliott, J. Walter. *Economic Analysis for Management Decisions.* Homewood, Ill.: Irwin, 1973.

Houthakker, H. S., and Taylor, Lester D. *Consumer Demand in the United States, 1929–1970: Analyses and Projections.* 2nd ed. Cambridge, Mass.: Harvard University Press, 1970.

Robinson, Joan. *The Economics of Imperfect Competition.* London: Macmillan, 1933.

Scherer, Frederic M. *Industrial Market Structure and Economic Performance.* Chicago: Rand McNally, 1980.

5

PRO-
DUCTION

We have now completed a careful investigation of consumer demand and elasticity and their implications for the firm's revenue. But revenue is only one component in the profit equation. Equally important is the firm's costs of production. Now we may develop a general model of business behavior capable of directing and organizing firms' decisions, including the quantity of output to supply, the relative quantities of productive factors to employ, and the price to charge. The analytical toolkit used to investigate these cost- and supply-related decisions is referred to as the "theory of the firm."

The development of supply analysis is a lengthy procedure. For example, identifying the correct rate of output for the firm to supply presupposes knowledge about the firm's production costs. But costs depend in part on the technical relationship between inputs and the final output. Accordingly, the progressive steps to be followed in developing a theory of competitive firm decision making and behavior are:

Production (Chapter 5) → costs (Chapter 6) → supply (Chapter 7)

As you embark on this journey, two comments may help you. First, production theory—the material in this chapter—is the main building block in the theory of the firm. When the cost and supply discussions in later chapters begin to elude you, return to this chapter and use it as a lifeline. Cost curves and supply curves, which we will encounter throughout the book, do not merely materialize as though pulled from a magician's hat. Nor are they orphans without a recognized parentage. In fact, production curves are the progenitors of cost curves.

Second, it is helpful to distinguish between engineering problems and economic problems. Production theory is a description of engineering relationships between inputs and final outputs. It assumes knowledge of engineering solutions, using current technology, applied to the problem of squeezing the maximum output from a given mix of inputs. Having a technician determine the alternatives for combining inputs to produce 5,000 television sets is an engineering problem. Deciding whether to produce 5,000 sets or 3,000 sets, whether to use mostly labor or mechanization, whether to operate the plant 8 hours per day or around the clock, or whether to sell off the physical equipment and abandon the television industry—these are economic decisions that go beyond the mere physical relation of inputs and output. This chapter focuses on the typical engineering production processes of firms. It lays the foundation for the managerial choices to be studied in virtually every remaining chapter.

Firms' Objectives and Constraints

In order to study the theory of the firm, we must seek a model of business firm behavior that managers can use in decision making. Business firms are so diverse that no single definition can capture their true nature and purpose. For our modeling, however, we can regard a firm as a business organization that hires factors of production, combines the factors in a production process to create output, and sells the resulting output. The firm organizes its production and sales activities so as to achieve certain objectives. Some possible objectives are to maximize profit, maximize output, or maximize the entrepreneur's utility.

Of course, the firm faces constraints in its decisions. Possible constraints on the firm include the following:

1. Bureaucratic constraints
   a. Price controls
   b. Antitrust regulation
   c. Rate-of-return regulation
   d. Taxation

2. Market constraints
   a. Prices of labor, capital, raw materials, and other inputs
   b. Demand for the firm's product
   c. Degree of competition

3. Technological constraints: the production function—the ways that labor, capital, raw materials, and other inputs can be combined to produce useful final goods

We will have abundant opportunities to consider all of these constraints on the firm's behavior in due course. For now we will

limit ourselves to the technological constraints inherent in the transformation of inputs into final output. This is the essence of **production theory.**

Total Product Curve

Firms combine inputs to produce final, salable goods. The rudiments of production analysis were introduced in Chapter 3 so we
could develop intuitively the concept of marginal productivity. We
can now become more rigorous about those ideas. Recall that the
firm's production function identifies the amounts of output that can
be produced from specific combinations of variable and fixed inputs. Using labor (L) as a generic term for all variable inputs and
capital (K) for all fixed inputs, and fixing capital at the level $\overline{K}$, the
production function associated with this level of capital is

$$Q = f(L, \overline{K}) \tag{5.1}$$

Suppose our engineers have told us that

$$Q = f(1, \overline{K}) = 10$$
$$Q = f(2, \overline{K}) = 30$$
$$Q = f(3, \overline{K}) = 40$$
$$Q = f(4, \overline{K}) = 44$$

The data points relating labor (L) and output (Q) are plotted two-
dimensionally in Figure 5.1, holding capital fixed at $\overline{K}$. The graph,

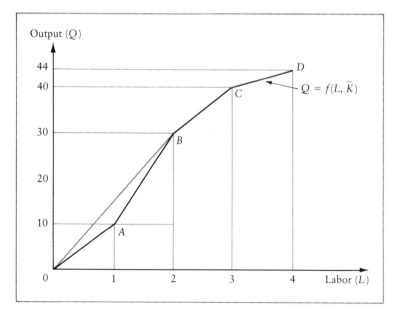

Figure 5.1
Total Product Curve

A graph can be used to show the
amount of output that various
quantities of labor can produce
when limited to a fixed amount of
capital.

an illustration of the production function holding capital fixed, is called a **total product curve.** Data points A, B, C, and D are joined with straight lines to form it. The total product curve shifts with increases or decreases in capital, because the labor input–final output relationship changes if workers have a different endowment of capital at their disposal.

Average Product of Labor and Marginal Product of Labor

The total product curve relates total output to total labor input. All such "total" curves in economics—total output, total utility, total revenue, and so forth—have corresponding average and marginal curves that arrange the data in a useful manner. You can greatly ease the burden of learning the theory of the firm by mastering the total-average-marginal relationships in the context of production theory. If you do so, the analogous relationships for cost and revenue curves—to be encountered later—will seem like old friends.

The **average product of labor,** AP_L, is defined as the average units of output that each worker produces, or[1]

$$AP_L = \left.\frac{Q}{L}\right|_K \tag{5.2}$$

The first two columns of Table 5.1 contain the labor and total output figures used to draw the total product curve in Figure 5.1. The third column records the AP_L associated with each size of the labor force. As the labor input is increased, the average product of labor rises for a time and then falls. The countervailing forces of specialization of labor and capital fixity, which were emphasized in Chapter 3, are in evidence here.

Table 5.1
Total, Average, and Marginal Products of Labor

Labor (L)	Output (Q)	$AP_L = Q/L$	$MP_L = \Delta Q/\Delta L$
1	10	10.0	10
2	30	15.0	20
3	40	13.3	10
4	44	11.0	4

A convenient graphic method for measuring AP_L from a total product curve is to draw a ray from the origin to any point on the curve and to evaluate the slope of the ray. Recall that slope equals rise/run. The slope of ray $0B$ in Figure 5.1 is $\Delta Q/\Delta L = 30/2 = 15$. Thus $AP_L = 15$ at point B. The AP_L at points, A, C, and D can be derived similarly. The slope of the ray from the origin always produces the ratio Q/L, which defines the AP_L.

---

1. The notation $A|_{(x, y, z, \ldots)}$ has already been used to denote that the value of A is determined for fixed values of $(x, y, z, \ldots)$. Hence, K is a constant in Equation 5.2.

The AP_L tells us, on average, how much output each worker produces. A related but distinct measure of labor's productivity tells us how much extra output one extra worker adds. This value is important when we contemplate hiring more workers, and it leads to a marginal, rather than average, productivity concept. This idea was also presented intuitively in Chapter 3.

The marginal product of labor, MP_L, is defined as

$$MP_L = \frac{\Delta Q}{\Delta L}\bigg|_K \qquad (5.3)$$

The marginal product of labor is the change in output resulting from a one-unit change in the variable labor input, holding capital fixed. Keep in mind that the computation of "averages" involves the ratio of total output and total labor used, whereas the computation of "marginals" involves the ratio of small changes in these total output and labor values.

The last column of Table 5.1 lists the MP_L values for the preceding example. The MP_L rises in the initial stages of production; then, starting with the third worker, it begins to diminish. We will study this result in detail shortly. For now, simply note that the efficiencies inherent in dividing tasks increase labor's marginal product until the congestion on the fixed factor introduces enough production inefficiencies to force marginal product to decline. In principle, therefore, both the AP_L and the MP_L rise and later fall for the same reasons: division of tasks and capital fixity.

All marginal concepts are defined as changes in the value of a dependent variable in response to changes in the value of an independent variable. To measure such changes, we must observe movements along the relevant curves. For example, to measure the marginal product of labor we must consider a move along the total product curve, as between points A and B in Figure 5.1. The slope of the line $\overline{AB}$ is $\Delta Q/\Delta L = 20/1 = 20$; between points A and B, $MP_L = 20$. The MP_L along other sections of the total product curve is calculated in the same way.

As an exercise, measure the AP_L and the MP_L values from the total product curve in Figure 5.1 and compare your answers to the figures in Table 5.1. The AP_L is the slope of a ray from the origin to each point on the curve; the MP_L is the slope of the total product curve itself between data points. Logically, measurement of the MP_L requires a small move along the total product curve to produce the changes in labor and output called for by the definition $MP_L = \Delta Q/\Delta L$. No movement is required to measure $AP_L = Q/L$, since total values (as opposed to changes in totals) are used.

Smoothing the Total Product Curve
The total product curve in Figure 5.1 is made up of several straight-line segments of different slopes. This is because we considered

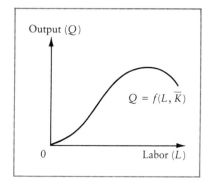

Figure 5.2
Smooth Total Product Curve

The curve is smooth when the labor force and the final output are continuously divisible.

discrete adjustments in labor and output. For most purposes, a continuous, smooth total product curve is more convenient in the analysis of firm behavior. Such smoothing is a valid first approximation in the light of two facts. First, labor is a flow variable, measured per unit of time. The firm cannot hire 1 1/2 workers, but it can hire 3 workers for 2 years, or 1 1/2 workers per year. Second, labor is infinitely divisible if measured in hours of labor services rather than numbers of workers. Figure 5.2 shows a smooth total product curve, which assumes that the labor force and the resulting output are all continuously divisible.

We may now generate the average and marginal product curve that correspond to the smooth total product curve. Only the method of measuring the marginal product is affected somewhat by changing from discrete data points to a smooth curve.

Consider the AP_L curve first. Figure 5.3a contains a smooth total product curve, from which the AP_L curve in Figure 5.3b is derived. As before, the AP_L at any rate of production equals the

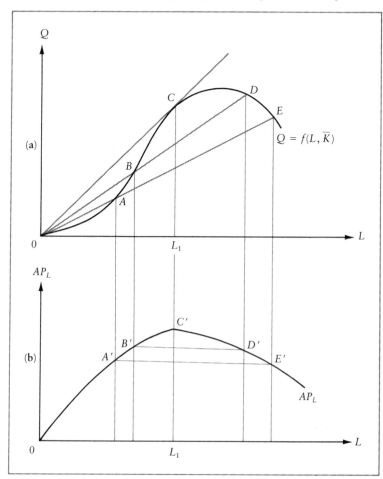

Figure 5.3
Deriving the Average Product of Labor Curve

(a) AP_L is the slope of a ray from the origin to any point on the total product curve. The AP_L rises as labor is expanded to L_1, then diminishes with further labor expansion. **(b)** The slope of the ray that is tangent to the total product curve at C is the maximum value of AP_L at C'.

slope of a ray drawn from the origin to a given point on the total product curve. In panel a, rays are drawn to points A through E. Each point on the AP_L curve in panel b is plotted at a height equal to the slope of the corresponding ray above.

As the labor force expands from zero to L_1, the AP_L rises; ray $\overline{0A}$ is flatter than $\overline{0B}$, which in turn is flatter than $\overline{0C}$. Ray $\overline{0C}$ is tangent to the total product curve at C; the AP_L achieves its maximum value at C, when L_1 workers are hired. The AP_L falls when labor is expanded beyond L_1, since the slope of ray $\overline{0D}$ exceeds that of $\overline{0E}$. Hence, the AP_L curve is an inverted U-shaped curve. It demonstrates graphically that the production efficiencies inherent in specialization of the labor force are eventually offset by the congestion resulting from capital limitations.

The economic meaning of the marginal product of labor is captured by the mathematical definition of the slope of the total product curve: slope $= MP_L = \Delta Q / \Delta L$. For a discontinuous total product curve, MP_L is the slope of each linear segment of the curve (see Figure 5.1). Although a smooth total product curve calls for a slightly more sophisticated technique to accommodate the curve's constantly changing slope, the essence is unchanged: The slope of the total product curve equals MP_L.

Figure 5.4 shows how the MP_L curve (panel b) is related to the total product curve (panel a). The total product curve is divided into three segments: $\overline{0A}$, $\overline{AB}$, and the segment beyond B. The corresponding segments on the MP_L curve are $\overline{0A'}$, $\overline{A'B'}$, and the segment beyond B'.

Consider segment $\overline{0A}$. Each tangent has a positive slope, so the MP_L is positive. Also, the tangents' slopes rise as point A is approached. Thus, MP_L increases when the labor force is expanded to A. The segment $\overline{0A'}$ of the MP_L curve shows these same results: positive and increasing MP_L.

It is impossible to draw a tangent to point A in Figure 5.4a, because it is an **inflection point,** the place where the curve ceases rising at an increasing rate and begins rising at a decreasing rate. The inflection point A identifies the maximum MP_L, denoted A' in panel b.

To evaluate slope at any point on a nonlinear total product curve, and hence to measure MP_L, draw a tangent to the given point and measure the slope of the tangent. Because the slope of the tangent is constant and the given point lies on the tangent, the slope of the tangent determines the slope of the total product curve at the given point—and hence the marginal product of labor. The slope measures how much output rises when labor is increased a small amount, precisely the definition of MP_L.

Throughout segment $\overline{AB}$ in Figure 5.4, each tangent is positively sloped, but the slopes get flatter as point B is approached. Hence MP_L diminishes each time more labor is hired between A and

Figure 5.4
Deriving the Marginal Product of
Labor Curve

(a) MP_L is the slope of a tangent drawn to any point on the total product curve. The MP_L rises along segment $\overline{0A}$, is at its maximum at point A (the inflection point), diminishes along segment AB, is zero at B, and is negative beyond B, as indicated by the slopes of the tangents. **(b)** These results are shown explicitly in the MP_L curve.

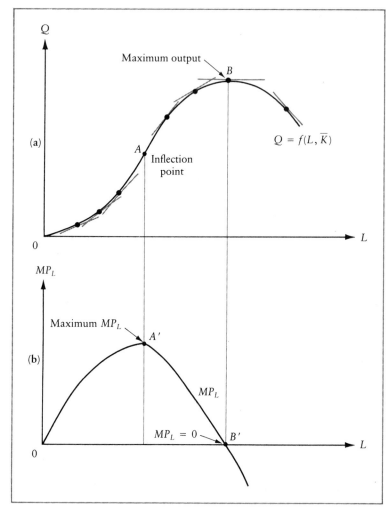

B. The corresponding segment $\overline{A'B'}$ of the MP_L curve therefore diminishes as the labor force expands. Congestion on the fixed factor (capital) is in evidence.

The slope of the tangent drawn to the total product curve's maximum at point B is zero; hence MP_L is zero at B'. Because more labor reduces total output beyond B, the tangents are negatively sloped. Thus the MP_L is also negative, as shown to the right of B' in Figure 5.4b.

To summarize:

The MP_L is positive up to B, equals zero at B, and is negative beyond B.

The MP_L increases up to A, the inflection point, and diminishes beyond A.

The MP_L curve, derived from the total product curve in Figure 5.4, is an inverted U-shaped curve.

Fitting Average and Marginal Product Curves Together

Now that we know how to derive the AP_L and MP_L curves from a total product curve, we still must learn how to fit the average and marginal curves together properly. All average and marginal measures follow a rule of arithmetic, which can be described in the following three-part rule applied to production theory:

Whenever $MP_L > AP_L$, the AP_L must be rising.

Whenever $MP_L < AP_L$, the AP_L must be falling.

Whenever $MP_L = AP_L$, the AP_L is neither rising nor falling but is at its maximum.

Think of the arithmetic of the average-marginal relationship in a less technical context first. Suppose a mother has two children whose average weight at birth is 7 pounds. If her third child (the marginal child) weighs 50 pounds at birth, the average birthweight must rise (when marginal weight is greater than average weight, the average weight rises). If the third baby weighs only 2 pounds, the average weight falls. If the new baby weighs exactly 7 pounds, the average and marginal weights are equal and the average weight is unchanged.

Now apply the idea to the average and marginal products of labor, where the three-part rule has its graphic counterpart in Figure 5.5.

1. $MP_L > AP_L$ up to point A. Since each worker's marginal product exceeds labor's existing average product, the average product must rise.

Verify this result using the tangent-ray test. Between the origin and point A, a tangent drawn to any point has a steeper slope than a ray drawn from the origin to the same point. Hence, $MP_L > AP_L$ at every point on the curve up to (but not including) point A.

2. $MP_L = AP_L$ at point A. The marginal product of the last worker at A equals the average product of labor. Hence AP_L neither rises nor falls but stays the same—and thereby achieves its maximum value. MP_L intersects AP_L at the maximum AP_L.

Applying the tangent-ray test to point A, $MP_L = AP_L$ because the tangent and the ray from the origin are the same line and hence have equal slopes.

3. $MP_L < AP_L$ beyond point A. The average product of labor

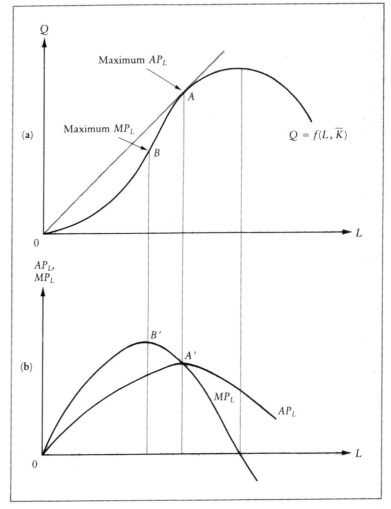

declines because each worker hired causes an increase in total output smaller than the existing average product of labor. The average
must therefore decline.

Using the tangent-ray test, a tangent drawn to any point to the
right of A is flatter than a ray from the origin to point A. Thus $MP_L
< AP_L$ beyond A, and AP_L must fall.

These results are illustrated in Figure 5.5b.

To summarize the story told by Figure 5.5:

1. $MP_L > AP_L$ up to A', hence AP_L rises.

2. $MP_L = AP_L$ at A', hence AP_L is constant.

3. $MP_L < AP_L$ beyond A', hence AP_L declines.

Production theory is a complex subject that is very difficult to master. This chapter presents an intuitive treatment. But the purpose of this application is to give you four examples of how production theory can be used to organise thoughts—even for problems that are not usually thought amenable to the application of production theory. To demonstrate the power and unity of the theory, the same figure is used for each example; it shows a total product curve with inputs K and L.

Business Documents

There is a revolution underway in the production of business documents sparked by computer-based word processors. In the typical firm, the production of documents requires both typists and word-processing equipment. Armed with the machines, the

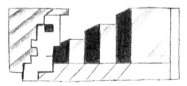

typists work much faster and more accurately. Hence the machines and the typists are complementary factors of production.

Therefore, we can write

Q = document pages produced per day
K = number of word-processing machines
L = typists, measured in hours per day

The number of word processors is the fixed factor.

As typists are added, the number of documents produced increases—initially at an increasing rate, as the typists share work and divide such tasks as copying, typing, and proofreading. But as more typists are added, the fixity of the number of

5.1

Potpourri of Production Theory Examples

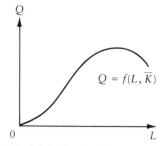

Standard Total Product Curve
Production theory, and the total product curve, can be applied to a wide range of activities.

machines becomes a constraint, and so the rate of increase in document production falls. Hence the usual production pattern emerges, as in the figure.

Elections

Here again, output must be measured as a continuous variable. The most meaningful output measure is not the outcome of the election—win or lose—but the number of votes. The fixed factor is the size of the paid staff, and the variable factor is the

amount of money spent on the media campaign. Therefore, we can write

Q = votes for our hero
K = size of the staff
L = money spent on the media campaign

As the amount spent rises, the number of votes also rises—but

subject to eventual diminishing returns to the fixed factor. Thus the media campaign is subject to the law of diminishing returns.

Note that the unit for measuring input is money spent. We do not need to limit ourselves to physical inputs.

Police Protection

The protection of citizens in a city involves a tradeoff between inputs. Let there be two inputs: patrollers in squad cars and patrollers walking the beat. The output, the probability of avoiding a mugging, is unusual. Therefore, we can write

Q = probability of avoiding a mugging
K = squad car hours
L = beat patrol hours

A managerial economist is always looking for continuous variables and for opportunities to label the axes with benefits that

will increase along the axes. The use of the probability of avoiding a mugging as a variable provides a measure of benefits because the avoidance of the cost is a benefit. (One caution, however: The limit of probability for avoiding a mugging is the number 1.)

Industrial Accidents

In another unusual application, the probability of avoiding an accident in the workplace is the output measure. The inputs are the precaution levels exercised by management and the workers. Therefore, we can write

Q = probability of avoiding an accident
Continued on page 100

K = precaution level of
     management
L = precaution level of
     the workers

For any fixed level of precaution by management, the
probability of avoiding an accident is enhanced by increased
worker precaution. For example,
the management of a firm producing leather goods can provide equipment shields, clear instructions to the workers on the
safe operation of the machines,
frequent checks of the safety-

related gauges and equipment,
safer solvents for reducing the fat
content of the hides, rigid work
rules, restrictions on the use of
dangerous compacting equipment, and so on. The workers can
observe safety rules, report safety
problems, avoid drinking alcohol
or taking powerful medicines

while on the job, get plenty of
sleep before reporting to work,
read carefully the plant manuals
about safety on the job, observe
fellow workers when working in
teams, pile leather properly, and
so on. But production theory requires that we restrict our analysis to two dimensions, so all of
these activities are subsumed under the word *precaution*. Just as
both capital and labor are necessary to the production of goods
and services, both management
and labor must contribute to
safety in the workplace.

Law of Diminishing Returns

Chapter 3 defined the law of diminishing returns in terms like the
following: When the intensity of a fixed factor of production is
increased by adding more and more units of a variable factor to the
production process, the resulting increases in total output must
eventually get smaller and smaller. In other words, the law of diminishing returns asserts that the marginal product of labor must eventually diminish because of the inevitable congestion of the fixed
factor of production as variable inputs are expanded. This law is
frequently called the **law of variable proportions,** because labor and
capital are combined in different proportions whenever the labor
force changes and capital is fixed.

Diminishing returns to labor inputs, or the **diminishing marginal product of labor,** begin at points B and B' in Figure 5.5. If
more workers are hired, the resulting increases in output will rise at
an ever-decreasing rate, as seen in the decreasing slope of the total
product curve beyond B. Diminishing returns show up directly in
the negative slope of the MP_L curve to the right of B'. Diminishing
returns—falling MP_L—occur for the same reason that AP_L falls
eventually. Indeed, we could just as well define returns in average
rather than marginal terms. Note that the AP_L begins to fall at point
A, whereas the MP_L begins to fall sooner, at point B. Diminishing
marginal returns begin sooner than diminishing average returns
because $MP_L > AP_L$ between B and A. Although the MP_L is falling
between B and A, it still exceeds the AP_L, which forces the AP_L to
rise at the same time the MP_L falls. Thus the exact point at which
diminishing returns begin will vary with the arbitrary choice of
defining "returns" in marginal or average terms. But either way,
diminishing returns occur because of capital fixity. In short, the
average and marginal productivity of labor both fall whenever the
congestion of labor on the fixed factor more than offsets the efficiencies created by labor specialization.

Three Stages of Production

Given the "sideways" and elongated S-shape of the smooth total product curve, can we use it to say anything about the ranges in which a firm is most likely to produce? The answer is yes. The total product curve (or the AP_L and MP_L curves) can be divided into three stages, and one stage alone can be identified as an efficient stage of production.

The three **stages of production** are illustrated in Figure 5.6. Stage I is characterized by a rising AP_L, stage II by a diminishing but positive AP_L and MP_L, and stage III by a negative MP_L. Stages I and III are manifestly inefficient; by implication, stage II is the only efficient zone of production.

The key to understanding the distinction among stages is to recognize that the firm uses two inputs, labor and capital, and that production is inefficient whenever these inputs are combined in proportions that hinder production. Stage III is inefficient because it entails a negative MP_L. If production temporarily falls into stage

Figure 5.6
Stages of Production

Stage I exhibits a rising AP_L (inefficient). Stage II exhibits a diminishing but positive MP_L and AP_L (efficient). Stage III exhibits a negative MP_L (inefficient).

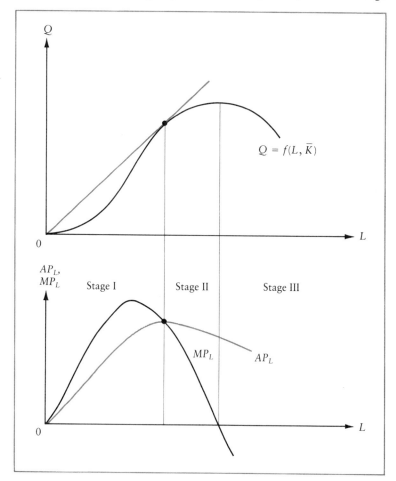

III, the firm can increase output by firing workers. By reducing labor inputs, costs fall and output and revenue rise. When the MP_L is no longer negative, stage III is abandoned. Stage III is clearly inefficient; MP_L is negative because the fixed capital inputs are overloaded.

Whereas stage III features too much labor for the available capital, stage I is inefficient because of too little labor being employed. In stage I, the AP_L rises when the labor force expands. Because of a small labor force relative to the firm's fixed capital, there is little if any congestion on the fixed factor. As a result, the productivity gains achieved by specializing the tasks of the increasing work force increase the workers' average productivity. But by remaining in stage I, a firm fails to exploit these gains. A firm would be inefficient if it stopped hiring workers in the midst of these productivity improvements. Stage I represents unexploited opportunities and should be avoided.

The profit-maximizing firm should hire enough workers to be out of stage I but few enough to avoid stage III. By a process of elimination, stage II is the only range of production for which labor and capital are not combined in inefficient proportions. Production theory by itself cannot determine the exact quantity of inputs to hire or output to produce within stage II, because these decisions depend on the prices of inputs and quantity of output. We will study these decisions in other chapters. Still, we can rule out stages I and III merely by understanding the way that variable inputs influence the production of physical ouput.

Note that the only efficient range of production, stage II, exhibits diminishing marginal (and average) returns throughout its entire range. The lesson is clear: Far from avoiding diminishing returns, profit-maximizing firms should seek them out.

Long-Run Production Functions

Up to now we have been involved in short-run production analysis. The **short run** is the period of time in which the firm's capital stock is fixed. (The short-run total product curve with capital fixed is the major building block in the construction of short-run cost curves in Chapter 6.) Given such fixity of capital, we were able to define the average and marginal product of labor, become acquainted with the concept of diminishing returns, and identify stages of efficient and inefficient production.

We may now discuss production when both the labor and capital inputs are allowed to vary. Indeed, the **long run** is defined as that period of time in which all factors are infinitely variable.

Total Product Curve Approach

Consider the rudimentary production function $Q = f(L, \overline{K})$. For short-run production analysis, we assigned a constant value to the firm's employment of capital, then constructed a total product curve that shows how output varies with labor. In the long run, however, capital is continuously variable. Since the amount of output that a given labor force can produce depends on the amount of capital available, each value of capital gives rise to a unique total product curve: Capital is a shift parameter for the total product curve. One method of charting the firm's long-run production function is to illustrate a family of total product curves, each curve dependent on a given amount of capital. This depiction of the production function allows labor, capital, and output to vary in a two-dimensional format.

Inefficiency of Stage I in the Long Run

We have already seen why a profit-maximizing firm will not know-ingly operate in stage I of production in the short run, when altering capital is not possible. Here we will see why a firm will not use stage I in the long run, when capital is variable. In particular, stage I operations are undesirable if the production function exhibits **constant returns to scale**—that is, when a proportionate increase in all inputs increases output by the same proportion. For example, doubling both labor and capital inputs results in a doubling of output under constant returns to scale.

Figure 5.7 presents two total product curves, each related to a different employment of capital. Consider the curve labeled

Figure 5.7
Constant Returns to Scale: The Total Product Curve Approach

For long-run constant returns to scale, doubling both labor and capital doubles output. Each level of capital generates a separate total product curve. The maximum AP_L must always equal the slope of ray $\overline{0AA'}$, and the maximum total output must occur on ray $\overline{0BB'}$.

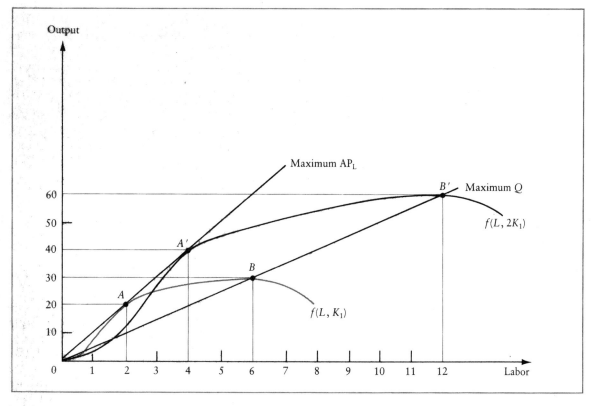

$f(L, K_1)$, drawn for the fixed amount of capital K. The average product of labor reaches a maximum at point A, where the ray from the origin becomes tangent to the total product curve. At point A, $AP_L = Q/L = 20/2 = 10$.

Now suppose the firm doubles its capital to $2K_1$. The total product curve shifts to $f(L, 2K_1)$. Under constant returns to scale, a doubling of both inputs also doubles output. Thus if labor goes from 2 to 4, output must rise from 20 to 40. This is a move from point A on the initial curve to point A' on the new one. Point A' represents the maximum average product of labor after capital and labor double. At A', $AP_L = Q/L = 40/4 = 10$. Because all inputs and output have doubled, all average products, including the maximum average products, remain constant. Thus, the slope of the ray $\overline{0AA'}$ measures the maximum average product of labor for different capital intensities, such as points A and A'. The maximum average product of labor does not change under constant returns to scale, since all total values simply increase in proportion. Thus the ray $\overline{0AA'}$ must be a straight line.

For capital equal to K_1, maximum output occurs at B, where the slope of the total product curve is zero. At point B, maximum output is 30 and is achieved by hiring 6 units of labor. When capital doubles, maximum output must also double when labor doubles. Thus, increasing labor from 6 to 12 increases output from 30 to 60. This is a move from point B to point B'. The ray $\overline{0BB'}$ connects all points that represent maximum output. Because inputs and output change proportionately under constant returns to scale, this ray must also be a straight line.

With these properties as background, it can be shown that the firm will not operate in the long run in stage I under constant returns to scale, because stage I entails a negative marginal product of capital. Figure 5.8 illustrates.

Consider point A, which lies in stage I of curve $f(L, \overline{K_2})$. Using the properties of constant returns to scale, we can construct another curve $f(L, \overline{K_1})$, $K_1 < K_2$, that becomes tangent to the maximum AP_L ray at A', vertically above A. A move from A to A' increases output by decreasing capital. Thus the marginal product of capital, $MP_K = \Delta Q/\Delta K$, is negative at point A.

Repeat the argument starting at B. Another total product curve can be drawn that becomes tangent to the maximum AP_L ray at B', implying less capital than K_2 yet more output. (For convenience, this curve is not drawn.) Thus MP_K is negative at point B. As you move closer to point C, the increase in output that can be obtained by reducing capital gets smaller and smaller; the negative marginal product of capital approaches ever closer to zero. Exactly at C, no curve can be drawn for less capital that will become tangent to the maximum AP_L ray vertically above C. Just at C the marginal product of capital ceases to be negative and becomes zero.

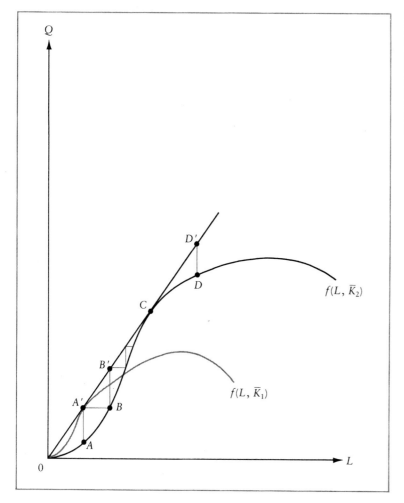

Figure 5.8
Inefficiency of Stage I When Capital Is Variable

For a constant-returns-to-scale long-run production function, stage I is inefficient because it entails a negative marginal product of capital. For any stage I point like A, the firm can increase output by reducing capital, *ceteris paribus*.

Now consider point D, which lies in stage II. In order to draw a contour tangent to D', more capital must be employed. Accordingly, the movement from D to D' increases capital and output; thus the marginal product of capital is positive. Any point such as D in stage II is characterized by positive marginal products of both labor and capital inputs.

Conclusion: All stage I production points, such as A and B, exhibit a negative marginal product of capital. Under constant returns to scale, any such rate of output can be produced with the same labor force but less capital. Stage I is just as inefficient as stage III. Both entail a negative marginal product of an input.

Isoquant Approach

One major theme of managerial economics is the central role of substitution by economic agents. In production theory, firms substitute one input for another, and the graphic device that captures these technical tradeoffs is the **isoquant curve.** *Iso-quant* means "equal-quantity." An isoquant curve connects all labor and capital combinations capable of producing the same quantity of final output.

Isoquant curves are an alternative to the family of total product curves as a graphic exhibit of the firm's long-run production function. Both visual displays—the family of total product curves and the isoquant curves—contain the same technical production information about the relationship between inputs and output. It is helpful to understand both methods of displaying the production function because both are used in firm decisions.

The curve labeled Q_0 in Figure 5.9 is an isoquant curve. It incorporates all labor and capital combinations capable of producing Q_0 units of output using the best available technology. It assumes that labor can be substituted for capital in production without changing total output. The curve is smooth because we have assumed that all inputs are infinitely divisible and adaptable.

Isoquant curves are derived from the production function $Q = f(L, \overline{K})$, but output is held constant while labor and capital vary. The engineers tell us the alternative ways labor and capital can be combined to produce a stipulated rate of output. Output is a shift parameter for the isoquant curve; there is a different isoquant for each level of output.

Isoquant curves possess four important characteristics:

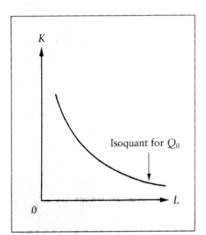

1. Isoquant curves are negatively sloped in the efficient ranges of production.

2. Isoquant curves are everywhere dense.

3. Isoquant curves are nonintersecting.

4. Isoquant curves are convex from the origin.

Figure 5.9
Isoquant Curve

An isoquant curve shows the many labor-capital combinations that result in the same total output.

These properties are discussed more fully in the sections that follow.

PROPERTY 1. NEGATIVELY SLOPED IN THE EFFICIENT RANGES   The first step in understanding isoquant curves is to define their slope, which is called the **marginal rate of technical substitution** (*MRTS*):

$$MRTS = \left.\frac{\Delta K}{\Delta L}\right|_Q \qquad (5.4)$$

The *MRTS* is the rate at which labor can be substituted for capital in the production process without changing the rate of output.

Figure 5.10 shows two isoquant curves. The curve on the left depicts the labor-capital combinations needed to produce Q_0 units of output, and the curve on the right is for Q_1 units of output, where

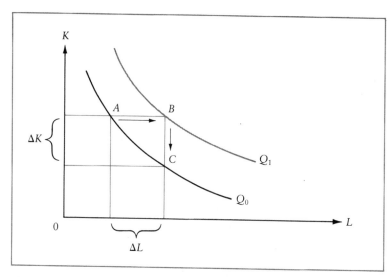

Figure 5.10
**Marginal Rate of Technical
Substitution**

The $MRTS$ is the slope of the isoquant curve: $MRTS = \Delta K/\Delta L = MP_L/MP_K$.

$Q_1 - Q_0$ is a very small change in output. Suppose that the movement from point A to point C on isoquant Q_0 is very small. What is the slope of the curve between A and C, and what is its significance?

The move from A to C can be studied "as if" it occurred in two steps: Step 1 is the move from A to B, and step 2 is the move from B to C. For step 1, capital is constant and labor increases by ΔL. The resulting increase in output is $\Delta Q = Q_1 - Q_0$. The change in output, ΔQ, equals the number of new workers hired, ΔL, times the marginal product of these workers, MP_L. Thus

$$\Delta Q = Q_1 - Q_0 = MP_L \cdot \Delta L \qquad (5.5)$$

In step 2, the move from B to C, output falls by $Q_0 - Q_1$, since capital is reduced by ΔK while holding the labor force constant. Output falls by the reduction in capital, ΔK, times the marginal product of capital, MP_K:

$$\Delta Q = Q_0 - Q_1 = MP_K \cdot \Delta K \qquad (5.6)$$

Let's summarize these steps:

	movement	change in output	(5.7)
step 1	A to B	$(+)\Delta Q = (Q_1 - Q_0) = MP_L \cdot \Delta L, (\Delta L > 0)$	
step 2	B to C	$(-)\Delta Q = (Q_0 - Q_1) = MP_K \cdot \Delta K, (\Delta K < 0)$	
steps 1 and 2	A to C	$\Delta Q = \quad 0 \quad = MP_L \cdot \Delta L + MP_K \cdot \Delta K$	

When steps 1 and 2 are added (moving from A to C), the change in output equals zero. Hence, the increase in output due to hiring more labor, $MP_L \cdot \Delta L$, must equal the reduction in output from a smaller employment of capital, $MP_K \cdot \Delta K$. Solving Equation 5.7 for $\Delta K / \Delta L$ produces

$$\frac{\Delta K}{\Delta L} = -\frac{MP_L}{MP_K} = MRTS \qquad (5.8)$$

The slope of the isoquant curve, $\Delta K / \Delta L$, called the $MRTS$, equals the negative of the ratio of marginal products of labor and capital.

Now let's see why the isoquant curve must have a negative slope when production takes place in the efficient stage II. Consider the isoquant curve in Figure 5.11. The curve has three ranges: $\overline{AB}$ and $\overline{CD}$ are positively sloped, and $\overline{BC}$ is negatively sloped. Since the slope of the isoquant, or the $MRTS$, equals $-MP_L / MP_K$, it follows that the slope is positive only when the marginal product of one of the factors is negative and is negative only when both marginal products are positive.

Consider a movement up the positively sloped segment of the isoquant from C to D. Both inputs are increased, yet production is constant at Q_0, implying that the marginal product of one of the inputs is negative. The same is true for a move from B toward A. The marginal product of one of the factors must be negative, because both inputs have increased without changing total output. If both inputs were increased and both exhibited positive marginal products, output would rise. This does not happen along a positively sloped isoquant. Upward-sloping isoquants are inefficient, because both inputs can be reduced without reducing output.

A moment's reflection reveals that segment $\overline{CD}$ in Figure 5.11 exhibits a negative MP_L and that segment $\overline{BA}$ shows a negative MP_K. The slope at point C is $\Delta K / \Delta L = -MP_L / MP_K = 0$. The slope is zero at C because the numerator, or MP_L, is zero. If labor is expanded beyond C, MP_L is negative. Thus range $\overline{CD}$ is production stage III, for which $MP_L < 0$.

Similarly, the slope at point B equals $\Delta K / \Delta L = -MP_L / MP_K = \infty$. The slope is infinite only when the denominator, MP_K, is zero. If capital rises above B, its MP_K becomes negative. Thus range $\overline{BA}$ is production stage I, for which $MP_K < 0$.

Having eliminated the upward-sloping portions of the isoquant as inefficient, it follows that efficiency pertains only to the negatively sloped segment, $\overline{BC}$. Any movement along a downward-sloping isoquant represents more of one input and less of the other, producing a constant output. Such a result requires positive marginal products for both factors, or production stage II.

A convenient method for identifying the efficient stage of production (stage II) is the use of **ridge lines**. A ridge line separates the

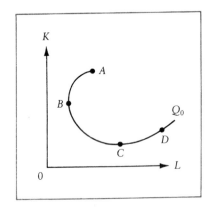

Figure 5.11
Isoquants: Negatively Sloped

$MRTS = MP_L / MP_K$ is negative and production is efficient only when MP_L and MP_K are both positive, as along segment $\overline{BC}$. Along segment $\overline{AB}$, the $MRTS > 0$ because $MP_K < 0$. For segment $\overline{CD}$, the $MRTS > 0$ because $MP_L < 0$.

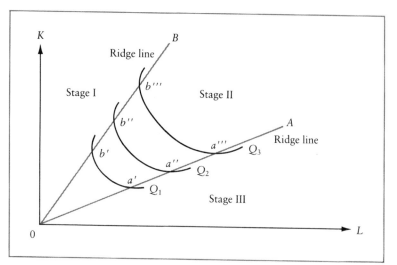

Figure 5.12
Ridge Lines

Ridge lines separate the efficient and inefficient ranges of the isoquant map. Each point on ridge line $\overline{0A}$ entails zero MP_L, and any point to the southeast lies in stage III, where $MP_L < 0$. The $MP_K = 0$ along ridge line $\overline{0B}$, and points to the northwest lie in stage I, where $MP_K < 0$. The space between the ridge lines is the efficient stage II: $MP_L > 0$ and $MP_K > 0$.

negatively sloped portions of isoquant curves from the positively sloped portions. In Figure 5.12, lines $\overline{0A}$ and $\overline{0B}$ are ridge lines. Line $\overline{0A}$ intersects all isoquants at their zero slope, such as point a', a'', and a'''. Production along any of the positively sloped isoquant segments to the southeast of ridge line $\overline{0A}$ constitutes operation in production stage III, the formal name for negative marginal product of labor.

Ridge line $\overline{0B}$ is formed when the isoquants intersect at the other extreme, where their slopes are infinite and just about to become positive, as at points b', b'', and b'''. Operation along any positively sloped isoquant segments to the northwest of ridge line $\overline{0B}$ also indicates production inefficiency, this time in the form of a negative marginal product of capital. This area corresponds to production stage I.

In summary, negatively sloped isoquants indicate efficiency. Furthermore, production stages have their counterparts in isoquant analysis; the ridge lines establish the boundaries between efficient and inefficient stages of production.

PROPERTY 2: EVERYWHERE DENSE   Every point in capital-labor input space is intersected by an isoquant curve. A single isoquant curve refers solely to a given output level. The selection of other levels of output would produce additional isoquant curves. Three of the infinite number of isoquants are drawn in Figure 5.13. The isoquants lying farther to the northeast, in the direction of the arrow, represent higher levels of output, because both inputs are increased and both exhibit positive marginal products. Thus $Q_3 > Q_2 > Q_1$. The family of all such isoquant curves is called the **isoquant map**. The isoquant map is a visual image of the firm's long-run production function.

Figure 5.13
Isoquant Map

Each isoquant curve pertains to one rate of output. Three of the infinite isoquant curves making up the isoquant map are illustrated here. Output rises in the direction of the arrow: $Q_3 > Q_2 > Q_1$.

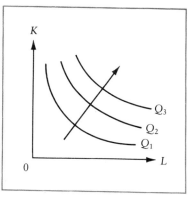

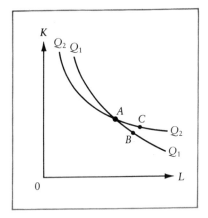

Figure 5.14
Isoquants: Nonintersecting
Because input combinations C and B are both comparable to A, they should lie on the same isoquant. Yet they do not, because of the contradiction created by the intersection of isoquants.

PROPERTY 3: NONINTERSECTING   Intersecting isoquants involve a logical contradiction. Consider the two intersecting isoquants, Q_1 and Q_2, in Figure 5.14. Input combinations A and C are on isoquant Q_2; combinations A and B are on isoquant Q_1. Combinations B and C, both equivalent to A, should therefore be equivalent to each other and be on the same isoquant curve. But they are not. Combination C produces more than B because C lies to the northeast of B. Intersecting isoquants can be ruled out because of these logical contradictions.

PROPERTY 4: CONVEX FROM THE ORIGIN   The marginal rate of technical substitution, $MRTS = \Delta K/\Delta L = -MP_L/MP_K$, is the slope of the isoquant curve. The isoquant is convex when the slope becomes smaller in absolute value as labor is substituted for capital. Thus the convexity property is frequently called the **diminishing marginal rate of technical substitution**.

Convex isoquants arise when labor and capital are imperfect substitutes in production. Consider two movements along the convex isoquant in Figure 5.15: the move from A to B and then the move from D to E. The MRTS along each segment is $(\Delta K/\Delta L)|_{Q_0}$, the rate at which the firm can substitute labor for capital while holding output fixed. Figure 5.15 is constructed so that the two increases in labor are equal: $\overline{CB} = \overline{FE}$. And yet the MRTS between A and B is greater than between D and E.

Starting at A, expanding the labor force by $\Delta L_1 = \overline{CB}$ permits a relatively large reduction in capital, $\Delta K_1 = \overline{AC}$. Thus $MRTS = \overline{AC}/\overline{CB}$ between A and B. However, the rate of exchange between labor and capital is smaller between D and E. Starting at D and

Figure 5.15
Convexity Property of Isoquants

Convexity means that the MRTS falls in absolute value as labor is substituted for capital along an isoquant. $MRTS = \Delta K_1/\Delta L_1$ between A and B and falls to $MRTS = \Delta K_2/\Delta L_2$ between D and E. When inputs are imperfect substitutes, MP_L falls and MP_K rises when labor is substituted for capital, causing $|MRTS| = |MP_L/MP_K|$ to fall.

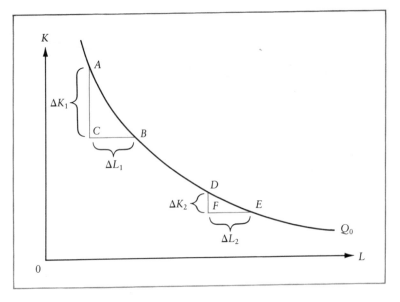

increasing by $\Delta L_2 = \overline{FE}$ (the same increase in the amount of labor as before), the firm can still reduce its use of capital, but the reduction, $\Delta K_2 = \overline{DF}$, is less than before. The $MRTS = \overline{DF}/\overline{FE}$ between D and E. Convexity implies a diminishing $MRTS$ as labor is expanded.

So long as inputs are not perfect substitutes, labor cannot be substituted for capital at a constant rate, because capital becomes increasingly scarce relative to labor. The law of variable proportions informs us that the inputs' marginal products change when their proportions vary. The slope of a convex isoquant falls in absolute value as labor is expanded, because the marginal products of inputs change.

Each time labor is substituted for capital, the input proportions vary; more labor is combined with less capital. When the labor force increases, MP_L falls, even when capital is fixed. But here capital is falling, giving additional force to the falling MP_L. Similarly, reducing capital increases the MP_K. Hence, the absolute value of the slope of the isoquant must fall as labor is substituted for capital, since $|\text{slope}| = |MP_L/MP_K|$ and since the numerator falls and the denominator increases.

If inputs are perfect substitutes in production, labor can be exchanged for capital at a constant rate, regardless of the relative scarcities of the factors. In this case, the $MRTS$ is constant and the isoquant is linear, as shown in Figure 5.16a. Note that the output Q_0 can be produced using combinations on the axes—that is, using all capital, K_0, or all labor, L_0, a feature that is rare among production functions.[2]

Another extreme case is a production function with fixed proportions. In this case, the isoquants are right angles, as shown in

2. Such combinations on the axes are also called corner solutions.

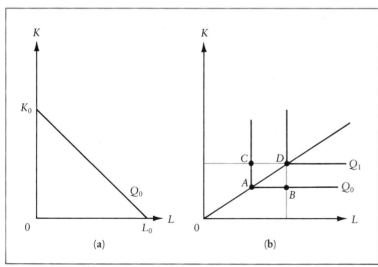

Figure 5.16
Linear and Fixed-Proportion Isoquants

(a) Linear isoquants indicate that factors are perfect substitutes.
(b) Right-angle isoquants reveal that factors must be used in fixed proportions; hence they are not substitutes at the margin.

Figure 5.16b. Input combination *A* is the only efficient way to produce Q_0 units of output. Moving to *B* is pointless, because extra labor has a marginal product of zero as long as capital is fixed. Point *C* is equally senseless, because extra capital adds nothing to output if labor is not increased also. Expanding output to Q_1 requires a proportional increase in both inputs, to combination *D*. Whereas linear isoquants suggest perfect substitutability, right-angle isoquants reveal that no substitution between inputs is feasible at the margin.

Linear and right-angle isoquant curves are limiting cases. For most production functions, labor and capital are imperfect substitutes and isoquants are convex.

A P P L I C A T I O N

5.2

Physicians and Their Aides

One setting that is not usually subjected to production analysis is the doctor's office. The greater the efficiency of such an office, the better the health of the patients, the faster patients get in to see a doctor, and the more time the doctor has with each patient. These factors in the health of patients dovetail nicely with the doctor's drive to make a lot of money.

The inputs used in producing a visit are a waiting room, a secretary, a nurse, a doctor or two, and two or three examination rooms that act as staging areas where the patient is denuded while waiting for the doctor.

The interesting question for the managerial economist is the tradeoff between the doctor's time and that of the doctor's aides. Consider the isoquant curve in the adjacent figure. The axes represent office hours per week and aides per physician (measured in hours on the job). The isoquant curve shows the level of output as measured in visits per week.

The shape of the curve in the

Aides per physician

Visits per week

0   Office hours per week

Isoquant Curve for Producing a Doctor Visit

Production (visits per week) is a function of the number of office hours per week and the number of aides per physician.

figure implies that visits to the doctor can be provided with a great deal of substitutability between the major inputs. The doctor can spend a lot of time per patient or see more patients by

giving them a lot of time with aides.

In an empirical study, Uwe Reinhardt discovered a wide range of substitutability in this production setting; the data could also be assembled along an isoquant like that shown in the figure.[*] Reinhardt also discovered that the position of the visit isoquant curve varies significantly depending on the type of practice the doctor is engaged in. The isoquant curves for the solo practitioner are higher than that for the group practitioner. Apparently, a solo practitioner is not able to produce visits with the same efficiency as a group practitioner, who can employ a variety of aides by pooling resources with the other doctors in the group. We can smooth out the isoquant curve by choosing as our unit of measurement hours per week, but the solo practitioner cannot smooth out the use of assistants.

[*]Uwe E. Reinhardt, *Physician Productivity and the Demand for Health Manpower* (Cambridge, Mass.: Ballinger, 1975).

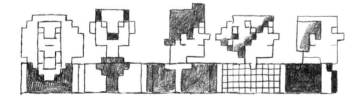
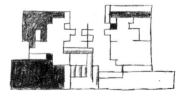

Returns to Scale: Constant, Increasing, and Decreasing

In studying the properties of long-run production functions, managerial economists have found it useful to ask this question: If all inputs are increased by the same proportion, will output rise proportionately, less than proportionately, or more than proportionately? For example, if all inputs double, output must respond in one of three ways: exactly double, less than double, or more than double. The way that output responds to proportionate, scaled expansions in inputs identifies the production function's "returns to scale."

A production function displays constant returns to scale if a doubling of all inputs exactly doubles output.[3] For example, look at Figure 5.17a:

$$f(2L, 2K) = 2 \cdot f(L, K)$$
$$f(2, 2) = 2 \cdot f(1, 1)$$

For **decreasing returns to scale,** a doubling of all inputs results in a less-than-doubled output. This case is shown in Figure 5.17b:

$$f(2L, 2K) < 2 \cdot f(L, K)$$
$$f(2, 2) < 2 \cdot f(1, 1)$$

Under **increasing returns to scale,** shown in Figure 5.17c, a doubling of all inputs more than doubles output:

$$f(2L, 2K) > 2 \cdot f(L, K)$$
$$f(2, 2) > 2 \cdot f(1, 1)$$

3. Doublings are used for ease. Any proportionate increase in inputs is adequate for checking returns to scale.

Figure 5.17
Returns to Scale

(a) With constant returns to scale, doubling all inputs exactly doubles output. **(b)** With decreasing returns to scale, doubling all inputs less than doubles output. **(c)** With increasing returns to scale, doubling all inputs more than doubles output.

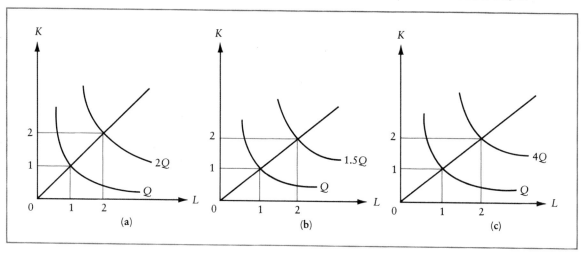

The concept of constant returns to scale is an appealing beginning point because it incorporates the reasonable presumption that an entrepreneur can duplicate the production process—with double the quantities of all factors—and derive twice the output as before. If 1 carpenter, 1 hammer, 40 nails, 10 boards, and 20 square feet of elbow room can produce 1 doghouse per day, then 2 carpenters, 2 hammers, 80 nails, 20 boards, and 40 square feet of elbow room should produce 2 doghouses per day, if all inputs are homogeneous. If all inputs could be cloned and put to work in identical fashion, output should rise in proportion to the increase in factors.

What, then, are the explanations for increasing and decreasing returns to scale? Increasing returns may arise from the specialization of labor and capital that occurs with an increase in the size of the firm. In small firms, workers and machinery are of necessity generalists, whereas these inputs can become specialists in certain timesaving, repetitive tasks as the firm grows. The single employee of a mom-and-pop grocery store stocks shelves, cuts meat, checks out customers, and trims lettuce. In large chains these tasks are specialized, thereby raising the physical productivity of labor. Similar specialization is open to capital. In a small store, a single two-wheel dolly may be the only means of hauling case goods, regardless of the size and weight of the loads, but larger stores have dollies of various sizes, including forklift trucks, that are scaled to specific needs.

Increasing returns to scale may also occur because of arithmetic. For example, doubling the dimensions of a cube more than doubles the volume in cubic feet. The volume of a cube that is 2 feet by 2 feet by 2 feet is 8 cubic feet. Doubling the dimensions to 4 feet by 4 feet by 4 feet increases the volume to 64 cubic feet. Likewise, doubling the diameter of a sewage or water pipe more than doubles the flow capacity of the pipe, resulting in increasing returns to scale.

Decreasing returns to scale may arise when it is impossible to expand all inputs proportionately, even though every effort is made to do so. Suppose an insurance company doubles all labor and capital inputs, including the sales force, fleet cars, order pools, and computer facilities to process policies. When a firm is just starting to grow, such an expansion may more than double output, for reasons already mentioned. In addition, the ability of the owner to manage and coordinate its inputs will be affected. If the management function itself improves with size, increasing returns to scale are fortified. But if management loses its effectiveness in training, supervising, and coordinating all components of an increasingly complex firm, decreasing returns to scale could result. (This problem is quite apart from the practical matter of finding homogeneous inputs.) As a firm expands, it hires workers who require training and whose productivity is lower than that of current workers.

Returns to scale are defined as the empirical relationship between output and inputs when all inputs are homogeneous and expanded proportionately. Curiously, most examples of increasing and decreasing returns to scale involve either inputs that are not homogeneous or input expansions that fail to increase all factors proportionately, such as management skills, weather, goodwill, and other intangibles.

Managerial economists often use **homogeneous production functions** in empirical and theoretical work, the essential characteristic of which is a linear expansion path. A production function is homogeneous to degree j if a proportional increase in all inputs equal to λ increases output by the jth power of λ:

$$f(\lambda L, \lambda K) = \lambda^j f(L, K) \qquad (5.9)$$

A special class of homogeneity occurs when a doubling of all inputs doubles output. In this case, $\lambda = 2$, the increase in output is $\lambda^j = 2^1$, and the production function is **linear homogeneous** (or homogeneous to degree 1). A production function demonstrating constant returns to scale is linearly homogeneous, and in addition to having a linear expansion path, it displays equidistant isoquants. Such homogeneous production functions are used by managerial economists studying the behavior of firms not because they are believed to be the most realistic but because their underlying assumptions have convenient analytical properties.

Chapter 6 shows how returns to scale influence the firm's long-run cost curves. There is no doubt about the importance of returns to scale, in spite of the difficulty of defining the concept. It has implications for the optimal size of firms, the tendency for industries to become monopolized, the ability of small firms to compete with large ones, and many other problems in firm and government decision making.

Summary

Every issue on the supply side of output markets (and hence on the demand side of input markets) involves the technical ability to combine the factors of production with the alteration of raw materials for the production of final goods. Every remaining chapter in this book is keyed to the concepts of production theory presented in this chapter.

In drawing two-dimensional graphs of relationships that exhibit more than two dimensions, we must always fix the values of all but two variables. In our simple production function, three variables are important: output, labor, and capital. To draw the production function in two dimensions, we must select one of these values as a shift parameter. By holding capital constant, we can construct the total product curve, the slope of which is the marginal product of labor. By holding output constant, we produce an isoquant curve, the slope of which is the

Key Terms

marginal rate of technical substitution. These are alternate methods of solving the problem of drawing in two dimensions a production function that is really multidimensional. You should be well acquainted with both conventions, because they both have important functions and applications.

An essential concept for both short-run and long-run production functions is the distinction between the diminishing marginal product and returns to scale. The diminishing marginal product of labor derives from the eventual restraint on production imposed by the fixity of capital. In contrast, returns to scale result when both capital and labor inputs increase proportionately. The diminishing marginal product involves a change in the proportions of the factors that are used as labor changes against a backdrop of fixed capital; returns to scale keep the ratio of input use constant by considering scaled changes in inputs in order to measure their effect on output. The former is displayed by the total product curve, the latter by the spacing of the isoquant map. The theoretical uses and policy implications of these production concepts will unfold in future chapters.

Problems

1. a. Explain why 4 months is sufficient to make plans to construct a car wash but not a steel plant.
   b. For what kinds of production functions is capital alterable in 20 minutes? In 5 years?

2. The chancellor of a small midwestern university stated in a speech, "In the past decade we have doubled the number of classrooms and doubled the number of professors, but the number of students has increased only 50 percent. Therefore, we should expand no more, because we have reached the level of diminishing returns." Comment on this statement.

3. Noted physicists have shown that huge satellites with photovoltaic cells can transmit via laser beams to the earth electricity that is equivalent to 10 percent of the sun's energy that falls on the cells. The efficiency of ground-based photovoltaic cells is only 5 percent.
   a. Would the ground-based cells ever be more efficient than the satellite cells?
   b. How are you defining efficiency in your answer to part a?
   c. What do you say to a physicist who insists that the satellite cells are always more efficient?

4. Real-life examples of stage III production are exceedingly rare because it is so easy to spot and so easy to eliminate. Can you cite examples of stage III production? Is it more common in the public than in the private sector?

5. Early kidney patients needing dialysis treatment paid about $50,000 per year for the service. New techniques, learned with the cooperation of these early patients, have lowered the price of kidney dialysis to about $12,000 a year. Should these people have paid for dialysis as consumers or been paid as factors of production?

6. The probability of an automobile accident is a function of drivers' caution levels. Let there be two drivers, driver A and driver B. Let $P(A,B)$ be the probability of avoiding an accident.

a. Draw probability isoquant curves analogous to the production isoquant curves discussed in this chapter.

b. Draw probability total product curves analogous to those discussed in this chapter.

c. In production theory, we can always increase output by expanding all inputs. But we can never produce an accident avoidance probability greater than 1, no matter how cautious drivers A and B become. How does this fact affect the shape of your iso-probability map and your probability total product curves?

d. Caution is costly; it requires time, effort, and resources. Explain why drivers do not take complete caution, even when mature and sober. (Hint: Do physicians eliminate all risks in surgery? Why or why not?)

7. Consider college education to be a form of production:

a. List all fixed and variable factors in the production of college education.

b. Are tenured faculty members fixed or variable inputs?

c. Are untenured faculty members fixed or variable inputs?

d. If buildings and tenured professors are fixed factors and taxpayers demand a reduction in costs, can costs be reduced without reducing efficiency?

8. Consider the economics of pothole repair. Let the output be the number of potholes repaired and the inputs be a truck, asphalt, shovels, and workers. It has been noted that one worker often fills potholes while two workers rest on their shovels.

a. Does this imply production in stage III, which is characterized by a redundancy of labor and excessive labor costs? (Hint: What if some streets have many potholes and others have only a few?)

b. Asphalt is partly a petroleum distillate that emits a gas in hot weather. Prolonged exposure to this gas makes strong men weak. Discuss "resting on shovel" as a factor of production.

9. Presidents of the United States have played golf, sailed, played the piano, and played touch football. Is such leisure a factor of production?

10. Show that, for production functions involving constant returns to scale, the ridge lines are straight lines.

11. Draw the isoquants when factors of production are perfect substitutes; perfect complements. Using these as limiting cases, draw the isoquants when factors are highly substitutable; poor substitutes.

12. Draw an isoquant curve. How does it shift if the quality of the product is increased? The quantity?

13. Draw a total product curve for the quantity of capital K_0. Now send all the workers to a training program to make them more productive. Redraw the total product curve.

14. Table 5.2 contains production data for a given capital stock. Compute the corresponding MP_L and AP_L values and check to see whether the following conditions hold true: (1) MP_L begins to fall before AP_L falls; (2) $MP_L = AP_L$ at the minimum of AP_L; (3) Q is maximized at the level of labor use for which $MP_L = 0$; (4) Q diminishes when MP_L is negative. (Hint: These conditions will only be approximate because of the use of discrete data. The postulated

Table 5.2

Figuring Average and Marginal Products of Labor

Labor (L)	Output (Q)	AP_L	MP_L
1	2		
2	5		
3	9		
4	12		
5	14		
6	15		
7	15		
8	14		
9	12		
10	9		

properties hold exactly only when the data are continuous and the curves are smooth.)

15. Suppose the short-run total product curve is linear. Derive the corresponding MP_L and AP_L curves. How might you explain such production responses?

16. Use what you have learned about isoquants to draw the following graphs:

    a. Draw an isoquant map that exhibits increasing, constant, and decreasing returns to scale over different ranges of production.

    b. Draw and interpret an isoquant that is concave from the origin.

    c. Draw an isoquant map whose isoquants are nearly but not totally vertical. Interpret the meaning of the implied $MRTS$.

    d. Draw an isoquant curve that is negatively sloped, is convex from the origin, and intersects both the labor and capital axes. Are the inputs perfect substitutes, considering that the same output can be produced using either all capital or all labor?

17. As a certain firm expands its labor force with capital fixed, output rises first at an increasing rate, then at a constant rate. Draw the total product curve and the MP_L and AP_L curves of this curious production function.

18. Being as original as possible, develop a list of explanations for increasing and decreasing returns to scale. Now cross out those entries that involve either nonhomogeneous inputs or a failure to expand all inputs proportionately. How many items are left on your list?

19. How would you estimate the marginal product of a piece of equipment you own?

20. Suppose that the total product curve of a firm rises to twice its original height.

    a. What must happen to the slope of the curve?

    b. Will it be twice the original slope at every level of output?

21. Draw a total product curve on a sheet of paper. Now suppose that the marginal product of labor falls by half everywhere along the curve. Redraw the curve.

22. Draw a total product curve. Now suppose that the curve rises to twice its height at every level of labor input. Will the new curve's inflection point be directly above the original one? Why or why not?

23. Draw an isoquant curve. Now suppose that the marginal product of labor falls to half its original value at each level of labor utilization. Redraw the isoquant curve in proper relation to the original one.

24. Show that two isoquants can intersect if the curves represent different production technologies.

25. Draw a production curve for the output of a teacher's classroom performance. What is the output? What are the inputs? Which are fixed and which are variable? What are the units of measurement?

26. Consider the doctor's office described in Application 5.2. Suppose that the office visit isoquant shifts outward by 10 percent when the office changes from a fee-for-service policy to a prepaid policy. Interpret the shift.

27. Suppose that a firm has forty workers who are identical in ability. If the firm hires an additional worker who is twice as able as the others, what happens to the marginal product of the fortieth worker?

28. Suppose that a firm's labor force undertakes a training program in order to double output for any given number of workers. What will happen to the number of workers needed to push the firm into stage III of production?

29. Explain why the marginal product of the nth worker is not unique to that worker.

30. Why does the marginal product of labor fall as workers are added even if the workers are equally qualified?

31. Output is held constant along an isoquant. Why is the isoquant not linear?

32. Explain how the production curve acquires its shape. Why does the curve slope downward beyond some point?

33. If a baseball player's batting average rises for a month, is it possible that the player does a little worse each week during the month?

34. Use your production theory to illustrate the change that takes place in housing construction due to prefabrication.

35. Explain why firms will not operate in stage III of production. How will they know if they are?

36. Explain how the principles of production can be discovered by people who run a business but who do not have a course in managerial economics under their belts.

37. What are the capital and labor inputs in the production of church services? What is the output? Is there substitutability among the inputs?

38. What are the capital and labor inputs in the production of legal services? What is the output? Does it make sense to draw a production curve to illustrate the production?

39. Explain why the isoquant analysis is more suitable for illustrating capital-labor substitution than for illustrating the production contour.

40. Consider the peak point on the production contour. What economic forces will cause the point to move to the right or the left?

Suggested Readings

Baumol, William J. *Economic Theory and Operations Analysis*. 4th ed. Englewood Cliffs, N.J.: Prentice-Hall, 1977.

Douglas, Paul H. "Are There Laws of Production?" *American Economic Review* 38 (March 1948): 1–41.

Ferguson, C. E., and Gould, J. P. *Microeconomic Theory*. 4th ed. Homewood, Ill.: Irwin, 1975.

Henderson, J. M., and Quandt, R. E. *Microeconomic Theory: A Mathematical Approach*. 3rd ed. New York: McGraw-Hill, 1980, chap. 4.

Levenson, A. M., and Solow, Babette S. "Returns to Scale and the Spacing of Isoquants." *American Economic Review* 56 (1966): 501–505.

Stigler, George J. "The Division of Labor Is Limited by the Extent of the Market." *Journal of Political Economy* 59 (1951): 185–193.

Stigler, George J. *The Theory of Price.* New York: Macmillan, 1966, chap. 6.

Tangri, Om P. "Omissions in the Treatment of the Law of Variable Proportions." *American Economic Review* 61 (1966): 484–493.

Vickrey, William S. *Microstatics.* New York: Harcourt, Brace Jovanovich, 1964, chap. 4.

6
COSTS OF PRODUCTION

A primitive Eskimo tribe is said to have devised a diabolical method of torture and eventual execution. The victim was seated on a large block of ice, beneath which was positioned a sharp spear. As the ice melted, the victim was slowly impaled. In similar fashion, you confront two ice blocks: production theory (Chapter 5) and the conversion of production curves into cost curves (this chapter). Only after these two ice blocks are melted away by the heat of your study will you begin to get the point of all the curve bending you have endured. Do not despair. The analysis and applications of this chapter will reveal how useful **production-cost analysis** can be in guiding managers' decisions.

This chapter transforms production concepts into their cost equivalents. Here dollar signs are attached to the labor and capital inputs that a firm employs, and **cost curves** are formulated. (So far, only the physical relationship between inputs and output has been discussed.) Cost curves are powerful decision-making tools when properly understood.

Meaning of Costs

Economists and accountants define *costs* differently. Both definitions are correct, because they are designed for different uses. Suppose a firm incurs $10,000 of labor costs per year. Furthermore, assume that the firm owns machines that cost $20,000 when purchased five years ago. What are the current costs of production?

Accountants include the $10,000 labor expense in current costs. Capital costs are more difficult to determine, but a portion of the original purchase price ($20,000) would be assigned to current costs by reference to a depreciation formula. For example, if the machines are depreciated evenly over a 10-year period, the annual capital cost would be $2,000 per year for 10 years and then would fall to zero. Thus the **accounting cost** would be $12,000 for the current year (labor expense plus one year's capital depreciation).

The economist proceeds differently. **Economic cost** means opportunity cost—the value of forgone options, or the amount of money given up by using resources in a certain way instead of in their next-best use. What are the forgone alternatives in the previous example? The wages of labor are determined broadly by the alternative uses of labor. Thus the economist includes the $10,000 labor cost as a surrogate for the value of the labor in alternative employment. The economist and the accountant treat labor costs the same way.

But what about capital costs? Economists measure capital costs as the value of the machines in alternative uses. Suppose the machines could be rented out to other firms for $40,000 per year. The economist measures the capital costs as $40,000—the forgone value of the machines in alternative uses. Note that the historical cost of $20,000 is irrelevant to the economist. It is a **sunk cost** and does not represent a measure of the opportunity cost of the machines. For example, the accountant's capital cost of the machines falls to zero once the machines are fully depreciated, whereas the economist's capital cost continues to reflect the forgone rental value of the machines.

Economists are interested in still another cost component—the **entrepreneurial opportunity cost.** Just like any other factor of production, entrepreneurs must earn an income, called a profit, at least as great as they could earn in their next-best alternative employments. Thus a profit equal to the entrepreneur's next-best alternative—the entrepreneurial opportunity cost—is a necessary cost of keeping the entrepreneur in the current activity.

Let's summarize our results. In our example, the accountant records the current expenses of hiring labor and the current year's share of the historical costs after allowing for depreciation. The economist measures the value of the labor, capital, and entrepreneurial services in their alternative uses. These are vastly different measures. Economic costs exceed accounting costs because they include the value of the entrepreneur in alternative employments. Hence the owner of a bicycle repair shop that reports accounting profits of $20,000 is actually earning negative economic profits if he or she is worth $25,000 to Schwinn as a bicycle mechanic.

This chapter develops the cost curves of labor and capital; entrepreneurial opportunity costs are added in Chapter 7. This addition is easily accomplished and allows a deeper understanding of contemporary managerial problems. Also, accounting costs differ from economic costs, so it follows that accounting profits differ from economic profits. We will study this distinction in detail in Chapter 7. Meanwhile, train yourself to include all opportunity costs and ignore all sunk (historical) costs when considering decisions in the current period. The economist's definition of cost is one of economic theory's outstanding contributions to human knowledge.

Total Costs in the Short Run

By now, you should be accustomed to regarding the short run as the analytic period in which at least one factor of production cannot be varied. It is natural to begin by treating capital as the fixed factor. When capital is fixed, the firm experiences diminishing marginal returns. Now let's study the firm's costs of production when other factors are fixed.

Total Variable Cost Curve

Figure 6.1a contains a short-run total product curve that, for convenience, ignores the negatively sloped portion corresponding to inefficient production stage III. To develop the desired cost concept, it is convenient to redraw the product curve with output (Q) on the horizontal axis and labor (L) on the vertical axis. There are at least two ways to visualize the effect of such a switch:

1. Trace the total product curve on thin paper, turn the paper over, hold it up to a light, and position the axes so output is measured on the horizontal axis.

2. Imagine grasping the vertical axis (Q) from beneath with the thumb and forefinger of your right hand and the horizontal axis (L) with your left and then exchanging the position of the axes.

Either method results in a total product curve with the slope illustrated in Figure 6.1b. Panels a and b illustrate the same relationship between input and output. The difference in the curves' appearance is due solely to an arbitrary change in the axes.

Next suppose that the firm pays $1 for each unit of labor service it hires. The total production curve in panel b is transformed into a cost curve in panel c by multiplying the units of labor on the vertical axis by the per-unit cost of labor, or the **wage rate** (w). For example, point A in panel b reveals that producing 30 units of ouput requires 10 workers. This is a production statement. In contrast, point A' in

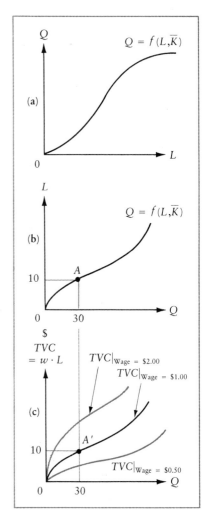

Figure 6.1
Total Variable Cost Curve

(a) The total product curve is $Q = f(L, \overline{K})$. **(b)** This panel shows the same curve as in panel a but with the labor and output axes reversed. **(c)** All three TVC curves shown here depend on a given wage rate. The TVC curve is derived by multiplying the marginal labor force by the wage at each output.

panel c tells us that 30 units of output require a labor cost outlay of $10 ($w \cdot L = \$1 \cdot 10$).

Variable costs are those that change when the rate of output changes. The cost curve in Figure 6.1c is thus called the **total variable cost** (TVC) curve because it traces out the relationship between output (Q) and the cost of hiring the variable resources necessary for such production. TVC may be expressed as

$$TVC = w \cdot L \tag{6.1}$$

where

    w = wage rate
    L = units of labor

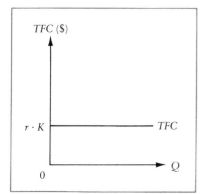

Figure 6.2
Total Fixed Cost Curve

Total fixed costs do not vary with a change in output. Hence, the *TFC* curve is horizontal.

There are four things to note about the *TVC* curve. First, its shape is determined by the shape of the firm's total product curve. Thus the various stages of production have their counterparts in the *TVC* curve. Second, a shift in the total product curve—due perhaps to a change in capital—shifts the *TVC* curve. Third, each *TVC* curve pertains to a unique wage rate. A reduction in wages shifts the *TVC* curve downward, as panel c illustrates. Increasing the wage rate has the opposite effect. Fourth, the *TVC* curve emanates from the origin, because variable costs can be eliminated by ceasing production.

Total Fixed Cost Curve

Fixed costs are those associated with the factors of production that are useful for a long time and hard to modify once in place. Thus fixed costs have two essential characteristics: (1) They cannot be avoided in the short run, and (2) they do not change as a result of expansions or contractions in output. Firms may have such fixed expenses as property tax liabilities, lease payments, monthly bank loan obligations, and management service contracts, which are independent of firms' rates of output and cannot be avoided in the short run. Since fixed costs are independent of the firm's output, the **total fixed cost** (TFC) curve is a horizontal line, as shown in Figure 6.2.

Recall that *capital* is a generic term representing all fixed factors. Thus TFC is defined as

$$TFC = r \cdot \overline{K} \tag{6.2}$$

where

    r = the per-unit rental rate of capital
    $\overline{K}$ = units of capital input (the bar over the K representing short-run fixity)

If a firm rents its capital, the **rental rate of capital**, r, is an explicit out-of-pocket expense. If the capital is owned outright, r is the forgone rental value of the capital, an implicit opportunity cost.

Short-Run Total Cost Curve

The short-run **total cost** (TC) is simply the sum of the variable and fixed cost components, as illustrated in Figure 6.3. The TVC curve emanates from the origin, whereas the TFC curve is a horizontal line. The short-run total cost curve (TC) is derived by vertical summation, that is, by adding the two cost components at every level of output. TC in Figure 6.3 exceeds TVC by exactly $100—the amount of fixed costs. For example, when output is zero, $TC = TFC$. At all other outputs, such as Q_1 and Q_2, TC is plotted by adding the $100 of fixed costs to the variable costs. The only difference between TC and TVC is the vertical displacement of TC due to the addition of fixed costs. Although the positions of the two curves are different, their slopes are the same.

Average and Marginal Cost Curves

You know by now that every total magnitude must have its average and marginal counterparts. We may now derive the average and marginal cost curves that correspond to the three total cost curves presented in the previous section.

Average Variable Cost Curve

The **average variable cost** (AVC) is defined as

$$AVC = \frac{TVC}{Q} = \frac{w \cdot L}{Q} \tag{6.3}$$

The AVC is the cost of obtaining the variable factors of production per unit of final output. This value is derived by dividing the TVC by Q, the units of final output produced. The AVC is the slope of a ray drawn from the origin to an arbitrary point on the TVC curve. In Figure 6.4a, three such rays are drawn to points A, B, and C of the TVC curve. The slopes of these rays measure the AVC for each level of output. (Refer to the derivation of AP_L in Chapter 5 if the reason for this statement escapes you.) The slope of the ray $\overline{0A}$ is TVC_1/Q_1, which equals AVC at point A. The value $AVC_1 = TVC_1/Q_1$ is plotted as point A' on the AVC curve in panel b. All other points on the AVC curve are derived similarly.

The slope of ray $\overline{0A}$ exceeds that of $\overline{0B}$ and equals the slope of $\overline{0C}$. The ray $\overline{0B}$ is tangent to the TVC curve and is thus the flattest ray that can be drawn to the TVC curve in Figure 6.4. Because the slopes of the rays define the AVC, we may conclude that the AVC falls up to output Q_2 and rises thereafter. The AVC is a U-shaped

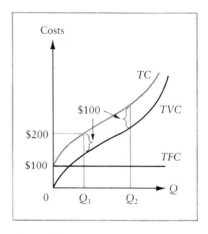

Figure 6.3
Short-Run Total Cost Curve

The total cost curve is the sum of total variable and total fixed costs. The TC curve lies above the TVC curve by the amount of total fixed costs. These curves have identical slopes.

Figure 6.4
Average Variable Cost Curve

(a) The *AVC* curve is the slope of a ray from the origin to any point on the *TVC* curve. **(b)** The *AVC* declines up to output level Q_2, then rises. It is a U-shaped curve.

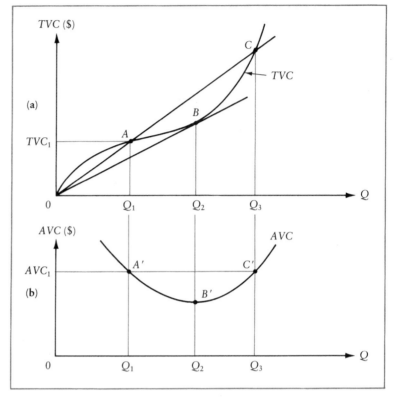

curve that reaches its minimum at the rate of output at which a ray from the origin becomes tangent to the *TVC* curve.

Intuitively, the *AVC* curve declines in the early stages of production because labor becomes increasingly efficient with the specialization of tasks. Eventually, the loss of efficiency caused by the congestion of labor on the fixed inputs forces *AVC* to rise. Hence, the *AVC* curve's U shape is directly traceable to diminishing returns.

Average Fixed Cost Curve

The **average fixed cost** (*AFC*) is defined as

$$AFC = \frac{TFC}{Q} = \frac{r \cdot \overline{K}}{Q} \tag{6.4}$$

Let's use the same familiar technique to derive the *AFC* curve from the *TFC* curve. Because the *TFC* curve is a horizontal line, the slopes of the rays drawn to the curve at larger quantities of output fall continuously. Thus the *AFC* curve continues to fall toward the horizontal axis without ever actually touching it, as seen in Figure 6.5b. The *AFC* curve is a rectangular hyperbola, because the product of *AFC* and *Q* always equals the constant *TFC*.

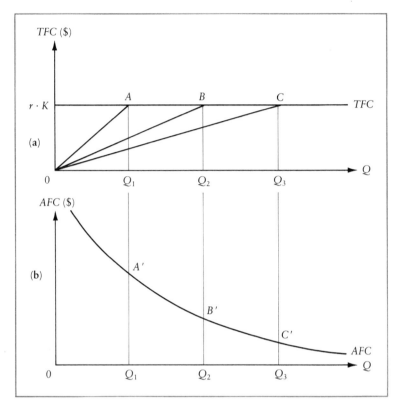

Figure 6.5
Average Fixed Cost Curve

(a) Using the ray technique to measure *AFC*, we can see that it declines throughout, because the slopes of the rays decline continuously. **(b)** The *AFC* curve is a rectangular hyperbola.

Suppose the firm has the following costs per month, which must be paid regardless of the firm's rate of output:

Property taxes	$ 1,000
Janitorial service	3,000
Legal and consultant retainers	2,500
Bank loan	3,250
United Way contribution	250
Total fixed costs	$10,000

The *AFC* equals $20 when the firm produces 500 units per month, only $2 if production is 5,000 units, and a miniscule $0.20 if 50,000 are produced. The firm spreads its overhead expenses over more units of output by increasing production.

Short-Run Average Total Cost Curve
The **short-run average total cost** (*ATC*) is defined as

$$ATC = \frac{TC}{Q} = \frac{TVC + TFC}{Q} = AVC + AFC \qquad (6.5)$$

Figure 6.6
Average Total Cost Curve

The average total cost (*ATC*) curve is the vertical sum of the *AVC* and *AFC* curves. The *ATC* achieves its minimum at Q_2; the *AVC* is minimized at the smaller output, Q_1. The vertical distance between the *ATC* and *AVC* curves is the *AFC*.

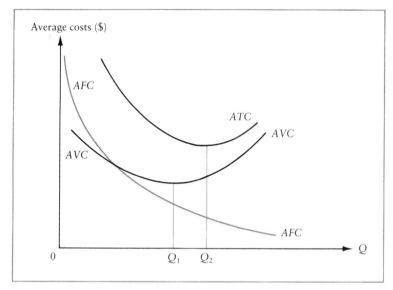

The *ATC*, which is often referred to as simply the **average cost**, is derived by summing its two components vertically at each output rate. As shown in Figure 6.6, this summation involves the U-shaped *AVC* curve and the negatively sloped *AFC* curve (which is drawn as a gray line). For small levels of output, both the *AVC* and *AFC* decline as output expands; thus the *ATC* must also fall initially. The *AVC* reaches its minimum at Q_1; but because the *AFC* still falls, the *ATC* must continue to fall beyond the output at which *AVC* attains its minimum value. Between output levels Q_1 and Q_2, the *AFC* is falling faster than the *AVC* is rising. During this phase, the *ATC*—the sum of *AVC* and *AFC*—must continue to fall. At output Q_2, the *AVC* curve is rising at exactly the same rate that the *AFC* curve is falling; when this occurs, the *ATC* curve attains its minimum level. Beyond Q_2, the increase in the *AVC* exceeds the decrease in the *AFC*; the net effect is to cause the *ATC* curve to rise.

Thus the *ATC* curve is U-shaped, lies above the *AVC* curve by the amount of *AFC* (which gets continually smaller), and achieves its minimum at a larger level of output than does the *AVC* curve. That is, the minimum of the *ATC* curve occurs to the right of the minimum of the *AVC* curve.

From the construction of the *ATC* curve in Figure 6.6, it should be clear that the vertical distance between *ATC* and *AVC* is *AFC*. This fact has two implications:

1. The *ATC* and *AVC* curves get closer together as output increases, because *AFC* gets smaller with larger output.

2. *AFC* shows up twice in Figure 6.6; once in the hyperbolic *AFC* curve itself and again as the difference between *ATC* and *AVC*.

It is convenient to eliminate this redundancy by dropping the explicit representation of the *AFC* curve. No information is lost, and the diagram becomes less cluttered. Thus the standard depiction of the firm's short-run average cost curves includes only the two U-shaped *ATC* and *AVC* curves.[1]

Short-Run Marginal Cost Curve

Chapter 3 defines *marginal cost* as the change in total cost resulting from a small increase in output, holding capital fixed. We may now study the properties of marginal cost in more detail.

Total cost is the sum of variable and fixed costs. Since fixed costs are independent of the firm's rate of output, any change in total cost due to a change in production must arise from a change in variable costs. Accordingly, **short-run marginal cost** (*SMC*) is

$$SMC = \frac{\Delta TC}{\Delta Q} = \frac{\Delta TVC}{\Delta Q} \qquad (6.6)$$

As usual, the definition of the marginal concept is equivalent to the mathematical definition of slope. Thus marginal cost is the slope of the corresponding total cost.

Although there are three total cost curves (*TC*, *TVC*, and *TFC*), there is only one relevant marginal cost curve. The *TFC* curve is horizontal; its slope is always zero. This is another way of saying that changes in output do not change *TFC*. But the *TC* curve has the same slope as the *TVC* curve, and so marginal cost may be derived by evaluating the slope of either curve. Thus there is only one *SMC* curve to be concerned with; it is the slope of both the *TVC* and *TC* curves.

We have seen in other contexts that the slope of a curvilinear function is measured geometrically by constructing tangents to different points of the total curve and measuring the slopes of these tangents. Figure 6.7 shows how to use this method to derive the *SMC* curve. Tangents are drawn to points *A*, *B*, *C*, *D*, and *E* of the *TVC* curve in panel a. The slope of the tangent at *A* exceeds the slope of the tangent at *B*. These marginal cost values are plotted as *A'* and *B'* in panel b; *SMC* is falling in this range of output. The slope of the *TVC* curve (which equals *SMC*) continues to fall up to the inflection point *C*. Beyond *C* the slopes of the tangents increase, as illustrated by the tangents drawn to points *D* and *E*. But no tangent can be drawn to the inflection point, because the curve is changing direction at that level of output. Thus the *SMC* curve falls up to the inflection point and rises thereafter; short-run marginal

---

1. Rather than summing *AFC* and *AVC* to derive *ATC*, we could have derived *ATC* directly from the *TC* curve. As an exercise, try constructing rays to the *TC* curve in Figure 6.3, deriving an *ATC* curve, and proving that (1) the *ATC* is a U-shaped curve, (2) it lies above the *AVC* curve, (3) its minimum point occurs to the right of the minimum of the *AVC* curve, and (4) the vertical distance between the *AVC* and *ATC* curves diminishes at larger levels of output and equals *AFC*.

Figure 6.7
Short-Run Marginal Cost Curve

(a) The slopes of tangents drawn to the *TVC* curve decline to the inflection point *C*, then rise. **(b)** The *SMC* curve reflects the slope of the *TVC* curve. Hence, the *SMC* curve declines up to output Q_3, then rises.

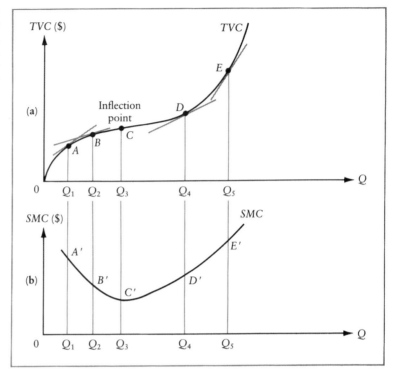

cost is a U-shaped curve. (This is the formal derivation of the marginal cost curve derived intuitively in Chapter 3.) The *SMC* curve plays an especially important role in the firm's decisions, because it measures the cost changes that result from output changes.

Fitting Average and Marginal Cost Curves Together

By now you should be comfortable with the idea that average and marginal curves derived from any total curve must not only show the proper relationship to the total curve but also to each other. Using *AVC* and *SMC* to illustrate, the rules of arithmetic governing average and marginal costs are as follows:

When $SMC < AVC$, *AVC* must fall.

When $SMC > AVC$, *AVC* must rise.

When $SMC = AVC$, *AVC* neither rises nor falls, but remains at its minimum value.

The same three-part rule applies to the relationship between *SMC* and *ATC*. This is a matter of arithmetic; averages are influenced by new (marginal) observations. For example, no student ever succeeded in raising a test-score average by scoring lower than average on the next (marginal) exam. To raise an average, the marginal value must exceed the present average.

Figure 6.8 shows the graphic relationship between TVC, AVC, and SMC. The SMC curve is the slope of the TVC curve and is a U-shaped curve that attains its minimum at the inflection point of TVC (point A in Figure 6.8a). The AVC is represented by a U-shaped curve that reaches its minimum at the output level at which a ray from the origin becomes tangent to the TVC curve (point B). You should satisfy yourself that, for any point on the TVC curve up to point B, the marginal cost (the slope of the TVC curve) is less than average variable cost (the slope of the ray from the origin to the TVC curve). And because $SMC < AVC$, AVC falls up to point B. To the right of B, $SMC > AVC$ (the slope of the TVC curve > the slope of the rays to the TVC curve), and the AVC rises. Just at B, the slope of the TVC curve and the slope of the ray are the same. Thus $SMC = AVC$ at point B. The SMC curve must therefore intersect the AVC curve from below at precisely the minimum point of the AVC.

These average and marginal curves are drawn in Figure 6.8b. You should forswear all other activities in life until you are able to

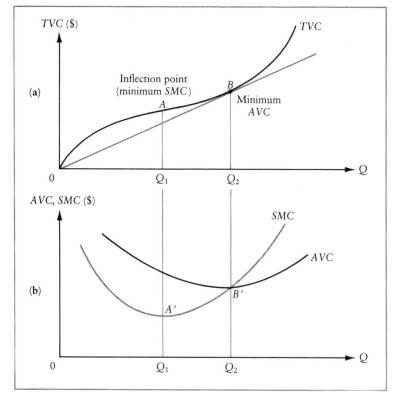

Figure 6.8
Combining the *AVC* and *SMC* Curves

(a) The *TVC* curve can be used to derive the *SMC* curve as well as the *AVC* curve. **(b)** When *SMC* < *AVC*, as between 0 and Q_2, the *AVC* curve falls. When *SMC* = *AVC*, as at Q_2, the *AVC* achieves its minimum value. When *SMC* > *AVC*, as beyond Q_2, the *AVC* curve rises.

derive the average and marginal curves from the total curve.

We have only one more step to take before leaving this discussion of short-run cost relationships: connecting *SMC* and *ATC*, just as we have done with *SMC* and *AVC*. The relationships are identical; the marginal cost will be below *ATC* when *ATC* is falling, will intersect the *ATC* curve from below at exactly the minimum of *ATC*, and will lie above *ATC* when *ATC* is rising.

Figure 6.9 presents the complete set of short-run marginal and average cost curves associated with the employment of variable (labor) and fixed (capital) resources. Because the *AFC* curve is the vertical distance between the *ATC* curve and its variable component, *AVC*, Figure 6.9 actually shows four cost relationships, not just the obvious three.

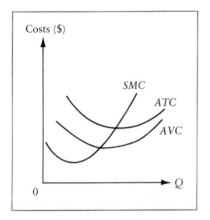

Figure 6.9
Family of Short-Run Average and Marginal Cost Curves

The *ATC*, *AVC*, and *SMC* curves are shown here explicitly. The *AFC* is implied by the vertical distance between the *ATC* and *AVC* curves. Hence, four cost relationships are illustrated, not just three.

Production-Cost Duality

Before we lose sight of the forest for the trees, let's take stock of what we have done so far in this chapter. We have been examining a common production problem, in which some inputs (and costs) can be varied while others remain fixed. If the firm faces constant prices for all inputs, the costs of hiring the variable factors change when output changes; however, the costs of the fixed factors are independent of output.

So far so good. But a proliferation of curves soon begins to make a relatively easy idea appear complicated. Each of the total cost components has a marginal and average cost curve of its own. Still, after the dust settles we'll have a manageable cost package (exhibited in Figure 6.9), comprising two U-shaped average curves and a U-shaped marginal curve.

The key point of this section: All the cost curves (except for fixed costs) owe their shapes to the firm's production curves. Chapter 3 showed intuitively that the marginal product of labor is the basis for marginal cost; this chapter reinforces the idea that the cost curve is dependent on the product curves, a phenomenon known as **production-cost duality**.

In Equation 6.6 short-run marginal cost has been defined as $SMC = \Delta TVC/\Delta Q$. Because $TVC = w \cdot L$, we can write

$$SMC = \frac{w \cdot \Delta L}{\Delta Q} \qquad (6.7)$$

For a given wage rate, output and marginal cost can change only if the quantity of labor hired changes. The term $\Delta L/\Delta Q$ in Equation 6.7 is the inverse of the marginal product of labor; $\Delta L/\Delta Q =$

$1/(\Delta Q/\Delta L) = 1/MP_L$. Thus Equation 6.7 may be rewritten as

$$SMC = \frac{w}{MP_L} \qquad (6.8)$$

Now the production-cost duality is explicit. The wage rate, w, is the change in labor cost from hiring an additional unit of labor, and the MP_L is the additional output from using an extra unit of labor. Thus marginal cost, the ratio of the wage rate and the marginal product of labor, measures the change in labor costs resulting from an increase in production.

Suppose that the wage is constant at $10 per worker per time period and that the marginal product of labor is 2. The marginal cost is therefore $5, because hiring a marginal worker adds $10 to costs but yields 2 extra units of output: $MC = w/MP_L = \$10/2 = \$5$.

Equation 6.8 shows how production affects cost. When the MP_L rises, the SMC must fall, because the denominator in Equation 6.8 rises. Conversely, the SMC rises when the MP_L falls. Note also that the level of labor that maximizes the marginal product of labor determines the level of output for which marginal cost is minimized. Thus the SMC is a mirror image of the MP_L. The SMC curve reflects the productivity of variable factors as incorporated in the MP_L curve.

An equivalent duality may be shown between the AVC curve and the AP_L curve:

$$AVC = \frac{TVC}{Q} = \frac{w \cdot L}{Q} \qquad (6.9)$$

The term L/Q is the inverse of AP_L: $L/Q = 1/(Q/L) = 1/AP_L$. By substitution,

$$AVC = \frac{w}{AP_L} \qquad (6.10)$$

For a constant wage, the AVC depends uniquely on the AP_L. If $w = \$10$ and $AP_L = 5$ units, then $AVC = \$10/5 = \$2$. The cost of hiring workers per unit of output (the AVC) is $2.

In sum, increasing and diminishing returns underpin all the short-run cost curves except the AFC and TFC curves. Understanding this point can help you cope with the proliferation of curves. Meanwhile, rest assured that dividing costs into variable and fixed components is a useful managerial tool.

6.1

Progressive Income Taxes and Marginalist Reasoning

There is considerable confusion about the income tax rates under a progressive tax structure. We can use our knowledge of average-marginal relationships to organize our thinking on many tax issues, including these two: (1) If an income increase pushes one into a higher tax bracket, can the higher tax rate actually reduce the individual's after-tax take-home pay? (Many people use this argument as a reason to limit their work effort and, no doubt, to underreport earned income.) (2) Can an income tax be fashioned that is both progressive and does not discourage higher-income groups from working harder?

The figure presented here illustrates a total tax curve, TT, for which total income tax payments, T, are a rising function of the level of taxable income, Y. No tax is paid on income less than $\overline{0A}$ because of exemptions, exclusions, deductibles, and so forth.

The tax rate can be stated in both marginal and average

terms. The **average tax rate,** t_a, is the percentage of total taxable income paid in taxes. Thus $t_a = T/Y$. The **marginal tax rate,** t_m, is the tax levied on the last dollar of taxable income. Hence $t_m = \Delta T/\Delta Y$. Remember that average measurements are always ratios of total magnitudes and that marginal measurements always refer to changes in total magnitudes. We have seen this in production and cost analysis. The same is true of average and marginal tax rates.

The figure presents a simple way to identify these tax rates. The slope of the total tax curve measures the marginal tax rate, whereas the slope of a ray drawn from the origin to the total tax curve measures the average

tax rate. Thus the figure depicts a constant marginal tax rate (TT is linear) and an increasing average tax rate (ray $\overline{0C}$ is steeper than ray $\overline{0B}$). The arithmetic rule governing average-marginal relationships is therefore satisfied: t_a increases with income because $t_m > t_a$ at all levels of taxable income.

Can earning more taxable income actually reduce take-home pay under a progressive tax structure? Under the constant tax structure used in the figure, a higher taxable income would increase the tax liability and the average tax rate, t_a. The important thing, however, is the marginal tax rate, t_m. As long as the trajectory of the total tax curve is flatter than the 45-degree line, t_m is less than 1 and each new dollar of taxable income is taxed at less than 100 percent. Thus more taxable income means more after-tax take-home pay.

But what if the marginal tax rate is not constant, as shown in

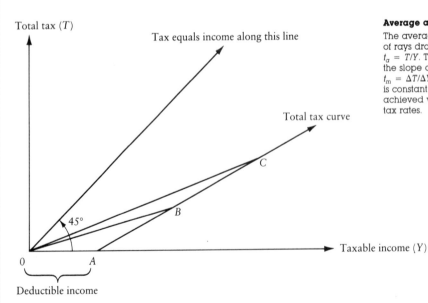

Total tax (T)

Tax equals income along this line

Total tax curve

C

B

45°

0   A

Taxable income (Y)

Deductible income

Average and Marginal Tax Rates

The average tax rate, t_a, is the slope of rays drawn to the total tax curve: $t_a = T/Y$. The marginal tax rate, t_m, is the slope of the total tax curve: $t_m = \Delta T/\Delta Y$. Thus t_a rises although t_m is constant. Progressivity can be achieved without increasing marginal tax rates.

the figure, but rises with income, as in the case of the U.S. income tax? The same analysis applies. If t_m rises, the total tax curve rises at an increasing rate. But as long as t_m is less than 1, the higher rates cannot lower after-tax income. Such a result would require a marginal tax rate greater than 1.*

*If taxpayers are moved into higher average (and marginal) brackets merely by inflation, such "bracket creep" can rob real income. Suppose that the increase in nominal taxable income is just offset by inflation, so that the worker's real income in unchanged. By moving into a higher tax bracket, the worker pays a higher average tax rate on the same real income. Hence inflation bites twice: It erodes the purchasing power of nominal income and increases tax liability on the same real income.

Now let's turn to the second issue: the degree to which a progressive tax discourages work. An income tax is progressive when higher-income groups pay a larger percentage of their income in taxes than lower-income groups do. Thus

progressivity implies a rising t_a but not necessarily a rising t_m. (The figure depicts progressivity with a constant t_m.) If a sense of "fairness" calls for progressive taxation and hence increasing average tax rates, this social goal can be accomplished without the rising marginal rates that produce work disincentives for higher-income groups.

This is an important lesson in marginalist reasoning. President Ronald Reagan used just such logic in promulgating a reduction in marginal tax rates for upper-income taxpayers. His was not an argument for eliminating the progressive income tax. Instead, he sought to preserve progressivity while promoting positive work incentives for upper-income groups.

Long-Run Costs

All costs are variable in the long run. Given sufficient time to adjust, firms can increase or decrease their employment of capital, buy or sell buildings, renegotiate bank loans, discount financial paper, and even declare bankruptcy. Managers' thinking must therefore encompass both the short run and the long run. Although many decisions are made on short notice and on the assumption that many costs are fixed, firms must also pursue long-run strategies pertaining to plant size, production runs, product lines, plant locations, and marketing.

There are two ways to study long-run costs, both useful to managers. First, the long run can be taken as a planning horizon made up of a series of short runs. This method analyzes long-run costs using the short-run curves we have already encountered. The second method is to use isoquants to achieve a more explicit representation of long-run costs when all factors are variable.

Envelope Curve

To begin, let's regard the long run as a planning horizon for the firm in which different combinations of labor and capital inputs may be contemplated. To simplify, suppose the firm is considering just three **scales of plant** (plant sizes), each determined by the amount of the capital input. Because the quantity of capital is a shift parameter to the total product curve and because each total product curve translates into a unique set of short-run cost curves, the assumption of three alternative levels of capital gives rise to the three *ATC* curves

Figure 6.10
Long-Run Average Cost Curve

The *LAC* curve is composed of the least-cost segments of three short-run scales of plant: ATC_1, ATC_2, and ATC_3. The *LAC* curve implies least-cost production when all inputs are variable.

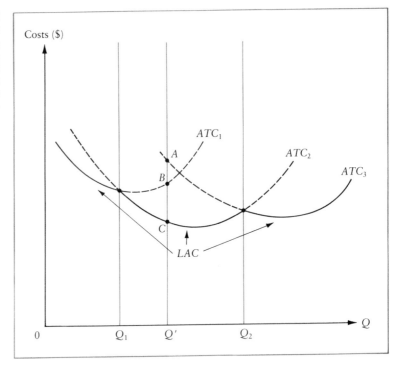

depicted in Figure 6.10. ATC_1 is the cost curve associated with the smallest scale of plant; ATC_2 is next largest; and ATC_3 is the largest.

Which scale of plant the firm should build depends on the expected rate of output. If the firm wishes to produce in the range $\overline{0Q_1}$, it may produce that quantity at least cost by employing the smallest scale of plant, ATC_1. Output in the range $\overline{Q_1Q_2}$ is produced at least cost by the scale of plant ATC_2. Any rate of output larger than Q_2 should be produced with the largest scale of plant, ATC_3.

The **long-run average total cost** (*LAC*) is the per-unit cost of production when the scale of plant is adjusted to produce a given output at least cost. The *LAC* curve represents average cost as a function of output, assuming that cost-minimizing adjustments in its combination of factors are made. The *LAC* curve in Figure 6.10 is the scalloped curve, composed of the solid, least-cost segments of the individual *ATC* curves. The dashed segments of the *ATC* curves are irrelevant to the *LAC* curve, because any output on the dashed segments can be produced cheaper by adopting a different scale of plant. For example, output Q' may be produced at a unit cost of $\overline{Q'A}$ using the largest scale of plant and $\overline{Q'B}$ using the smallest. But the least-cost method of producing Q' is to adopt the intermediate scale of plant, ATC_2, and to reduce unit cost to $\overline{Q'C}$. Points A and B are therefore not part of the *LAC* curve, because they do not represent least-cost methods of producing output Q'.

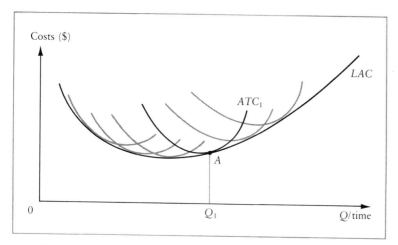

Figure 6.11
Envelope (*LAC*) Curve

If inputs are infinitely divisible, the curve is smooth. Each scale of plant contributes a single point to the *LAC* curve; the *LAC* curve is an envelope of all cost-minimizing scales of plant. *ATC₁* is the "optimum" scale of plant because it results in overall minimization of average costs.

When the number of plant sizes is small, the *LAC* curve is scalloped. But when a larger number of potential scale adjustments are considered, the *LAC* curve smooths out, as illustrated in Figure 6.11. With an infinite number of scales of plant, each plant contributes only one point to the *LAC* curve rather than a whole segment, as before. For example, output Q_1 in Figure 6.11 is produced at least cost by the adoption of scale of plant ATC_1. Point A is the only output for which scale of plant ATC_1 is the least-cost alternative and is therefore the only point that scale of plant ATC_1 contributes to the *LAC* "envelope." Each of the infinite scales of plant contributes a similar point. The *LAC* curve is the "envelope" of all such cost-minimizing points.

The *LAC* curve has several names: the **envelope curve**, because it envelops all the least-cost components of the short-run *ATC* curves; the **planning curve**, because it helps the firm plan the correct plant size for alternative rates of production; and the **Viner-Wong envelope curve**, named after its principal investigators.[2]

Long-Run Marginal Cost Curve

Long-run marginal cost (*LMC*) is the change in **long-run total cost** (*LTC*) resulting from a small change in output when all cost-minimizing adjustments in all resources have been accomplished:

$$LMC = \frac{\Delta LTC}{\Delta Q} \qquad (6.11)$$

The *LAC* and *LMC* curves must fit together in standard fashion, as shown in Figure 6.12. Any further elaboration of the average-marginal relationship would surely be monotonous.

Figure 6.12
Combining the *LAC* and *LMC* Curves

The average-marginal rules of arithmetic also apply to long-run costs.

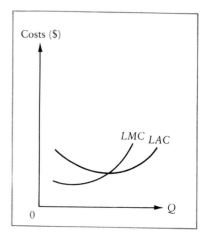

2. Jacob Viner, "Cost Curves and Supply Curves," *Zeitschrift für Nationalökonomie* 3 (1931): 23–46. Reprinted in George J. Stigler and Kenneth E. Boulding, eds., *Readings in Price Theory* (Homewood, Ill.: Irwin, 1952), pp. 199–232.

At this point, however, it may be helpful to bring together the numerous cost definitions. Note that the distinction between fixed and variable costs is dropped once we move into long-run analysis; all costs are variable to the firm in the long run. Fixed costs are a characteristic solely of the short run.

Short-run costs:

$$TVC = w \cdot L$$

$$TFC = r \cdot \overline{K}$$

$$TC = TVC + TFC = (w \cdot L) + (r \cdot \overline{K})$$

$$AVC = \frac{TVC}{Q} = \frac{w \cdot L}{Q} = \frac{w}{AP_L}$$

$$AFC = \frac{TFC}{Q} = \frac{r \cdot \overline{K}}{Q}$$

$$ATC = \frac{TC}{Q} = \frac{TVC + TFC}{Q} = AVC + AFC$$

$$SMC = \frac{\Delta TC}{\Delta Q} = \frac{\Delta TVC}{\Delta Q} = \frac{w \cdot \Delta L}{\Delta Q} = \frac{w}{MP_L}$$

Long-run costs:

$$LTC = (w \cdot L) + (r \cdot K)$$

$$LAC = \frac{(w \cdot L) + (r \cdot K)}{Q}$$

$$LMC = \frac{\Delta LTC}{\Delta Q}$$

Isoquants and Isocosts

We may now reinforce and expand the analysis of long-run costs by developing cost curves directly from the isoquant analysis presented in Chapter 5. Recall that an isoquant shows all labor and capital combinations capable of producing a given quantity of output. When many output levels are considered, the resulting family of isoquant curves is called the isoquant map. The isoquant map illustrates the firm's technical production possibilities when all factors are variable.

THE ISOCOST LINE. In the long run, a firm can alter the size of its labor force as well as its capital stock. To maximize profit, its managers must get the greatest possible production from a given budget by combining labor and capital inputs in the correct proportions. Naturally, the ratio of labor to capital will depend in part on the prices of wages (w) and the rental rate of capital (r). Thus factor prices limit the quantity of inputs that a firm can purchase for a given expenditure.

The total cost of production is

$$C = wL + rK \tag{6.12}$$

If we know the total outlay of the firm, C, and the values of w and r, we may construct the necessary constraint on production. This constraint, pictured in Figure 6.13, is called an **isocost line** ("equal-cost" line). An isocost line illustrates, for given factor prices, the different combinations of factors that can be purchased for any given cost outlay.

Suppose a firm spends C_1 dollars to buy inputs. If the firm uses its entire cost outlay to purchase capital, C_1/r units of capital can be purchased. Thus C_1/r is the vertical intercept of the isocost line. If only labor is purchased, C_1/w units of labor are available, which is the horizontal intercept. The isocost line is constructed by connecting the two intercepts with a straight line. This line represents the rate at which the firm can exchange purchases of capital for labor. Each isocost line represents a given outlay. If the cost outlay increases to C_2, for given factor prices, the isocost line shifts parallel to the right, as Figure 6.13 shows.

The linear equation for the isocost line is easily derived by rearranging the total cost equation, $C = wL + rK$. Solving for K yields

$$K = \frac{C}{r} - \left(\frac{w}{r}\right)L \tag{6.13}$$

In this form, the vertical intercept of the isocost line is C/r and the slope is $-w/r$. Thus the rate at which the firm can substitute labor

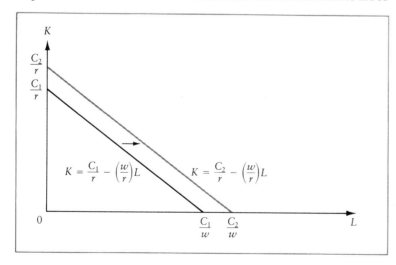

Figure 6.13
Isocost Line

An isocost line shows the different combinations of factors that the firm can purchase for a given cost with given factor prices. The linear equation is $K = C/r - (w/r)L$. The vertical intercept is C/r, and the slope is $-w/r$.

for capital while holding total outlay constant is determined by the ratio of factor prices.

EFFICIENT FACTOR COMBINATIONS.   Now let's combine the isoquant map with the isocost constraint to describe **producer optimization,** the condition prevailing when firms combine labor and capital in efficient combinations. Recall from Chapter 5 that the slope of the isoquant, called the marginal rate of technical substitution (*MRTS*), defines the technical rate at which labor and capital can be substituted in order to maintain a constant output. Recall further that the *MRTS* equals the negative of the ratio of marginal products of factors. Thus $|MRTS| = MP_L/MP_K$.

Figure 6.14 contains an isoquant map and a linear isocost line. The maximum output that the firm can produce with a cost outlay of C_0 at given factor prices is determined by the tangency of the isocost line with the highest attainable isoquant curve, Q_2. At the tangency, point A, the firm employs K_0 units of capital and L_0 units of labor. Also at the tangency, the slope of the isoquant in absolute value (MP_L/MP_K) equals the slope of the isocost in absolute value (w/r). In other terms, the condition for producer optimization is

$$\frac{MP_L}{MP_K} = \frac{w}{r} \tag{6.14}$$

Any adjustment in factor combinations at tangency point A pushes production along the isocost line, which inevitably generates intersections with lower isoquants. For example, points B and D represent reduced producer efficiency; without spending another penny on resources, the firm could increase its total output from Q_1 to Q_2 by adjusting its factor combination to A. Once the tangency

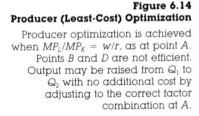

Figure 6.14
Producer (Least-Cost) Optimization

Producer optimization is achieved when $MP_L/MP_K = w/r$, as at point A. Points B and D are not efficient. Output may be raised from Q_1 to Q_2 with no additional cost by adjusting to the correct factor combination at A.

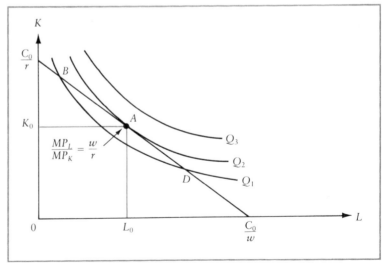

is achieved, no further changes in factor proportions can increase total output. Thus producer optimization requires the firm to allocate costs so that the ratio of marginal products equals the ratio of factor prices. When this is done, the firm maximizes its output for the given cost outlay.

The producer optimization condition in Equation 6.14 can be rewritten algebraically as follows:

$$\frac{MP_L}{w} = \frac{MP_K}{r} \qquad (6.15)$$

In order to maximize output with a given cost outlay at stipulated factor prices, the firm must combine inputs so that the marginal products per dollar spent on all inputs are equal. If $MP_L/w > MP_K/r$, the firm can increase output without increasing resource costs by buying more labor and less capital until the marginal products per dollar spent on each input are equated.

Producer optimization has been presented as though the firm's objective is to produce the maximum output for a given cost outlay. This is output maximization subject to cost constraint. The firm could also seek the least costly means of producing a given output, a method known as cost minimization subject to an output constraint.

EXPANSION PATH.   The direct link between isoquant-isocost analysis and long-run cost curves is the **expansion path.** As you should recall, long-run cost is the cost of producing a given output when all cost-minimizing factor adjustments are made. These adjustments have been described in terms of adjustments in the scale of plant. Now they can be described in isoquant-isocost language.

Suppose the firm is considering output levels of Q_1, Q_2, and Q_3, where $Q_1 < Q_2 < Q_3$. The isoquants representing these output levels are illustrated in Figure 6.15a. The tangencies of the three isocost lines with the isoquants representing these three output levels identify the least-cost methods of producing these outputs. For given factor prices, output must be produced so the ratio of factor prices equals the ratio of the factors' marginal products. For output Q_1, a cost outlay of C_1 is required; for Q_2 an outlay of C_2 is necessary; and so on. As output rises, employment of labor and capital inputs must rise; as long as factor prices are constant, the factor combinations must be adjusted to keep the ratio of their marginal products constant.

The expansion path shows all least-cost factor combinations for all possible output levels, given factor prices. It shows the factor combinations the firm should select as it expands (or contracts) output. For given factor prices, producer optimization requires that the factor combination be adjusted to keep the ratio of marginal

**Figure 6.15
Expansion Path and Long-Run
Costs**

(a) The expansion path shows all least-cost factor combinations for all possible output levels, given factor prices. **(b)** The LTC curve may be derived from the expansion path. **(c)** The LMC and LAC curves are derived from the LTC curve. Each expansion path underpins a set of LTC, LMC, and LAC curves.

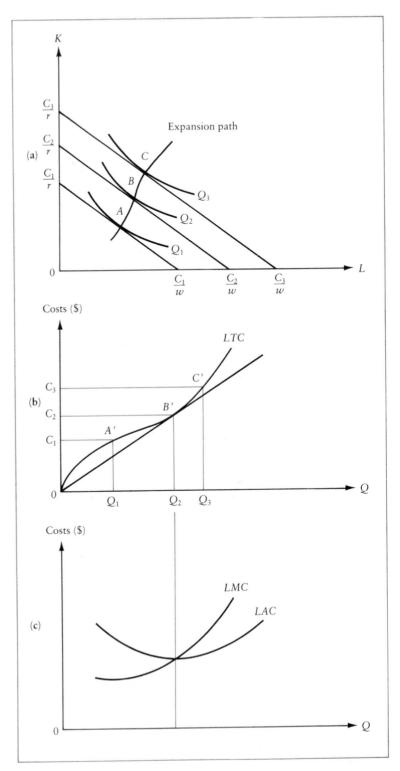

products constant and equal to the ratio of factor prices. The expansion path reflects the factor adjustments made necessary by expanding (or contracting) output, hence its name.

The long-run total cost curve (LTC) relates the lowest total cost of producing alternative levels of output when the factor prices are given and when all factors are variable. This same information is contained indirectly in the expansion path diagram. Thus we can derive the LTC curve from the information contained in the expansion path. For example, output Q_1 in Figure 6.15a can be produced with the minimum expenditure outlay of C_1 if labor and capital are hired in the ratio defined by the tangency at point A on the expansion path. Thus the combination (C_1, Q_1) is one point on the long-run total cost curve, plotted as point A' in Figure 6.15b. Similarly, output Q_2 can be produced with a minimum cost outlay of C_2 if the factor combination dictated by point B on the expansion path is achieved. Thus the cost-output combination (C_2, Q_2) is another point on the LTC curve, plotted as B' in panel b. Point C' is derived in the same way for output Q_3. The collection of such least-cost points is the LTC curve, as shown in panel b. From the LTC curve, the corresponding LAC and LMC curves in panel c are easily derived, using methods you are already familiar with.

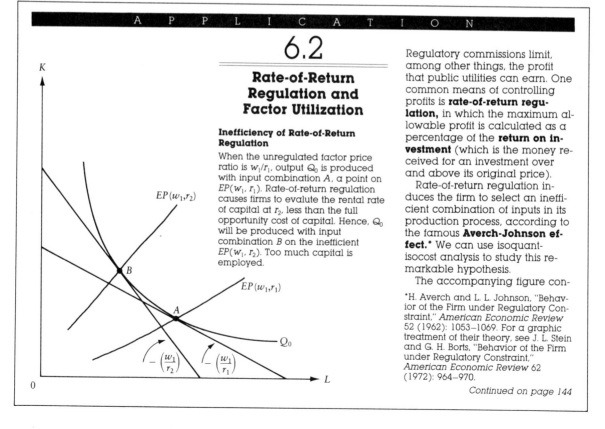

A P P L I C A T I O N

6.2

Rate-of-Return Regulation and Factor Utilization

Inefficiency of Rate-of-Return Regulation

When the unregulated factor price ratio is w_1/r_1, output Q_0 is produced with input combination A, a point on $EP(w_1, r_1)$. Rate-of-return regulation causes firms to evaluate the rental rate of capital at r_2, less than the full opportunity cost of capital. Hence, Q_0 will be produced with input combination B on the inefficient $EP(w_1, r_2)$. Too much capital is employed.

Regulatory commissions limit, among other things, the profit that public utilities can earn. One common means of controlling profits is **rate-of-return regulation,** in which the maximum allowable profit is calculated as a percentage of the **return on investment** (which is the money received for an investment over and above its original price).

Rate-of-return regulation induces the firm to select an inefficient combination of inputs in its production process, according to the famous **Averch-Johnson effect.**[*] We can use isoquant-isocost analysis to study this remarkable hypothesis.

The accompanying figure con-

[*] H. Averch and L. L. Johnson, "Behavior of the Firm under Regulatory Constraint," *American Economic Review* 52 (1962): 1053–1069. For a graphic treatment of their theory, see J. L. Stein and G. H. Borts, "Behavior of the Firm under Regulatory Constraint," *American Economic Review* 62 (1972): 964–970.

Continued on page 144

tains the standard isoquant–isocost–expansion path apparatus. Let the wage rate equal w_1 and the rental rate of capital equal r_1. If w_1 and r_1 are market-determined factor prices that reflect true opportunity costs of the resources, output Q_0 is produced at least opportunity cost with factor combination A. Similarly, any other rate of output would be produced efficiently with a factor mix along the expansion path EP (w_1, r_1), since the ratio of marginal products equals the ratio of factor prices everywhere on the expansion path.

Now let the regulatory commission set a profit limit equal to some percentage return on the firm's invested capital. Because profits are regulated as a percentage return on capital (and not as a limit on total profits), the firm can gain total profit by increasing the size of the capital stock on which the rate of return is based. In effect, the firm can consider the cost of purchasing capital to be less than r_1; extra capital expansion increases allowed profit. Thus rate-of-return regulation drives a wedge between the true opportunity cost of capital and what the firm perceives as the lower price of capital. This perceived price is what the firm uses in decision making.

If r_2 is the rental rate of capital that the firm perceives, $r_2 < r_1$, then the isocost line rises in slope, and output Q_0 will be produced with the inefficient factor combination B. Indeed, any rate of output will be produced with input mixes along the inefficient expansion path $EP(w_1, r_2)$. Firms will produce any rate of output with a capital stock that is too large from society's point of view.

Because public utilities are naturally large, and because rate-of-return regulation tends to enlarge the scale of plant even more, the impact of rate-of-return regulation on capital markets and markets for loanable funds cannot be ignored by the general business community.

Cost Analysis and Profit Maximization

Figure 6.16
Profit Maximization and Producer Optimization

(a) The firm maximizes profit by equating MR and LMC at point A and producing output Q_1. **(b)** Output Q_1 is produced at least cost by using input combination A'.

Profit-maximizing output decisions for firms require information about marginal costs and marginal revenues of production. If a firm is competitive and can sell any amount of output it desires at the same price, its marginal revenue (MR) equals price and is depicted as a horizontal line, as in Figure 6.16a. Figure 6.16a also shows the firm's long-run marginal cost curve (LMC), which measures the addition to total cost of expanding sales by one unit at a time.

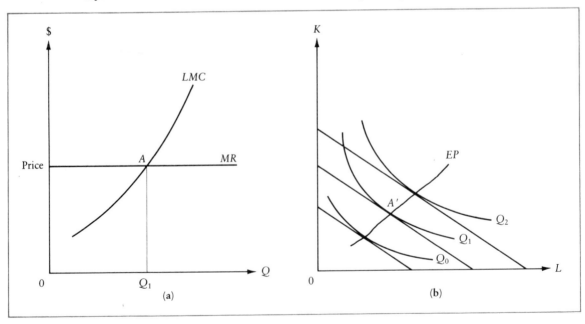

The $MR = LMC$ profit-maximizing rule is achieved at output Q_1 in Figure 6.16a. Profit will fall if output is either expanded or contracted from Q_1. If output falls, the extra cost savings (LMC) is less than the extra revenue forgone (MR). If output rises above Q_1, the extra costs incurred (LMC) exceed the additional revenue obtained (MR). Hence Q_1 is the firm's best rate of production, because it is the only output for which marginal revenue equals marginal cost. The firm maximizes profit by producing and selling Q_1 units of output, since $MR = LMC$ at Q_1.

Note the relationship between the LMC curve in Figure 6.16a and the isoquant map in panel b. Once the firm's profit-maximizing rate of output, Q_1, is established, isoquant-isocost analysis determines the factor combinations needed to produce output Q_1 at least total cost. Point A on the LMC curve in panel a corresponds to point A' on the expansion path in panel b; production-cost analysis by itself is too weak to set the firm's rate of output and hence its factor combinations. The marginal revenue—in conjunction with marginal cost—is needed to determine the best rate of output.

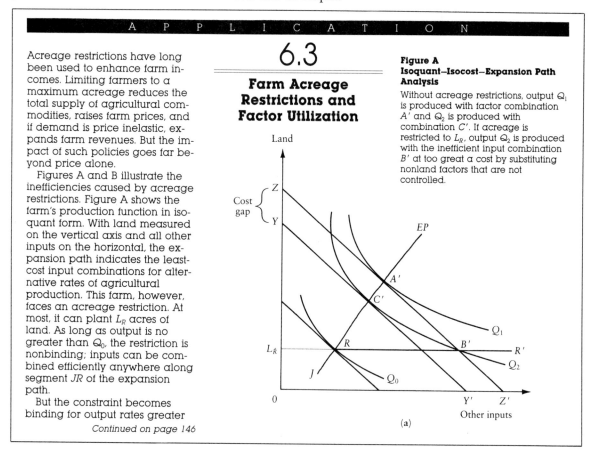

APPLICATION

6.3

Farm Acreage Restrictions and Factor Utilization

Acreage restrictions have long been used to enhance farm incomes. Limiting farmers to a maximum acreage reduces the total supply of agricultural commodities, raises farm prices, and if demand is price inelastic, expands farm revenues. But the impact of such policies goes far beyond price alone.

Figures A and B illustrate the inefficiencies caused by acreage restrictions. Figure A shows the farm's production function in isoquant form. With land measured on the vertical axis and all other inputs on the horizontal, the expansion path indicates the least-cost input combinations for alternative rates of agricultural production. This farm, however, faces an acreage restriction. At most, it can plant L_R acres of land. As long as output is no greater than Q_0, the restriction is nonbinding; inputs can be combined efficiently anywhere along segment JR of the expansion path.

But the constraint becomes binding for output rates greater

Continued on page 146

Figure A
Isoquant–Isocost–Expansion Path Analysis

Without acreage restrictions, output Q_1 is produced with factor combination A' and Q_2 is produced with combination C'. If acreage is restricted to L_R, output Q_2 is produced with the inefficient input combination B' at too great a cost by substituting nonland factors that are not controlled.

(a)

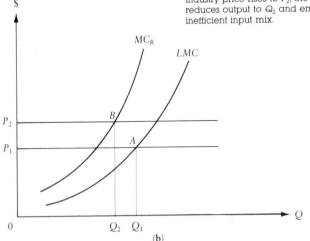

Figure B
Cost Analysis

When price is P_1, the farm produces Q_1. ($P_1 = LMC$ at Q_1.) Acreage restrictions increase marginal cost to MC_R as a result of inefficiencies. If industry price rises to P_2, the farm reduces output to Q_2 and employs an inefficient input mix.

(b)

than Q_0. The horizontal line $\overline{RR'}$ depicts the intput combinations that will be required to produce output rates in excess of Q_0 when L_R units of land is the farm's maximum plantable acreage. Note that any rate of production greater than Q_0 is achieved with factor combinations off the efficient expansion path. This means that land will be used too intensively as labor, machinery, fertilizer, pesticides, and so forth are used to boost yields.

Figure B shows the farm's marginal cost curves. The LMC curve shows the long-run marginal cost of production when the farm is free to combine inputs efficiently as output changes. Let price P_1 be the original industry price before acreage restrictions are imposed. The farm equates LMC and P_1 at point A by producing output Q_1. The LAC curve has been omitted to reduce clutter, but the total cost of producing Q_1 is indicated by the height of the isocost curve $\overline{ZZ'}$ in Figure A when the efficient input combination A' is selected.

Acreage restrictions, by encouraging inefficient use of the factors of production, increase marginal costs to the level of the curve labeled MC_R. At the same time, if acreage restrictions are imposed on all farmers, the industry supply of some crops will decrease and prices will increase to, say, P_2.

The farmer can equate MC_R and P_2 at point B by cutting production to Q_2. But is this output cut accomplished by moving to the efficient combination C' in Figure A? Not at all. Instead, combination B' is selected. The acreage restriction induces the substitution of inputs whose uses are not controlled.

Input combination B' in Figure A is of course a technically feasible way of producing Q_2. But it is economically wasteful at the prevailing factor prices. In fact, as Figure A is drawn, the smaller output (Q_2) requires the same cost outlay as the larger output (Q_1). Inefficient use of factors is the cause.

Note that the government is not able to reliably cut farm output by cutting land use. Output will fall below unregulated levels, to be sure, but not in proportion to the cut in usable land. Farmers partially offset the intent of the government policy by substituting productive resources that are not restricted.

Also, output Q_2 becomes too costly. This result can be seen in Figure A and Figure B. In Figure A, the vertical gap between isocost $\overline{ZZ'}$ (the actual cost of Q_2 using the inefficient input mix B') and isocost $\overline{YY'}$ (the cost of Q_2 using the efficient input mix C') measures the excessive cost of producing Q_2 due solely to acreage restrictions. In Figure A, $MC_R > LMC$ for output Q_2. This inequality is another reflection of the economic waste attributable to restrictions.

In addition to stressing the importance of the agricultural issue, this application also emphasizes the link between isoquant curves and cost curves. Both are important managerial tools. Isoquants illustrate factor utilization; cost curves focus attention directly on the costs of production.

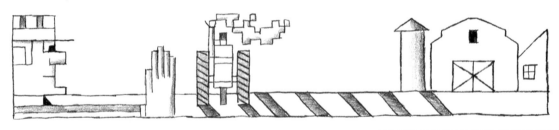

6.4

Producing Rust Prevention

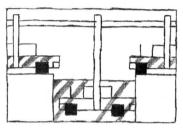

The use of production-cost analysis is not limited to problems that entail physical output. The model can just as easily be used to study the quality of goods as well as quantities. For example, automobile manufacturers are concerned with the number of cars produced per month, but they must also pay attention to the quality of cars—for example, the ability of car bodies to withstand rust. How does a firm "produce" rust prevention? How much rust protection should be built into each car? And how can a manager select the least-cost method of achieving a given amount of rust prevention?

Two inputs are especially important in guarding cars against rust: (1) the thickness of the metal in the frame and (2) the thickness of the rust-preventive material applied to the metal. Metal thickness and rust preventive are substitute factors: More rust preventive is needed to maintain the same rust rate if thinner metal is used for fenders.

Figure A contains an isoquant curve, Q_0, showing the combinations of these two inputs that are capable of yielding the same level of rust protection. Protection is measured as the number of cars per 1,000 that do not rust in the first 5 years; $Q_0 = 0.99$. The isoquant map is suppressed to avoid clutter, but a higher rate of rust prevention would be depicted by an isoquant to the right of Q_0.

Suppose the relative prices of metal and rust preventive fix the slope of the initial isocost line, $\overline{AA'}$. A 0.99 rust-prevention rate is achieved at least cost by using input combination C. If more rust prevention were desired, the cost-minimizing factor combination would lie to the northeast of point C on expansion path EP_1. The curve labeled LMC_1 in Figure B represents the marginal cost curve associated with expansion path EP_1. If the marginal

benefit of rust prevention is MB, the efficient rust-prevention rate is $Q_0 = 0.99$. (This conclusion follows from the marginal logic for maximizing net benefit, which was set forth in Chapter 3.)

If the price of metal rises, *ceteris paribus,* the isocost curve becomes steeper, as in isocost $\overline{BB'}$ in Figure A. The same rust-prevention rate, 0.99, is produced at least cost with the factor combination E along expansion path

EP_2. With the price of metal at this level, total cost is higher for any prevention rate, and therefore a lower ratio of metal to rust-preventive material will be used.

The change in relative factor prices due to an increase in the price of metal moves the firm to a new expansion path, changes factor utilization, and produces a new LMC curve, labeled LMC_2 in Figure B. The rise in marginal cost reduces the profit-maximizing rust-prevention rate from 0.99 to 0.98. Thus an increase in the price of metal increases the incidence of rust.

This application shows the importance of understanding both isoquant analysis and cost-curve analysis. In strict mathematical terms, they are equivalent formulations, yet they provide different emphases. Isoquants focus our thoughts on the technical trade-offs of one input for another and on efficient factor combinations; cost curves direct our attention to output and costs.

Figure A
Isoprobability–Isocost Analysis
To be efficient, the firm seeking to produce a quality attribute such as rust prevention should select factor combination E when the isocost line is $\overline{BB'}$ but combination C when the isocost line is $\overline{AA'}$.

Figure B
Cost Analysis
The efficient rate of output for rust prevention is at the level where marginal benefit equals marginal cost.

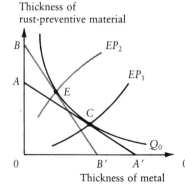

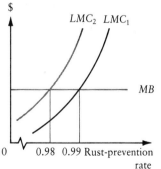

Firm Size and Average Costs

Different plant and firm sizes have their advantages and disadvantages. **Economies of scale** are the efficiencies and cost savings that lead to lower per-unit costs when the firm expands its scale of operations. **Diseconomies of scale** result in higher per-unit costs when the scale of operations expands because of certain problems caused by size. These scale characteristics have their counterparts in the *LAC* curve: Economies of scale are present along the downward-sloping segment, and diseconomies of scale take over when *LAC* rises. Let's examine the sources most likely to give rise to economies and diseconomies of scale.

Economies of Scale

Perhaps the most important source of scale economies is specialization of tasks. In small firms, workers lose effectiveness by switching among numerous tasks. For example, a single worker in a small dry-goods store must leave customers to answer the phone and accept deliveries. Economies can be captured if the dry-goods firm is large enough to specialize its sales force, switchboard, and warehouse facilities. In larger firms, machinery and equipment can be specialized in the same way. Forklift trucks, elevators, and conveyor systems of various capacities can be installed and devoted to their best uses. On the other hand, small firms are frequently limited to machinery that must serve a more general need and, for this reason, is often too big or too small for a given task at hand.

Closely related to the gains from specialization are the gains from learning by doing. If a firm can order a production run of significant size and duration, workers become more adept at performing repetitive tasks. This gain reflects the celebrated learning-curve effect. An increase in the size of production runs can lower unit costs as workers find shortcuts, improve manual dexterity, and become more familiar with technical equipment.

Economies of scale can result from arithmetic relationships as well. As noted in Chapter 5, doubling the dimensions of a cube more than doubles its volume. A storage company that doubles the outside dimensions of its warehouse would more than double its storage capacity. Per-unit costs fall when growth results from such engineering and technical gains.

Like specialization of resources, diversification of production may lead to economies of scale. Large, vertically integrated, multiplant firms can protect themselves somewhat from market aberrations in input prices by diversifying production. Cost increases in some departments can be offset by cost reductions in others. Similarly, a firm with 200 plants may insure itself against fire; paying for the occasional fire may be less expensive than insuring each plant. A small firm, however, is not sufficiently diversified to insure itself.

Finally, large firms can find cost savings in their reserves and inventories. Professor William Baumol has used an inventory model to show that firms' inventories should rise only in proportion to the square root of sales volume.[3] Thus inventory costs fall per unit of sales as sales are increased. In addition, firms often hold some machinery idle, ready to replace machines that unexpectedly break down or that are removed from use for planned maintenance checks. There are frequently economies of scale in such reserves, because a single reserved machine can back up many on-line units. But a small firm may require roughly the same backup capacity as a larger firm, which causes per-unit costs of production to be higher for smaller firms, other things being equal.

Diseconomies of Scale

Although size appears to be advantageous, there may be a limit beyond which increases in scale cease to reduce unit costs—and perhaps even raise them. For example, after a firm reaches a certain size, the economies of scale achieved during the firm's growth may fade and even reverse themselves if further increases in size are attempted. The most frequently mentioned source of diseconomies is the eventual tendency for management skills to become inadequate for a larger firm. Large firms require more coordination among departments and closer supervision of middle management than small firms do. If "entrepreneurship" is a fixed factor of production, then expansion of firm size will ultimately lead to rising average costs.

Transportation costs can also account for scale diseconomies. Two factors are important here. If a firm's growth forces it to hire workers who live a greater distance from the plant than current workers, a wage premium may be necessary to obtain a work force. Also, firm expansion may require shipping final goods to more distant markets, which raises transportation costs.

Other factors are at work to raise average costs when size increases too much. Workers can become overly specialized in large firms. This loss of flexibility may inhibit worker productivity if carried too far. Worker loyalty may also suffer in a large, impersonal corporation, and wage premiums may be required to induce workers to join the firm. Also, the gains achieved by learning by doing must eventually fade out in a large firm, since the greatest learning usually takes place in the earlier phases of production. Finally, some types of production are simply better done on a smaller scale, because machines and equipment can become unmanageable if too large.

---

3. William J. Baumol, *Economic Theory and Operations Analysis*, 4th ed. (Englewood Cliffs, N.J.: Prentice-Hall, 1977).

Figure 6.17
U-Shaped *LAC*

For output below point *A*, the *LAC* slopes downward, reflecting economies of scale. In the range $\overline{AB}$, the *LAC* curve is relatively flat, indicating no significant economies or diseconomies. To the right of point *B*, the *LAC* curve slopes upward, reflecting the diseconomies that may afflict a larger firm.

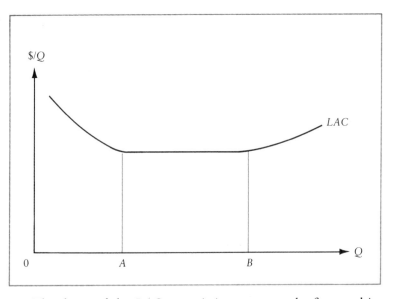

The shape of the *LAC* curve is important to the firm, and its shape is determined by economies and diseconomies of scale. The *LAC* curve in Figure 6.17 is typical. Economies of scale are common during a firm's initial growth, depicted as range $\overline{OA}$. In the range $\overline{AB}$, increases in scale do not affect unit costs much. Beyond *B*, after the firm has become very large, diseconomies may occur. However, it seems that the *LAC* and *LMC* remain relatively constant over broad ranges of output. Managers are apparently painstaking and ingenious in overcoming diseconomies of scale.

Summary

The firm's costs of production are determined not only by the market prices for its inputs but also by how well the firm is able to combine the inputs to produce goods and services. Therefore, anyone who wishes to study the costs of the firm must well understand production theory. This chapter weds production and cost.

The first fundamental distinction made in this chapter is that between short-run and long-run costs. In production theory, the inputs are divided into capital, which is relatively fixed, and labor, which is relatively variable. By holding the capital costs fixed, we can derive the short-run cost curves. These curves have meaning when analyzing periods too short to allow changes in the firm's capital.

A second major distinction made in this chapter is that between the marginal and average cost curves. These curves must have the same arithmetic relationship to each other as the marginal and average product curves have (as explored in Chapter 5).

The third major point of the chapter is that the long run is a time period long enough to allow the firm to alter its use of any factor of production. The long-run average and marginal cost curves are related to isoquant curves, which indicate the substitutability of capital and labor.

The powerful theory of costs has many applications. For example, the profit-maximizing response to farm acreage restrictions is to substitute other factors of production for the land. In a less tangible case, the probability of rust avoidance can be analyzed in terms of factor combinations and the efficient level of factor prices.

Problems

1. Why can't we tell the shape of the long-run average cost curve from the law of diminishing returns? We can for the short-run average cost curve.
2. Consider a U-shaped long-run average cost curve for inputs. What does such a curve imply about the isoquant map?
3. a. Assume a U-shaped LAC curve. At what level of output would a firm choose a scale of plant that is (1) underutilized; (2) overutilized; (3) properly utilized?
   b. How would you define "properly utilized"?
   c. Assuming a horizontal LAC curve, at what level of output would a firm choose a scale of plant that is (1) underutilized; (2) overutilized; (3) properly utilized?
   d. What does a horizontal LAC curve imply about the isoquant map?
4. Explain the relationship among ATC, SMC, LAC, and LMC at a given level of output.
5. a. What is the average cost of trips across a bridge? What is the marginal cost?
   b. What is the average cost of jogging through a park? What is the marginal cost? Does it matter which park?
   c. What is the shape of the marginal cost curve as a function of total output and as a function of the rate of output? (Hint: Does production and cost theory make any sense if output is not measured in flow terms?)
6. Show that, as prices of inputs rise, the LMC and LAC curves shift upward proportionally but not in parallel fashion. Show that this response from LMC and LAC curves means that the penalty for choosing the wrong scale of plant for a given rate of output is more severe the higher factor prices are.
7. Suppose you are the owner of a firm producing jelly beans at the average costs per box indicated in Table 6.1. Initially you produce 200 boxes of jelly beans per time period. Then the President calls you long distance and places an order for a box, requiring you to increase your output to 201 boxes. He offers you $350 for the box. Should you produce it?
8. Prove that a constant average tax rate beyond some income level Y_1 requires either no deductible or a regressive marginal tax rate.
9. This chapter defines an average tax rate, t_a, and a marginal tax rate, t_m.
   a. Use these terms to define a progressive income tax structure.
   b. If t_m is positive but diminishing, will extra taxable income result in a lower total tax liability? A lower average tax rate? A regressive tax structure?

Key Terms

accounting cost 122
average cost 128
average fixed cost 126
average tax rate 134
average variable cost 125
Averch-Johnson effect 143
cost curve 121
diseconomies of scale 148
economic cost 122
economies of scale 148
entrepreneurial opportunity cost 122
envelope curve 137
expansion path 141
fixed costs 124
isocost line 139
long-run average total cost 136
long-run marginal cost 137
long-run total cost 137
marginal tax rate 134
planning curve 137
producer optimization 140
production-cost analysis 121
production-cost duality 132
rate-of-return regulation 143
rental rate of capital 125
return on investment 143
scales of plant 135
short-run average total cost 127
short-run marginal cost 129
sunk cost 122
total cost 125
total fixed cost 124
total variable cost 124
variable costs 124
Viner-Wong envelope curve 137
wage rate 123

Table 6.1

Jelly Bean Production

Units of Output	Average Cost
200	$200
201	201
202	202

Table 6.2
Computing Costs

Output (Q)	Labor (L)	TVC	TFC	TC	AVC	ATC	SMC
1	11						
2	19						
3	24						
4	32						
5	46						
6	64						
7	88						
8	119						
9	158						
10	206						

10. Let Q = units of output, L = units of labor, w = wage rate per worker per time period = \$1, TFC = \$10. Capital is fixed. Using these data, fill in the blank spaces in Table 6.2. Check for the following properties: (1) U-shaped average and marginal cost curves; (2) an SMC curve that intersects both the AVC and ATC curves from below at their minimum points; (3) an AVC that attains a minimum at a smaller level of output than the ATC. (Hint: Some of these conditions will be satisfied only approximately because of the discrete nature of the data.)

11. Show graphically that lower-income groups pay a higher average tax rate on the same income if they have fewer exemptions and deductibles.

12. Prove that a *ceteris paribus* doubling of the wage rate
    a. Shifts the AVC curve upward proportionally and not in parallel fashion.
    b. Does not change the rate of output at which the AVC is minimized.
    c. Shifts the ATC curve upward and causes it to achieve its minimum at a larger rate of output.
    d. Shifts the SMC upward.

13. Prove that a *ceteris paribus* doubling of the rental rate of capital:
    a. Does not shift the AVC or SMC curves.
    b. Shifts the ATC curve upward and increases the rate of output for which the ATC is minimized.

14. Derive the short-run TVC, TC, AVC, ATC, and MC curves under these assumptions:
    a. Production exhibits a constant marginal productivity of labor.
    b. Production exhibits a diminishing marginal productivity of labor.
    c. Production exhibits an increasing marginal productivity of labor.
    d. All costs are fixed.
    e. All costs are variable.

15. Suppose that a firm produces a good using, among other things, a machine that is useful in an alternative industry and that has a

market price of $20,000. The value of the machine in the current industry is also $20,000. Why?

16. Labor services are available in a market for $5 per hour.
    a. If the workers organize and raise that wage to $6 per hour, how will the firm's cost curves be affected.
    b. How will the expansion path be affected?

17. Suppose that the total fixed costs in a firm are $40,000 and that the total variable costs are $20,000 at a particular level of output, which is in stage I of production. What would happen to the average total costs if output were to rise from that level?

18. The term *capital* refers to resources that can be invested in one period to produce benefits in many future periods. The demand for such capital depends on the demand for the product it will produce. Suppose that the demand for the product falls to half. What will happen to the rental rate of the capital and to the use of this capital?

19. Consider the typical family of cost curves. If the average variable cost curve shifts up vertically to twice its original height, what must happen to the position of the marginal cost curve and the average fixed cost curve?

20. a. Suppose that the total variable cost of production rises by $6 as output rises by 40 units. If production is in stage I, what do you expect to happen to the average variable cost?
    b. Suppose that the total variable cost of production falls by $2 as output falls by 6 units. The average variable cost falls as well. What will happen to the total fixed cost?

21. As output rises by 1 unit, the total variable cost rises by 50 cents and the average variable cost rises from 35 cents to 36 cents.
    a. Is production in stage I or stage II?
    b. What is the marginal cost?

22. If the marginal product of the labor force in a plant is 16 and the wage rate is $5, what is the marginal cost of production? What would happen to the marginal cost if the marginal product rose to 20?

23. If the slope of the production isoquant is 6 and the ratio of factor prices is 4, what can the firm do to increase profits?

24. Reconsider the farm example in Application 6.3.
    a. What will happen to the marginal product of land as the land use restriction is applied?
    b. Suppose that the farmer can sell the idle land to another farmer who does not have to hold the land idle. What price can the first farmer charge for the land?

25. Suppose that a firm's *LMC* curve crosses its price line at an output of 50 units.
    a. If the *LMC* curve rises to twice its original height, what can you say about the output level at which it will cross the unchanged price line?
    b. Can you determine an upper and lower limit for output? Why or why not?

26. What would happen to the price of farm implements if the land available for cultivation were reduced by 25 percent as a result of

acreage restrictions? Make some assumptions about the demand for food and the substitutability of nonland factors for land.

27. a. Suppose that the efficient level of rust-prevention probability is 99 percent. If the cost of the rust-preventive paint rises relative to the cost of the car, how would the efficient level of rust-prevention probability change?

b. Suppose that the frequency of washing the car is a factor in the probability of rust prevention. If the price of the rust-retarding paint doubles, what happens to the efficient rate of washing the car?

Suggested Readings

Baumol, William J. *Economic Theory and Operations Analysis*. 4th ed. Englewood Cliffs, N.J.: Prentice-Hall, 1977.

Brumberg, Richard E. "*Ceteris Paribus* for Supply Curves." *Economic Journal* 63(1953): 462–467.

Friedman, Milton. *Price Theory: A Provisional Text*. Chicago: Aldine, 1963, chaps. 5, 6.

Stigler, George. *The Theory of Price*. New York: Macmillan, 1966, chaps. 6–9.

Viner, Jacob. "Cost Curves and Supply Curves." *Zeitschrift für Nationalökonomie* 3(1931): 23–46.

Walters, A. A. "Production and Cost Functions." *Econometrica* 31 (1963): 1–66.

7

COMPETI-
TION

In Chapters 5 and 6, we saw that the firm's costs are rooted in
its production technology. Those chapters distinguished between short- and long-run production adjustments, showed
the relationship between the short- and long-run cost curves,
and described the logic by which firms choose the optimal combination of labor and capital inputs in the production of a given quantity
of output. Production-cost analysis is the first step in understanding
the economic behavior of firms.

A firm is an institution that combines inputs to produce final
output and sells that output to consumers. Raw materials do not
spontaneously combine to produce the great variety of outputs that
consumers desire, and consumers cannot economically produce for
themselves all the goods they actually consume. Thus the firm acts
as an intermediary between consumers and raw materials. Firms
also play an important role in capturing the efficiencies that result
from the specialization and division of tasks; these efficiencies
would be lost if all consumers had to be self-sufficient.

This chapter is principally concerned with the following three
decisions of firms: (1) the level of output that maximizes profits in
the short run (capital stock fixed), (2) the level of output that maximizes profits in the long run (capital stock variable), and (3) the
decision to enter or exit an industry. It concentrates on competitive
firms—to be defined shortly—and covers the price and output of
both the competitive firm and the industry to which it belongs.

A full understanding of competitive behavior requires a careful definition of *profit,* which is the central focus of this chapter.[1] **Profit** (π), also called **accounting profit,** is the difference between total revenue and total cost:

$$\pi = TR - TC \qquad (7.1)$$

Total revenue, a concept discussed in Chapter 4, is merely price times quantity; it is easily handled in models of the competitive firm. Total cost is a subject broached in Chapter 6. To evaluate the firm's profit, can't we just perform the algebraic subtraction called for in Equation 7.1 and call it a day? No, we cannot, and here's the reason. The costs defined in Chapter 6 are merely the costs of acquiring the variable and fixed resources. If entrepreneurs have valuable alternatives to their present occupations, the highest-valued forgone alternative is also a cost of producing in their current industries. This alternative cost is what economists call entrepreneurial opportunity cost. Failure to include all production costs—resource costs and opportunity costs—introduces error in the calculation of economic profit, flaws internal management decision making, and limits our understanding of the managerial decision to enter or exit an industry.

Perfect Competition versus Pure Competition

This chapter is about competitive firms and industries. Competitive equilibrium involves the decentralized coordination of many firms and consumers and can be very hard to explain. In order to explain competition, many authors over the years have presented a paradigm case called **perfect competition.** Under perfect competition, each firm's output is so small relative to the industry output that the firm cannot affect industry price by expansion or contraction of its own output. Accordingly, the competitive firm is a price taker; it cannot affect the market price of its output. The competitive price is set at the industry level, and each firm takes this price as a parameter. (Price-taking behavior is often called parametric pricing, as explained in Chapter 3.)

The paradigm of perfect competition further assumes that all firms in a particular industry are identical in all dimensions, including production functions and technologies, costs, management skills, location, and entrepreneurial opportunities. In addition, re-

---

1. An immigrant businessperson was visited one Christmas by his eldest son, an accountant. The son noticed that his father's accounts receivable were placed in a shoebox under the counter, that cash went into his father's pockets, that bills were paid haphazardly, and that there was no inventory control, no double-entry accounting, not even a systematic way of filling out the bank deposit slip. The son criticized his father's management techniques and asked whether he even knew if he was making a profit. The father answered in broken English: "Son, when I came to this country, all I had was the pants I wore off the boat. Now I have a home that's paid for, three children graduated from college, a summer cottage, two cars, and a fat bank account. Take all that and subtract the pants, and that's my profit." This chapter moves toward a more precise, if less charming, definition of profit.

sources are assumed to be freely mobile in the economy, which permits identical firms to freely enter and exit the industry. With these assumptions, the paradigm model of perfect competition is a fruitful method for exploring many important short-run and long-run aspects of the competitive mechanism. It is the model employed in the first half of this chapter.

As useful as the model of perfect competition is, excessive concentration on it has led to confusion about several aspects of competition, including the definition and economic significance of profit, the question of how output is distributed to the factors of production in competitive markets, the entry and exit decision, and the question of how such a simplistic theory can guide the decisions of real firms and government policy makers. **Pure competition** is a less restrictive model; the only assumptions retained from the model of perfect competition are parametric pricing and free entry and exit. This definition of pure competition corresponds to that of Paul Samuelson.[2] In pure competition, firms are allowed to differ in respect to such factors as entrepreneurial skills and opportunities, location, and production techniques. Thus pure competition emphasizes parametric pricing without requiring firms to be identical in anything except price. Parametric pricing is the key to pure competition and the key to applying its concepts to the real world of nonidentical firms.

Competition is frequently given short shrift in managerial economics textbooks, presumably out of the conviction that it represents an extreme form of market structure. Although the competitive model is useful to economists in evaluating social policy, it is not considered useful in guiding managers' decisions. This book takes a far different approach. Competitive analysis is laden with substance for managers, especially once the relatively simple transition from perfect to pure competition has been made.

The first part of this chapter is confined to the paradigm case of perfect competition (identical firms and parametric pricing). The latter part extends the analysis to pure competition (nonidentical firms and parametric pricing). There is much to be gained by studying both models, because there is a lesson to be learned from each.

Competitive Firms' Revenue Curves

The revenue curves of all competitive firms—regardless of the distinctions between perfect and pure competition—reflect price-taking behavior. These revenue curves are depicted in Figure 7.1. Price is set by industrywide supply and demand forces, as panel c shows. Each firm uses the industry price as a parameter; hence the horizontal line extending from panel c into panel b is the firm's demand curve. It is perfectly elastic, because the competitive firm

2. Paul A. Samuelson, *Foundations of Economic Analysis* (New York: Atheneum, 1965), p. 82.

Figure 7.1
Revenue Curves in Competition

(a) In competition, total revenue is linear. **(b)** The horizontal price line is the firm's *MR* and *AR* curve. **(c)** Price is set at P_1 by market forces.

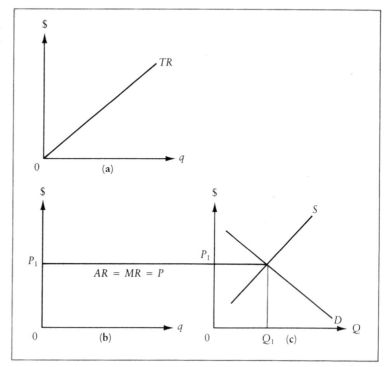

can adjust its rate of output without changing price. Since the firm can capture extra sales without lowering price, the horizontal demand curve is also the firm's marginal revenue curve (see Chapter 3). Since price is fixed for the firm, each unit sold adds a constant amount to the firm's total revenue, $TR = P \cdot q$.[3] Thus the total revenue curve, *TR*, is linear, as in panel a.

Revenue curves obey the arithmetic rules that govern total-marginal-average relationships. Marginal revenue is the slope of total revenue. Since total revenue is linear, its slope, and hence marginal revenue, is constant. **Average revenue** (AR) is

$$AR \equiv \frac{TR}{q} \equiv \frac{P \cdot q}{q} \equiv P \qquad (7.2)$$

Average revenue equals price, which in turn equals marginal revenue. Thus the competitive firm is characterized by a perfectly elastic demand curve, the value of which equals the firm's marginal revenue, average revenue, and price.

With the revenue curves in hand, we are prepared to combine the costs and the revenues of a competitive firm to study the rules for profit-maximizing decisions and their implications for short- and long-run competitive equilibrium.

---

3. The lowercase *q* denotes the output of any single firm; the uppercase *Q* represents industry output.

Short-Run Competitive Equilibrium

To proceed in an orderly fashion, we must begin our analysis of perfect competition by taking into account only the firm's labor and capital costs (studied in Chapter 6). This naive assumption provides an "engine" for investigating the rudiments of short-run competitive behavior. Later, we may add entrepreneurial opportunity costs to our analysis of the firm's entry/exit decision.

Short-Run Profit Maximization

Figure 7.2 combines the revenue, cost, and profit curves of one of many identical firms in a competitive industry. In panel a, the linear total revenue curve tells us that the firm is a price taker. Profit, as you may recall, is defined as the residual of revenues over costs. It may be positive, zero, or negative and is represented in Figure 7.2a by the vertical distance between the total revenue and total cost curves. This vertical distance is maximized by producing output q_3. The profit residual $\overline{AB}$ is the largest available to the firm, given its cost and revenue constraints.

Figure 7.2b explicitly shows the firm's **total profit curve.** Each point on the total profit curve (designated π) is plotted at a height equal to the difference between total revenue and total cost. Thus, profit is zero at q_2 and q_4, where total revenue equals total cost. The total profit curve reaches its maximum at output q_3: The maximum profit $\overline{AB}$ in panel a equals $\overline{q_3C}$ in panel b.

Chapter 3 defines *profit maximization* in terms of marginal revenue and marginal cost. Profits rise whenever the production of an extra unit of output adds more to revenue than it adds to cost. In other words, profits rise when $MR > SMC$. Conversely, profits fall when additional output adds more to costs than to revenue, that is, when $SMC > MR$. Thus the firm achieves its greatest available profit by continuing production until marginal revenue equals marginal cost, or

$$MR = SMC \qquad (7.3)$$

This equation is known as the short-run **profit maximizing rule.**

Since every marginal magnitude equals the slope of its total curve, marginal cost equals marginal revenue at output q_3 in Figure 7.2. In panel a, point A (the slope of which equals SMC) and point B (the slope of which equals MR) lie on parallel tangents; their slopes are therefore equal. If the firm lowers output to, say, q_2, its profits will fall. At q_2, $MR > SMC$; the firm is not fully exploiting its profit potential. Conversely, if the firm tries to increase profits by increasing output to q_4, it will fail, because extra production serves only to raise marginal cost above marginal revenue.

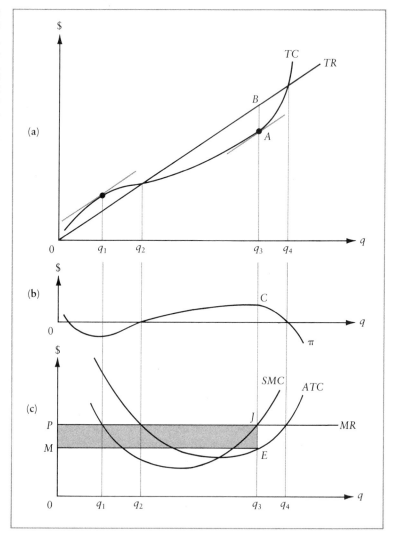

Profits are at a maximum only when marginal revenue equals marginal cost, which occurs only at output q_3 in Figure 7.2. The total profit curve in panel b confirms that q_3 is the profit-maximizing output rate.

The short-run profit-maximizing rule, $MR = SMC$, appears more explicitly in Figure 7.2c. The firm should equate marginal revenue and marginal cost at point J, thereby producing output q_3. Panel c contains average curves, so total costs and revenues are obtained by multiplying the average values by the quantity produced. Thus the **average total cost** (ATC) at q_3 equals $\overline{q_3 E}$. It is transformed into total cost as follows:[4]

---

4. Remember that vertical distances in a graph with totals measured on the vertical axis translate into areas on graphs with averages measured on the vertical axis.

$$TC = ATC \cdot q = \overline{q_3E} \cdot \overline{0q_3} = 0MEq_3$$

Similarly,

$$TR = AR \cdot q = \overline{q_3J} \cdot \overline{0q_3} = 0PJq_3$$

Also,

$$\pi = TR - TC = 0PJq_3 - 0MEq_3 = MPJE$$

The total profit, $MPJE$, is depicted in Figure 7.2c as the shaded rectangular area. The vertical distances $\overline{AB}$ in panel a and $\overline{q_3C}$ in panel b are the equivalents of the profit area $MPJE$ in panel c.

There is one qualification to the short-run profit-maximizing rule, $MR = SMC$. Note that the rule is satisfied at two levels of output in Figure 7.2: q_1 and q_3. But at output levels slightly to the right of q_1, $P > MC$; hence the firm has a chance to increase profits further. The firm should therefore expand output to q_3. The marginal cost curve must cut the marginal revenue curve from below, as at point J.

Short-Run Loss Minimization and the Shutdown Decision

A competitive firm's short-run cost and revenue curves are depicted in Figure 7.3. Marginal revenue equals short-run marginal cost at point J. However, the price is too low to permit positive profits because it is everywhere below the average total cost (ATC). By

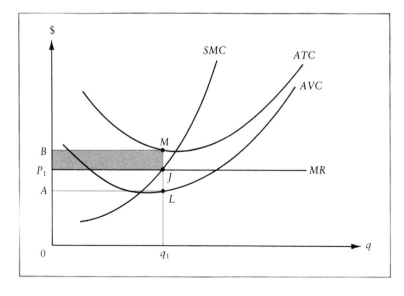

Figure 7.3
Short-Run Loss Minimization

A firm should produce at a loss in the short-run when $ATC > P > AVC$. The loss is P_1BMJ, which is less than the total fixed cost $ABML$, the loss from shutting down.

equating marginal revenue and marginal cost, the firm incurs negative profits equal to P_1BMJ, the shaded area. Is there any other output level that would make the firm's losses smaller than P_1BMJ? No. If the firm produces at all, it should produce q_1; losses get larger with any other output owing to the same logic described for positive profits. For example, if the firm produces one less unit, marginal cost is less than marginal revenue: The firm gives up more revenue (MR) than it saves in costs (SMC), and so its loss will be larger. Thus the profit-maximizing rule, $MR = SMC$, where the marginal cost curve cuts the marginal revenue curve from below, is also the rule for **loss-minimization,** providing the firm decides to stay in business in the short run.

But the firm in Figure 7.3 is incurring a loss, so should it not shut down altogether? Not necessarily. This decision must be made by comparing the loss incurred at output q_1 with the loss that would be incurred at zero output. If the firm shuts down, it eliminates its sales revenues as well as its total variable costs. Accordingly, its total loss will be the fixed cost. In Figure 7.3, the total fixed cost is $ABML$, which is greater than the loss incurred by producing q_1 units of output, P_1BMJ. Thus the firm incurs a smaller loss by producing q_1 units than by shutting down completely.

We must conclude that a firm producing at a loss should continue to do so in the short run if price exceeds average variable cost (AVC). If $P > AVC$, as in Figure 7.3, then $TR > TVC$. Total revenue is sufficient to pay all variable costs ($0ALq_1$) and to pay AP_1JL toward the fixed costs of $ABML$. Only if total revenue exceeds total variable cost can losses be minimized by continued production.

Consider Figure 7.4, where price is below the average variable cost. If the firm selects output q_1 by equating MR and SMC at point L, it incurs a loss (P_1BML) greater than the fixed cost ($ABMJ$). This firm should shut down in the short run, because its total revenue does not pay the total variable cost. A firm need never lose more than its fixed costs.

Shutdown analysis of this sort is strictly a short-run exercise. It points up the firm's fixed costs, which must be paid even if the firm stops operating. Naturally, however, a firm that is forced to operate at a loss to minimize short-run losses will make every effort to eliminate the fixed costs. This may require renegotiating leases, paying off bank loans, selling or depreciating capital equipment, or even initiating bankruptcy proceedings. But these are long-run adjustments. As long as firms have fixed-cost obligations, operating at a loss is cost-minimizing when $TR \geq TVC$.

A complete statement of the firm's short-run profit-maximizing and loss-minimizing conditions may now be given: The firm maximizes profits and minimizes losses by producing the rate of output

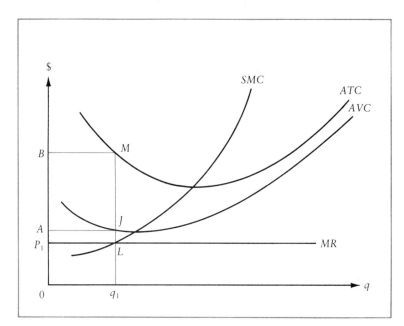

for which $MR = SMC$ if the SMC curve intersects the MR curve from below and if $TR \geq TVC$. If the SMC curve intersects the MR curve from above, profits are minimized instead of maximized. If $TR < TVC$, the firm should shut down. These statements make up the **shutdown rule.**

Short-Run Firm Supply

The short-run rules outlined in the previous section permit us to generate the firm's short-run supply curve. Figure 7.5 displays the firm's short-run cost curves and four possible prices, $P_4 > P_3 > P_2 > P_1$. Price P_1 is the lowest price that brings forth any output; for any lower price, $TR < TVC$ and the firm shuts down. Thus price P_1 is called the **shutdown price.** Similarly, point A, the minimum average variable cost, is referred to as the **shutdown point.** At the shutdown point, the firm can either shut down or produce, because the loss will equal the total fixed cost for either decision. For any price less than P_1, it will surely shut down, and for any price greater than P_1, it will produce. If price is P_2, the firm produces q_2 units of output and incurs a loss. When price is P_3, total revenue just covers total cost at output q_3, and profits are zero. (This last sentence is clarified several times in this chapter.) Any price greater than P_3, such as P_4, where the firm produces q_4 units of output, yields positive profits.

Points A, B, C, and D on the marginal cost curve in Figure 7.5 are derived from profit-maximizing rules and represent the amounts of output that the firm wants to sell at various prices, for given input prices, capital inputs, and technology. In other words, the short-run

Figure 7.5
Short-Run Firm Supply Curve

The short-run supply curve is the
SMC curve above point *A*, which is
the minimum *AVC*. For $P < P_1$, the
firm closes. For $P > P_1$, the firm
produces where $P = SMC$.

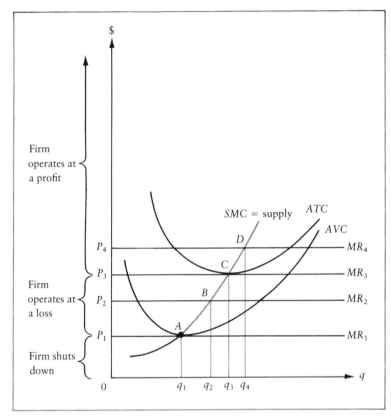

marginal cost curve above the minimum average variable cost is the
short-run firm supply curve. The black portion of the marginal cost
curve, drawn below the shutdown point in Figure 7.5, does not
establish supply points, because output is zero for any price less
than the minimum average variable cost. The upward-sloping short-
run supply curve, developed intuitively in Chapter 2, is now revealed to be the result of the profit-maximizing and loss-minimizing
decisions of firms facing diminishing marginal returns in production.

Short-Run Industry Supply

We have seen that the firm's short-run supply curve is the portion
of its short-run marginal cost curve that lies above the minimum
average variable cost. The horizontal summation of all firms' supply
curves produces a curve suitably close to the competitive **short-run
industry supply curve.** Although there are technical reasons why
this summation may produce a curve that differs somewhat from
the true industry supply curve, nothing is lost here by ignoring this
difference. For our purposes, the short-run industry supply curve
can be regarded as the horizontal summation of all firms' short-run
supply curves.

7.1

Inefficiency of Stage I Production

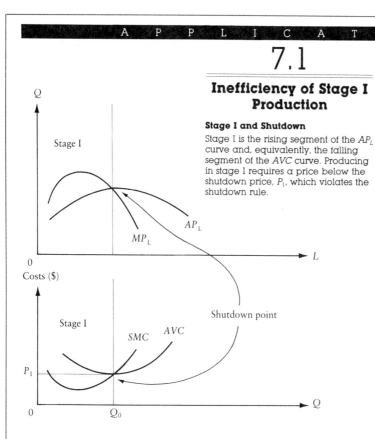

Stage I and Shutdown

Stage I is the rising segment of the AP_L curve and, equivalently, the falling segment of the AVC curve. Producing in stage I requires a price below the shutdown price, P_1, which violates the shutdown rule.

Chapter 6 shows intuitively that firms should not operate in production stage I. We may now prove this assertion. Stage I is the region of a rising average product of labor, diagramed in the adjacent figure. We know that the AP_L and the AVC are related as follows:

$$AVC = \frac{w}{AP_L}$$

Thus when AP_L is at a maximum, as it is at the beginning of stage II, the AVC curve is at a minimum. For the firm to produce, price must equal or exceed the average variable cost; otherwise the firm will shut down. Notice in the figure that no output below Q_0 will be produced, because price is wholly below the AVC for these outputs. *Stage I corresponds to the shutdown region.* Thus the conclusion that competitive firms should not operate in stage I follows directly from the loss-minimizing behavior of firms. Producing in stage I violates the shutdown rule.

7.2

Shutdown and Labor Fringe Benefits

Payments for labor are seldom as simple as a straight hourly wage. Typically, payments include a fringe benefit package with such items as contributions to unemployment insurance, various forms of insurance coverage, and free parking privileges. Many of these benefits are negotiated so that the employer has a continuing obligation to pay them even if the plant shuts down—at least for a time. Therefore, such payments tend to shift the cost structure in favor of keeping the plant open, because these components of worker's compensation are fixed costs to the firm.

The accompanying figure illustrates. Suppose initially that the firm's average variable costs

Continued on page 166

Fringe Benefits and Shutdown

If the fixed-cost components of fringe benefits rise by the same amount that wage payments fall, the AVC curve shifts downward, lowering the shutdown point from A to B. Labor's risk of layoff is thereby reduced.

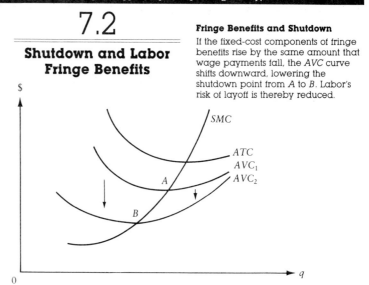

are AVC_1. If labor succeeds in negotiating a compensation package that reduces wage payments and increases the fixed-cost forms of fringe benefits by the same amount, AVC_1 will fall to AVC_2; the ATC curve is stationary. The firm's total costs are the same, but the shutdown point falls from A to B.

Hence, workers have a vested interest in receiving part of their compensation in fringe benefits. There are, of course, obvious income tax advantages. But in addition, the more fixed labor costs there are, the lower the shutdown point and the lower labor's risk of layoff.

Firms' Long-Run Adjustments

In the long run, firms make two kinds of decisions. First, the firm can vary all its factors of production and thereby adjust its output and factor combinations in order to maximize profits in its present occupation. Second, the firm can choose between its present activity and alternative activities; that is, the firm can decide whether to enter another industry (by exiting the present one) or to stay put.

Choosing a Scale of Plant

The first method a firm can use to adjust long-run production is to select the most efficient factor combinations and scale of plant. For the time being, let's continue to ignore the entry/exit decision by assuming that entrepreneurs are unfit to work in any other activity or industry.

Figure 7.6 exhibits the firm's LAC curve—the envelope curve, derived in Chapter 6—and two short-run scales of plant, ATC_0 and ATC_1. Suppose the industry price is P_0 initially. The firm maximizes short-run profit by equating P_0 and SMC_0 at point A. The firm selects the scale of plant ATC_0, because it is the least-cost means of producing output q_0. Because it represents the lowest possible unit costs, ATC_0 is called the "optimum scale of plant."

Now let the industry price rise to P_1 in response to an increase in industry demand. In the short run, the firm is locked into scale of plant ATC_0. Thus it maximizes short-run profit by expanding output to q_1, which brings P_1 and SMC_0 into equality at point B. However, if price P_1 is regarded as permanent, the firm will take steps to enlarge its output to q_2, where $P_1 = LMC$ at point C.

But output q_2 could not be produced with scale of plant ATC_0 without enormous losses, because it entails excessive congestion of the variable factor on the fixed factor; SMC_0 greatly exceeds price P_1 at output q_2. However, the firm can move to output q_2 and increase its total profit by adopting a larger quantity of capital; that is, output may be expanded by increasing the use of all inputs—capital and labor. Thus the profit-maximizing long-run adjustment

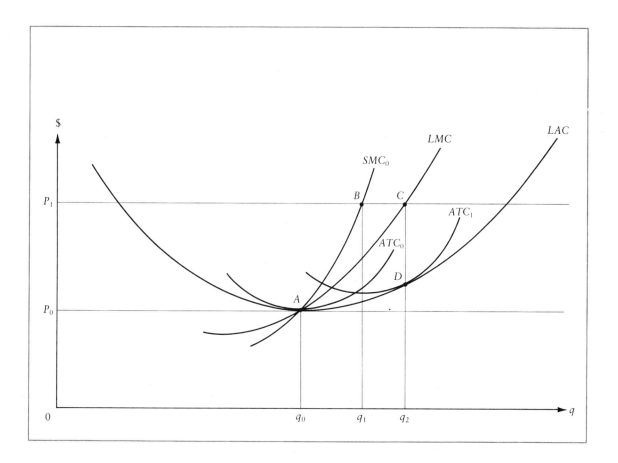

Figure 7.6
***LAC* Curve and Short-Run Scales of Plant**

The *LAC* curve is the envelope of the two short-run average cost curves. It represents the lowest cost for each level of output.

for the firm for any given price is to equate price with long-run marginal cost, as at output q_2. Output q_2 is produced at the lowest unit cost with the scale of plant ATC_1, as evidenced by the tangency between ATC_1 and the LAC curve at point D. And $P_1 = LMC$ at q_2, so the firm can make no further profit-increasing adjustments in its factor combinations or its output level.

Each point on the firm's long-run marginal cost curve depicts the profit-maximizing rate of output at a given price when sufficient time is allowed for the firm to select the most efficient scale of plant and the proper ratio of capital and labor. When price rises, the firm has impulses to increase its output by enlarging its scale of plant; its goal is to move up the stationary LMC curve until $P = LMC$ at the higher price. The **long-run firm supply curve**, therefore, is the segment of its long-run marginal cost curve that lies above the minimum long-run average cost.

The reason for this qualification will become clear in the next section, which introduces the second long-run adjustment of firms: the entry/exit decision. For now, note that prices below the minimum *LAC* cause negative profits, which will induce the firm to leave the industry, releasing its labor and selling or scrapping its capital. Thus industry prices below the minimum *LAC* do not generate long-run supply in the present industry when all adjustments are completed.

Deciding to Enter or Exit an Industry

One of the firm's long-run decisions involves the selection of a scale of plant. The other long-run decision that firms must make is whether (and when) to enter or exit an industry. The **entry/exit decision** is extremely important from the standpoint of any individual firm and is the driving force in the competitive industry's move toward long-run equilibrium.

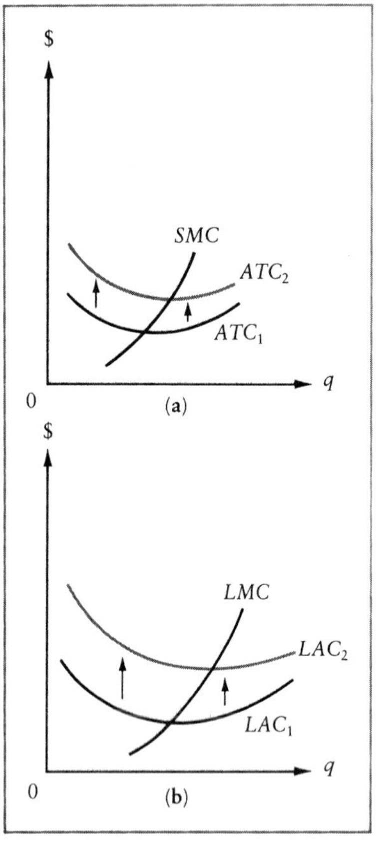

ENTREPRENEURIAL OPPORTUNITY COST.   In order to streamline the presentation of certain components of perfect competition, thus far this chapter has included only the firm's explicit costs of hiring resources. But since entrepreneurs have valuable economic alternatives, staying in a given industry entails opportunity costs as well. These costs must be taken into account when choosing the most profitable industries to produce in.

As Chapter 6 explains, entrepreneurs invest funds in their businesses, funds that could have been used elsewhere. The forgone returns on invested capital are an important component of the entrepreneurial opportunity cost. In addition, many entrepreneurs devote time and energy to the day-to-day operations of their businesses. The forgone value of the time spent running the firm is another component of opportunity cost. Thus the entrepreneurial opportunity cost equals the forgone value of invested capital and time. When ownership takes the form of holding corporate stock, the opportunity cost is merely the market rate of return on other financial investments. But entrepreneurs who invest time as well as money must take account of both components.

Our model of the firm's costs will be complete once we have added the entrepreneurial opportunity cost to labor and capital cost. The entrepreneurial opportunity cost enters our cost calculations as a fixed cost, since the entrepreneur's forgone options in other industries are the same regardless of the firm's rate of production in its present industry.

Figure 7.7 illustrates the effect on short- and long-run cost curves of including the entrepreneurial opportunity cost as a component of fixed cost. In either case, the average cost curves shift upward, just as they would with the addition of any fixed cost. In the short run, depicted in Figure 7.7a, a change in a fixed cost does not alter the marginal cost of output expansion. Hence the *ATC* curve merely slides up along a stationary short-run marginal cost

Figure 7.7
Entrepreneurial Opportunity Cost

Opportunity cost enters the cost curves as a fixed cost. The *ATC* and *LAC* curves shift upward, but the *SMC* and *LMC* curves do not change when opportunity costs are added.
(a) These are short-run costs.
(b) Long-run costs are presented in this panel.

curve, as in the shift from ATC_1 to ATC_2. (Remember that fixed costs do not change decisions at the margin.)

As for the long run, shown in Figure 7.7b, introducing the entrepreneurial opportunity cost shifts the LAC curve upward. The LAC curve is an envelope of all short-run ATC curves. But we now have a new set of ATC curves, each of which has shifted upward. An envelope of these new short-run scales of plant, which include opportunity cost as a fixed cost, can be constructed just as before. The new envelope curve, LAC_2, lies above LAC_1 and reaches its minimum at a larger level of output. We know this is so because the addition of the fixed cost does not shift the long-run marginal cost curve, LMC. Thus the new envelope curve must slide up the LMC curve, just as the short-run ATC curve slides up the SMC curve when opportunity costs are included.

It is important to realize that every short-run ATC curve and long-run LAC curve includes the opportunity cost of the entrepreneur.

ECONOMIC PROFIT.   **Economic profit** is the money that the firm has left over when it uses its revenues to pay all costs, including entrepreneurial opportunity cost:

$$\text{Economic profit} = \text{total revenue} - \text{explicit costs} \qquad (7.4)$$
$$- \text{entrepreneurial opportunity costs}$$

Economic profit can be positive, negative, or zero, and each of these values carries significance for the entry/exit decision.

To investigate the entry/exit decisions of firms, let's first consider the behavior of one firm in isolation from its industry. Figure 7.8 shows the long-run costs of a competitive, price-taking firm. The

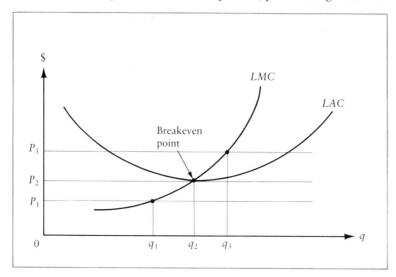

Figure 7.8
Entry/Exit Decision

If $P > LAC$, as at q_3, economic profit is positive and the firm is in the correct industry. If $P = LAC$, as at q_2, economic profit is zero and the firm just breaks even by exactly covering entrepreneurial opportunity costs. If $P < LAC$, as at q_1, economic profit is negative and the firm exits the industry in the long run.

short-run average and marginal costs have been suppressed to avoid clutter. When price is P_3, the firm maximizes long-run profits by choosing the scale of plant and level of output that equate price and long-run marginal cost. This point occurs at output q_3, where $LMC(q_3) = P_3$. At q_3, $LAC(q_3) < P_3$. Thus the firm earns positive economic profits, since the difference between total revenue and all the firm's costs, including the entrepreneurial opportunity cost, is positive. *Positive economic profit* means that the entrepreneur has net revenue left over after paying explicit and opportunity costs; that is, the entrepreneur earns more with his or her resources in this industry than in the best forgone industry. Earnings exceed the entrepreneurial opportunity costs when economic profits are positive.

If price falls to P_2, the firm adjusts its output to q_2, where $LMC(q_2) = P_2$. A smaller scale of plant is called for. At q_2, $LAC(q_2) = P_2$, and economic profit is zero. Here we must take care to interpret **zero economic profit** properly: It means that the total revenue of the firm is just sufficient to pay all labor and capital costs and to pay the entrepreneur an amount equal to his or her opportunity cost. Nothing is left after these costs are paid; thus the entrepreneur "breaks even" by earning a return equal to the value of forgone options. Zero economic profit—the **breakeven point**—simply means that the entrepreneur can earn the same amount in both the current industry and the next-best alternative.[5]

If price should to fall to P_1, the firm adjusts its scale of plant and output to $LMC(q_1) = P_1$. However, the firm earns negative economic profit at output q_1 because $LAC(q_1) > P_1$. The firm should therefore exit this industry. *Negative economic profit* means that, after the explicit costs are paid, there is not enough revenue left to pay the entrepreneur an amount as large as could be earned in an alternative employment. In the event of negative economic profits, the entrepreneur should find another industry that offers higher profits. The firm should exit its current industry at price P_1 or, more generally, at any price below P_2.

In Figure 7.8, P_2 is the breakeven price, and the minimum LAC is called the breakeven point. Exit is called for whenever the industry price falls below the minimum LAC.

Long-Run Industry Supply

We have seen that the firm will maximize long-run profits by selecting the scale of plant and producing the output that equates industry price and long-run marginal cost (LMC). We have also seen that the firm will exit the industry when industry price is less than the

---

5. During the 1960 Presidential election campaign, candidate John F. Kennedy quipped about the farmer who "hoped to break even this year because he really needed the money." This got a good laugh in the Farm Belt. Yet in economic terms, a breakeven entrepreneur is making money—in an amount just equal to the best-available alternatives.

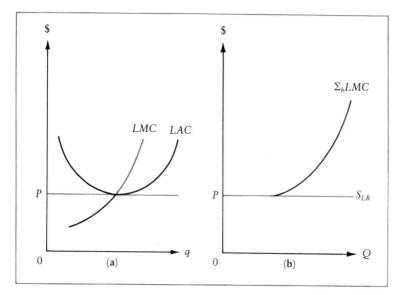

Figure 7.9
Long-Run Supply of the Firm and the Industry

The supply curve for the firm is the *LMC* curve above the minimum *LAC*. However, the long-run industry supply curve is not the horizontal summation of the firm supply curves. Because of the entry of new firms, it is instead the horizontal line at the competitive price level.

minimum *LAC*; under these circumstances, the entrepreneur earns higher profits elsewhere. However, this information is not enough to allow us to conclude that the **long-run industry supply curve** is the horizontal summation of the firm's long-run marginal cost curves above the minimum *LAC*.

The long-run industry supply curve, $\Sigma_h LMC$, is illustrated in Figure 7.9. (The term Σ_h is a reminder that the summation is horizontal.) No industry output is produced at a price less than the minimum *LAC*; instead, firms exit. By the same token, no industry output is produced at a price greater than the minimum *LAC* in the long run, because firms will enter, produce more output, and force the industry price down to the minimum *LAC*. Because all firms are assumed to exhibit identical resource and opportunity costs, the breakeven price, P, is the same for all firms. We may conclude that the long-run supply curve is the horizontal S_{LR} curve.

Long-Run Competitive Equilibrium

Equilibrium in the short run is established when industry supply and demand curves intersect and each firm in the industry maximizes profits with its prevailing scale of plant. However, **long-run competitive equilibrium** is not such a simple matter. It requires that sufficient time pass to permit all firms in the industry to adjust their scales of plant in order to set long-run marginal cost equal to price and to permit firms to either enter or exit the industry until there is no further incentive for entry or exit.

The scale-of-plant adjustment is complete when $P = LMC$ for firms. Entry and exit will occur whenever economic profits do not equal zero. If economic profits are positive, firms in this industry are earning more than they could earn in any alternative industry. En-

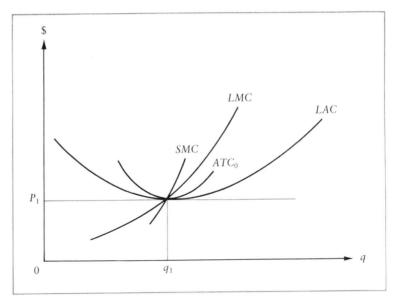

trepreneurs from these other industries will enter the industry in search of these positive economic profits. If economic profits are negative, entrepreneurs can do better in other industries—and so they exit. The incentive to enter or exit is fully eliminated when the economic profit for all firms is zero, or $P = LAC$. For these two conditions to be satisfied simultaneously, the "optimal" scale of plant must be selected by each firm, as illustrated by ATC_0 in Figure 7.10. Each firm is operating its optimal scale of plant at the minimum of its long-run cost curve, LAC. The long-run equilibrium conditions can be met only at the minimum of the LAC curve, because only there does $LMC = LAC$. Full long-run equilibrium occurs when all firms earn zero economic profit. The equation for long-run competitive equilibrium:

$$P = LMC = \text{minimum } LAC \qquad (7.5)$$

This equation holds true only in perfect competition, where all firms are identical; the long-run equilibrium condition for pure competition is introduced in a later section.

Long-Run Adjustments to an Increase in Demand

So far, we have assumed that all firms have identical production functions, resource costs, and opportunity costs. Now we will study the response of a competitive industry to an increase in demand. This exercise will reinforce the definition of long-run competitive equilibrium that we have been using.

It is convenient to divide the response to demand increases into two parts: increased output by existing firms and the entry of new firms. Figure 7.11b illustrates an original industry demand curve, D; an original short-run supply curve, $\Sigma_h SMC$; and the resulting equilibrium price, P_0. Panel a displays the behavior of one of the identical competitive firms in initial long-run zero-profit equilibrium, where $P = LMC = $ minimum LAC. The short-run marginal cost corresponding to the "optimal" scale of plant is denoted SMC_0; its short-run average total cost curve is omitted for convenience. The industry initially produces Q_0 units of output; each firm's contribution, measured on a smaller scale, is q_0 units; $\Sigma q_0 = Q_0$.

Now let industry demand increase to D_1. Price initially rises to P_2, causing the firm to adjust output along its short-run marginal cost curve to q_1 units. We may assume that this industry output expansion does not affect the price of resources or the position of the firm's cost curves. Output q_1 is only temporary. Because $P_2 > LMC(q_1)$, the firm will expand its scale of plant in order to produce q_3 units and maximize long-run profits. Such long-run output adjustments move the firm along its LMC curve and the industry along the curve $\Sigma_h LMC$. Clearly $\Sigma_h LMC$ is more elastic than $\Sigma_h SMC$; but when all firms produce q_3 units, the industry output $\Sigma q_3 = Q_3$ exceeds the quantity demanded at price P_2. This surplus is eliminated by a price reduction to P_1. Firms maximize long-run profits at price P_1 by cutting output to q_2 through suitable reductions in their scales of plant.

Price P_1 is the **market-clearing price**, the price at which the quantity supplied equals the quantity demanded in the long run. At that price, each firm is maximizing long-run profit with the condition $P_1 = LMC(q_2)$. This appears to be an equilibrium position.

Figure 7.11
Firm and Industry Response to an Increase in Demand

(a) The firm's response to an increase in demand is to expand output in the short run by hiring labor and to expand further in the long run by increasing the scale of plant. **(b)** An increase in industry demand from D to D_1 raises the price to P_2. Eventually, positive economic profits attract entry, which reduces price. In equilibrium, the firm is left with zero economic profit, having earned positive profits during the adjustment period.

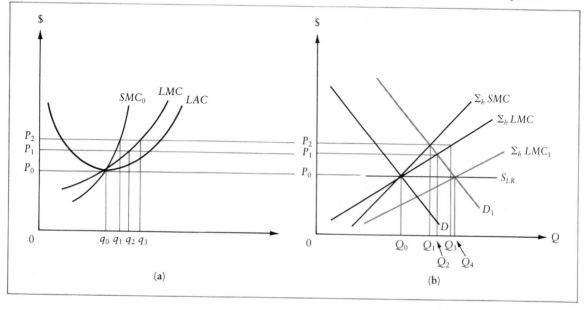

(a)   (b)

Figure 7.12

Time Trends and Adjustments to Demand Increases

(a) Price rises initially, then falls because of entry. **(b)** Capital is fixed until time period t_1, then rises as scales of plant are increased. Entry reduces price and eventually capital. **(c)** Firm output rises initially, then falls as entry reduces price and profit. **(d)** Industry output rises, in part from expansion of the initial firms' output and in part from entry.

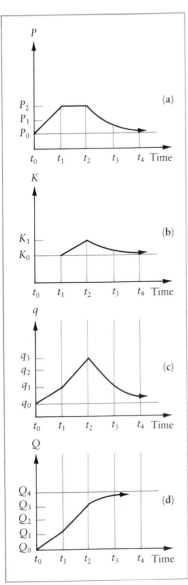

However, note that $P_1 > LAC(q_2)$; economic profits are positive, and entrepreneurs earn higher returns than they forgo in their best alternative. For this reason the seeming equilibrium at (P_1, q_2) cannot be sustained; positive economic profits attract the entry of competing firms. As new firms enter, they add their supplies to existing supplies. The $\Sigma_h LMC$ curve begins to shift to the right to reflect the supply of the new firms. Prices are forced down, gradually and simultaneously causing each firm to reduce its capital stock and to experience falling economic profits. Entry will continue to increase industry supply, increase $\Sigma_h LMC$, reduce price, and squeeze out economic profit until all economic profit is eliminated, at which time entry will stop.

Economic profits return to zero when $P =$ minimum LAC for each firm. Thus new entry will continue until the industry marginal cost curve, $\Sigma_h LMC$, reaches $\Sigma_h LMC_1$, reducing price to P_0. At price P_0 all economic profits have been eliminated, the incentive to enter the industry has been totally exploited, and the output adjustments have run their course. Long-run competitive equilibrium is reestablished. Industry output rises to Q_4 when price P_0 is reachieved (price has risen and fallen again in the interim). Note that each firm has returned to its original output q_0, to its optimal scale of plant, and to zero economic profit. The original firms contribute the same industry output as before, Q_0, leaving the output $Q_4 - Q_0$ to be supplied by new firms.

Two kinds of industry long-run cost curves are shown in Figure 7.11. The curves $\Sigma_h LMC$ and $\Sigma_h LMC_1$ are the horizontal summations of all firms' LMC curves. These curves measure the supply response to price changes before and after the competitive market adjusts to full equilibrium. The long-run industry supply curve, S_{LR}, is the collection of price and industry output combinations for which all scale-of-plant and entry adjustments are made. Each point on the horizontal supply curve is compatible with long-run competitive equilibrium.

The time-trend graphs in Figure 7.12 summarize the essential adjustments from one long-run equilibrium to another. The horizontal axes all measure time; the vertical axes measure price (P), firm purchases of capital (K), firm output (q), and industry output (Q).

Time period t_0 represents the variables in initial equilibria at P_0, K_0, q_0, and Q_0. At time period t_1, demand increases and price rises from P_0 to P_2. The firm sets $P_2 = SMC$ without altering the scale of plant K_0. Firm output rises from q_0 to q_1, while industry output rises to Q_1.

In the next round of adjustment, to time period t_2, firms expand capital to K_1 in order to set $P_2 = LMC(q_2)$. Firm output rises to q_3 and industry output rises to Q_3. By time period t_3, the effect of the increased capital expansion in the previous period begins to lower prices, causing firms to reduce capital stocks and output in order to reduce *LMC* to the lower price. In addition, entry starts to reduce prices, erode profits, and induce additional sell-off or depreciation of capital. By time period t_4 the process of adjustment is complete. Price has returned to its original level, $P_0 = \text{minimum } LAC$; the buildup of capital stock by existing firms in order to capture initial profits has all been sold off or depreciated; and each firm has returned to its optimal scale of plant, K_0. The additional industry output, $Q_4 - Q_0$, is produced by the entry of new firms.

The speed and ease of entry into an industry affects the nature of time trends like these. If high entry costs cause entry to be slow, existing firms may increase capital quickly, in order to capture the profits at the initially elevated prices, and later sell capital gradually, as entry dictates. Or the speed of entry may be so fast that existing firms do not have time to adjust their scales of plant at all. In this case, entry would be the primary mode of returning the industry to competitive equilibrium.

A P P L I C A T I O N

7.3

Patent Protection

The competitive mechanism and production-cost analysis provide a useful foundation for the study of patents. Research and new-product development are expensive, time-consuming, and—since they may not result in a useful product—inherently risky. Moreover, once the new invention is on the market, rival firms can easily break it down and scrutinize its inner workings. The fruits of inventive activity, whether a new design, a secret formula, or a novel application, can be laid bare for rival engineers to examine. Compared to the inventing firm, which "starts from scratch," the rival firm faces lower costs. We can use competitive theory to investigate the economic consequences of product piracy.

Without some form of patent protection, the price of the invention would be driven down to just production costs; price would not include a return to the inventor. Knowing this in advance, the inventor would be greatly deterred from engaging in inventive activity in the first place. And firms would surely be reluctant to pay high salaries to creative people if their inventions could be reproduced at lower cost by rival firms. Competition would stifle creativity and would certainly lose its claim to be a stimulus of efficiency. Clearly, government must provide an incentive to invent. But how? Let's discuss three possibilities: grants, prizes, and patents.

Grants are paid in advance as a way of encouraging creative effort. But success can never be guaranteed. Past success is often used as a guide to the future, a practice that does not encourage the budding young genius or the elderly tinkerer. Hence grants are ineffective incentives, because there is no direct link between the payment and the ultimate

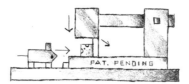

value of the invention.

Prizes solve the problem inherent in grants by allowing an assessment of the worth of the invention after it is accomplished. Awarding a prize to the inventor targets the incentive and rewards success. The drawback is that prizes are typically awarded in predetermined categories. Another limitation is the size of the prize. Presumably, it should bear some relation to the value of the contribution. But this is rarely the case. In fact, the dollar value of prizes is usually announced in advance.

The use of patents skirts all these problems. Patents reward inventive activity by providing for a period of monopoly control over the invention. The "prize" is in proportion to the value of the achievement, as measured by the profit earned during the life of the patent. Furthermore, and most important, the nature of the achievement need not be known in advance in order to offer a prize. With the patent, both the size of the prize and the nature of the achievement are determined after the fact, but the incentives are in place beforehand.

7.4

Advertising in Competitive Markets

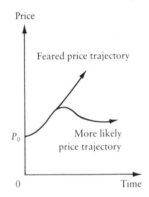

In perfect competition, the firm has no incentive to advertise. The advantage to advertising is the higher price the firm can charge if advertising increases product demand. But this advantage is dissipated by the costless entry of new firms selling an identical product. Furthermore, since consumers often treat the products of different manufacturers as perfectly substitutable, a firm cannot advertise its own product without simultaneously advertising its competitors' products. Finally, the firm that advertises has little chance of influencing industry demand, because one firm is just a small part of the industry. The incentive to advertise is therefore subject to many of the same problems as the incentive to invent.

Departure from perfect competition creates the incentive to advertise. In fact, the purpose of advertising is often to force a departure from competition by convincing consumers not to treat the products of all sellers alike.

7.5

Price Controls and Competitive Adjustments

Price controls are often imposed when fear of runaway prices runs high. Controlling the profits of firms experiencing rapid price hikes is another motive for instituting controls. Figure A compares the time trend of the price that policy makers fear with the more likely time trend that the analysis of long-run competitive equilibrium suggests: Entry will eventually cause prices to moderate.

It is useful to know what impact government-established price controls will have on the long-run adjustment process and on firms' profits during the transition. Beginning with the original equilibrium price P_0 in Figure B, let demand rise to D_1 and, accordingly, the equilibrium price to P_1. If price is allowed to rise to P_1, the resulting profits attract entry, supply rises to S_1, and the adjustment process proceeds normally over time, as depicted by the solid time-trend line in the right-hand panel of Figure B. However, if a price ceiling is set at P_C, the entry adjustment process is slowed down; prices tend to follow the dashed trend line instead. Let's study the implications of dis-

turbing the long-run adjustment process by price controls.

The horizontal axis in the right-hand panel of Figure B divides time into four zones: $\overline{T_0 T_A}$, $\overline{T_A T_B}$, $\overline{T_B T_C}$, and $\overline{T_C T_D}$.

1. $\overline{T_0 T_A}$: In this zone, the market price is allowed to rise in response to the shift in demand.
2. $\overline{T_A T_B}$: Now the controlled price, P_C, is below the price that would prevail without controls. Shortages emerge during this time period.
3. $\overline{T_B T_C}$: During this period, the equilibrium price that would have prevailed but for the controls falls below the control price. Shortages persist.
4. T_C: Entry, albeit slowed by the controls, is finally great enough to bring the market price below the price ceiling, P_C.
5. $\overline{T_C T_D}$: Entry continues until the price falls low enough to assure firms a fair rate of return. When economic profits are eliminated, entry stops and long-run equilibrium is achieved.

Figure A
Price Trajectories When Demand Increases

The rising price trajectory is feared, although prices will probably taper off and fall. The initial high prices tend to attract competition.

Thus, in respect to price controls, we see that

1. It cannot be said that price controls keep *costs* down, because the transaction costs resulting from the shortage exceed the price the market would have produced.

2. It cannot be said that price controls keep *prices* down, because (as Figure B indicates) there are some periods in which the controlled price is above the market price that would prevail without controls.

3. It cannot be said that price controls prevent capitalists from obtaining unfair profits, because during period $\overline{T_B T_C}$, prices and profits are higher under controls than they would be in a free market.

Price controls not only distort economic relationships in the short run, as discussed in Chapter 2, but also inhibit the transfer of resources among industries in the long run and thereby distort the best allocation of productive re-

Figure B
Long-Run Adjustments to Price Controls

Price controls slow entry yet keep prices and profits above the free-market levels during time period $\overline{T_B T_C}$.

sources. Of course, price controls are often defended on the grounds that many industries are not competitive and will not adjust according to the analysis presented here. However, very few industries are so monopolized that profit incentives do not attract competitors. And whatever tendency these industries may have to adjust is greatly hampered by price controls. Perhaps the resources used to implement and enforce price controls in such industries could more usefully be employed in eliminating other structural and legal hindrances to competition.

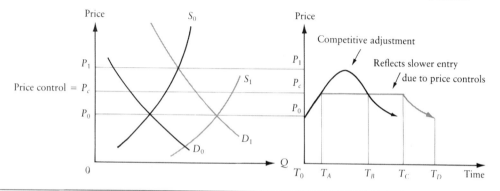

Pure Competition

Firms are not identical. Fortunately, the model of identical firms (perfect competition) can easily be adjusted to incorporate the more general case of nonidentical firms (pure competition). The model of pure competition takes a giant step toward the real world by drawing a distinction of vast significance: among marginal, inframarginal, and extramarginal firms (to be defined shortly).

Suppose that firms are identical in every regard except the opportunity costs of the entrepreneurs. Under this assumption, the long-run competitive equilibrium condition must be amended. When entrepreneurs have differing opportunity costs, it is not true that all firms earn zero economic profit in the long run. It may seem to you that we have merely set up a straw man and will now knock it over. But the zero-profit issue runs deeper than this. The notion that long-run competitive equilibrium must produce zero economic profits for all firms is important because of its implications for economic efficiency, because economists and lawyers commonly hold it to be true, and because it leads to the incorrect conclusion that when positive economic profits exist, competition is absent.

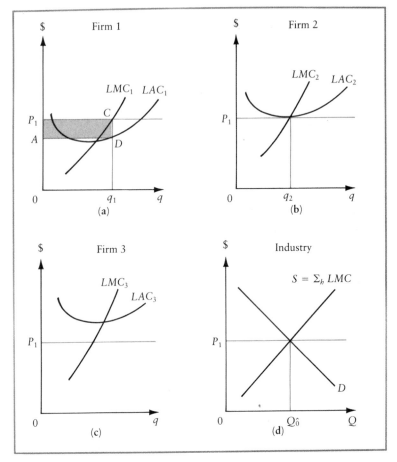

Figure 7.13 illustrates long-run competitive equilibrium when
firms still have identical production functions and resource costs but
when entrepreneurs have varying opportunity costs. The cost curves
of three firms are depicted in panels a, b, and c. The labor and
capital costs of all three firms are identical, because of their identical
production functions and their lack of control over per-unit input
prices (w and r). So the difference in the positions of the LAC curves
is due solely to the different entrepreneurial opportunity costs. The
owner of the firm in panel a has few alternatives and hence low
opportunity costs. The LAC curve in panel b is higher than the one
in panel a, reflecting the higher opportunity costs of forgone alternatives. The LAC curve in panel a is highest of all, an indication of
still-greater opportunity costs. (Opportunity costs are a fixed cost,
so they do not affect the firms' marginal cost curves.) Figure 7.13
shows that firms can have different cost structures even when they
face identical production functions and input prices.

Figure 7.13d displays the industry supply and demand curves; their intersection establishes industry price, P_1. Firm 1 (in panel a) produces q_1 units of output and earns the positive economic profit AP_1CD; firm 2 produces q_2 units of output ($q_1 = q_2$) but earns zero economic profit; firm 3 would earn negative economic profit by producing in this industry and therefore seeks higher accounting profits elsewhere.

Any firm that, like firm 1, earns positive economic profits in long-run equilibrium is an **inframarginal firm.** Firm 2 earns zero economic profit; it is earning just enough accounting profit to keep producing in the present industry. Such a firm is called a **marginal firm.** Firm 3 does not produce in the industry at price P_1 because of the negative economic profits that would result. This kind of firm is an **extramarginal firm.**

You may ask why the presence of positive economic profits for firm 1 would not invite more firms to enter the industry, shift the industry supply curve to the right, reduce industry price, and continue to squeeze economic profits until all remaining firms earn zero profits in equilibrium, as in perfect competition. In moving to the industry price, P_1, these are exactly the adjustments that occur. But at price P_1, all entry and exit have ceased. Only firms that have lower opportunity costs than firm 2 (lower LAC curves) could profitably enter the industry at price P_1. When all such inframarginal firms have entered, no other firms have entry prices below P_1. Also, all extramarginal firms—those earning negative economic profits at price P_1—have exited. The industry supply curve, $S = \Sigma_h LMC$, will not be shifted by further entry or exit. Thus price P_1 is the long-run equilibrium price, the industry is in long-run equilibrium, and inframarginal firms earn positive economic profits. Only the marginal firms earn zero economic profits.

We may now restate the conditions for long-run competitive equilibrium more accurately, if somewhat more loosely: Equilibrium occurs when no firms are entering or exiting the industry at the prevailing industry price. The marginal firms—those just willing to remain in the industry rather than produce elsewhere—earn zero economic profit; the inframarginal firms earn positive long-run economic profits resulting from lower costs (in the present example, lower opportunity costs). The commonly held view that long-run economic profit is zero for all firms applies only to the special case of perfect competition, in which all entrepreneurs have identical production functions, resource costs, and opportunity costs. When firms have different costs, they have different entry and exit prices. Thus the industry's long-run equilibrium can coexist with positive economic profits for the inframarginal, low-cost firms.

Inframarginal firms earn positive economic profit, that is, a return in excess of available alternatives. Although we have started with an example in which firms' costs differ solely because of different opportunity costs, inframarginal profits may result from any source of cost differences, such as efficient management, access to superior resources, location advantages, better production technologies, and newer physical plants. Relatively low-cost, inframarginal firms can produce along the positively sloped segment of their *LAC* curves. The higher-cost, marginal firms operate at the minimum *LAC* and earn zero economic profit. Inframarginal profits are thus perfectly compatible with competition. The key is that each firm is small relative to industry output. Understanding this point is essential to both management and public policy making.

A P P L I C A T I O N

7.6

Potpourri of Marginal, Inframarginal, and Extramarginal Concepts

The distinction among *marginal, inframarginal,* and *extramarginal* is a powerful concept incorporating succinct, compact language. Consider the demand curve in Figure A. At price *P* the

Figure A
Demand and Marginal Benefit
The price line crosses the demand curve at the marginal unit. Units to the right are extramarginal, those to the left inframarginal.

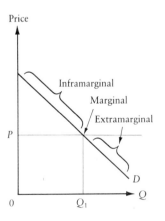

consumer purchases Q_1 units. The Q_1th unit is the marginal unit, because only for that unit is the marginal benefit to the consumer equal to the price paid. All units up to the Q_1th unit are in-

Figure B
Supply and Marginal Benefit
The price line crosses the supply curve at the marginal unit. Units to the left are inframarginal, those to the right are extramarginal.

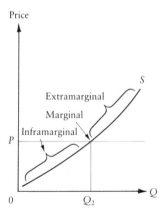

framarginal, because the marginal benefit to the consumer exceeds the price actually paid. All units in excess of Q_1 units are extramarginal, because the price *P* exceeds the marginal benefit for all such units. Note that the marginal, inframarginal, and extramarginal concepts are directly tied to a given price.

Figure B continues the example with a supply curve. At price *P*, the Q_2th unit is the marginal unit, because only for the Q_2th unit does the price charged exactly cover the firm's marginal cost of production. Units up to Q_2 are inframarginal ($P > MC$), and all units in excess of Q_2 are extramarginal ($P < MC$). Again, the distinction is only relevant with respect to a given price.

Finally, the terms can be attached to price-taking firms as well as to production units. In Figure C price is set at the industry level. Firms that earn a normal return equal to their entrepreneurial opportunity costs are marginal firms; lower-cost

Figure C
Identifying Marginal Firms

The equation of the minimum average cost and the price level identifies the marginal firm. Firms that earn positive economic profits at that price are inframarginal; firms that lose money are extramarginal.

firms that earn profits in excess of opportunity costs are inframarginal firms. Extramarginal firms have costs too high to allow entry at the prevailing price.

These examples illustrate that the terms *marginal, intra-* *marginal,* and *extramarginal* can be used in all cases involving optimization by economic agents at a given price. Furthermore, the concepts add content to the analysis of competition.

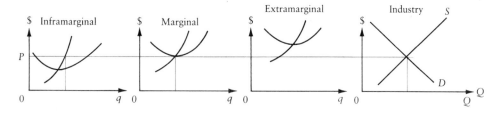

A P P L I C A T I O N

7.7

Hunting for Monopolies

One major activity of the government is the regulation of monopoly profits. Indeed, a principal item in President Jimmy Carter's energy bill was identification and control of the monopoly profits of energy-producing firms. The analysis of inframarginal competitive long-run profits shows that the presence of positive economic profits—a greater-than-normal (or fair) return—is not a valid test for the existence of monopoly. Although the competitive marginal firm earns zero profit,

the inframarginal firm earns positive profits. Still, this is the usual test applied by political subcommittees in search of monopolies.

To identify an inframarginal competitive firm as a monopolist solely on the evidence of positive

economic profits and then to tax away the profits or otherwise regulate the firm as a monopolist is both bad economics and bad politics. Yet the model of perfect competition—often the only competitive model presented—promotes such misguided policies by its theorem of zero long-run economic profits for all firms. Excessive reliance on this model has important consequences for public policy and hence for the regulatory environment of competitive firms.

A P P L I C A T I O N

7.8

Proposition 13 and Apartment Rental Rates

Not too long ago, a California referendum limiting property taxes to 1 percent of market value passed by a 2-to-1 vote. This remarkable public support was due in part to the votes of apartment dwellers, who were told that their landlords' tax savings would be passed on to them.* After all, the rental housing market is quite competitive. In competitive markets, aren't

cost reductions passed on to customers in the form of lower prices?

Applying the theory of pure competition, we can see that the

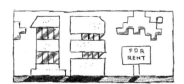

promise made to California renters cannot be kept at all in the short run and not completely in the long run either. The price that landlords can charge for apartments is determined by industry supply and demand at the minimum of the marginal landlords' *LAC* curves. The inframarginal firms (apartment houses) earn positive economic profits because

*There is considerable debate about the property tax on dwellings: Is it a tax on profits, hence not passed on to the consumer? Or is it largely shifted to the consumer in the long run, much like an excise tax? It seems to be a

combination of both after industry supply responds fully to the tax reduction. For a detailed theoretical treatment of this issue, see Peter Mieszkowski, "The Property Tax: An Excise Tax or a Profits Tax?" *Journal of Public Economics* 1 (1972): 73–96.

Continued on page 182

of such factors as prime location or better management. These profits are reflected in the property value of the inframarginal apartment house. For the marginal, zero-profit firms, property value is strictly the book value of the apartment; it includes no economic profit. Therefore, the property value of the inframarginal apartment house is greater than that of the marginal apartment house, and hence any percentage decrease in property taxes will be bigger in absolute terms for the inframarginal landlord than for the marginal landlord.

Now let's use competitive theory to see how much of a rent reduction will follow a tax reduction. The initial industry price is set at P_1 by supply and demand, as shown in Figure A. Figure B shows three types of apartment-owning firms before the passage of Proposition 13: inframarginal firm 1 (on the left), marginal firm 2 (in the middle), and extramarginal firm 3 (on the right). Now let Proposition 13 pass and property taxes be reduced. In the short run, property taxes are fixed costs. Reducing property taxes shifts the *LAC* curves down without affecting the firms' marginal cost curves or the industry supply curve, $\Sigma_h LMC$. Note that the profitable, inframarginal apartments (the left-hand panel) receive a larger tax reduction than the less-profitable apartments. The remarkable result is that there will be no impact on

Figure A
Supply of Housing

The industry supply of housing tends to increase in the long run in reponse to measures like California's Proposition 13. Price tends to decrease.

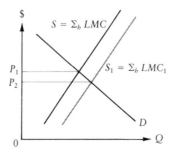

rental rates in the short run.

In the long run, previously extramarginal firms like firm 3 will enter the industry, shifting the industry supply curve to $\Sigma_h LMC_1$. Entry reduces price to P_2, but by virtue of the higher costs of the entering firms, entry cannot bring price into line with firm 2's costs and certainly not with firm 1's

Figure B
Long-Run Response of Individual Landlords

Given the demand and supply curves in Figure A, housing firm 1 is inframarginal. Firm 2 is marginal before the property tax cut and inframarginal after. Firm 3 is extramarginal before the property tax cut and marginal after.

costs. Although there is long-run entry, it bears little relation to the size of the cost reductions of the inframarginal firms. Rent reductions depend only on the number of previously extramarginal firms that can enter under the new tax formula.

To summarize, property tax reductions will produce no rental-rate relief in the short run and some reduction only in the long run. With a percentage reduction, property taxes will be reduced more on the more profitable apartments, which have greater property value. But this rental-rate reduction will be smaller than the property tax reduction. The competitive market will not pass through the cost savings. Instead, any rental-rate reduction will be due to the entry of new higher-cost or poorly located apartments that could not survive under the previous rates.

This analysis changes if demand shifts outward or if there is inflation. If there is inflation, the entry of new landlords will reduce rental rates in real terms but not in nominal terms. If, as recent data indicate, people continue to move to warmer climes, California will experience an increase in the demand for housing. If this development shifts the demand curve by more than the entry of new firms shifts the supply curve, rental rates will go up, not down. This analysis reinforces our point: Rental rates have little to do with taxes on inframarginal apartments.

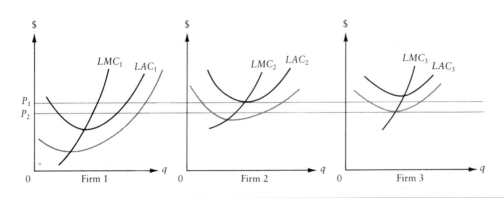

Economic Rent: A Price-Determined Cost

The model of pure competition allows for the fact that in-framarginal firms can earn positive economic profits in long-run equilibrium. A concept that helps explain this fact is the **rent-inclusive long-run average cost curve** (LAC^*). Throughout the discussion that follows you must make a clear distinction between LAC and LAC^*.

Consider Figure 7.14 (and ignore the dashed LAC^* curve for now). When price is P_1, the inframarginal firm produces q_1 and earns a positive economic profit of AP_1BC. This economic profit arises from some cost advantage over marginal firms; perhaps the firm has a location advantage, a newer and more efficient physical plant, or simply lower opportunity costs. Economic profit is a surplus bestowed by a valuable resource in scant supply.

The economic profit of the inframarginal firm has various names, including *inframarginal profit, economic rent,* and *in-framarginal rent.* It is important to understand the intellectual heritage of the term *rent.* It was used originally to describe the surplus paid to the owners of land, a surplus that accrued because land was in scarce supply. The term has now been broadened to include the surplus resulting from any scarce factor of production. **Economic rent** is therefore the surplus of a specialized resource's earnings over what the resource could earn in its most valuable forgone use; this difference equals the previous definition of *economic profit.* (Note

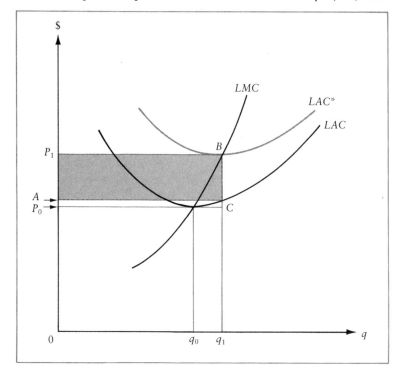

**Figure 7.14
Inframarginal Firm's
Rent-Inclusive Long-Run Average
Cost Curve**

By definition, all firms operate at the minimum level of the LAC^* curve.

that *economic rent* is unrelated to *contractual rent*, a sum of money that a renter pays to a landlord.)

Now let's return to the curve labeled LAC^* in Figure 7.14. It is sometimes argued that the inframarginal firm's profits are positive because not all relevant costs are included. Specifically, it is said, the entrepreneur always has the option of selling the firm. The selling price of the firm would equal the inframarginal rent, AP_1BC. As long as the entrepreneur does not sell, the forgone option to sell is an opportunity cost. If the forgone opportunity to sell the firm (rent AP_1BC) is added to the firm's other costs, already captured in the LAC curve, the dashed rent-inclusive LAC^* curve is attained. It would appear that the firm earns a zero profit at price P_1 if the opportunity cost of selling the firm for AP_1BC is counted as a cost.

There are two reasons to be wary of the rent-inclusive LAC^* curve. First, zero economic profit is a tautology if it is achieved by including rent as a cost. Furthermore, this tautology applies to all firms, not just competitive firms. Imagine Howard Hughes's attorneys arguing before a tax court or regulatory agency that the economic profits of the Hughes Corporation are zero because of the high opportunity cost of selling the firm. But the most important concern is that indiscriminate use of the LAC^* curve may lead to incorrect analyses of entry/exit decisions. Let's see why.

Managers and managerial economists are interested in costs principally as they affect industry price, profit maximization, and entry/exit decisions. The LAC and LMC curves are relevant to these decisions; the LAC^* curve is not. The reason is that rent is a **price-determined cost**, whereas all other costs we have studied are **price-determining costs**. We have already seen how labor, capital, and entrepreneurial opportunity costs help to determine prices. If wages rise as entrepreneurs develop more valuable alternatives in other industries, the industry supply curve shifts to the left and price rises.

In contrast, economic rent is price-determined, not price-determining. Economic rent rises whenever price increases. In Figure 7.14 the firm produces q_0 at price P_0 and earns a zero economic profit. If prices rises to P_1, the firm expands output to q_1, and economic profit AP_1BC appears. This area also represents economic rent, and it results from a higher product price; it is therefore price-determined. If price falls, economic rent falls too. But the change in economic rent plays no role in determining price.

A price-determined cost does not affect profit-maximizing decisions about production or entry/exit. Suppose that Figure 7.14 did not include rent in the firm's costs. At price P_1, the firm would produce q_1 units, because $P_1 = LMC(q_1)$. Its revenue would exceed the return in the next-best alternative, because $P_1 = LAC(q_1)$; its profits would be higher in this industry than anywhere else. Now include rent in the firm's cost curve, increasing average costs to

LAC^* and giving the illusion that the firm earns zero economic profit. Will the firm change its output? No; $P_1 > LMC(q_1)$. There is still no alternative that offers higher profits.

In short, including economic rent in the firm's costs gives us no information about firm and industry behavior that we do not already have, and it hides the tautology in the argument that all firms operate at zero long-run profits. Thus economic rent should not be included in the firm's costs if we are trying to construct models of the firm's decisions. Calling economic rent a price-determined cost is perhaps the most difficult concept yet presented in this book. But its importance is commensurate with its difficulty.

A P P L I C A T I O N

7.9

Taxi Medallions

We can use the theory of pure competition to understand the taxi industry. In most large cities there are enough taxicabs to force each one to be a price taker. However, there is also usually a restriction on entry, because taxi owners are required to register their cabs.

The ostensible purpose of taxi registration is to screen drivers so that corrupt, antisocial, and potentially dangerous men and women do not get licensed. (The passenger can't gather accurate information by asking the driver, "Are you incompetent, a nut, on parole, or a pervert?") It has long been argued that such quality control is best handled at the licensing stage. A successful applicant is required to purchase a taxi medallion, the medallion serving as evidence to customers

of legitimate registration.

Aside from the safety aspects of taxi licensing, the medallions have been used to limit the supply of taxis and drive up fares. The following analysis helps us see who gains and loses from taxi regulation.

Assume that the initial industry supply and demand curves in the figure determine the long-run

Effect of Taxi Regulation on Production and Exit Decisions

Entry restrictions in the form of limits on the number of medallions issued in the taxicab market create economic rent as demand increases. The LAC^* curve rises and falls with price.

equilibrium price P_0. The firm in the left-hand panel is a marginal firm earning zero economic profit in long-run equilibrium. The firm produces q_0 units of output (taxi rides) and operates at the minimum LAC. The taxi owner has a taxi medallion, acquired at zero cost from the regulatory agency, but assume, for simplicity, that it can be sold on the open market to anyone presenting a valid registration form.

Now let demand increase over time from D_0 to D_1, while the number of medallions that the regulatory agency issues remains fixed. The industry price rises to P_1, and the firm responds by increasing service to q_1. The increase in demand and price gives the medallion owner a rent of AP_1BC. The price-determined

Continued on page 186

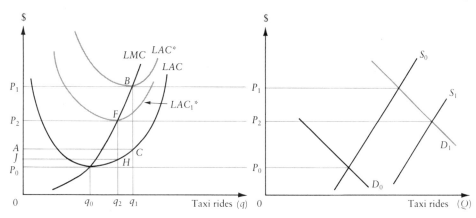

rent results from the limited supply of licensed taxi drivers. The customers pay a higher price.

Now suppose the medallion is sold on the open market to a person approved by the regulatory agency. How much will the medallion sell for? Its price will equal the present value of the expected economic profits that the medallion makes possible, the economic rent AP_1BC. Note, however, that the new owner's LAC curve does not rise to LAC^*, because he or she must pay the lump sum AP_1BC for the medallion. The new owner's correct average cost curve is the same as the old owner's.

The old owner could have constructed a rent-inclusive LAC^* curve by including the rent as an opportunity cost of sale. The new owner would have discovered that the rent had actually been extracted, and so the new owner's rent-inclusive cost curve is also LAC^*. But the costs of the commonly available capital (cab) and labor (hours roaming the streets) resources are unchanged, as are the entrepreneurial opportunity costs. If the new cab owner's opportunity cost is roughly the same as the initial owner's, the LAC curve is the same for both.

Say that the regulatory agency increases the supply of medallions, so that the supply of taxi service increases to S_1 (see the right-hand panel). Price falls to

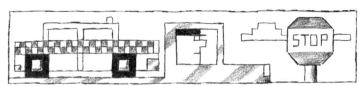

P_2. The firm reduces rides to q_2. The rent-inclusive LAC^* curve shifts down to LAC_1^*. The rent from the medallion was originally AP_1BC, a lump sum that the new owner paid. But the rent has now fallen to JP_2FH, because of the reduction in the commodity price. The new owner has suffered a reduction in the asset value of the medallion.

Does the cabbie lose money as a result of the loss in rent? Yes, because the total payments (including labor and capital costs, entrepreneurial opportunity costs, and the loan payment on the medallion purchase) exceed total revenue: $P_2 < LAC^*(q_2)$.

Does the cabbie exit the industry? If you regard the firm as operating at zero economic profit at point B on the LAC^* curve, it would seem that any price below P_1 would generate negative economic profits and cause the owner to exit. But wait: $P_2 > LAC(q_2)$. The lower price P_2 still exceeds the per-unit cost of labor, capital, and entrepreneurial opportunity. Thus economic profits are positive—and the taxi industry is still the best of the cabbie's alternatives. To be sure, he or she is worse off because the

medallion has lost value, but this is a sunk cost. If the cabbie exits the taxi industry, he or she will still have to pay the loan on the medallion purchase. The loss in the medallion's value does not affect the decision to exit the taxi industry. That loss is now a cost to the owner's life, not to the selection of a particular industry. It is therefore a sunk cost and not an appropriate inclusion in the firm's average cost curve for the purpose of making an entry/exit decision.

As long as price stays above P_0, the new owner should stay in the taxi industry (and regret the medallion's lost value at every stop sign), because the opportunities are worse elsewhere. If price falls below P_0, exit is called for. The cabbie should enter the next-best industry, say truck driving (and continue to regret the medallion's lost value at every stop sign).

Note carefully that the cabbie's production and exit decisions are not related to the firm's economic rent or its loss of rent. The rent-inclusive LAC^* curves move about with changes in price and are not relevant in the cabbie's profit-maximizing output and exit decisions.

7.10

Academic Entry and Exit

The concept of pure competition provides useful insights into academic markets. Consider each professor a firm producing a roughly homogeneous composite of university services, including classroom instruction, research, and public service. If the market for professors is competitive, the price they charge for services is set by supply and demand forces and is uniform for all. Hence, market price is P_0 in Figure A.

Figure B depicts the cost curves

of three professors. Assume that the only important cost difference among professors is the opportunity cost of forgone alternatives, and remember that these opportunity costs are contained in the cost curves. Professor Able's LAC curve (in the left-hand panel) is

low because he has few if any alternatives. Professor Baker (in the center panel) has better alternatives in nonacademic positions, which is reflected in a higher LAC curve. Professor Charles (in the right-hand panel) has even more valuable alternatives and hence a higher LAC curve.

At the initial price, P_0, Professor Charles is marginal; her profit as a professor equals the best forgone option. Professors Able and Baker, however, are infra-

Figure A
Market for Professorial Services

As in other industries, supply interacts with price to determine the demand for professorial services.

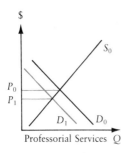

Professorial Services Q

Figure B
Marginalist Reasoning for Professors

For professionals like professors, being inframarginal or marginal is inversely related to opportunities elsewhere. At price P_1, the marginal Professor Charles leaves her profession for private industry. Thus *marginal* does not mean "worst"; in fact, it may mean "best."

marginal. Supply and demand forces provide them with a return in excess of their opportunity costs. The market price, in combination with low opportunity costs, bestows economic rent on Professors Able and Baker.

Now let the demand for professors fall to D_1, *ceteris paribus,* which reduces price to P_1. Professor Charles is immediately extramarginal; she exits the academic market in the long run. Note carefully that Professor Charles is not extramarginal because she is less efficient. Quite the contrary. Professor Charles leaves first because she has skills that are valuable in business and/or government. *Extramarginal* doesn't always mean "inefficient." It just means that costs (including opportunity costs) are too high to allow participation in the industry at the current price.

The exit of extramarginal professors who have nonacademic

opportunities reduces industry supply and brings price up somewhat. Long-run equilibrium (not shown in the figures) is reestablished when the only remaining professors are those who cover their opportunity costs. But Professors Able and Baker never once think of exiting. Falling prices have reduced their economic rent, to be sure, but the paucity of alternatives keeps them in place.

The model of pure competition, which describes nonidentical firms, provides insight into the dynamics of entry and exit. In the model of perfect competition, in which firms are identical, all firms would become extramarginal when prices fell and, logically, all should exit. Pure competition, on the other hand, emphasizes an orderly and predictable exit mechanism, starting with the highest-cost, most extramarginal firms and proceeding downward. The model also shows why some industries take so long to die in the face of falling demand. The decision to exit depends on better alternatives elsewhere. If industries are made up of firms whose entrepreneur's alternatives are limited, falling demand and prices merely reduce economic rents without triggering exit, thereby producing a relatively sustained death rattle.

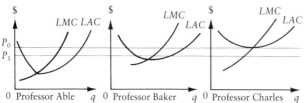

APPLICATION

A simple exercise in the use of cost curves is the analysis of the impact of criminal fines—say for antitrust violations or fraud—on the firm's decision to exit an industry. Since a fine, as opposed to a payment for a resource, is a sunk cost, it is completely independent of the decision to exit. The fine therefore does not shift the *LAC* curve, which is the only cost curve relevant to entry and exit.

A fine must be paid regardless of the industry the firm selects. Hence the imposition of a fine should not be allowed to

7.11

Criminal Fines and the Entry/Exit Decision

influence the selection of an industry.

The only exception occurs when the asset value of the firm must be drawn on to help pay the fine. Although the entrepreneur may be forced to liquidate in order to pay the fine, the physical assets will remain in the industry under the control of a new entrepreneur.

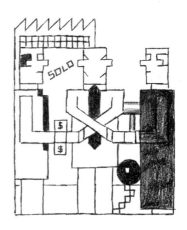

Competition and Efficiency

The economic efficiency of competitive markets is a widely heralded claim and can be demonstrated by drawing on our knowledge of the equal marginal cost and revenue principles, which were set forth in Chapter 3. The **equal marginal benefit principle** states that each point on an individual demand curve measures the consumer's marginal benefit of purchasing one more unit. Total **societal welfare**—the net economic benefits of the allocation of resources—is maximized when the marginal benefits are equal for all consumers.

Figure 7.15 contains five panels. The marginal benefit (demand) curves of two representative consumers are shown in panels a and b. The marginal cost (supply) curves of two representative firms are displayed in panels d and e. Panel c exhibits the industry supply and demand curves. The industry demand curve, labeled $D = \Sigma_h MB$, is the horizontal summation of all consumers' demand curves. Also, the marginal cost curve above the shutdown point is each firm's supply curve. Adding the supplies of all firms together by horizontal summation gives us the industry supply curve in panel c, labeled $S = \Sigma_h MC$. Competitive market forces lead to an equilibrium price of P_c and an equilibrium quantity exchanged of Q_c.

The key characteristic of competitive markets is that neither buyers nor sellers have any control over price. All buyers and sellers are price takers. Consumers arrange their purchases so that price equals the marginal benefit of the marginal unit bought. But since all buyers face the same price, their marginal benefits are equated automatically. In Figure 7.15, the equal marginal benefit principle is satisfied when consumer 1 (panel a) buys q_1 units and consumer 2 (panel b) buys q_2 units. Competition assures that the industry output Q_c is allocated among consumers so as to achieve maximum total benefit. This allocation is one dimension of efficiency in competition.

Figure 7.15
Efficiency of Competitive Markets

(a) Consumer 1 has marginal benefit equal to the price. **(b)** Consumer 2 has marginal benefit equal to the price and, therefore, equal to the marginal benefit of consumer 1. **(c)** In the industry as a whole, marginal benefit equals marginal cost, because supply and demand are in equilibrium. **(d)** For firm 1, marginal cost equals price. **(e)** For firm 2, marginal cost equals price also; hence, the marginal cost for firm 2 equals that of firm 1 and equals the marginal benefit for consumers 1 and 2.

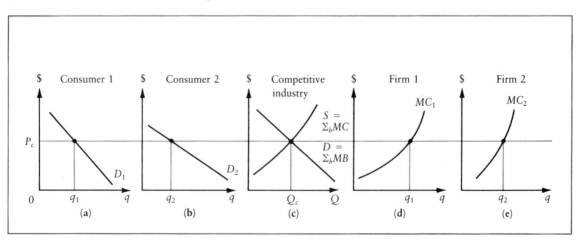

Sellers are also price takers in competition. Firms 1 and 2 (and all others not shown) maximize their individual profits by adjusting production until price equals marginal cost. But since they all face the same price, they all produce at the same marginal cost. Industry output Q_c is therefore produced at the lowest possible total cost. This fact is the second component of efficiency in a competitive market.

Competition is efficient because its output is produced at the lowest cost and is distributed among consumers so as to maximize total consumer benefit. These conditions apply to the competitive output Q_c. But we have one final efficiency question to ask: Is output Q_c the best quantity of output for this industry? That is, do consumers value the output produced more than the alternative products that the same resources could have produced elsewhere? If so, we have a fully efficient solution.

Panel c shows that Q_c is in fact the best industry output. Each point on the industry demand curve measures the extra benefit that consumers receive for the marginal unit. Likewise, each point on the industry supply curve measures the extra cost of producing the marginal unit. The competitive market produces each unit of output for which the marginal benefit to society exceeds the marginal cost of production. Society's net welfare is improved every time it makes a decision for which marginal benefit is greater than marginal cost. But in competitive equilibrium, marginal benefit equals marginal cost. Thus all welfare gains are totally exhausted in competition, and output Q_c is efficient. It is the same output that an omniscient "higher power" or "benevolent dictator" would allocate to the industry on the basis of the same information on marginal costs and benefits.

Let's review the three efficiency rules that are satisfied by competitive markets:

The equal marginal benefit rule assures that competitive output is divided among consumers so as to maximize total benefit.

$$MB_1 = MB_2 = \ldots = MB_n$$

The equal marginal cost rule assures that competitive output is produced at the lowest total cost.

$$MC_1 = MC_2 = \ldots = MC_n$$

The third condition assures that the competitive rate of output is more valuable to consumers than the value of any alternative goods that the same resources could produce. When resources are properly allocated,

$$MB = MC$$

We have seen that competitive equilibrium achieves efficiency in the use of resources. But competitive equilibrium generates efficiency only when the firm pays the full social cost of its resources. For example, if pollution damages are not incorporated into the firm's costs, competition from "dirty" firms will force "clean" firms to adopt dirty production techniques or exit the industry. In addition, firm marginal costs will be understated, which in turn induces firms to produce too much output and consequently to generate excessive pollution, both in the production and consumption of goods.

Another example of the undesirable results of competitive equilibrium occurs when profitable pornographic movies and magazines attract the entry of competing firms that allow material to get increasingly obscene in order to keep "down" with the competition. Because the full social cost of such material is not paid by producing firms, marginal costs are understated, industry supply is overstated, prices are too low, and an excessive quantity of output is produced as long-run adjustments move the industry to equilibrium.

Many of the problems associated with the incomplete reflection of full societal costs in product prices are solved by property right systems, which are discussed in Chapter 15. For now, note that competitive efficiency must be limited to the minimization of private costs.

A P P L I C A T I O N

7.12

Marginal Benefit Curves and Price Controls on Gasoline

Marginal benefit (demand) curves differ among consumers and among areas. Consider the demand curves for gasoline in the figure: the left-hand panel depicts demand in an urban area, and the center panel depicts demand in a rural recreation area. The demand curve for the urban area is flatter because urban drivers have access to a wider array of substitutes for buying gasoline, including mass transit and car pooling. Thus when gasoline prices rise, urban drivers find it easier to cut back on consumption. The right-hand panel shows the industry supply and demand curves for gasoline and the initial equilibrium price, P_0, and equilibrium quantity, Q_0. Rural users purchase q_0^r gallons of gasoline, and urban users purchase q_0^u gallons.

Now suppose that the gasoline supply curve falls from S_0 to S_1,

ceteris paribus, forcing the equilibrium price up to P_1. We would expect more drastic cutbacks in the urban area than in the rural area, given these demand curves. Marginal benefit is a measure of the willingness to pay for marginal units. Consumers with readily available substitutes will cut back more at the margin for a given price rise than will those with fewer substitution possibilities.

But suppose the government imposes price controls at the original price, P_0. The shortage is $\overline{Q_2 Q_0}$. Price controls thus force a larger cutback for both groups

than the price increase would have required.

What policies could the government employ to allocate the gasoline shortages induced by price controls between these two groups? Let's consider three possibilities:

1. Nonmarketable ration coupons provided equally to all drivers, resale illegal
2. Marketable ration coupons provided equally to all drivers, resale legal
3. Elimination of price controls and a return to equilibrium at a higher price

Nonmarketable Ration Coupons

Under this plan, the rural user will be forced to cut back the same amount as the urban user. But the rural user will suffer more, because of the higher forgone mar-

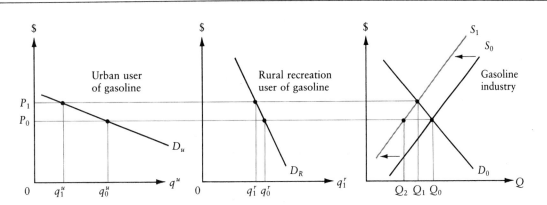

ginal benefit of the cutback. This policy violates the equal marginal benefit principle and thereby fails to maximize the total consumer benefit of the available gasoline output. Also, this policy requires the government to allocate the available gasoline, because gasoline companies would otherwise sell "too much" gasoline in the cities, where transportation costs per gallon are lowest.

Marketable Ration Coupons

With this scheme, we could expect rural users to buy some coupons from urban users, because rural users place a higher marginal benefit on gasoline. The exchange of coupons would make the marginal benefits of the two groups of consumers more alike but would not clear the market,

Effect of Price Controls on Different Users

Price controls on gasoline affect urban and rural recreation users differently, as shown in the left-hand and center panels. To ration the shortage induced by the price controls, the market must cut back supply.

because suppliers cannot use the coupons as cash to invest in more production and exploration. Nor can suppliers use the coupons as an incentive to shift supplies from areas with the least shortage to areas with the greatest. Hence white markets in coupons do not alleviate the shortage. Equal marginal benefits can be achieved for the given output, but the actual output will be too low. Marginal benefit exceeds marginal cost, and efficiency requires an expansion of output un-

til these marginal values are equal.

Equilibrium

Abandoning price controls would allow the shortage to be eliminated by price adjustments. Consumers in all areas could adjust their purchases to the market price, according to their demands and substitution possibilities, and thereby equate their marginal benefits. Gasoline companies would also have a profit incentive to properly allocate the total gasoline sold among the markets. If they tried to sell "too much" gas in the cities, their revenues would fall, because city users value gas less at the margin than rural users do. Allowing economic agents to follow such incentives is a powerful component of social policy.

Labor, Capital, and the Entrepreneur

Production-cost theory begins with some striking oversimplifications, including the following:

Resources are of two distinct types: labor (variable) and capital (fixed).

Labor is homogeneous.

Capital is homogeneous.

Labor and capital are the resources devoted to production. The entrepreneur, in contrast, is the risk taker and decision maker whose compensation takes the form of profit, a residual of revenues over costs.

These simplifying assumptions allow managers to separate issues and derive many useful relationships, such as the shapes of production functions and cost curves, the technical tradeoffs among inputs, diminishing returns, returns to scale, shutdown rules, and entry/exit considerations.

These relationships are more than mere mechanical exercises and sources of unjust enrichment for purveyors of economics books. Rather, the ability to think rigorously about tradeoffs, relative fixities, and short-run versus long-run effects is enhanced by seeing the analysis illustrated on paper. But paper is two-dimensional and hence can only start the process of thinking about multidimensional tradeoffs.

At this point it is necessary, albeit disheartening, to declare these beginning assumptions a fiction. Labor is not homogeneous, nor is capital. Moreover, the distinction between labor and capital is artificial. Labor is not always completely variable nor capital completely fixed. Relative fixities overlap, in that some workers are more permanent than some equipment (vice presidents tend to last longer than trucks).

The distinction between the entrepreneur and the labor and capital inputs is also artificial. The skills embodied in the entrepreneur are akin to equipment, just as the specific skills of labor are (see Chapter 12). And the entrepreneur's effort, at least for an owner-operated business, is in part a form of labor. Separating labor, capital, and entrepreneurship is not the simple procedure implied by the model.

Entrepreneur is the time-honored term for risk taker and decision maker. In the simplest of firms, these roles often coincide. However, the more complex and sophisticated the financial structure of the firm, the looser the link between ownership (and the implied assumption of risk) and decision-making responsibility. This latter role need not be played by investors-stockholders-entrepreneurs, and managerial theory should not be so narrowly focused as to imply that it is. The cost curves, the competitive mechanism, and other constructions can be used to study modern, sophisticated firms in which the investor-entrepreneurs are disparate and far removed from any decision making authority. As long as the *LAC* curve includes the investors' opportunity costs, it will be living up to its main job of organizing the analysis of long-run entry/exit decisions.

To summarize, the entrepreneur is often a composite of labor, capital, risk bearer, and decision maker. At other times, the entrepreneur is the source of invested capital and little else. In either case, entrepreneurs must receive a **fair rate of return**—a monetary and/or psychic payment at least as great as their evaluation of the next-best opportunity for the application of the same skills, time, invested capital, and risk factors. Every *LAC* curve, properly constructed, will include a fair rate of return to the entrepreneur as a cost of doing business.

In studying the entry/exit mechanism in competition, we have focused on an entrepreneur whose main job is to search for the industry that will yield the greatest profit. Some textbooks have attributed much more complex roles to the entrepreneur. So will this one later. But for now, it's sufficient to understand the rules governing entry into and exit from industries.

Summary

The key to competition is parametric pricing: Each competitive firm's supply is so small relative to industry supply that the firm cannot affect industry price by its own expansion or contraction of output.

This chapter presents two general models of competition: perfect and pure. These are accepted terms among economists but are not well understood by others and, indeed, are often used interchangeably. Perfect competition is characterized by firms that are identical in all dimensions. In this model, all firms earn zero economic profit in long-run equilibrium.

Although the model of perfect competition is a highly abstract approach to a description of the real world, it can be used as a building block in the construction of the more realistic and useful model of pure competition. In pure competition, entrepreneurs' abilities, location advantages, production techniques, and other factors giving rise to different cost structures are allowed to vary. Pure competition is a model of nonidentical firms except for product price, which all firms take as a parameter. The model of pure competition gives rise to the distinctions among marginal, inframarginal, and extramarginal firms. Here the zero-profit theorem of long-run equilibrium applies only to the marginal firms; inframarginal firms earn positive economic profits in the long run.

It is important to realize that every marginal concept is associated with a given price. At a given price along a demand curve, units of demand are either marginal, inframarginal, or extramarginal. The same is true along a supply curve. That idea may also be extended to include firms of various cost structures: At the industry price, firms are either marginal (zero economic profit), inframarginal (positive economic profit), or extramarginal (not in the industry because costs are too high).

The model of pure competition may be used to clarify the meaning of price-determined costs and the rent-inclusive cost curve. This chapter applies the model to many specific problems, such as the taxi industry, price controls, California's Proposition 13, monopoly versus inframarginal competitive profits, advertising, patents, and criminal fines. As you can see, competitive analysis takes on broad significance to managers once the paradigm model of perfect competition is modified to allow for nonidentical firms.

Key Terms

accounting profit 156
average revenue 158
average total cost 160
breakeven point 170
economic profit 169
economic rent 183
entry/exit decision 168
equal marginal benefit principle 188
extramarginal firm 179
fair rate of return 192
inframarginal firm 179
long-run competitive equilibrium 171
long-run firm supply curve 167
long-run industry supply curve 171
loss minimization 162
marginal firm 179
market-clearing price 173
perfect competition 156
price-determined cost 184
price-determining costs 184
profit 156
profit-maximizing rule 159
pure competition 157
rent-inclusive long-run average cost curve 183
short-run firm supply curve 164
short-run industry supply curve 164
shutdown analysis 162
shutdown point 163
shutdown price 163
shutdown rule 163
societal welfare 188
total profit curve 159
zero economic profit 170

Problems

1. You run a hamburger palace that is open from 11 a.m. to midnight. You are considering adding a breakfast menu that would require the same griddle space, seating area, cash register space, and so forth.

   a. What costs are relevant to your decision?

   b. What costs are irrelevant?

2. You run a large midwestern university. Many of the students are from other states that have their own large universities. Most state schools are losing enrollments because the baby-boom bulge is ending. The losses in enrollment result in reduced funding. A popular idea among state legislators is to recoup some of the lost revenue by raising tuition for out-of-state students. Analyze such a policy, paying attention to the marginal cost of extra students and the elasticity of demand.

3. A major increase in property taxes is announced to pay for a new sewer system. Before the announcement, there is a brisk market for homes on your block—homes sell quickly at an average price of $70,000. After the announcement, some homeowners say, "I'm fed up with taxes; I'll sell my $70,000 home, move to exurbia with a septic tank, and avoid those new taxes." For Sale signs remain up for months, and many discouraged would-be sellers give up and stay in the neighborhood. Explain the forces at work in this example.

4. A home is built in 1903 at a cost of $7,500. Over time it deteriorates badly and begins to require frequent maintenance of all kinds. In 1975 it sells for $35,000, and in 1978 it is appraised at $65,000. No major improvements—such as garages, additions, a finished basement, or an attic—have been made.

   a. Show how the appreciation in value of the home can be explained by an increase in demand. Note that the increase from 1975 to 1978 was far faster than inflation.

   b. What supply response would you expect?

   c. Under what conditions would the price fall below $65,000? Below $35,000? Below any other price?

   d. Explain the impact of a new freeway on the price of this house (1) if it is located near employment centers and (2) if it is out in the boondocks, near the end of the new freeway.

   e. What effect does the 1903 price have on your answers?

5. You own and rent out a cabin in northern Wisconsin. It is booked solid from late May to the middle of September, after which bookings depend on the weather. Suppose you can anticipate demand accurately once you get the weather forecast. What cost components do you consider in your decision to stay open?

6. Miller Brewing Company has plants in Milwaukee, Wisconsin; Eden, North Carolina; Fort Worth, Texas; Azusa, California; and Fulton, New York—but none in Arizona or New Mexico, where population is growing. Suppose that the demand for beer grows in Arizona and New Mexico. As a result, Miller Brewing Company plans an expansion in output.

a. Suppose that transportation is costless (or costs very little compared to other production costs). A vice president of Miller suggests producing all the extra output in the plant closest to the expanding market. Is this a good idea? What has to be true of the company's cost curves for this to be a profit-maximizing move?

b. Suppose that transportation costs are 2 cents per thousand miles per bottle or can. Restate the equal marginal cost principle in light of these costs.

7. Former Secretary of Health, Education, and Welfare Joseph Califano quit smoking and would like to encourage others to do likewise. One of his proposals to discourage smoking is for the government to end the price-support program for tobacco. The American Tobacco Institute has chided Califano, saying "If you eliminate the price support for tobacco, the farmers will not cooperate with acreage restrictions and will plant more acres and increase the supply of tobacco, thus driving down the price of cigarettes and *encouraging smoking*." Surely Califano expects a different result. Which do you expect?

8. Because of rising prices for feed grains, the price of meat rose sharply in 1973. Various consumer groups, aided by access to TV and newspaper coverage, organized a meat boycott. Consumption dropped about 10 percent at the prevailing prices. Ranching is in fact competitive, so the boycott caused some ranchers to reduce their herd size and others to "sell out" (exit for good). Exit in any industry involves the sale or scrapping of capital, but in ranching a major portion of capital is cattle. So exit drove prices down in the short run.

a. Use managerial economic theory to trace the effect of the boycott over time on the price of meat and the size of herds.

b. Can such a boycott succeed? In the long run? In the short run?

c. What happens when the boycott is called off?

9. Paul Samuelson has noted that some economists use very strange logic to conclude that price equals average costs: "A typical form of the argument is as follows: (1) a firm will equate marginal cost to price; (2) it will also try to minimize its unit costs; (3) at the point of minimum unit cost average cost equals marginal cost; (4) hence, average cost must equal price (average revenue) and profits will be zero."[6] Using the theory of pure competition, demonstrate the failure of logic in the argument he quotes.

10. Construct time-trend lines for price that illustrate the long-run adjustment process arising from an increase in industry demand when

a. All firms are identical and the industry is a constant-cost industry.

b. All firms are identical and the industry is an increasing-cost industry.

c. Firms have various cost structures and the industry is an increasing-cost industry.

6. Paul A. Samuelson, *Foundations of Economic Analysis* (New York: Atheneum, 1965), p. 83.

11. The taxicab industry regulates supply by issuing a fixed number of medallions.
    a. Show that an increase in demand causes cabs to be used inefficiently.
    b. Why are New York City cabs both fairly new and worn out?
12. Does the ancient term *entrepreneur* have any equivalent in the modern corporation? What—or who—is a corporate "entrepreneur"?
13. Suggest reasons why predatory pricing (or "price wars") is suicidal under competitive conditions.
14. Draw the family of average cost curves for a firm. Now assume that the labor force negotiates a new compensation package that includes no wage increase but includes doubling of hospitalization coverage and a stipulation that the coverage cannot be discontinued for 2 years after a layoff.
    a. Redraw the average cost curves of the firm.
    b. Analyze the impact of the new contract on the shutdown decision.
15. Suppose that a firm in a competitive market experiences a doubling of labor costs but also shows a steady profit. Using the firm-industry diagram of this chapter, demonstrate how this outcome could come about.
16. What is the impact of price controls on the sale price of firms?
17. a. What will happen to the value of a taxi medallion after the cost of gasoline doubles?
    b. Can economic theory be used to predict the quantitative change in the medallion's value—or just the qualitative change?
18. Suppose that price controls on gasoline create shortages in urban areas but not in rural areas. Would a business incentive exist to attempt to alleviate this balance?
19. A firm faces a large fine arising from a court case.
    a. How will the size of the fine affect the firm's continued operations?
    b. How large can the fine be before it forces the sale of the company?
20. The patent system discussed in Application 7.3 has an additional feature: The workings of the invention must be disclosed after the patent period is over. Discuss the competitive impact of that part of the system. Is it inconsistent with the grant of temporary monopoly?
21. Suppose that the average cost curve of the typical firm in a perfectly competitive industry has its minimum point at $3.
    a. If the price of the product rises to $4, what is the likely industry adjustment?
    b. Draw the time-trend lines corresponding to this adjustment.
22. a. Why do managerial economists allow for a normal profit in the average total cost curve?
    b. If the rate of return on riskless government securities were to double, what would happen to the average cost curves for the typical firm? Describe the process that would bring about the change.

23. a. Are labor costs price-determined?
    b. If a firm's product price were to double, what would be the impact on the wages paid to labor?
24. Suppose that the slope of the total product curve is 4 and the wage rate is $6 per hour. What is the marginal cost of producing one more unit?
25. Suppose that the slope of the average variable cost curve is 5 when the output is 100 units. Do you have enough information to calculate the marginal cost of production?
26. Suppose that the government imposes price controls on rubber tires and that a shortage of 100,000 tires develops. If the government also sold ration coupons that had to be purchased in order to buy tires, what would be the purchase price of the ration coupons?
27. Suppose that the government were to impose a tax on the profits of competitive firms. Trace the impact of the tax on the entire economy using the firm-industry diagram of this chapter.
28. Suppose that the government places a price floor under the price of wheat in order to prop up farm incomes. Would you predict the need for additional acreage restrictions to also be imposed?
29. If an entrepreneur is able to cover his variable cost, but will never be able to pay off the loan which the bank provided in order to start the firm, how can he and the bank come to a mutually beneficial agreement in discharging part of his obligation to repay the loan? How will we know if it is mutually beneficial?
30. Explain why the competitive supply curve is a locus of marginal cost points.
31. How will the sale price of a restaurant be changed by the reduction of its property taxes?
32. Jimmy Carter determined that the energy crisis would be alleviated if corn were converted into gasohol. Analyse the impact of this policy on the market for corn. What would happen to the market for soybeans if the gasohol program was a success?
33. Suppose an entrepreneur owns a patent on a better mousetrap and makes a handsome profit for several years. News comes of an alternative way of catching mice which is under development and will hit the market in a few years. Should the owner of the patent increase or decrease production?
34. Explain why the firms in a competitive industry will equate their marginal costs without collusion.
35. Explain why the firms in a competitive industry will have an incentive not to adopt every new technological innovation which is developed.
36. Why do farmers rent out some of their land instead of growing their own crops on it? What does economic theory tell you about the rental rate on such land?
37. Suppose that an entrepreneur wants to sell his business. What does economic theory predict about the selling price of the firm? Suppose the workers wanted to buy the firm. What would they be willing to offer that the rest of the market might not?
38. Why does competition induce entrepreneurs to enter industries for which they are most suited?

39. Suppose that due to the entry of new firms price falls below the minimum average cost for all firms in a competitive industry which employ a certain old technology. What will happen to the wages of the workers in those older firms? What must the workers do in order to bolster their wages?

Suggested Readings

Becker, Gary S. *Economic Theory*. New York: Knopf, 1971, chap. 5.

Coase, R. H. "The Nature of the Firm." *Economica* 4 (1937): 386–405.

Ellis, H. S., and Fellner, W. "External Economies and Diseconomies." *American Economic Review* 33 (1943): 493–511.

Knight, F. H. "Some Fallacies in the Interpretation of a Social Cost." *Quarterly Journal of Economics* 38 (1924): 582–606.

Samuelson, Paul A. *Foundations of Economic Analysis*. New York: Atheneum, 1965, chap. 4.

Stigler, George. *The Theory of Price*. New York: Macmillan, 1966, chap. 6.

8

RISK

In practice, a firm's overall operations—and every business decision—contains an element of risk; there is always some doubt about the outcome. There are numerous examples. An order for a shipment of coal may not arrive because of a strike at the mine. A fire may destroy productive resources. Prices of inputs or outputs may change a bit—or a lot. Nevertheless, a manager must make decisions that may be affected by events beyond his or her control or ability to predict.

In pure competition, the concept presented in Chapter 7, all relevant variables are known or exactly predicted. This chapter builds on the powerful implications of pure competition and treats risk as an extension of the theory of the firm. If you read several books on the subject of risk (as you should), you will find that the approach to risk in this book differs considerably.

Usually, risk is treated as a highly mathematical subject based on statistics and probability. Such treatment is important but certainly more rigorous than necessary for our purposes. This chapter, in contrast, treats risk as a cost and examines the ways that market forces impose these costs on managers, as well as provide opportunities to reduce the costs. Chapters 6 and 7 demonstrate how managers seek efficiency in a riskless environment; this chapter provides a framework for efficient decision making when risk is present.

Let's begin with an operational definition of **risk:** an economic cost that arises because of the unpredictability of outcomes. The emphasis in this definition is on **cost.** As they would with any cost, managers try to reduce or avoid risk; it is a cost they would like to bear efficiently. At the market level, competition forces firms to be efficient about risk lest they be replaced by firms that are.

Consider an example: Firms often insure against the loss of an executive from illness or death because of the unique knowledge that individual has accumulated. Although few people are uniquely gifted, it is quite common for people of normal ability to acquire indispensable skill and insight within a particular firm or agency.

Large firms reduce this risk by moving people around. Small firms reduce the risk by taking out an executive insurance policy. By paying a price, an **insurance premium,** a firm can reduce the financial unpredictability arising from the loss of a key executive. Note that the outcome itself, the health of the executive, may not be affected at all. But the risk, the financial consequence of the outcome, has been shifted to the insurance company, and the risk to the firm has been significantly reduced.

Not only are there a large number of market responses to the reality of risk, but much of contract and tort law can be viewed as a legal response to risk. A manager equipped only with conventional economic theory is likely to view the law as an interference with efficiency. But the law and the market economy are better viewed as partners in the pursuit of efficiency. Contracts are necessary for the efficient exchange of risks, and enforcement provisions of the law are necessary to make such contracts believable.

Short Course in Statistics

This section introduces, in the simplest terms, some statistical concepts that will help us understand risk. Fortunately, mathematicians have a well-developed vocabulary to complement the economic language we've been using. For our purposes, only the remarkable properties of a few statistical concepts need to be presented, not the formal mathematics.

One of the most basic terms is **random variable,** which refers to a variable, such as price, cost, or weather, that can take on values that are not exactly predictable. For example, the price of a specific four-bedroom house 4 years from now is a random variable. **Probability** is the likelihood, generally expressed as a percentage (or as a digit), that a random variable will have a given value. We may estimate a probability of, say, 75 percent that the house will be priced between $120,000 and $125,000 in 4 years. The set of probabilities associated with all of the possible values of a random variable is the **probability distribution.** If the random variable can take on only discrete values, the probability distribution takes the form of a list. If the random variable can take on an infinite variety of values, the distribution is better described as a mathematical function that summarizes the probabilities. The most familiar of these functions is the **normal probability density function,** which is best introduced diagramatically (see Figure 8.1). Note that the vertical axis is probability and that the horizontal axis is the value of the random variable, in this case P for price. Any point on the curve is the probability that the price will equal the value directly below it on the horizontal axis. If the random variable is distributed normally, the probability curve takes on the general shape of a bell. Thus the normal probability distribution is often called a bell curve.

The weighted average of the possible values that a random

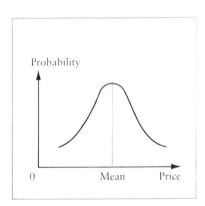

Figure 8.1
Normal Distribution Curve

Because of its shape, the normal distribution curve is also known as a bell curve. The price is not known for certain but could take on values above or below the mean. This curve illustrates that probability.

variable can take on (where the weights are the corresponding probabilities) is the **expected value.** To get the expected value, or mean, merely multiply each value that the random variable can take by the corresponding probability and then add all of the results.[1] For example, suppose a random variable can take on the value 10 with probability $P_{10} = 0.5$ and the value 20 with probability $P_{20} = 0.5$. The expected value is $(0.5 \cdot 10) + (0.5 \cdot 20) = 15$. (Ironically, the expected value in this example is a kind of average, but the variable can take on only the values 10 and 20—not the expected value itself.) It might help you to think of the expected value as the average amount of money won in repeated gambles. Suppose a game of chance offered $5 every time heads came up from a coin flip and $10 every time tails came up. The average amount per flip is obviously $7.50. If you were to pay $7.50 every time you played the game, you could expect to break even after several games. Of course, if you were to play only once, it would be impossible to break even; you could only gain $2.50 or lose $2.50. Still, the expected value is the value that would allow you to break even.

The statistical measure of the amount by which the actual value of a random variable differs from the expected value is the **deviation.** Say that, after six coin flips, you've had five heads and a tail. At $7.50 per coin flip, you would have paid $45 to play; you would have received $35. The deviation is $10.

The **standard deviation** is a measure of the reliability of the expected value.[2] Look at the two bell curves in Figure 8.2. Price is on the horizontal axis, and the probability of each possible price is on the vertical axis. The bell curve in panel a is broader and flatter than the "spiked" one in panel b. These two shapes represent the relative reliability of the mean. The lower, flatter bell curve in panel a represents lower probabilities to either side of the mean than the "spiked" curve does but higher probabilities a little farther away from the mean. Therefore, the reliability—or standard deviation—of the price is much less in panel a than in panel b. This difference may mean two things:

The price in panel a is truly subject to greater fluctuations about the mean than is the price in panel b.

The two curves represent different perceptions of the same fluctuation. Economic incentives induce people to shift risks to those who are better able to bear risks and to purchase information from those who are better able to estimate risk.

The reliability of the average is central to a manager's or firm's ability to plan.

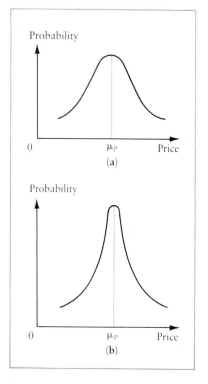

Figure 8.2
Standard Deviation

Simply put, standard deviation is a measure of the reliability of the mean. Panel a has a less reliable mean price than panel b.

---

1. The mean is generally represented by the Greek letter μ (mu).

2. The standard deviation, or reliability, is generally represented by the lowercase Greek letter σ (sigma).

Risk Aversion

There is a cost inherent in holding any risky asset. In this case, the opportunity cost is the forgone opportunity to hold an asset that is riskless or, at least, less risky than others. **Risk aversion** is the preference for less-risky assets of lower expected value over riskier assets of greater expected value. In other words, a risk-averse person is willing to pay a premium to avoid risk. For example, if a $100,000 house has a 0.01 probability of total loss due to fire, wind, pestilence, or earthquake, the expected value of the house is $99,000. A risk-averse person would be willing to pay more than $1,000 to have either the house or $100,000 should the house be lost. A risk preferrer is a person who would not be willing to pay $1,000 to avoid the loss; a risk-neutral person would be willing to pay just $1,000 to avoid the risk. Clearly, only the risk-averse person would ever buy insurance, since the premium must cover expected losses plus costs, including a fair rate of return.

Modern discussion of risk aversion was spawned by a famous article in which Milton Friedman and Leonard Savage linked the concept of risk with the concept of marginal utility.[3] Their argument is best recounted with the aid of Figure 8.3. The total utility of money is a function of money. Line $\mathscr{L}_1$ depicts the total utility of the various amounts of money in the range from A to B. In particular, points U_A and U_B represent the total utility of A and B, respectively.

Line $\mathscr{L}_2$ introduces risk. Suppose that a gambler presupposes the possibility of only the two extreme outcomes in the diagram, A

3. Milton Friedman and Leonard J. Savage, "The Utility Analysis of Choices Involving Risk," *Journal of Political Economy* 56 (August 1948): 279–304.

Figure 8.3
Total Utility as a Function of Money

Line $\mathscr{L}_1$ represents the certainty of receiving money in a gamble. $\mathscr{L}_2$ represents the weighted utility of the gamble.

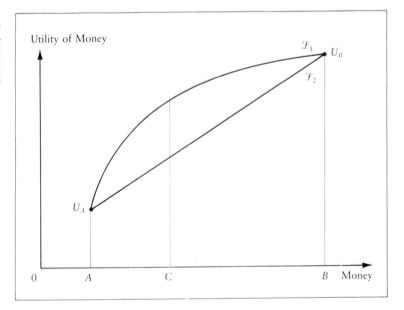

and B, and that there is probability P of winding up with A and probability $1 - P$ of winning B. Then line $\mathcal{L}_2$ can be used to determine the expected utility: $PU_A + (1 - P)U_B$. Note that $\mathcal{L}_1$ is curved and $\mathcal{L}_2$ is straight but that both begin and end at the same point. In addition, $\mathcal{L}_1$ lies above $\mathcal{L}_2$ between A and B, which means that the slope of $\mathcal{L}_1$ (the marginal utility of money) must initially exceed the slope of $\mathcal{L}_2$ (the average utility of money).

Now consider point C, where marginal utility equals average utility (because the slopes of $\mathcal{L}_1$ and $\mathcal{L}_2$ are the same). To the right of point C, marginal utility is less than average utility; the marginal utility of uncertain dollars (the slope of $\mathcal{L}_1$) is less than the marginal utility of certain dollars (the slope of $\mathcal{L}_2$). The gambler represented in Figure 8.3 would be willing to sacrifice the possibility of winning amount B in order to eliminate the possibility of ending up with only A.

This willingness to pay for risk avoidance is illustrated in Figure 8.4, which is a more complicated version of Figure 8.3. Figure 8.4 also shows that there are bounds to the willingness to pay for risk avoidance. Suppose that P is such that $PA + (1 - P)B = D$. D is thus the expected value of the gamble. The utility of amount D is represented by point G. But winning D is not a certainty, so the expected utility of the gamble is represented by point F, which lies below G because of the diminishing marginal utility of money. Now consider point H, which is the utility of amount E. Since point H is at the same height as point F, it represents the same utility as the gamble; hence, receiving amount E with certainty is just as attractive as gambling on the higher expected value. Even though the gamble has expected value D, it is worth no more than the certain

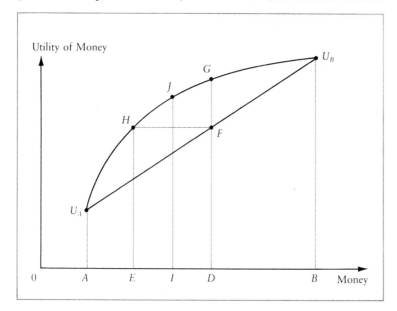

Figure 8.4
Risk Aversion

People are willing to pay to avoid a gamble. They would rather pay $\overline{DE}$ to have the certainty of receiving E than gamble to get B with the chance of winding up with A.

receipt of the smaller amount E. A person with these preferences would be willing to pay up to the difference $\overline{ED}$ as an insurance premium.

Suppose that a fair rate of return requires a premium represented by $\overline{ID}$. Competitive insurance companies would charge $\overline{ID}$ to absorb the risk and allow the gambler to enjoy the certainty of amount I. The utility of the certain receipt of I is represented by point J. Since J is higher than F, the availability of insurance has demonstrably made the gambler better off.

Note that risk aversion follows directly from the idea of diminishing marginal utility of income. The last increment of income is worth less than the average increment. Hence the risk-averse individual is willing to sacrifice several of the last group of units of income, in the form of an insurance premium, in order to achieve a greater certainty of keeping the inframarginal units.

Risk Spreading

Because risk is viewed as undesirable, people have an incentive to purchase relief from it. **Risk spreading** allocates risk to those who can bear the risk at lower cost. Managers are constantly assessing risky options in order to determine which to bear and which to spread to others.

A common way to spread risk is to group risky activities. The ratio of the standard deviation to the mean value of the activities is thereby reduced. This reduction, called the **portfolio effect**, follows from two statistical facts:

1. As more assets of equal standard deviation and mean value are added to a portfolio, the probability distribution gets closer and closer to the normal distribution. Once the number of such assets reaches ten or so, the normal distribution is an excellent approximation. Therefore, the owner of such a portfolio gains greater and greater confidence in the mean and standard deviation of the total portfolio as more assets are added.

2. As more assets are added, the ratio of the standard deviation to the mean value (σ/μ) falls according to the inverse square root of n, where n is the number of assets. As Figure 8.5 illustrates, riskiness drops as n rises. Thus the holder of a large number of risky assets can offer to absorb more risk in exchange for a premium.

The economic incentive for such risk-bearing activities as insurance and banking and lending services are grounded in these two statistical facts describing the portfolio effect.

In the case of insurance, for example, the "activity" is home or business ownership. The possibility of fire, however remote, affects the value of that activity. Among a large number of homes, we can be sure that some will burn down, but we cannot know which ones.

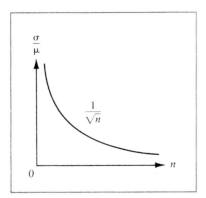

**Figure 8.5
Portfolio Effect**

When one accumulates a large number of risky assets of equal mean and variance, the ratio of variance to mean falls according to the inverse square root of the number of such assets. Simply put, risk falls when risks are spread over a number of assets.

The insurance company assembles small payments from each of a large number of homeowners to place in a fund that will pay the unfortunate few whose homes actually burn. That is, the insurance company holds a portfolio of risky homes and passes the benefits of its risk bearing to homeowners, in exchange for their insurance premiums. In this way the standard deviation of the asset value of homeownership is greatly reduced for all homeowners. Competition among insurance companies forces total premiums to cover the expected losses and to provide a competitive rate of return.

The risk-bearing activity of lending services is customer borrowing, or spending prior to earning. The risk element is that some borrowers, who cannot be identified in advance, will not repay. By holding a portfolio of loans, the standard deviation of the repayments per repayment is greatly reduced. Hence the cost of borrowing can be greatly reduced. Competition among lending services makes it necessary to pass these cost reductions on to customers.

Even conglomerate mergers represent risk spreading; the activity is the conduct of unrelated businesses. (Mergers are discussed in more detail in Chapter 13.) Each activity faces its own market vagaries, and so returns to investors are uncertain. By holding a portfolio of companies, a conglomerate reduces the uncertainty of its investment and hence attracts investment funds more readily than a single firm could.

Let's consider two more methods managers have for spreading risk. First, a firm may opt for **output contracts,** which allow the risk of demand fluctuation to be shared efficiently among producing firms and smaller suppliers. The activities are the output of the firm and the derived demand for the input. If the output firm is O and the supplier is S, then the element of risk is the fluctuation in demand for the output q_O and in demand for the input q_S. The small supplier sells the risk of fluctuation in the demand for q_S to the manufacturer of q_O by specifying the amount of q_S that will be purchased by O and the price. With such a contract, the risk is shifted to firm O in exchange for favorable terms elsewhere in the contract. Firm O thus exploits its superior risk-bearing position and sells the service to firm S. Firm O's superior ability to bear risk may derive from many sources, including the variety of products it sells, the warehouse space it has to accommodate fluctuating inventories, and its ability to predict and respond to fluctuations in the market by varying its sales effort. Firm O is decidedly better able than firm S to find additional markets for q_O.

The second method is the signing of **requirement contracts,** which allow suppliers to bear the risk of demand fluctuations. In this situation, firm S would be larger than firm O. For example, firm S could be a large-scale supplier of canned fruit, and firm O could be a local grocery store. With a requirement contract, firm O could order just what it could sell, and firm S would absorb any fluctuation. Since it has a portfolio of firms to sell to, firm S is well suited to absorb the risk. Sales at the small firms might fluctuate, but the variance in aggregate sales is much smaller than the variance at any one store.

Efficient Risk Bearing: The Role of Contracts

So far we have concentrated on the advantages of spreading risk for individual firms. Here we may concentrate on the efficiency aspects of risk. When two parties simultaneously trade goods with well-known characteristics, presumably neither party is worse off; at least one party (or both) is better off. This is the measure of **economic efficiency.**

The same efficiency criterion arises when trades involve exchange over time. For example, if A pays B now for a good to be delivered in the future, the agreement is expected to make at least one of them better off after its completion. But the trade is usually accompanied by a contract, of some level of complexity and formality, in order to provide recourse for A should B not perform. By providing such a recourse, the mutually advantageous—that is, efficient—trade is facilitated. Without it, A would be less willing (or unwilling) to make the agreement. Without contract enforcement, many agreements for future performance would be abandoned in favor of agreements for more simultaneous exchange.

Consider the production of two types of shirts. Type 1 shirts have an average cost of $5 and last 100 wearings; the new, improved type 2 shirts last 300 wearings but cost $10 to produce. Conventional economic theory predicts that the higher-quality shirt will drive the lower-quality shirt off the market and that free entry will force the price of shirts to $10. However, the higher-quality shirt cannot replace the lower-quality shirt unless consumers believe that it will last much longer. Consumers view the durability of the shirt as a risk. It is in the interests of the manufacturer to bear that risk for consumers by guaranteeing the shirt. Having made the shirt, the manufacturer is in a better position to assess its quality. Hence the durability of the shirt is subject to less standard deviation in the manufacturer's estimate. Furthermore, the manufacturer produces a very large number of shirts; the ratio of standard deviation to mean value of the portfolio of shirts is practically nil.

It is in the mutual interest of the manufacturer and the consumer for the manufacturer to guarantee a shirt. Such a contract facilitates efficient exchange over time. The market for the more durable shirts is expanded (or, in the extreme, made possible where it was not before) and sales of the inferior shirts are reduced (or perhaps eliminated). Similarly, special use and care labels allow high-quality garments that deteriorate under ordinary use and care to compete with lower-quality garments. Both cases illustrate the general principle: Contracts facilitate efficiency.

The shirt example illustrates another important principle: Risky transactions include a search for the efficient risk bearer or the superior risk bearer. Whenever risk is an element in a transaction, efficiency requires that the economic agent assess the risk who is in the best position to assess it and the agent bear the risk who is best able to bear it. Usually the same agent performs both functions. Some transactions, however, require that one party assess the risk and another bear it. For example, a car manufacturer can assess the risk of engine failure and provide instructions to the owner on ways to reduce the risk.

A   P   P   L   I   C   A   T   I   O   N

8.1

Spreading Risk through Insurance

Insurance policies generally have several features designed to spread risk. The three most common features are deductibles, coinsurance, and payment ceilings. Each of these instruments has a special impact on the sharing of risk. The figure will help elucidate the principles behind them.

A loss must be at least as large as the **deductible,** the portion of any loss covered by the insured, before the insurer pays anything. The lower the deductible, the higher the premium—because the insurance company bears more of the risk. An efficiency consideration of deductibles is that administrative costs, which are largely fixed costs (independent of the size of the claim), are reduced when there are higher deductibles and thus fewer claims. Furthermore, since a deductible is usually at the small end of the spectrum of possible losses, a higher deductible encourages the person or firm to prevent losses. The lower the deductible, the lower is this prevention incentive. In fact, the insurance literature has a term for this: "confounding of risks and incentives," or "moral hazard."[*] These terms actually pertain to behavior that economists would readily predict: When risk is

[*]The term *confounding of risks and incentives* is the formulation of Nobel laureate Kenneth Arrow, *Essays in the Theory of Risk Bearing* (Chicago, Markham, 1971).

shifted to another party, people reduce their loss-prevention effort.

Another key feature of risk sharing is **coinsurance,** the fraction of the amount above the deductible that the insurance company does not pay. In the figure, coinsurance is represented by the angle α. If α is 45 degrees, coinsurance is complete. If it is less than 45 degrees, the insured pays

Three Elements of Insurance Policies

The deductible, the coinsurance rate, and the ceiling can all be adjusted to spread the risk between the insurer and the insured.

part of the loss above the deductible and below the ceiling. Car insurance is usually written with zero coinsurance above the deductible. But health insurance often has a coinsurance feature to give policyholders an incentive to economize in their choice of physicians and hospitals.

An **insurance ceiling** places an upper limit on coverage—hence on the risk borne by the insurance firm. It guards against an open-ended drain of resources resulting from a poor estimate of the likelihood of disaster. Of course, the market provides incentives for firms to offer policies with different ceilings and premiums, higher premiums in exchange for higher ceilings. Ceilings on auto insurance coverage are common.

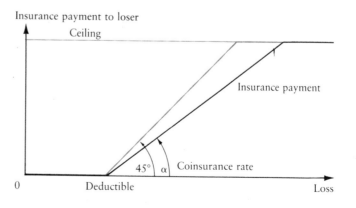

8.2

Farming: A Risky Business

Farming is a risky business, (1) because once the crop is planted, weather may cause considerable deviation from the expected yield and (2) because the demand for farm output is price inelastic. How can farmers deal with the risk they face?

It is instructive to consider each crop a risky asset. As with any earning asset, the riskiness can be reduced by spreading the risk. There are many nonfarm examples of risk spreading; one is fire, automobile, and life insurance. We do not know in advance which house will burn down, which car will crash, or which life will be shortened, but we can pool these risks so that each of those who do not suffer calamity can make a small contribution toward a large payment to those who do. Insurance, therefore, is a way of reducing risk by spreading it over many participants.

A second nonfarm example of risk spreading is diversification. Business firms diversify their product lines so that losses on unfortunate investments can be outweighed by gains on others. A loss is less likely to force an entrepreneur out of business and workers out of their jobs if the firm has a well-diversified product line. The same is true for financial investments. Risk spreading is the application of the principle of not putting all one's eggs in the same basket.

Risk spreading is essential in the farm industry. There are at least three ways a farmer can spread risk: (1) plant a diversified portfolio of crops, (2) use the futures markets, and (3) use the loan markets. We have already seen how diversification spreads risk. The futures market works like this: The farmer sells the risk to a company that can pool such risk. For example, Continental Grain Corporation may buy a diversified portfolio of farm crops in advance (while the crops are still growing) and take the risk on the harvest-time price. The buyer of farm futures spreads risk by buying diversified crops and, in the process, reduces the risk to each farmer who sells crops in advance. In contrast, access to loan markets allows risk to be spread over good and bad years. Loans may be taken out in bad years and repaid in good years.

The farmer with small landholdings has disadvantages in terms of spreading risk that the larger farmer or corporation farm does not have. For example, farmers have an incentive to plant large acreages for each crop in order to capture economies of scale. If the farmer does not have much land, this goal is at odds with crop diversification. For the small farmer, there must be a tradeoff between diversification and economies of scale. Similarly, the futures market can be of great importance in spreading risk, although it is actually more expensive for the small farmer than for the large farmer because of economies in transaction costs. The information costs and bargaining costs are less-than-proportional to the size of the transactions and hence are less on average for large sales than for small sales. Finally, loan markets may offer the small farmer high interest rates and the danger of foreclosure after several bad years in succession. A large farmer with lower costs due to economies of scale and less risk resulting from greater diversification and less-costly participation in futures markets is a better loan prospect and can get lower interest rates.

So in farming, the word is "Get big or get out." Risk-spreading advantages allow larger farms to be comfortably inframarginal while the smaller farmer struggles to break even.

Competition and Risk

Competitive forces reinforce the incentive to spread risk and reduce risk. Indeed, the search for the best combination of risk bearing is part of the process of cost reduction inherent in the competitive process. Recall from Chapter 7 that competitive firms must continually seek cost-reducing combinations of capital and labor or be driven out of business by firms that are more successful in this endeavor. The result is that consumers obtain the output at a price reflecting the opportunity cost of the inputs.

Firms seek out not only the optimal capital and labor combinations but the best combination of risk-bearing strategies as well, including insurance, contracts, product timing, and risk-resistant production techniques. Thus risk may be considered a cost. This approach does not contradict the earlier theory; instead, it enriches it.

Consider Figure 8.6, which illustrates the cost curves for firm 1 (panel a) and firm 2 (panel b) and a temporary industry price, P_0 (panel c). Suppose that firm 1 has lower costs because of its superior ability to spread risk. Unless firm 1 is the only firm that can avail itself of the superior risk-bearing technique, other firms will adopt it, and the price will fall below P_0. Firm 2 must then exit the industry or cut costs by becoming more sophisticated in its own treatment of risk. The savings are passed on to customers when firm 2 matches the price of its competitors.

Efficient Levels of Risk

There is an element of risk in any economic activity. The manager's job is to determine the efficient level of risk to accept. Fairly standard economic principles can be applied to the problem.

In general, the attempt to reduce risk to zero is too costly; usually, zero risk is not even attainable. As a result, debates about

Figure 8.6
Competition and Risk Bearing

Risk is a cost. Competition forces firms to reduce such costs by finding superior risk-bearing techniques or to be driven out of business by firms that do. **(a)** Firm 1's costs are low because of its superior ability to bear risk. **(b)** Firm 2 must cut costs or exit the industry **(c)**.

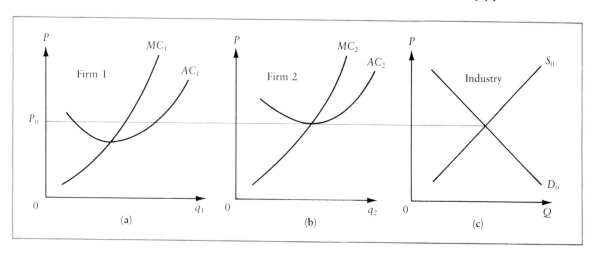

product reliability or safety or contract performance are properly concerned with attaining efficient (nonzero) levels of risk.

Single Failure-Rate Determinant

Elementary economic analysis often helps to organize ideas, but one must abstract from reality. Let's start with a very simple product that can fail in only one way—say a car engine that can fail only if the pistons become welded to the cylinder walls because of poor lubrication. (Obviously, there are thousands of ways an engine can fail. We assume that there is only one way, however, in order to pose a problem that can be analyzed using two-dimensional diagrams.)

The manager must balance the benefits and costs of reducing the engine's **failure rate.** Ultimately, of course, the consumer bears all costs. Figure 8.7 relates failure rates and costs. The failure rate of the engine is plotted on the horizontal axis. The failure rate declines to the right until it reaches the 0-percent level. (No product can fail less than zero times; failure rates are never negative numbers.) The failure rate falls to the right since it is conventional for the horizontal axis to show improvement to the right. The vertical axis is a monetary measure of marginal benefit and marginal cost.

The curves in Figure 8.7 take a rather conventional shape. The marginal cost curve depicts the increasing difficulty of improving the failure rate as perfection—0-percent failures—is approached. The marginal benefit curve represents the declining benefit associated with reducing the failure rate as perfection is approached. Marginal benefit declines because risk-averse individuals become less willing to pay for risk reduction as the risk shrinks. (A risk-neutral individual would be willing to pay equal amounts for suc-

Figure 8.7
Costs and Benefits of Reducing Failure Rates

The efficient failure rate equates the marginal costs and marginal benefits of failure-rate reductions. This point is seldom zero.

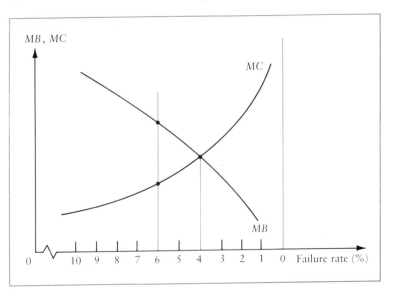

cessive increments, and the *MB* curve would be horizontal. But otherwise, the analysis would not change.)

Clearly, perfection is inefficient. The efficient failure rate, according to Figure 8.7, is 4 percent. At that level, the marginal benefit of reducing the failure rate is equal to the marginal cost of reducing the failure rate. A failure rate greater than 4 percent, say 6 percent, is inefficient because the marginal benefit of an incremental reduction in the failure rate exceeds the marginal cost. Similarly, any failure rate lower than (to the right of) 4 percent is inefficient, since $MC > MR$.

Of course, the cost of reducing the failure rate is passed on to consumers. But the point where $MC = MB$ is the level at which the sum of the purchase price plus repair costs plus risk costs is minimized.

Two Failure-Rate Determinants

Now consider products that can fail in only one way but whose probability of failure can be affected by two determinants. Further assume that these determinants are operated by different economic agents. For example, the probability that a car engine will fail depends on how well it is made by the manufacturer and how well it is maintained by the owner.

Figure 8.8 reproduces Figure 8.7 but with an important modification. The new feature is the use of two cost curves, *SMC* and *LMC*. (The use of the labels for short-run marginal cost curves and long-run marginal cost curves is deliberate.) In Figure 8.8, *SMC*

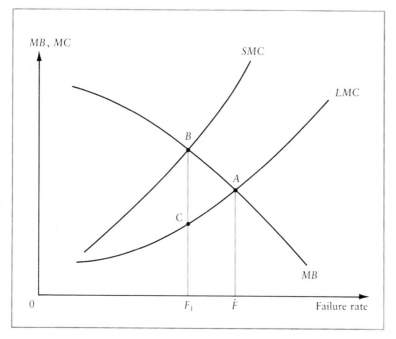

Figure 8.8
Two Failure-Rate Determinants

When two activities that determine failure rates are coordinated, the result is akin to operating on the long-run marginal cost of production. Uncoordinated failure-rate reduction, which is analogous to operating above the *LMC* on an *SMC*, is more costly and results in an inefficiently large number of failures.

represents one party's marginal cost of reducing the failure rate when the other party's effort level is fixed. *LMC* represents the marginal cost of reducing the failure rate when both parties are efficiently coordinated.

The intersection of *MB* and *LMC* at point *A* represents the efficiency point, at failure rate $\hat{F}$. The central position of point *A* along *LMC* indicates that both activities are coordinated. From the theory of cost, we know that the *SMC* curve lies above the *LMC* curve; in this context, *SMC* lies above *LMC* because the effort by one party costs more when it is not efficiently coordinated with the other party's effort. The effort level chosen in a unilateral effort would be at a point like *B*, the intersection of *SMC* and *MB* at failure rate F_1. Clearly, F_1 is an inefficiently high failure rate compared to $\hat{F}$.

Failure rate F_1 corresponds to the inefficient failure rate that would result if the car manufacturer assumed that the owner would not exercise an efficient level of care and that the manufacturer would have to repair failures. The failure rate is inefficiently high because the car would actually be made too well (at too great a cost). At the efficient failure rate, $\hat{F}$, the effort made by the manufacturer and the owner would be coordinated, the total cost of reducing the failure rate would be less, and the failure rate would be less. Hence the risk would be less, for both manufacturer and owner. The manufacturer can gain a competitive advantage by passing the lower cost on to the consumer in the form of a lower purchase price.

Product Liability

Any product presents a risk to our wallets, health, and safety. Yet people prefer these risks to the production of only riskless but prohibitively costly products. If only perfect products could be produced and sold, the standard of living would fall greatly—if society were to survive at all. This surprising statement is a variant of the economic theory of efficient levels of risk: Products generally have an optimal level of imperfection or a positive failure rate. In other words, efficiency requires that products fail from time to time and that consumers bear some of the associated physical and financial risk. Such contracts as guarantees allow manufacturers and consumers to share risk efficiently.

But what if the consumer cannot be informed sufficiently at reasonable cost to enter into efficient contracts? Legal rules can provide recourse to aggrieved consumers when products fail. When liability is not covered by prior agreement, legal rules provide guidance to lawyers, judges, and juries in deciding whether the consumer or manufacturer pays for product failures.

This section applies the elementary theory of risk to the analysis of the efficiency of four such rules, which cover absolute producer liability, strict liability, negligence, and information disclosure. The emphasis is on the incentives created by such rules and not on the actual legal mechanism.

Absolute Producer Liability

The rule of **absolute producer liability** is an extreme used largely as a benchmark; it requires the producer to bear the liability for any product problem. Such a rule is generally inefficient, since the user's incentive to engage in efforts to reduce the failure rate is blunted. The rule is efficient only when manufacturer effort is the sole determinant of failure rates.

Strict Liability

Under the rule of **strict liability,** the producer bears the liability of failure unless the consumer is deemed to be negligent. If juries hold consumers to an efficiency standard, such as a reasonable maintenance schedule, this rule works much like an efficient guarantee. The consumer bears the liability if the efficiency standard is not met, and the producer has the incentive to produce the product as if the consumer performs efficiently to optimize risk.

Negligence

Under the **negligence** rule, the producer bears the liability if the producer is negligent and the consumer is not. Otherwise, the consumer bears the liability. This rule is efficient if the jury holds both parties to a standard of negligence equivalent to the efficiency standard. The producer has a strong incentive to be efficient, since efficiency absolves the producer in all cases. The consumer also has a strong incentive to meet the efficiency standard. If the producer is negligent and the consumer meets the standard, liability shifts automatically to the producer; if the producer is nonnegligent and hence not liable, the consumer can bear the liability efficiently only by meeting the standard.

Both the strict liability and negligence rules are efficient when, and only when, juries apply a negligence standard equivalent to the efficiency standard—that is, if they hold producer and consumer to the level of effort where the marginal benefit of failure avoidance equals the marginal cost in design, manufacture, use, and maintenance. Properly applied, then, these rules form an efficient incentive structure when efficient contracts are impractical or impossible to arrange.

Information Disclosure

One of the great difficulties in implementing liability rules is determination of the efficient failure rate. Marginal cost curves shift all the time. Marginal benefit curves are known only through approximations based on preferences revealed by consumers. Hence the exact point where the marginal benefit and marginal cost curves of reducing the failure rate intersect is never known with certainty and is surely a moving target. Strict liability and negligence rules therefore have another serious limitation: they can only be implemented in cases of large, "unreasonable" departures from efficiency.

Theoretically, if consumers knew the failure rates associated with products on the market, and the cost of their maintenance and repair, the forces of competition would govern quality as well as price. **Information disclosure** about product quality is, of course, part of the competitive process. In reality, however, information disclosure is often less than complete. The harm that may be visited on consumers due to inaccurate expectations or improper use and care is often severe and unnecessary. The problem is addressed in section 5 of the Federal Trade Commission Act, various sections of the Uniform Commercial Code, and evolving interpretations of the common law. The law often steps in to force disclosure of information that is material to consumers (that affects their decisions) but that is not produced automatically.

Information disclosure is intended to unleash market forces to improve the efficiency of products. Thus disclosing the nicotine and tar content of cigarettes has improved competition in the cigarette market. The addition of labeling, of course, adds negligible marginal cost to the producer once the information is known. Another example is the use and care labeling of garments. Such labels are now sewn into garments, but the information used to be part of the discardable packaging material. Any boob can save hundreds of pieces of paper that contain use and care information for the family clothing and place them neatly in a binder for easy reference, next to the television warranty, car owner's manual, settlement cookbook, and family copy of *Managerial Economics*. But it is obviously more reliable and incredibly cheap for the garment label to carry the information.

The problems of cigarette or garment labeling pale when compared to information disclosure about such complicated products as automobiles or television sets. People generally do not understand how these products work, and information about the failure rate of each major component would be incredibly cumbersome, costly, and hard to understand. It would be inefficient to require disclosure of such minutiae; competition does not take place at that level except for the most expert buyers. For general disclosures, it is more appropriate to use summary statistics, such as average operating costs, average repair costs, and reasonable use and care instructions.

If this information disclosure is all so reasonable, why doesn't the market provide it automatically? Of course, the market does provide information through consumer groups and magazines like *Consumer Reports*. Such secondary sources of information rely on the experiences of product users and provide very accurate information for products that don't change much over time. Problems arise when products continually change. In these cases, the manufacturer, through testing and sales of repair parts, knows about significant changes in repair costs or in use and care far in advance of the secondary market. But there is a strong incentive to withhold the information. By the time the secondary market receives and publishes the information, improved models (with the problem cured) can be rushed to the market. Meanwhile, a large number of sales can be made on mistaken information.

The legal system provides protection for consumers who purchase a product that is sold using such "unfair and deceptive practices" as withholding of material facts. However, a serious problem of economic efficiency arises: Aside from the expense of litigation, consumers cannot tell, on the basis of their own experience, that the item they bought failed to live up to expectations. This problem results from the statistical nature of failures. The efficient failure rate is seldom zero. When it is nonzero, some failures are expected. But the individual product either fails or it does not. Similarly, an individual product may be a lemon even though the product line succeeds in meeting the average repair rate or other reasonable quality targets. Perfect production is inefficient, so some lemons are optimal. A larger-than-average repair bill is therefore the "downside risk" of the purchase of a risky asset.

If a product line is unreasonably faulty, the consumer will not find out merely by experience. The relevant information is the failure rate or, in the case of a multiple-component product, the average repair cost, as well as the standard deviation from what these quality measures are reasonably expected to be at the time of sale. That information is better known to the manufacturer than the general public unless disclosure obligations are imposed on the manufacturer. Thus disclosure laws are an aid to the efficient functioning of the market, because the manufacturer has a monopoly on the relevant information and has an incentive to conceal it. Unlike strict liability and negligence rules, rules requiring disclosure of information are based on the recognition that efficient levels of risk can only be obtained as the outcome of informed markets.

Summary

Risk is an element in virtually any personal or business decision. Statisticians provide useful terms for describing and assessing the riskiness of decision outcomes.

The portfolio effect demonstrates why certain firms and individuals are better risk bearers than others. Economic incentives induce superior risk bearers to seek risk in exchange for a price, or premium, paid by inferior risk bearers. The knowledge that contracts will be

Key Terms

enforced facilitates such advantageous exchange.

Efficiency often requires that risks be shared. The only way to achieve an efficient level of risk is often to induce people and firms to coordinate their efforts. Liability rules and information disclosure aid the process of generating risk levels and sharing risk.

Problems

1. Young men generally pay higher auto insurance rates than older men, even when they have never had an accident or traffic violation. Use economic theory to explain why young men as a group are classified as a greater risk when only a subset are poor drivers. Why doesn't competition lead to treatment of drivers according to their ability and not their age?

2. As cars become smaller (to increase gas mileage), what happens to the efficient death rate? Is this result fair? (What is fair?)

3. According to the theory of risk, the negligence rule and the rule of strict liability are both efficient and will lead to the same number of accidents or failures. However, the loser in the event that no negligence is proven is the consumer under the negligence rule and the manufacturer under the rule of strict liability. Use the theory of inframarginal profit (if necessary, refer back to Chapter 7) to explain this fact.

4. What is the impact of third-party (say, insurance company) payments on the efficiency of efforts to reduce failure or accident rates? Include in your analysis the fact that insurance premiums usually leap, and policies are sometimes terminated, after a claim.

5. "An automobile is a risky asset. But the owner can contribute to its longevity and reliability through proper maintenance and care. Therefore, the owner should bear the loss whenever a problem arises after the warranty expires, and the warranty limits should be set freely by the manufacturer." Criticize this statement, integrating the following terms into your analysis: *negligence, efficiency,* and *efficient allocation of tasks.*

6. Why do large orders for a firm's output delivered in batches reduce marginal costs for a firm?

7. a. Explain the difference between an output contract and a requirements contract.
   b. Explain why a small firm will generally buy productive inputs on a requirements contract but sell its output on an output contract. (Hint: Your explanation should include a discussion of both the incentives of the firm and the functioning of the market.) Bolster your argument with a rigorous hypothetical example.

8. Explain why a risk-averse individual faced with a gamble determined by the flip of a coin (the probability of heads equaling 0.5) would prefer a sum less than the expected value of the gamble.

9. a. Farm crops are risky assets. Why?
   b. List three ways farmers can spread risk.
   c. Large farms have an advantage in spreading risk. Why? Why then are not all farms large?

10. U.S. domestic onshore oil exploration is conducted by 10,000 or so independent oil "wildcatters." However, offshore exploration is done by large firms, often in joint ventures. Explain this phenomenon. (Hint: Sheer expense is not a complete answer.)

11. A agrees to supply coal to B on an output contract for 20 years at the prevailing market price in each year. A's coal mine runs out of coal in year 10, so A announces that he will not be able to perform the contract obligations. What economic considerations would lead to the conclusion that A has no obligation to provide coal from some other source?

12. a. Suppose your building is worth $1 million and has a 0.001 probability of burning down in a given year. Would you turn down fire insurance if the yearly premium was $1,000 per year? $2,000 per year?
    b. Suppose you own 500 such buildings. Would you be willing to pay more than $1,000 to insure each one?

13. In a recent trial, a major automobile company was accused of producing an unsafe car.
    a. What is an unsafe car?
    b. Should all cars be equally safe?
    c. Will the market induce an efficient level of safety?

14. a. Explain the role of the limitation of a car warranty.
    b. Why should the limit be the same for all buyers?
    c. Why do manufacturers offer extended warranties for an additional price?

15. Why do small businesses take out insurance to protect themselves against the loss of key personnel even though large firms do not?

16. a. What is the role of a coinsurance provision in an insurance policy?
    b. Why would coinsurance survive in a competitive market?

17. Why do state highway patrols have no car insurance on their vehicles? (Hint: The danger of the job is not an answer. Why not?)

18. Why do some firms charge lower prices to customers who will guarantee the purchase of fixed amounts of output?

19. What is the correlation between failures and production theory? Is the correlation exact?

20. Does strict liability ever reduce the occurrence of accidents below what it would be under the negligence rule? Why or why not?

21. Information disclosure rules require use and care labeling of clothing. Do these rules actually provide information that the manufacturer would not have an incentive to provide in any case? Why or why not?

22. Some manufacturers are reluctant to provide certain information about their products. Can we conclude that the disclosure of such information would harm the firm? Why or why not?

23. Will a firm always disclose all favorable information? Why or why not?

24. a. Explain why consumers generally have incomplete information about a product.
    b. What does this fact imply about the preconditions for competitive efficiency?

25. Would you expect consumer magazines competing for subscriptions to provide efficient information? Why or why not?
26. a. Explain why a zero failure rate in cars is generally not desirable.
    b. What market forces guide manufacturers to the efficient level of failures?
27. Banks are getting into the bull-renting business. The banks rent bulls to their rancher customers for a few hundred dollars per month. The ranchers use the bulls for breeding purposes and find they work out better than artificial insemination or painstaking herd development. Use the theory of competition and risk to explain why the ranchers would prefer this method of breeding.
28. Would a firm ever be willing to trade off economies of scale for the risk-spreading effect of a larger range of products?
29. Explain how the mortgage loan market acts as a risk-spreading device for the homeowner and the lender.
30. Explain why the competitive market will induce people to accept risk when they are the best risk bearer and buy relief from the risk when it is cheaper to do so.

Suggested Readings

Arrow, K. *Essays in the Theory of Risk Bearing*. Chicago: Markham, 1971.

Brown, J. P. "Toward an Economic Theory of Liability." *Journal of Legal Studies* 11 (June 1973): 323–350.

Friedman, Milton. *Price Theory*. Chicago: Aldine, 1976.

Posner, Richard. *Economic Analysis of Law*. 2nd ed. Boston: Little, Brown, 1977, chap. 4.

9

MONOPOLY

We have been studying the behavior of firms under competitive conditions, in which all firms are price takers and thus lack the market power to set industry price or output. We may now turn our attention to the monopolist. The competitive firm cannot influence industry price or output, but the monopolist, being the only seller in the industry, must set both price and output. Major economic consequences arise from the monopolist's control over price and output.

We may now begin our study of the monopolist with the simplest assumptions: The monopolist firm (1) charges the same price to all customers, (2) produces a single output, (3) produces its output in a single plant, and (4) is not regulated by government. These assumptions allow us to explore the essentials of monopoly behavior without undue complexity. Later we can relax these assumptions in order to probe deeper into the behavior and implications of monopoly.

The monopoly analysis that begins here provides a point of departure for many related topics of critical importance to managerial economists. For example, this chapter covers the multiplant monopolist and monopoly regulation. Multiproduct monopoly and monopoly price discrimination—the ability to charge different prices to different customers—are given extensive coverage in Chapters 11 and 12. This chapter also sets the stage for studying **cartels,** groups of potentially competing firms that coordinate their market decisions in order to approximate the profit-maximizing behavior of the monopolist. Cartels play an important role in our present domestic and world economy and thus deserve careful scrutiny, which is accomplished in Chapter 13.

Explanations for Monopoly

The dictionary tells us that *monopoly* is of Greek derivation and means "single seller." There are many reasons a firm may lack rival competitors in its industry; six of these reasons deserve special mention here.

First, and most trivial, is the monopoly that exists because industry demand is not sufficient to support more than one producer. For example, an American firm producing mustache cups will have few if any competitors due to limited consumer demand.[1] Second, firms are given government-awarded patents and copyrights that protect against competition for many years (17 years for patents and 50 years after the author's death for published material). Third, a firm may have control over an essential resource or have unique knowledge of a production process, making it difficult for other firms to compete in the industry. However, neither patents nor sole command over resources is a perfect barrier to entry, because competing firms can often produce close substitutes without violating patent laws.

Fourth, a firm's production function may be characterized by decreasing costs—that is, by a negatively sloped long-run average cost curve. In such cases, the firm can always lower its per-unit production costs by expanding output. If other firms have U-shaped long-run average cost curves, the monopoly firm can eliminate its competitors by increasing its output and placing itself in a more favorable cost position compared to the competition. By eliminating all competitors in this way, the firm becomes the industry's only seller and gains complete control over its price and output.

Firms that exist because of the special characteristics of their production functions are called **natural monopolies** or **technological monopolies**. The electric power utilities, local telephone companies, and municipal water and sewage systems are typical examples of such decreasing-cost industries. They are inconsistent with long-run competitive equilibrium; because competition cannot be achieved, the government often awards them exclusive production franchises in exchange for the right to regulate and monitor their pricing, output, and quality decisions. Thus government franchise and regulation, the fifth reason for monopoly, is closely related to the presence of natural monopoly.

Finally, monopoly behavior occurs in industries that have neither decreasing costs nor important barriers to entry. In some cases, otherwise competing firms choose to coordinate their pricing and output decisions in order to become an effective monopoly. Such collusive arrangements among firms have been illustrated most pointedly in recent years by the Organization of Petroleum Exporting Countries (OPEC) cartel.

---

1. A mustache cup has a straight piece inside, just below the rim, for holding back a man's mustache while he is drinking.

Let's begin our investigation of monopoly by assuming that the monopolist's cost curves are substantially the same as the competitor's—U-shaped *ATC* and *LAC* curves—and thereby concentrate on monopolistic behavior resulting solely from the absence of competition. Then we may give special attention to the aspects of monopoly that arise from decreasing long-run average costs.

Simple Monopoly

The essential distinction between a competitive firm and a monopoly firm lies in the demand curves that the two firms face. The competitive firm faces a perfectly elastic demand curve, cannot influence price, and therefore adjusts only its output in seeking its profit-maximizing equilibrium. In contrast, the monopolist faces the industry demand curve as the only seller in the industry. The simple monopolist must therefore set its price and output within the bounds established by consumer demand.[2]

Although the monopolist sets both price and output, these are not set independently. The industry demand curve in Figure 9.1 illustrates this dependency. If the monopolist sets a price of $5, the most output it can sell at that price is 1 unit. Point *A*, representing sales of 3 units of output at a price of $5, is outside the bounds set by demand. Thus the typical criticism levied against monopolies— their unbridled ability to sell any quantity of output at any price—is absurd and ignores the demand constraint that monopolists face.

The profit-maximizing rule for competitive firms was defined in Chapter 3: *MR* = *MC*, with *MC* rising. The monopolist must also equate marginal revenue and marginal cost to maximize profits. However, the monopolist's revenue characteristics differ from the competitor's. Because the monopolist faces the industry demand curve, it must lower its price to sell more output. In monopoly, price cannot equal marginal revenue.

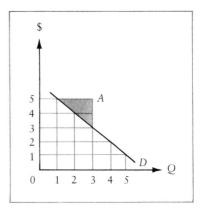

**Figure 9.1
Downward-Sloping Monopoly
Demand Curve**

Increased sales require a lower price. Point *A* is not possible.

Price and Marginal Revenue

It is difficult to overstate the importance of the inequality of price and marginal revenue in the theory of monopoly. The rule for the monopolist is $P > MR$. To see why, refer to the formal definition of marginal revenue in Chapter 3:

$$MR = P + Q\left(\frac{\Delta P}{\Delta Q}\right) \qquad (9.1)$$

Marginal revenue is the sum of the two terms in Equation 9.1. The increase in total revenue resulting from the sale of an additional unit of output, the first term in Equation 9.1, equals the price at which

2. A simple monopolist faces arbitrage for its products, meaning that efforts to sell the product at two different prices will be frustrated by people buying at the lower price and reselling the product at a price that is still below the monopolist's higher price. Thus a simple monopolist charges uniform prices to all customers.

the marginal unit is sold. The reduction in total revenue resulting from the reduction in the price of all units sold previously at a higher price, the second term in Equation 9.1, is the product of the slope of the demand curve, $\Delta P/\Delta Q$, and the number of inframarginal units to which the price reduction applies, Q.

In competition, price equals marginal revenue because of the special assumption that the firm need not reduce price to sell more output. The slope of the perfectly elastic demand curve that the competitor faces, $\Delta P/\Delta Q$, is zero. Thus the second term in equation 9.1, $Q(\Delta P/\Delta Q)$, is zero; marginal revenue for the competitor equals price.

For the simple monopolist, the algebraic sum of the two effects in Equation 9.1 is always less than price, except in the trivial case of the first unit sold. Consider Figure 9.1. When the price is $4, the monopolist sells 2 units and has total revenue of $8. To sell an additional unit, the monopolist must lower the price to $3 on all units sold, pushing total revenue to $9. Note that price ($3) exceeds marginal revenue ($1). According to Equation 9.1, marginal revenue is the algebraic sum of $3 (the price received on the last unit sold) and $-$2 (the loss in revenue of $1 each on units 1 and 2, which previously sold for $4 instead of $3): $Q(\Delta P/\Delta Q) = 2(-1/1)$ $= -$2.

Table 9.1 contains revenue data corresponding to the demand curve in Figure 9.1. You may use Equation 9.1 to verify the marginal revenue figures in the last column of Table 9.1. There is no use reading farther into this chapter until you know why $P > MR$ for the monopolist, a result that shows up directly in Table 9.1 for all units except the first one.

Table 9.1

Revenue Data Corresponding to
the Demand Curve in Figure 9.1

Price	×	Quantity Sold	=	Total Revenue $(P \cdot Q)$	Marginal Revenue $(\Delta TR/\Delta Q)$
5		1		5	5
4		2		8	3
3		3		9	1
2		4		8	-1
1		5		5	-3

Price, Marginal Revenue, and Price Elasticity of Demand

The discussion of price elasticity of demand in Chapter 4 showed that marginal revenue is related to the price elasticity of demand according to the following formula:

$$MR = P\left(1 - \frac{1}{|\varepsilon|}\right) \tag{9.2}$$

In this equation, ε refers to the price elasticity of demand. We may now use these relationships to derive the monopolist's family of revenue curves: marginal revenue (MR), average revenue (AR), and total revenue (TR).

Table 9.2 arranges the relationships among P, MR, and ε in a useful manner. The first column shows the possible values for the price elasticity of demand (ε). If we know ε, we can deduce all the other relationships.

Table 9.2
Effect of the Price Elasticity of Demand ($|\varepsilon|$)
on the Monopolist's Revenue Curves

When $|\varepsilon|$	$MR\left(\dfrac{\Delta TR}{\Delta Q}\right)$	$P = AR$	TR
> 1 (elastic)	> 0	> MR	Rises
= 1 (unit elastic)	= 0	> MR	Attains its maximum
< 1 (inelastic)	< 0	> MR	Falls

Consider the demand curve D in Figure 9.2a. It will help to recall that price is equal to average revenue: $AR = TR/Q = (P \cdot Q)/Q = P$. The demand curve measures the average revenue (or price) that can be charged for different levels of output. Thus the demand curve is the average revenue curve and equals price at every point on the curve.

The demand curve in Figure 9.2a is linear, so price ranges from elastic to inelastic. At point A, $|\varepsilon| > 1$; thus marginal revenue must be positive and less than price. The marginal revenue value corresponding to the demand point A is plotted as point A' on the marginal revenue curve. At point B on the demand curve, $|\varepsilon| = 1$, and marginal revenue must be zero (see point B'). At point C, $|\varepsilon| < 1$, and the marginal revenue is negative (see point C'). The marginal revenue curve lies entirely below the demand (average revenue) curve, because $P = AR > MR$ in a simple monopoly. Thus at any point on the demand curve, we know the price and can compute the price elasticity of demand. With this information and Equation 9.2, we can also calculate the marginal revenue.

The marginal revenue curve is the slope of the total revenue curve, so we can work backward to derive the total revenue curve. By definition, if MR is positive, the slope of TR must be positive; if MR is zero, the slope of TR is zero; and if MR is negative, the slope of TR is negative. In Figure 9.2, when the firm lowers price from P to P_0, demand is price elastic. The additional units sold at the lower prices between P and P_0 cause total revenue to rise, as shown in

Figure 9.2
**Monopolist's Marginal, Average,
and Total Revenue Curve**

(a) For a straight-line demand
curve, marginal revenue is a
straight line with twice the slope.
(b) The total revenue curve is a
parabola.

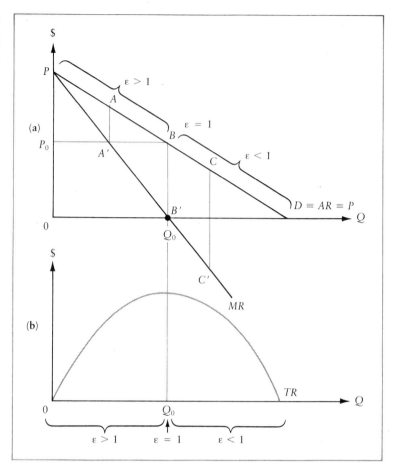

Figure 9.2b. At price P_0, $|\varepsilon| = 1$, marginal revenue is zero, and total revenue is at its maximum. Further price reductions from P_0 to 0 cause total revenue to fall, because demand is price inelastic at prices below P_0. Thus the total revenue curve for the monopolist is an inverted bowl-shaped curve and is uniquely related to the demand and marginal revenue curves. Observe that the total-average-marginal relationships that pertain in other contexts are preserved in the monopolist's revenue curves.

Profit-Maximizing Equilibrium of the Simple Monopolist

We may now identify the monopolist's profit-maximizing equilibrium. Faced with the industry demand curve, the monopolist selects the price-quantity combination that maximizes profit. Figure 9.3 displays the profit-maximizing equilibrium using total curves in panel a and marginal curves in panel b. The profit-maximizing rule for the monopolist, as for the competitor, is

$$MR = MC \qquad (9.3)$$

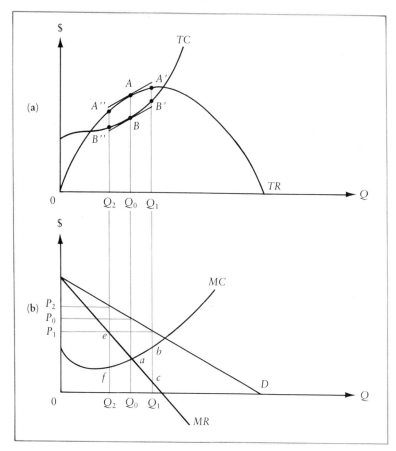

(a)

(b)

Figure 9.3
Monopoly Profit-Maximization Condition: $MR = MC$

Any output other than Q_0, where $MR = MC$, yields a lower profit. **(a)** The profit-maximizing equilibrium can be shown with total curves. **(b)** It can also be shown with marginal curves.

In Figure 9.3 the monopolist selects the level of output Q_0, for which marginal revenue equals marginal cost, and simultaneously sets price to clear the market at P_0. Note that the $MR = MC$ intersection at point a in panel b occurs at the same level of output, Q_0, for which the slopes of the total revenue and total cost curves are equal in panel a. Profit is illustrated as the vertical distance $\overline{AB}$ between the total revenue and total cost curves.

If the monopolist sets the price-quantity combination at (P_1, Q_1), profit falls, because each unit of output between Q_0 and Q_1 is produced and sold at a marginal cost exceeding the marginal revenue. Panel a shows profits falling from $\overline{AB}$ to $\overline{A'B'}$. In panel b the additional output $Q_1 - Q_0$ adds costs of $Q_0 a d Q_1$ (the area beneath the marginal cost curve) but revenues of only $Q_0 a c Q_1$ (the area beneath the marginal revenue curve). Therefore, increasing output from Q_0 to Q_1 reduces total profit by the area abc. If the price-quantity combination (P_2, Q_2) is selected, profits are reduced to $\overline{A''B''}$ or, equivalently, by the area aef, because for the units $Q_0 - Q_2$, $MR > MC$. Output reductions give up more revenue than is saved in costs. Thus profits are maximized when $MR = MC$ and

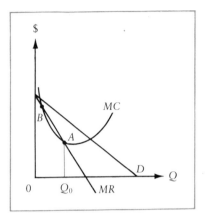

Figure 9.4
Monopoly Profit Maximization

To maximize profits, a monopolist must set $MR = MC$, and the MC curve must cut the MR curve from below.

price is set to clear the market. This profit-maximizing rule is perfectly generalizable to all market structures.

We qualified the $MR = MC$ profit-maximizing condition for competition by requiring that the marginal cost curve cut the marginal revenue curve from below. Because the marginal revenue curve is horizontal in competition, requiring the marginal cost curve to cut the marginal revenue curve from below is equivalent to requiring marginal cost to be rising. Monopoly still requires that the marginal cost curve cut the marginal revenue curve from below. Now, however, because marginal revenue falls for the monopolist, this condition may be satisfied even with marginal cost falling, as long as marginal cost is falling more slowly than marginal revenue. In Figure 9.4, the MC curve cuts the MR curve from below at point A, satisfying the profit-maximizing condition. At point B, however, MC cuts MR from above. Thus output should be expanded to Q_0.

Figure 9.5 is a more complete representation of monopoly equilibrium. The monopolist sets $LMC = MR$ (point e) by selecting a level of capital so that $ATC = LAC$ (point h) and consequently $SMC = LMC = MR$ (point e). The price that clears the market when Q_m is produced is P_m, determined by point f on the demand curve. Thus Figure 9.5 helps organize our thoughts on several variables at once: output (Q), price (P), capital (K), labor (L), revenue (R), cost (C), and profit (π).

The positive economic profit $P_m fha$ can exist in long-run equilibrium as long as competition and entry are barred. As you can now see, effective barriers to entry are important in keeping the industry monopolized and in permitting long-run rates of return in excess of opportunity costs.

Figure 9.5
Welfare Loss Triangle

Because of underproduction, $P > MC$. The value lost to the economy is measured by the area efb.

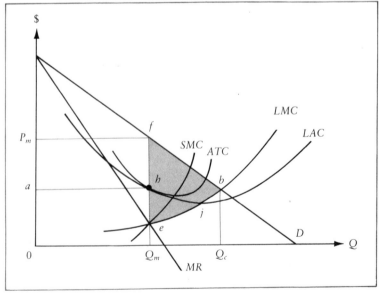

It is essential to the existence of monopoly that the profits $P_m fba$ in Figure 9.5 not be dissipated by entering firms. Positive economic profits can exist in long-run equilibrium as long as effective barriers to entry are erected and maintained.

Properties of Monopoly Equilibrium

We have seen that long-run profit maximization requires the monopolist to equate short- and long-run marginal cost, as at point e in Figure 9.5. The condition $SMC = LMC$ implies that the firm has selected the correct combination of inputs for the production of the selected output. The short-run ATC curve is tangent to the long-run LAC curve at output level Q_m, and the input efficiency condition $MP_L/MP_K = w/r$, described in Chapter 6, is achieved. There is no way to reduce the cost of producing this level of output by rearranging capital and labor inputs.

The long-run competitive equilibrium condition, $P = LMC$, is not satisfied in monopoly. Because profits are maximized in monopoly when $MR = LMC$ and $P > MR$, price must exceed LMC, as shown in Figure 9.5. This condition implies that the monopolist produces too little output. Recall that price measures the additional benefit of the last unit purchased by consumers. Recall also that long-run marginal cost is the marginal benefit forgone in the next-best use of the capital and labor diverted to the production of one more unit of the monopolist's output. Therefore, the condition $P > LMC$ implies that the marginal benefit of producing one more unit of the monopolist's good is greater than the value of the forgone uses of the resources that would be drawn from elsewhere in the economy to produce the additional unit. Because $P > MR$ for the simple monopolist, production stops before all the efficiency gains implied by $P > LMC$ have been exploited. Therefore, monopoly causes too few resources to be withdrawn from other activities and used to produce the monopolist's product. In short, the monopolist misdirects the economy's resources by producing too little output.

A convenient measure of this loss is presented in Figure 9.5. If output increased to Q_c, where $P = LMC$ at point b, all the gains generated by producing output whenever $P > LMC$ would be exhausted. (Because this is the competitive equilibrium condition, the output is denoted Q_c.) The total benefit of increasing output from Q_m to Q_c is the area $Q_m fbQ_c$ beneath the demand curve. The total cost of using the capital and labor resources to increase output from Q_m to Q_c—the opportunity cost of the resources—is the area $Q_m ebQ_c$ beneath the LMC curve. The net benefit of such output expansion—total benefit minus total cost—is the shaded area efb. Because monopoly prevents output from increasing from Q_m to Q_c, the area efb measures the monopoly-induced loss in societal welfare; it is referred to as the **welfare loss triangle**. It is often said that the monopolist produces too little and charges too much. This is true, as you can see from Figure 9.5: $Q_m < Q_c$ and $P_m > P_c$. But these are not independent problems; both arise because $P > MR$ in monopoly, and both contribute to the welfare loss attributed to monopoly and measured by the welfare loss triangle.

There are other sources of inefficiency inherent in simple monopoly. The complete absence of entry by competing firms, which is necessary for the existence of monopoly, means that price may exceed average cost in the long run. There is no market mechanism to push the firm to the optimal scale of plant and hence to the minimum long-run average total cost, such as point j in Figure 9.5. (Of course, inframarginal competitive firms also do not operate with cost-minimizing scales of plant, as we saw in Chapter 7.)

In addition, the $P > LAC$ condition makes long-run profits available for use in ways that may perpetuate the inefficiencies of the monopoly. For example, some tempting uses of monopoly profits include buying up firms that produce substitute products, buying up resources essential to competitors, lobbying for legislative protection of the monopoly, and bribing politicians. Any or all of these uses of monopoly profits can lead to even greater inefficiencies.

In summary, monopoly equilibrium, $MR = LMC$, implies the following:

$ATC = LAC$: efficient input combinations for the output produced.

$P > LMC$: welfare losses caused by too little production.

$P > LAC$: positive long-run economic profits.

$P > $ minimum LAC: optimal scale of plant not adopted.

9.1

Vertical Integration: Monopolistic or Risk-Spreading Practice?

American business enterprises are frequently criticized as anti-competitive when they are vertically integrated. Managers and industry representatives must be able to respond to this oft-repeated attack.

Individuals have the option of renting or purchasing such items as cars, houses, clothing, and bicycles. So why is it that we rent a car very infrequently, usually when we are far from home, or rent clothing only for a wedding or a wake? Why do so many people own instead of rent their dwelling? And why do those who rent prefer long-term leases (using daily leases only to occupy motels and hotels)?

The answer is that it is desirable to make long-term arrangements as a substitute for frequent market activities. Long-term contracts and outright purchase reduce the risk of a home, car, or bicycle not being available when desired. Also, the sheer numbers of transactions—and hence transaction costs—are reduced. Information-gathering costs are also reduced. A variety of cost reductions take place

from outright ownership or long-term contracting.

There is a direct application of these observations to the concept of vertical integration. Typically, there are several stages of production between raw materials and finished goods. A firm is vertically integrated when it owns the means of production in two or more successive stages. For example, an oil company could own all of the following:

1. Exploratory vessels
2. Drilling equipment
3. Wells
4. Tankers
5. Pipelines
6. Refineries

7. Distribution trucks
8. Storage tanks
9. Gas stations

Such firms are called major oil companies. Alternatively, an oil company could own just the last four and rely on other companies to provide crude oil to its refineries, as do the "independents." Or a company could own just a few gas stations.

What are the advantages of vertical integration—owning several stages of production? A chief benefit is the certainty of supply, which allows for the more efficient use of capacity at the various production stages. Idle refineries and tankers are costly, and the certainty of supply arising from vertical integration reduces this cost. The same is true for pipelines, which are fixed capacity-in-place and are most economically used at high volumes of flow. Owning several stages of production therefore substitutes for frequent market transactions and cuts costs by spreading risk and diminishing the number of transactions and the information required to make the transactions.

Vertical integration may thus be a procompetitive, not an anticompetitive, tactic. Competition is a process in which economic agents, acting in their own interests, seek technological and organizational improvements to reduce costs and raise profits. These cost reductions are passed on to consumers if many independent firms compete. The competitive paradigm is closely mimicked when many vertically integrated firms compete.

APPLICATION 9.2
Tie-in Sales and Reciprocity

A **tie-in sale** is the sale of one good contingent on the sale of another. A **reciprocity agreement** binds sellers and buyers to the purchase of each others' products. Both of these sales arrangements have been used by firms for mutual gains in efficiency, yet both have been fought successfully under the antitrust laws on the theory that they allow monopolists to extend their monopoly in one product into another market. Closer analysis disputes this contention.

Suppose a firm had a monopoly in widgets (the economist's all-purpose good) at a monopoly price of P_0 (refer back to Figure 9.3). Suppose further that the widget monopolist also sells gadgets in a competitive market at the market price of $10 apiece. An attempt to tie the sale of widgets to the sale of gadgets cannot increase the profit from the profit level of independent sales. There is a willingness-to-pay or demand curve for widgets and a profit-maximizing price. The tie-in can only change the composition of payments.

For example, in the tie-in sale the monopolist could raise the price of gadgets to, say, $2 above the competitive price—but only by compensating the buyer by lowering the price of widgets below P_0 by the same $2. There is no possibility of selling the combination for a higher total price without a reduction in profit, because the monopoly is not transferred from widgets to gadgets. The gadget market is still competitive, and widgets are still monopolized. The monopoly power in widgets can only be exercised once.

Similarly, monopoly power does not increase when the monopolist engages in reciprocal buying. Suppose the widget manufacturer will buy rackets for use in producing widgets only if the racket producer purchases some widgets. The widget monopolist cannot, through such a reciprocity requirement, increase its monopoly power by obtaining better terms for rackets. Monopoly power can only be exercised once and is restrained by the demand curve. The profit-maximizing price does not change as a result of reciprocity.

Nonexistence of the Monopoly Supply Curve

Under competition, the marginal cost curve is the firm's supply curve and an important building block of industry supply and long-run equilibrium. Although much of the competitive analysis carries over into monopoly, this phenomenon does not. The marginal cost curve of the monopolist is not the monopolist's supply curve. Indeed, there is no curve that establishes a unique relationship between price and output supplied for a monopolist—the monopoly supply curve simply does not exist.

Figure 9.6 shows why the monopolist's marginal cost curve is not a supply curve. When the demand and marginal revenue curves are D_1 and MR_1, marginal revenue and marginal cost intersect at point A; the firm maximizes profits by selling output Q_0 at price P_1. However, if demand and marginal revenue are D_2 and MR_2, the optimal output is still Q_0 but the price is P_2. Point A on the marginal cost curve, which equates marginal revenue and thereby determines output Q_0, is consistent with many different prices, each determined by the demand curve. Accordingly, the marginal cost curve is not the monopolist's supply curve. The monopolist does not have a supply curve as it is conventionally defined.

Figure 9.6
Nonexistence of the Monopoly Supply Curve

There can be no two-dimensional relationship between price and quantity in a monopoly, because the market-clearing price depends on the demand curve.

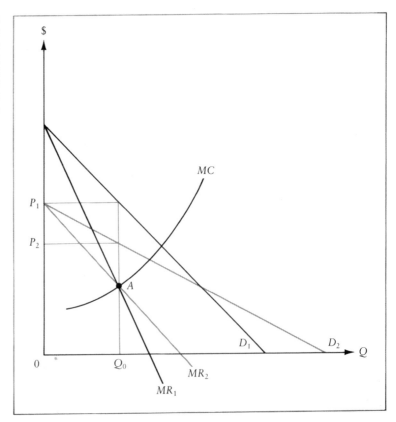

Multiplant Monopoly

Up to now, we have assumed that the monopolist operates only one plant. A more realistic case is for the monopolist to own many plants. Because the competitive equilibrium is also a multiplant equilibrium, albeit with many owners, we have a useful basis for comparing competition and monopoly. In fact, the only meaningful comparison of monopoly and competition must involve competition at the industry level and **multiplant monopoly.**

The key building block in the model of multiplant monopoly is cost minimization. A monopolist wants to produce any given rate of output at minimum total cost; to do otherwise would involve forgone profit. Chapter 3 demonstrates how the equal marginal cost principle can be employed to seek a cost minimum. A multiplant monopolist's production of a given total output should be allocated among the various places of production (plants) so that all plants are producing at the same marginal cost. If marginal costs are not equal in all plants, the multiplant monopolist can reduce the total cost of producing any rate of output by switching production from plants with a higher marginal cost to those with a lower marginal cost. When the marginal costs in all plants are equal, the multiplant monopolist's total costs are minimized.

Multiplant Monopoly's Marginal Cost Curve

We may use the equal marginal cost principle to derive the multiplant monopolist's marginal cost curve. Each point on the marginal cost curve represents a distribution of production that equates marginal costs in all plants: $MC_1 = MC_2 = \ldots = MC_n$.

Figure 9.7 illustrates this important principle. The marginal cost curves of two of the many plants are shown in panels a and b, and the monopolist's marginal cost curve is shown in panel c. For the firm to produce a total output of $0Q_1$ at least cost, it must

Figure 9.7
Multiplant Marginal Cost Curve

(a) Plant 1 has marginal cost curve MC_1. **(b)** Plant 2 has marginal cost curve MC_2. **(c)** The horizontal summation of marginal costs is the multiplant monopolist's MC curve, when and only when the equal marginal cost principle is followed.

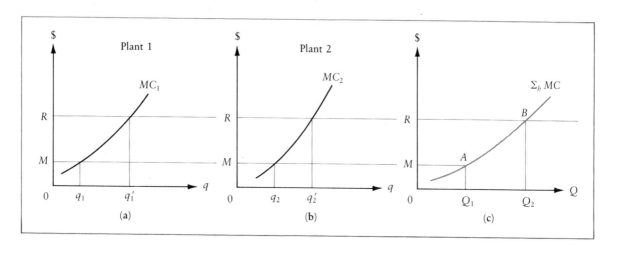

allocate production among the many plants so that marginal costs are equal in all plants. Suppose the equal marginal cost principle is satisfied in Figure 9.7. The output $0Q_1$ is the sum of the outputs $0q_1$ in plant 1, $0q_2$ in plant 2, and the individual outputs of all other plants not shown in the figure. Point A is the horizontal sum of the various plants' output when and only when the equal marginal cost principle is satisfied. Similarly, point B, another point on the monopolist's marginal cost curve, is the horizontal sum of the output of the individual plants when all plants produce their part of the total output Q_2 at the same marginal cost $0R$.

Points A, B, and all other similarly derived points make up the multiplant monopolist's marginal cost curve; in Figure 9.7c it is labeled $\Sigma_h MC$. Note carefully that the marginal cost curve $\Sigma_h MC$ has meaning only if each level of output satisfies the equal marginal cost principle: $MC_1 = MC_2 = \ldots MC_n$. Of course, the equal marginal cost principle derives from underlying economic forces related to profit maximization; the multiplant monopolist has a profit incentive to follow the equal marginal cost principle.

Profit-Maximizing Equilibrium and Multiplant Monopoly

In order to compare competitive and monopoly equilibrium, we must make the following assumptions:

> The monopolist buys up all firms in a competitive industry and effectively blocks further entry.
>
> Each previously competitive firm is operated as a separate plant by the monopoly.
>
> The production functions of all firms (plants) are identical.
>
> The opportunity costs of the competitive firms' owners equal the opportunity costs of the managerial skills needed to operate the monopolist's plants.

These assumptions allow us to keep the plant cost curves the same and to study the effect of monopoly ownership in an otherwise perfectly competitive industry.

PERFECT COMPETITION VERSUS MULTIPLANT MONOPOLY   Figure 9.8 gets us started in this analysis. Under competition, the intersection at point A of the industry supply curve ($\Sigma_h LMC$) and the industry demand curve (D) establishes the competitive price P_c and output Q_c. Each identical price-taking firm produces output q_c and earns zero long-run profits by adopting the optimal scale of plant and producing at the minimum of its long-run average cost curve, LAC (see Figure 9.8a).

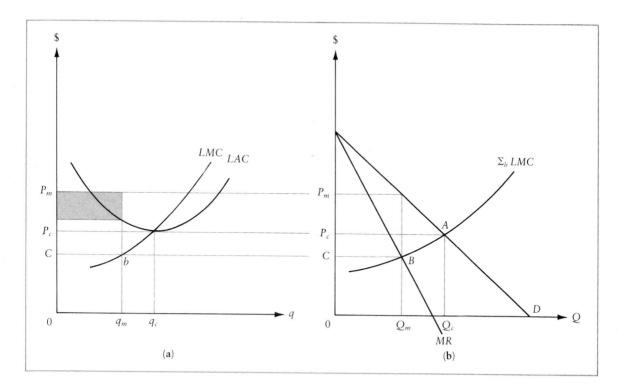

(a)

(b)

Figure 9.8
Perfect Competition versus
Multiplant Monopoly

(a) In competition, each plant
produces q_c; but in monopoly, each
produces q_m. **(b)** Using the same
number of plants, the monopolist will
cut total output from Q_c to Q_m, and
the output in each plant from q_c to
q_m. Price will rise from P_c to P_m.

When the industry is monopolized and all previously competitive firms are under the same ownership, the monopolist changes the equilibrium price-quantity combination in the **aggregate** as well as for each plant. The monopolist's profit-maximizing rule is $MR = \Sigma_h LMC$, which occurs at point B. The monopolist reduces total output to Q_m and increases price to P_m. It is the monopolist's ability to restrict output and raise prices that generates monopoly profits.

The monopolist will operate each plant at the output level for which the monopolist's marginal revenue equals the plant's long-run marginal cost. Marginal revenue at output Q_m is $0C$; accordingly, the plant illustrated in panel a equates MR and LMC at point b and produces q_m units of output. Each plant earns an economic profit equal to the shaded area by reducing its scale of plant and operating at an output rate below the minimum LAC. The monopolist's total economic profits are the sum of the economic profits earned in each plant.

Figure 9.8 does not present the complete long-run profit-maximizing adjustment of the multiplant monopolist. In final equilibrium there are further adjustments in the scales of plant and plant closings. Specifically, the multiplant monopolist closes down some plants and operates the others at their optimum scales of plant. As it makes these adjustments, the monopolist selects levels of aggregate output (Q), price (P), output in each plant (q_i), capital (K), labor (L), and the number of plants (N). The full power of the cost curves can be seen in the final equilibrium. Now let's derive the rules for the proper selection of these levels.

In Figure 9.8b the curve $\Sigma_h LMC$ is the horizontal summation of the marginal costs of the original number of plants, N_0. If the monopolist chose to operate all N_0 plants, it would select the total output Q_m, where $MR = \Sigma_h LMC$. Assuming that all plants are identical (an assumption we will abandon in the following section), each plant produces $Q_m/N_0 = q_m$ units of output, and marginal costs are equal in all plants. Note, however, that none of the plants now operate at minimum long-run average cost. There is an advantage to closing some plants altogether and shifting their production to the remaining plants, because this rearrangement reduces the long-run average costs of production for the same output rate. The profit-maximizing number of plants for the given output Q_m is achieved when all producing plants operate at minimum long-run average cost and produce output q_c.

But this still is not the final equilibrium. The plant closings shift the $\Sigma_h LMC$ curve to the left, as shown by the shift to $\Sigma_h LMC_1$ in Figure 9.9b. But note that $\Sigma_h LMC_1 \neq MR$ at output Q_m; specifically, $\Sigma_h LMC_1(Q_m a) > MR(Q_m b)$. Although the monopolist minimizes the cost of producng Q_m units by closing plants and rearranging output until all plants operate at the minimum LAC, output Q_m is no longer the profit-maximizing output. Instead, output should be cut to Q_{m1}, because $\Sigma_h LMC_1(Q_{m1}) = MR(Q_{m1})$.

We now face the same adjustments with output Q_{m1} that were just described for output Q_m. The monopolist should close down entire plants and push their output toward the remaining plants, thereby permitting the remaining plants to adopt the scale of operation that yields lowest average cost. For any given output, profit maximization requires that all plants produce at the minimum average cost, which the multiplant monopolist can achieve by suitable closings of superfluous plants. But these closings again shift the $\Sigma_h LMC$ curve leftward, again changing the correct output level of the firm and requiring additional plant closings.

After many such adjustments, the final equilibrium is found where $LMC = $ minimum LAC in the remaining plants and $\Sigma_h LMC = MR$. These two conditions, both required for equilibrium, eliminate any further profit increase resulting from plant closings. In Figure 9.9, equilibrium occurs at point B, where $\Sigma_h LMC_2 = MR$. Each plant produces q_{m0} units of output at minimum long-run average cost and contributes an economic profit of $P_c P_{m0} hj$ (see panel a).

Note that the monopolist depicted in Figure 9.9 moves from point A (the competitive equilibrium) to point B (the multiplant monopolist's equilibrium) by closing down entire plants. There is a convenient interpretation for this movement. The horizontal line

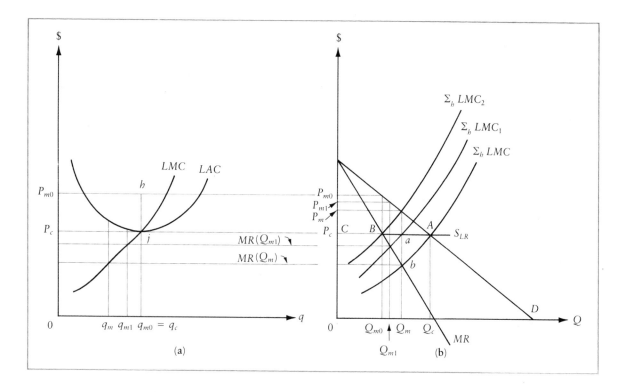

Figure 9.9
Long-Run Adjustment of Multiplant Monopolist

(a) Plants that are absorbed by a monopolist reach equilibrium at point j. **(b)** After the closing of excess plants, the monopolist will produce q_{m0} in each of the plants it operates and set $MR = \Sigma_h LMC_2 = S_{LR}$ and $P = P_{m0}$.

$\overline{AB}$ is equal to the long-run supply curve of the competitive industry, S_{LR}. Its height is equal to the height of the competitive firm's minimum LAC curves. When demand rises or falls, the competitive long-run equilibrium moves horizontally along the curve S_{LR} by entry or exit of competitive firms. The long-run supply curve, S_{LR}, is therefore the "marginal cost of entry or exit," or in the language of the multiplant monopolist, the **marginal cost of plant openings or closings.** The monopolist moves along the curve S_{LR} and continues to close plants whenever $S_{LR} > MR$; at such points the firm saves more in total costs from a plant closing than it sacrifices in total revenue from the lost production. When $S_{LR} = MR$, as at point B in Figure 9.9, the optimal number of plant closings has been accomplished; all remaining plants operate at minimum LAC. Thus the monopolist's profits are maximized at B. Because S_{LR} is horizontal in the case of perfect competition, output must fall enough to drive marginal revenue up to the competitive price P_c.

If the demand curve is linear, we may be more specific about the number of plant closings. Because the demand and marginal revenue curves in Figure 9.9 are linear, the distances $\overline{CB}$ and $\overline{BA}$ are equal. The output of the multiplant monopolist is exactly half the competitive output. And because each remaining plant operates at the competitive level, it follows that the monopolist will use only half the competitive number of plants. The multiplant monopolist facing a linear demand curve represents a special case of the general model.

This section has discussed the special case of identical plants in order to study the idea of plant closings and some essential differences between the paradigm cases of perfect competition and multiplant monopoly. The next section generalizes the analysis to the more likely case of nonidentical plants. But there is an important lesson to be retained: Unlike the case of competitive equilibrium, the multiplant monopolist will reduce output by closing plants even when all plants exhibit identical costs. In the paradigm model of multiplant monopoly, plants aren't closed because they are inefficient. They are closed because this is the cost-minimizing method of cutting production to the profit-maximizing rate. Presumably the plants targeted for closing could be selected at random.

PURE COMPETITION VERSUS MULTIPLANT MONOPOLY   This section can be relatively brief, because the tone of the analysis has been set in the discussion of multiplant monopoly using perfectly competitive assumptions. Now let's permit some of the original competitive firms (and later the monopolist's plants) to earn inframarginal profits by virtue of cost advantages, as discussed in Chapter 7. Does the presence of inframarginal firms change the results?

Figure 9.10
Long-Run Equilibrium of
Multiplant Monopolist with
Inframarginal Plants

(a) Firm 1 is inframarginal in competition and in monopoly.
(b) Firm 2 is inframarginal in competition, marginal in monopoly.
(c) Firm 3 is marginal in competition, extramarginal (and thus not operated) in monopoly.
(d) The aggregate output of the multiplant monopolist is therefore Q_m, where $S_{LR} = MR$.

Figure 9.10 shows the equilibrium of the multiplant monopolist in the presence of inframarginal plants. Competitive equilibrium occurs at point A in panel d, where $P = \Sigma_h LMC = $ minimum LAC of the marginal firms. At this point, the monopolist closes plants, reduces output, and increases price in order to maximize profits. The highest-cost plants, initially the marginal competitive firms like the plant in panel c, will be closed first; plant closings continue in descending order of cost, until output falls to Q_m, where $S_{LR} = MR$. The plant closings move the monopolist along S_{LR}, the marginal cost curve of plant closings. At point B the optimal number of plant closings is achieved, because $S_{LR} = MR$.

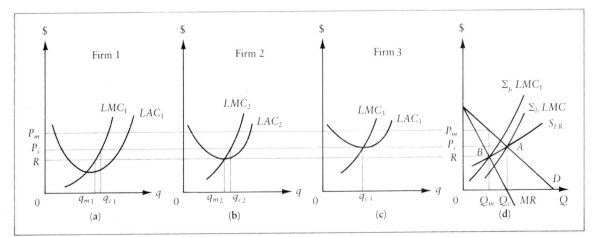

(a)   (b)   (c)   (d)

Remember that the height of the S_{LR} curve equals the height of the minimum point of the highest-cost plant's LAC curve. In equilibrium at point B, firm 2 (panel b) is the "marginal" plant, operating its optimal scale of plant where $MR = LMC_2$. Firm 1 (panel a) continues to be inframarginal in long-run equilibrium, whereas firm 3 (panel c)—and all other plants with a minimum LAC greater than marginal revenue $(0R)$—is closed.

In the case of identical plants, the monopolist reduces output only by closing entire plants and allowing the remaining firms to produce at the competitive rate of output. In the case of non-identical plants, where we allow for inframarginal plants, output falls for two reasons: (1) closings of entire high-cost plants and (2) reductions in the output of inframarginal plants. In Figure 9.10, plants 1 and 2 both reduce output by reducing their scales of plant.

9.3

Taxing the Multiplant Monopolist

Monopoly profits are of great concern to many people. Professor John Kenneth Galbraith, in discussing the market power of monopolists over price and profit, tells us, "In the English language only a few words—fraud, defalcation, subversion, and sodomy—have a greater connotation of nonviolent wickedness."[*] One proposed method to control monopoly is to tax away the profits. Will the monopolist absorb the losses of a tax, or can the firm shift these tax costs to customers by further reductions in output and increases in product price?

For simplicity, assume that all the monopolist's plants are identi-

[*]John Kenneth Galbraith, The New Industrial State (New York: Signet Books, 1967), p. 190.

cal. In the right-hand panel of the figure, the monopolist maximizes profits by producing output Q_n, where $MR(Q_n) = \Sigma_h LMC(N \text{ plants}) = S_{LR}$. Each of N plants produces $q_n = Q_n/N$ units of output at the minimum LAC, as shown in the left-hand panel. Commodity price is P_n, and the initial pretax profit is $abcd \cdot N$.

Assume that half the monopoly

Effect of Lump-Sum Tax

Exactly half of each plant's profits is taxed away. But for the multiplant monopolist, such a tax does not affect output, price, or the number of plants.

profits are taxed away with a single levy—that is, in a **lump sum.** The tax, a fixed cost to the firm, shifts the average cost curve up to $LAC + tax$. The new $LAC + tax$ curve must intersect point f, which is half the distance between points d and c. This requirement assures that exactly half the profit is taxed away. Should the monopolist continue to operate each plant at the optimum scale of plant and maintain the same output Q_n and price P_n by holding the number of plants constant at N? Or should the firm raise output to q_m in each plant in order to operate at the minimum of the $LAC + tax$ curve, cut total output to Q_m by reducing the number of plants to M, and raise price to P_m?

Continued on page 238

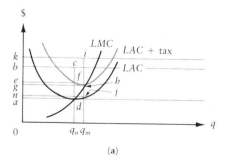

(a)

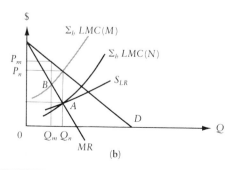

(b)

The profits resulting from these two strategies are as follows:

$$\pi(Q_n) = ebcf \cdot N = \frac{1}{2}(abcd) \cdot N$$

$$\pi(Q_m) = gkih \cdot M$$

The untaxed monopolist always had the option to produce $Q_m = q_m \cdot M$ (point B, where $\Sigma_h LMC(M$ plants$) = MR(Q_m)$) but instead chose to produce $Q_n = q_n \cdot N$ (point A, where $\Sigma_h LMC(N$ plants$) = MR(Q_n) = S_{LR}$). The implication is that

$$abcd \cdot N > gkih \cdot M$$

But by construction,

$$nkij \cdot M > gkih \cdot M$$

Hence

$$\pi(Q_n) = \frac{1}{2}(abcd) \cdot N > gkih \cdot M$$
$$= \pi(Q_m)$$

The monopolist will therefore produce the same output (Q_n) after taxes, use the same number of plants (N), and charge the same price (P_n). The monopolist will absorb the lump-sum tax and not pass it on to consumers in the form of further output restrictions, plant closings, or price increases.

This result is perfectly generalizable to the case of infra-marginal plants. Lump-sum taxes on the monopolist's profits do not affect the monopolist's profit-maximizing rate of output or the commodity price. The proof just presented is a formal elaboration of marginalism. Since the lump-sum tax is a fixed cost to the firm, neither the LMC curve for each plant nor the $\Sigma_h LMC$ curve shift. Marginal revenue equals marginal cost at the same rate of output before and after the tax. The monopolist can only reduce its profits by altering price and output in a misguided effort to shift the tax to customers.

9.4

Labor Union Objectives

It is often assumed that the labor union's objective is to maximize the net benefits of the employed workers. Elementary analysis makes it apparent, however, that this is only one of several plausible union objectives. For example, the union may want to maximize the total wage earnings of its membership. Or it may seek to maximize the number of its members who find work. Another possibility is for the union to seek the highest wages for a select group of union members, such as members with seniority or members with special skills. The achievement of these various objectives requires different wage and employment goals.

The adjacent figure exhibits these possibilities. The labor demand curve facing the union employees is D_L. The curve labeled MR_L is associated with D_L in the same manner as all MR curves are tied to their average revenue curves. If the union wishes to maximize the total wage income of its members, it should expand the employment of members until the MR_L of additional employment is zero. In the figure, $MR_L = 0$ and total wage earnings are therefore maximized when L_2 workers are employed at wage w_2.

If union membership equals L_2, the objectives of maximizing workers' earnings and maximizing employment are consistent.

tent. But suppose union membership is L_3. Employing all L_3 workers requires a wage of w_1, which is inconsistent with the wage w_2 needed to maximize earnings. Moreover, suppose the union wants to maximize the wages of a special group of

Alternative Union Objectives
Maximum employment occurs at w_1 and L_3; maximum income occurs at w_2 and L_2. The maximum level of wages of a particular-sized group occurs at L_1 and w_3.

workers, L_1. This policy requires a wage of w_3, also inconsistent with the other two goals.

Unions, like firms, seek to achieve more than a single objective. But unlike firms, unions have no one-dimensional objective with the basic intuitive appeal to analysts that profit maximization has. Thus despite the prominence of the labor input in U.S. industry and the obvious importance of unions in labor organizations, the analysis and prediction of union behavior is not so well developed as the theory of the firm.

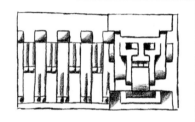

Monopoly Regulation

The last major topic in this chapter is the regulation of monopoly firms, specifically public utilities. Chapter 13 contains a broader discussion of antitrust legislation and regulation.

Figure 9.11 shows the unregulated monopolist's equilibrium and the resulting welfare loss triangle, ABC. Price measures marginal benefit, and marginal cost measures the marginal benefit forgone. Monopoly results in too little output. In monopoly equilibrium, there are units of output not produced for which $P \equiv MB > MC \equiv MB$ forgone. Each marginal unit not produced when $P > MC$ is a maldistribution of resources resulting in a welfare loss. The sum of these welfare losses equals the welfare loss triangle, ABC. How can society discourage such welfare losses?

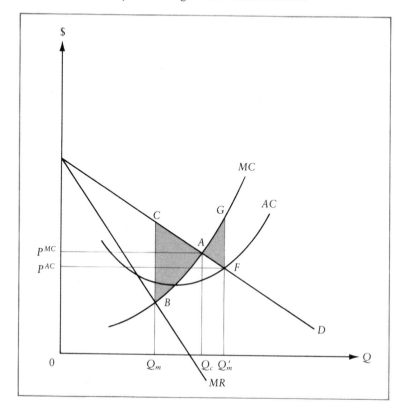

Figure 9.11
Efficiency of Marginal-Cost Pricing

Production of output greater or less than Q_m creates a welfare loss triangle.

Marginal-Cost Pricing versus Average-Cost Pricing

One means of addressing the economic distortions caused by monopoly is for regulatory agencies to institute a form of price regulation called **marginal-cost pricing**. As demonstrated in Figure 9.11, requiring the monopoly to charge the competitive, marginal-cost price P^{MC} (and to serve the resulting market quantity demanded, Q_c) is a way of eliminating the welfare loss triangle. If the monopolist's maximum price is set at P^{MC}, its marginal revenue equals price P^{MC} up to output Q_c. Marginal-cost pricing induces the monopolist to equate MR and MC at point A. The welfare loss disappears because the pricing policy induces the monopoly to select the efficient, competitive rate of output characterized by $P = MC$.

In spite of the gains in welfare promised by marginal-cost pricing, the history of U.S. utility regulation is littered with attempts at **average-cost pricing**. Regulatory authorities often claim that their major responsibility is to allow the monopoly a "fair rate of return," a term suitably close to the economist's definition of zero economic profit. In Figure 9.11, zero economic profit is achieved by charging price P^{AC} equal to average cost $Q'_m F$ and selling Q'_m units of output. Their concentration on a fair rate of return demonstrates that regulatory authorities are usually more concerned with eliminating monopoly profit than with achieving economic efficiency. Note that average-cost pricing creates a welfare loss triangle of its own, area AGF, and therefore moves the monopolist from one inefficient state to another. Apparently, monopoly profits are regarded as being so evil that their elimination takes precedence over other goals.

Five Applications at the end of this chapter explore the regulatory alternatives to marginal-cost pricing and average-cost pricing. Before turning to these examples, however, it is essential to study another dimension of the monopoly regulation problem.

Decreasing-Cost Firms

The fundamental analytic issue of **decreasing-cost firms** can be illustrated by the "bridge problem." Bridge costs are primarily construction, maintenance, and police patrol costs. Construction costs are independent of the number of cars that actually use the bridge—actual volume being independent of planned volume.[3] Even maintenance costs are nearly fixed with respect to car volume, because weather—not car travel—causes the bulk of the damage. Thus the marginal cost of an extra trip across the bridge is virtually zero. The use of bridge services does not use up the bridge. Efficiency calls for a zero (or near-zero) price equal to marginal cost.

The bridge problem is shown graphically in Figure 9.12. Assume that all bridge costs are independent of travel. The average

---

3. In Milwaukee, a bridge over the harbor was planned for 160,000 cars per day, but actual volume is far less. The average cost per car is therefore greater than planned.

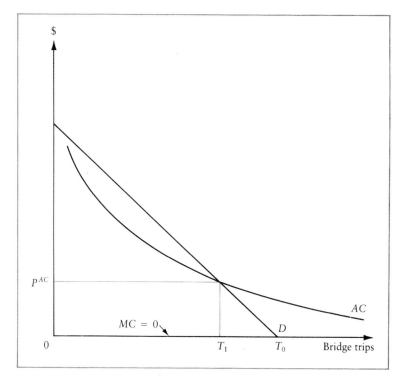

Figure 9.12
Bridge Problem

Marginal-cost pricing achieves efficiency; average-cost pricing merely covers the cost of financing the bridge.

cost is thus the curve AC, and the marginal cost is zero (running along the horizontal axis). Economic efficiency requires a zero price, allowing the number of trips to rise to T_0. However, the bridge must be financed somehow. An average-cost price of P^{AC} is required to finance the bridge, provided perhaps by driver tolls. But tolls reduce bridge travel from T_0 to T_1, which is clearly inefficient: The forgone trips, $T_0 - T_1$, could have been provided at zero marginal cost. Thus the presence of decreasing costs drives a wedge between efficient pricing and the financing necessary for providing the services.

Now let's consider a case closer to the firms that may actually be targets for monopoly regulation. Certain firms differ from the bridge example only by degree. That is, if fixed capital costs dominate the firm's cost structure, costs are largely, but not entirely, independent of output. In such cases, the marginal costs of expanding production are low and below the average costs throughout the range of output demand. As a result, average costs fall. The public utilities—including electricity, sewage, natural gas, and local telephone service—are examples of decreasing-cost firms whose costs are largely fixed with respect to the services produced.

A decreasing-cost firm with positive but low marginal costs is illustrated in Figure 9.13. Efficiency requires the output Q_e and the marginal-cost price $P^{MC} = Q_eA$. But now we have a variant of the

Figure 9.13
Regulation of Decreasing-Cost Firms

The marginal-cost price, P^{MC}, results in negative economic profits for the firm.

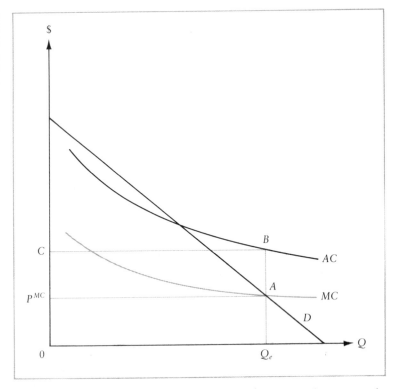

bridge problem. Marginal-cost pricing results in negative economic profits equal to the area $P^{MC}CBA$. Marginal-cost pricing, which is necessary for efficiency, does not allow the firm to recover enough revenue from users to cover all production costs. The firm will require a subsidy equal to the loss $P^{MC}CBA$ in order to break even. But general subsidies may also be inefficient if they are paid by persons who gain no benefit from the service. Thus the regulation of decreasing-cost monopolies by marginal-cost pricing presents special analytical and practical problems. The following Applications address many of these issues.

A P P L I C A T I O N

9.5

Two-Part Pricing: A Method for Regulating Decreasing-Cost Firms

The two-part tariff is one way to remedy the difficulties that arise from marginal-cost pricing in a decreasing-cost monopoly. Customers are charged in two steps, as Figure 9.13 helps to illustrate:

1. Divide the loss $P^{MC}CBA$ equally among all users and charge them all an "entry" price equal to a per-capita share of the loss.

This is a lump-sum payment independent of use; its sole purpose is to recover the firm's loss and allow it to break even.

2. Charge each user the marginal-cost price P^{MC} for each unit purchased.

Such a **two-part pricing** policy has the merit of getting the efficient output Q_e produced (because of the second step) and allowing the firm to cover costs (because of the first step). In Figure 9.13, revenue $0P^{MC}AQ_e$ is received from consumers in the form of user charges, and revenue $P^{MC}CBA$ is received as an "entry fee," or a lump sum that gives the individual the "right to purchase" units at marginal cost. (An example is telephone service.) If the entry fee does not reduce any user's quantity demanded to zero, the two-part pricing scheme is efficient.

However, the two-part tariff has been criticized as inequitable. Users differ in their incomes and

wealth, and the fixed entry fee constitutes a larger percentage of income and wealth for the poor. Thus the entry fee has the same regressive effect as any lump-sum tax or head tax. Also, con-

sumers differ in their use of the service. Even if everyone had equal income and wealth, we would still have an equity problem: Consumers who use more face a lower average fixed charge.

Two-part pricing is the perfect solution for regulating decreasing-cost industries if economic efficiency is the only criterion of societal welfare. But if equity is also important, the two-part tariff needs modification.

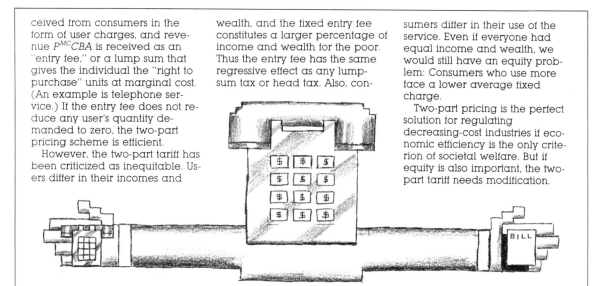

A P P L I C A T I O N

9.6

Optimal Two-Part Tariff Combining Efficiency and Equity

The simple two-part tariff can be modified to increase equity.[*] The adjacent figure is helpful in clarifying this variant of a two-part pricing policy.

We know efficiency is achieved by charging the marginal-cost price, P^{MC}, and selling $\hat{Q}$ units of output. However, the total loss is area $P^{MC}stg$, which must be raised by imposing the same entry fee on all users.

The entry fee is the same to all users regardless of income and is therefore regressive, meaning that the fixed charge as a percentage of income rises as income falls. The term *equity* refers to the lack of a regressive burden on poor users. By this definition, and for a given income distribution, equity worsens when the fixed entry fee is raised and improves when the entry fee is lowered. Of course, even when the entry fee is eliminated, the rich

[*]This section is a graphic interpretation of Martin Feldstein, "Equity and Efficiency in Public Sectors Pricing: The Optimal Two-Part Tariff," *Quarterly Journal of Economics* 86 (1972): 175–187.

and poor still pay the same user fee, which many would argue is also inequitable. (It might be asserted that the poor should pay a lower price than the rich to achieve equity.) As a practical matter, however, the phone company or electric company cannot know individuals' incomes but can know the distribution of income. Hence they could try to balance efficiency and equity by adjusting the size of the fixed entry fee.

The fixed charge may be reduced by raising the price per unit (the user fee). For example, say that price has been set at P^{AC} allowing the firm to produce Q_0 units of output and exactly cover costs. At point h, the lump-sum entry fee vanishes, because the firm's loss disappears. Thus point h (average-cost pricing) is the optimal output from one view-

point: Everybody pays the same user fee, and nobody pays a fixed fee. However, the firm has moved away from the efficient output $\hat{Q}$. This is a good example of the basic tradeoff between efficiency and equity.

The key to establishing an optimal two-part tariff is to balance equity and efficiency considerations. Thus in the figure a movement along the demand curve to, say, point w reduces the firm's output to Q_1, causing an efficiency welfare loss equal to area wcg. However, the higher price also reduces the difference between total cost and the revenues obtained from use-related charges. Thus the total loss falls from $P^{MC}stg$ to the smaller area $slzw$, and the per-capita entry fee is reduced—a clear gain in equity.

Given our society's concern for equity, there is some price between P^{MC} and P^{AC} (some point along the demand curve between g and h) that would balance the gains in equity and the losses in efficiency at the margin. But if equity doesn't matter, P^{MC} is

Continued on page 244

the correct price. If only equity matters, P^{AC} is the correct price. If they both count, the optimal two-part tariff lies between these extremes at a point like w.

This example is especially pertinent to public-sector managers. Given the public's growing concern for equity and justice, managers (and regulators) of public utilities must not only be able to explain the advantages of economic efficiency to a wary public but must also be prepared to blend efficiency with equity considerations.

More Equitable Variant of Two-Part Pricing

Point w represents a compromise between the most efficient price (P^{MC}) and the most equitable price (P^{AC}). It is thus a combination of entry (lump-sum) fees and user (per-unit) fees.

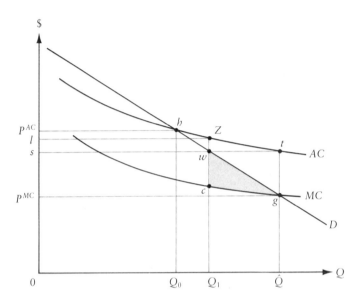

9.7

Block Pricing

Block pricing is a first cousin to the two-part tariff. Its purpose is the same: to allow decreasing-cost firms enough revenue to cover costs (the entry fee) but to use marginal-cost pricing to assure efficiency.

Consider the case of electricity. Under block pricing, the customer is charged a high price for the first block of consumption of electricity and is charged lower prices (perhaps equal to marginal cost) for all additional units of electricity purchased. Block pricing thus results in a lower per-unit price for large-scale users.

Suppose that Bill uses 200 kilowatts of electricity per month and that Steve uses 2,000. Let a block price of $10 be charged for the first 100 kilowatts used, or 10 cents per kilowatt, and 5 cents per kilowatt be charged on all units purchased in excess of 100 kilowatts. Bill's total electric bill is $15, or 7.5 cents per kilowatt. Steve's total bill is $105, or 5.2 cents per kilowatt.

Clearly, block pricing results in lower average prices for those who use more electricity. If use is positively related to income and wealth, block pricing is therefore a regressive pricing policy.

Of course, the government can impose some equity in two-part tariff and block pricing schemes by lowering the entry fee for the poor. However, measurement, reporting, and administrative problems make such equity measures difficult to implement.

Peak-Load Pricing

The regulation of public utilities is beset with another major problem: serving the peak load. Although public utilities are decreasing-cost industries, sudden increases in demand can put such burdens on production that average and marginal costs rise as the firm expands output on a short-term basis. **Peak-load pricing** is a regulatory attempt to handle the problem of serving the peak load.

Let's again use the electric utilities as an example. Electricity-generating capacity typically comes from a variety of plants; for simplicity, we will consider three (and abuse some technical terms in the process):

Primary generators: These are usually large coal-fired or nuclear-powered steam generators. Primary generators spin constantly because they are too costly to stop and start. Thus additional electricity is available from these generators at very low marginal cost. Within the range of the capacity of the primary generators, electric utilities are certainly decreasing-cost firms.

Secondary generators: These are typically smaller steam generators and jet turbines that can be stopped and started on short notice. They act as backup for peak-demand periods. The marginal cost of electricity from secondary generators is higher than from the primary generators. When they must be used, costs rise.

Borrowed electricity: Capacity is borrowed from other regions to meet peak demand and as insurance against brownouts and blackouts. (Borrowing is a form of spreading risks.) This is the most expensive source of electricity, because it must be transmitted over long distances and is often produced from inefficient backup generators at its source.

Given these cost characteristics of electricity-generating capacity, the cost curves of an electric utility appear like those exhibited in Figure 9.14. The off-peak demand is represented by the demand curve $D^0_{off peak}$ and the peak demand by D_{peak}. What pricing strategies are optimal now?

Without attempting a definitive answer, we can at least confront certain issues that follow naturally from the pricing strategies discussed so far. Average-cost pricing is the norm in regulating electric utilities. But because demand fluctuates, the average cost of electricity also changes. Which average-cost price should regulatory authorities select? Consider the average-cost price P^{AC}. When demand is $D^0_{off peak}$, price P^{AC} exceeds the average cost of providing Q_1 units of output by the distance $\overline{ab}$. During those off-peak periods, positive economic profits are earned. But during peak demand, the

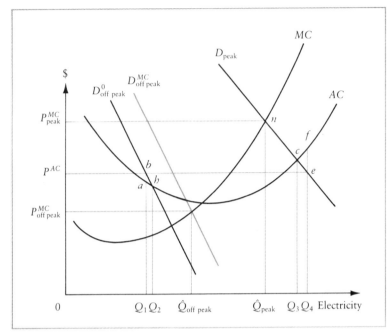

average cost of service rises. If price P^{AC} is kept constant, the utility
will earn negative economic profit at output Q_4, because the average
cost exceeds price P^{AC} by $\overline{ef}$. Thus the strategy of using a single price
for all times and seasons is a way of shooting for an average normal
return over the peak/off-peak cycle. This is the strategy most regulatory authorities adopt.

9.8

Seasonal Rates

Electricity use is higher on average in the summer than in the
winter, primarily because of the
energy requirements of air-
conditioning units. Some regulatory authorities have adopted
seasonal rates to make consumers pay a higher price for the
higher-cost electricity brought on
line during peak summer periods. This policy is certainly a step
in the direction of letting prices
reflect the opportunity cost of
production. However, seasonal
rates cannot reflect marginal-cost
pricing very closely. They merely
recognize the higher average
cost of providing summer electricity due to the greater frequency of summer peaks.

Seasonal rates may be viewed
as a "floating" average-cost
price, which allows prices to rise
in the summer months enough to
cover the higher average costs of
summer electricity. Such prices
respond only to seasonal demand fluctuations but not to
hourly shifts. Thus in Figure 9.14,
winter (off-peak) rates and output of Q_2h and Q_2 and summer
(peak) rates and output of Q_3c
and Q_3 would allow the utility to
earn a fair rate of return year-
round and would cut electricity
use somewhat during the sum-

mer as customers seek substitutes
in the face of higher electricity
prices.

Comparing year-round
average-cost pricing to seasonal
average-cost pricing, seasonal
rates cause a cutback along the
demand curve D_{peak} from e to c
at the peak. Thus peak electric
capacity needs fall from Q_4 to Q_3.
The quantitative difference between Q_4 and Q_3 depends on the
price elasticity of demand for
peak electricity use, which in turn
depends on the availability of
substitutes.

Here we see the essential
weakness of seasonal rates. The
price elasticity of demand for
electricity under seasonal rates

reflects primarily the substitution of electricity for alternative sources of energy. Under seasonal rates, consumers are not given the option of waiting until after the peak to run their electrical appliances. Who can save their dirty dishes and dirty clothes from June to September in order to wash them in the off-peak period? In short, seasonal rates do not present customers with many money-saving incentives to switch electricity use to the off-peak period. (Of course, customers can sell their electrical appliances and switch to natural gas. But then they would have the wrong appliance when costs are low again.) We should expect very little switch in consumption patterns to result from seasonal rates.

This problem brings us to another implication of seasonal rates. For technical reasons, an electric utility must have enough reserve capacity to meet the peak—or it must shut down entirely. The system cannot be run on overload for more than a few seconds without resulting in total loss of power. This technical fact limits the usefulness of seasonal rates. Higher summer rates may reduce the use of air conditioning on average but may have no effect on the "actual peak." A customer may respond to seasonal rates this way: "I used to turn on the air conditioner to maintain a temperature of 80 degrees or less. With summer rates I will shoot for 85 degrees or less." Seasonal rates may simply alter

the average customer's breaking point. Average capacity requirements over the summer will be less under seasonal rates, but the utility must have enough excess capacity to handle the rare 101-degree day when all air conditioner switches go on regardless of summer rates. Thus summer rates are not so effective as marginal-cost pricing in lowering the excess-capacity requirements of the utility.[*]

_____

[*]Sewage systems exhibit the same excess-capacity requirements. Excess capacity must be sufficient to handle the single heaviest rainstorm expected. It takes only one electrical blackout or one basement full of sewage to learn the need for such capacity.

A P P L I C A T I O N

9.9

Time-of-Day Rates

Marginal-cost pricing allows consumers the option of saving money by using electricity during off-peak periods. Thus **time-of-day rates** are a better solution to the peak-load problem than seasonal rates are. For example, time-of-day pricing encourages consumers to wash their dishes in the off-peak evening hours, when electricity is generated at low marginal cost and when the price of electricity is correspondingly low. And consumers may even forgo some daytime air conditioning if they can look forward to some low-cost evening relief.

In Figure 9.14, the correct marginal-cost price at the peak is P_{peak}^{MC}, because $P = MC$ at point n. The peak capacity $\hat{Q}_{peak}$ is smaller than Q_3, the peak capacity needed under seasonal rates. Again, the quantitative difference between $\hat{Q}_{peak}$ and Q_3 depends on the price elasticity of electricity under time-of-day pricing, the major determinants of which are the substitutes available to consumers when price rises at the peak.

Under time-of-day pricing, we

would expect to see considerable shifting of electricity consumption from daytime to nighttime. Thus the difference between $\hat{Q}_{peak}$ (capacity needed under time-of-day pricing) and Q_3 (capacity needed under seasonal rates) is likely to be quite large, because there is a great deal of discretion in home appliance use. Proper marginal-cost pricing reduces the excess capacity needed to serve peak demand. (Environmentalists should favor marginal-cost pricing, because it implies fewer power plants.)

Time-of-day pricing exhibits another useful feature. The demand for off-peak electricity is a

function of, among other things, the prices of substitutes. Under time-of-day rates, peak and off-peak electricity are substitutes. Thus the effect of a marginal-cost price of P^{MC} at the peak tends to increase the off-peak demand to $D_{off peak}^{MC}$. This demand shift is beneficial because it increases electricity use during off-peak hours, when marginal cost is low. Thus under time-of-day rates, the excess capacity required to serve the peak falls to $\hat{Q}_{peak}$, and the off-peak price $P_{off peak}^{MC}$ generates $\hat{Q}_{off peak}$ units of electricity consumed, thereby spreading the capacity more evenly over peak and off-peak periods.

There are clear economic gains in both of these results. Un-

Continued on page 248

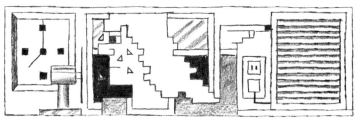

der seasonal rates, peak and off-peak electricity are not substitutes. Thus seasonal rates do not shift the off-peak demand for electricity, and the excess capacity cannot be so evenly spread over the peak/off-peak cycle.

Time-of-day rates come closer to the marginal-cost pricing ideal than seasonal rates do because of the substitutes that time-of-day rates offer consumers. Of course, time-of-day pricing is not perfect marginal-cost pricing either. Ideally, home consumers or plant supervisors should be able to consult a meter that measures the actual marginal cost of use at any given time. They could then compare that marginal cost with the marginal benefit of use. Such perfectly calibrated information systems are not now in place, and time-of-day pricing is an imperfect attempt to convey such information. The technology of marginal-cost metering is now well under development. Meanwhile, most municipalities could benefit by the simple expedient of replacing flat average-cost and seasonal rates with time-of-day pricing.

Key Terms
aggregate 233
average-cost pricing 240
block pricing 244
decreasing-cost firms 240
lump sum 237
marginal cost of plant openings or closings 235
marginal-cost pricing 240
multiplant monopoly 231
natural monopolies 220
peak-load pricing 243
reciprocity agreement 229
seasonal rates 446
technological monopolies 220
tie-in sale 229
time-of-day rates 247
two-part pricing 242
welfare loss triangle 227

Summary

The core concept in the analysis of simple monopoly is the relationship between price and marginal revenue. Specifically, $P > MR$. This is so because, to sell a marginal unit of output, the firm must lower price on all inframarginal units as well.

The model of multiplant monopoly provides a useful means of comparing the allocative efficiency of competition and monopoly. Even more important, multiplant analysis helps organize the decisions of managers whose production takes place in several geographical locations.

Monopoly regulation is typically viewed as a means of creating competition in the regulated industries. Marginal-cost pricing and average-cost pricing are alternative means of social control in several areas of public policy making, including the regulation of decreasing-cost firms, two-part pricing, peak-load pricing, seasonal rates, and time-of-day rates. Marginal-cost pricing captures the efficiency aspects of competitive pricing, even though its implementation often requires special care because of the decreasing-cost nature of the regulated firms. If $P = MC$, then $P < AC$ and firms lose money. Two-part pricing policies are designed to promote efficiency while generating sufficient revenue to avoid losses.

Problems

1. Many textbooks compare competition and monopoly using one plant by equating marginal cost and marginal revenue to depict monopoly equilibrium and by equating average cost and demand to depict competitive equilibrium. Why is this wrong?
2. In this chapter's discussion of the naive case of identical firms, it was shown that the monopolist will operate half as many plants as under competition when there is a linear demand curve. What if the demand curve is convex? Concave?
3. Show that a tax on accounting profits will be passed on to the consumer in a competitive market but absorbed by the monopolist.
4. Suppose that you had 75 percent of a market and that several other firms shared the other 25 percent equally. Under what circumstances would this be a stable equilibrium? (Hint: Think inframarginal.)
5. "Many oil firms are holding oil off the market, waiting for oil prices to go up. This is evidence of monopoly power." Comment

on this statement. (Hint: Look up *evidence* in the dictionary. Would competitive firms hold oil off the market?)

6. Demonstrate graphically and verbally that peak-load pricing of electricity will result in lower total capital requirements and lower average electric bills.

7. The French use electric pumps to pump seawater into mountain reservoirs at night and then drain the reservoirs during the day to produce electricity. It takes more electricity to pump the water up than is generated on the way down. So why do they do this?

8. Should a firm producing a "necessity," such as electricity, water, or automobiles, be restricted to a "fair" rate of return?

9. Say that average cost is a constant at 10 cents per unit and that demand is represented by the numbers in Table 9.3. What price will maximize profit?

10. A telephone company faces a tremendously fluctuating demand for long-distance phone calls. For years, American Telephone & Telegraph responded with peak-load pricing. Recently MCI, Sprint, and other long-distance telephone companies have entered the market with peak-load prices of their own. What do you expect to happen to AT&T's rate structure?

11. Why is mail delivered to the home by a regulated monopoly while food is provided by competing firms that seldom deliver?

12. Suppose that a monopolist faces a demand curve and a total cost curve that trace the data shown in Table 9.4. What is the profit-maximizing price and quantity?

13. Suppose that you have a handicapped child and that the modern-day cuts in government educational expenditures make it necessary for you to send your child to a private school—even though you still pay public school taxes.
   a. What does the theory of monopoly indicate about the efficiency of this outcome?
   b. How is your problem any different from the problem faced by Catholics, Jews, or vegetarians who want to send their children to private schools?

14. Suppose that one person owned all the land in a particular country but wanted to sell some of it.
   a. Draw a demand curve for land and demonstrate the profit-maximizing price and quantity of land to be sold.
   b. Once the sale was completed, would the monopolist have the incentive to sell more? Why or why not? (Hint: See Ronald Coase, "Durability and Monopoly," *Journal of Law and Economics* 15 (1972):143.)

15. Suppose that a labor union had the objective of maximizing the number of jobs. How would its goal differ from the number of jobs that would be provided in a competitive market?

16. a. If a labor union wanted to maximize the income of its workers with 20 years' seniority, how would it react to an offer of increased health and life insurance for all members?
   b. Would the labor union prefer to have additional benefits in the form of higher wages or in the form of fringe benefits? Why?
   c. How would the benefits package affect the number of jobs?

Table 9.3
Price and Quantity Demanded for Good with Average Cost per Unit of 10 cents

Price	Quantity
1.00	1,000
0.90	1,100
0.80	1,200
0.70	1,300
0.60	1,400
0.50	1,500
0.40	1,600
0.30	1,700
0.20	1,800

Table 9.4
Sample Demand and Total Cost Data for a Monopolist

Quantity	Price	Total Cost
0	1.00	20
10	0.95	21
20	0.90	22
30	0.85	23
40	0.80	24
50	0.75	25
60	0.70	28
70	0.65	32
80	0.60	38
90	0.55	50
100	0.50	80

17. Often a tire store will not sell a tire without installing it. Is this a monopolistic practice?

18. The multiplant monopolist's marginal cost curve is the horizontal summation of the individual plants' marginal cost curves. If one plant is taken out of production and replaced by a more efficient plant, how will the aggregate marginal cost curve shift?

19. The multiplant monopolist's marginal revenue curve is independent of the number of plants; the marginal cost curve is not. Explain.

20. Suppose the electric utility that you manage serves 5,000 identical customers and faces a demand curve represented by the equation $Q = 200,000 - 5P$. Devise a three-block pricing system that will maximize profits.

21. Seasonal rates for electricity shift some activities to the low-priced season. Name some of those activities.

22. Suppose that a small chemical firm owns its own oil wells and is therefore vertically integrated with its "feeder" fuel. Why would this arrangement be better for the firm than purchases of oil on the open market?

23. Suppose that a million people purchase IBM Personal Computers. Does IBM then have a monopoly position with respect to those people? If so, how does their owning IBMs differ from the habit of going to the same barber? If not, how does their owning IBMs differ from purchasing natural gas from the gas company?

24. Suppose that you are called in to help the local bus company (a monopoly) increase revenue. You find that some bus routes have inelastic demand and that some others have elastic demand. The city fathers and mothers want the fare to be the same on all bus routes and at all times of the day. What do you say to them?

25. Price exceeds marginal revenue in the simple textbook illustration of monopoly equilibrium.
    a. How would a monopolist who is ignorant of the theory know that fact and react to it?
    b. Is the textbook theory of any value if it applies only to the behavior of people who know the theory and not to those who are ignorant of it? Why or why not?

26. The welfare loss triangle represents a loss to society as a whole caused by the exercise of monopoly power. Is it in the interest of any individual company experiencing part of this loss to attempt to eliminate the loss altogether? Why or why not?

27. a. If you were the only owner of a fleet of oil tankers, how much monopoly power would you have?
    b. Would your power be greater if the oil producers were competitive or, like you, a monopoly?

28. a. The hardware business provides many opportunities to integrate vertically. Name several.
    b. What is the relationship between the theory of fixed costs and that of vertical integration?

29. How can vertical integration be a procompetitive tactic when practiced by monopolists?

30. a. Why does $P > MC$ imply that the marginal benefit of additional production exceeds marginal costs?
    b. Would the consumer ever know this? Why or why not?
    c. If the consumer were a large firm, would it be in a better position than an individual is to break down monopoly power? Why or why not?
31. Suppose that a firm that possesses a monopoly in widgets vertically integrates into the market for gadgets. If the market for gadgets is competitive, can the firm gain monopoly profits by such a move?
32. In 1983, OPEC reduced its price in a price war. The price, at this writing, had fallen to $28 per barrel from $34 per barrel. Is $28 a competitive price?
33. Does the sole producer of wooden barber poles have a monopoly?
34. If we tax the monopolist who holds a patent monopoly, what will happen to inventive activity?
35. Will resale price maintenance lead to an increase in monopoly power if it is imposed on the dealers in order to prop up a dealer's cartel? If so, what would be the incentive for the manufacturer to so prop?
36. Does dealer inventory provide market information? If so, how would dealer inventory be affected by resale price maintenance? How would the manufacturer have to deal with the potential entrant in order to maintain the price? How would the dealer decide whether the potential entrant will generate more business than the old established firms?
37. Suppose that firm A buys some of firm B's output and pays for it with some of its own output. Does this reciprocal arrangement reduce the competitiveness of either firm's industry?
38. Would you expect more charitable giving to the cultural arts by monopolists or competitors?
39. Firms must register their trademarks in order to protect them from use by other firms. Do trademark restrictions constitute a monopolistic practice propped up by the government?
40. Professors generally get promotional copies of textbooks in the mail from book publishers. The publishers are anxious to have their books adopted for classroom use, but much to their chagrin, some professors sell the free books to their local bookseller. Does this impose an extra burden on the student? Is the answer different when the seller is a student who sells the book after using it in a class?
41. Does a publisher who gets exclusive rights to publish a book have a monopoly? How would the power of that monopoly depend on the popularity of the book?
42. Suppose that the marginal cost curve in one plant owned by a multiplant monopolist shifts to the right because of the skill of a new manager. Demonstrate how the output will be shifted in all of the plants that are in operation. What will happen to the number of plants in operation? What will happen to the product price?
43. What will happen to the average costs of production if the demand for a monopolist's product shifts out to the right?

Suggested Readings

Baumol, William J. *Economic Theory and Operations Analysis.* 4th ed. Englewood Cliffs, N.J.: Prentice-Hall, 1977.

Hicks, J. R. "The Theory of Monopoly." *Econometrica* 3 (1935): 1–20.

Lerner, Abba P. "The Concept of Monopoly and the Measurement of Monopoly Power." *Review of Economic Studies* 1 (1934): 157–175.

Machlup, F. "Monopoly and Competition: A Classification of Market Position." *American Economic Review* 27 (1937): 445–451.

Naylor, Thomas H., and Vernon, John M. *Microeconomics and Decision Models of the Firm.* New York: Harcourt, Brace and World, 1969.

Patinkin, Don. "Multiple-Plant Firms, Cartels, and Imperfect Competition." *Quarterly Journal of Economics,* 1947, pp. 173–205.

Sherman, Roger. *The Economics of Industry.* Boston: Little, Brown, 1974.

Stigler, George. *The Theory of Price.* 3rd ed. New York: Macmillan, 1966, chap. 13.

Vickrey, William S. *Microstatics.* New York: Harcourt, Brace and World, 1964, chaps. 3, 5, 7.

10

IMPERFECT COMPETI-TION

The magnitude of the economic hardships endured during the depression years of the 1930s caused the free world's economic intelligentsia to take stock of itself. The cause for alarm was the apparent unsuitability of the profession's main engine of analysis—the competitive model. The contradictions between the predictions of the competitive model and the observed facts during the 1930s were set out in bold relief. One such contradiction pertained to the macro economy. The competitive model predicted that labor (or any other) market surpluses would be self-eliminating in the long run through wage and price adjustments. But the Great Depression made it clear that unemployment was not so easily disposed of. This disparity between theory and fact motivated Britain's Lord John Maynard Keynes to formulate an alternate theory of the macro economy, a theory capable of explaining the root causes of unemployment and of providing relevant policy options.[1] Keynes's reformulation took on such far-reaching intellectual, theoretical, philosophical, and political dimensions that it has justifiably been called the "Keynesian revolution." The impact on world affairs of Keynes's ideas about macroeconomic theory and countercyclical economic policy can scarcely be overstated.

At the same time the seeds of the Keynesian revolution were germinating, other troubled winds were blowing over economic theory. In brief, the competitive and monopoly models could not explain some behavior, such as product differentiation, advertising strategy, price wars, price leadership, tacit and open collusion, stra-

1. The theory was first set down in John Maynard Keynes, *The General Theory of Employment, Interest, and Money* (New York: Harcourt, Brace and World, 1964).

tegic behavior among competitors, and excess capacity of firms. Such behavior could readily be observed in the economy. Additional theory was clearly required to improve understanding of the workings of the market.

Thus was born the study of **imperfect competition,** a catchall term comprising all the models that purport to analyze the middle ground between the two polar models of competition (many sellers) and monopoly (one seller). Models of imperfect competition take into account the fact that nearly every firm has some monopoly power over its product. The pure monopoly model was already well in place by the 1930s, and so it was a natural transition to adapt certain aspects of the model of monopoly behavior whenever firms' demand curves displayed the least bit of price elasticity.

Among other things, these new models explained why a firm may exhibit excess capacity, something the competitive model could not do. Remember that perfect competition requires all entrepreneurs to adopt the optimum scale of plant and thereby produce up to capacity in the long run. Joan Robinson, a giant figure in the analysis of imperfectly competitive markets, reminisced about the felt need for new models during the depression years:

> Here we were, in 1930, in a deep slump, and this is what we were being asked to believe. Under perfect competition, any plant that was working at all must be working up to capacity. . . . [But] in the world around us, more or less all plants were working part time.[2]

In this climate, the search for more compelling explanations of observed market behavior was launched. The initial burst of enthusiasm about the potential usefulness of models of imperfect competition was tempered by the fact that many of the methods proved to be intractable from both a methodological and empirical point of view. As we are soon to see, the links from demand and costs to price and output are much less precise here than we have come to expect in the competitive and monopoly models. Thus if we expect too much from the models of imperfect competition, we are sure to be disappointed. Even so, the intellectual world of imperfect competition is quite rich and useful in many areas where the competitive model simply does not apply. That there is much room for improvement is beyond dispute. Still, a study of competing firms under less than perfectly competitive conditions is well worth the effort.

Models of imperfect competition break down into two groups: (1) oligopoly, in which the number of firms is small and the emphasis is on the interdependence of rivals' decisions, and (2) monopo-

---

2. Joan Robinson, *The Economics of Imperfect Competition,* 2nd ed. (New York: St. Martin's Press, 1969), p. vi.

listic competition, in which the number of firms is quite large and the emphasis is on product differentiation. In addition to these topics, this chapter covers the cartel.

Cartels

It is natural to bridge the gap between the discussions of pure monopoly and imperfect competition with cartel analysis. A **cartel** is a group of potentially competitive firms that coordinate their output and pricing decisions in order to reduce industry output below competitive levels, raise prices and profits, and act insofar as possible like a multiplant monopolist.

Collusion, the cooperation among cartel members to fix prices at an artificially high level, is subject to prosecution in the United States under the Sherman Antitrust Act of 1890. Paradoxically, the U.S. government sponsors some forms of cartelization, as when agricultural prices are boosted above competitive levels by crop-restriction programs. But cartels do not have the legal or moral stigma in many foreign countries that they have in the United States. One of these international cartels—the Organization of Petroleum Exporting Countries—has been unique in its influence in international politics and economics.

Major economic difficulties arise in the organization and perpetuation of a cartel. The cartel's adjustment to long-run profit-maximizing equilibrium is the same as the multiplant monopolist's except that the cartel does not have single ownership of all plants. As with multiplant monopoly, cartel profit maximization—compared to competitive equilibrium—requires that (1) each producing firm be given an output quota smaller than its competitive rate of output and (2) some firms be closed down.

Just as the multiplant monopolist operates fewer than the competitive number of plants, so does the cartel aim to reduce output by closing down the highest-cost firms. But are these entrepreneurs willing to exit? Exiting firms must be paid a suitable exit fee out of the expected cartel profits. The remaining firms may be reluctant to make these payments out of fear that the cartel will break down and eliminate their profits. The choice of which firms to close and the reluctance to pay for their exit creates organizational difficulties for the cartel right from the beginning.

If the cartel is successfully organized, the next obstacle is its inherent instability. Consider Figure 10.1, which displays the equilibrium of the cartel (panel b) and the cost curves of one participant firm (panel a). The cartel's optimal output is Q_m; the inframarginal firm that produced q_c under competitive equilibrium is given a quota of q_m by the cartel. (The individual firm must produce where cartel $MR = LMC$ of the firm at point A.)

Each firm's profits are higher under the cartel quota than under competitive conditions; otherwise the firm would not join the cartel.

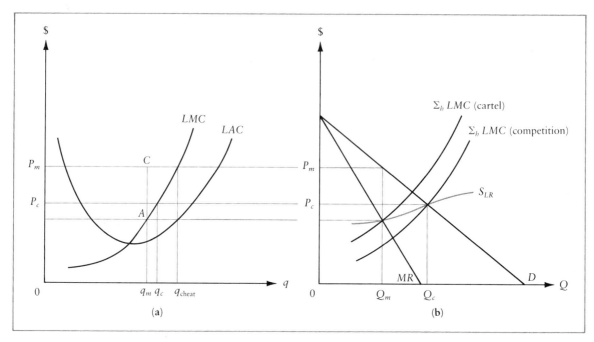

Figure 10.1
Inherent Instability of Cartels

(a) At q_m, the cartel price at C is greater than the LMC at A. Because P_m is greater than the LMC, the firm has an incentive to cheat. **(b)** The competitive price, P_c, is established where $\Sigma_h LMC$ (*competition*) crosses D and S_{LR} at Q_c. Cartel price is established with less plant capacity where $\Sigma_h LMC$ (*cartel*), MR and S_{LR} intersect at Q_m, forcing price above competitive levels.

So why is the cartel inherently unstable? Because at q_m the cartel price P_m exceeds long-run marginal cost by the distance $\overline{AC}$. The seller, happy to have the cartel profits, can increase profits even more by expanding output to q_{cheat}, where cartel price equals long-run marginal cost. The seller has a profit incentive to exceed the cartel output quota, particularly if such cheating cannot be detected and punished. But what is sauce for the goose is sauce for the gander. If enough members exceed production quotas in response to these latent profit impulses, the cartel will break down. Cheating is more likely the greater the number of sellers, the smaller the output of each firm compared to total cartel output, the more heterogeneous the product, and the easier it is to distribute the produce under alternative brand names.

The greater the number of sellers, the less significant the effect of one firm's cheating on market price, because the firm views itself as a price taker. Cheating is also more difficult to detect when each firm represents a small portion of the total market. Thus small firms are more likely to cheat and less likely to get caught.

When products are heterogeneous, quality can be improved without incorporating the increased cost into the price. When price exceeds long-run marginal cost, a firm has an incentive to increase output, even if it means shaving the price a bit to attract customers. A similar response is to raise the quality a bit or to improve guarantees without raising the price. Both price reductions and quality improvements lead to increased sales and higher profits. To solve these problems, cartels often require complex pricing schemes and market-sharing agreements. But when the products of cartel members are marketed under a variety of brand names, an immense problem of detection is created; it is very difficult to know which producers are cheating.

So if you ever work for the Justice Department's Antitrust Division and your office has limited funds for the investigation and prosecution of price-fixing cases, note carefully these forces of instability in cartels lest you prosecute cartels that will collapse of their own weight before your case is closed.

Aside from instability and cheating, another cartel problem is the establishment of the right price and quantity. This problem is particularly troublesome in the extractive industries, where different firms—or countries—have vastly different reserves and hence different time horizons. The longer the firm's time horizon, the greater the threat that the cartel monopoly price will induce technical change or the discovery of new sources of output. Hence members with longer time horizons will perceive greater elasticity of demand and argue for a lower price than the members with shorter time horizons. This fact explains in part why Saudi Arabia, with immense known oil reserves and a long time horizon, usually argues for lower OPEC price increases than the other member countries.

This discussion of cartels would not be complete without mention of one strategy available to firms that must bargain with cartels. Firms and countries that purchase goods from cartels can prey on their inherent instability by adopting **secret bidding.** Periodically, the purchaser can accept bids from individual cartel members that are sealed to prevent producers from finding out the other bids. Nor should the winning bid be announced after the decision. This practice gives each cartel member an extra incentive to cheat. As distrust grows, the cartel is pushed closer to breakdown.

A P P L I C A T I O N

10.1

Basing-Point Pricing

An important problem in cartel pricing arises when rival producers are geographically separated. Then the prices charged to customers contain two components: the mill price and the transportation costs. One common pricing system is **FOB pricing** (the initials stand for "free on board"), under which all prices quoted are mill prices. The customer pays the transportation costs to the point of delivery.

Holding cost and technology constant for all firms, each customer has an incentive to buy from the closest producer in order to keep transportation costs low. In other words, strict adherence to FOB pricing prevents firms from selling in their rivals' market areas. Indeed, the only way a firm can expand its market area is to engage in price-cutting initiatives. Under these conditions price wars can break out at any moment—the very

thing that threatens the stability of the cartel.

One way to eliminate such geographical price competition is the use of **basing-point pricing.** Under this system, all producers quote the same prices to a given customer, regardless of the distance between the producer and the consumer. The figure illustrates this system. The horizontal axis measures geographical distance, and the vertical axis measures the price of output. Point X is the basing

Continued on page 258

point; all firms, regardless of location, quote delivered prices as if the goods were shipped from point X.

Suppose that the mill price is the same for goods produced at X and Y: $\overline{XA} = \overline{YB}$ = mill price. The transportation costs rise with distance, along line $\overline{AF}$ from point A and along $\overline{BE}$ from point B. Under FOB pricing, the total price charged to a customer at point Z—including the mill price and transportation costs—would depend on the origin of the output. If goods are shipped from X to Z, the price would be $\overline{ZF}$; but if they are shipped from Y, the price would be only $\overline{ZE}$. Under basing-point pricing, the firm at Y charges the price $P_{cartel} = \overline{ZF}$ by including a transportation charge from X (the base point) instead of from the actual origin point, Y. The price gap $\overline{EF}$ is called "phantom freight," because it is based on a travel distance from X even though goods actually traveled only from Y. Thus the system forces the customer at Z to buy from sellers at either X or Y at the same price.

Competition among cartel members may now proceed in more familiar and comfortable forms, with emphasis on such nonprice elements as product quality, ser-

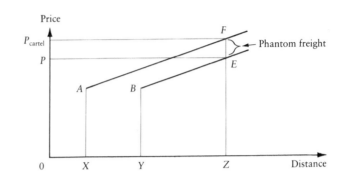

Eliminating Geographical Price Competition

Locational advantages among cartel members can be eliminated by calculating transportation costs for all firms from a base point. Thus customers are charged "phantom freight" rates.

vice agreements and warranties, and promptness of delivery. Price wars are averted, and cartel profit maximization can continue in an atmosphere of price stability.

The most celebrated case of phantom freight occurred in the U.S. steel industry when Pittsburgh was selected as the base point. Thus arose the "Pittsburgh-plus"

pricing system of the early twentieth century; all steel prices included a transportation charge from Pittsburgh regardless of actual shipping origin.

Basing-point pricing is such an obvious form of collusion that it has been illegal in the United States for over 30 years. The effects of such pricing seem quite clear: It requires collusion and tends to achieve the higher prices and cartel profits for which it was devised.[*]

[*]For a comprehensive discussion of basing-point pricing, refer to F. M. Scherer, *Industrial Market Structure and Economic Performance*, 2nd ed. (Chicago: Rand McNally, 1980), pp. 325–334.

10.2

Resale Price Maintenance: Evidence of Cartels?

Resale price maintenance is a device a manufacturer uses to place a floor under the price that its retailers (which may or may not be otherwise independent) may charge at the point of sale. It is now illegal in most cases on the grounds that it restrains price competition among dealers—or worse, that it is a device used to aid a collusive dealer cartel.

But there is one nagging argument in defense of resale price maintenance—the "point-of-sale service" defense. In a nutshell, this defense concerns the incentive that retailers have to provide information—expert explanation

or showroom display and demonstration—when that information can be gained from one dealer but the product can be purchased from a second dealer with no payment to the dealer that provided the information.

Providing information about a product is expensive; the second dealer can provide the product (without information) at lower

cost than the first dealer and hence charge a lower price to attract customers away from the first dealer. In this way, the second dealer acts as a "free rider" (a concept discussed in more detail and in many contexts in Chapter 15). The first dealer thus has an incentive to cut expenses by cutting the information services, which bring no return. In this circumstance, the information is a collective good, and each dealer has an incentive to provide too little of it. So the product is provided with too little information at a dealer price that is too low. For any price set at the factory gate, the manufacturer wants the dealers to maximize sales. But this sort of competition among dealers produces less-than-maximum sales.

Resale price maintenance provides a remedy to the free-rider problem. Dealers that under-provide information cannot offer a price below that offered by dealers that provide the efficient level of information.

This defense of resale price maintenance is quite plausible. But as economists and lawyers point out, there are other institutional arrangements designed to

prevent free riding.* The simplest is for the dealer to charge for presale services or for the manufacturer to provide information

*See Robert H. Bork, "The Rule of Reason and the Per Se Concept: Price Fixing and Market Division," *Yale Law Journal* 75 (1966): 373; Ward S. Bowman, "The Prerequisites and Effects of Resale Price Maintenance," *University of Chicago Law Review* 22 (1966): 825; Richard A. Posner, *Antitrust Law: An Economic Perspective* (Chicago: University of Chicago Press, 1976), especially pp. 67–68; and Lester G. Telser, "Why Should Manufacturers Want Fair Trade?" *Journal of Law and Economics* 3 (1962): 86.

through advertising. Furthermore, not all dealers' services are so completely substitutable that free riding is feasible.

This issue is unresolved at the theoretical level. As a matter of law, however, the beneficent incentives of the competitive market to keep consumer prices down are apparently considered a stronger force than whatever inefficiencies are caused by free riding. The point-of-sale service defense has been roundly rejected, and resale price maintenance has been used as evidence of a dealer cartel.

Models of Noncollusive Oligopoly Pricing

Oligopoly is an industry structure made up of more than one firm but of few enough so that the decisions of any one influence market price. For example, the U.S. automobile-manufacturing and copper-producing industries are typical oligopolistic industries. Gone are the competitive, price-taking firms without any control over industry price. Gone also are the pure monopolists that set price and output without rivals to breathe down their necks. In their places are oligopolistic firms whose decisions must take into account the expected behavior of rival firms. "If I raise my price, how will my competitors respond?" "If I raise my output, how will my competitors respond?" The answers to such questions are the basis on which firms make decisions. Thus the core of oligopoly analysis is the interdependence among firms.

To be more concrete, each firm in an oligopoly must base its price and output decisions on its rivals' expected reactions to such decisions. In terms of output, each firm must place a value on the following term:

$$\frac{\Delta q_i}{\Delta q_j} \tag{10.1}$$

This term, the **conjectural variation in output,** measures the expected change in output of the ith firm in response to an output change of the jth firm. Its value represents the conjecture that the jth firm makes about how its own output decisions will be met by its rivals, the ith firms. If $\Delta q_i / \Delta q_j = 0$, the jth firm believes that its rivals' rates of output are fixed. The **conjectural variation in price** is the price analogue of the conjectural variation in output:

$$\frac{\Delta p_i}{\Delta p_j} \tag{10.2}$$

Assumptions about these conjectural variations have played a critical role in the development of oligopoly models.

Oligopoly models can be divided into two broad groups: (1) models that assume firms act independently and (2) models that take into account some degree of collusion. This section discusses noncollusive oligopoly behavior; models of tacit collusion are covered later in the chapter.

Early Oligopoly Models

Oligopoly analysis has a checkered past. The first model was published in 1838 by a French mathematical economist, Augustin Cournot. (The fact that no one paid it the least attention for 45 years may have been due to his strict mathematical exposition.) In 1897, Professor F. Y. Edgeworth published an alternative oligopoly model, which took issue with Cournot's. But both models employ curious assumptions and, not surprisingly, generate curious results.

A comprehensive exposition of these models is beyond the scope of this book, but a brief summary of the models' assumptions and results will help to put the modern theories in better perspective.[3]

COURNOT'S MODEL   Cournot assumed that oligopoly behavior was noncollusive: Each firm believed it could change its output decisions without causing its rivals to respond by changing their rates of output. Formally, this idea is the equivalent of letting the conjectural variation in output equal zero for all firms. Each firm acts as if all rivals' output rates are fixed. Cournot concluded that, in equilibrium, oligopolists would jointly produce a rate of output greater than would a monopolist serving the same market and would earn less than the full monopoly profit.

EDGEWORTH'S MODEL   Professor Edgeworth took issue with Cournot by asserting that the firm's decisions are based on price, not quantity of sales. In other words, Edgeworth assumed that each firm's conjectural variation in price equals zero; firms set their prices with the conviction that rivals' prices remain fixed. Edgeworth concluded that such a noncollusive oligopoly can never reach equilibrium. Prices fall and rise through continuing rounds of price wars and eventual upward readjustments. Profits likewise oscillate.

The Cournot and Edgeworth models share a flaw: Both assume that firms never learn from experience and never adjust their behavior to accommodate new information. In the Cournot model, all firms adjust output as they adjust to equilibrium. Nevertheless, each

---

3. For a full treatment of the Cournot and Edgeworth models, along with modern applications and extensions, see Steven T. Call and William L. Holahan, *Microeconomics*, 2nd ed. (Belmont, Calif.: Wadsworth, 1983), chap. 10.

firm continues to regard rivals' output as fixed. In the Edgeworth model, the continuous price oscillations should alert firms that rivals' prices aren't fixed. But firms continue to base their decisions on the constantly violated assumption that rival prices are rigid. In short, both models assume that entrepreneurs are dumber than stumps.

This was the state of oligopoly analysis at the turn of the century. The naivete of Cournot's and Edgeworth's assumptions brings their results into question. Even so, an important lesson emerges from these rudimentary oligopoly models: Oligopoly firms are better off colluding than competing. Independent action causes loss of profit.

Chamberlin's Model

Professor Edward Chamberlin's oligopoly model is a criticism of both the Cournot and Edgeworth solutions. Chamberlin insisted that the assumption of zero conjectural variation made by Cournot and Edgeworth is a denial that a firm considers its total influence on price and output, both direct and indirect. In evaluating the assumption of zero conjectural variation, Chamberlin remarked, "When a move by one seller evidently forces the other to make a counter move, he is very stupidly refusing to look further than his nose if he proceeds on the assumption that it will not."[4] Zero conjectural variation forces oligopolists to compete as if their actions are independent—an assumption that ignores the essential oligopoly characteristic of interdependence.

So Chamberlin assumed that firms consider the total consequences of their pricing and output policies. When they do so, it is clear that Cournot- and Edgeworth-type responses are self-defeating. Thus the profit-maximizing solutions implied by the monopoly equilibrium can be achieved by firms without collusion, provided the owners are minimally intelligent and can see the danger of ignoring the effect of their actions on their competitors. Under these conditions, no rival will undertake price and quantity adjustments that lead away from the monopoly ideal. Actions are not collusive, yet the monopoly results are obtained. Here the partial loss of monopoly profits implied by the Cournot model and the complete instability of the Edgeworth solution are replaced by an uncoordinated monopoly result.

Chamberlin's criticism of the Cournot and Edgeworth models is no doubt a step in the right direction: Firms will find a way to avoid the loss of profits implied by Cournot and Edgeworth. However, Chamberlin does not give us a clue as to how the firms interact in order to maximize the profits of all. Let's try to fill that gap.

4. Edward H. Chamberlin, *The Theory of Monopolistic Competition* (1933; reprint, Cambridge, Mass.: Harvard University Press, 1962), p. 46.

Dominant-Firm Price Leadership

A major component of any communications network among competing oligopolistic firms is the **price leader**. Price leadership takes two general forms. First, in the dominant-firm structure, one firm clearly dominates the market and a collection of price-taking firms operates beneath the umbrella of the major firm. Second, in barometric price leadership, the oligopolistic industry "selects" a firm to act as the initiator of price changes, and other firms follow the leader. A barometric price leader may or may not hold a dominant position in the industry.

Dominant-firm price leadership, also called the **leader-follower model**, works like this: The dominant firm sets the industry price; the price-taking, competitive firms sell their desired outputs at that price. The dominant firm serves the market that remains after the competitors have adjusted their sales to the profit-maximizing levels. In Figure 10.2a, the demand curve labeled D is the aggregate demand for the industry's output. The curve labeled $S = \Sigma_h MC$ is the horizontal sum of the competitive firms' marginal cost curves. Thus $S = \Sigma_h MC$ is the industry supply curve of the price-taking competitors. The dominant firm's demand curve (D_d), shown in panel b, is derived by subtracting the quantities supplied by the competitive firms from the industry demand curve. Thus the de-

Figure 10.2
Leader-Follower Model

(a) $S = \Sigma_h MC$ is the supply curve of the followers. **(b)** The leader faces demand equal to the difference between total demand and the supply of the followers. The leader sets output at B, where marginal cost and marginal revenue are equal, and sets price at P_2, which the followers take as a parameter.

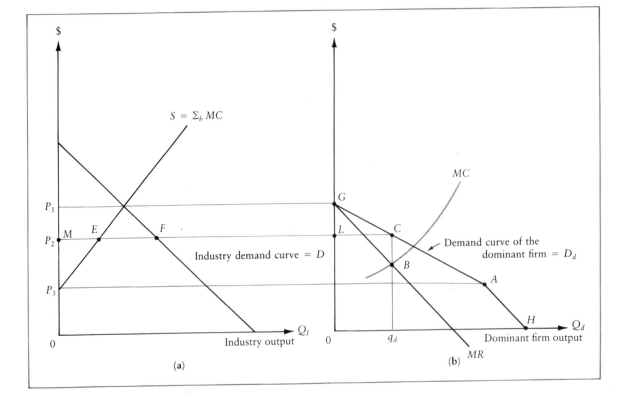

(a)   (b)

mand curve faced by the dominant firm is $\overline{GAH}$. At price P_1 the competitive firms serve the entire market, and at price P_3 the dominant firm serves the entire market. Thus between prices P_1 and P_3 the dominant firm's demand curve, D_d, is this horizontal subtraction:

$$D_d = D - \Sigma_h MC \qquad (10.3)$$

For prices below P_3, the dominant firm faces the industry demand curve segment $\overline{AH}$, because follower firms do not produce below price P_3.

The marginal revenue curve, MR, is related to the demand curve segment $\overline{P_1A}$ of the dominant firm. The gray curve labeled MC is the marginal cost curve of the dominant firm. The dominant firm maximizes profit by equating MR and MC at point B and thus selects price P_2. At price P_2 the dominant firm sells $\overline{0q_d} = \overline{LC}$ units of output. Competing firms sell $\overline{P_2E}$ units of output. Changes in the industry demand curve, the competitive supply curve, or the dominant firm's marginal cost curve will cause the price and quantity to change.

Many industries fit this model, including the drug and grocery markets, where one major chain often competes with numerous small neighborhood stores. Application 10.3 uses the model to study the OPEC cartel and the advisability of imposing well-head taxes on domestic oil production.

10.3

Taxes on Old Oil and the OPEC Cartel

The oil industry presents us with two facts: (1) OPEC is a principal force in determining oil price and output in the United States, and (2) domestic U.S. petroleum producers are earning vast economic profits resulting in part from the high price of petroleum products. Many people have favored limiting petroleum producers to a normal return on investment by taxing away these monopoly profits and distributing them to consumers. Here we will see that taxing U.S. oil companies, far from benefiting U.S. consumers, actually strengthens the OPEC cartel's position in world energy markets at the expense of domestic producers and consumers.

Let's use the dominant-firm (leader-follower) model to analyze the pricing and output deci-

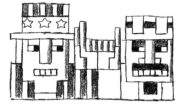

sions of the OPEC monopoly cartel (the leader) and non-OPEC producers (the followers). This is a plausible model, because it considers the OPEC cartel the price-setting leader in the industry and the domestic oil producers as price takers at the price set by the cartel. Cartels

can survive competition if they have monopoly power over the lowest-cost production processes. Then only higher-cost competitors, whose entry cannot entirely wipe out the cartel's profits, can enter. This mechanism works in the oil industry because OPEC oil is produced at much lower cost than domestic U.S. oil is.

The demand curve labeled D_{US} in Figure A represents the U.S. demand for oil, and the curve labeled S_{US} is the aggregate supply of U.S. oil producers. Price P_2 is the lowest price that generates domestic production. The supply curve S_{US} is anchored at this minimum price.

The curve D_0 is the demand faced by the leader, OPEC, and is derived as a residual of the total U.S. demand and the supply

Continued on page 264

Figure A
Dominant-Firm Model of OPEC/U.S. Petroleum Producers

In the left-hand panel, D_{US} is the U.S. demand for oil and S_{US} is the supply provided by U.S. oil producers. OPEC's demand curve, D_0, is the difference between D_{US} and S_{US}. MR_0 is OPEC's marginal revenue curve, derived in conventional fashion from the demand curve D_0.

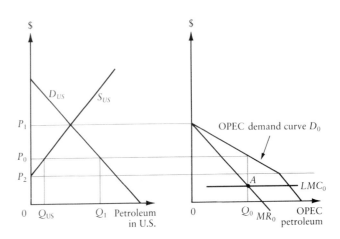

of the followers (the U.S. domestic producers): $D_0 = D_{US} - S_{US}$. Thus OPEC's demand curve extends between price P_1, at which all U.S. demand is satisfied by U.S. suppliers, and the lower price P_2, at which U.S. supply vanishes and the entire U.S. demand is met by OPEC producers.

OPEC's marginal revenue, MR_0, is derived from the demand curve D_0. The OPEC marginal cost, LMC_0, is drawn below P_2, the minimum price for U.S. output, to reflect the lower costs of OPEC oil compared to U.S. oil. For exposition, LMC_0 is drawn horizontally, although a positive slope produces the same qualitative results.

OPEC maximizes total cartel profit by producing where $MR_0 = LMC_0$ (at A) and by setting the OPEC price at P_0. At price P_0, OPEC produces Q_0 units for the United States; the additional demand, $Q_1 - Q_0$, is produced by domestic sellers. Neither OPEC nor domestic U.S. suppliers can set price without regard to market conditions. Each group is confronted by the consequences of the other's decisions.

Let's examine domestic oil supply more closely. Oil suppliers face differing costs because of differing well depths, geological structures, distances from distribution facilities, and so forth. For any given price for the final product, there will be marginal wells that just break even, inframarginal wells that earn economic rent, and extramarginal wells that would lose money if brought into production. As firms enter the market, supply increases and price falls. Equilibrium is established when price

is equal to the minimum LAC of the marginal wells and when no more inframarginal wells are left. The marginal wells break even, but the inframarginal wells gain rents that cannot be competed away, because there are no more inframarginal wells left that can enter and bring the price down further. It is these inframarginal rents that the well-head tax is designed to reduce.

The well-head tax is an effort to extract U.S. domestic producers' inframarginal profits. As we saw in Chapter 9, a lump-sum tax does not affect monopoly pricing and production. However, as a practical matter we lack good information on the oil-extraction costs of different firms, information we would need to institute a perfectly calibrated well-head tax suitable to extract the rent from each producer.

As a compromise, the well-head tax could be levied on "old" oil, meaning oil discovered prior to a given year. Such a "hands-on," practical tax could be used to hold the net reward to, say, $6 per barrel of old oil. The idea behind taxing "old" oil is the presumption that it is low-cost oil from which rents are generated as oil prices rise. But what impact will such a tax have on the petroleum market and, in particular, on the behavior of the

OPEC cartel and its relatively competitive domestic rivals in the United States?

Figure B illustrates the effect of the old-oil well-head tax on the cost curves and on supply. The left-hand panel contains the cost curves of firm 1, which produces old oil; the center panel shows the cost curves of firm 2, which produces new oil; and the right-hand panel shows the industry supply curves, which are, as usual, horizontal summations of producers' marginal cost curves.

When no taxes are levied, the industry long-run supply curve is the sum of all producers' long-run marginal cost curves, labeled $\Sigma_h LMC(all\ oil)$ in the right-hand panel. Now suppose that firm 1 is taxed so that the net return on old oil cannot rise above $6 per barrel. Such a firm expands output when prices rise to $6.

There is never an incentive to raise the rate of production above q_1, however, because the returns from doing so will be eliminated by the tax. Thus at prices above $6 per barrel, the slope of the industry supply curve merely reflects the horizontal sum of the marginal cost curves of firms producing new, untaxed oil. This curve, labeled $\Sigma_h LMC(tax)$, rises at the same rate as the $\Sigma_h LMC(new\ oil)$ curve, which is the horizontal sum of the mar-

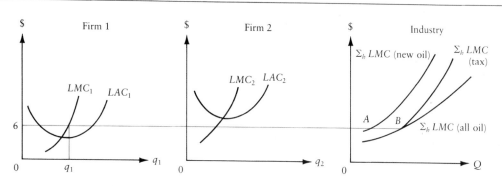

Figure B
Effect of Well-Head Taxes on Industry Supply

Firm 1 (left-hand panel) produces "old" oil. Firm 2 (center panel) produces "new" oil. The industry supply curve (right-hand panel) includes all oil suppliers. Producers of old oil have no incentive to produce more output than q_1, because the tax holds the net return to $6. The quantity AB in the right-hand panel is the fixed sum of all old oil that firms will produce. The total supply is $\Sigma_h LMC(tax)$.

ginal cost curves of owners producing new oil. The horizontal distance $(\overline{AB})$ between $\Sigma_h LMC(new\ oil)$ and $\Sigma_h LMC(tax)$ at prices above $6 reflects the constant output of the taxed firms, such as q_1 for firm 1.

To summarize, the well-head tax on old oil shifts the U.S. supply curve to the left, from $\Sigma_h LMC(all\ oil)$ to $\Sigma_h LMC(tax)$.

Now consider Figure C. It looks imposing but is actually quite easy to interpret. The black lines are the cost and revenue curves from Figure A. OPEC sets the price P_0, and the United States imports the amount Q_0 from OPEC in order to satisfy the total quantity demanded at price P_0.

What is the effect of the tax on the old oil of U.S. domestic producers? We have seen that the tax causes the supply curve S_{US} to rotate to the left, to S'_{US}. If the S_{US} curve pivots around P_2, the OPEC demand curve D_0 pivots around point B to D'_0 and becomes relatively more inelastic. And because the demand curves D_0 and D'_0 intersect at B, the marginal revenues of each must pass through point C—half the distance of $\overline{EB}$. Also, because MR_0 begins at P_1 and MR'_0 begins at the higher price, P_3, the marginal revenue curves must cross at C.

As a result of the domestic price control on oil, the OPEC cartel will set marginal cost equal to its new marginal revenue curve, MR'_0. This adjustment requires a reduction in cartel output from Q_0 to Q'_0 and allows an increase in the world oil price from P_0 to P'_0. Thus U.S. well-head taxes allow the OPEC cartel to exaggerate the very output reductions and price increases that constituted the incentive to organize the cartel in the beginning. The well-head tax on U.S. producers actually solidifies the cartel and strengthens its economic and political power.

The well-head tax does extract a portion of the profit from the inframarginal firms as they reduce their output in response to the tax. However, these profits are not eliminated; rather, they are exported to the monopoly OPEC producers.

One may not approve of the distribution of income inherent in the free-market pricing of oil, but to attempt income redistribution through well-head taxes in a market dominated by foreign governments can only redistribute income across national borders. Well-head taxes replace domestic millionaires with foreign millionaires—and raise prices for U.S. consumers.

Figure C
Industry Supply and Demand for Oil

The impact of the tax is a leftward shift of domestic supply, which causes a rightward shift of demand for OPEC oil.

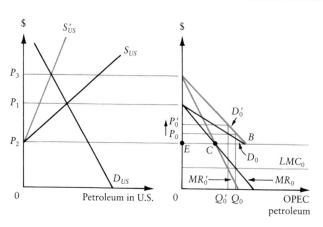

10.4

Inventory Profits versus Created Shortages

The oil crises of the 1970s allowed consumers to take note of two simultaneous events: shortages in the supplies of oil products and rising profits among U.S. oil companies. Many observers believe that oil companies created the shortages in order to jack up profits. Here we encounter an example in which the oil companies' profits rise when they expand domestic production.

Consider the adjacent figure, which exhibits the cost curves of a marginal oil producer earning a normal return at price P_1 by producing Q_1 units of output. Suppose the OPEC cartel votes to increase world prices to P_2. The domestic firm, facing price P_2, will increase output to Q_2, which increases the firm's profit from zero to AP_2BC. This profit is an **inventory profit**; it arises because the value of the firm's inventories rises through forces external to the firm's decisions. It is similar to the capital gain that homeowners receive when the demand for housing increases and housing prices appreciate.

In the long run these inventory profits will fall, because the firm's extraction costs rise as depletion takes place. The arrows in the figure indicate rising costs due to depletion. Thus domestic firms' profits will rise whenever the

OPEC cartel raises prices and then will tend to fall as depletion costs rise in the long run. Here we see a case where prices and profits rise among the firms that have no control over world shortages. Indeed, these firms actually increase output during the period of rising profits.

Even though U.S. domestic oil producers may not be involved directly in OPEC cartel pricing

and output decisions, they may nevertheless be reluctant to participate in weakening the cartel. In fact, oil producers in Scotland pray for OPEC price increases. Of course, the entry of new firms in response to OPEC price increases is risky because of the rising costs as depletion occurs. If the government taxes the inventory profits of well owners, there will be less incentive for domestic exploration and production, and the goal of domestic energy independence will be retarded. Similarly, if gambling winnings are taxed without allowing losses to be written off, there will be few poker players.

Effect of Industry Price on Inventory Value

The value of such inventories as stored oil rises, if the industry price rises.

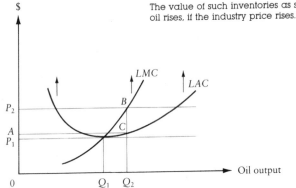

Barometric Price Leadership

The dominant-firm model of price leadership is a hybrid of monopoly and competitive analysis. Perhaps more in keeping with this chapter's emphasis on the interdependence of oligopoly firms is **barometric price leadership**. This form of price leadership occurs in industries where instability in pricing policies threatens to erode the firms' aggregate profits. The barometric firm is the first firm in the industry to make price changes; the rivals, anxious to avoid destructive price competition, follow its lead. The price leader may or may not be a dominant force in the market. Regardless, the firm taking the role of price leader must be able to assess accurately the changing demand and cost conditions in the industry and to set its pricing policies accordingly. Barometric price leadership allows firms to respond in an orderly fashion to cost and demand shifts without interpreting competitors' price changes as hostile acts of economic aggression. If a barometric price leader emerges, all firms may benefit.

Unlike competitive, price-taking firms, oligopoly firms are large compared to industry output and must set price. Because of the interdependence of firms, the pricing policies of one firm may set off retaliatory pricing by rivals. Hence firms must experiment with their pricing structures in order to arrive at the best prices, taking into account rival response. *Experimentation* is the key word in oligopoly pricing.

Oligopoly industries often exhibit the following characteristics: (1) long periods of stable prices that are uniform across firms; (2) prices that change quite a bit when they do change; (3) price experimentation that may begin with any one of a number of firms; and (4) a lengthy period of stable prices that emerges after a period of price jockeying. The theory of barometric pricing explains this price bahavior.

To understand barometric pricing, it is useful to recognize three facts. First, price changes are costly. Often a large sales staff must be coordinated. Furthermore, determining the "right" price is expensive. Second, price changes are risky. If rivals do not match price increases, significant erosion of market share could result. In fact, the price experiment is to see if rivals will match or, through counter moves, "suggest" a different price. Third, firms in the industry face similar cost pressures, particularly for labor, energy, materials, and capital. It is reasonable for one firm to assume that its cost pressures are hurting rivals also.

Figure 10.3 traces the prices of two rival oligopoly firms, for convenience named Solid Citizens, Inc. (the solid line) and Dashed

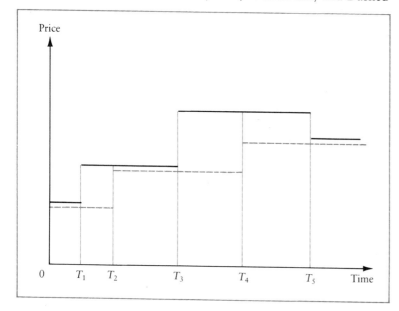

Figure 10.3
Barometric Pricing over Time

Price changes are expensive, risky experiments for an oligopoly. Therefore, they are large and infrequent. The solid lines show time trends of price for Solid Citizens, Inc.; the dashed lines show time trends for Dashed Hopes, Ltd. In time blocks $\overline{0T_1}$, $\overline{T_2T_3}$, and beyond T_5, the prices are equal (although shown here slightly apart).

Hopes, Ltd. (the dashed line). Suppose that both firms begin to feel cost pressure. With equal prices in the time block $\overline{0T_1}$, there is an initial reluctance to raise the price because of the inherent costs and risks of doing so. Eventually, however, rising costs lead to price experimentation. At time T_1, Solid Citizens raises its price. Dashed Hopes now faces a choice: Meet Solid Citizen's price or undercut it. If Dashed Hopes calculates that it can earn a fair rate of return at Solid Citizen's new price, it may choose to match the price increase. At time T_2, Dashed Hopes matches Solid Citizen's price. Thus Solid Citizens acts as the barometric price leader, does the initial price experimenting, and invites other firms to follow if they choose.

But say that at time T_3 Solid Citizens raises its price again but that Dashed Hopes sees an opportunity to gain customers and make fuller use of its plant capacity by not matching the new price. At time T_4, Dashed Hopes decides to undercut Solid Citizen's price increase. As a result, Solid Citizens suffers customer erosion and revises prices downward at time T_5. Price experimentation may be risky. Rivals tend to return to a stable, uniform price.

In barometric pricing, price jockeying takes place as firms attempt to find, without collusion, a price that will accomplish two goals (1) last a long time, so as to avoid the cost and risk of price changes and to avoid the loss of customer goodwill; and (2) earn a fair rate of return for investors, lest managers be replaced.

Kinked Demand Curve Model

Price stability is a hallmark of oligopolistic industries. Is price stability evidence of collusion? Two studies that appeared almost simultaneously have demonstrated how price stability in oligopolistic markets may be the natural result of the noncollusive, uncoordinated behavior of rival firms.[5] These studies presented a **kinked demand curve.**

The central feature of the kinked demand curve model is that each firm has a term for asymmetrical conjectural variation in price. Consider a firm selling at a particular price. If the firm lowers its price, it expects competitors to follow the price reduction in order to retain their customers. Thus for price reductions, the conjectural variation term, $\Delta P_i / \Delta P_j$, equals unity. Price reductions are expected to be matched by the rival firms. But for price increases, the firm does not expect competitors to follow; rival firms will be content to allow the price-raising firm to price itself out of the market. Thus for price increases, $\Delta P_i / \Delta P_j = 0$.

It is this asymmetry that produces the kink in the demand curve. In Figure 10.4, the beginning price-quantity combination is represented by point A. If the firm lowers price, it expects other firms to

---

5. See R. L. Hall and C. J. Hitch, "Price Theory and Business Behavior," *Oxford Economic Papers*, no. 2 (1939), pp. 12–45; and Paul M. Sweezy, "Demand under Conditions of Oligopoly," *Journal of Political Economy* 47 (1939): 568–573.

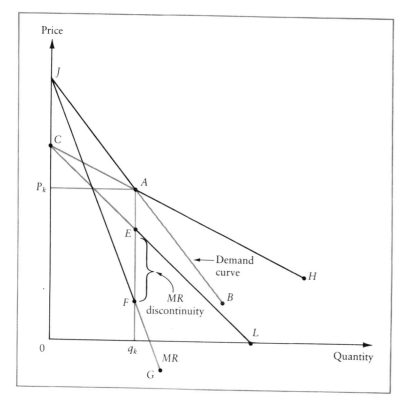

Figure 10.4
Kinked Demand Curve

The demand curve is $\overline{CAB}$, with a kink at A. Starting at price P_k, the firm perceives that rivals will follow price cuts but not price increases. The marginal revenue curve has two segments, $\overline{CE}$ and $\overline{FG}$, with a discontinuity of $\overline{EF}$ at output q_k.

follow. Thus for prices below P_k, the firm perceives a relatively inelastic demand curve, such as $\overline{AB}$. But if price is raised above P_k, the firm anticipates large losses of customers, because it believes that its competitors will not follow the price increase for the express purpose of stealing its customers. For this reason, the firm perceives a relatively elastic demand curve for prices above P_k, such as segment $\overline{CA}$. Thus the firm really faces two demand curves: curve $\overline{CA}$ and another curve $\overline{AB}$. Another way to express the same thing is to say that the single demand curve $\overline{CAB}$ has a kink at point A. And it is this kink that produces the price and output stability so utterly lacking in many oligopoly theories, notably the Edgeworth model.

The stability implications are most easily seen by deriving the firm's marginal revenue curve. This derivation is a little trickier than usual because, like the demand curve, the MR curve has two segments. For ease in construction, suppose temporarily that the firm faces the demand curve $\overline{JAB}$; the black segment $\overline{JA}$ is merely an imagined extension of the actual demand segment $\overline{AB}$. The marginal revenue curve corresponding to the demand curve $\overline{JAB}$ is $\overline{JFG}$. Next make an imagined extension of $\overline{CA}$, resulting in the demand curve $\overline{CAH}$. The corresponding marginal revenue curve is $\overline{CEL}$. Now erase the imagined demand segments, drawn as black lines, and the black marginal revenue segments to which they pertain. After the erasures are cleared off, the marginal revenue curve that remains comprises the two segments $\overline{CE}$ and $\overline{FG}$, as shown in Figure 10.4.

Note that the marginal revenue curve is discontinuous at exactly the output corresponding to the kink; that is, there is no unique marginal revenue at output q_k. This discontinuity is illustrated by the dashed vertical segment $\overline{EF}$. The kink in the demand curve at q_k forces a discontinuity in the firm's marginal revenue curve at the same output level.

Figure 10.5 illustrates the stability characteristics of the model. Let the firm's marginal cost curve be MC_1. Strictly speaking, the $MR = MC$ profit-maximizing principle is not satisfied, because MR is not defined at output q_k, where the MC curve "intersects" the discontinuity. Still, taking discrete changes in output away from q_k in either direction reveals that q_k is the best output available. $MR > MC$ at outputs less than q_k, and $MR < MC$ at outputs greater than q_k.

Now consider the effect on price and quantity of moderate increases or decreases in the firm's marginal cost, as shown by MC_2 and MC_3. Because all three marginal cost curves intersect the line segment $\overline{EF}$, P_k and q_k continue to be the profit-maximizing price and output of the firm. Moderate cost changes do not result in price and output adjustments, as they would in models of competition

Figure 10.5
Kinked Demand and the Stability of Oligopolistic Pricing

When MC_1 is the firm's marginal cost curve, MC_1 intersects the MR discontinuity between E and F. P_k and q_k are the profit-maximizing price and output. If MC_1 rises to MC_2 or falls to MC_3, profit maximization calls for the same price and quantity.

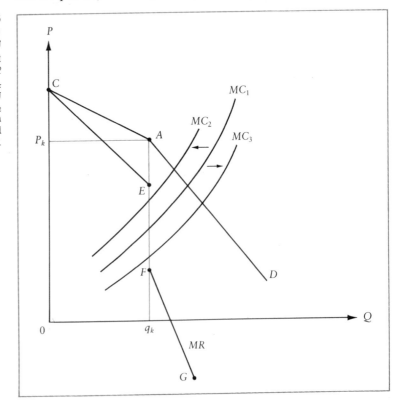

and monopoly. The kink produces unusual price stability.

Figure 10.6 demonstrates a similar price stability when demand shifts. Assume that the firm experiences a marked increase in demand, from D_0 to D_1. If the kink occurs at the same price, P_k, this demand shift would give the firm no incentive to change price, although its rate of output would increase in response to higher demand.

Thus kinked demand curves put the analysis of oligopoly on a much different footing in comparison to Edgeworth's model. For Edgeworth, noncollusive oligopoly results in unstable price and output patterns, even when costs and demand are stable. With the kinked demand curve, moderate cost and demand shifts can occur without causing firms to alter their prices and output rates.

The kinked demand curve model enjoyed a pleasant honeymoon; many economists came to regard it as "the" model of oligopoly behavior. The honeymoon was over, however, when Professor George Stigler questioned the theoretical and empirical relevance of the kink.[6] Stigler studied the historical pricing policies

6. George J. Stigler, "The Kinky Oligopoly Demand Curve and Rigid Prices," *Journal of Political Economy* 55 (1947): 432–449. Both Sweezy, "Demand under Conditions of Oligopoly," and the Stigler criticism are reprinted in G. J. Stigler and K. E. Boulding, eds., *Readings in Price Theory*, vol. 6 (Homewood, Ill.: Irwin, 1952).

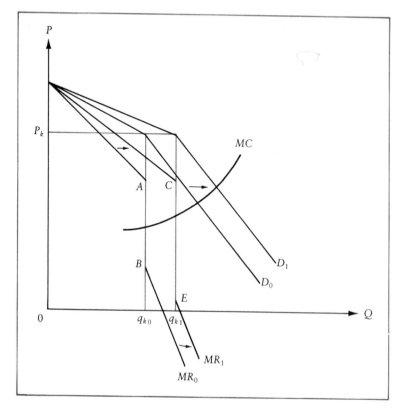

Figure 10.6
Kinked Demand Shifts and Pricing Stability

The original demand curve is D_0, giving rise to an *MR* curve with the discontinuity $\overline{AB}$. Shifting the demand curve to D_1 results in the *MR* curve with discontinuity $\overline{CE}$. Moderate shifts in demand may leave price largely unaffected while changing the quantity sold.

and dynamics of seven oligopolies in search of behavioral evidence that price decreases are followed more regularly and quickly than price increases. He was not able to observe any systematic behavior that could be attributed to firms by the theory. On the basis of his empirical results, Stigler concluded that there is no proven basis in experience for oligopolists to believe that a kink exists in their demand curves—that rivals will match a price decrease but not an increase.

Perhaps the most disconcerting aspect of this theory is its inability to explain how the price gets set in the first place. Most of the models we have dealt with explain the determination of price and output, but this one does not.

Thus the model exhibits some striking limitations. It does not explain very well its curious results. It cannot predict price and output. Its results run counter to the empirical evidence provided by Stigler. And it is surely unsuitable as a description of long-run equilibrium, in which cost and demand shifts must ultimately be reflected in industry prices and output rates.

The main use of the theory may be in describing the predicament of a small, fledgling firm. When a new competitor enters the industry and is unacquainted with its competitors' business practices, the theory may be a suitable explanation of its pricing policies while it is becoming established. But there is a limit to how long the kink could remain. The kink can be regarded as a hindrance to profits, because it prevents firms from raising prices along what would otherwise be a relatively inelastic segment of the demand curve. Stigler marveled at the naivete of those who questioned the ability of the business community to "iron out" the kink if it ever presented itself:

> The kink is a barrier to changes in prices that will increase profits, and business is the collection of devices for circumventing barriers to profits. That this barrier should thwart businessmen—especially when it is wholly of their own fabrication—is unbelievable. There are many ways in which it can be circumvented.[7]

Oligopoly Profits

It has been observed that profits and the number of firms in an industry are inversely related. In particular, the lower the **industry concentration** (measured by the percentage of total output sold by the industry's eight largest firms), the lower the return to investors.[8] Many theories have been advanced to explain this feature of oligopoly profits.

---

7. Stigler, "Kinky Oligopoly Demand Curve," p. 435.

8. See Joe S. Bain, "Relation of Profit Rate to Industry Concentration: American Manufacturing, 1936–1940," *Quarterly Journal of Economics* 65 (August 1951): 293–324.

Tacit Collusion

One theory suggests that the greater the concentration, the more the rivals recognize both their interdependence and the advantages of following a barometric price leader toward the industry profit-maximizing price. Such collusion is "tacit" as opposed to express or explicit, as if the industry were a cartel attempting to maximize the aggregate or **joint profits** of member firms.

Either by firsthand experience or through formal training in economics and business administration, entrepreneurs learn about the inherent dangers of price wars and noncooperative solutions to price and output dilemmas. Among competing firms that are too large to be considered price takers, profit maximization resulting from coordinated price and output policies becomes an ideal. Adam Smith long ago recognized the potential benefit of collusive behavior among firms when he noted, "People of the same trade seldom meet together, even for merriment and diversion, but the conversation ends in a conspiracy against the public, or in some contrivance to raise prices."[9] Collusion is illegal in the United States, but a steady stream of prosecutions and convictions under the Sherman Antitrust Act of 1890 bears witness to its attractiveness.

If firms are to keep prices high and output correspondingly low in order to achieve the monopoly ideal, a communication system that can glue the oligopolists together must evolve. Price shaving that leads to price wars and excessive profits that attract new competitors must be avoided. To maximize profits for all, pricing must be an industry matter.

Tacit collusion is a theory of "guilt by profitability." Profits are taken as evidence of deliberate departures from competition rather than as manifestations of hard work, cleverness, foresight, efficiency, and luck. To be fair, collusion should never be considered the full source of oligopoly profits. There are alternative, less conspiratorial explanations.

Lumpy Entry

The nature of products often determines the efficient size of firms necessary to produce them. In oligopoly, firms are large with respect to the aggregate industry output. Thus a would-be entrant must enter with a large amount of new productive capacity. That entrant must look not merely at the profits being earned by the firms in the industry but at the postentry profits as well. If a firm's entry would itself depress prices so that postentry profits were negative, entry would be deterred, even if preentry profits were quite high. Naturally, this effect is greatest in industries that are already quite concentrated. The problem does not arise in competition because each

9. Adam Smith, *An Inquiry into the Nature and Causes of the Wealth of Nations* (New York: Modern Library, 1937).

APPLICATION

10.5

Focal-Point Pricing

Focal-point pricing is one form of communication that oligopolists use to avoid the legal risks of overt collusion while gaining some of the treasures such collusion would yield.* The theory of focal-point pricing follows from this general premise: Certain prices communicate information better than other prices.

For example, pretend that you and your best friend are both shopping for a new car. You arrive together at the car lot and each are attended by a different sales representative. You select identical cars and option packages. Your sales representative quotes you a price of $6,999.99, but your friend gets a quote of $7,035.42. These price quotes say a lot. Your price, $6,999.99, says in effect, "I have done everything I can for you to keep the price under $7,000. I cannot do much better than this." The price of $7,035.42 says, "You can bargain me down to $7,000."

Oligopolists use the "language of numbers" to talk to each other in similar fashion. Certain price points are standard in the industry: Denim pants sell for $14.99, and electric drills sell for $19.99. Price leaders can jump to such focal points in the process of changing prices as a signal to the rest of the industry that they are shooting for a stable price at the new level. The use of focal points in price adjustments is an invitation to industry stability, an expression that "we had to change prices this much for market-related reasons, but we will not go any further. Please follow."

*The basic reference on focal-point pricing is Thomas C. Schelling, *The Strategy of Conflict* (Cambridge, Mass.: Harvard University Press, 1960).

prospective entrant is small and cannot influence industry price by its entry.

Figure 10.7 illustrates this problem of **lumpy entry**. Initially, suppose there are four firms of the same capacity serving the demand curve D, charging the price P_1, and selling an aggregate output of Q_4. Each firm sells a fourth of the industry output, or $Q_4/4$ units. The LAC and LMC curves represent the typical costs of the firms. At price P_1, all four firms earn a positive economic profit equal to the shaded area.

Now suppose that a new firm enters with similar capacity, which is a requirement for producing the good in question. If its entry drives the price down to P_2, the entering firm (and also the original firms) are pushed to a rate of output $Q_5/5$ and, given the cost structure, negative economic profit. Thus the new firm is deterred from entering despite the current positive economic profits.

If it were the same size as the first four firms, a fifth firm would represent 20 percent of the postentry capacity. With ten firms, the eleventh would make up only 9.1 percent of postentry capacity and would be less likely to depress the price into the negative economic profit range.

Figure 10.7
Lumpy Entry

Large-scale entry requirements can result in positive economic profits but no entry. Here four firms can produce profitably—but five cannot.

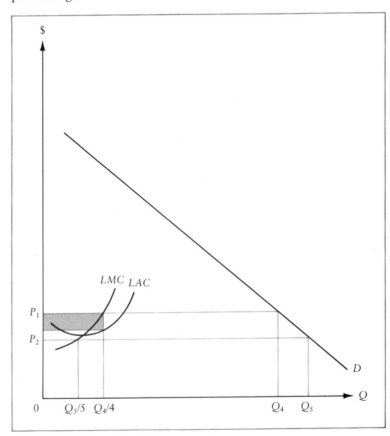

In competition, where the number of firms is very large, new entrants need not worry about the effect of their own entry on postentry profits. They are too small to have any impact. Thus lumpy entry is important in oligopoly but not in competition.

Regional Monopoly

Lumpy entry may limit the number of oligopolists that profits can attract to a given industry. Another limiting factor to entry arises from the geographic dispersal of firms. If the product has significant transportation costs, nearby customers will essentially face just one seller. This **regional monopoly** will not be eroded by entry if entry is at all profitable for other reasons, because the most profitable entry location is generally not next door to an existing rival. Hence, again, entry will not wipe out profits. And again, the greater the concentration, the greater the effect. If an industry can support many firms, the effect of regional monopoly is less.

Barriers to Entry

Regardless of the exact nature of oligopolistic interdependence, one thing is clear: If the industry is to retain aggregate profits suitably close to the monopoly ideal, the entry of competing firms must be avoided. Thus the probability of long-run profit maintenance depends in part on the strength of the industry's **barriers to entry.**

There is considerable confusion over the meaning of *barriers to entry*. One approach is to point to the high fixed costs in oligopoly industries as effective barriers because of the sheer magnitude of capital needed by prospective entrants. It is true that large capital requirements make it difficult to enter. Yet effective management of firms already in the industry does also. Are we to list efficiency as a barrier to entry?

We must therefore distinguish between requirements of entry and barriers to entry. Because of the nature of most oligopoly products, high fixed costs are a requirement of entry, not a barrier. Fixed costs are no more a barrier to entry than any other costs necessary to attract and satisfy customers, such as those for advertising, labor, and entrepreneurial skills. After all, is a factory a barrier to building cars? Is a good voice a barrier to operatic success? If we equate requirement and barrier, *barrier* loses its operational meaning.

A barrier to entry exists when a firm is barred from an industry even though it can meet all cost and production requirements. For example, the barring of superior black athletes from professional baseball prior to the 1950s was a true barrier to entry. However, sixty-year-old men are not considered to be barred from baseball, because they simply do not meet the industry requirements for entry. If a firm could enter the taxi business in New York City but for the artificial cost of a medallion (see Application 7.9), it faces a barrier to entry.

In summary, the term *barriers to entry,* to be operational, must refer to artificial barriers that may be imposed by government, organized crime, or the oligopoly firms themselves. Examples would include import barriers, licensing restrictions not based on legitimate economic considerations, government-supported cartel protection, discrimination, certain forms of industry predation, and threats. Managers must be able to argue persuasively that requirements are not barriers, for such a distinction plays a large part in the administration of antitrust law. We will return to this topic in Chapter 13.

Monopolistic Competition

Somewhere between competition (many sellers with no influence over price) and monopoly (one seller with complete influence over price) lies the uncertain world of imperfect competition. There is no single theory of imperfect competition. Instead, there are numerous approaches to the study of this middle ground. So far in this chapter, we have encountered various models of oligopoly, with the emphasis on the interdependence of rivals' market decisions. Now we will study **monopolistic competition,** which stresses the role of small product differences in otherwise competitive markets.

Consider the soap industry. We know from watching television commercials that the firms in this industry are very aggressive in differentiating their products and in communicating these differences to consumers via elaborate advertising ("Buy our soap with the green dots instead of the soap with the lower-quality blue dots"). Paper products, tobacco, liquor, gasoline, restaurants, automobile sales and service, retail grocery and drug stores, insurance, and toothpaste are representative of the many industries that differentiate products and advertise. Neither the competitive nor the monopoly model explains this behavior. Competitors sell closely substitutable products and hence have no reason to advertise. And the monopolist's product specification and advertising are not rivalrous. Thus reliance on competitive and monopolistic models leaves us with unexplained behavior in important industries.

We may begin our study of monopolistic competition by listing the assumptions of the most prominent model:[10]

> *Product differentiation:* Each producer sells a product that is a close but not perfect substitute for its rivals' products. **Product differentiation** can take many forms: changes in the physical attributes of the good, differences in packaging, changes in location, differences in warranties and service, or merely a fancied difference in the minds of consumers.

---

10. These assumptions were first outlined by Chamberlin, *Theory of Monopolistic Competition.* Robinson published a related work in the same year: see the first edition of *Economics of Imperfect Competition* (London: Macmillan, 1933).

Product group: There is assumed to exist an identifiable cluster of firms whose products are quite similar. The collection of such firms constitutes a **product group.** This formulation is an attempt to define an industry among firms whose products are not identical.

Competition in the group: Competition within the group is atomistic; there are many firms, and entry and exit are virtually free—as free as in perfect competition.

Uniformity: All firms in the group are assumed to exhibit identical cost curves and to face identical demand curves for their products.

Symmetry: One firm's adjustment in any of its decision variables (price, product variation, advertising) is distributed evenly over the large number of rivals in the group so that the effects of one firm's decisions on any rival firm are negligible.

These assumptions have met with sharp criticism from the theory's detractors, most notably Professor Stigler. Stigler is especially critical of the assumption that firms producing differentiated products are identical and of the concept of the product group. It seems that the concept of identical firms, in particular, is as unnecessary in the model of monopolistic competition as it is in the competitive model. Thus the following analysis drops the myth of the identical firm.

But what about the product group? The most straightforward way to collect firms into groups is by the degree of substitutability of their products. Consider the cross-price elasticity of demand, θ_{XP_Y}, of products X and Y:

$$\theta_{XP_Y} = \frac{\% \, \Delta \text{ in good } X \text{ sold}}{\% \Delta \text{ in price of good } Y} = \frac{\Delta X}{\Delta P_Y} \cdot \frac{P_Y}{X} \qquad (10.4)$$

The cross-price elasticity of demand measures the percentage change in the sales of one good in response to a percentage change in the price of another good. If θ equals zero, the goods are not substitutions, because a change in relative price does not induce any substitutions. At the other extreme, two goods are perfect substitutes if θ is infinite, because complete substitutions between the goods can occur without any change in relative prices. Thus the larger the cross-price elasticity of demand (θ), the greater the substitutability of products. The product group is an imprecise but useful way of aggregating those firms whose products are reasonably good substitutes.

Stigler rejects the concept of the product group by observing:

It is perfectly plausible . . . that the group contain only one firm, or, on the contrary, that it include all of the firms in the economy.

This latter possibility can readily follow from the asymmetry of substitution relationships among firms: taking any one product as our point of departure, each substitute has in turn its substitutes, so that the adjacent cross-elasticities may not diminish, and may even increase, as we move further away from the "base" firm in some technological or geographical sense.[11]

Stigler's caution is wise counsel. But the concept of the product group should not be dismissed too cavalierly. Firms can be grouped together by a reasonable, commonsense evaluation of the substitutability of their products. Even though the grouping cannot be precise, products do fall into broad groups. Detergent and chopsticks are obviously not in the same group. Detergent and shampoo are also not in the same product group, despite their similarities as cleaning agents, as witnessed by the small number of people who wash their clothes with shampoo. The large number of differentiated detergent and shampoo products separate quite naturally into two distinct product groups. (This statement is true at current prices, but consumers might well wash clothes in shampoo if detergent became too expensive relative to shampoo.) Color television sets and electronic typewriters are not close substitutes either. Although both are electronic devices, you cannot watch the World Series on your typewriter. Similarly, automobiles and horses are no longer in the same product group in the United States; for most uses they are very imperfect substitutes. Yet some ranchers may still consider them substitute modes of transportation in checking fences and riding herd on animals. In such cases, the automobile and horse would be in the same product group, and relative prices would determine whether the cowhand rides the range in a Mustang or on a mustang.

With these introductory remarks in mind, we may begin an analysis of monopolistic competition. The three decision variables available to a profit-maximizing monopolistic competitor that are not open to a competitive firm are changes in price, changes in product, and changes in advertising and sales effort. Because the monopolistically competitive firm has a small degree of monopoly power, because of the differentiation of its product, it is a price setter. Reductions in price expand sales by movements along the firm's demand curve. Product differentiation and advertising are ways of increasing the size of the firm's market by shifting the demand curve.

Short-Run Price and Output Equilibrium

Suppose we are able to identify a product group by reference to the substitutability of the firms' products. We assume that these firms

11. George J. Stigler, *Five Lectures on Economic Problems* (London: Longmans, Green, 1949), p. 15.

differ in the demand curves and cost curves they face. Thus we abandon the fiction of identical firms and focus our analysis on the marginal firm in the group, just as we did in the analysis of pure competition in Chapter 7.

The description of price and output equilibrium employs two demand curves, both displayed in Figure 10.8. The curve labeled d_f is the demand curve the firm faces when its own price reductions occur *ceteris paribus* —that is, with the prices of all substitute products held constant. Because the firm knows it is a small component of a large product group, it can hope its own price adjustments will not be met by similar price changes by rivals. The demand curve d_f is relatively elastic, because the numerous products in the group are reasonably close substitutes.

The less elastic demand curve, labeled D_g in Figure 10.8, measures the changes in quantity demanded when the firm's price reduction is copied by other firms in the group. Curve D_g is a **mutatis mutandis** demand curve, the Latin phrase meaning "the necessary changes having been made." Thus points on D_g measure the quantities that the firm can sell when its price reductions occur simultaneously with similar (but not necessarily identical) price cuts by other (but not necessarily all) firms in the group. The subscript g stands for *group* and reminds us that D_g is the firm's share of total group demand when other firms in the group reduce their prices at the same time. The entrepreneur knows the other firms will change their prices if their demand and cost curves call for it. But the firm cannot know the position of its rivals' demand and cost curves and thus cannot know how the position of the D_g curve will change in response to changes in the economy, except vaguely. The ultimate equilibrium must occur at a point on D_g, because the firm's sales will depend in part on its rivals' pricing policies. But because D_g is not known to the firm, equilibrium must be found by trial and error.

Now let's trace the move to an equilibrium price and quantity in Figure 10.9. While examining the pricing decision of the firm, we will temporarily ignore the entrepreneur's production and advertising decision. Advertising is easily omitted by assuming that consumer wants are given and that consumers have perfect knowledge about substitutes. Advertising is pointless in such a simple model; it raises costs without increasing firm revenues or consumer benefits.

Let point A in Figure 10.9 be our arbitrary starting point, where price is P_3 and quantity sold is Q_1. Beginning at P_3, the firm attempts to find its profit-maximizing price by trial and error. The firm may, for example, attempt to maximize profit by finding the optimum position on the demand curve d_f, which passes through point A. The curve labeled MR_f is the marginal revenue curve associated with the demand curve d_f. Using this strategy, the firm selects the price and output combination P_2 and Q_5, because $MR_f = MC$ at B. But if other firms face similar incentives because of their demand and

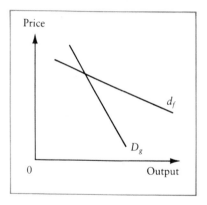

Figure 10.8
Demand Curves of Monopolistic Competitor

The firm's *ceteris paribus* demand curve is d_f; D_g is the *mutatis mutandis* demand curve facing the firm when rivals can adjust to price changes.

Figure 10.9
Price and Output Adjustment in
Monopolistic Competition

The firm must experiment with
prices to find D_g. Each price
and quantity choice induces
responses by rivals.

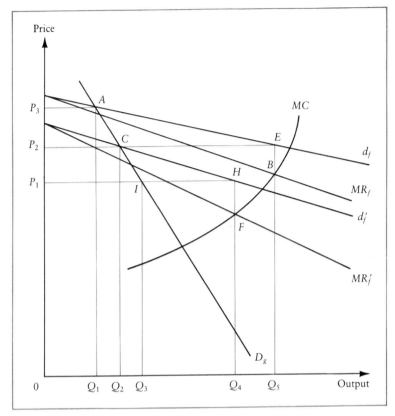

cost structures, they will be reducing their prices too. Thus the firm
expects to sell Q_5 units at price P_2 (point E on d_f) but instead sells
only Q_2 (point C on D_g). In this way the firm moves from A to C
on the demand curve D_g. Point C on the demand curve D_g is only
known to the firm after it gets there.

But point C does not maximize profits, because price P_2 doesn't
produce the anticipated sales of Q_5 units. Additional price changes
are required. Beginning now at C (P_2 and Q_2), the firm perceives
another curve, d_f, that measures the change in sales resulting from
a price change away from P_2, assuming all rivals' prices are fixed. In
other words, there is a d_f curve intersecting each point of the D_g
curve. When price falls along D_g, the perceived curve d_f slides down
the D_g curve. Beginning at C, the *ceteris paribus* demand curve d'_f
is available to the firm for repetitions of the process. The relevant
marginal revenue curve, MR'_f, corresponds to the demand curve d'_f.
The firm now equates MR'_f and MC at F and sells Q_4 units at price
P_1. As before, rivals' price reductions limit the firm's sales to Q_3 at
price P_1. Point I on demand curve D_g is now revealed to the firm.
The firm is led once again to continue its search for the best price
along these same lines, always faced with a lack of information
about rival responses.

Equilibrium is the final result of this search for a profit-maximizing price. The firm has an incentive to change its price and output whenever the D_g and d_f curves intersect at a different rate of output from that where $MR_f = MC$. Each time the firm lowers its price, the d_f curve slides down the D_g curve. Ultimately, the equilibrium depicted in Figure 10.10 is reached. The d_f curve intersects D_g at A, and price and output are P_0 and Q_0. Because $MR_f = MC$ at Q_0, the firm finally achieves a price and output combination that maximizes profits. The firm has no further incentive to change its price and output. Thus, when the intersections at points A and B in Figure 10.10 occur at the same output level, the firm attains short-run equilibrium.

The short-run equilibrium described in Figure 10.10 does not contain an average cost curve; economic profits are not indicated. Clearly, economic profits can be positive, zero, or negative in the short run for monopolistically competitive firms. If profits are negative in the short run, the shutdown analysis of Chapter 7 applies: Revenue must cover variable costs in order to justify producing with short-run losses.

Long-Run Price and Output Equilibrium

The long run allows for two kinds of adjustments not permitted in the short run: (1) changes in the firm's scale of plant and (2) entry or exit of firms. Thus long-run equilibrium in monopolistic competition requires two conditions in addition to those necessary for short-run equilibrium: Each firm must be operating at the least-cost scale of plant for the output selected, and entry or exit must have driven economic profit to zero for the marginal firms, thereby eliminating further entry or exit.

Suppose that positive economic profits exist initially for most of the firms in a product group. Positive profits attract entrants, and since the demand curve D_g reflects the firm's share of the group market, the entry of new firms shifts D_g leftward by reducing the firm's share of sales. Entry continues to shift D_g until the economic profits of marginal firms are zero.

The establishment of a long-run equilibrium price and quantity proceeds along the lines outlined in the previous section, except that the long-run cost curves apply. Figure 10.11 illustrates this equilibrium. The firm continues to adjust its price, output, and scale of plant until the intersection of the D_g and d_f curves once again intersect at the same output level at which $MR_f = LMC$. These intersections occur at output Q_m at points A (for D_g) and B (for d_f). For Q_m to be a true long-run equilibrium quantity, D_g must have stopped shifting, which occurs only when economic profits are zero for the marginal firms and entry ceases. Profits are zero at Q_m for the marginal firm depicted in Figure 10.11 because the LAC curve is tangent to the demand curve d_f at output Q_m. Thus all conditions

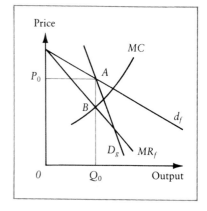

Figure 10.10
Short-Run Price and Output Equilibrium of Monopolistic Competitor

D_g and d_f intersect at the same output as the MC and MR_f intersection.

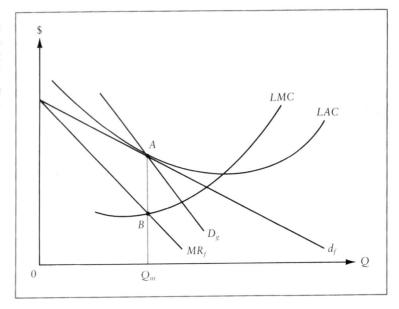

for long-run equilibrium are attained at Q_m: (1) $MR_f = LMC$ and $D_g = d_f$; (2) the firm selects the least-cost scale of plant for output Q_m, thereby operating on the LAC curve at A; and (3) economic profits are zero for the marginal firm.

We have now seen the equilibrium that results from the ability of each monopolistically competitive firm to set its own price. In addition to price competition, firms attempt to enlarge their markets by selling products that differ from the products of competitors within the group and by advertising those products. The economic incentive to differentiate products arises from the fact that consumers' preferences vary so widely. One firm may cater to a price-conscious clientele by offering a "no-frills" product that perhaps sacrifices some quality in order to keep prices low. Another firm serves the customer whose main interest is a high-quality product, even if it costs a bit more. Firms are constantly on the lookout for ways to "position" their products in order to gain a larger share of the market and increase profits.

Previous discussions of price and output equilibrium assumed that the firm's decisions about product characteristics and advertising were already made. It would be nice to hold price and quantity constant and adjust product characteristics instead, but no useful graphic method of performing such an analysis exists, because product quality is so varied. It is clear, however, that product differentiation and advertising, as well as entry and exit, shift all the demand and cost curves in Figure 10.11. Curve D_g shifts if the variation in product characteristics is successful in capturing a larger share of market sales. And the cost curves must shift when the firm changes its product. Nevertheless, the final equilibrium condi-

A P P L I C A T I O N

10.6

Trading Stamps, Bingo Night, and a Day at the Races

Retail food stores are relatively few in a given neighborhood. Generally, consumers' choices are further limited because the available stores belong to a small number of chains. Food stores provide a service that is physically quite substitutable for the services of rivals; a 16-ounce can of stewed tomatoes is much the same at Safeway and IGA. So how can food stores differentiate their products? One answer, of course, is promotions.

Here is a random sample of common promotions:

1. *Trading and redemption stamps* (such as S&H Green Stamps).
2. *Bingo night:* For every $100 of food purchased, you receive a bingo chip. Fill a row, column, or diagonal and you win a cash prize or gift. Many people love these games.
3. *A day at the races:* For every $100 of food purchased, you get a ticket linked to a horse that will be in a long-forgotten race televised the following week. If the horse wins, places, or shows, you get a prize. This game is especially exciting, since it is usually rigged so that

the horse most people are backing leads the race until the last 20 yards and then falls flat on its nose.

To analyze the effectiveness of promotions like these, let's start by assuming that no store has a promotional gimmick and that all stores earn a normal rate of return. Then store 1 adopts a gimmick, say redemption stamps. If this ploy is successful, the demand for store 1's product will rise. Store 1 may raise prices, but

it can profit without price increases merely by the greater volume of customers its gimmick has attracted away from rivals. Remember: The food is the same, but the gimmick is not.

One by one, other food stores retaliate by adopting gimmicks of their own. Of course, product differentiation calls for gimmick differentiation. The percentage of stores employing gimmicks rises over time. But the profits are squeezed out, because the promotions tend to cancel one another out. Eventually, prices must rise throughout the industry to pay the promotion costs.

What is the best way to differentiate when many stores have promotions? Cancel the promotion, cut costs, and cut prices! Advertise lower prices at exactly the same time the bingo games or races are having their grand finale. The profit incentives underlying the institution and eventual cessation of promotions indicate that the percentage of stores using gimmicks should rise and fall cyclically. From a managers' viewpoint, success depends on knowing when to start and, just as important, when to stop the gimmick.

tions are the same as before. The firm is inclined to experiment with various products and to produce the most profitable ones. The firm also has an incentive to advertise in order to establish and maintain consumer preferences for its products rather than those of competing firms.

Summary

Oligopoly is an industry structure in which there are few enough firms that each must worry about competitors' reactions. In competitive industries, where firms are tied together by parametric pricing, competitors' reactions are not at issue. In monopoly and cartel structures, single or joint decision making makes rival reactions unimportant.

The study of oligopoly and cartel behavior is at once intriguing and puzzling. Comparative statics—so useful a method in the analysis of competition and pure monopoly—is somewhat less useful in the study of oligopolies and cartels because of the indeterminacy of certain results. Of course, a perfectly determinate and general theory of oligopoly is out of the question, because each industry presents its own problems and characteristics. Thus this chapter has presented several approaches to the analysis of oligopoly behavior. Managerial economists must choose from among these tools of analysis to understand the industry their firm is in. But many problems simply cannot be handled in the abstract. Industry-by-industry case studies are often the most fruitful avenues for oligopoly research.

Theories of monopolistic competition have been developed to elucidate the behavior of firms that compete on several levels: price, product differentiation, and advertising. Product differentiation gives the firm a negatively sloped demand curve for its product and yet some market power over its price. Advertising is a method for communicating product differences to potential customers.

Problems

1. Price wars often occur in industries whose firms exhibit high capital costs as a component of total costs. Why should these cost factors make a difference?
2. Discuss the changes that occur in a leader-follower industry when the leader experiences a reduction in costs due to technological change.
3. a. Derive the kinked demand curve for a firm and its associated marginal revenue curve assuming that price reductions will not be followed by rivals but that price increases will be.
   b. In such a case, how does the firm decide which price to charge?
   c. Would you expect such an assumption to be verified by experience?
4. The theory of the kinked demand curve may be flawed, but it does serve the pedagogical role of forcing students to understand that MR is a function of Q. Explain why.
5. Use the model of dominant-firm price leadership to show that a tax on U.S. supplies of domestic oil will strengthen OPEC whereas a tax on U.S. consumers will weaken OPEC.
6. Suppose that a multiplant monopolist's high price encourages entry by new firms but that entry is slow because of heavy investment costs. Should the monopolist
   a. Close plants and reduce output in order to keep the price up?
   b. Expand output to lower the price in order to slow down entry?
   c. Buy out the entrants?
   Explain your choice.
7. Why are car manufacturers reluctant to advertise safety features?
8. a. What incentive is there for an individual competitor to provide truthful information about its product?
   b. Compare the equilibrium of the competitive market and the monopoly firm when the provision of information is an important variable in the demand function. Show that monopoly output can be greater than competitive output.
   c. Suppose that the government provides the efficient level of information in a competitive market. Compare output and price to that of a monopoly equilibrium.

9. A famous aspirin company advertises the highest-quality aspirin and charges a high price. Suppose this high quality derives not from superior chemical compounds but from stock rotation that guarantees freshness. Why would the company not reveal in its advertising the reason for its higher-quality product?

10. a. Distinguish between the marginal revenue associated with a price change and the marginal revenue of advertising.
    b. Distinguish between the marginal cost of production and the marginal cost of advertising.

11. The concept of a product group relates to substitutability in demand. Is substitutability in production irrelevant to the definition of *product group?*

12. The Federal Trade Commission has charged major cereal manufacturers with producing so many brands of cereal that shelf space is unavailable to small producers. This situation creates a barrier to entry. Concentrating on the store owner's incentives, develop a counterargument.

13. Is product differentiation desirable to the consumer? Why or why not?

14. a. Is the automobile industry more competitive now than in 1960?
    b. What changes have occurred in the industry?
    c. What technical innovations do you expect now that you would not have expected in 1960?

15. The larger the number of member firms, the more likely a cartel is to collapse. Explain why.

16. Suppose that purchasers use a secret bidding procedure to encourage lower prices from a suspected cartel but that they still receive identical bids from the suppliers. Show how the buyers can use stockpiled goods to respond to this development and thereby encourage cartel cheating in the next round of bidding.

17. Show how cartel members can cheat by varying product quality or warranty conditions.

18. Many institutional arrangements are available for preventing free riding at the retail level, such as charging for point-of-sale services and for general media advertising. Using production theory, show that such measures do not completely solve the problem of free ridership.

19. Suppose that we place a tax on all inventory profits. How would such a tax affect the spreading of risk?

20. If an oligopolist finds that its price is higher than its rivals' prices but that its product quality is also higher, it does not feel the need to match the rivals' prices. How can the oligopolist decide whether the price difference is excessive?

21. Oligopoly profits may exceed normal profits merely because of the relationship between economies of scale and the position of the demand curve (entry can be lumpy). Does the elasticity of demand have any bearing on this relationship?

22. Does the superior efficiency of a firm resulting from the age of the firm and the experience of the entrepreneurs constitute a barrier to the entry of new, relatively inexperienced firms?

23. How do gasoline stations differentiate their product?

24. a. Are paper bags and wooden crates in the same product group? Explain your answer.
    b. What about wooden crates and cardboard boxes?
    c. What about paper bags and cardboard boxes?
25. Suppose that an oligopoly consists of firms having a minimum average cost at 100 units of output. The demand for the product is represented by $Q = 5,000 - 50P$.
    a. What levels of price and quantity would result in normal profits in the industry?
    b. How many firms would there be at those levels?
26. Suppose a firm believes that it would lose 5 percent of its sales if it raised its price by 10 percent and would increase its sales by 10 percent if it lowered the price 10 percent. According to the kinked demand curve theory, which course should the firm take?
27. Suppose that the supply of follower firms falls. Using the leader-follower model, show what would happen to the profit-maximizing output and price of the leader.
28. Suppose that the industry price for power drills is $29.95. What danger faces a firm that charges $25.00 in an effort to gain customers?

Suggested Readings

Bain, J. *Barriers to New Competition.* Cambridge, Mass.: Harvard University Press, 1956.

Bishop, Robert L. "The Theory of Monopolistic Competition after Thirty Years: The Impact on General Theory." *American Economic Review* 54 (1964): 33–43.

Chamberlin, E. H. *The Theory of Monopolistic Competition.* Cambridge, Mass.: Harvard University Press, 1933.

Fellner, W. *Competition among the Few.* New York: Knopf, 1950.

Stigler, George. "The Kinky Oligopoly Demand Curve and Rigid Prices." *Journal of Political Economy* 55 (1947): 432–449.

Stigler, George. "Monopolistic Competition in Retrospect." In *Five Lectures on Economic Problems,* 12–24. New York: Macmillan, 1949.

Sweezy, Paul M. "Demand under Conditions of Oligopoly." *Journal of Political Economy* 47 (1939): 568–573.

11

MULTI-PRODUCT FIRMS

The competitive model set forth in Chapter 7 deals with firms that produce a single output. This simplification is extremely useful for approaching the ideas of competitive efficiency, profit maximization, the short-run shutdown decision, entry and exit, fair rates of return (zero economic profit), and so forth. Now we extend our analysis to encompass firms producing and selling multiple products, a more typical case. Even firms selling a single output face the potential of adding product lines. Thus managers need a model of firm behavior that takes account of multiproduct competitive firms.

The models presented in this chapter lend richness to the study of managerial economics; they do not contradict but rather extend previous analyses into concrete areas of actual managerial problem solving. This extension is quite easily managed and intuitively appealing, and the extra decision-making power it provides is well worth the effort.

The two multiproduct models presented here are joint production and alternative production. The **joint production** model is used to study firms producing goods that, by their nature, must be produced together, such as beef and hides, mutton and wool, oil and natural gas. The **alternative production** model, in contrast, applies when all the products produced by a firm require a common factor of production and must compete for this common factor in the production scheduling. For example, various grades and sizes of paper can be produced with the same machinery but not at the same time. A firm must choose the correct output mix of paper and allocate the common factor to the production of the competing paper grades. Leather, cement, farm goods, retail sales in department stores, and many other products are subject to alternative production considerations.

Joint Production

When goods are produced jointly—as beef and hides are—we encounter a problem that is fundamentally different from any problem we face using single-product models: In producing such goods, the firm faces the market forces in several markets at once. The analytical tool that captures this difference is vertical summation, which is useful for both industry-level and firm-level analyses.

Industry-Level Analysis

Figure 11.1 illustrates the technique of vertical summation of demand on the industry level, using beef and hides as an example. The

Figure 11.1
Vertical Summation of Demand Curves

To aggregate demand curves of jointly produced goods, vertical summation is required. Here the demand for steers is the vertical summation of the demands for the components, beef and hides.

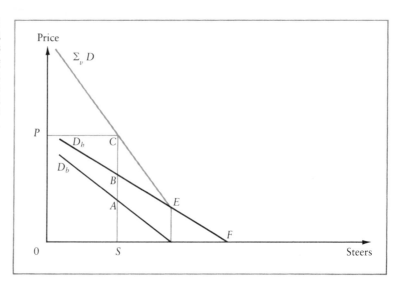

curve labeled D_b is the demand curve for steers by beef users, and curve D_h is the demand curve for steers by hide users. Our goal is to construct an aggregate demand curve for steers, a curve that shows the maximum price that can be obtained for each steer. Horizontal summation of the two demand curves is not meaningful here, because unlike previous demand analyses, each steer contributes to the benefits of both classes of users. Rather than sum horizontally the number of steers demanded at each price, we must sum vertically the amounts of money that all users are willing to pay for each additional steer. This is the essence of vertical summation.

To illustrate the technique using Figure 11.1, say that beef users are willing to pay $\overline{SA}$ for the Sth steer and that hide users are willing to pay $\overline{SB}$ for the same Sth steer. Because the two demands are for different uses of the same steer, the total price that will be offered for the Sth steer by both classes of users is $\overline{OP} = \overline{SA} + \overline{SB} = \overline{SC}$. Point C is the vertical summation of points A and B for the Sth steer.

Similar vertical summation for all other quantities of steers produces the aggregate demand curve labeled $\Sigma_v D$. (The subscript v is carried with the summation sign to signify vertical summation.) In Figure 11.1, the aggregate demand curve for steers, $\Sigma_v D$, has a kink at point E, the output level at which the beef users' demand vanishes. Line segment $\overline{EF}$ is a component of both the hide users' demand curve and the aggregate demand curve, $\Sigma_v D$.

Figure 11.2 illustrates the market equilibrium for joint production. The beef and hide demand curves, together with the vertically summed steer demand curve, $\Sigma_v D$, are like those in Figure 11.1. The industry supply curve for steers is the horizontal summation of all steer-producing firms' marginal cost curves, $\Sigma_h MC_S$. Market equilibrium is achieved at point A, the intersection of the

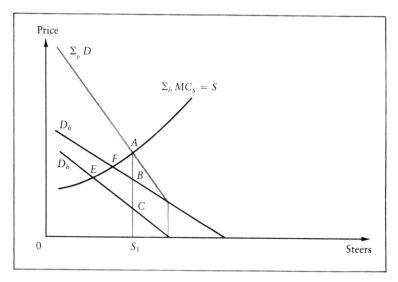

Figure 11.2
Market Equilibrium in Joint Production

Supply and demand are equated at price $\overline{S_1 A}$, the sum of the price of beef, $\overline{S_1 C}$, and the price of hides, $\overline{S_1 B}$.

**Figure 11.3
Firm and Industry Equilibrium in
Joint Production**

(a) The competitive steer producer
takes P_b and P_h as parameters and
sets their sum equal to marginal
cost: $P_b + P_h = P_s = MC_s$. **(b)**
Market forces establish industry
prices P_h and P_b, the price
parameters for each firm in the
industry.

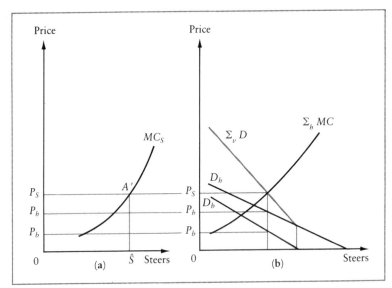

steer supply and demand curves. Note that the competitive efficiency implied by marginal-cost pricing is achieved at the equilibrium rate of industry output, S_1:

$$P_b + P_h = P_s = MC_s$$

where
$$P_b = \text{price of beef} = \overline{S_1 C}$$
$$P_h = \text{price of hides} = \overline{S_1 B}$$
$$P_s = \text{price of steers} = \overline{S_1 A}$$
$$MC_s = \text{marginal cost of steers} = \overline{S_1 A}$$

Firm-Level Analysis

Now let's study the competitive firm's joint production equilibrium.
Figure 11.3 shows the industry supply and demand curves for steers
(panel b) and the corresponding curves for the firm (panel a). Market forces will establish these industry prices: price of steers = P_s;
price of beef = P_b; price of hides = P_h. All three prices are taken
as parameters by each competitive firm. Hence the competitive
firm-relevant demand curves for beef, hides, and steers are the perfectly elastic price lines P_b, P_h, and P_s. Note that the firm's demand
curve for steers, P_S, is the vertical summation of the beef and hide
demand curves. Profit maximization is achieved when the firm produces the rate of steer output for which $P_S = MC_S$, as at point A'.
The firm sells $\hat{S}$ steers and receives a total price of P_S for each steer,
paid partly by beef customers and partly by hide customers.

11.1

Defining the Term *Subsidy*

In the beef and hide example of joint production, the price of beef is lower than it would be in the absence of the demand for hides. In Figure 11.2, the price of beef is $\overline{S_1C}$. However, save for the demand for hides, beef prices would be set at the higher level consistent with point E, the intersection of the beef demand curve and the steer supply curve. Do hide users therefore subsidize beef eaters? Or do beef eaters subsidize hide users? After all, the price of hides in Figure 11.2 is $\overline{S_1B}$, lower than the price at point F that would prevail if there were no demand for beef.

In fact, neither group of users subsidizes the other; they affect each other's prices symbiotically.

The presence of both demand components keeps both prices lower than would otherwise be the case.

A rigorous definition of *subsidy* will clarify the issue. A subsidy occurs when one economic agent allows another to purchase goods at a price less than the marginal cost. In our example, firms equate the price of steers and the marginal cost of producing steers: $P_s = P_b + P_h = MC_s$. But users don't buy the steer; they buy beef or hides. Thus the producer's marginal cost of beef is the marginal cost of the steer less the proceeds for the hide, or

$$MC_b = MC_s - P_h = P_b$$

Similarly, the marginal cost of hides can be expressed as:

$$MC_h = MC_s - P_b = P_h$$

Because the market has no trouble allocating goods according to these rules, $P_b = MC_b$ and $P_h = MC_h$. Hence there is no subsidy.[*]

[*]Chapter 15 shows that the question of subsidies is especially nettlesome when dealing with collective goods that the market cannot allocate efficiently but that are jointly produced nonetheless.

11.2

Allocating Costs of Jointly Produced Goods

Suppose you own a cattle ranch that earns a normal economic profit. You raise steers and sell the jointly produced beef and hides to separate users. You want to know how much of your total cost should be attributed to beef and how much to hides. Unfortunately, any such **cost allocation** is impossible. The costs of joint production, fixed or variable, cannot be attributed to either product. Furthermore, the prices of the joint products cannot be used meaningfully to allocate costs.

The adjacent figure depicts your firm at zero-profit equilibrium (the left-hand panel) and the steer industry (the right-hand panel). The price of steers, P_S, is set by the intersection of the industry supply and demand curves for steers at point E. Industry output is $\hat{S}_{ind}$. Beef and hide prices are demand-determined, because they depend on the height of the respective demand curves at output $\hat{S}_{ind}$. Your firm,

Continued on page 292

Joint-Cost Allocation

In economic logic it is impossible to attribute joint costs uniquely among joint products. The necessary accounting rules of thumb are usually based on the demand-determined price proportions.

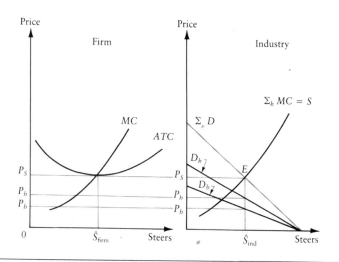

being competitive, takes all prices as parameters and, by assumption, earns zero economic profit by raising and selling $\hat{S}_{firm}$ steers.

Initially, the price of hides is greater than the price of beef. But these prices do not reflect costs. We cannot conclude that the average cost of hides exceeds the average cost of beef, for two reasons: (1) beef and hides are produced jointly, not separately, and (2) prices reflect only the height of the component demand curves.

Suppose we exchange the industry demand curves for beef and hides. The vertically summed demand curve is unchanged, which means that the number of steers and hence the amount of beef and the number of hides are all unchanged. Therefore, neither variable nor fixed costs change. The prices of beef and hides bear no relation to the average variable cost and average fixed cost, except that the totals must be equal in the case of a zero-profit firm. Any allocation of costs is therefore arbitrary and lacks a logical basis. Accountants must make cost allocations for tax purposes, of course, but this example illustrates how crude and unscientific such allocations must be.

A P P L I C A T I O N

11.3

Price Controls and Jointly Produced Goods

Price Controls on Joint Products
Price controls on one product affect the market for jointly produced goods. Here a control on natural gas results in an increase in the price of oil.

At several points in previous chapters we have examined the impact of price controls. Now we may extend the analysis to joint production. Oil and natural gas are often jointly produced. How does a price control on natural gas affect both the natural gas industry and the oil industry?

The figure exhibits the standard joint-product analytics before and after the imposition of the price control on natural gas. The horizontal axis measures the number of wells drilled. (Wells are similar to steers: Each well contains the jointly produced oil and natural gas.) The demand curve for wells ($\Sigma_v D$) is the vertical summation of the demand curves for oil (D_{oil}) and natural gas (D_{ng}). The industry supply curve for wells is labeled $\Sigma_h MC = S$. The market clears at point E. $\hat{W}$ wells will be drilled in equilibrium, and the prices of natural gas and oil are $\hat{W}A$ and $\hat{W}B$ respectively.

When the price ceiling equal to $\overline{OH}$ is imposed on natural gas, the effective demand curve for natural gas becomes the dashed horizontal line; the vertically summed demand curve becomes the dashed curve labeled $\Sigma_v D$. The price control on natural gas distorts the vertical summation of demand and hence the markets for both natural gas and the jointly produced good, oil.

The imposition of price controls forces a reduction in wells from $\hat{W}$ to W_1 and a concomitant re-

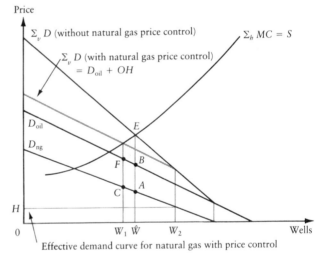

duction in the production of both natural gas and oil. Note that the price of oil rises from $\overline{WB}$ to $\overline{W_1F}$, whereas the (money) price of natural gas falls from $\overline{WA}$ to the controlled price $\overline{W_1C}$. The diagram reveals that there is no shortage of oil; buyers demand less oil in response to the higher price. There is, however, a shortage of natural gas. At the controlled price, buyers want to buy more natural gas than is available.

It must be emphasized that the imposition of price controls distorts both markets, even though technically no shortage exists in the oil industry. Although oil shortages are avoided by price adjustments, the market cannot avoid the ultimate economic distortion of producing an inefficient rate of output. Price controls in one market (natural gas) can create waste, not only in its own industry but in related markets (oil) as well—even when the related markets are not themselves subject to the price restraints.

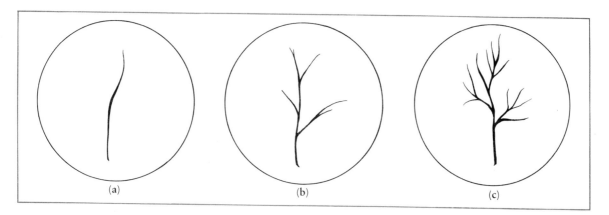

Figure 11.4
Effect of Beating on Wood Fiber

This microscopic depiction shows
(a) a fiber before beating; **(b)** a
fiber plus fibrils after some beating;
and **(c)** a fiber, fibrils, and fibrilae
after beating.

Alternative Production

We may now return to the subclass of multiproduct models called alternative production, in which a firm's various products must compete for the use of a common factor of production. Single-product firms are nearly as rare as the dodo bird, so modern managers must be able to extend the concepts of marginal analysis to the more complex case of multiple products.

Firm-Level Analysis

Consider a paper mill that makes two grades of paper. Although each grade of paper requires some unique inputs, both paper grades can make use of the same pulp-beating equipment. (Figure 11.4 shows what a pulp beater does to wood fibers.) All factors of production fall into two categories: **special factors of production** are those that are unique to a product; **common factors of production** are those that, like the pulp-beating equipment, can be used to produce more than one product. Both the special factors and the common factors are costly. Thus the manager of our paper mill must decide how much of each paper grade to produce and how much of the common factor (the beating equipment, in this example) to devote to each paper grade.

The manager's first step is to use the profit-maximizing principles to derive each paper grade's demand curve for the common factor. Figure 11.5 illustrates how this is achieved for paper grade 1. In competition, the price of paper, a parameter, is depicted as a horizontal line; P_1 is the competitive price in this example. The upward-sloping curve in Figure 11.5 ($MSFC_1$) is the **marginal special factor cost curve**, which shows the marginal cost of expanding the output of paper grade 1 attributable solely to the hiring of special factors. The **common factor demand curve** (labeled CFD), in Figure 11.5, is derived by a process of **vertical subtraction**. For each marginal rate of output, $MSFC_1$ is vertically subtracted from P_1. The result is the negatively sloped CFD_1, which depicts demand gener-

Figure 11.5
Common Factor Demand Curve

The common factor demand curve for paper grade 1 is derived by vertical subtraction: $CFD_1 = P_1 - MSFC_1$.

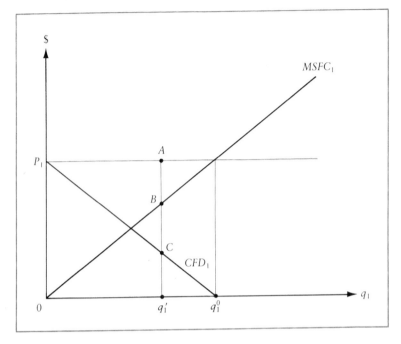

ated by paper grade 1 for the common factor of production.

How does vertical subtraction create a curve like CFD_1? Consider the rate of output q_1^0 in Figure 11.5, where $P_1 = MSFC_1$. Since the price of the marginal unit of output equals the marginal cost of special factors in this case, there is no residual to spend on the common factor. Thus the vertical subtraction $P_1 - MSFC_1 = 0$ is one point on CFD_1. The firm will not be willing to pay any opportunity cost for the use of the common factor in the production of the q_1^0th unit of paper grade 1.

For output q_1', however, $P_1 - MSFC_1 = \overline{AB} = \overline{q_1'C}$. P_1 exceeds $MSFC_1$ by $\overline{AB} = \overline{q_1'C}$, which represents the maximum marginal outlay that the firm would be willing to provide for the q_1'th unit in order to equate price and the full marginal cost. Each point like C on CFD_1 measures the maximum amount that the firm will devote to obtaining enough of the common factor to bring a marginal unit of paper grade 1 into production. As with any demand curve, it is useful to think of CFD_1 as a marginal benefit curve of the common factor for the product in question.

The next modeling step is to generate a common factor demand curve for paper grade 2 by vertically subtracting the marginal special factor cost for paper grade 2, $MSFC_2$, from the price, P_2. The new common factor demand curve, CFD_2, is derived in exactly the same fashion as CFD_1 is derived in Figure 11.5. If the firm sold more than two products, a CFD curve would be similarly derived for each. Each point on each CFD curve measures the marginal benefit

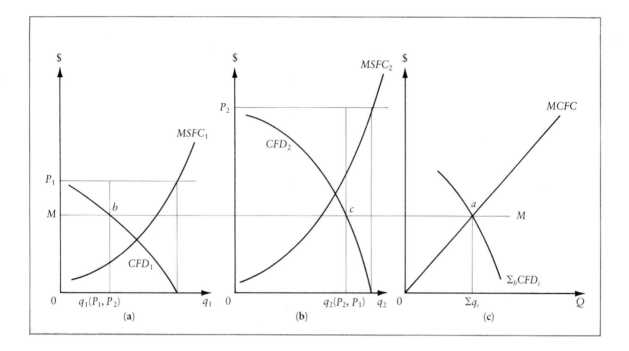

(a)   (b)   (c)

Figure 11.6
Firm Output of Two Alternative Products

Paper output levels q_1 and q_2 can be determined when the prices P_1 and P_2 are taken as parameters. **(a)** The firm produces $q_1(p_1,p_2)$ of one product. **(b)** The firm produces $q_2(p_2,p_1)$ of the alternative product. **(c)** The opportunity cost of the common factor can be determined by noting where the $MCFC$ equals the horizontal summation of the CFD_i.

of devoting the common factor to the production of a marginal unit of each product.

Figure 11.6 shows the $MSFC$ and CFD curves for two products (panels a and b). In addition, panel c introduces the **marginal common factor cost curve** ($MCFC$). With this figure, we are in a position to analyze the profit-maximizing level of output for each type of paper and the requirements of each for the use of the common factor. The product prices, P_1 and P_2, are determined outside the firm (the next section will show how).

The central theme of the ensuing analysis is that the two products are alternatives competing for the firm's common factors of production. They essentially "demand" some of the common factor. It is simple enough to horizontally sum the demand curves for the common factor to come up with aggregate demand. The curve labeled $\Sigma_h CFD_i$ in Figure 11.6c is this aggregate demand. It is derived as all horizontal summations are: For any vertical height, it is the sum of the horizontal distances of CFD_i.

Note that $\Sigma_h CFD_i$ crosses $MCFC$ at point a. At this level of output, the familiar rule $MB = MC$ is satisfied for the common factor. The firm can therefore maximize profits by using enough of the common factor to produce a total output Σq_i, as depicted in Figure 11.6c. Output Σq_i also establishes the opportunity cost, at the margin, of the common factor.

Efficiency requires that the firm's individual products generate sufficient marginal benefits to pay marginal costs. In Figure 11.6, the satisfaction of this requirement is shown with the use of line $\overline{MM}$, which is drawn horizontally through point a. Line $\overline{MM}$ intersects CFD_1 at point b, the profit-maximizing level of output for paper grade 1, designated $q_1(p_1,p_2)$. Similarly, line $\overline{MM}$ intersects CFD_2 at point c, from which the profit-maximizing level of output for paper grade 2, $q_2(p_2,p_1)$, can be derived. The expressions $q_1(p_1,p_2)$ and $q_2(p_2,p_1)$ remind us that each product supply within the firm is dependent not only on its own price but also on the price of the other product.

The interdependence of the two alternative products is further illustrated in Figure 11.7. Essentially, the diagram illustrates equilibrium between products when there are two different prices for paper grade 2, P_2^0 and P_2^1. (The superscripts 0 and 1 are used to distinguish the two different prices and the associated equilibrium curves.) It is easy to see that the shift from P_2^0 to the lower price, P_2^1, causes a shift from CFD_2^0 to CFD_2^1. Each CFD_2 is the vertical subtraction of the marginal special factor cost curve from P_2. Since one of its components has shifted to the left, $\Sigma_h CFD$ must shift left. The intersection of $MCFC$ and $\Sigma_h CFC_i$ occurs at a lower level, thus providing an increased incentive to produce q_1. Meanwhile, the production of q_2 falls. The net result can be expressed in symbolic notation:

$$q_1(P_1^0,P_2^0) < q_1(P_1^0,P_2^1) \text{ and } q_2(P_2^1,P_1^0) < q_2(P_2^0,P_1^0)$$

Figure 11.7
Rearrangement of Output When the Price of One Alternative Product Falls

(a) The production of paper grade 1 rises when the price of paper grade 2 falls. **(b)** The production of paper grade 2 falls. **(c)** The opportunity cost of the factor also falls, causing less total product to be produced.

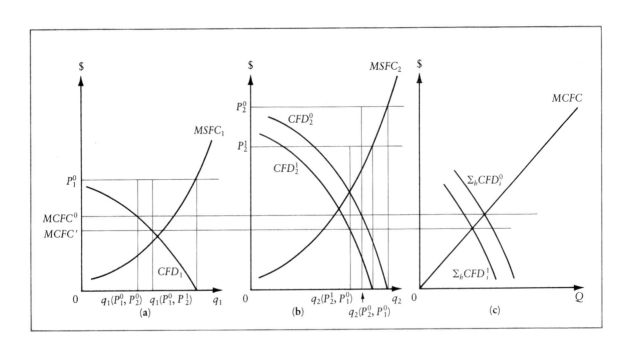

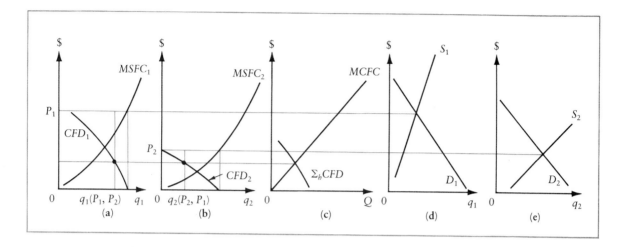

The equal marginal principle that always accompanies efficiency calculations can readily be seen in this example, albeit in modified form. The firm, to maximize profits, will equate $MCFC$ and the CFD_i for all products. But CFD_i is $P_i - MSFC_i$. Therefore, profit maximization requires this rule: $P_i - MSFC_i = MCFC$ for all products. In other words, the benefit from selling a unit of a product, minus the marginal cost of special factors, must equal the marginal cost of the common factor. Is the rule $P = MC$ violated? No, it is merely rewritten as $P = MSFC + MCFC$. Hence, the analysis of alternative products does not contradict standard economic theory.

Figure 11.8
Industry Supply and Demand and Firm Production of Alternative Goods

(a) Output of paper grade 1 lies where common factor demand equals the marginal cost of the common factor. **(b)** Output of paper grade 2 is determined in the same way. **(c)** The opportunity cost of the common factor is equal to the marginal common factor costs. **(d)** Supply and demand determine price P_1. **(e)** Supply and demand also determine price P_2.

Industry-Level Analysis

The previous section analyzes alternative production without explaining how industry prices are determined. The competitive model assumes that industry prices are determined by the forces of supply and demand adjusting to shortages and surpluses. Competitive firms engaged in alternative production encounter much the same industry forces. Observe Figure 11.8, which repeats the three panels of Figure 11.6 and adds two panels to show supply and demand for good 1 and good 2. The prices P_1 and P_2, which the firm regards as parameters, are determined at the market level. All else remains the same.

The critical tool in industry-level analysis of alternative production is the adjustment of prices to shortages and surpluses and the consequent readjustment of firms to the changes in prices. Consider Figure 11.9, in which the prices of two products are equal. The $MSFC_i$ curves are equal too, but the position of curves D_1 and D_2 is such that at $P_1^0 = P_2^0$ there is a shortage of Q_1 and a surplus of

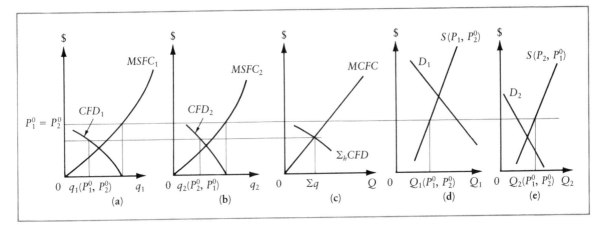

Figure 11.9
Multiproduct Firm Industry in Disequilibrium

Assume that P_1 and P_2 are equal, causing a shortage of Q_1 and a surplus of Q_2. **(a)** Output q_1 is determined as before. **(b)** Output q_2 is determined likewise. **(c)** The opportunity cost of the common factor is also determined as before. **(d)** At the given price, there is a shortage of Q_1. **(e)** At the given price, there is a surplus of Q_2.

Q_2 (see panels d and e). The result is upward pressure on P_1 and downward pressure on P_2.

The firm's response to these price changes is shown in Figure 11.10. The supply curves of the two goods shift as individual firms rearrange their output. The S_1 curve shifts to the right, from $S_1(P_1, P_2^0)$ to $S_1(P_1, P_2^1)$, and the S_2 curve shifts to the left, from $S_2(P_2, P_1^0)$ to $S_2(P_2, P_1^1)$. Shifting continues until the surpluses and shortages that initiated it are eliminated. As in single-product markets, prices give firms the incentive they need to allocate internal resources efficiently. The noncollusive aggregate result is an industry price level that eliminates shortages and surpluses.

A   P   P   L   I   C   A   T   I   O   N

11.4

Minimum Markup Laws

During and following the Great Depression of the 1930s, a number of laws were passed to protect small businesses. Among the holdovers are **minimum markup** laws, which require firms to mark up their products at retail by some minimum amount. The markup is essentially the difference between the retail price and wholesale price. For example, in Wisconsin the minimum markup is 6 percent, which means that the retail price must be at least 6 percent above wholesale. Laws like these make it difficult for multiproduct retail stores to offer goods at the efficient prices dictated by the equal marginal revenue principle.

The purpose of minimum markup is to protect the small stores that are competing with stores carrying a wider assortment of products. Liquor stores, camera shops, and gasoline stations, for example, are insulated by these laws from competition with department stores, supermarkets, and the like.

Minimum markup laws have considerable impact on the pricing of "high-volume" items. For example, in the few days before Thanksgiving and Christmas, the efficient markup rate of turkeys falls dramatically. Because turkeys are being sold so quickly, the marginal common factor cost attributable to each is reduced.

In the grocery store, the common factor for poultry is shelf space per unit of time. The faster the pace of turkey sales, the less time spent on the shelves per turkey $P - MSFC = MCFC$ falls since $MCFC$ falls.

Thus we may add another economy to our vocabulary: **economies of scope** permit supermarkets and department stores to provide high-volume items at low markup. However, if the markup is kept high artificially (that is, through minimum markup laws), consumers may be denied the efficient price provided by multiproduct firms.

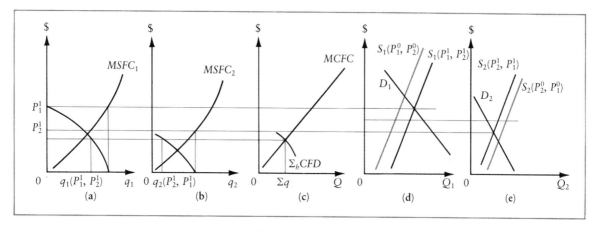

Multiproduct Monopolists

So far, the discussion of the theory of multiproduct firms has assumed that the firm has no control over its price. This section extends the analysis to cases of monopoly in which the firm does have control over price. The symbol of this control is a downward-sloping demand curve.

Figure 11.10
Adjustment to Equilibrium Prices
Assume **(a)** the equilibrium q_1, **(b)** the equilibrium q_2, and **(c)** this opportunity cost for the common factor. **(d)** The aggregate supply of good 1 rises to alleviate the shortage. **(e)** The aggregate supply of good 2 shifts to alleviate the surplus.

11.5

Entry and Exit in Product Markets

The conventional theory of the firm, which deals exclusively with single-product firms, gives us insight into the entry/exit process. A firm will remain in its industry as long as price covers opportunity cost. In the short run, opportunity cost is the average variable cost; in the long run, it is the average cost, including a fair rate of return to investors. If price does not cover these costs, the firm will exit the industry—or not enter in the first place.

In the theory of the multiproduct firm, the concept of the entry and exit of firms is ex-

tended to the entry and exit of products. The rule is that a firm will produce the same combination of products as long as the revenues from all products cover all opportunity costs. Each product must contribute an equal marginal profit to the firm, so that **net marginal revenue,** or *NMR* (the difference between *MR* and

MSFC) equals marginal common factor cost. Any product that cannot match the others in net marginal revenue will be dropped—"exit the industry"—and any that can match the others will be retained or added.

The message is that management should consider products to be competitive entities within the firm. The survival of those products should be governed by the same rules governing the survival of the firm in the market. The accompanying table demonstrates the unity of economic theory on the issue of entry and exit.

Comparative Theoretical Equilibria

Criterion	Single Product	Joint Products	Alternative Products
Production	$P = MC$	$P_1 + P_2 = MC$	$P_1 - MSFC_1 = P_2 - MSFC_2 = MCFC$
Entry/exit (investor fair rate of return)	$P = AC$	$P_1 q_1 + P_2 q_2 = TC$	$P_1 q_1 + P_2 q_2 = TC$

Joint Production

Let's begin with the example of beef and hides. The monopolist depicted in Figure 11.11 faces a downward-sloping demand curve for beef and hides and hence the marginal revenue curves MR_b and MR_h. In order to find the level of output that equates marginal benefit and marginal costs, the firm must vertically sum these marginal revenue curves. (The vertical summation is necessary since the same steer contributes to both revenue flows.) The profit-maximizing level of steer production is that where $\Sigma_v MR = MC$. The market-clearing prices at that level of output are P_h^M and P_b^M.

Alternative Production

The monopolist that produces alternative products with a common factor of production must perform calculations similar to those of a competitor producing alternative products. We have already learned that the competitive firm must subtract *MSFC* from price to obtain the demand for the common factor of production. The only difference here is that the monopolist must be aware that increases in output will affect price; hence marginal revenue lies below price.

To determine the proper allocation of the common factor within the firm, the monopolist must subtract *MSFC* from *MR* to derive the net marginal revenue associated with the product. This

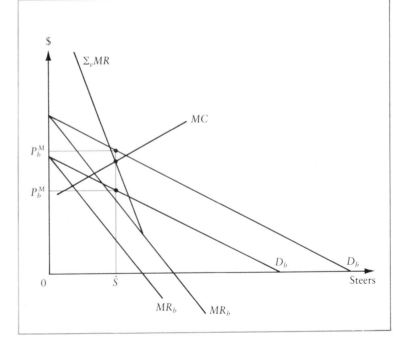

Figure 11.11
Determination of Joint Production Levels in a Monopoly

The demand for steers is derived from the demand for beef and hides. Both generate marginal revenue for the monopolist. The vertical summation of marginal revenue is equal to marginal cost at the profit-maximizing level of steers and the given prices for beef and hides.

11.7

Price Controls on Alternative Products

Once you appreciate the interdependence of alternate products, it should be easy to extend the usual analysis of price controls and resulting shortages to the multiproduct firm. Placing a price control on alternative products is much like trying to compress a balloon by squeezing it in your hands: The balloon bulges out wherever it can, as do profit opportunities.

If the government were to freeze product prices without preannouncement, a firm would limit the production of whichever products experienced greater increases in input prices. If the government price controls created a short-age of a common factor of production, such as meat in a multiproduct meat-packing plant, the amount of meat still available would be devoted to producing products with high net marginal revenue.

If, on the other hand, the government were to pre-announce a price control, firms would anticipate the control period by raising prices, in accordance with perceived elasticities of demand.

11.8

When to Destroy a Joint Product

Ironically, it may be in the monopolist's interest to produce joint products and then destroy one or more of them. This tactic is not merely a matter of holding an accidental overrun off the market to keep the monopoly price high but instead a deliberate destruction of deliberate production.

Consider the adjacent figure, which repeats the analysis of Figure 11.11 but rearranges the positions of the demand curves and marginal revenue curves. The figure here shows that at point d, and the level of steer production $\hat{S}$, the rule $MR = MC$ is satisfied. However, MR_h is negative at $\hat{S}$ (and represented there by point e). It is therefore profit maximizing to reduce sales of hides until MR_h rises back to zero, at point f. The monopolist destroys the hides of the number of steers represented by distance $f\hat{S}$ in order to raise the revenue from hide sales at price P_h. At the same time, the beef from the entire production of steers, $\hat{S}$, is sold at price P_b.

Thus we have the general rule

modified. The marginal revenue curve for joint products is the vertical summation of the component parts, except for components with a negative MR. Enough products that have a negative MR where $\Sigma_h MR = MC$ should be destroyed so that their individual MR rises to zero. In this example, the hides should be buried or shredded for use as fertilizer or an alternative product.

Destruction of a Deliberately Produced Joint Product

The monopolist will not sell hides for which the marginal revenue is negative. Here, distance $f\hat{S}$ represents the steers whose hides are destroyed.

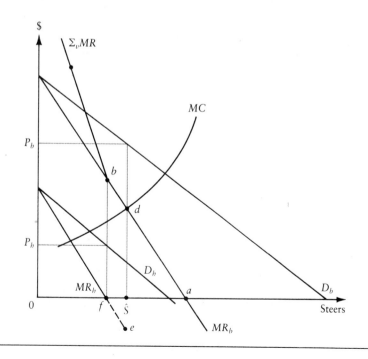

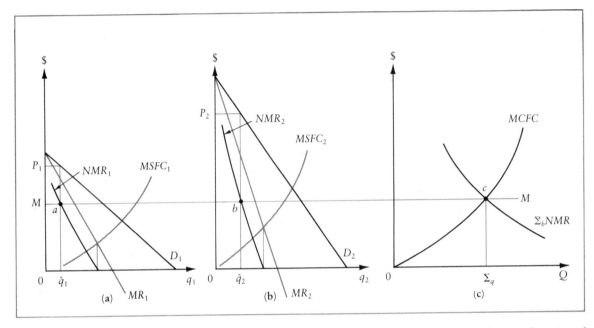

Figure 11.12
Alternative Production by a Monopolist

(a) The marginal revenue less the marginal special factor costs, NMR_1, is set equal to the opportunity cost of the common factor. Quantity q_1 is produced. **(b)** NMR_2 is equated to the opportunity cost of the common factor, and q_2 is produced. **(c)** The marginal common factor cost is equated to the horizontal summation of the net marginal revenue curves to determine the opportunity cost of the common factor.

vertical subtraction is depicted in Figure 11.12a for product 1 and Figure 11.12b for product 2. The NMR curves are the common factor demand curves for the monopolist.

The rest of the analysis is exactly like that of the competitor. The horizontal summation of the NMR curves, $\Sigma_b NMR$, intersects $MCFC$ at point c in panel c. This manipulation establishes the profit-maximizing level of common factor use. The allocation of that level of common factor is depicted as the intersection of NMR_1 and line $\overline{MM}$ at point a in panel a and the intersection of NMR_2 and line $\overline{MM}$ at point b in panel b. The monopolist will produce $\hat{q}_1$ and $\hat{q}_2$ and charge P_1 and P_2 to clear the market.

In its multiproduct form, the general rule for the single-product monopolist, $MR = MC$, is extended to

$$NMR_i = MR_i - MSFC_i = MCFC \qquad (11.1)$$

11.9

Judicial Use of Multiproduct Pricing Theory

The fact that fixed costs cannot be allocated precisely is of immense importance in the internal accounting of firms and in the judicial examination of those accounts when firms are defendants in antitrust suits. Such defendants are typically accused of lowering the price on one product to drive rivals out of business while subsidizing this predation with profits on other products.

Phillip Areeda and Donald Turner have proposed a defense for firms accused of predatory pricing. They suggest that such firms show that the prices of their products are above the average variable cost, not the average cost.[*] But economists have trou-

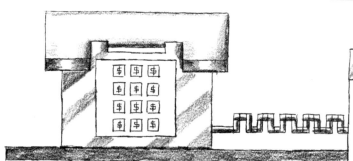
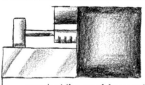

ble with this calculation, since average variable costs—much less average costs—cannot be allocated precisely for joint products. However, the Areeda-Turner rule is a great improvement over the rules requiring fully allocated costs.

A recent case in the telephone industry provides a useful illustration of the Areeda-Turner rule.

*Phillip Areeda and Donald Turner, "Predatory Pricing and Related Practices under Section 2 of the Sherman Act," *Harvard Law Review* 88 (1975): 697.

Northeastern Telephone Company sued Ma Bell and in particular its affiliate, Southern New England Telephone Company, for the predatory pricing of equipment.[†] What concerns us here is judicial appreciation of the complexity of multiproduct firms. No more eloquent state-

[†]Northeastern Telephone Company v. American Telephone and Telegraph Company _____ F.2d _____ (2nd Cir. 1981). (The blank lines in the citation indicate that the decision has been handed down but that its place in the 2nd Circuit Reporter was not set at the time of this writing.)

ment of the problem exists than that of Circuit Judge Kaufman in this case:

Northeastern's argument in favor of a fully distributed cost test is based on a misunderstanding of the economic notion of subsidization. Northeastern seems to believe that whenever a product's price fails to cover fully distributed costs, the enterprise must subsidize that product's revenues with revenues earned elsewhere. But when the price of an item exceeds the costs directly attributable to its production, that is, when price exceeds marginal or average variable costs, no subsidy is necessary. On the contrary, any surplus can be used to defray the firm's nonallocable expenses.

Summary

In a departure from the typical emphasis on single-product firms, this chapter considers the firms that produce more than one product. There are two kinds of multiproduct firms: The joint-product firm produces products that cannot be produced separately; the alternative-product firm uses common factors of production to produce goods that essentially compete for the common factor.

The basic theory of multiproduct firms can be used to examine their reaction to such problems as price controls and minimum-markup laws. The usual categories of analysis are applicable here: the entry/exit decision, price setting, and competitive versus monopoly equilibrium conditions. Competitive firms have no difficulty in allocating resources to the various products. But monopolies have the usual efficiency problem of artificial scarcity and may even destroy some of their products in order to raise the marginal revenue of the products they do sell.

The study of firm economics is not contradicted by multiproduct-firm analysis but instead enriched by it. In particular, the notion of entry and exit can be expanded: With a capacity to produce multiple products, firms can enter new markets and exit old ones while staying in existence. In fact, the most common type of entry or exit in our economy is that resulting from rearranging the product mix within an existing firm.

Key Terms

alternative production 288
common factor demand curve 293
common factors of production 293
cost allocation 291
economies of scope 298
joint production 288
marginal common factor cost curve 295
marginal special factor cost curve 293
minimum markup 298
net marginal revenue 299
special factors of production 293
vertical subtraction 293

Problems

1. a. Are men's and boys' haircuts alternative or joint products or simply a single product? Explain your answer.
   b. Why do we often see lower prices for children's haircuts despite higher marginal squirming costs?
2. The telephone companies formerly amalgamated into American Telephone & Telegraph were restricted to a "fair" rate of return. They produced both long-distance calls and local calls. But now that they may no longer compete in the long-distance market, what will happen to local rates?
3. A marina provides slips, which are parking spaces for pleasure boats with pedestrian access, and moorings, which are anchoring spots with rowboat access.
   a. Are these joint or alternative products? Why?
   b. How would you advise a firm or municipal marina authority to price the two services?
4. Banks use different price structures for business and personal checking accounts. Why?
5. a. Why do new-car dealerships usually sell used cars also?
   b. How should they decide whether to sell used cars indoors or outdoors?
   c. How should they decide on the mix of used and new cars?
6. Universities offer huge undergraduate classes and tiny graduate classes.
   a. Are these joint or alternative products?
   b. Is it "fair" or "efficient" to price them the same per student?
7. Ace Construction Company has spent $100,000 to develop a bid on a municipal building. Its final bid covers costs plus a 10-percent markup:

Development of bid	$ 100,000
Materials	5,000,000
Labor	10,000,000
Overhead (67 percent of labor)	6,700,000
Total costs	$21,800,000
Markup	2,180,000
Total bid	$23,980,000

   The city refuses all bids and offers to award the contract to the first firm that will bid $22 million. What should Ace do?
8. Suppose that your backyard oil well produces both oil and natural gas in fixed proportions. Show how an increase in the price of oil will affect your output of natural gas.
9. A grocer has 10 feet of shelf space to devote to two cereals: Wheaties and Cheerios. The two cereals are priced the same. The cereal shelves are restocked by the distributor once a week. The grocer knows nothing about revenue or cost curves but has learned to adjust the order so that only two boxes of each cereal are left when the distributor restocks the shelves.
   a. Can you show that the equal marginal revenue principle is satisfied?

b. How did the grocer decide to devote 10 feet of shelf space to cereals in the first place?

c. Derive a general rule for determining the amount of space to devote to all products in the store. Translate this general rule into a rule of thumb for the grocer. What economic forces would lead the grocer to discover the rule by himself or herself? (Hint: What would happen if the grocer did not follow the rule?)

10. An auto firm produces two cars, the Deluxe and the Custom, in its Hoboken works. They are substitutes in production; the relevant production costs are shown in Table 11.1. The two cars also sell to distinctly different clientele; the demand data are shown in Table 11.2.

a. How many of each car should be produced? At what prices?

b. Suppose the Deluxe and the Custom are substitutes in consumption. How would your answer change?

Table 11.1
Production Costs for Deluxe and Custom Autos

Quantity	$MSFC_D$	$MSFC_C$	MCFC	Quantity	$MSFC_D$	$MSFC_C$	MCFC
100,000	5,000	5,000	2,000	650,000	5,550	5,100	3,100
150,000	5,050	5,010	2,100	700,000	5,600	5,120	3,200
200,000	5,100	5,020	2,200	750,000	5,650	5,130	3,300
250,000	5,150	5,030	2,300	800,000	5,700	5,140	3,400
300,000	5,200	5,040	2,400	850,000	5,750	5,150	3,500
350,000	5,250	5,050	2,500	900,000	5,800	5,160	3,600
400,000	5,300	5,060	2,600	950,000	5,850	5,170	3,700
450,000	5,350	5,070	2,700	1,000,000	5,900	5,180	3,800
500,000	5,400	5,080	2,800	1,050,000	5,950	5,190	3,900
550,000	5,450	5,090	2,900	1,100,000	6,000	5,200	4,000
600,000	5,500	5,100	3,000				

Table 11.2
Demand Data for Deluxe and Custom Autos

P_D	Q_D	P_C	Q_C
10,000	100,000	8,000	250,000
9,500	125,000	7,500	300,000
9,000	200,000	7,000	375,000
8,500	300,000	6,500	450,000
8,000	350,000	6,000	550,000
7,500	375,000	5,500	700,000

11. Your firm produces three joint products in equal fixed proportions. The demand data are summarized in Table 11.3; the production costs for the common factor are summarized in Table 11.4.

a. What level of output should be set?

b. What price should be charged for each product?

c. Recalculate the level of output and prices assuming that the fixed proportions are $3Q_B$ to $2Q_B$ to $1Q_C$.

Table 11.3
Demand Data for Three Joint Products

P	Q_A	Q_B	Q_C	P	Q_A	Q_B	Q_C
100	0	0	0	40	5	6	14
90	0	0	0	30	25	7	16
80	0	0	6	20	50	8	18
70	0	3	8	10	60	9	20
60	0	4	10	0	100	10	22
50	0	5	12				

Table 11.4
Production Costs for the Common Factor of Three Joint Products

Quantity	Total Cost
0	0
10	50
20	60
30	75
40	95
50	105
60	110
70	120
80	140
90	170
100	210

Table 11.5

Demand Data in
an Imperfectly
Competitive Foreign
Market

P_A^f	Q_A^f
0	50
10	40
20	30
30	20
40	10
50	0

d. Recalculate again, this time assuming that there is a competitive foreign market for product A, which has a price $P_A = 20$.

e. Now assume that the foreign market for product A is imperfectly competitive. (The demand data are summarized in Table 11.5.)

12. Explain why a multiproduct firm in an imperfectly competitive market could be offered a positive price for a unit of output but choose to destroy that output.

13. Explain why a multiproduct firm may face identical special factor costs and identical common factor costs but still charge significantly different prices for two products.

14. Explain why excess economic profits in a multiproduct firm cannot be attributed to any one of the products.

15. Explain why the manager of a large-chain grocery store would want to have a lower markup on Easter lilies than on hamburger.

16. Suppose a paper firm that is producing two alternative products with a common paper machine develops a third product. This product is well accepted by the market, and the firm is a monopolist in that market. Analyze graphically how the firm should price the product and allocate machine time to its production.

17. a. When an airline pays the same price per landing at an airport as a single-engine private plane does, which one is being subsidized? Why?

    b. Explain how the definition of *subsidy* helps you answer this question.

18. Suppose a firm producing two different grades of cement opens a new plant that can produce only one grade of that cement. Should the original plant begin to specialize in the grade that the new plant does not produce?

19. Suppose that the common factor costs of two different products were to double.

    a. How would the cost increase be reflected in the short-run decisions of the firm?

    b. How would the cost increase be reflected in the long-run equilibrium of the industry?

20. How would price controls affect the incentive to destroy a deliberately produced joint product?

21. Would a member of a cartel or a competitive firm be more likely to destroy a deliberately produced joint product? Explain your answer.

22. Economies of scale reduce long-run average costs when larger amounts of a single product are produced. Economies of scope do not require that large amounts of any product be produced. Explain the relationship between these two concepts.

23. a. What does a hardware store produce?

    b. How does a hardware store decide to allocate shelf space to its various products?

    c. Why do some hardware stores sell pots and pans whereas others do not?

24. Refer to Figure 11.2. If the demand curve for hides were to rise to twice its original height, how much beef and hides would be produced? Explain your answer.

25. Demonstrate that a price control on established products will induce a monopolist producing alternative products to expand its product assortment.

26. A leather-goods firm produces garment leather from one side of a cow hide and shoe leather from the other side. Suppose that the firm gets a shipment of leather that is too thin to make both products so that one or the other must be chosen. Use your joint product theory to determine which of the two products will be chosen for production.

27. A firm that produces two alternative goods will be given an order for Q units of product A, only if it can produce the entire amount. Use your theory of alternative product firms to illustrate how the firm should decide whether to take the order.

28. If a firm contracts to buy 40,000,000 units of product A and later reneges, how do you calculate what the firm has lost?

29. When the joint product firm experiences an increase in fixed costs, how does that affect the mix of outputs it produces?

30. What is the impact of the discovery of a new use for cow brains, previously unmarketable, on the price and quantity of meat and leather?

31. A gasoline station sells retail gasoline and repair services. Identify the common factors of production and whether the goods are alternative or joint products. During a period of price controls on gasoline, what incentive does the station have to favor repair customers in the allocations of scarce gasoline?

32. A television retailer sells many brands of televisions. Describe the calculation that would be used to determine whether to add or subtract a brand.

33. Movie theaters can show either one film over and over or double features. Are these joint products or alternative products? What factors go into making the decision? Would you expect more double features with first run movies or older movies?

34. Del Mar Associates produces magnificent books and hilarious phone calls to authors. Are these alternative products or joint products, or is one an input into the production of the other?

35. Suppose that the cost of labor were to rise relative to the cost of capital. You know from the theory of production that the firm will tend to shift away from labor toward capital for any level of output. Describe how the multiproduct firm will also shift toward alternative products that are less labor intensive in their production.

36. A firm produces forty-seven different products and claims that it is too hard to follow marginalist rules. Instead, it uses average costs allocated to all products, fills orders if the price covers costs, and refuses orders if they don't. Can you suggest ways in which the firm could more easily follow marginalist rules? Can you determine which products are overproduced under this firm's strategy and which are underproduced?

Suggested Readings

Hayne, Henry. *Managerial Economics Analysis and Cases.* 4th ed. Dallas: Business Publications, 1978, chap. 12.

Scherer, F. M. *Industrial Market Structure and Economic Performance.* 2nd ed. Chicago: Rand McNally, 1980, chaps. 7, 8.

Stigler, George J. *The Theory of Price.* New York: Macmillan, 1966, chaps. 8, 9.

12

SPECIAL
TOPICS
IN PRICING

We have already studied many pricing practices—such as dominant-firm price leadership, barometric price leadership, and peak-load pricing. These approaches tend to fall rather naturally within the framework of the marginalist approach to the theory of the firm. By contrast, the "special topics" in pricing that are the focus of this chapter seem to depart from the predictions of the marginalist approach. Actually, however, they are marginalist responses that the firm may employ in the face of special market conditions.

Note that this chapter contains no Applications. Instead, the entire chapter is an application of the theory that came before.

Cost-Plus Pricing

There is no better example of a seeming departure from marginalist reasoning in the annals of special pricing practices than **cost-plus pricing**, or markup pricing. Cost-plus pricing is apparently neither price-taking behavior nor monopolistic $MC = MR$ pricing.

Cost-plus pricing is an effort to establish price at some fixed percentage—or **markup**—above average variable costs. An accountant would call the markup the **contribution margin** (CM), signifying that it is the portion devoted to the fixed costs of the firm. The markup must be large enough to sustain the firm in the long run by providing the investors with a fair rate of return but small enough to retain customers in the competitive marketplace. Hence the profit maximizing markup swings so that $MC = MR$; the markup cannot be set independently of economic conditions.

To understand how the markup is determined, consider the AVC and MC curves in Figure 12.1. If there are many competitors in the market, the firm will face a very elastic demand curve at the competitive price level P.

If the firm attempts a markup in excess of CM, customers will look for less expensive alternatives; a price cut is the firm's best response. If the markup is less than CM, the resulting explosion of orders will reveal that the price is too low. Thus the markup is an experimental number. If the markup that can be achieved does not permit a fair rate of return to investors, then the firm will produce something else or exit the industry—a failed experiment. Otherwise, the firm may consider its experiment a success.

Cost-plus pricing can easily be reconciled with marginalist reasoning. Note, however, that *marginalist reasoning* may describe the thought processes of a managerial economist but not necessarily those of an entrepreneur. Rather, marginalist theory describes the results of decisions made by entrepreneurs who are ignorant of the theory but who have the capacity to adapt to economic conditions. If you ask the manager of a hardware store if she sets $MR = MC$, she will probably not know what you mean. But try asking instead how her intuitive business decisions are made: "Do you try to build sales in tools and home-improvement fixtures when you can? Do

Figure 12.1
Markup over Average Variable Cost

The contribution margin (CM) is the difference between MC and AVC.

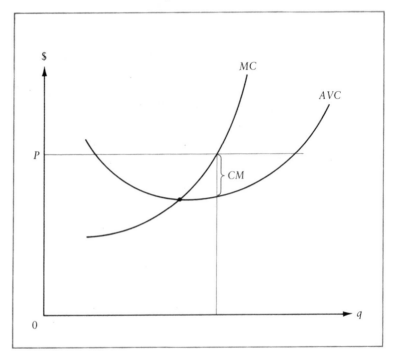

you try to save costs? Do you keep track of prices at nearby hardware stores?'' In the course of these common practices, she uncon-
sciously equates $MR = MC$.

Limit Pricing

A firm that has market power obviously will try to maintain that
power over time. Such a firm is typically not a pure monopoly, so
it must take into account in its pricing decisions the existence and
strength of real and potential rivals. New rivals will enter the market at a rate positively related to the difference between the price
charged by the firm and the average cost of all firms in the market.
Limit pricing, as the name implies, is an effort to place a limit on the
price charged in order to deter or slow down entry.

In Figure 12.2, time is the variable on the horizontal axis and
profit per unit of time is the variable on the vertical axis. Trajectory
T_0 represents the profits per year of a firm that sets short-run profit-
maximizing prices throughout the period (in other words, that does
not engage in limit pricing). Trajectory T_L denotes the acceptance of
lower short-run profits, up to year A, in anticipation of higher
profits beyond year A due to the slower entry of rivals (in other
words, a firm engaged in limit pricing). Trajectory T_L, with a lower
slope, intersects T_0 at point A.

In many respects, limit pricing is like dominant-firm price leadership, which is introduced in Chapter 10. However, limit pricing
includes both short-run and long-run analysis, whereas dominant-

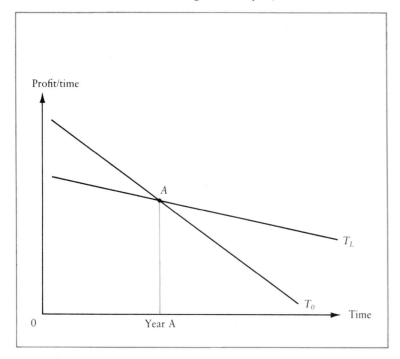

Figure 12.2
Profit Trajectories in Limit Pricing

A firm with market power may
curtail profits in the short run in
order to deter entry and protect
longer-run profits. The strategy pays
off if the present value of trajectory
T_L (with limit pricing) exceeds that
of T_0 (without limit pricing).

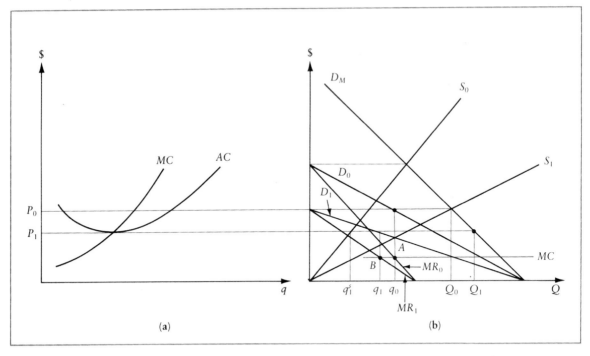

(a)   (b)

Figure 12.3
Scale Economies of Limit Pricing

(a) The strategy of limit pricing allows the capture and retention of scale economies only if the firm is able to set price below the minimum AC of the potential entrant. **(b)** The retention of scale economies requires the production of Q_1 in order to clear the market at price P_1.

firm price leadership is a longer-term concept. Look at Figure 12.3. The market demand curve, D_M, and the short-run supply curve, S_0, appear in panel b. They determine the demand curve for the price leader, D_0, and the associated marginal revenue curve, MR_0. The short-run profit-maximizing price and quantity for the limit pricer are therefore P_0 and q_0, located where $MR_0 = MC$ (point A).

The problem that arises for the limit pricer is that (P_0, q_0) is not a stable equilibrium. This problem becomes obvious in Figure 12.3a, which contains the cost curves of the potential entrant. The minimum of the average cost curve lies below the short-run profit-maximizing price (P_0). So this potential entrant would enter. But over time, firm entry will shift the supply curve from S_0 to S_1, the demand curve from D_0 to D_1, and the marginal revenue curve from MR_0 to MR_1. The new short-run profit-maximizing price and quantity would be P_1 and q_1, where the MR_1 and MC curves intersect (point B).

The limit pricer attempts to keep the price at P_1 initially, rather than P_0, in order to keep the potential entrant from committing its capital resources and expertise. But price can be lowered to P_1 only if the limit pricer produces $Q_1 - q_1^s$, so that the market can be cleared at price P_1. Thus output must exceed the short-run profit-maximizing output in order to prevent the fall of both price and output.

Figure 12.3 shows the price leader as having significant economies of scale. But to capture these scale economies, the leader must employ limit pricing. Note also that, from the consumer's point of view, limit pricing attains and keeps lower prices and does it sooner than the entry of other firms would.

Predatory Pricing

Predatory pricing is the pejorative term applied to the act of lowering a firm's product price for the purpose of driving a rival firm out of business and then raising the price to take advantage of the enhanced market power. The objective is to reduce the price below a rival's average total cost long enough to cause the rival to exit the market. Such a practice is often called a "price war." As with any war, the promise of the rosy "post-war" period must be sufficiently better than the reality of the prewar period to make the war worthwhile. Furthermore, the "predatory" firm cannot benefit unless consumers also benefit.

Predatory Pricing by Identical Firms

When firms have identical costs, predatory pricing is suicidal. To see why, observe Figure 12.4. Panel a shows the cost curves of the predatee, and panel b shows those of the predator. The initial break-even equilibrium for the two firms is at output levels q_0^R (predator) and q_0^E (predatee) and price P_0.

In order to decrease price to P_1, the predator must increase output. With the glut of products on the market, the predatee loses money, of course, but can minimize those losses by setting $MC = P_1$ at point b and producing q_1^E. That is, the predatee responds to the predator by reducing output.

Figure 12.4
Cost Curves of Two Firms with the Same Minimum AC

In order for **(a)** the predatee to be driven out of business by **(b)** the predator, the predator must incur greater costs than it imposes on its rival. In such a case, predation is suicide.

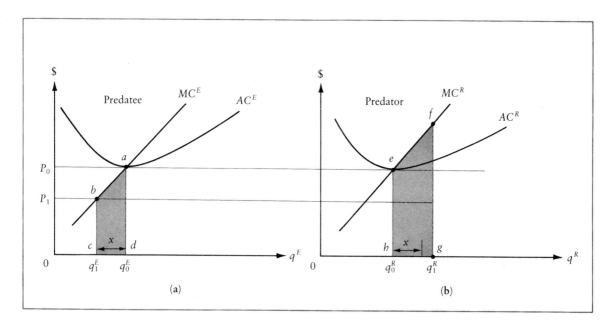

(a)   (b)

The predatee's response creates problems for the predator, since the lower price can be preserved only through *greater* aggregate output. But the predatee has cut output by an amount labeled x. Thus the predator must increase output by substantially more than x in order to keep the price below P_0. In doing so, the predator incurs much larger losses than the predatee does, because the predator must extend production further into the zone of diminishing returns, and hence higher MC, whereas the predatee can cut back both output and marginal cost. The predatee can cut total costs by the area *abcd*; the predator, if required to increase output to q_1^R in order to sustain the lower price, P_1, experiences an increase in total costs equal to area *efgh*.

You can see from Figure 12.4 that both firms suffer losses as a result of a price war. It should also be obvious from Figure 12.4 that the predator lost the most.

Predatory Pricing by Firms with Different Costs

This case of predatory pricing is simply stated. One firm adopts a new scale of plant entailing economies of scale that can only be captured if the firm lowers the price. Thus it attracts customers for its increased output. Given the position of the demand curve, firms that adopt the new scale of plant survive. Those that do not will exit the industry.

There is considerable confusion in the literature of economics (and in antitrust law, as Chapter 13 shows) over the relationship between the number of firms in an industry and the degree of competition. It is often supposed that an industry has become less competitive if the number of firms in the industry falls because of price reductions by the price leaders. But Figure 12.5 shows that such is not always the case.

Figure 12.5 exhibits the cost curves of firms employing different technologies and the industry demand curve served by the firms. The MC_1 and AC_1 curves permit five firms to exist at price P_1; the related output level is $5q_1$. The MC_2 and AC_2 curves depict the costs of firms using a more advanced technology entailing greater economies of scale. But these economies can only be captured by attracting customers via price reductions. Only three technologically advanced firms serve the market demand, but they produce output $3q_2$. So paradoxically, consumers are better off with fewer firms, because of the greater output and lower price associated with economies of scale.

The competitive process can lead to greater industry concentration as firms adopt new technologies. For example, the refrigerator car led to higher industry concentration in meat packing, and the interstate highway system induced greater competition in beer brewing but fewer firms. Modern electronic technology permits branch banking. And mom-and-pop stores started to die out when

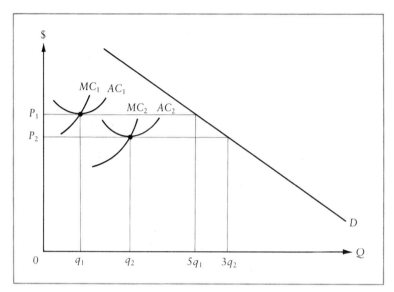

Figure 12.5
Oligopoly Equilibrium

The equilibrium of an industry with five firms is superceded (following a round of predatory pricing) by a new equilibrium with three lower-cost firms. These efficiencies can only be achieved through price cuts.

the automobile made it possible for consumers to drive to super-markets. These examples all represent vigorous competition, lower prices, improved consumer welfare, and fewer firms.

Competition and industry concentration via price cuts are not necessarily antithetical. The negative connotations of the term *predatory* hide the benefits to consumer welfare of weeding out the inefficient.[1]

Final note: Predatory pricing presupposes oligopoly. In a com-petitive market, no firm can drive out a rival by expanding output to reduce price.

Price Discrimination

Chapter 9 analyzes simple monopoly, in which the monopolist charges uniform prices to all customers. This construct allows us to discuss monopolies that sell a product subject to arbitrage. Under arbitrage, any attempt to sell a commodity at two different prices is frustrated by those who buy at the low price and undercut the monopolist by reselling the product at a higher price. However, even casual observation reveals that firms with monopoly power often sell their output at different prices: Movie houses have adult and child tickets; universities charge different tuition rates to in-state and out-of-state students; barbers set differential prices ac-cording to age; doctors charge wealthy patients more than poor patients for similar health care; some firms sell in foreign markets

---

1. Those who fear predation nearly always point to predatory pricing by John D. Rockefeller's Standard Oil Trust as an example of the evils of the practice. This time-honored interpretation is challenged on both theoretical and empirical grounds by John McGee, "Predatory Price Cutting: The Standard Oil (N.J.) Case," *Journal of Law and Economics* 137 (1958): 168.

at lower prices than in domestic markets. But such products are not subject to arbitrage. A customer cannot very well view a movie and then resell it. So let's find out how **price discrimination,** the practice of selling the same good at different prices comes about.

Charging Different Prices to Different Customers

One type of price discrimination occurs when different markets are charged different prices—a practice known as **market separation.** But the mere observation of price differentials in different markets is not sufficient to identify price discrimination, because cost differences may account for price differences, as when transportation costs are higher for one market than for another. Price discrimination occurs only when cost differences cannot explain the differentials in price charged in different markets. A variety of conditions favor such price discrimination.

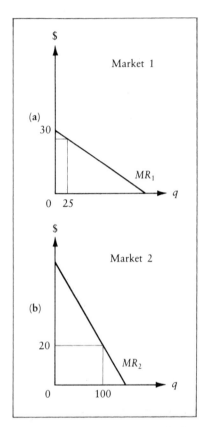

Figure 12.6
Equal Marginal Revenue Principle

To maximize revenue from a given level of output, the monopolist must equate the marginal revenues from various markets: $MR_1 = MR_2 = MR_n$.
(a) Market 1 has a higher marginal revenue than market 2. **(b)** Sales should be shifted from market 2 to market 1.

EQUAL MARGINAL REVENUE PRINCIPLE   Discussions of competition and multiplant monopoly elsewhere in the book demonstrate that the total cost of producing a given quantity of output is minimized by allocating production so that the marginal costs in all plants or firms are equal (equal marginal cost principle). Similarly, if the monopolist is able to sell its output in different markets that have differing demand, marginal revenue, and price elasticity, it should distribute its sales of a given output to each market so that the marginal revenue is equal in all markets (equal marginal revenue principle). If marginal revenues are unequal, total revenue can be increased by switching sales from the market of low marginal revenue to one of higher marginal revenue.

Figure 12.6 demonstrates the equal marginal revenue principle. Suppose that a monopolist initially sells 25 units in market 1 and 100 units in market 2, for a total of 125 units. But the marginal revenue in market 1 ($30) exceeds the marginal revenue in market 2 ($20). If the monopolist transfers 1 unit of sales from market 2 to market 1, the combined output remains the same, but there is a revenue increase of $10. Revenue falls by $20 in market 2 but rises by $30 in market 1.

By transferring sales from the market with low marginal revenue to the market with high marginal revenue, the firm gains total revenue for a given output equal to the difference in marginal revenues. All such gains are exhausted when sales have been divided so that marginal revenues are equal in both markets.

SIMPLE MONOPOLISTIC SELLING IN TWO MARKETS   The equal marginal revenue principle ensures that a given output is sold at a price permitting the maximum total revenue. But the monopolist must still decide how much total output to sell and what prices to charge. In order to understand the behavior of a discriminating monopo-

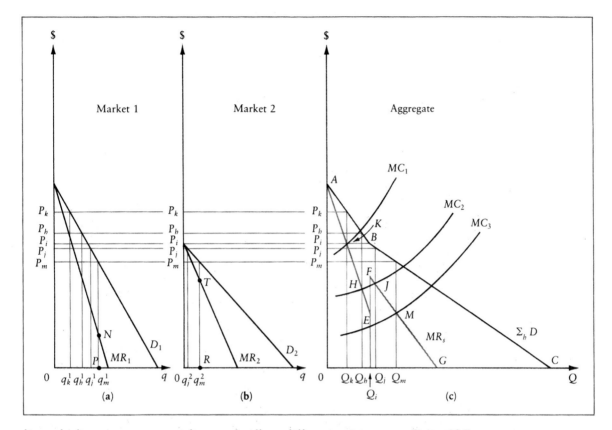

Figure 12.7
Simple Monopolist Selling in Two Markets

(a) Market 1 demands quantity q_m^1 at price P_m. **(b)** Market 2 demands quantity q_m^2 at the same price. **(c)** The marginal revenue curve for the aggregate market consists of segments $\overline{AE}$ and $\overline{FG}$, not the horizontal summation of MR_1 and MR_2.

list, which can separate markets and sell at different prices, we must understand the behavior of the simple monopolist, which may also serve different markets but cannot discriminate because of arbitrage.

Say that the simple monopolist sells in two markets; the demand and marginal revenue curves of these two markets are illustrated in Figure 12.7a and 12.7b. The simple monopolist derives the aggregate demand of the two markets (Figure 12.7c) by horizontally summing the individual demand curves, a familiar procedure by now. The horizontal summation of the demand curves D_1 and D_2 produces the curve labeled $\Sigma_h D$ in panel c. This aggregate demand curve is made up of two kinked segments, $\overline{AB}$ and $\overline{BC}$. The segment $\overline{AB}$ corresponds to the demand curve in market 1, because at prices above P_i market 2 does not contribute any quantities demanded. For prices below P_i both markets contribute quantities demanded. The segment $\overline{BC}$ of the aggregate demand curve, $\Sigma_h D$, reflects the horizontal addition of demand curve D_2 to curve D_1.

The next step is to derive the simple monopolist's marginal revenue curve, MR_s. But we can't simply perform a horizontal summation of the individual markets' marginal revenue curves. Instead, marginal revenue must be linked properly to the demand curve. As shown in Figure 12.7, the marginal revenue curve lies below the demand curve at every output level. For linear demand curves, the marginal revenue curve falls twice as fast as the demand curve.

Now, however, the demand curve is kinked. Thus we must construct a marginal revenue segment for each demand segment. Proceeding as usual, the marginal revenue segment $\overline{AE}$ corresponds to the demand segment $\overline{AB}$; the marginal revenue segment $\overline{FG}$ corresponds to the demand segment $\overline{BC}$. Thus the simple monopolist's marginal revenue curve is $\overline{AEFG}$, or the two segments $\overline{AE}$ and $\overline{FG}$. The discontinuity at output Q_i corresponds to the kink at point B on the demand curve.

The behavior of the simple monopolist selling in two markets subject to arbitrage depends on the position of the marginal cost curve. If the MC curve cuts only segment $\overline{AE}$ of the firm's marginal revenue curve, the monopolist should sell only in the stronger market. For MC_1 in Figure 12.7, $MC_1 = MR_s$ at point K; the monopolist sells output Q_k entirely in market 1 at price P_k.

Difficulty arises if the marginal cost curve cuts both segments, $\overline{AE}$ and $\overline{FG}$, of the marginal revenue curve, MR_s. Note that MC_2 intersects MR_s at points H and J. Should the firm sell output Q_h at price P_h exclusively in market 1? Or should the larger output Q_j be chosen and price reduced to P_j, allowing some sales in both markets? Both options determine a local profit maximum, as illustrated in Figure 12.8. The choice of the best of these two options can only be determined by experimentation.

If the marginal cost curve in Figure 12.7c cuts only the segment $\overline{FG}$ of the firm's marginal revenue curve, as when MC_3 cuts MR_s at point M, the simple monopolist will produce Q_m units and sell output in both markets at a uniform price of P_m. Specifically, q_m^1 units are sold in market 1 and q_m^2 units in market 2.

Before moving to another case of price discrimination, you should note that, whenever the simple monopolist charges the same price in both markets, the marginal revenue in these markets differs. For example, when the firm equates MC_3 and MR_s at point M and sells output Q_m at price P_m in both markets, output q_m^1 is sold in market 1 and q_m^2 is sold in market 2. But $MR_1(q_m^1) = \overline{PN} < MR_2(q_m^2) = \overline{RT}$. Output Q_m could be sold at a larger profit if the monopolist could separate the two markets, charge different prices, and switch sales between the markets until $MR_1 = MR_2$. But for the simple monopolist facing arbitrage, such profit improvements cannot be achieved.

SIMPLE MONOPOLIST VERSUS DISCRIMINATING MONOPOLIST   The key distinction between simple and discriminating monopolists lies in the derivation of their marginal revenue curves. When the monopolist's price is taken from the aggregate demand curve, $\Sigma_h D$, the only

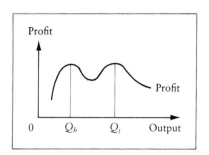

Figure 12.8
Multiple Profit-Maximizing Outputs

When a simple nondiscriminating monopolist serves two markets, the profit-maximizing condition $MR = MC$ may occur at more than one level.

meaningful construction of marginal revenue is to tie MR directly to $\Sigma_h D$, as in the case of the simple monopolist. However, the discriminating monopolist does not select a price from the aggregate demand curve; instead, it equates marginal revenues in all markets and selects prices in the individual markets from the individual curves D_1 and D_2. Thus we need a different method of calculating the discriminating firm's aggregate marginal revenue curve. Because the price discriminator always allocates sales so as to equate marginal revenue in all markets, a convenient derivation presents itself: Horizontally sum the marginal revenue curves MR_1 and MR_2 to derive the aggregate marginal revenue curve labeled $\Sigma_h MR$. A movement along the $\Sigma_h MR$ curve means that output and sales are always expanded by selling each incremental unit in the market yielding the highest marginal revenue. This procedure keeps marginal revenue equal in both markets.

Figure 12.9 illustrates the price discriminator's aggregate marginal revenue curve, $\Sigma_h MR$, which is also made up of two disjointed line segments, $\overline{AL}$ and $\overline{LG}$. The price discriminator's marginal revenue curve coincides with the simple monopolist's marginal revenue curve, MR_s, everywhere except between points L and F. For outputs between these points, the simple monopolist moves along the MR_s segment $\overline{LE}$, producing only in market 1. In contrast, the price discriminator finds it profitable to sell in both markets and to equate marginal revenue in both markets by suitable price differentials.

We may now compare the behavior of the simple monopolist to

Figure 12.9
Comparing Simple and Price-Discriminating Monopolies

(a) When $MC = MC_1$, only market 1 is served; Q_K units are sold. If $MC = MC_2$, the simple monopolist sells Q_J in market 1. The discriminating monopolist serves both markets: q_H^1 at P_H^1. **(b)** Market 2 is served only by the discriminating monopolist when $MC = MC_2$; q_H^2 units are sold at P_H^2. **(c)** If $MC = MC_1$, the simple monopolist and the price discriminator will both produce the same output, Q_K. If $MC = MC_2$, the simple monopolist charges P_J and sells in only one market; the price discriminator produces Q_H and sells in both markets.

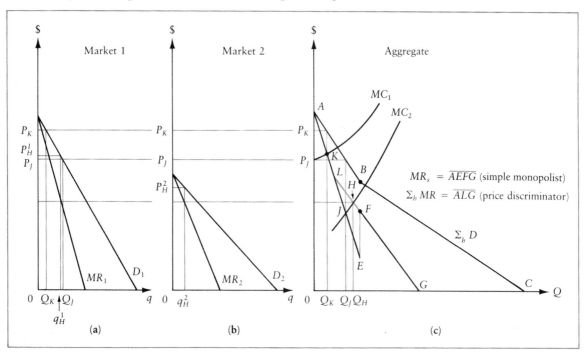

that of the price discriminator. Not surprisingly, the comparison depends on the position of the marginal cost curve. There are four basic positions for marginal cost, as illustrated in Figure 12.9 and Figure 12.10. (The comparison causes clutter unless two diagrams are used.) In Figure 12.9c, when the marginal cost curve cuts segment $\overline{AL}$ of either MR_s or $\Sigma_h MR$, both monopolists behave the same. For MC_1 in Figure 12.9c, $MC_1 = MR_s = \Sigma_h MR$ at point K; both monopolists produce output Q_K and sell all the output in market 1 at price P_K. Even though the two markets are separable, it does not pay the monopolist to lower the price in market 2 enough to bring the weaker market into service.

Next suppose that the marginal cost curve intersects segment $\overline{LE}$ of MR_s and segment LF of $\Sigma_h MR$, as when MC_2 in Figure 12.9c intersects points J and H. The simple monopolist would choose output Q_J, would sell only in market 1, and would charge a uniform price of P_J. In contrast, the price discriminator could profitably serve market 2 by charging different prices. Specifically, the firm should select output Q_H, where MC_2 equals $\Sigma_h MR$ at point H, and should equate marginal revenues in both markets by selling q_H^1 at price P_H^1 in market 1 and q_H^2 at price P_H^2 in market 2. Conclusion: When the marginal cost curve cuts $\Sigma_h MR$ in the range $\overline{LF}$ (for which $\Sigma_h MR = MR_s$), the discriminating monopolist sells in two markets,

Figure 12.10
**Comparing Simple and
Price-Discriminating Monopolies**

(a) Price and quantity in market 1
follow the same demand and *MR*
curves presented in Figure 12.9.
(b) Market 2 has its own set of
demand and *MR* curves, with a
different combination of prices and
quantities. **(c)** If *MC* = *MC₃*, there is
once again output ambiguity for the
simple monopolist. The price
discriminator earns a greater profit
and produces *Qᵧ*. If *MC* = *MC₄*, both
produce *Qᵣ*.

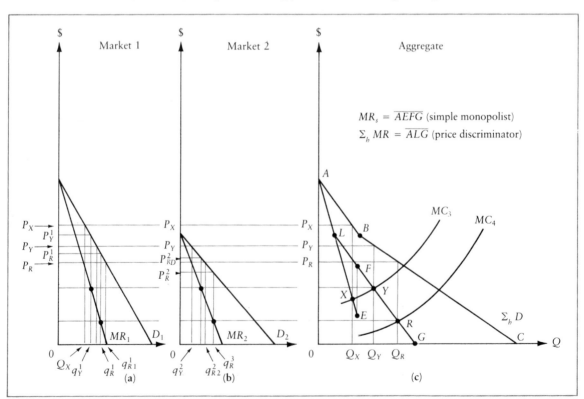

sells more output, charges different prices, and earns a greater profit than the simple monopolist, which sells all its output at a uniform price in the strongest market.

Now turn to Figure 12.10 to continue the comparison. Assume that the marginal cost curve intersects both segments of the MR_s curve, $\overline{AE}$ and $\overline{FG}$, as when MC_3 intersects MR_s at points X and Y. In this case, the simple monopolist must choose between selling the entire output Q_X at price P_X in the stronger market or selling output Q_Y in both markets at the lower price P_Y. The price discriminator has no such ambiguity; it equates MC_3 and $\Sigma_h MR$ at point Y, produces output Q_Y, and equates MR in both markets by selling q_Y^1 at price P_Y^1 in market 1 and q_Y^2 at price P_Y^2 in market 2. Conclusion: Price discrimination solves the problem of price and output ambiguity faced by the simple monopolist. The price discriminator maximizes profit by operating along the $\Sigma_h MR$ curve.

Finally, a marginal cost curve may intersect the marginal revenue curve only at a point for which $\Sigma_h MR = MR_s$ (segment $\overline{FG}$), as when MC_4 intersects $MR_s = \Sigma_h MR$ at point R. In this case, the optimal output is the same for both types of monopoly. However, the simple monopolist sells all output at price P_R, selling q_{R1}^1 units in market 1 and q_{R2}^2 units in market 2. The discriminating monopolist can increase profits by reducing the units sold in market 1 to q_R^1 units at the higher price P_R^1 and by increasing sales in market 2 to q_R^2 units at the lower price P_R^2. These prices equate the marginal revenues in the two markets and maximize the total profit of output Q_R. Conclusion: When the MC curve intersects only segment $\overline{FG}$ of the marginal revenue curve, total output is the same for both types of monopoly, but prices and individual market sales differ.

Most textbook analyses merely show that the price discriminator can increase profits of a given level of output by equating marginal revenue in all markets. But we have seen that price discrimination often leads to a different total output for the simple monopolist as well as differential prices in each market. These conclusions are summarized in Table 12.1, which is directly related to Figures 12.9 and 12.10.

The price discrimination described here is feasible only if the price elasticities of demand differ in the different markets. Recall the relationship among price, marginal revenue, and elasticity:

$$MR = P\left(1 - \frac{1}{|\varepsilon|}\right) \tag{12.1}$$

The equal marginal revenue principle, necessary for profit maximization under price discrimination, requires that

$$MR_1 = P_1\left(1 - \frac{1}{|\varepsilon_1|}\right) = P_2\left(1 - \frac{1}{|\varepsilon_2|}\right) = MR_2 \tag{12.2}$$

Table 12.1

Comparison of Simple and Discriminating Monopolists
(see Figures 12.9 and 12.10)

When the MC curve intersects only segment $\overline{AL}$, where $MR_s = \Sigma_h MR$, simple and discriminating monopolists produce the same output, charge the same price, and sell in only the stronger market.

When the MC curve intersects both MR_s in segment $\overline{AE}$ and $\Sigma_h MR$ in segment $\overline{LF}$, the simple monopolist sells only in the stronger market at uniform prices. The discriminating monopolist produces more output than the simple monopolist, sells in two markets at different prices, and earns a higher profit.

When the MC curve intersects both segments of the MR_s curve, $\overline{AE}$ and $\overline{FG}$, the simple monopolist must choose between selling in one or both markets. Both choices maximize profits locally. The global maximum is determined by experience. The discriminating monopolist selects the larger output and sells in both markets at different prices. Profits exceed those of the simple monopolist.

When the MC curve intersects only segment $\overline{FG}$, where $MR_s = \Sigma_h MR$, both simple and discriminating monopolists select the same output. The discriminating monopolist sells at different prices in the two markets and earns higher profits than the single-priced monopolist does.

Equation 12.2 may be rewritten as

$$\frac{P_1}{P_2} = \frac{\left(1 - \dfrac{1}{|\varepsilon_2|}\right)}{\left(1 - \dfrac{1}{|\varepsilon_1|}\right)} \tag{12.3}$$

In the special case of price elasticities being the same in each market ($\varepsilon_1 = \varepsilon_2$), marginal revenues must be the same in both markets, as must prices. The equal marginal revenue principle is satisfied when the prices in both markets are the same. Separating markets and charging differential prices in markets with identical price elasticities of demand can only reduce profits.

In summary, price discrimination requires (1) that the monopolist's product not be subject to arbitrage and (2) that demand elasticities differ between markets. Medical services, movie tickets, and many other markets appear to satisfy these criteria. However, preventing the arbitrage that price discrimination tends to induce is costly, and firms will not bother to separate markets and charge different prices when the benefits of price discrimination are less than the costs incurred in preventing arbitrage.

Charging Different Prices in the Same Market

The previous discussion of price discrimination was limited to the case of market separation—selling the same commodity in different markets at different prices. In some cases, a monopolist may even be able to charge the same customer different prices for different quantities of the good. Although such market power is rare, the implications of such monopoly behavior are interesting and important to study. The exercise of such monopoly power is called **perfect price discrimination**.

Refer to the demand curve in Figure 12.11, which illustrates perfect price discrimination. The consumer is forced to pay P_1 for the first unit, P_2 for the second, and so forth. When prices and outputs are infinitesimally small, such a pricing policy extracts the maximum revenue but eliminates the inefficient reduction of output for which nondiscriminating "simple" monopolies are famous.

Another pricing procedure, much simpler to administer, amounts to the same thing. A monopolist can make a consumer an "all or nothing, take it or leave it" offer. For example, in Figure 12.11, the monopolist might offer the consumer Q_0 units at a total price equal to the area $0ABQ_0$ (or maybe just a little less to sweeten the deal). If the consumer accepts, the end result is the same as if the consumer had purchased one unit at a time at continuously falling prices: All consumer surplus is extracted from consumers and ends up in the monopolist's profits.

In the typical case of the nondiscriminating simple monopolist, a price reduction causes price to be lowered on all units previously sold at a higher price. We have seen previously in this chapter that under these circumstances price exceeds marginal revenue and that the area below the marginal revenue curve equals total revenue. But under perfect price discrimination, in which the monopolist lowers price on the marginal unit but not on the inframarginal units, the demand curve itself defines the marginal revenue from an extra unit sold. For the perfect price discriminator, price equals marginal revenue, as it does in competition. Thus both price and marginal revenue are measured by the demand curve. The demand curve—the "marginal willingness to pay" curve—is the marginal revenue curve for the perfect price discriminator. The area beneath the demand curve measures the monopolist's total revenue and the consumers' total benefit, which are equal under perfect price discrimination.

In Figure 12.12, let the demand curve, D, equal the horizontal summation of all the individual consumers' demand curves. (Assume that the individual demand curves are identical.) If the monopolist is not a perfect price discriminator, output Q_1 is produced, because $LMC = MR$ at Q_1; the marginal revenue curve measures the additional revenue resulting from the sale of an extra unit of output when uniform prices are charged. If the monopolist is able to extract the maximum revenue from consumers by perfect price discrimination, the relevant marginal revenue curve is the demand curve itself. The fact that prices on previous units are not lowered under perfect price discrimination makes the usual MR curve irrelevant to decision making. Accordingly, the monopolist will maximize profit by expanding output to Q_c, where LMC equals price at

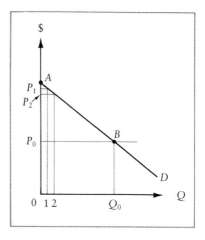

Figure 12.11
Perfect Price Discrimination

All consumer surplus is extracted from the market when the monopolist has the power to exercise perfect price discrimination.

Figure 12.12
Demand and Perfect Price
Discrimination

The demand curve, *D*, is also the
marginal revenue curve, *MR*.
Average revenue, *AR*, has half the
slope of *D*. The competitive level of
output is profit-maximizing.

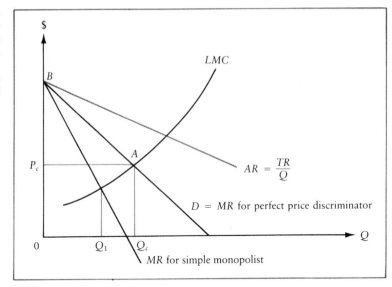

point *A*. The monopolist will charge price P_c for the last unit sold
and higher prices for previous units.

Note that output Q_c is the optimal competitive output. Paradoxically, when monopolists can completely exploit their market
power through perfect price discrimination, the usual output-
reducing evil of monopoly does not exist. Perfect price discrimi-
nators do not sell too little output; rather, they produce the competitive optimum rate of output but at higher prices for all but the
marginal unit.

Note too that the demand curve facing the perfect price discriminator is no longer the average revenue curve. In Figure 12.12, total
revenue for output Q_c is not OP_cAQ_c but rather the larger amount
$0BAQ_c$, the area beneath the demand curve. Thus the average revenue (defined as $AR \equiv TR/Q$) must exceed P_c, the price charged for
the last unit sold; the average revenue curve must lie above the
demand curve. These relationships are shown in Figure 12.12.

Transfer Pricing

The modern firm is usually composed of several small "firms" called
divisions or **profit centers.** Just as prices coordinate entire economies, the modern firm can use prices internal to the firm, called
transfer prices, to coordinate its profit centers.

The subject of transfer pricing combines several elements of the
theory of the firm and of markets—particularly the principles of
marginalist reasoning and supply and demand—for the purpose of
analyzing the internal workings of the firm as a market substitute.
Ronald Coase set the theme for such study in his article "The
Nature of the Firm," in which he cautions against considering the

firm as merely a combiner of inputs to produce an output.[2] Instead, the firm constantly evaluates its position through a sequence of production decisions. As basic materials are combined and changed into increasingly complex intermediate goods in a chain leading to final goods, the firm must constantly decide whether to process its intermediate output more completely or to sell it to external buyers who will process it further and whether to make more of its own inputs or to buy them in external markets. Such buy/make and sell/use decisions affect not only the use of the factors of production but also the nature of the product itself. As firms seek to lower costs and maximize profits, comparative advantages, specialization of labor, and location relative to suppliers or output markets all become important. Furthermore, a firm facing many such decisions has the incentive to divide the organization into more manageable and specialized profit centers.

Since management is seeking to maximize the profits of the entire organization, the goals of the profit centers must be coordinated to be compatible with the firm's interests. But the coordination of large organizations is usually not treated in the study of microeconomics; the closest approach is a discussion of the shape of the long-run average cost curve as it slopes upward, because of coordination problems, beyond some level of output. However, the study of *managerial* economics does try to show how economic theory can be applied to coordination problems. **Transfer pricing,** the coordination of a firm's subdivisions using prices as information devices, is the tool. Essentially, the firm's divisions are told to maximize profits (or minimize losses) as if they were separate firms and to use the prices of goods transferred from other divisions the same way that external market prices would be used. The proper determination of transfer prices allows the firm to convey an enormous amount of information among divisions much more cheaply and quickly than it could by sending copious memos and directives.

The topic of transfer pricing may be treated rather comprehensively by analyzing a firm that has two divisions. One division produces an intermediate good that is sold to an external market and to a second division, which uses that intermediate good as one input in the production of a final good. Examples abound. The spark-plug division of an automobile firm may sell spark plugs to both the engine division of the parent corporation and to the replacement-part market. The engine is the final good, and the spark plug is the intermediate good. (When you have finished this section, you might apply this analysis to the engine as an intermediate good in the production of the final automobile.) The question is which spark-plug price is most efficient for both the transfer of spark plugs within the corporation and for the sale of spark plugs externally.

---

2. Ronald Coase, "The Nature of the Firm," *Economica*, new ser., 4 (1937): 386.

Corrugated paper firms confront buy/make and sell/use decisions at several production stages. The firm begins with a rather rough, semirefined brown paper. This "kraft" paper is generally produced on rolls that can be sold to the external market. Alternatively, the paper can be processed further in a process called lamination. Laminated "kraft" paper, consisting of two or more sheets glued together, can then be sold on the external market or formed into corrugated paperboard by gluing layers of laminated paper on either side of fluted laminated paper. The corrugated paperboard can be sold in reams or rolls or processed further to form boxes for customers. At each of these stages, the marginal benefit and marginal cost of the options must be considered.

Buy/make and sell/use decisions can be broken into six categories, depending on whether the external market for the intermediate good is competitive, imperfectly competitive, or nonexistent and whether the market for the final good is competitive or imperfectly competitive. The six possible cases are outlined in Table 12.2.

Table 12.2
Transfer Pricing and Market Structure

Case	Final-Good Market	External Market for Intermediate Good
A	Competitive	None
B	Competitive	Competitive
C	Competitive	Imperfectly competitive
D	Imperfectly competitive	None
E	Imperfectly competitive	Competitive
F	Imperfectly competitive	Imperfectly competitive

Case A, with no external market for the intermediate good and a competitive market for the final good, is the simplest circumstance. As in Chapter 11, analysis of this case will rely on horizontal and vertical summation of marginal revenue and marginal cost curves. Consider Figure 12.13.[3] The horizontal axis measures the total output of the intermediate good, Q_I^{TOT}. The vertical axis measures money prices. The competitive market for the final good is represented, as usual, by a horizontal demand curve, D_F. The marginal cost of producing the intermediate good, MC_I, is different from the marginal cost of processing the intermediate good into the final good, MC_P. The full marginal cost of producing the final good (MC_F) is therefore the vertical sum $MC_I + MC_P$.

To derive the net marginal revenue of processing the intermediate good into the final good, NMR_P, MC_P must be vertically

---

3. In the transfer pricing analyses that follow, the uppercase Q stands for total output and the lowercase q stands for the output sold within the firm to another division.

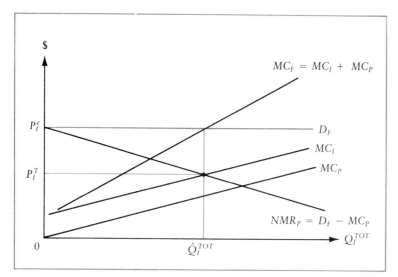

Figure 12.13
Transfer Price Determination, Case A

When there is a competitive market for the final good and no external market for the intermediate good, the correct transfer price is the marginal cost of the intermediate good.

subtracted from D_F. The intersection of NMR_P and MC_I determines the efficient quantity of the intermediate good to produce, $\hat{Q}_I^{TOT}$. The marginal cost at that quantity is the correct transfer price, P_I^T. The two profit-seeking divisions, each facing P_I^T, will act to maximize the profits of the corporation.

Now consider the complications present when there is a competitive external market for the intermediate good. This is case B, corresponding to Figure 12.14. The competitive external market for the intermediate good is represented in panel a by a horizontal demand curve, D_I, and the internal market for the intermediate good is represented in panel b by the horizontal demand curve D_F. In panel b, MC_P is vertically subtracted from D_F to derive NMR_P, as in case A. The internal and external markets are substitutes, so the marginal revenues must be horizontally summed. This operation has been accomplished in the curve labeled MR_I in panel c. Note

Figure 12.14
Transfer Price Determination, Case B

When there is a competitive market for the final good and for the intermediate good, MR_I is derived as the horizontal summation of **(a)** D_I and **(b)** NMR_P. **(c)** The correct transfer price is the marginal cost of the intermediate good.

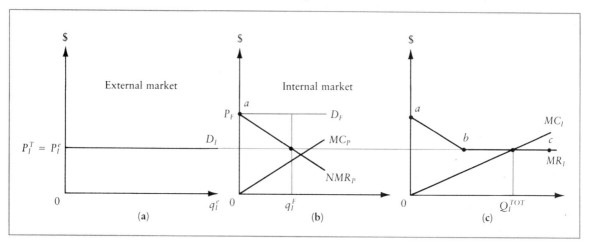

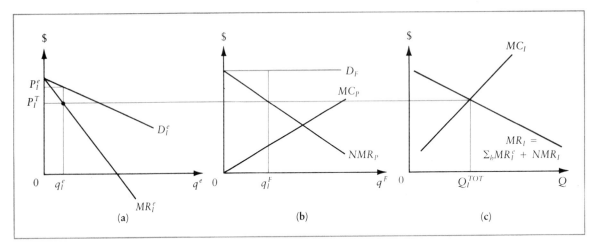

Figure 12.15
Transfer Price Determination,
Case C

When there is **(a)** an imperfectly competitive external market for the intermediate good and **(b)** a perfectly competitive market for the final good, the transfer price is **(c)** P_I^T = MC_I. But the price to the external market is $P_I^e > P_I^T$.

that portion $\overline{ab}$ of MR_I is the translation of $\overline{ab}$ from panel b. Portion $\overline{bc}$ is the graphic representation of the firm's ability to sell as much of the intermediate good as it wants in the external market. The intersection of MR_I and MC_I in panel c depicts the efficient level of output, Q_I^{TOT}. The transfer price P_I^T equals MC_I at that level of output and is equal to P_I^e. The quantity sold to the division producing the final good is q_I^F.

Case C introduces the complication of an imperfectly competitive external market for the intermediate good and a competitive market for the final good. External demand is represented by a downward-sloping demand curve, D_I^e, and its associated marginal revenue curve, MR_I^e (see Figure 12.15a). Demand for the final good is represented in Figure 12.15b by the horizontal line D_F. As in cases A and B, the NMR_P curve represents marginal revenue minus MC_P. The efficient level of output is determined in panel c at the intersection of MC_I and MR_I. Note that MR_I is the horizontal sum of MR_I^e and NMR_I. This result should remind you of the analysis of the price-discriminating monopolist. Corporate divisions can obviously prevent arbitrage between internal and external consumers and hence will find it profit maximizing to equate the marginal revenues in each market. Thus we may horizontally sum the MR curves. The transfer price thus derived is $P_I^T = MC_I$. The price to the external market for the intermediate good is $P_I^e > P_I^T$. At price P_I^e, the quantity sold is q_I^e; at price P_I^T, it is q_I^F.

Case D is that of an imperfectly competitive market for the final good and a nonexistent external market for the intermediate good. As in case A, this case can be analyzed with a one-panel diagram, Figure 12.16. The downward-sloping D_F and MR_F curves represent demand for the final good, as before. Similarly, NMR_P is derived as the vertical subtraction $MR_F - MC_P$. The equation $NMR_P = MC_I$ locates $\hat{Q}_I^{TOT}$ and the final-good price P_F as well as the transfer price $P_I^T = MC_I$ at the $\hat{Q}_I^{TOT}$ level of output.

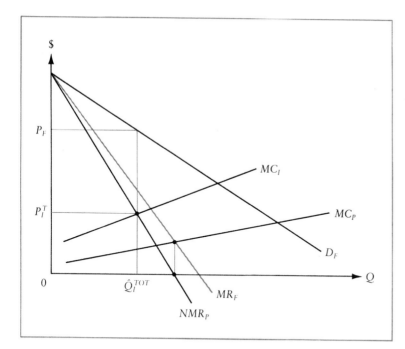

Figure 12.16
Transfer Price Determination,
Case D

When there is an imperfectly
competitive market for the final
good and no external market for the
intermediate good, the firm should
equate $NMR_P = MC_I$ in order to
determine price P_I^T.

Case E, an imperfectly competitive market for the final good
and perfectly competitive external market for the intermediate
good, is represented in Figure 12.17. In panel a, competitive demand for the intermediate good is depicted by the horizontal D_I
curve. Panel b is the by now standard derivation of NMR_P. Panel c
shows the MR_I curve intersecting the MC_I curve to locate the efficient output level Q_I^{TOT} and the transfer price P_I^T. Note that, if the
marginal cost of the intermediate good is sufficiently high, the transfer price will rise above the price available in the external market—
as with the gray line MC_I^2. In such a case the firm will sell none of
its intermediate good to the external market.

Figure 12.17
Transfer Price Determination,
Case E

When there is **(a)** a perfectly
competitive external market for the
intermediate good and **(b)** an
imperfectly competitive market for
the final good, the firm should
(c) equate the price in the external
market with MC_I and NMR_P.

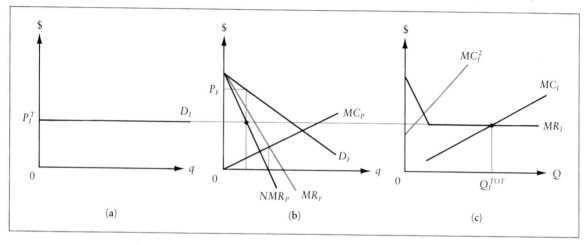

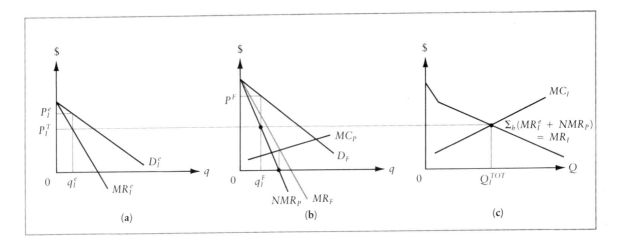

Figure 12.18
Transfer Price Determination,
Case F

When there is an imperfectly competitive market for both **(a)** the intermediate good and **(b)** the final good, the output of the intermediate good is determined by equating $\Sigma_h MR_I + NMR_P = MC_I$. **(c)** The transfer price is $P_I^T = MC_I$.

The last of the six cases, case F, has imperfect competition in both the external market for the intermediate good and the final-good market. Both markets are represented by downward-sloping demand and marginal revenue curves (see Figure 12.18), and NMR_P is derived in panel b as before. As in case E, Q_I^{TOT} is located at the intersection of $MR_I = MC_I$ (panel c). The transfer price is determined to be equal to MC_I at that level of output, and the quantities sold to each market are determined by equating $MR_I^e = P_I^T$ and $NMR_P = P_I^T$ to derive q_I^e and q_I^F and P^F. But unlike case E, the price in the external market exceeds the transfer price: $P_I^e > P_I^T$.

In all of these cases, the use of transfer prices coordinates the use of goods within a corporation by forcing decision makers to evaluate the goods' marginal opportunity costs.

Regional Pricing

Another dimension of managerial pricing policy asks where the product will be consumed in relation to the production site. When the distances between points of sale and production represent significant transportation costs, special pricing strategies must be employed in order to maximize profits and retain and expand markets.

Regional pricing, which is concerned with locational factors, includes a number of pricing strategies. The most common are mill pricing, often called FOB pricing (see Chapter 10), uniform delivered pricing, and spatial price discrimination. All are strategies for determining the relationship between the price charged at the "plant gate" and the price of the good as delivered to the point of sale or consumption.

Mill pricing, the simplest of these strategies, entails charging a price independent of transportation costs. Transportation may then be provided by the seller as a separate service at an additional charge or provided by the buyer or some third party. This form of regional pricing is common when transportation costs are a small part of

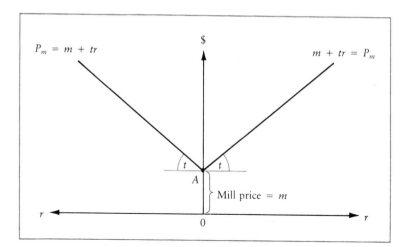

$P_m = m + tr$

$$m + tr = P_m$$

\$

t t

A

Mill price $= m$

r r

0

Figure 12.19
Mill Pricing

The firm located at point 0 charges a price of m at the point of sale. Transportation is arranged separately at a rate of t per unit of distance. The full price rises with distance, r.

total price, and hence its manipulation is not a significant marketing strategy. Mill pricing is also used when customers readily provide their own transportation in order to thwart the imposition of other, more onerous types of regional pricing strategies.

To understand mill pricing, consult Figure 12.19. The horizontal axis, in both directions from point 0 (where the firm is located), shows distance away from the firm, labeled r. The vertical axis (this time in the middle of the diagram) represents price. The mill price charged at the plant gate is represented by the vertical height labeled m. The two rays emanating from point A represent the full prices that customers would pay, the sum of mill price plus transportation costs, at various distances from the firm. Note that the slope of these rays is t, the transportation cost per unit of distance. The diagram demonstrates that the full price rises as a linear function of distance.

Uniform delivered pricing is a strategic attempt to charge less than mill prices to distant customers by charging more than mill prices to nearby customers. This tool is especially attractive when nearby customers cannot provide alternative transportation. When many customers can be served by a single truck route, some economies of scale are likely to be realized in the transportation of the product. If customers cannot organize to provide such multiple deliveries—and no third party can profit by providing multiple deliveries to nearby customers—the seller can maintain what is in fact a form of price discrimination. Uniform delivered pricing has the advantage of allowing a firm to compete more effectively for customers far from its plant gate.

The axes in Figure 12.20 are the same as in Figure 12.19, and the mill price trajectory is repeated. P_u, the uniform delivered price, is drawn as a flat line because the delivered price is the same regardless of distance.

The third regional pricing strategy that we will consider is profit-maximizing **spatial price discrimination.** Under this scheme,

Figure 12.20
Comparison of Three Pricing
Strategies

Mill pricing (P_m), uniform delivered price (P_u), and profit-maximizing spatial price discrimination (P_s) are related as shown here.

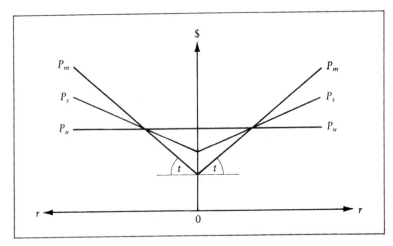

the firm attempts a kind of hybrid between mill pricing and uniform delivered pricing. In an attempt to maximize profits at each delivery location, the firm takes account of the greater elasticity of demand at higher prices by passing along only part of the increased transportation costs to customers at greater distances. Consider Figure 12.21, in which the demand and marginal revenue curves of typical customer groups are drawn. The profit-maximizing price is, of course, located where the marginal cost plus marginal transport costs, T, equals MR. Note that for any change in T, as from T_1 to T_2, there is a corresponding but smaller increase in price, as from P_1 to P_2. This effect is more pronounced the greater the elasticity of demand.

Figure 12.21
Spatial Price Discrimination

Because of the downward-sloping demand curve, increased transportation costs due to distance are only partially absorbed by the firm. Thus profit-maximizing spatial price discrimination follows a trajectory between those of mill pricing and uniform delivered price (see Figure 12.20).

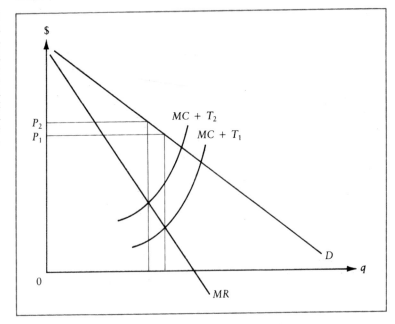

Returning to Figure 12.20, you can see that the trajectory of the spatial discriminatory price, P_s, must lie between those of P_m and P_u. The reason is that mill pricing (P_m) requires all of the transportation costs to particular locations to be borne by customers in those locations. In extreme contrast, uniform delivered pricing (P_u) makes no distinction among customers at different locations. But under spatial price discrimination, the firm absorbs part of the transportation cost differences and the customers in those locations pay the rest. Hence the profit-maximizing strategy is to partially absorb transportation costs and to let nearby customers subsidize distant customers. Spatial price discrimination allows the firm even greater competitive flexibility at the boundary of the market area, since it allows greater subsidization of fringe areas from the interior.

Summary

The theories presented in other chapters underlie discussion of special topics of pricing. In particular, cost-plus pricing may be viewed as an extension of the theory of profit maximization; the percentage markup is chosen to equate marginal revenue and marginal cost. Limit pricing sets a price so low that entry is deterred.

Predatory pricing is the pejorative term used to describe the reduction of price intended to drive rivals out of business. Economic theory shows that such a "price war" will not achieve its goal unless there are economies of scale to be gained. Then it benefits consumers. Predatory pricing must achieve sufficiently better profits in the "postwar" period than in the "prewar" period to pay for the war. Thus predatory pricing is generally suicidal.

Price discrimination, the practice of charging different prices to different customers or of charging different prices in the same market, can only be accomplished if the product cannot easily be transported or resold so as to eliminate the price differences.

The subject of transfer pricing illustrates how firms can use prices internally. The firm is a generator of supply and demand within itself and can use prices to coordinate a tremendous amount of economic activity into simple summary numbers.

Finally, regional pricing, which sets prices according to the distance between customer and firm, further embellishes the usual pricing model (which does not consider space). Under mill pricing, the customer pays all transportation costs; uniform delivered pricing allows all customers to pay the same price, regardless of transportation costs (in effect, a subsidy of distant customers by close customers). The profit-maximizing strategy lies between these two extremes: Partial freight costs are absorbed under spatial price discrimination.

Key Terms

contribution margin 309
cost-plus pricing 309
limit pricing 311
market separation 316
markup 309
mill pricing 330
perfect price discrimination 323
predatory pricing 313
price discrimination 316
profit centers 324
regional pricing 330
spatial price discrimination 331
transfer prices 324
transfer pricing 325
uniform delivered pricing 331

Problems

1. Supermarkets have lower markups than corner grocers do. Yet supermarkets enjoy a greater return on investment. Explain why.
2. Textbook authors typically want their publisher to charge lower textbook prices than publishers do. However, homeowners gener-

Table 12.3

Costs of Distribution
and Production for a
Competitive Firm

Q	TC_D	TC_P
300	1,000	850
350	1,050	1,000
400	1,150	1,200
450	1,300	1,450
500	1,500	1,750
550	1,750	1,250
600	2,000	1,750

Table 12.4

Demand Data for
Outside Distributor

P	Q
$10	0
9	0
8	100
7	1,000
6	2,000
5	4,000
4	10,000
3	20,000

Table 12.5

Demand Data
for North American and
South American Markets

P	Q_{NA}	Q_{SA}
50	55	50
45	60	75
40	65	100
35	70	125
30	75	150
25	80	170
20	85	180
15	90	190
10	95	195
5	100	200

ally want to sell their homes for more than real estate agents do. Explain why.

3. a. Should insurance agents working on a commission basis prefer higher or lower prices than the insurance firms they work for?
   b. Would your answer be the same for an independent insurance agent selling policies for several different companies?

4. It is often argued that predatory pricing is more likely to succeed when there are high capital costs than when there are low capital costs. Why is this argument wrong?

5. Suppose a multidivision firm that uses transfer pricing suffers the loss of an overseas division due to nationalization by its host country. In which of the cases of transfer pricing discussed in this chapter can transfer prices be used to measure the value of lost inventories?

6. Suppose that a multiplant monopolist is also a price discriminator. Draw a multipaneled diagram to demonstrate equilibrium.

7. Suppose that your firm faces a competitive price for its output of $P = \$10$ per unit. The total costs of distributing the product, TC_D, rise as more is sold. The costs of production, TC_P, also rise with output. Table 12.3 shows these data.
   a. Determine the profit-maximizing level of output.
   b. Suppose that an outside distributor is willing to purchase your output and retail it. Her demand curve plots the points shown in Table 12.4. How much will you sell to the distributor at what price?

8. Suppose that your firm's mill price is $500 per unit and that transportation costs are 5 cents per mile.
   a. What is the price for a customer 100 miles away?
   b. Suppose there is a competitor 50 miles from this customer with the same costs as yours. Now what is your price?

9. If your firm's customers are virtually uniformly distributed along the coastline of a country, as on the East Coast of the United States, are you more likely to employ mill pricing or uniform delivered pricing than if the customers are arranged in clusters at various distances from your plant?

10. Your firm can sell output in two separate markets, North America and South America. The demand curves are summarized in Table 12.5, and marginal cost is a constant at $MC = \$15$. Find the simple monopoly price and the profit-maximizing discriminatory price.

11. a. Explain why profits are higher when firms practice price discrimination.
    b. Explain why price discrimination cannot take place in a competitive market.

12. a. "Predatory pricing is less feasible the lower the entry costs." Explain this statement.
    b. "Predatory pricing is less feasible the higher the exit costs." Explain this statement. (Hint: Is there a symmetry between entry and exit costs?)

13. a. Suppose that a firm prices a product at 25 percent above its wholesale costs. How will the firm know if the price is too high or too low?

b. Suppose the firm uses the same markup for every product in the store. What information would you expect the manager to be faced with relatively quickly?

14. A cartel consisting of ten identical firms tries to charge a limit price to deter the entry of an eleventh identical firm.
    a. What price must the cartel charge, and how does the price compare to the price that would prevail in the market if the eleventh firm were to enter?
    b. What alternative strategy would be more profitable to the cartel?

15. Can one analyze limit pricing in a model assuming costless and instantaneous entry? Why or why not?

16. Reductions in gasoline prices at the pump in the early months of 1983 were often labeled price wars by newscasters. Is it accurate to call such price reductions predatory price wars? Why or why not?

17. Through price reductions by competitors, some firms are driven out of business.
    a. From the viewpoint of competitive theory, is this an anti-competitive result? Explain your answer.
    b. How would the advantages of technological change ever be passed on to consumers in the form of lower product prices?

18. The number of eighteen-year-olds in the population will peak in 1983 and then plummet until about 1988. Universities will suffer enrollment declines and associated budgetary complexities. Would you anticipate more price (tuition) discrimination, in the form of scholarships for the needy, as this demographic decline unfolds? Explain your answer.

19. Suppose that you manufacture canned soup.
    a. Explain why you can increase profits by placing different labels on the high-quality brand of soup and the "store brand" of the same soup.
    b. What must be true about the consumers of your soup in order to maintain these differentials?

20. a. Explain the similarity between the equal marginal revenue principle and the equal marginal cost principle.
    b. Show why both are satisfied in competitive markets.

21. Explain why an increase in marginal cost might induce a price-discriminating monopolist to stop the practice.

22. The fundamental problem of economics is scarcity, which creates opportunity costs. Does the price-discriminating monopolist create more or less scarcity than the simple monopolist? Explain your answer.

23. a. What is the relationship between the multiproduct firm and the multidivision firm?
    b. What is the relationship between adding a new product and adding a new division?

24. Suppose that a firm is seeking to maximize the output of the entire organization. How does the principle of transfer pricing change?

25. A paper firm produces corrugated paper liner and paper for paper bags. One of its divisions uses the liner paper. Show how a reduction in demand for cardboard boxes would change the transfer

price for liner and also change the output mix of liner and bag paper.

26. Cement firms usually employ uniform delivered pricing, whereas paper firms usually employ mill pricing. Explain why.

27. Why do some movie theaters charge lower prices for couples than for single ticket buyers?

Suggested Readings

Hirschleifer, Jack., "On the Economics of Transfer Pricing," *Journal of Business,* July 1956, pp. 172–184.

Koch, J. V., *Industrial Organization and Prices.* Englewood Cliffs, N.J.: Prentice-Hall, 1980.

Scherer, Frederick M., *Industrial Market Structure and Industry Performance.* Chicago: Rand McNally, 1980.

Stigler, George J., *The Theory of Price.* London: Macmillan, 1956.

13

ECO-NOMICS OF ANTITRUST ISSUES

The antitrust laws of the United States (summarized in the Appendix) are generally viewed as the chief manifestation of government intervention into the economy for the purpose of strengthening competition. Strengthening competition is a laudable goal, but it is debatable whether the antitrust laws, as they have evolved, actually accomplish it. In practice, the government's antitrust efforts are often anticompetitive and anticonsumer. However, they do express the general public's belief in the competitive market as the source of material benefits to consumers.

We expect competitive forces to coordinate, without collusion, demand and supply; prices are the coordinating device. As firms compare price and marginal cost, they are induced to produce at the efficient level, where price equals marginal cost. Firms comparing price and average cost can determine whether to invest in particular industries (the entry/exit decision). They also assess various technologies and their use of the factors of production in a continual effort to discover cost advantages and generate profits. We expect that the final result of these profit-seeking activities will not be excessive profits but benefits to the consumer in the form of lower prices, better products, and better service.

These benefits of noncollusive coordination are threatened when potential competitors form cartels. The market power that results forces prices above marginal costs and above average costs without countervailing entry to erode such profits. The antitrust laws were intended to attack practices like these, which restrain competition and prevent consumers from enjoying its benefits.

Antitrust laws encourage the judiciary to scrutinize the conduct of firms (pricing practices, merger attempts, trade practices), the industrial structure of firms (competitive, monopolistic, or oligopolistic), and their performance (growth in market share and the size and longevity of profits). Data drawn from these categories are blended with economic theories to determine the legality of various acts and practices. Practices that may have redeeming consumer benefits but that may also be destructive are judged in **rule of reason** proceedings. Consistent judicial rulings against certain practices have put them in the category of **per se violations,** which are practices with so little likelihood of consumer benefit to countervail the greater likelihood of harm that judicial resources are not invested in determining their legality case by case.

This chapter examines the antitrust laws in a rather novel way. The usual treatment consists of a litany of laws and dry readings from cases to trace the development of legal interpretations. By contrast, this chapter focuses on the economic analysis of those acts and practices that attract the attention of the antitrust forces. The purpose is to arm you with an economic understanding of those business practices—not to teach you about legal practice.

This chapter comes with a limited warranty: Except for advice against participation in overt price fixing, it does not supply a list of dos and don'ts for avoiding prosecution. Nor should you consult any textbook for such a list. The law in the area of business practices is in a state of flux, and material about acceptable and unacceptable practices would probably be out of date by the time you read it. Thus there is no substitute for an astute lawyer who is trained to keep pace with such change. The economic analysis supplied here is meant to help you develop an articulate relationship with the business attorneys who advise you and with legislators in the event you wish to pursue changes in the law.

Horizontal Price Fixing and Territorial Division

Horizontal price fixing is collusion by potentially competing firms for the purpose of affecting product prices. Product prices may be raised to increase profits, kept low to limit entry, or timed to meet special market conditions.[1] The model of the cartel presented in Chapter 10 illustrates the ideal: Output quotas are fixed for cartel members so as to equate marginal cost and marginal revenue. In practice, however, it is more common for firms to agree on how far prices should rise and when. A division of the market into geographic areas—**territorial division**—may accompany the price-fixing agreement or may be used alone to reduce competition.

Horizontal price-fixing agreements and territorial division are per se violations of the law. That is, the reasonableness of the prices charged is not an issue in the determination of illegality, even if it could be shown that the prices and/or territories are exactly the same as would result from unfettered competition. The theory, as expressed in the Socony-Vacuum Oil case, is that firms capable of setting up a benign conspiracy can affect economic conditions in a malign manner later on.[2] Competition is an ongoing process, and the antitrust laws should protect the *process*—not an act that temporarily produces comparable results.

Horizontal price fixing and territorial division may enhance competition, however, as in the case of partnerships. Such partnerships as law offices, small-scale grocers, and small banks in effect agree not to compete in an effort to capture partnership efficiencies. But similar practices by other businesses are not so clear and must be judged by a rule of reason.

One way to tell whether a business practice or act constitutes price fixing is to distinguish between naked and ancillary restraints, as Justice Taft did in the Addyston Pipe and Steel case.[3] **Naked restraints** are those with no redeeming procompetitive impact. Firms enter into them solely for the purpose of injuring competition. On the other hand, **ancillary restraints** are those with elements that enhance efficiency or output and that can therefore be weighed against the restraint on competition. Justice Taft argued that, because there was no ancillary effect in the Addyston Pipe and Steel case, it should not be tried on a rule of reason; the price fixing and market division that took place were per se violations. The rule of reason was similarly rejected in the Trenton Potteries case.[4]

Since price fixing is illegal per se, the U.S. Justice Department must merely show that the act was committed, not that there was any economic damage. For example, if an industry is losing money and the firms in it agree to fix prices merely to raise returns on investment to a normal rate, the reasonableness of these prices

---

1. The evidence demonstrates that price fixing occurs mainly in low-profit industries. This does not mean that price fixing does not increase profits but instead that it is often tried by desperate people seeking to survive encroachment by a new competitor. See G. Hay and D. Kelly, "An Empirical Survey of Price-Fixing Conspiracies," *Journal of Law and Economics* 17 (1974): 13.

2. United States v. Socony-Vacuum Oil (1940).

3. United States v. Addyston Pipe and Steel (1898).

4. United States v. Trenton Potteries Company, 273 U.S. 392, 47 Sup. Ct. 377, 71 L. Ed. 700 (1927).

would not be allowed as evidence.

Horizontal price fixing and territorial division are generally viewed as per se violations unless there is some associated benefit. Territorial division without a price-fixing agreement can still increase prices by reducing or eliminating competition within a given territory. However, Justice Warren Burger, in his dissent to the decision in the Topco case, recognized that territorial division may help thwart the free-rider problem.[5] We will return to this argument in a later section.

5. United States v. Topco Associates, Inc. (1972).

13.1

"Reasonableness" of Collusive Prices

Firms caught in the act of price fixing often argue that the prices they were charging under the agreement were reasonable because the rate of return on investment was no higher than a normal rate. But using the adjacent figure, we can easily counter this argument.

The left-hand panel of the figure shows the cost curves of a typical firm. The industry demand curve is represented in the right-hand panel. Suppose the market-clearing noncollusive price is P_0. Because it does not generate a

market rate of return, this is obviously not a long-run equilibrium price. For the long-run market-clearing price P_1 to be achieved, some firms must exit the industry.

If the firms agree to help each other remain in business, they can set the price at $P_2 = AC$ in order to generate a fair rate of return. But the consumer is hurt,

because $P_2 > P_1 > P_0$. The appropriate competitive adjustment would result in prices lower than P_2. In fact, prices would fall from P_1 to P_0 while exit is occurring.

It seems obvious that a "normal" rate of return has the effect of hurting consumers. Therefore, price P_2 is unreasonable.

Collusive Prices and Rate of Return

Collusive prices are not "reasonable" if they yield only the normal rate of return on investment. Collusive price P_2 yields a normal return higher than the noncollusive price, P_1, which also yields a normal return.

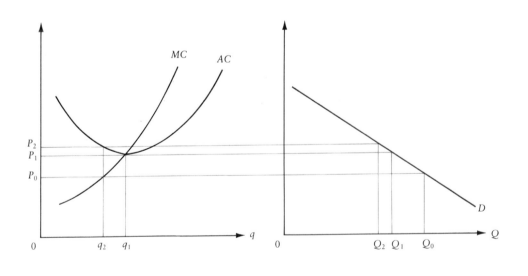

Price Fixing and Trade Associations

Price fixing sometimes arises out of business associations with quite legitimate purposes. Among other things, trade associations permit firms in the same industry to provide general information to the public while avoiding the free-rider problem. (Generally, a **free rider** is one who enjoys without charge the unintended benefits of another's economic activity.) For example, the mobile camper industry can more effectively compete against tent campsites, motels, and other forms of recreation by advertising to the public the virtues of dragging a camper behind the family car. It can also establish mailing lists for use by members, hold conventions, sponsor short films on campers, and promote itself in other ways. An individual firm cannot provide this type of general information without benefiting competing firms without charge (thus the term *free rider*). Once general advertising has been used to "compete *for* the field," more specific advertising can be used by individual firms to "compete *in* the field." Thus the trade association may be a procompetitive force.

But the trade association also provides occasions for executives with pricing authority to meet to discuss markets and the general economy. It is not uncommon for price-fixing efforts to coalesce at such meetings. Because written price-fixing agreements provide concrete evidence of the intent to break the law, oral communication concerning price movements is the preferred method.

Aside from providing convenient times and places for in-person delivery of price-fixing messages, trade associations may also provide facilities for the exchange of price information, including the publication of price lists, prices of recent transactions, or average prices and total sales volume. Members can use this information for the legitimate purpose of meeting competitive prices and discovering potential markets. But such information exchanges may also be used to verify compliance with prior collusive agreements. Thus United States Gypsum unsuccessfully argued that it used such information exchanges and verifying telephone calls to competitors to meet competitors' prices, in accordance with the laws governing price discrimination.[6] The courts have looked with increasing disfavor on price information exchanges, and now even the exchanges of information between competitors about past transaction prices, either directly or through a trade association, is illegal.[7] The reasoning is that the threat of discovery will tend to encourage compliance. Historic price information can be used to coordinate changes in accordance with prior agreements, since firms can swiftly send signals to each other through the price reporting mechanism.

6. United States v. United States Gypsum (1978).

7. A case in point is United States v. Container Corporation of America (1969).

Price Discrimination

Chapter 12 discusses price discrimination in the context of pricing policy. Our concern here is its antitrust implications. Legally, price discrimination has been attacked for its deleterious effect on the competitors of the price discriminator, and on the customers of the firm that buys from the price discriminator.

Section 2 of the Clayton Act and the Robinson-Patman Act are the chief laws covering price discrimination. For example, section 2 of the Clayton Act (1914) attacked price cutting at the local level in an effort to prevent large firms from invading markets served by existing small firms. The impact of price discrimination on consumers was merely implied by the law: The greater the number of suppliers, the better the consumer is served. Price cutting may eliminate some local suppliers, and so its prohibition benefits consumers.

The Robinson-Patman Act (1936) prohibited more general price discrimination. Born in the Great Depression, it was an effort to retard the growth of chain stores.[8] Although chain stores enjoy economies of scale in purchasing and can pass these efficiencies on to consumers in the form of lower product prices, the profits of smaller stores are squeezed.

The Robinson-Patman Act is asymmetrical in its effect. Price discrimination may take the form of price differences that do not correspond to differences in marginal cost or of equal prices when marginal costs are different, but the act attacks only cases involving price differences. Still, the seller that is offering a commodity for sale at different prices may defend against the charge of price discrimination if it can prove that the price differences can be fully (not just partially) explained by cost differences or by the need to meet (not approach or undercut) a competitor's price.

The rules against price discrimination are puzzling—if not infuriating—to the modern managerial economist because they are largely anticompetitive. Thus it is important to realize that they were primarily intended to protect small businesses. We may know from our study of managerial economics that the consumer is best served by protection of the competitive process and not competitors, but framers of the Robinson-Patman Act erroneously equated the two. They felt that maintaining a large number of suppliers in the market was the best way to foster competition.

This view is a misinterpretation of the economist's model of perfect competition, with its emphasis on equilibrium. The model explains how the monopolist that can avoid arbitrage can also

---

8. The Robinson-Patman Act applies only to commodities of like grade and quality. Sellers cannot violate the act unless they are selling similar commodities to two different customers. Services and such intangibles as electricity are not considered commodities under the terms of the act. Furthermore, to be considered commerce, sales transactions must take place across state lines.

discriminate in price by equating marginal revenue rather than price across markets. In competition, however, arbitrage is automatic. The competitive model assumes that the cost of entry into a competitive market is negligible, and hence price discrimination cannot exist in competitive equilibrium.

But it is important to realize that, although price discrimination cannot exist in competitive equilibrium, it can exist in the industry's move toward competitive equilibrium. In fact, price discrimination may play a very useful role in the approach to equilibrium. For example, temporary shortages in one location give rise to an increase in the equilibrium price there. In response to the higher price, firms produce more, and the price drops as a consequence. If price discrimination is prohibited, firms lack the price incentive to respond to shortages. Thus the competitive process is slowed down, not enhanced, by the prohibition of price discrimination. Similarly, local surpluses justify "below-cost" sales, a desirable result slowed down by the rules.

In the longer run, price discrimination may help a firm in an oligopoly decide whether to enter a new market or to install new equipment in order to boost production. Specifically, price discrimination allows the firm to test the elasticity of demand—by examining the response to price changes in one market without instituting price changes in all markets. This sort of information helps reduce the risks of entering new markets. Risk is a cost, as Chapter 8 explains; hence reduction of risk encourages entry, enhances output, and in turn serves customers.

The Utah Pie case provides an example of how the laws against price discrimination have been used.[9] In this case, Utah Pie Company charged Pet Mills Company, Carnation Milk Company, and Continental Baking Company with selling pies in the Salt Lake City market at prices below the prices at which they were selling pies in California. As Table 13.1 illustrates, the Salt Lake City pie eater was doubtless too busy enjoying the fruits of competition to detect any "anticompetitive" practices: Sales of pies quintupled in 3 years. Although Utah Pie's large market share fell, its total sales quadrupled. The Supreme Court found in Utah Pie's favor.

Another case limited the use of economies of scale as an argument for price discrimination. Morton Salt Company offered salt to wholesalers and retailers at prices reflecting the quantity bought; the greater the quantity, the lower the price.[10] Such price differences could result in different resale prices. To apply the Robinson-Patman Act to the Morton Salt case, according to the Supreme Court, "the Commission need only prove that a seller charged one purchaser a higher price for like goods than he had charged one or

Table 13.1
Pie Sales in Salt Lake City

| | Year | |
Factor	1958	1961
Total pies sold in Salt Lake City	57,000	267,000
Utah Pie market share	66.5%	45.3%
Total pies sold by Utah Pie	37,905	120,951

9. Utah Pie Company v. Continental Baking Company, 386 U.S. 685 (1967).

10. Federal Trade Commission v. Morton Salt Company, 334 U.S. 37 (1948).

more of the purchaser's competition." Thus the advantages provided by economies of scale were considered less important than the impact of price discrimination.

Tie-in Sales and Reciprocity

Tie-in sales and reciprocity are related practices attacked by the antitrust laws for the largely erroneous reason that they transfer monopoly power from one product to another. As Chapter 9 explains, tie-in sales require the purchaser of one product (the **tying product**) to purchase another (the **tied product**). Reciprocity is an agreement between parties to purchase each other's goods.

Examples of tie-in sales include IBM's rental of business machines with the tied-in obligation to purchase a flow of IBM punch cards for use in their machines.[11] Similarly, United Shoe Manufacturing Corporation required shoe manufacturers to use only its equipment if they used any.[12] Also, Jerrold Electronics, the pioneer in cable TV, required towns and villages in mountainous areas to purchase not only the mountaintop receiving antenna but also the cable to town, the home hookup equipment, and associated amplifiers; substitute equipment could not be used at any stage without violating the contract.[13] And International Salt, which manufactured a machine to spew salt into canned goods, required the renters of such equipment to purchase the salt as well.[14]

Objections to tie-in sales are supported by one of two theories: the "transfer of power" theory and the "price discrimination" theory. The idea behind **transfer of power** is that a firm with a monopoly on a product due, say, to a patent or mere novelty can extend that monopoly to the tied product to the detriment of consumers. The price discrimination argument is that the firm can monitor the sales of the tied product to gauge demand for the tying product and then charge higher prices to heavier users.

Let's consider the transfer of power theory more carefully. It assumes that a firm with monopoly power can increase that power by tie-in sales. But basic economic analysis reveals that this cannot be the case. The guiding principle is that a monopolist can only extract monopoly power once. For example, suppose that a firm has a monopoly in the tied product but faces competition in the tying product. It would try to find the profit-maximizing price for the tied product but would face a parametric price for the tying product. Any attempt to charge a price above the competitive price for the tying product would have to be offset by a reduction in the price of the tied product; otherwise, the firm would not be able to sell the

---

11. United States v. International Business Machines, Inc., 293 U.S. 131 (1936).

12. United States v. United Shoe Manufacturing Corporation, 347 U.S. 521 (1954).

13. United States v. Jerrold Electronics Corporation, 365 U.S. 567 (1961).

14. United States v. International Salt Company, 332 U.S. 392.

profit-maximizing quantity of the tied product. What if the firm has monopoly power over both products? The analysis is largely the same: Any price charged for one of the products that is different from the profit-maximizing price must be offset by corresponding differences in the price of the other product in order to maximize profits on both.

Now let's analyze the price discrimination theory. If the firm uses the tying product to meter the use of the tied product, it can more readily estimate the elasticity of demand—and hence derive a basis for price discrimination. The price discrimination theory is particularly relevant when the tying product is used with the tied product, such as punch cards in the use of business machines. Such price discrimination is decried on the grounds that it increases monopoly profit. But as Chapter 12 explains, output with price discrimination is either the same as or larger than without it. Thus the usual economic problem created by monopoly, output reduction, is not aggravated but is alleviated by price discrimination. And after all, the basic concern is monopoly, not price discrimination.

Reciprocity also concerns the courts, since it appears to foreclose sales by competitors. However, reciprocity is subject to exactly the same analysis as tie-in sales; the transfer of power theory is no more applicable. A firm engaged in reciprocity either has market power or has not. The value to it of reciprocity is incorporated in the price of the goods sold. And the argument that reciprocity forecloses sales by other firms has no merit: Sales by one firm always foreclose those of another. Nevertheless, the Supreme Court chose the opposite argument in a case brought against Consolidated Foods Corporation:

> reciprocity . . . results in an irrelevant and alien factor intruding into the choice among competing products. . . . [T]hreatened withdrawal of orders if products of an affiliate cease being bought, or a conditioning of future purchases on the receipt of orders for products of that affiliate, is an anti-competitive practice.[15]

Vertical Restraints of Resale Price Maintenance and Territorial Divisions

Chapter 12 covers the complexities of coordinating a multidivision firm through transfer pricing. The need for similar coordination also exists among firms that are not formally integrated. Like a multidivision (or vertically integrated) firm, the independent manufacturer has an interest in the prices charged by retailers selling its products as well as in their territorial boundaries. Some manufacturers have therefore attempted to set retail prices and divide sales

---

15. Federal Trade Commission v. Consolidated Foods Corporation, 380 U.S 592 (1965).

territories among retailers, which are both forms of **vertical restraint.** Such resale price maintenance (also discussed in Chapter 10) and territorial division have been attacked under the antitrust laws.

The objection to these practices is that they stifle competition. Resale price maintenance is thought to stabilize price fixing among retailers by preventing price concessions. Similarly, territorial division can be used to enforce the quotas of a cartel agreement.

Recently however, the courts have begun to realize that the sale of products requiring point-of-sale services or promotions is likely to be afflicted by the free-rider problem. Consider the purchase of a television set, an expensive, complex product that people shop around for. Not only are they looking for a good deal, but they also need to gather information about product features prior to purchasing a TV. A dealer that wishes to respond to this desire for information incurs the costs of hiring expert service and sales people, installing attractive displays, and providing informational brochures. Consumers, however, need not purchase a TV set at the same store where they gather information. Instead, they may visit one store for information, then search for the store with the lowest price. Thus they end up buying from a relatively uninformative store, such as a discount house or department store. The uninformative store is a free rider on the effort of the informative store. If it continually loses sales in this fashion, the informative store must cut prices and costs—by cutting its selling effort. The end result is a lack of consumer information, which hurts consumers, dealers, and manufacturer alike.

Resale price maintenance and territorial division can be viewed as a response to this free-rider problem. For example, when the resale price is set by the manufacturer and cannot be undercut by retailers, television dealers have an incentive to compete on the grounds of superior point-of-sale service. The manufacturer can raise or lower the maintained price in order to induce the correct amount of point-of-sale service. More specifically, an increased markup encourages retailers to attract customers by promotion and service. Their increased selling efforts incur higher costs, of course, so eventually profits fall to a normal rate of return. By controlling the selling effort of "independent" dealers, the manufacturer fosters a relationship like that found in vertically integrated, multidivision firms.

Territorial division has much the same effect on the free-rider problem. By restricting dealers from invading one another's territories to make sales, it assures that all dealers receive adequate returns for their selling efforts. Resale price maintenance is generally used for items that are transported from the point of sale by the customer. Territorial division would not solve the free-rider problem for such products, since customers could easily cross the territorial boundaries. But for items that must be delivered or for which economies of scale require fewer dealers spread out over greater distances, territorial division is more likely to be used.

The antitrust implications of resale price maintenance and territorial division would therefore appear to be best decided on a case-by-case basis. The central question is whether they are instituted to prop up a dealer cartel or to avoid the free-rider problem. As usual, the answer lies in the structure of the industry and not in the practices themselves. In an oligopoly, competition is actually enhanced when the manufacturers employ such tactics. And if the manufacturer has a monopoly, these tactics do not provide more monopoly power by allowing the manufacturer to reduce output. To the contrary, a monopolist's resale price maintenance and territorial division may result in greater consumer welfare than if the free-rider problem eliminated or reduced point-of-sale information. If the monopoly itself is a problem, antitrust enforcement may be in order. But if the monopoly is legitimate, (for patent protection, for example), resale price maintenance and territorial division should be ignored, because they serve to increase, not decrease, output.

The rule against resale price maintenance is so firmly established that firms are even prohibited from establishing maximum prices.[16] However, territorial division has been lifted out of the category of per se violations and placed in the rule of reason category. The most prominent case in this development is Continental TV, Inc. v. GTE Sylvania, Inc., wherein the procompetitive efficiencies of resale price maintenance and territorial division were explicitly recognizied.[17]

Mergers

The monopoly problem is, of course, that it tends to reduce output below competitive levels, causing an increase in price above marginal cost. There are few examples of pure monopoly, and so the monopoly problem most often appears in the form of collusion among firms trying to mimic the pure monopoly. The likelihood of collusion generally increases when the number of firms in the industry falls.

In the early 1980s, "merger mania" became a hot topic. Rather than start new divisions from scratch, many large corporations bought up existing firms. The resulting **mergers** had the overall effect of reducing the number of firms in many industries. Mergers would appear to automatically weaken competition and also to enhance the opportunities for collusion. It would seem, therefore, that consistent application of the antitrust laws would require the prohibition of mergers.

But instead of prohibiting mergers, the antitrust laws permit a

---

16. See Kiefer-Stewart Company v. Joseph E. Seagram & Sons, Inc., 340 U.S. 211 (1951).

17. Continental TV, Inc. v. GTE Sylvania, Inc., 433 U.S. 36 (1977).

rule of reason in determining their legality. After all, mergers may enhance the entry/exit process, which is so vital to competition. When a firm decides to exit an industry, it naturally tries to sell its assets to the highest bidder. This bidder is often another firm with some knowledge of the market—and in fact may be a competitor. The opportunity to exit via such a merger raises the value of a company from the beginning and hence the incentive to enter in the first place. Thus mergers can enhance competition and must be evaluated case by case.

There are three kinds of mergers: horizontal, vertical, and conglomerate. A **horizontal merger** takes place between firms that are in the same stage of production in the same industry, such as two firms producing glassine paper. A **vertical merger** takes place between firms in different stages of producing some final good, such as a pulp producer and a paper manufacturer. A **conglomerate merger** takes place between firms in unrelated markets, such as a paper firm and an oil company.

Let's consider the horizontal merger first. Obviously, any horizontal merger gives the new entity a larger market share than either of the original firms had prior to the merger. It is often thought that this increased concentration is dangerous. However, the relationship between concentration and competition, as discussed in Chapter 11, is not direct. Technical changes in production, finance, management, and marketing may change the efficient size and product mix of any firm over time. Two firms may merge to exploit such changes faster than they could through internal growth. Hence, although the potential for collusion may rise with industry concentration (even this statement will be qualified shortly), a merger may also present opportunities to enhance efficiency. And the potential for collusion may actually fall after a merger if the result is less dominance by one or two top firms.

For example, suppose an industry has two giant firms, such as Miller Brewing and Anheuser Busch in the beer industry. A merger between the third-largest firm and some smaller competitor may increase the rivalry sufficiently to decrease the danger of collusion between the top two firms. That is, the existence of a stronger third firm may destabilize the tacit or explicit price-fixing arrangements of the top two. Merely looking at industry concentration is obviously not enough to judge the competitive effects of a merger.

Vertical mergers are often undertaken to coordinate production and sales in a manner superior to what is possible through resale price maintenance and territorial division. Economies of scale due to superior management control and reduction of risk due to greater certainty of supply provide strong motivation for vertical mergers. In spite of these procompetitive results, vertical mergers have been under attack by virtue of the transfer of power theory. But if a firm has monopoly power, a vertical merger with another firm will not reduce output. Instead, the monopolists will find that $MC = MR$ at a lower price and a greater level of output, and the cost reductions will partially be passed on to consumers.

Conglomerate mergers usually are undertaken to diversify investment portfolios and to share superior management skills. A conglomerate can spread risks over firms in independent markets and thus protect itself from disaster in any one industry. For the same reason, a conglomerate is also more attractive to investors. Furthermore, successful management in one industry is often transferable to another, since modern management combines intuition; training in managerial economics, statistics, and computer science; and knowledge of banking and insurance markets. Conglomerate mergers may also be pursued by firms that use the capital acquired in the merger to finance ventures in unrelated markets. Finally, the threat of takeover implied by conglomerate mergers tends to keep management efficient.

A P P L I C A T I O N

13.2

Assessing Industry Concentration

For assessing mergers, concentration is typically measured by concentration ratios and the Herfindahl index. The **n-firm concentration ratios** are merely the share of the market held by the top *n* firms. Usually four or eight firms are considered.

The **Herfindahl index** is a bit more subtle in that it is the sum of the squared market shares of the firms (ΣS_i^2, where S_i is the share of the *i*th firm. The Herfindahl index can range from a high of 1 to a low of 1/(number of firms in an industry composed of firms of equal shares). The index reflects the share of the largest firms. For any given concentration ratio, the index will be higher the more unequal the shares are. Thus the Herfindahl index is sensitive to the problem of price leadership.

Consider a horizontal merger between the largest firm in an industry and another large firm. The Herfindahl index is large and will grow considerably when the merger is accounted for if the largest firm has a substantial share initially. But it is not large and will not grow considerably if the largest firm does not have a substantial share initially.

The following example illus-

trates this principle. Suppose that industry A has fifteen firms with market shares of one at 11 percent, four at 10 percent, nine at 5 percent, and one at 4 percent—for a total of 100 percent. The Herfindahl index is therefore $H = (0.11)^2 + 4(0.10)^2 + 9(0.05)^2 + (.04)^2 = 0.0762$. If the leading firm merges with the fifth-largest firm, one of the 5-percent firms, $H = (0.16)^2 + 4(0.10)^2 + 8(0.05)^2 + (0.04)^2 = 0.0872$. Both the initial Herfindahl index and the postmerger Herfindahl index are quite low.

Now consider the more concentrated industry B, which also has 15 firms. The five largest firms have market shares of 40 percent, 30 percent, 10 percent, 8 percent, and 5 percent, and the remaining ten each have a market share of 0.7 percent—for a total of 100 percent. In industry B, the Herfindahl index is $H = (0.40)^2 + (0.30)^2 + (0.10)^2 + (0.08)^2 + (0.05)^2 + 10(0.007)^2 = 0.26939$. Clearly this is a much more concentrated industry. If the largest firm merges with the fifth-largest firm, which has a 5-percent share before the merger, $H = (0.45)^2 + (0.30)^2 + (0.10)^2 + (0.08)^2 + 10(0..007)^2 = 0.30939$. The Herfindahl index jumps substantially when an already-large firm merges. Thus the index is very sensitive to additional concentrations in an already concentrated market.

However, the Herfindahl index is unreliable when assessing mergers between firms that have substantially smaller shares than the leaders in a concentrated industry. Consider the merger attempt between Schlitz Brewing Company and Heileman Brewing Company, which was aban-

Continued on page 350

doned when the Justice Department sued to block it. In the beer industry in 1981, Anheuser Busch and Miller accounted for 51 percent of the total sales in the country; Schlitz and Heileman controlled roughly 8 percent apiece. It was thought that a merger between Schlitz and Heileman "might substantially lessen competition in the beer industry in violation of section 7 of the Clayton Act. . . . (I)t would significantly increase the industry's Herfindahl index by .0118

from .1664 to .1762."[*]

This reliance on the Herfindahl index is misplaced. The industry has lopsided shares, with Anheuser Busch and Miller way ahead of the pack. The theory of cartels indicates that the anticompetitive danger comes from express or tacit collusion between these two leaders. Because they

[*]Assistant Attorney General W. Baxter to Congressman Henry Reuss, 23 April 1982.

are so large, the Herfindahl index is naturally large. And because Schlitz and Heileman are also large companies, although quite small relative to the leaders, their merger must make a numerically significant difference. But all of this discussion misses the most crucial point: The merger between Schlitz and Heileman would actually have loosened the tight oligopoly structure at the top of the industry. This element of theory is not captured by the index.

13.3

Minimum Efficient Size and Merger/Deconcentration Policy

In determining public policy toward mergers and the general problem of industry concentration, there has long been a debate about the size of the firms that should be permitted to merge. The logical extension of that debate is the question of whether existing firms should be broken into smaller firms. The theoretical theme that has been used to organize the debate is the notion of the **minimum efficient size** of firms, minimum efficient level of output, and hence minimum efficient market share that will minimize the average cost of production.[*] It is useful to examine the strength of this theme by considering the shapes of the short-run and long-run average cost curves that it engenders.

Geometrically, the minimum efficient size of a firm is the output at which average costs are minimized. In Figure A, this level of output is q_a. The U shape of the *ATC* curve represents the effect of the law of diminishing returns on the variable factors of production (presented in Chapter 6). In Figure B, the long-run average cost (*LAC*) envelope, which summarizes a firm's costs, also has a U shape. This shape represents the firm's difficulties in coordi-

[*]See White House Task Force on Antitrust Policy, *The Neal Report*, report 1, in *Trade Regulation Reporter*, supplement to number 415 (Washington, D.C.: Government Printing Office, 26 May 1969).

nating a larger and larger scale of production. Beyond output q_b, the firm in Figure B experiences diseconomies of scale. Thus increased output is more expensive—not because of the law of diminishing returns but because of organizational difficulties.

The *LAC* curve need not take the gradual U shape of Figure B; it may take a flatter shape (as in Figure C) or a more pronounced, steeper U shape (as in Figure D). It is important to realize that the *LAC* curves will differ from firm to firm, because management teams vary in their principles and competence—and thus in their ability to organize activities of different scales. The *LAC* curves are useful reflections of a firm's organization ability, but a curve drawn to reflect one firm's experience cannot be used to predict another's.

E. A. G. Robinson has noted that the ability to organize large-scale production depends on five forces, none of which are likely to be identical among firms.[†]

[†]E. A. G. Robinson, *The Structure of Competitive Industry* (Chicago: University of Chicago Press, 1958), p. 12.

1. *Technical forces:* Engineering and the state of the production arts.

2. *Managerial forces:* Either available in the market or developed over a considerable period of time within the firm. This category includes skills that are quite specific to each firm.

3. *Financial forces:* Relationships with the banking and insurance industries as well as the ability to finance ventures and spread risks internally.

4. *Marketing forces:* Deployment of marketing personnel and the development of their knowledge and skills over time.

5. *Forces of risk and fluctuation:* Ability of the firm to respond to forces that must be taken as parameters; ability to introduce new products, extinguish old ones, and price them efficiently (a particularly useful concept in multiproduct firms, which is the predominant form of business enterprise, because the firm can spread risk internally over its portfolio of products).

Obviously, these forces will not be equally developed in all firms in an industry. Firms that do better at developing these forces will tend to be larger through internal growth. Firms that merge to produce superior "forces" combine to produce desirable efficiencies.

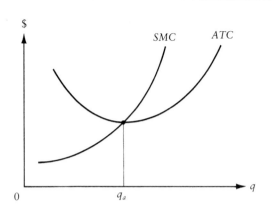

Figure A
Economies of Scale and Minimum Efficient Size

The efficient level of output lies at the intersection of the *SMC* and *ATC* curves.

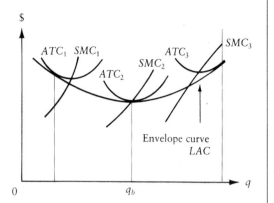

Figure B
Short-Run and Long-Run Costs

Diseconomies of scale appear beyond output q_b.

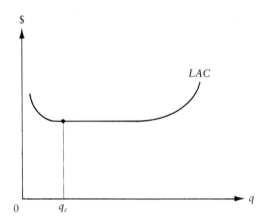

Figure C
Potential Shape of *LAC* Curve

The greater management's efficiency at running a large firm, the flatter the *LAC* curve.

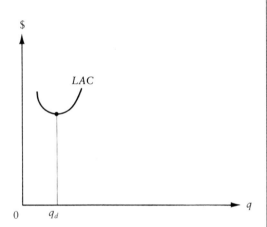

Figure D
Potential Shape of *LAC* Curve

The *LAC* curve of a less efficiently managed firm is relatively steep.

The concept of minimum efficient size ignores the underpinnings of the *LAC* curve. If a firm with 5 percent of a market can survive in an industry where the leader has 40 percent of the market, it does not follow that the larger firm can be broken down into eight (40/5) survivable firms. The efficiencies that helped the leading firm grow are likely to be lost by such a "deconcentration."

It is therefore important for managerial economists to realize that average cost curves are drawn for the purpose of organizing thoughts about the incentives inherent in the competitive process. It is wrong to attribute greater explanatory power to the curves: The cost-minimizing outputs are not invariant over time, nor do they have prescriptive value in merger/deconcentration questions.[‡]

[‡]For more on this and other difficulties with the Neal Report, see Robert Bork, *The Antitrust Paradox: A Policy at War with Itself* (New York: Basic Books, 1978), especially chap. 6.

13.4

Market Definition in the "Cellophane Case"

In the famous "Cellophane case," the U.S. Justice Department accused Du Pont, former holder of the patent for Cellophane, of monopolizing the cellophane market.* The evidence of monopoly included Du Pont's share of the cellophane market (70 percent) and its large rate of return on investment for a long period of time.

Du Pont argued in its defense that Cellophane faced intense competition from other flexible wrapping materials, including glassine and greaseproof papers, pliofilm, and kraft papers. Du Pont's market share fell to 21 percent when these products were included in the overall market for flexible wrap. Du Pont won the case, but the economic logic of the decision was flawed, as can be demonstrated by an analysis based on the leader-follower model.

*United States v. E. I. Du Pont de Nemours and Company, 351 U.S. 377 (1956).

Consider the accompanying figure. Du Pont is the leader in the flexible-wrap market, and the producers of all other flexible wraps are the followers. Du Pont's demand curve for Cellophane, D_{cello}, is drawn in the right-hand panel as the horizontal difference between the total demand for flexible wrap and the competitors' supply of noncellophane wrap (in the left-hand panel). Du Pont's marginal revenue curve, MR_{cello}, is derived from D_{cello}, as usual. If MC_{cello} is Du Pont's marginal cost curve, Du Pont maximizes profit by equating MR_{cello} and MC_{cello} at point A, producing W_0^C units of cellophane and charging price P_0. Other suppliers—the followers—produce W_0^{ND} units of wrap at

price P_0. The total production of flexible wrap at P_0 is W_0^{TOT}

Now consider Du Pont's argument, keeping in mind that antitrust laws are intended to benefit consumers. Du Pont's large profit, it said, was a consequence of the fact that its many plants could produce Cellophane at less cost than other manufacturers could produce flexible wrap and of its ability to achieve market power, despite the competition from other wrap manufacturers.

But Du Pont's small share of the flexible-wrap market was not the result of intense competition, as the company argued, but instead derived from the fact that it restrained output in order to raise the price of Cellophane. Furthermore, nothing can be learned from the theory of cross-elasticity of demand, because a firm with monopoly power will always price its goods so that demand is elastic. In a dominant-firm price leadership, elasticity must arise from the substitutability of other products.

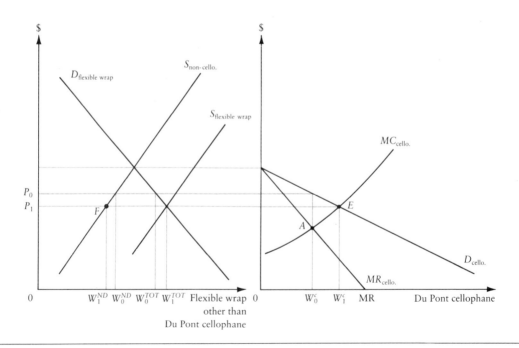

The question for policy makers was whether Du Pont should be required to divest itself of plants so that the plants could compete individually. If all Du Pont plants were free to act independently, as competitors, the MC_{cello} curve could be added horizontally to $S_{noncello}$ to produce the total flexible-wrap supply curve, $S_{flexible\ wrap}$. In the absence of monopoly power, market forces would have set price at P_1, determined by the intersection of supply and demand at point E. At the lower price P_1, the sale of Cellophane would have risen to W_1^C ($P_1 = MC_{cello}$ at point E), and the sale of flexible wrap would have fallen to W_1^{ND} ($P_1 = S_{noncello}$ at point F). Total flexible-wrap sales would have risen to W_1^{TOT}

The leader-follower model shows that Du Pont's low market share for flexible wrap, rather than resulting from vigorous competition, could have resulted from the output restrictions made possible by its market position. It is just as reasonable to argue that Du Pont had such a small market share precisely because it was exercising market power to the detriment of consumers. Cross-price elasticity is not enough.

13.5

Legality of Motion Picture Splits

Motion picture split agreements, which have been used for decades by movie exhibitors, have been challenged by the U.S. Justice Department as violations of the antitrust laws prohibiting restraint of trade.

Under split agreements, exhibitors in a particular market collude to determine which of them has the sole right to negotiate for films offered by distributors. At first blush, such collusion would indeed appear to have the common evil ingredients of a cartel, with the resulting higher prices to consumers. Such an analysis has been provided by Professor James Gordon:

It is therefore beyond cavil that splitting interferes with the pricing mechanism by substituting private agreements not to compete for competitive price making. The net effect is a misallocation of some of the nation's economic resources and a distortion of the normal investment pattern. . . . To the extent that the antitrust laws are meant to remedy misallocations of economic resources and the frustration of consumer wants, the motion picture exhibitors' agreement not to compete would seem the paradigm case for the invocation of the per se rule against market division and price fixing.[*]

[*]James S. Gordon, "Horizontal and Vertical Restraints of Trade: The Legality of Motion Picture Splits under the Antitrust Laws," *Yale Law Journal* 75 (1965): 239, 250–251.

The refutation of Gordon's approach requires recognition that the problem is one of bargaining between distributors (who offer to rent the film for exhibition) and exhibitors (who use the film to attract customers who rent seats in a theater). Thus the film is a factor of production for the exhibitor.

The Gordon argument, that splits interfere with competitive efficiency, is misplaced: Competition does not exist in the movie industry, with or without splits, because of the monopoly power of the distributor. The distributor's monopoly power over the movie must be protected by the copyright laws because of the technical ease with which films can be copied. Competition from the distributors of such pirated films would quickly erase the return to the film's creator.

Because of the need for copyright monopoly, the correct comparison in this case is not between competition and collusion but between unilateral distributor monopoly without exhibitor splits and bilateral bargaining with splits. The splits would provide exhibitors with greater bargaining power and hence the ability to obtain film at a price no higher (since the distributor would not negotiate for a price higher than the profit-maximizing price) and probably much lower than would prevail under distributor monopoly. Hence the motion picture split system provides a countervailing force to distributor monopoly and helps the consumer by putting a lid on prices.

Summary

The antitrust laws are intended to help consumers but are not always successful in execution. Several business acts and practices are under attack by the antitrust forces. Rather than emphasizing the recitation of laws and statutes, this chapter focuses on economic analysis of the laws and develops a balanced view of the success of these laws.

Among the practices considered in this chapter are horizontal price fixing and territorial division, methods of cartel stabilization. In addition, in considering the antitrust approach to price discrimination, this chapter points out that the static model of price discrimination is not up to the job of predicting its anticompetitive effects.

Tie-in sales, reciprocity, and vertical territorial division do not harm consumers economically, but they can harm individual competitors.

Finally, horizontal, vertical, and conglomerate mergers affect industry concentration but do not necessarily destroy competitiveness. In particular, they create problems of market definition. The famous "Cellophane case" shows how economic analysis can be used to focus market definition questions.

Problems

1. Prices for steel ingots are generally identical except during periods of market adjustment. Does this fact prove that collusion is taking place?
2. Suppose that all cement firms agree to raise the price of cement by $2 per ton on January 1. When January 1 arrives, they all raise the price by $2. Is the economic damage to their customers greater than, less than, or equal to $2 per ton? Explain your answer.
3. a. What changes in the production and distribution of beer would you expect to have resulted from the construction of the interstate highway system and the development of unpasteurized beer that does not require refrigeration?
   b. Would competition lead to an increase or a decrease in the number of beer firms as a result? (Hint: How does your answer depend on demand elasticity?)
4. Consumer watchdog Ralph Nader has recommended that any industry with a 50-percent four-firm concentration ratio or a 70-percent eight-firm concentration ratio be broken up.
   a. Can any blanket formula like this apply to all industries without costs to society? Why or why not?
   b. As noted in this chapter, the beer industry would certainly be broken up under Nader's proposal. Would you predict efficiency losses or gains? Why?
   c. If the top four firms in an industry controlled 48 percent of total sales, would their incentive to collude increase or decrease under Nader's proposal? Why? What would happen to prices?
5. In calculating the market share in the Cellophane case, should the huge market for cigarette wrappers be excluded on the grounds that cigarette manufacturers would never substitute waxed paper or glassine paper wrappers? Why or why not?

6. "Cartelization is more likely, *ceteris paribus,* if the entry of new firms is fast than if it is slow." Analyze this statement.

7. "Identical bids to produce a nonstandardized product, such as a building design, a road, or a nuclear power plant, provide a strong inference of collusion." Analyze this statement using marginal cost curves.

8. "All other things being equal, it is more feasible for a cartel member to cheat on the agreement when there are few buyers than when the buyers are numerous." Analyze this statement.

9. Consider an industry with a four-firm concentration ratio of 80 percent. Is cartelization more likely if the six-firm concentration ratio is 100 percent than if the twenty-five-firm concentration ratio is 92 percent? Why or why not?

10. The provision of environmental protection is subject to a free-rider problem. If one firm incurs costs to reduce pollution, it must pass those costs on to consumers in the form of higher product prices. A firm that pollutes more can charge less. Do the antitrust laws against collusion on prices stand in the way of environmental protection? Why or why not?

11. The following is a quote from the "findings of fact" in the famous Cellophane case: "Cellophane has always been higher-priced than the two largest-selling flexible packaging materials, wax paper and glassine, and this has represented a disadvantage to sales of cellophane." Does the fact that Cellophane had a higher price per square inch refute the analysis in this chapter? If so, repair it. If not, defend it.

12. Uniform delivered pricing provides the same price to all customers regardless of transportation costs. Thus customers near a plant gate subsidize distant customers. Yet uniform delivered pricing is not a target of the Robinson-Patman Act. Comment.

13. Fallstaff Brewing Company, the nation's fourth-largest brewery in the 1960s, had no sales in New England. Nevertheless, it was blocked from acquiring Narragansett Beer Company, which was the leading seller in New England. Supreme Court Justice Byron White argued that, even though Fallstaff executives did not plan to enter the New England market with new capacity, thus rendering that market more competitive, the threat of potential entry would by itself make the market more competitive. Analyze this argument using the leader-follower model and the idea of limit pricing.

14. Should the antitrust laws be designed to preserve small firms, even if greater costs are the result? Support your argument.

15. Dealers' point-of-sale services often include not only information but also large (and expensive) inventories to choose from. Does resale price maintenance play a role in optimizing the size of the inventory? Why or why not?

16. Suppose that a firm holds a patent on an invention and exercises price discrimination in the sale of that product. Is the owner of the patent overcompensated? Why or why not?

17. Analyses of markets always face the problem of market definition: How many sellers should be included? Is it accurate to include only

the sellers that are in the market and actually selling? Why or why not?

18. The enforcement of antitrust laws against cartels depends on proof of an agreement. Proof may include written documents with their "gotcha paragraphs" and "smoking guns" as well as testimony by frightened cartel members testifying against the others. Do these tactics tend to focus too much attention on relatively harmless cartels? Why or why not?

19. Suppose a gasoline station sells gas only to customers who buy tires. Is this an anticompetitive tie-in sale? Explain your answer.

20. What is the difference between a manufacturer dividing a sales territory among its dealers and the dealers dividing the territory themselves?

21. The Utah Pie case uncovered an enormous increase in the total number of pies sold during the period of price discrimination under attack in the case. Use that fact to critique the court's decision.

22. If perfect competition requires competition among a very large number of firms, why is it that competition is not lessened but in fact increased.when technological change, resulting in economies of scale, eliminates some firms.

23. Does a price-control policy strengthen or weaken cartels? Explain your answer.

24. Suppose that your boss decides to tie the sale of your company's cement to the sale of its concrete burial vaults in an effort to stimulate sales of the vaults. Write a memo to your boss on the wisdom of that idea.

25. Suppose an industry is composed of one firm, A, with 60 percent of the market; two firms, B and C, each with 10 percent of the market; and an assortment of smaller firms. What would you predict would happen to price and output in the industry if B and C merged?

Suggested Readings

Asch, Peter. *Industrial Organization and Antitrust Policy.* Rev. ed. New York: Wiley, 1983.

Bork, Robert H. *The Antitrust Paradox.* New York: Basic Books, 1978.

Elzinga, Kenneth G., and Breit, William. *The Antitrust Penalties.* New Haven, Conn.: Yale University Press, 1976.

Phillips, Almarin. *Market Structure, Organization, and Performance.* Cambridge, Mass.: Harvard University Press, 1962.

14

CAPITAL BUDGETING AND MULTI-PERIOD DECISIONS

Thus far, we have studied principles of managerial decision making as if the ramifications of decisions were confined to a single time period. This simplification has allowed us to fix ideas, but more realistically, benefits and costs occur over time. This chapter introduces the time value of money and explores numerous decisions where time plays an important role. **Intertemporal analysis** (also called multiperiod analysis) extends economic principles to decisions that span multiple time periods.

Multiperiod choices are all around us. Consumers may spend less than their current income and sock the rest into savings for consumption in the future. Or they may spend more than current earnings by borrowing against their future incomes. Teachers saving for the lean summer months, individuals purchasing life insurance, medical students spending future income in the present, and squirrels storing up nuts for the winter are all making intertemporal choices. Society makes intertemporal decisions when it forgoes some current consumption in order to build up the capital stocks needed to enhance future productive capacity.

This chapter concentrates on the intertemporal choices of firms. Firms must often choose between supplying output in the present at current prices or in the future at future prices. For example, timing the sale of such nonrenewable resources as oil and natural gas is an intertemporal choice. Business firms may also choose to purchase financial capital (stocks and bonds) and physical capital (trucks and production lines) whose returns accrue only in the future. Thus managers must select the most profitable investment projects and determine the best time to initiate them. Some assets won't pay off for many years; others pay off quickly. Managers must therefore understand the value of dollars received or paid in the future.

So far, we have considered labor and capital to be broad surrogates for factors that are relatively variable (labor) and fixed (capital). It will become clear in this chapter that capital and labor differ more in degree than in kind. For example, the returns on capital investment accrue to the firm over several years because of the long-lived nature of capital. Thus an important component of capital analysis is the multiperiod returns. But these multiperiod returns have their analogy in labor analysis: Expenditures made to train and educate human beings are investments in human capital and yield multiperiod returns similar to the returns on capital investments. Because investments in human beings give the labor force some characteristics of capital, such investments may be studied within the framework of capital theory.

Intertemporal Evaluation

This chapter gives special emphasis to capital budgeting, project selection and timing, and investment in physical and human capital. The first step in studying multiperiod choices, however, is to see how flows of costs and benefits occurring in different time periods are made comparable. The interest rate is an integral mechanism in making such intertemporal comparisons.

Compounding and Future Value

Given the choice of receiving $1 today or a year from today, which would you choose? You would probably take the dollar now, because you can invest it at the current interest rate and end up with more than $1 by next year: $1 (today) ≠ $1 (next year).

Sums of money cannot be compared intertemporally without first making them commensurate. Let P_0 represent a sum of money you possess now. How much is P_0 worth a year from today? If you invest P_0 at the rate of interest i, P_0 will grow in value by next year to P_1, according to this formula:

$$P_1 = P_0 + P_0 i = P_0(1 + i) \tag{14.1}$$

In other words, the value P_1 is next year's value of P_0 if invested at interest rate i; P_1 thus equals the original principal (P_0) plus the interest earned on the principal ($P_0 i$). The process whereby money sums increase over time because of the addition of interest is called **compounding.**

Consider an example: $1,000 invested at 5-percent interest.

$$P_1 = \$1000(1 + 0.05) = \$1050$$

In a year, $1,000 grows to $1,050.

What is the compounded value of P_0 in 2 years if both the principal and the interest earned in the first year continue to earn interest in the second year? P_2 is $P_1 = P_0(1 + i)$ plus the interest on P_1 in year 2. The second year's interest is $P_1 i = P_0(1 + i)i$. Thus,

$$P_2 = P_1 + P_1 i = P_0(1 + i) + P_0(1 + i)i \qquad \textbf{(14.2)}$$

Factoring $P_0(1 + i)$ yields

$$P_2 = P_0(1 + i)(1 + i) = P_0(1 + i)^2 \qquad \textbf{(14.3)}$$

For example, $1,000 invested at 23-percent interest for 2 years grows to $1,512.90:

$$P_2 = \$1,000(1 + 0.23)^2 = \$1512.90$$

The formula for computing 2-year interest may be generalized: The compounded value of P_0 after t years, P_t, is

$$P_t = P_0(1 + i)^t \qquad \textbf{(14.4)}$$

For example, $1,000 invested at 16.5-percent interest for 30 years grows to $97,673.73:

$$P_{30} = \$1,000(1 + 0.165)^{30} = \$97,673.73$$

The formula in Equation 14.4 allows us to compute the future compounded value of any sum of money invested in the current period when principal and accumulating interest payments continue to earn interest for a given number of years. But this formula is accurate only for **simple compounding,** in which interest is computed only once per year. More complex—yet conceptually similar—formulas are required if interest is compounded semiannually, monthly, daily, or continuously. Hand-held business calculators spin out these computations in a moment. The same information is published in compound interest tables.

Discounting and Present Value

We may reverse the logic of compounding analysis to ask how much a future sum of money (P_t) is worth today (P_0). For example, we may want to know how much money must be invested today in order to end up with the sum P_1 by next year. The answer is derived by solving Equation 14.1 for P_0:

$$P_0 = \frac{P_1}{1 + i} \qquad (14.5)$$

If the interest rate is 5 percent and you want to have $1,050 in a year, you must invest $1,000 today, because $1,050/(1 + 0.05) = 1,000$.

The process of finding today's value of a future sum is called **discounting**. In computations of this sort, P_0 is called the **present value**, or the **discounted value**, of the future sum P_1.

The present value of any future sum is computed by solving Equation 14.4 for P_0:

$$P_0 = \frac{P_t}{(1 + i)^t} \qquad (14.6)$$

In other words, the present value of an amount P_t to be received in t years is P_t divided by the discount factor $(1 + i)^t$. Say that you are twenty years old today. On your fortieth birthday, you want to receive $2 million in a lump-sum payment so that you can retire. The present value of this $2 million depends on the interest rate used for discounting. If $i = 12$ percent,

$$P_0 = \frac{\$2,000,000}{(1 + 0.12)^{20}} = \$207,333.53$$

If $i = 25$ percent,

$$P_0 = \frac{\$2,000,000}{(1 + 0.25)^{20}} = \$23,058.43$$

Note the importance of the interest rate in determining present values of future sums. The higher the interest rate, the lower the present value of a given future sum.

If you want to receive a string of equal payments in the future and wish to determine the present value of the investment that will allow you to do so, you must use this formula:

$$P_0 = \sum_{t=1}^{n} \frac{P_t}{(1 + i)^t} \qquad (14.7)$$

Suppose you win a 1-million prize as a contestant on a TV game show. The prize is to be paid to you in $100,000 installments for 10 years, starting a year from today. What is the present value of your winnings? If $i = 10$ percent,

$$P_0 = \sum_{t=1}^{10} \frac{\$100,000}{(1 + 0.1)^{10}} = \$614,456.71$$

If $i = 20$ percent,

$$P_0 = \sum_{t=1}^{10} \frac{\$100,000}{(1 + 0.2)^{10}} = \$419,247.21$$

When prizes are paid in installments, the time value of money ensures that the present value of the prize is less than its advertised amount.

A P P L I C A T I O N

14.1

Estimating Losses Due to Personal Injury

In this litigious age, a manager must constantly be on guard against firm-caused injuries to workers or to people outside the firm. Chapter 8 points out that one must weigh the marginal benefits and costs of adjusting accident rates. Too many accidents impose net costs, but zero accident rates are impossible to attain. The manager should therefore seek to equate the marginal benefits and marginal costs of accident reduction.

What if an accident happens? The notion of present value gives the manager a formula for calculating the expected loss of earnings of an injured worker—and thus the appropriate compensation. The exact calculation is quite complicated and must be tailored to individual cases, but a manager may retain an economist to make the calculation and then analyze the "bottom line" of the economist's report.

The amount to be paid an injured worker, called **compensatory damages,** has two components: (1) expected loss of earnings over the employee's work life and (2) medical expenses, punitive damages, awards for pain and suffering, and so forth. The second com-

ponent, which is frequently larger than lost earnings, is usually determined by documentation of actual costs and by court precedent. Lost earning power must be calculated anew for each individual.

Every calculation of **expected lost earnings** is a projection, because the accident interrupts an earnings flow and thus prevents us from observing it. Commonly, the lower bounds of the award are calculated by projecting a growth path of future wages

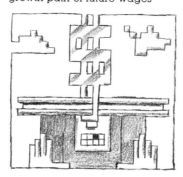

based on the wage at the time of the accident and then discounting those wages to their present value. The formula for this calculation is

Expected lost earnings =

$$\sum_{t=1}^{n} \frac{w_0(1 + g)^t}{(1 + i)^t}$$

where

n = expected remaining work years
t = time period
w_0 = wage at time of accident
g = percentage growth rate of wages
i = long-term interest rate
$w_0(1 + g)^t$ = wage in any time period t

In the postwar period, the growth rate of wages within occupations has been remarkably close to the interest rate.* Indeed,

*U.S., Department of Labor, Bureau of Labor Statistics, *Monthly Labor Review* 103 (May 1980): 30.

Continued on page 362

setting $i = g$ is a useful simplification for obtaining an approximate estimate of liability. If $i = g$, the formula for calculating expected lost earnings reduces to

Expected lost earnings $= w_0 \cdot n$

Say that a forty-nine-year-old worker's wages and fringe benefits are $30,000 per year at the time of an accident and that 15 additional years of work life are a normal expectation. The lower bound of the present value of the worker's projected (forgone) income is $30,000 $\cdot$ 15 = $450,000.[†] Therefore, a lump-sum payment of $450,000 today is appropriate compensation for the worker's projected losses in the future.[‡]

[†]This figure is a lower bound since persons may change occupations, particularly if they are young. Thus the projected w_0 is an underestimate. For a useful work-life expectancy table, see U.S. Department of Labor, Bureau of Labor Statistics, "A Work-Life Expectancy Table for Men, 1968," by Howard Fullerton, Monthly Labor Review 94, 2 (1971): 3–11.

[‡]For more on the subject of damages for loss of earning capacity, see Richard Posner, Economic Analysis of Law, 2nd ed. (Boston: Little, Brown, 1977): 144–149.

Capital Budgeting and Project Evaluation

Capital budgeting is the term used to describe the calculations and decisions involved in evaluating and selecting investment projects and the timing of those projects. As you know, a capital good is one that can be purchased in one period for the purpose of deriving benefits in the future. A warehouse, an electric motor, a lawsuit, and an education are all capital goods and are therefore amenable to analysis using capital budgeting.

The principal use of capital budgeting is the comparison of contributions to a firm's net worth supplied by various capital investments. This section introduces several criteria that have been advanced for determining the best investments. The best is always net present value.

Net Present Value

The **net present value** (*NPV*) of a capital investment project is simply the sum of the discounted benefits of the project minus the sum of the discounted costs:

$$NPV = \sum_{t=1}^{n} \frac{B_t}{(1 + i)^t} - \sum_{t=1}^{n} \frac{C_t}{(1 + i)^t} \qquad (14.8)$$

where
$\quad B_t =$ benefits in period t
$\quad C_t =$ costs in year t
$\quad i =$ cost of loanable funds used to discount benefit and cost time streams
$\quad t =$ time period
$\quad n =$ life span of the project

Let's consider a concrete example of calculating *NPV*. Suppose a project has the expected benefits and costs shown in Table 14.1. These benefits and costs yield different *NPV*s, depending on the discount rate. If benefits and costs are not discounted at all ($i = 0$), *NPV* after 5 years is $10,100. *NPV* is $6,691.83 after 5 years when future benefits and costs are discounted at 10 percent and

Table 14.1
Calculating Net Present Value

Year	B_t	C_t	NPV $i = 0$	NPV $i = 10\%$	NPV $i = 20\%$
1	$ 0	$4,000	$– 4,000.00	$– 4,000.00	$– 4,000.00
2	0	100	– 100.00	– 90.11	– 83.33
3	5,000	300	+ 4,700.00	+ 3,884.30	+ 3,263.89
4	6,500	500	+ 6,000.00	+ 4,507.89	+ 3,472.22
5	4,500	1,000	+ 3,500.00	2,390.55	+ 1,687.89
			$ 10,100.00	$ 6,691.83	$ 4,340.67

$4,340.67 when the discount rate is 20 percent. Net present value is quite sensitive to the discount rate, as these figures illustrate.

Figure 14.1 permits us to analyze a typical investment project in the abstract. There are two time trajectories in the figure: R is revenue to be obtained from a project, and C is costs of the same project. These trajectories are hypothetical but follow a typical pattern. Investments usually generate very few benefits in the beginning, build to a peak in the middle years, then drop off as projects are abandoned, become obsolete, or are sold. Costs, on the other hand, are generally high in the beginning, during construction and the payment of other start-up costs, then fall substantially to a maintenance level, and then rise again as the facility deteriorates or requires demolition—as in mine closings, decommissioning of nuclear power plants, building demolition, or highway abandonment. Automobile purchases also follow this cost pattern. Initially, down payments and financing costs dominate; then a period of lower costs

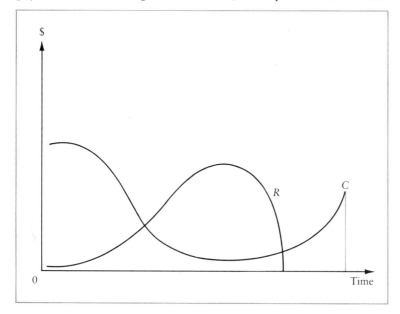

Figure 14.1
Trajectories of Revenue and Cost Curves over Time

Costs are usually higher at the beginning and end of a project; revenue is generally higher in the middle years. Proper discounting must be employed to evaluate such money flows.

Figure 14.2
Net Present Value as a Function of Interest Rates

Ironically, the *NPV* does not simply fall as interest rates rise if there are substantial future costs.

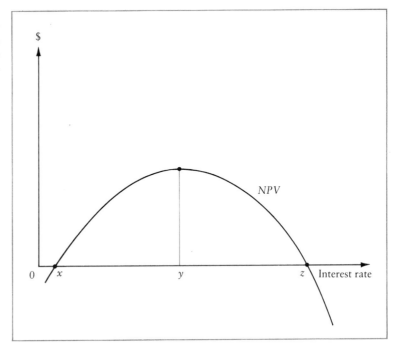

ensues, after which repair costs soar. The *NPV* formula permits us to compare these benefit and cost time streams even though their trajectories are considerably different.

Net present value depends crucially on the interest rate. Since the interest rate appears in the denominator of the discount factor, larger interest rates discount delayed costs and benefits more heavily than those in the near term. As Figure 14.2 shows, if the interest rate is low, the tail-end closing costs plus the near-term start-up costs outweigh the revenue stream; the *NPV* is negative for interest rates to the left of *x*. At higher rates of interest, between *x* and *y*, *NPV* rises, because the closing costs are more heavily discounted. At still higher rates, to the right of *y*, *NPV* falls, because the middle-term revenues are heavily discounted. *NPV* falls to zero at *z* and is negative to the right of *z*.

Net present value is also useful in choosing among mutually exclusive projects. Since the goal of management is to maximize the net worth of the firm, managers aim to choose projects that maximize *NPV*.

Internal Rate of Return

Analysts often use an alternative to net present value called the **internal rate of return** (*IRR*) to evaluate projects. This idea is best presented with an example. Suppose a firm is contemplating the purchase of a machine that lasts only a year.

14.2

NPV and
Project Timing

Choosing the timing of a given project is subject to the same rules as choosing among mutually exclusive projects. Suppose a project can be initiated in any of three years—t_1, t_2, or t_3. The best year is selected by ranking the three net present values. Specifically, the manager must pick the largest of the three terms that follow:

$$\sum_{t=t_1}^{\infty} \frac{(B_t - C_t)}{(1 + i)^t}$$

$$\sum_{t=t_2}^{\infty} \frac{(B_t - C_t)}{(1 + i)^t}$$

$$\sum_{t=t_3}^{\infty} \frac{(B_t - C_t)}{(1 + i)^t}$$

Project timing frequently boils down to this problem: Build a large plant now or build a small plant with the option to expand it later. The cost flows of the two al-

ternatives are considerably different. Say that

C_1 = cost of building larger plant now = $1 million
C_2 = cost of building smaller plant now = $0.8 million
C_3 = cost of future expansion = $0.4 million
i = interest rate used for discounting = 10 percent

To make the problem interesting, we are assuming that $C_2 + C_3 > C_1$ and that $C_2 < C_1$.

If the present value of revenues is roughly the same for either

decision, we can determine the appropriate timing of plant construction by evaluating the present value of costs. The decision depends on the solution to this equation:

$$C_1 \gtrless C_2 + \frac{C_3}{(1 + i)^t}$$

If C_1 exceeds the cost of C_2 plus the present value of expansion costs, the smaller plant should be built. Otherwise, the larger plant should be built.

Using logarithms and the same cost figures, the previous equation can be solved for t. The solution value is $t \gtrless 7.27$ years. In other words, if the larger plant is needed within the next 7.27 years, it should be built now. Otherwise, the smaller plant should be built now and expanded later.

P = purchase price of machine = $800

R = expected revenues from machine = $1,200

C = expected costs of machine upkeep = $200

Assume that P is paid today and that all revenue is received and all costs are paid a year from today, at the end of the machine's useful life.

What is the internal rate of return on the machine, denoted m? Intuitively,

$$m = \frac{\$200}{\$800} = 0.25$$

The firm pays $800 for the machine. Next year, after earning $1,200 with the machine and paying $200 to keep it going, the firm has $1,000 free and clear. That $1,000 minus the $800 purchase price yields a rate of return on the machine of 25 percent.

Formally, the internal rate of return is the rate of discount that yields a zero net present value. This condition holds when

$$\frac{R - C}{(1 + m)} - P = 0 \qquad (14.9)$$

Using the figures in the previous example, the solution value for m is 0.25. Hence, NPV is zero if future revenues and costs are discounted at 25 percent. The IRR is therefore 25 percent.

Should the machine be purchased? This decision depends on whether there are better investment opportunities. The opportunity cost of buying the machine for $800 is the forgone return on the $800 invested in something else. The market interest rate, i, measures this opportunity cost, since funds used for capital investments are diverted from investments in financial assets. Hence, the profitability of the machine boils down to a comparison of m and i.

Suppose $i = 10$ percent and $m = 25$ percent. Investing $800 in financial paper at 10-percent interest would yield $80, whereas buying the machine yields $200. When $m > i$, the capital investment is profitable. But if $i = 30$ percent and $m = 25$ percent, the machine is not profitable, because bonds return $240 and the machine returns only $200. The analyst selects projects whose internal rate of return exceeds the market rate of interest.

One problem that arises from using the IRR to make investment decisions is evident from Figure 14.2. Note that discount rates x and z both satisfy the definition of internal rate of return. Of course, if the market interest rate is y, then z is the relevant IRR — not x. But note why: The net present value of the project is positive at the rate of interest y. If NPV is positive, m must exceed i. In effect, then, the analyst using the IRR criterion is actually using the NPV criterion.

Another comparison of the IRR and NPV criteria yields a prob-

Figure 14.3
Revenue and Cost Trajectories for Two Hypothetical Projects

The choice between two projects must be made on the basis of *NPV* in order to maximize the profits of the firm.

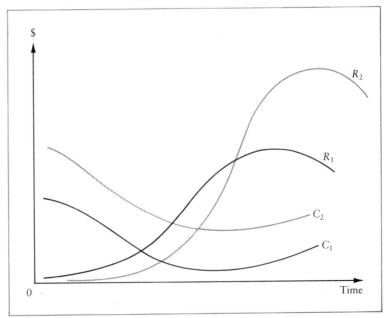

lem that is not so readily dismissed. Consider the revenue and cost trajectories for projects 1 and 2 in Figure 14.3. Project 1 has lower costs and generates less revenue than project 2; but project 1 generates revenue sooner. As a result, the NPV trajectories take the form of those in Figure 14.4: NPV_1 is greater than NPV_2 at interest rates up to and less than the interest rates of NPV_2. But the IRR of project 2 is i_3; the IRR of project 1 is i_2. Using the IRR criterion, project 2 is the preferred project. Thus ranking the projects according to the IRR is consistent with the profit-maximizing NPV criterion only for market interest rates higher than i_1.

Payback Period

Another dangerously seductive criterion for making investment decisions is the **payback period.** Using this criterion, the analyst asks how quickly the project will pay for itself. Thus this criterion prejudices the choice toward projects that generate revenue more quickly, regardless of the net present value. However, this criterion is often used when the loan paying for the project has a time limit, as if the loan and the project must be linked.

Although the cost of capital may not be steady, it never rises to infinity—as such a fixed term implies. The NPV formula, with appropriate manipulation of the term for the cost of capital, is the best way to account for the time limits of loans.

Benefit/Cost Ratio

Another error-prone criterion for ranking projects is the **benefit/cost ratio** (B/C ratio), or **profitability index.** Generally, investment

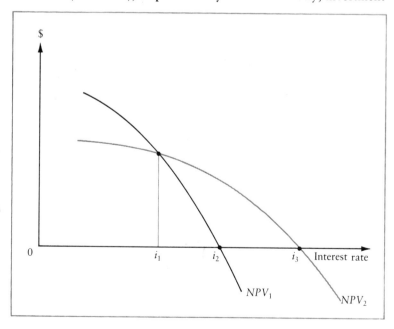

Figure 14.4
NPV of Two Hypothetical Projects as Function of Interest Rates

The *NPV* curves of two different projects may cross, making the internal rate of return criterion unreliable for choosing between the projects.

projects are rated in terms of their additions to the net worth of the firm. We cannot always rely on the B/C ratio to provide this information.

Simple algebra indicates that a positive net benefit is equivalent to a benefit/cost ratio greater than 1:

$$(B - C) \gtreqless 0 \Leftrightarrow B \gtreqless C \Leftrightarrow B/C \gtreqless 1 \qquad (14.10)$$

(A mathematician would insist on noting that the last step requires that $C > 0$.) However, we cannot jump to the conclusion that a project with a greater B/C ratio is superior in terms of NPV to one with a lower B/C ratio.

Consider two mutually exclusive projects, 1 and 2. Let $(B_1 - C_1) > (B_2 - C_2)$. Is $B_1/C_1 > B_2/C_2$? Not necessarily. To see this, rewrite $(B_1 - C_1) > (B_2 - C_2)$:

$$C_1\left(\frac{B_1}{C_1} - 1\right) > C_2\left(\frac{B_2}{C_2} - 1\right) \qquad (14.11)$$

If $C_1 \leq C_2$, then

$$\frac{B_1}{C_1} - 1 > \frac{B_2}{C_2} - 1 \qquad (14.12)$$

and

$$\frac{B_1}{C_1} > \frac{B_2}{C_2} \qquad (14.13)$$

But if $C_1 > C_2$, then $B_1/C_1 > B_2/C_2$ does not follow from $(B_1 - C_1) > (B_2 - C_2)$. In other words, it may be that $B_1/C_1 < B_2/C_2$ even though $(B_1 - C_1) > (B_2 - C_2)$. Project 1 is preferred because of its greater NPV, even though it exhibits the lower B/C ratio.

A numerical example may help drive this point home. Consider the two projects evaluated in Table 14.2. Using the B/C criterion, we would choose project 2, even though project 1 bestows greater NPV. This example shows that the NPV method cannot accurately be approximated by using benefit/cost ratios.

Since other criteria are correct when and only when they yield the same decision as NPV, managers should use NPV in the first place. Fortunately, no additional information is required to make the right capital budgeting decision.

Table 14.2

Comparing *B/C* Ratios and *NPV*s of Two Projects

Characteristic	Project 1	Project 2
Present value of benefits	15	5
Present value of costs	5	1
B/C ratio	3	5
NPV	10	4

Input Selection

The subject of this chapter is managerial decision making when the benefits and the costs of decisions span several time periods. Now that we have studied intertemporal project analysis and capital budgeting decisions, we may consider a general model of input selection that also takes time into account. But first we need to lay some groundwork using single-period analysis.

For convenience, let's begin with the labor input. Identifying the correct number of workers to hire is an exercise in marginal reasoning. Each worker hired adds to the firm's total revenue and total cost. Revenue is enhanced by selling the extra output resulting from the employment of a marginal worker, but costs rise because the worker must be paid. Hence, the profit-maximizing work force is achieved by equating the marginal revenue of adding workers with the marginal cost of expanding the labor force.

The marginal revenue that comes from hiring an extra worker is called the **marginal revenue product of labor** (MRP_L). The MRP_L has two components: (1) the worker's marginal product, MP_L, and (2) the price for which the extra units of output can be sold:

$$MRP_L = MP_L \cdot P \qquad (14.14)$$

For example, if having one more worker adds 50 units of output and if the firm can sell each new unit for $10, the marginal revenue product of labor is $500.

Table 14.3 illustrates the calculation of MRP_L. The first two columns relate the firm's total output to the size of its labor force. The middle column records the marginal product of labor, or the new output produced by each new worker. The fourth column lists the price of each unit of output. Since the price is $2 regardless of sales, the firm is a price taker in output. The MRP_L figures, in the final column, equal the MP_L for each marginal worker times price.

Table 14.3
Calculating Marginal Revenue Product of Labor

Labor	Q	MP_L	P	MRP_L
1	10	10	$2	$20
2	16	6	2	12
3	19	3	2	6
4	21	2	2	4
5	22	1	2	2
6	22	0	2	0

The marginal revenue product curve is diagramed in Figure 14.5. It is negatively sloped because the extra revenue that a new worker contributes to the firm depends on the marginal product of labor, which diminishes in the efficient production stage II. Each point on the MRP_L curve is the marginal revenue of an additional worker.

Now let's return to the marginal cost of hiring workers. Labor markets are competitive if each firm hiring labor is too small to

Figure 14.5
Marginal Revenue Product Curve

The curve slopes downward because of the diminishing marginal product.

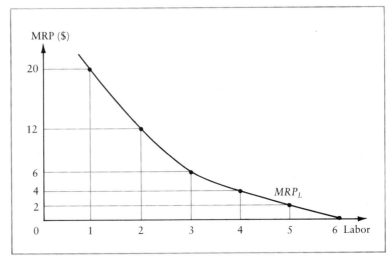

influence wages by its hiring decisions. In competitive labor markets, each firm is a wage taker. Thus the marginal cost of hiring workers in competitive labor markets simply equals the going wage.

Now we can study the marginal rule for employing workers. (Assume that the firm is competitive in its output and input decisions.) Figure 14.6 shows that the correct size of the work force depends on a comparison of the marginal revenue and marginal cost of hiring, or a comparison of the MRP_L and the wage. Figure 14.6 shows two wages. If $w = \$20$, one worker is hired, because $MRP_L = w$ at point A. If the wage falls to \$6, the firm expands hiring to 3 workers, since $MRP_L = w$ at point B. For each wage, the correct labor force is identified by a point on the MRP_L curve.

Figure 14.6
Marginal Revenue Product Set Equal to Wage for Profit Maximization

The marginal revenue product curve is essentially a demand curve for the factor of production.

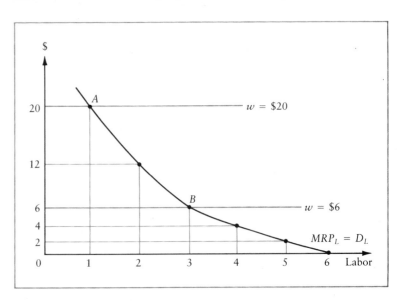

Notice that the MRP_L curve in Figure 14.6 is labeled D_L, or demand for labor. The MRP_L curve is the firm's labor demand curve because it tells the firm how much labor to hire at each wage, other things being equal.[1]

Let's summarize our results. If a firm sells its output and buys its labor inputs in competitive markets, the optimum employment of labor satisfies the following profit-maximizing condition:

$$MRP_L = MP_L \cdot P = w \qquad (14.15)$$

The same condition is required for the optimum employment of capital:

$$MRP_K = MP_K \cdot P = r \qquad (14.16)$$

MRP_K, of course, is the **marginal revenue product of capital;** r is the rental rate of a unit of capital per period. If the firm is a competitive, price-taking buyer of capital, r is a parameter to the firm. Equation 14.16 is the general formula for deriving the demand for capital, just as the demand for labor is derived from the profit-maximizing condition in Equation 14.15. Indeed, marginal analysis of the demand for labor is perfectly generalizable to the demand for capital or any other factor. The demand curves for all inputs are negatively sloped with respect to their prices.[2]

Multiperiod Analysis of Optimum Quantities

Treating labor and capital analogously masks an important characteristic of capital: A capital good is long-lived and generates multiperiod revenue flows. When a firm purchases a unit of capital, such as a machine, it either buys the machine with its earnings or borrows the money from a creditor. Either way, the price of the capital good to the firm is P_K.

The revenues the machine produces—its MRP_K—must be regarded as a time stream, the present discounted value of which is $\Sigma MPR_{K_t}/(1 + i)^t$. In evaluating how much capital to employ over time, the manager must compare the price of the capital good with the present value of the time stream of revenue. Thus the multiperiod analogue of Equation 14.16 is

---

1. Nothing of substance is lost by treating the MRP_L curve as the firm's demand curve for labor, even though this treatment is strictly valid only in the short run. For a complete discussion of input demand, see Steven T. Call and William L. Holahan, *Microeconomics,* 2nd ed. (Belmont, Calif.: Wadsworth, 1983), chap. 11.

2. The proof of this assertion exceeds the scope of this book. For a graphic proof that factor demand curves are negatively sloped, see R. R. Russell, "A Graphical Proof of the Impossibility of a Positively Inclined Demand Curve for a Factor of Production," *American Economic Review* 54 (1964): 726–732, and for a mathematical proof, see C. E. Ferguson, *The Neoclassical Theory of Production and Distribution* (Cambridge, England: Cambridge University Press, 1969).

$$\sum \frac{MPR_{K_t}}{(1 + i)^t} = \sum \frac{r_t}{(1 + i)^t} = P_K \qquad (14.17)$$

The purchase price of the last machine must equal the present value of the stream of revenues attributable to the machine. Note that the purchase price of the machine, P_K, must also equal the present value of the per-period rental payments of the machine, $\sum r_t/(1 + i)^t$ (or the present value of the multiperiod obligations incurred if the machine is financed).

Price of Capital, Rental Rate of Capital, and Interest Rate

It is easy to confuse the three variables— price of capital (P_K), rental rate of capital (r), and interest rate (i)— but they are not the same thing at all. We must be especially clear about the meaning of r, because it is used throughout the book to signify the rental rate of a unit of capital per period.

Suppose a firm purchases a unit of capital (a machine) at price P_K. Because of **depreciation**, the machine steadily loses a certain portion of its value for n years, after which it has no further value, either as a productive input or as scrap. During the machine's productive life, however, the firm may either use the machine itself or rent it to another firm. The amount of money for which the machine can be rented per period equals r, the rental rate of capital.

If the firm decides to rent out its machine, what is the rental rate per period it can charge for the machine? In economic equilibrium and in perfect capital markets, the rental rate of capital must provide the owner of capital a return equal to the forgone return that could have been earned by using the sum P_K to buy an earning asset that yields the market interest rate, i. (Note that P_K and r are dollar amounts; i is a percentage.) In other words, r must exactly cover the firm's total cost of owning capital, including the opportunity cost.

What are the costs of capital? First is the interest opportunity cost. For each period that the firm has P_K dollars tied up in a machine, it forgoes the chance to earn the market rate of interest on P_K if it were invested. The per-period interest opportunity cost equals $i \cdot P_K$. Second, the firm faces a depreciation charge. The firm must set aside a sum of money each period, the compounded value of which will equal the purchase price of the machine by the time it is fully depreciated at the end of the machine's life. This procedure, the equivalent of getting back the principal when investing in a money-earning asset, allows the firm to replace the worn-out machine. If d is the **depreciation rate**, or the proportion of P_K that must be set aside per time period, the per-period depreciation charge is $d \cdot P_K$.

The per-period rental rate of capital, r, must cover both the interest opportunity cost and the depreciation cost of owning capital. Thus

$$r = (i \cdot P_K) + (d \cdot P_K) = (i + d)P_K \qquad \textbf{(14.18)}$$

Equation 14.18 shows clearly that the variables r, P_K, and i are not equal; instead, they are interrelated. A change in the interest rate or the purchase price of capital would change the rental rate of capital.

If we assume that the machine is infinitely long-lived, then $d = 0$. In this case, Equation 14.18 reduces to

$$i = \frac{r}{P_K} \qquad \textbf{(14.19)}$$

Because the machine never wears out, it yields a perpetual annual return to the firm, r/P_K, equal to the rate of interest. This return is equivalent to the return on a financial perpetuity.

If the machine wears out the same year it is purchased, then $d = 1$ and Equation 14.18 reduces to

$$r = P_K \qquad \textbf{(14.20)}$$

But the rental rate of capital equals the purchase price of a capital good only in the extreme, atypical case of a short-lived, single-period capital investment.

Three points of special importance must be made here. First, labor and capital are commensurate in multiperiod analysis. The wage rate, w, is the price of the labor services provided by one unit of labor per time period. Similarly, the rental rate of capital, r, is the price of the capital services provided by one unit of capital per period. The demand for labor and capital is for the flow of services provided by these inputs. The respective prices of obtaining these service flows per period are w and r.

Second, the per-period rental rate of capital is r, whether the firm rents its capital inputs or purchases them outright. If the firm rents capital, r is an explicit payment per unit of capital rented. If the firm buys and uses its own units of capital, it forgoes the opportunity to rent them out to other firms at r dollars per period. In the latter case, r is an implicit opportunity cost. Either way, r is the cost of obtaining the services of a unit of capital per time period. The rental rate does not depend on the ownership of capital.

Finally, the multiperiod profit-maximizing condition contained in Equation 14.16 introduces a subtle but important distinction by comparison to the single-period condition in Equation 14.15. For capital to be profitable, the present value of the MRP_K time stream must equal or exceed the purchase price of the capital good. Even though $r < MRP_K$ in any given period, the capital good is profitable if the present value of the MRP_K flow equals or exceeds the present value of the per-period rent payments (which equal P_K).

Now we can distinguish between variable and fixed factors. A variable factor whose returns are generated largely in the same period as the employment of the factor will be hired only if the marginal revenue product of the factor equals or exceeds the price of the factor in each period. In contrast, a fixed factor like capital will be hired when the present discounted value of the MRP_K equals or exceeds the price of capital, even though $MRP_K < r_t$ in some periods.

Investment in Human Capital

Up to now we have assumed that labor is variable in the short run and exerts its influence on the firm's revenues in the present period and that capital is fixed in the short run and affects the firm's revenues primarily in future periods. Using this distinction, the labor market can be studied in the context of a single-period model. Only in studying the optimum employment of capital was it necessary to introduce a **multiperiod analysis,** comparing the revenues and costs of the marginal input in terms of the present discounted values of their respective time streams.

A moment's reflection reveals that certain aspects of the labor input exhibit characteristics strikingly similar to those of capital. For example, a firm can give special training to its work force and thereby increase the profits attributable to labor in future periods. In other words, investment by a firm in a piece of capital equipment and investment in the training, education, and productivity of the labor force are both undertaken in order to increase future profits. And surely the training received in a university or vocational school is desired, partially if not entirely, for the future returns to the educated worker such an education promises.

Consider dentists who wish to increase their time stream of profits. They can purchase higher-speed drills, go back to school for refresher courses, or train technicians to help in "four-handed dentistry." All three investments are made to increase future profits. The drill is an investment in physical capital. The training (either for the dentist or the technician) is an investment in **human capital.** Training adds a component of capital to the human being. There are, of course, important differences between the drill and the training and between capital and human capital. Barring acts of God, incredibly inept handling, or theft, the drill cannot suddenly "die" or "change jobs," as can human capital. Thus human capital is subject to "instantaneous" depreciation upon the death, disability, or job switch of the worker. Still, the analogy between investing in capital and in human capital is sufficiently close that economists have employed capital theory to study the optimum investment in human beings.[3]

When the returns to the investment in the training of people occur in future periods, we must employ a multiperiod analogue of

---

3. This section and Application 14.3 rely heavily on Gary S. Becker, "Investment in Human Capital: A Theoretical Analysis," *Journal of Political Economy* 70 (1962): 9–49 and Walter Y. Oi, "Labor as a Quasi-Fixed Factor," *Journal of Political Economy* 70 (1962): 538–555.

the single-period profit-maximizing equation used up to now in selecting the optimum quantity of labor. The multiperiod formula for optimum labor employment is akin to the formula for capital goods: For the last worker hired,

$$\sum \frac{MRP_t}{(1 + i)^t} = \sum \frac{w_t}{(1 + i)^t} \qquad (14.21)$$

(All references to costs and revenues in this section are related to labor. Thus the subscript L, denoting labor, has been dropped to avoid clutter.) In Equation 14.20, the equality of the last worker's costs and revenues are expressed in terms of the present value of their respective time streams. If $MRP_t = w_t$ in each time period, then their present discounted values are also equal. However, the discounted values of revenues and costs can be equal without equality between MRP_t and w_t in each (or in any) period. The firm may take losses on its human capital investment in some periods as long as the present value of the revenues equals or exceeds the present value of wage costs.

General Training

There are several ways to invest in human capital—including exercise programs, regular medical checkups, and the distribution of nutrition information—but we will pay particular attention to the "training" of workers. During the period of employment, typical employees increase their productivity either through learning by doing or through formal training programs. Thus the worker's MRP increases with training. If the skills acquired are general enough to be marketable to other firms, the competitive forces in the labor market will bid up the wages until $MRP_t = w_t$ in each time period. The newly acquired skills increase the MRP of the work force of all firms, not just of the firm providing the training. Some examples of general training are the acquisition of typing and clerical skills, the acquisition of machinist skills, and medical and legal training.

Because **general training** involves the equality of MRP_t and w_t in each period, the present discounted values of MRP and w must also be equal. When training is general, the wage rate rises to equality, with the higher MRP attributable to the training; in a competitive labor market, the workers will shift jobs to take advantage of better wage offers.

A firm has nothing to gain in providing general training to its work force, because the cost of training cannot be recouped by paying the workers a wage less than MRP in future periods. The firm therefore should not provide any general training at its own expense.

It is useful to have a profit-maximizing equation in which training appears explicitly. Consider the following:

$$MRP_0 + \sum_{t=1}^{n} \frac{MRP_t}{(1+i)^t} = w_0 + T_0 + \sum_{t=1}^{n} \frac{w_t}{(1+i)^t} \qquad (14.22)$$

where

T_0 = training costs, incurred entirely in period 0
MRP_0 = MRP during training period 0
w_0 = wage paid during training period 0
t = time periods, where $t = 0, 1, 2, \ldots, n$

The present value of the MRP in all periods equals the present value of all wage and training costs in all periods. If training is general, $MRP_t = w_t$ in each period after the training is completed. Hence

$$\sum_{t=1}^{n} \frac{MRP_t}{(1+i)^t} = \sum_{t=1}^{n} \frac{w_t}{(1+i)^t} \qquad (14.23)$$

which implies that

$$MRP_0 - T_0 = w_0 \text{ and } MRP_0 > w_0 \qquad (14.24)$$

Generally trained workers must "pay" for their own training by accepting a wage during the training period less than MRP_0 by the amount of the training costs incurred by the firm. Is this exploitation of the worker? No! The wage rate $w_0 < MRP_0$ is the value of the employment to the firm less the costs for training that enhances the worker's future wage rates. Because the firm stands to gain nothing from this investment in human capital, the trainee pays for the training in the form of depressed wage rates.

General training often takes place outside the firm, as in secretarial or engineering schools. If the worker's MRP during general training is negative, as might be the case for a barber or hairdresser, the training must take place in a school. The wage in period 0 would be

$$w_0 = MRP_0 - T_0 < -T_0 < 0 \text{ when } MRP_0 < 0 \qquad (14.25)$$

To be trained on the job, such a costly trainee would have to pay the firm. Better to go to barber school and pay only the training costs than to be trained on the job and pay training costs plus the lost revenue generated by nonprofessional haircuts.[4]

---

4. There is no analogy between the investment in general training and the collateral a bank requires when investing in physical capital. Hence a person without physical assets finds it hard, if not impossible, to finance an education through loans negotiated in an unregulated market. In contrast, a person with, say, a house can mortgage it to pay for an education. This unequal access to loans has led to the provision of government-guaranteed educational loans.

Specific Training

Specific training occurs when the acquired skills are not readily marketable to other firms. Specific training raises the MRP_t without raising the w_t, because the skills acquired in specific training are useful only to the firm providing the training and thus do not increase the marginal product of labor at the industry level, where wages are determined. Examples of specific training include gaining trade secrets that are not (legally) marketable, gaining specialized knowledge of a firm's workers, and learning certain military skills, such as repairing missiles and shooting M-16 rifles.[5] These skills cannot be transferred to other firms.

The firm must pay the costs of specific training, because such training adds to worker productivity without increasing wages and therefore is not a return to the worker. Thus Equation 14.22 may be rewritten as

$$MRP_0 - w_0 - T_0 = \sum_{t=1}^{n} \frac{w_t}{(1+i)^t} - \sum_{t=1}^{n} \frac{MRP_t}{(1+i)^t} \quad \textbf{(14.26)}$$

But because the worker is unwilling to invest in specific training, $MRP_0 = w_0$ in the initial period. Thus

$$T_0 = \sum_{t=1}^{n} \frac{MRP_t}{(1+i)^t} - \sum_{t=1}^{n} \frac{w_t}{(1+i)^t} \quad \textbf{(14.27)}$$

Equation 14.27 states that the firm pays the training costs, which equal the difference between the present values of revenues and costs of labor.

5. The ability to get along with, organize, and motivate workers is marketable and can be gained and demonstrated by successful experience. But knowledge of specific people and their abilities is not marketable.

APPLICATION

14.3

Economic Downturns and General versus Specific Training

The firm breaks even on generally trained workers in each period, as we have seen: $MRP_t = w_t$. Now suppose there is a reduction in the demand for the firm's product, which in turn reduces the price of output and hence the MRP of labor. When the MRP falls off a bit, the rational firm lays off some workers with general training. However long the downturn lasts, the firm can easily replace such workers with other workers of similar skills when market conditions improve. Typically, the rule followed in a downturn is "the last hired, the first fired," because the newest employees generally have accu-mulated the least specific training and hence are the most variable as a factor of production.

Let t_a refer to a time period in which MRP_L falls. Initially, $MRP > w$ for specifically trained workers. Even though MRP_{t_a} is off some, it may nevertheless still exceed w_{t_a}, in which event these workers will be retained. But suppose $MRP_{t_a} < w_{t_a}$. In a single-period analysis, labor would be laid off.

Continued on page 378

But the firm may still expect

$$\sum_{t=t_a+1}^{n} \frac{MRP_t}{(1+i)^t} > \sum_{t=t_a+1}^{n} \frac{w_1}{(1+i)^t}$$

If so, workers with specific training are retained, because the present value of MRP exceeds the present value of wage costs after the recession lets up. In this case, workers are retained even though $MRP_{t_a} < w_{t_a}$, just as a piece of physical capital that is already paid for and still promises future net profits would be.

Specifically trained labor resembles capital as a factor of production. The capital value of the training is already paid for, and so a temporary downturn in demand that generates losses in some periods will not cause layoffs (as happens with generally trained workers)—as long as the present value of the revenues equals or exceeds the present value of wage costs. Of course, whenever the time stream of costs exceeds the time stream of revenues, specifically trained workers will also be laid off. Even though the firm has invested training in the worker, there is no use throwing good money after bad. The training is paid for, but it is a sunk cost and is not considered in the decision to lay off a worker whose employment diminishes the present value of the firm's profits.

Firms are more reluctant to lay off workers with specific rather than general training because specifically trained workers may take other jobs, which results in the loss of the firm's human capital investment. Thus workers with specific training improve their chances of keeping their jobs during a recession by making it abundantly clear that they will seek alternative employment if laid off. The firm thereby has an extra incentive to keep such workers and avoid the total depreciation of its training investment. This way of thinking is especially prevalent if the downturn is expected to be of short duration or if it is merely a reduction in the demand for a particular product. If the recession affects the entire economy, there is less likelihood that even specifically trained workers can find work in other firms. If the firm believes that workers will not seek or cannot find alternative employment, it becomes less reluctant to lay them off during a recession.

Human capital analysis permits some broad generalizations in four areas. First, schooling is generally undertaken at an early age to spread the benefits over a longer period. (However, education also requires a certain maturity, so it should not be undertaken too early.)

Second, firms will not provide specific training to employees that they think will not be around long. Until recently, women were so considered. Such employees tend to receive only general training and must pay for it themselves in lower wages during training.

Third, the slogan "equal pay for equal work" must be interpreted in light of multiperiod analysis to mean "an equal time stream of payments for an equal time stream of MRP." It is analytically incorrect to debate the equal pay issue with reference to wage differentials in a given period. The time streams of revenues and costs of workers must be considered.

Finally, workers with specific training will be paid a wage less than their actual MRP but more than the competitive MRP. This strategy reduces labor quit rates and preserves the firm's investment in human capital.

Geographic and Intertemporal Resource Allocation

Other chapters show how the entry and exit of competitive firms allocates resources among industries. The general principle is that firms produce in the most profitable industries. This unifying concept may be extended to geographic areas and different time periods. Competitive entrepreneurs select the most profitable geographic markets to sell in, and many also have the option of selling their output in the present period or in a future period. The basic principles of entry and exit apply equally to switching supplies among industries, geographic areas, and time periods.

Geographic Allocation

Consider a product being sold by competitive firms in two geographic markets. If we assume the existence of arbitrage and zero transportation costs, there can be no price difference between the two markets in equilibrium. If prices differ, there are profit incentives to shift supplies from the lower-priced market to the higher-priced one, until the price differential that induced the shifts is eliminated. In fact, such responses make it difficult even to think of the two markets as separate. If transportation costs are positive and there are no barriers to entry, equilibrium prices in different geographic areas can differ only by the transportation costs.

Intertemporal Allocation

Intertemporal supply choices are especially interesting for firms selling such exhaustible, storable resources as oil, natural gas, and coal, because selling a ton of coal today forecloses the opportunity of selling it in any other period. Entrepreneurs selling storable resources have an asset that must be sold in the most profitable time period, taking into account the growth path of selling prices and storage costs over time.

To see how the prices of exhaustible resources compare in different time periods, consider the substitutability of two different stores of value: a financial asset (bond) and a ton of coal. The financial asset must rise in value over time in order to induce people to hold it. Similarly, the ton of coal must rise in value to induce storage. In fact, these assets must rise in value at the same rate over time, less the costs of storage and the financial transaction.

Suppose the stores of value for bonds and coal rise at different rates. Entrepreneurs holding the asset with the slower rate of increase will sell some of it and buy some of the faster-rising asset. These switches bring the relative rates of value increase closer together. The process stops when the two rates are equal. Thus the equilibrium price of exhaustible assets like coal must rise at the same rate as financial assets. This idea is the famous **Hotelling principle** of intertemporal resource allocation: Profit-maximizing entrepreneurship in competitive markets forces the prices of exhaustible resources to rise at the rate of interest, less transaction costs.[6]

Let's examine the intertemporal entry/exit mechanism more closely, assuming that the storage costs of holding coal in the ground are negligible. Intertemporal entry and exit equate the present value of the price of coal in all time periods. Suppose coal can be sold in period 1 or period 2. Period 2's price, P_2, must equal period 1's price, P_1, plus interest earned on P_1 between the current period and the next period, $P_1 \cdot i$. In symbols,

$$P_2 = P_1 + (P_1 \cdot i) = P_1(1 + i) \qquad (14.28)$$

or

$$P_1 = \frac{P_2}{1 + i} \qquad (14.29)$$

6. Harold Hotelling, "The Economics of Exhaustible Resources," *Journal of Political Economy* 39 (1931): 137–175.

The present value of price in the next period equals this period's price, which requires that P_2 exceed P_1 by the rate of interest.

Suppose that $P_1 < P_2/(1 + i)$ temporarily. The present value of price in period 2 is greater than the price in period 1, and so it is profitable for the individual firm to store more gas until period 2. However, the industry effect of many individual firm decisions to stop selling gas in the present period by storing for the future reduces current supplies, increases future supplies, and pushes the present value of the prices for different periods toward equality. These intertemporal adjustments continue until the price in period 1 equals the present value of the price in period 2; $P_1 = P_2/(1 + i)$.

Conversely, if $P_1 > P_2/(1 + i)$, firms have a profit incentive to sell more gas in the current period. But the increases in period-1 supplies and decreases in period-2 supplies force the different prices closer together, until $P_1 = P_2/(1 + i)$ once again. Thus the competitive market assures that nonreproducible resources will be stored for future use and sold in the current period in an orderly way.

Beginning in intertemporal long-run equilibrium, where $P_1 = P_2/(1 + i)$, let the interest rate rise to i' so that $P_1 > P_2(1 + i')$. In this case, firms have an incentive to switch output from the future to the present. This switch continues until the intertemporal supply changes reduce P_1 and increase P_2 to the point that $P_1' = P_2'(1 + i')$. Because a higher real interest rate implies that consumers place a higher value on current consumption than on future consumption, it is proper that the competitive market allocates a larger portion of the nonrenewable resource to present consumption. In contrast, a lower interest rate would reduce the current consumption rate of the resource and increase storage for the future.

14.4

Intertemporal Supply, Price Control, and Price Decontrol

Price controls were imposed on natural gas in the 1950s. We have seen how such controls misallocate resources and retard long-run equilibrium adjustments between industries. We will now discover how price controls may have distorted the intertemporal consumption of natural gas.

Surprisingly, controls may actually have increased supplies of natural gas in the short run. At any given time, natural gas is both stored and extracted. Price controls curtail investment in future extraction but give owners a greater incentive to deplete present stocks sooner (unless they believe the controlled price will be lifted soon). If price controls are such that $P_1 = P_2$ and costs are negligible, then $P_1 > P_2/(1 + i)$. It is more profitable to sell natural gas in the current period and invest in something other than resource storage and extraction than to store and sell natural gas later at the same price. Thus the supply of natural gas increases in the current period, perhaps enough to drive the current price below the controlled price. There may be no apparent shortages or upward pressure on prices in the early periods following the imposition of controls.

But stored gas is being depleted and exploration curtailed. This reduction of supplies will lead finally to severe shortages of the stored reserves and a shortage of invested capital and equipment for producing more when the stored gas is depleted.

Furthermore, the shortage hits consumers more suddenly than if prices rose gradually. With artificially low gas prices, consumers have less incentive to insulate, install solar panels, or relocate to smaller houses. All the markets for these substitutes have to adjust suddenly when the shortage of natural gas occurs suddenly. Sudden adjustments are more expensive than gradual adjustments.

Thus the initial reaction to price controls—an increase in supply—may seem very desirable, but it masks the true long-run impacts. An inherent danger in our political system is that politicians, seeking reelection in the short run, may have incentives to concentrate on the apparent short-run benefits of controls and to ignore the inevitable long-run shortages.

The counterpart of this argument arises during periods of de-

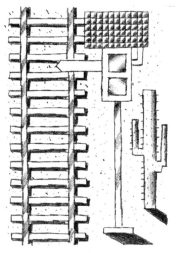

control. When prices are again to be market-determined after a period of price controls, suppliers will store their gas supplies in expectation of the higher prices to come. Prices are boosted as well

by the limited current investment in future exploration and storage. In short, the supply of gas in the current period may not be very elastic with respect to higher prices.

Members of Congress and Presidents have often assailed profiteering companies for storing gas while waiting for prices to rise. They have interpreted such behavior as evidence of monopoly. But this is a natural response to price decontrols, and both monopolists and competitors may respond in this way. The anticipatory storage of natural resources is neither a necessary nor sufficient test for monopoly power. Competitive firms sell natural gas at the most profitable time. If public policy raises the expectation that the present value of future prices exceeds current prices, price-taking competitors will store resources while prices rise.

14.5

Contracts and Intertemporal Efficiency

For many results in managerial economics, exchange can be treated as simultaneous, with no delay between agreements and their performance. But in fact, many actions of economic agents are separated in time, and economic theory would be of limited usefulness if it did not apply to intertemporal bargaining.

The simple purchase of a magazine may appear to be a simultaneous exchange of money and printed paper. But it may be days later that the buyer discovers that pages are missing. More complicated transactions—such as the exchange of labor services, equipment purchases, and the building of skyscrapers—require a great deal of time between agreement and performance. During such time periods, there is the potential for any party to regret the deal; among other reasons, relative prices may change or new products may not live up to durability

claims. These risks may make people reluctant to enter agreements in the first place.

Contracts facilitate intertemporal agreements. State enforcement of contract terms allows parties to rely on agreements prior to completion of their performance. It is important to realize that courts do not generally require parties to carry out the terms of an agreement. If the parties unilaterally renege, however, they must pay damages to restore the value of the contract to the injured parties. The role of contracts is therefore to provide incentives for care and efficiency in entering into agreements and to allow people to trust long-term agreements. These conditions are

a requirement for efficient intertemporal resource allocation.

Suppose a new firm wants to produce a higher-cost, higher-quality television set. By providing a guarantee, durability claims can be enforced by contract, allowing the higher-quality TV set to compete with low-priced sets. Similarly, contracts allow mail-order houses to compete with local stores. And because contracts make claims by new firms more believable and reliable, they facilitate the competitive entry/exit process.

In general, state enforcement of contracts facilitates sequential exchange. Without contracts, exchange would be more simultaneous and, as a consequence, less efficient.*

*For more on the economics of contracts see Anthony T. Kronman and Richard A. Posner, *The Economics of Contract Law* (Boston: Little, Brown, 1979).

Key Terms

Summary

Most management decisions take place within a time dimension. This chapter analyzes the major problems posed by the existence of a time dimension and the legal and economic responses to time that the manager must understand.

The chief problem posed by the time dimension is the fact that dollars change in value over time. They must therefore be calculated in terms of their value at the time they are received or spent. The usual method for comparing the present and future value of dollars is to calculate their value in the present period, or their present value. Calculating the net present value of business projects is the intertemporal analogue of calculating their marginal profit.

This chapter examines several methods of project evaluation, often called capital budgeting. Calculating net present value is the best method for capital budgeting. Other methods, such as calculating the internal rate of return or the payback period, are correct only when they agree with the net present value.

This technique can be applied not only to the analysis of physical investments but to the analysis of investments in people as well. In analyzing the net present value of human capital, one must pay special attention to the peculiar economics of general and specific human capital.

Finally, supply and demand analysis may be augmented by determining the intertemporal value of money. Such a tool has application to the law of contracts, which is essential to economic efficiency, and to the imposition of price controls, which shift resources intertemporally as well as reduce their quantity in any period.

Problems

1. Suppose a firm can purchase a building in downtown Manhattan for $50 million and lease office space in it for $2 million.
   a. Should the building be purchased if the interest rate is 5 percent? 10 percent? 15 percent? Explain your answer.
   b. Suppose the resale price of the property is expected to rise at a rate equal to half the interest rate. Should the building be purchased? Should it be resold? If so, when? (Again, solve the problem for interest rates of 5 percent, 10 percent, and 15 percent.)

2. Suppose the sale price for the right to clear-cut an area of forest rises 20 percent this year and is expected to continue rising at a rate that decreases by 1 percent a year (that is, next year it will rise 19 percent, the following year it will rise 18 percent, and so on). When should the rights be sold?

3. Assume that you can undertake one of two projects, A or B, which are mutually exclusive. On the basis of the facts in Table 14.4, answer the following questions:
   a. If the annual benefits of project A are $30,000 and the benefits of project B are $20,000, which project is preferable on

Table 14.4

Benefit/Cost Analysis
of Two Projects

Project	Life Span	Initial Cost	Scrap Value
A	5 years	$10,000	$ 500
B	10	20,000	1,000

benefit/cost grounds if the interest rate is 5 percent? 10 percent? 15 percent?

b. If the interest rate is 10 percent, what annual benefits from project B will equalize its present value with that of project A?

4. Using the present value formula, explain why a competitive industry's demand for loanable funds slopes downward.

5. Your firm must make a $50,000 payment in 6 years to replace a machine that will wear out by then. Your boss wants to invest equal monthly payments during the next 6 years.

   a. What is the monthly payment required if the interest rate is 5 percent? 10 percent? 15 percent?

   b. Can you suggest an alternative strategy that takes inflation into account?

6. Heating costs in your building have skyrocketed. Heat now costs $15,000 per year. You are offered the following deals. Comment on each alternative, using an interest rate of 6 percent.

   a. A contractor offers to fix air infiltration problems for $5,000. He estimates that the job will last 5 years and save $1,000 in heating cots per year. After 5 years, annual maintenance costing $500 will be required.

   b. A consultant offers to perform an energy waste audit for $500. This audit will save no heat, but most buildings can save 20 percent on their heating costs by following her advice.

   c. A contractor can convert your building from electric heat to natural gas at a cost of $10,000. You will save $1,100 per year.

7. a. If the property tax were to rise for the land your building is on, would your landlord attempt to pass the tax increase on to you?

   b. What economic factors should you take into account in answering the question?

8. A firm attempts a limit-pricing strategy in order to slow down competitive entry. The pricing managers anticipate the profit streams shown in Table 14.5 under short-run profit-maximizing pricing and under limit pricing.

   a. Which strategy is more profitable if the interest rate is 5 percent? 10 percent? 15 percent?

   b. What interest rate must prevail for the two strategies to be equally profitable?

9. Medical schools typically prefer applicants in their twenties rather than those over thirty-five. Does this preference necessarily constitute age discrimination?

10. Explain why a firm will provide executive training programs but not secretarial training programs.

11. The New York Yankees have an incredibly rich owner, one of the most lucrative TV contracts, and one of the best stadiums. Furthermore, the owner is not a strict profit maximizer. Still, the Yankees do not have the best player in every position. Explain why such a team will not buy up all the superstars from other teams, using marginal productivity theory. (Hint: Show that the Yankee's nth superstar is worth less to the Yankees than that player is worth to another team as its first superstar.)

Table 14.5
Short-Run Pricing
versus Limit Pricing

Year	Short-Run Pricing	Limit Pricing
1	$40 million	$25 million
2	35	25
3	30	25
4	25	25
5	20	24
6	15	23
7	15	22
8	15	21
9	15	20
10	15	20

12. Suppose that a personnel officer does not care, on noneconomic grounds, whether she hires a man or a woman for an important long-term management post in her firm. She is looking for a twenty-five- to twenty-eight-year-old person to be groomed for top management later on. She knows if she hires the woman, there is a chance the woman will spend 2 years on leave for family formation, after which she will return permanently. She also knows that a man has an equal chance of suffering from ulcers and heart attacks and therefore spending a similar period of time away from the firm to recover. Furthermore, she knows that the probability of the woman suffering the man's ailments is equal to the probability of the man having a baby. Retirement age is sixty-five for both, and productivity increases are the same for each, given the same years of experience. Yet the personnel officer determines that the woman candidate is worth less to the firm than the man and, if hired, should get a lower wage than the man. How can her decision be justified?

13. University professors hired in the period 1965–1969 enjoyed a very tight market due to the great expansion of enrollment that took place then. As a result, high salaries were paid and mobility was great. Tenure systems maintain these high incomes, even though market conditions are considerably different now.
    a. Did the salaries paid in those years exceed expected *MRP?*
    b. Do the protected incomes paid now exceed expected *MRP?* (Contrast the professor who has recently received offers to those who have not.)

14. A firm uses capital and labor. It calculates that the marginal product of capital is 17, whereas that of labor is 25. The rental price of capital is equal to the wage rate of labor.
    a. Should the firm change its input mix? Why or why not?
    b. Should it expand output? Why or why not?

15. U.S. auto workers complain about the low wages in Singapore, where some car parts are made. If the wages are lower there, why aren't more cars made in Singapore?

16. Suppose that a firm needs a warehouse and has a choice of one large warehouse that costs $250,000 or a smaller warehouse that costs $150,000 with the potential for a future addition costing $150,000. Forecasts indicate the eventual need for the larger space, but currently the smaller space is more than adequate.
    a. If the smaller warehouse will be too small in *T* years, should the firm build the larger warehouse now? Or the smaller one with the plan to add on when necessary? Explain your decision.
    b. How does your answer depend on the interest rate?

17. "Construction costs are rising; therefore, we should build now." Comment on this statement.

18. In many states, the award of damages in accident cases is not augmented by the value of prejudgment interest.
    a. Explain why this practice encourages insurance companies to drag out compensatory damage cases for years.

b. How is this incentive affected by changes in the interest rate?

19. Suppose that your employer doubles your pension benefits when you reach age fifty-five.

    a. How do you calculate the value now of that future event?

    b. If you were looking for another job, how would you compare the pension benefits provided by the new job with those provided by your present job?

20. Suppose that a bus company receives a capital grant from the U.S. Department of Transportation and then contracts with a bus manufacturer for the purchase of new buses. How could you calculate the economic harm to the bus company if the buses are delivered a year late?

21. Suppose a paper firm decides to install a new paper-making machine in the Midwest at a cost of $50 million. The machine will allow the company to produce paper at a profit of $2 million per year for 100 years.

    a. What is the internal rate of return?

    b. Calculate the net present value of the project if the interest rate is 5 percent; 10 percent; 15 percent.

22. When the *USA Today* newspaper made its debut across the nation, its chief marketing device was the mechanical dispenser boxes installed virtually overnight in every major city. Assuming that the paper does not have to pay for the dispensing sites, how would you calculate the capital value of the right to place the boxes in those locations?

23. a. Does a textbook have capital value?

    b. Does the copyright to *Gone with the Wind* have capital value?

    c. Does the copyright to "Getting Gertie's Garter" have capital value?

24. Beautiful wooden sailboats are for sale at very low prices, much less than it would cost to build them. Meanwhile, houses are for sale at prices comparable to what they would cost to build. Explain this difference. (Hint: The fact that sailboats are a luxury and that housing is a necessity is not an answer.)

25. Suppose the city condemns the sewer connected to your place of business and assesses your company $15,000 to defray the costs of repair.

    a. What would happen to the sale price of your company?

    b. How does your answer change if the tax is levied to pay for repairs of a city park a mile away?

26. Explain how the subject of transfer pricing, introduced in Chapter 12, can be modified to take the time dimension into account.

27. If the government places a floor under the price of wheat, how will the intertemporal allocation of wheat be affected?

28. a. Is the study of managerial economics general training or specific training?

    b. Does your answer depend on whether you take the course in a university or as part of a training program in a bank?

Suggested Readings

Baumol, William J. Economic Theory and Operations Analysis, 5th ed. (Englewood Cliffs, N.J.: Prentice-Hall, 1974.)

Hirschleifer, J. "On the Theory of Optimal Investment Decisions," *Journal of Political Economy* 66 (August 1958): 329–352.

Lorie, J. H., and Savage, L. J. "Three Problems in Capital Rationing," *Journal of Business* 28 (October 1955): 229–239.

15

PUBLIC-SECTOR MANAGE-MENT

revious chapters make the tacit assumption that all benefits and costs of production and consumption enter into decision makers' private comparisons of costs and benefits. Under such circumstances, the parties to a transaction enjoy all the benefits and pay all the costs of their decisions, no more and no less. The models that have already been presented are useful in studying markets characterized strictly by private benefits and costs.

However, many decisions and transactions benefit or injure people who are not voluntary parties to the transactions. Your decision to drive on the freeway during the rush hour increases the time it takes someone else to get to work. If you paint your house, you also enhance your neighbor's property value. Economists call these effects **externalities,** although there are numerous less forbidding and perhaps more descriptive synonyms, including *spillover effects, third-party effects, neighborhood effects*, and *external effects*.

Externalities are costs or benefits that do not enter fully and appropriately into decision makers' comparisons of costs and benefits. A key feature of externalities is their involuntary nature. If you contract to have 2 inches of manure spread on your lawn, no externality is present, because you voluntarily incur a cost in anticipation of receiving a benefit. But if Farmer Jones spreads 2 inches of manure on his field and the rain washes it onto your lawn, an externality occurs, because it is an involuntary transaction from your viewpoint. If the manure damages your property, you incur an **external cost.** If it enhances your property, perhaps replacing fertilizer that you expected to have to pay for, you receive an **external benefit.** Life is full of such third-party effects, ranging from the trivial (your lunch partner injures you by chewing with her mouth open) to the momentous (an upstream industrial chemical firm kills flora and fauna and accelerates the incidence of cancer by dumping its wastes into a river).

When transactions exhibit important external components, free-market production and exchange cannot allocate resources to their most valuable uses, as we are about to see. But questions abound. If the market ceases to send and receive the proper price signals because of externalities, by what means are resources allocated? Can public intervention improve efficiency in such markets? Are there ways to shore up the market mechanisms in order to achieve greater efficiency?

This chapter provides a systematic study of the problems and possible remedies in industries that display important externalities. Because externalities are present in so many public-sector services and because of the policies needed to regulate private-sector industries displaying significant externalities, the analysis in this chapter is replete with public policy implications. The economics of externalities is getting increasing attention as the public demands greater efficiency from its government.

Jointness in Production and Consumption

The beginning point in studying externalities is **jointness,** which may occur in production or consumption activities. A single production process often gives rise to multiple outputs: Steers provide beef and hides; sheep yield mutton and wool; oil wells emit oil and natural gas. In consumption, goods are often consumed jointly by many consumers: A tornado siren alerts everyone within hearing range; a national defense system protects all Americans collectively. Jointness in production or consumption makes these cases fundamentally different from those we have studied so far.

Jointness and Vertical Summation

The analytical tool that captures the differences associated with jointness is vertical summation of cost and benefit curves—rather than horizontal summation used to calculate the market values of most demands and supplies.

Figure 15.1 illustrates the vertical summation of demands, us-

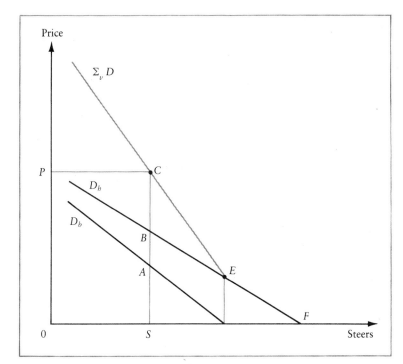

Figure 15.1
**Vertical Summation of Demand in
Joint Production**

For the Sth steer, the total willingness
to pay is $\overline{SC} = \overline{SA} + \overline{SB}$.

ing the beef and hide example.[1] The curve labeled D_b is the demand curve for steers by beef users, and curve D_h is the demand curve for steers by hide users. Our goal is to construct a demand curve for steers that measures the maximum price consumers will pay for each steer. Horizontal summation of the two demand curves is not meaningful, because unlike the situation we've encountered in previous demand analysis, each steer contributes to the benefits of both classes of users. Rather than horizontally summing the number of steers demanded at each price, we must sum vertically the amounts of money each user is willing to pay for additional steers.

In Figure 15.1, beef users are willing to pay $\overline{SA}$ for the Sth steer, and hide users are willing to pay $\overline{SB}$ for the same Sth steer. Because the two demands are for different components of the same steer, the total price that will be offered for the Sth steer by both classes of users is $\overline{OP} = \overline{SA} + \overline{SB} = \overline{SC}$. Point C is the vertical summation of points A and B for the Sth steer. Similar vertical summation for all other quantities of steers produces the market demand curve for steers, labeled $\Sigma_v D$. (The subscript v with the summation sign signifies vertical summation.) The demand curve for steers has a kink at E, the output level at which the beef users' demand vanishes. Line segment $\overline{EF}$ is a component of the hide users' demand curve and the market demand curve $\Sigma_v D$.

1. Vertical summation is explained in Chapter 11 in the process of describing competitive firms' profit-maximizing behavior when joint production arises. The next two paragraphs repeat that explanation for the benefit of those who have not studied the relatively advanced material in Chapter 11.

Jointness and Efficiency

Let's apply the joint production model to an industry exhibiting substantial externalities and see how the market outcomes described in other chapters are affected. Consider education, a service that, much like steers, produces two kinds of benefits to users: private benefits to students and public benefits to society. **Private benefits** are those that accrue directly to the individual attending school. These include the enjoyment derived from training the mind to operate at a high level; the excitement of learning new concepts, teaching them to others, and even discovering new knowledge; and graduates' enhanced streams of income. In contrast, the **public benefits** of education are those that spill over to society at large when its citizens are educated. One public benefit of education is an intelligent electorate that is capable of recognizing and avoiding errors in public policy. The maintenance and development of culture are another important public benefit of education. A knowledge of history and the ability to learn from past mistakes and triumphs are spillovers that carry benefits to society in addition to the private benefits that students receive.

Figure 15.2 displays the private marginal benefit curve of education, MB_P, and the public benefit curve, MB_u. We may assume that both types of benefits are a declining function of the number of years in school, measured on the horizontal axis. The total demand for education is the vertical sum of the private and public benefit, labeled $\Sigma_v MB$ in Figure 15.2. We may also assume that the marginal cost of additional years in school rises. The curve labeled MC is the marginal cost of schooling as a function of years in school.

In free-market transactions, buyers make payments for goods only when they anticipate receiving commensurate benefits. Thus, students pay for schooling because of the private benefits they expect. However, people are not likely to pay for the public benefits, in part because these benefits accrue to society at large and cannot be captured by any individual and in part because benefits can often be received without payment. Hence, the public marginal benefit curve for education does not represent effective demand for education. (This problem is discussed in greater detail in later sections.) Thus, only the private marginal benefit curve is relevant to private market decisions.

Private market allocation of education will result in a level of education Y_1, because $MB_P = MC$ at point A. This result is socially inefficient, because at Y_1, $\Sigma_v MB > MC$. If no public benefit externalities were created by privately purchased education, Y_1 would be efficient. But in the presence of these externalities, efficiency calls for the equality of $\Sigma_v MB$ and MC at point C and an educational output of $\hat{Y}$. When joint production generates external benefits for which there is no effective demand, the efficiency mechanisms of

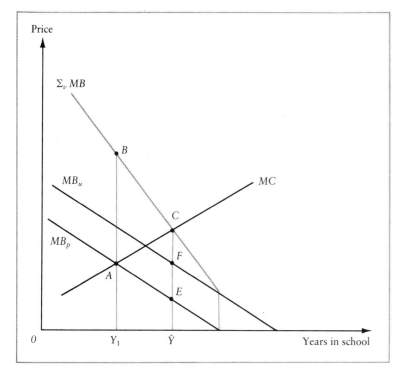

Figure 15.2
Joint Production and Externalities
Education yields both private and public benefits. These must be vertically summed to produce total marginal benefit.

the price system are restrained. Such externalities result in market failure.

One way to establish the efficient level of education $\hat{Y}$, where $\Sigma_v MB = MC$ at point C, is to lower the price that students pay for education from $\overline{Y_1 A}$ to $\overline{\hat{Y}E}$. The lower price encourages students to move from A to E along the private marginal benefit curve. For each small increase in schooling between Y_1 and $\hat{Y}$, $\Sigma_v MB > MC$, meaning that the marginal benefit of education, including private and public benefits, exceeds the value of the necessary resources in their most valuable alternative uses. Increasing education by price reductions allows society to capture the valuable external benefits. When $\hat{Y}$ is attained, society is receiving a marginal benefit—private plus public—equal to the marginal cost of resources, and the efficient amount of public benefits are produced. At $\hat{Y}$, $\Sigma_v MB \equiv \overline{\hat{Y}E} + \overline{\hat{Y}F} = \overline{\hat{Y}C} \equiv MC$. The lower price is not a transfer (welfare) payment. It is necessary to induce students to expand education beyond Y_1, to $\hat{Y}$ years, and thereby bestow the optimum public benefits that society desires. Lowering student prices is necessary to capture efficiency, but if prices are lowered accurately, the lower price is not a transfer.[2]

2. An excellent article on this subject is E. G. West, "An Economic Analysis of the Law and Politics of Non-Public School 'Aid,'" *Journal of Law and Economics* 19 (1976): 79–102. West extends the analysis to justify public aid to private schools because of their beneficial spillover effects.

15.1

Jointness and Mass Transit

Consider the benefits that derive from bus service. As in education, benefits are both private and public. Bus riders capture the private benefits of trips, but car drivers also benefit from less-congested roads, lower pollution levels, and a lower probability of accidents. Thus bus service generates joint products: private and public benefits of bus transportation.

The accompanying figure illustrates the two components of benefits resulting from bus transportation. The private benefits to the bus riders are shown in the marginal benefit curve labeled MB_b; the public benefits of bus transportation, which accrue in large measure to car drivers, are shown in the marginal benefit curve MB_c. The vertical summation of these marginal curves is $\Sigma_v MB$.

Because car drivers receive a benefit without making a payment, their demand for bus transportation does not enter into the bargaining process that sets price and quantity. Accordingly, the price system will establish B_1 bus trips at a fare of $\overline{B_1 A}$, because the private marginal benefit to bus riders equals marginal cost at A. The efficient level of bus trans-

portation is $\hat{B}$, at which $\Sigma_v MB = MC$ and at which all benefits of bus ridership enter into the decision. But $\hat{B}$ can be achieved only if the bus fare to riders is lowered from $\overline{B_1 A}$ to $\hat{B}E$, allowing riders to increase their quantities of bus travel demanded in accord with

private benefits and thereby bestowing the optimum quantity of public benefits as well.

How should the additional bus service be financed? Because car drivers are major beneficiaries of the additional bus service, some financing should come from automobile-related taxes, such as gasoline taxes and automobile registration taxes. Property taxes can also be appropriate sources of bus financing, especially if property values are enhanced by bus service.

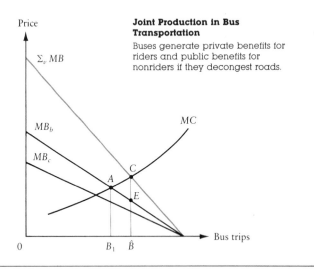

Joint Production in Bus Transportation

Buses generate private benefits for riders and public benefits for nonriders if they decongest roads.

Public Goods

The previous section shows how public benefit externalities interfere with efficiency and how pricing policies may help to restore a better allocation of resources to certain industries. Now we may become more rigorous about these ideas by distinguishing between private goods and public goods.

Private goods have two essential properties: rivalry and exclusion. **Rivalry** means that private goods are not consumed collectively. If you eat an apple, nobody else can eat the same apple. Eating one apple uses up that apple, so a new apple is needed each time. **Exclusion** refers to the ability of sellers to limit use to consumers who pay for products. Rivalry and exclusion allow private goods like apples to be produced and exchanged in market transactions, because buyers receive benefits for the goods they pay for and sellers can restrict the benefits of products to paying customers.

In contrast, **public goods** exhibit nonrivalry and nonexclusion. **Nonrivalry** means that a good can be consumed collectively. A public good can be shared, and unlike an apple, enjoyment of the good by one does not use up the good for others. Jogging through a park or driving over a bridge does not require the replacement of the park or the bridge after each use. **Nonexclusion** is the inability of sellers to restrict use to people who pay for the services. Private market production and exchange of public goods are not possible, and so some form of public intervention is necessary to divert the efficient amount of resources to their provision.

One important trait of public goods is their extremely low marginal cost of use. The average cost of building a bridge, TC/crossings, may be quite high. But the marginal cost of an additional crossing once the bridge is built, $\Delta TC/\Delta$ (crossings), is very close to zero. Only a minute change in the bridge's characteristics occur per crossing—perhaps a few cement molecules knocked out of place—surely not worth the measurement and collection costs.

Similarly, one more physical-fitness nut jogging through the park or one more viewer enjoying a fireworks display imposes zero marginal cost. Likewise, if a few more people move into a neighborhood that emphasizes education, they enjoy the public benefit of the school spillover at low or zero marginal cost. (Of course, marginal cost is zero in these examples only if the additional consumption does not cause congestion of the park, display grounds, or school system. Congestion costs are considered in Application 15.2.) So in the absence of congestion costs, efficiency calls for public goods to be provided at a price equal to marginal cost—that is, at a zero price.

Obviously, a zero price creates a problem: The public good must be financed somehow, or it will not be produced in the first place. This problem applies strictly to public goods, and not private goods, because

1. For private goods, price is used to finance production. The revenue per apple enables growers to cover the costs of its production. For public goods, where the price is zero, alternative sources of revenue are needed.
2. For private goods, the price system provides information: The price equals the marginal benefit of the last apple sold. Comparing price to costs, growers are guided into growing the efficient number of apples. For public goods, decisions about how much of the goods to provide must be made in the absence of price information. Votes are guides of sorts but are not fine-tuned to public wants.
3. For private goods, there is no incentive for consumers to under-declare their willingness to pay for the marginal unit. If apples are presently selling for 20¢ apiece and one more apple is worth 21¢ to

the eater, the eater would certainly lose by offering only 19¢. The eater who made such an offer would be excluded from buying the apple. But suppose there is no way to exclude an additional consumer from the public good once built. Or suppose exclusion is very costly or changes the nature of the good. In these cases, users have an incentive to underdeclare benefits, and there is no market in which consumer benefits can be observed.

A P P L I C A T I O N

15.2

Congestion of Public Goods

Public goods, like bridges, once constructed, allow additional use at near-zero marginal cost because they are not used up at each use. However, if a bridge becomes congested, this congestion imposes opportunity costs on users separate from the negligible number of cement molecules lost from the bridge on each crossing.

To study the effect of congestion on a public good, consider the case of a road built between two points. In Figure A, the horizontal axis measures the volume of cars on the road at any given time. The vertical axis measures time costs. Two demand curves are shown, each negatively sloped with respect to the time cost of driving on the road; along each demand curve drivers will reduce their driving by seeking substitutes when the price of driving, measured in terms of time spent, rises. Curve $D_{off peak}$ is the aggregate demand of drivers at off-peak hours; D_{peak} is the aggregate demand of drivers during the peak rush-hour periods.

Figure A also displays two cost curves: the marginal time cost of travel, MC, and the average time cost of travel, AC. Over the range of low-volume, off-peak traffic, $MC = AC$, because an additional car can enter the road without slowing down any other driver. For that range of volumes, the road is a public good.

For traffic volumes above V_0, an additional driver adds more to the time cost of other drivers than the previous driver did because of congestion. Now the

Figure A
Congestion Externalities
Drivers ignore the congestion costs that they impose on other drivers. Excessive traffic volume results.

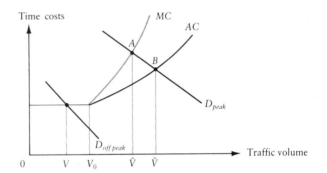

marginal and average time costs rise; as always, $MC > AC$ when AC rises. Each extra driver entering the road imposes a small extra delay on every other driver.

But no driver has an incentive to incorporate this marginal time cost into the decision to drive during the peak time versus the off-peak time. To each driver, the marginal time cost imposed on other drivers is an external cost for which the driver does not pay. Instead, each driver compares the private benefit and private costs of driving; that is, each compares the marginal benefit to the average time cost of travel. Drivers add their cars to the roadway whenever the marginal benefit of driving exceeds the average time cost of driving, or when $MB > AC$.

Equilibrium for all drivers occurs at the inefficient volume $\bar{V}$,

where D_{peak} intersects AC at point B. Thus the efficient volume of peak drivers, $\hat{V}$, at which D_{peak} equals MC at point A, is not achieved. The external costs that drivers impose on one another are not internalized, and excessive traffic volume is the result.

What remedies are available for such congestion of public goods? Policy options fall into three general categories: (1) expand road capacity, (2) impose tolls, or (3) stagger work hours to smooth out the peak demand.

Expanding Capacity
Figure B demonstrates the effect of expanding road capacity. Two problems arise. First, increasing the number of lanes shifts the average and marginal time cost curves down to MC_1 and AC_1. Thus more volume can occur be-

fore the external costs of congestion arise. However, drivers now equate their marginal benefits of driving during the peak (points on their demand curve) with their average time costs, points on the new AC_1 curve.

Second, the expansion of capacity shifts the equilibrium to traffic volume $\hat{V}_1$. But given the new road capacity, efficiency occurs at volume $\check{V}_1$. Thus a larger facility, while reducing the average driving time per driver, still creates excessive congestion, given the size of the facility. Volume increases beyond $\check{V}_1$, the new efficient level.

Also remember that traveling during peak and off-peak hours are substitutes for many drivers. The expansion of capacity reduces the price of peak travel time from $\overline{VB}$ to $\overline{V_1D}$. The price of peak travel is a shift parameter in the demand for off-peak travel. Therefore, when the price of peak travel falls, the demand curve for off-peak travel shifts to the left, and off-peak volume falls from V to V_1. Because the facility is larger, the roadway becomes increasingly empty during the off-peak hours, because demand is lower then. Thus a major limitation of facility expansion as a solution to congestion is the off-peak idleness of the public good.

Charging Tolls

Suppose that, instead of expanding capacity, an attempt is made to internalize the external congestion costs by charging an entry price into the roadway—a toll. The proper toll would be enough to bring the total entry price up to full marginal cost. The driver already pays the average time cost; so the toll, if properly calibrated, would equal $\overline{CA}$ in Figure C. The driver's total price, average waiting time plus toll, or $\check{VC} + \overline{CA}$, equals the marginal time cost of driving during peak hours, or $\check{VA}$.

Beginning at point B (volume

Continued on page 396

Figure B
Facility Expansion in Response to Congestion

Expansion lowers both the average and marginal time cost during peak use and shifts off-peak demand to the left.

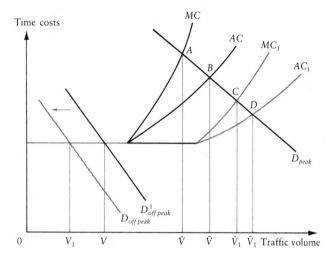

Figure C
Toll Charges in Response to Congestion

Peak-time tolls equal to $\overline{CA}$ produce efficient congestion, increase off-peak use, and provide demand elasticity data as well as revenue.

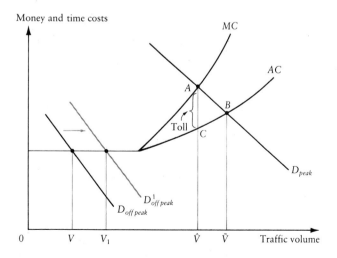

$\hat{V}$), the imposition of the rush-hour toll $\overline{AC}$ would increase the total price of driving and reduce the quantity of peak driving demanded from $\hat{V}$ to $\hat{V}$. At $\hat{V}$, the efficient traffic volume is achieved; $MB_{peak} = MC$.

This policy also makes better use of the road during off-peak hours. The increase in the price of peak-time driving, the result of the toll, increases the demand for its substitute—driving during the off-peak hours. Hence off-peak demand shifts to $D^l_{off\,peak}$, and off-peak volume rises from V to V_1. Other charges, such as higher parking prices for drivers who arrive downtown during peak hours, would have the same effect.

The toll system also provides information about the elasticity of demand for peak driving between points B and A in Figure C and hence information about benefits. For example, if demand at the peak is relatively elastic, the toll will reveal that capacity expansion is not warranted. A very inelastic peak demand would provide partial evidence that expansion is necessary. Still, capacity should be enlarged only if the marginal cost of expansion is less than the marginal time cost of drivers.

Staggering Work Hours

Staggering work hours shifts both demand curves: Off-peak demand increases as workers move to different travel hours, and peak demand falls for the same reason. Staggered work hours smooth out the demands for travel over the day. The failure to use a pricing mechanism prohibits determination of the efficient volume; yet this policy has the benefit of achieving a more uniform use of the facility, much like the toll method.

Staggering work hours is a move toward efficiency if either of the following two relationships is satisfied, where MC_s refers to the marginal cost of staggering work hours:

$$MC_s < MC \text{ of driver} \\ < MC \text{ of expansion}$$

or

$$MC_s < MC \text{ expansion} \\ < MC \text{ of drivers}$$

Figure D compares the expected results of the various policy options for handling traffic volume.

Figure D
Comparision of Three Congestion-Reducing Strategies

The effects on traffic volume of tolls, capacity expansion, and staggered work hours are shown here.

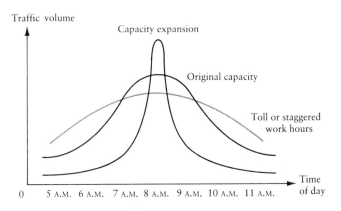

Free-Rider Problem

The **free-rider problem** describes the behavior of consumers of collectively consumed public goods and explains why the financing of such public goods on a private-payment basis is so difficult to achieve. To illustrate, suppose that 1,000 people will benefit if a park is built. Let the marginal cost per acre of construction be $500, as shown in Figure 15.3. Let the private marginal benefit curve for each participant be MB_i, with an intercept of $1 and a slope of $-(\$1/100)$. The vertical summation of all 1,000 MB_i curves produces the curve labeled $\Sigma_v MB_i = 1{,}000\,MB_i$. This curve marks the true marginal benefit to the group, with an intercept of $1,000 and a slope of -10. (Figure 15.3 is not drawn to scale.)

The efficient acreage for the park is found by equating $\Sigma_v MB$ and MC. Thus

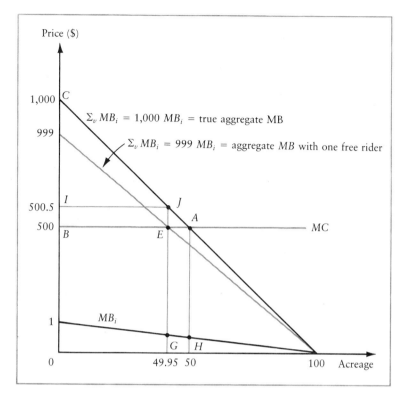

Figure 15.3
Free-Rider Problem
The incentive to underdeclare the
value of public goods is a hindrance
to efficiency. (This graph is not
drawn to scale.)

$$\Sigma_v MB \equiv 1,000 - 10X = 500 \equiv MC$$

where X equals park acreage. Solving for X, the efficient size of the park is 50 acres.

Under such "full revelation of benefits," where all consumers participate in the financing of the park according to their identical marginal benefits, each individual pays 0.001 of the total park cost and receives 0.001 of the total benefit. The total benefit equals area $0CAH$, or \$37,500. The total cost of the park is $0BAH$, or \$25,000. Thus the total net benefit or consumer surplus, area ABC, equals \$12,500; each individual's share of the net gain is \$12.50.

Now let's see the effect if one individual, a free rider, attempts to get the park developed without paying his or her share of the total cost. Suppose that only 999 out of the 1,000 original participants reveal their true marginal benefit curves and are willing to participate in the financing of the park. The new aggregate marginal benefit curve falls ever so slightly to $\Sigma_v MB_i = 999 \, MB_i$. When one individual is a free rider, less than full revelation of benefits results in a park size of 49.95 acres, fractionally smaller than the efficient size of 50 acres. This new acreage is derived by setting $\Sigma_v MB = MC$. Thus

$$\sum_{v}MB \equiv 999 - 9.99X = 500 \equiv MC$$

The value of X is now 49.95 acres, a 0.001-percent reduction in park size. By not participating in the payment scheme, the free rider saves $25 in expenses and enjoys the benefit of a park virtually indistinguishable from 50 acres.

But what are the exact benefits and costs of the free rider and of the remaining 999 participants? All 1,000 persons now share the total consumer surplus equally, but only 999 participate in the cost. The total benefit of the 49.95-acre park is the area $0CJG$, the area beneath the true aggregate marginal benefit curve, and it equals $37,474.98. Each individual, including the free rider, receives an equal share of the total benefits, or $37.47. Thus the free rider receives $37.47 in benefits at no cost instead of the $12.50 net benefits he or she receives by participating in the payment scheme. Each remaining participant receives a net benefit equal to the total benefit, $37.47, less his or her share of the total cost, which remains $25. Thus each paying participant receives a consumer surplus or net benefit of $12.47. The free rider gains $24.97 in net benefits (receiving $37.47 instead of $12.50 if he or she participates), whereas each paying participant is denied only 3¢ in net benefits ($12.47 instead of $12.50). These results dramatize two facts: the strong incentive to be a free rider and the weak incentive to prevent free riders.

This example makes it clear that financing public goods through voluntary payment schemes according to individual benefits has the same inherent instability problems as cartels do: Each participant is better off when the solution is achieved than when it is not; but while the solution is being arrived at, each member has an incentive to cheat (become a free rider). If there are enough free riders (500 or more in the park example), the private-payment scheme collapses and the public good may not be provided at all.

To summarize, the efficient solution calls for public goods to be allocated according to the condition $\sum_{v}MB = MC$; but private-payment schemes may break down in the presence of free riders.

If voluntary contributions cannot be counted on in the financing of public goods, what remedies are available? Compulsory taxation is the most common method of financing public goods. For example, citizens are taxed in order to provide national defense. In this way citizens are denied the option of understating or completely denying the existence of their marginal benefits and becoming in essence free riders. Property, income, and sales taxes are the major sources of tax revenue used to provide public goods.

Club memberships can also provide a solution to the free-rider problem. Memberships are usually sold on an all-or-nothing basis.

A person cannot buy just the option to use the sauna but must pay a lump sum that purchases access to the entire club. Individual services can then be sold to members at low prices, because the marginal cost of using the facility, once constructed, is low. But this solution is efficient only if the lump-sum membership fee does not exhaust the total consumer surplus of any prospective member of the club who can benefit from membership. Otherwise, such members would not join or the club would be too small. Perhaps it would not be formed at all. Obviously, to achieve the exact $MB = MC$ position is virtually impossible.

Church tithing, a system that gives members a moral obligation to contribute 10 percent of their income (or some other arbitrary amount) to the church, is another method of overcoming the free-rider problem. And although not a method of finance, the analysis of costs and benefits is a social-scientific method of selecting appropriate public-sector projects and of operating such projects at the correct levels. Such analysis is a way of replacing the information that a price system fails to provide for public goods.

To sum up, the collective enjoyment of public goods gives rise to the free-rider problem, which in turn prohibits production and financing of public goods by conventional pricing schemes. Alternative methods of measuring benefits and of financing public goods must be found.

Cost-Benefit Analysis

The public-sector analogue of capital budgeting is **cost-benefit analysis.** Chapter 14 explains how a business firm allocates capital over time and across projects. The same principles apply to government projects—but with complications.

Governments must determine which parks, dams, highways, schools, and so on will be provided within the limitation of the revenue generated by their taxing authority. Generally, economic principles are not in the forefront of the criteria used; decisions are often made on political grounds favoring lobbying groups. But as this section demonstrates, governments can use economic principles to make spending decisions.

The first difficulty that arises in public-sector cost-benefit analysis is measurement of the objective. Costs are usually easier to estimate in advance than benefits are. However, when environmental costs are high, as in the case of building a dam or highway, complications arise. Similar complications abound on the benefit side. Unlike the business firm, which assigns benefits only to those aspects of a project that contribute to the "bottom line," a public agency must serve a wide variety of people who will share unequally in a project's benefits and harms. For example, highway construction projects benefit people differently depending on the distance they must drive or the frequency of travel. Such projects require the removal of competing economic activity.

Another problem that arises is the absence of a market-determined price for the use of a public good, which (as you may recall from consumer theory) represents a lower bound of benefits. Therefore, benefits are hard to estimate. Also, public projects like highways are "lumpy" and, for all practical purposes, irreversible once built. Thus benefits are also lumpy and impossible to measure merely by prices (even if those prices could be ascertained). Therefore, the inframarginal benefits of a public project must be measured some other way. Carrying this point another step, the benefits of the project depend on the user charge applied to it, but the user charge need not be a breakeven price equal to average cost. As Chapter 9 indicates, when average cost is greater than marginal cost, the efficient user charge is equal to marginal cost and hence less than average cost: The project loses money. Still, the inframarginal benefits are often sufficient to make a project worthwhile, as with the typical bridge or tollway.

The calculations involved in making benefit and cost measurements for expensive, lumpy public projects are too numerous to set out here. Thus we will focus briefly on the need, as in private-sector capital budgeting, to maximize net present value (See Chapter 14 if you need to refresh your memory on this point). Furthermore, the marginal benefit of market goods can be measured by price. But for lumpy public projects, benefit must be measured as **consumer surplus,** the difference between the amount that consumers are willing to pay for a project or improvement and the amount they must pay to obtain it.

The French economist Dupuit noted that the price of a commodity does not always measure the value or benefit of that commodity to consumers. He observed that water—enormously important to the well-being of society—sold at very low prices. Because price did not appear to measure adequately the value or benefit of water, Dupuit set out to develop a measurement that he felt reflected such value. He called his measurement *consumer surplus.* [3]

In order to see how consumer surplus is measured, let's assume temporarily that the government passes a law requiring water to be sold only in 1-gallon buckets. (Stranger laws have been passed.) According to the demand curve for water in Figure 15.4, consumers are willing to purchase 1 gallon of water when the price is $5 per gallon. Consumer surplus is zero for the first gallon, because there is no difference between the amount consumers are willing to pay ($5) and the amount they do pay ($5). When the price is $4, con-

---

3. J. Dupuit, "De la mesure de l'utilité des travaux publics," *Annales des Ponts et Chenssees* 8 (1844). See also Alfred Marshall, *Principles of Economics,* 9th ed. (London: Macmillan, 1961), p. 124.

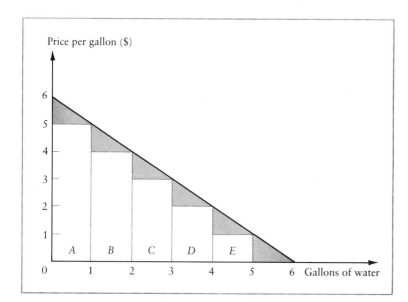

Price per gallon ($)

Figure 15.4
Consumer Benefit for Public Goods
When the price is zero, consumer surplus is approximated by the area beneath the demand curve.

sumers buy 2 gallons. Consumers are willing to pay $5 for the first gallon and $4 for the second gallon, but because they actually pay $4 for each gallon, there is a consumer surplus of $1 on the first gallon and nothing on the second. For a price of $3 per gallon, the quantity demanded is 3 gallons. At that price the total consumer surplus is $3: $2 on the first gallon, $1 on the second, and nothing on the third. When the price is zero, consumer surplus is $15, which equals the sum of the areas of rectangles A, B, C, D, and E. In this example, consumer surplus when the price is zero is approximately, but not exactly, equal to the area beneath the demand curve. The area below the demand curve but not included in consumer surplus is shaded in Figure 15.4.

Now let a new law be passed that permits water to be sold in half-gallon buckets. The demand curve in Figure 15.5 illustrates the effect of this new law on our measurement of consumer surplus. Consumers are willing to pay $5.50 on a per-gallon basis, or $2.75, for the first half-gallon. If the price of water is zero, consumers get the first half-gallon for nothing, so their consumer surplus on the first half-gallon (rectangle a) is $2.75. The consumer surplus on the second half-gallon (rectangle b) is $2.50.

Note that the consumer surplus for the first gallon of water at zero price is $2.75 + $2.50 = $5.25 when water is sold in half-gallon units and only $5 when sold in gallon units. Graphically, the area of rectangles a and b in Figure 15.5 exceeds that of rectangle A in Figure 15.4. In the second graph, the total consumer surplus for all units when the price is zero is $16.50 (the sum of rectangles a through k), versus a total consumer surplus of $15 when the water is sold in gallon units. You can see that more of the area beneath the demand curve is included in consumer surplus when water becomes

Figure 15.5
Size of Units and Consumer Surplus

The error involved in measuring consumer surplus as the area beneath the demand curve shrinks as the good is sold in smaller units.

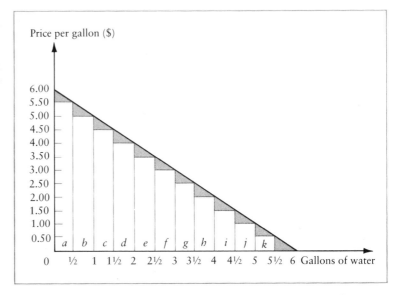

available in smaller units. The shaded area represents the error involved in using the area below the demand curve as the measure of consumer surplus. This error shrinks as water is sold in smaller units. We can completely eliminate all the error represented by the shaded area by allowing water to be sold in infinitely small units, thereby making the area below the demand curve a perfect measure of consumer surplus.

Each point on the demand curve measures consumers' willingness to pay for an extra unit of product. The demand curve is negatively sloped because consumers value extra units of output less and less. This principle—**diminishing marginal utility** or **diminishing marginal benefit**—asserts that the first unit consumed yields the most benefit and that each subsequent unit provides less marginal benefit than the last. The notion of diminishing marginal benefit derives from the generalization that the more of a good one already possesses, the less additional benefit an extra unit of the good can generate. Thus the demand curve is in fact a marginal benefit curve or, equivalently, a marginal willingness-to-pay curve.

Measuring consumer surplus as the entire area beneath the demand curve (or marginal benefit curve) is only correct when the commodity price is zero. What we have called consumer surplus when the price is zero is really a measure of the **total benefit** of consuming good. In Figure 15.6, the total benefit to consumers of consuming x_0 units of X is represented by the area beneath the demand curve up to x_0, or the area of the trapezoid $0abx_0$. This area is the sum of the expenditures that consumers are willing to make on units of X purchased one at a time and thus measures total consumer benefit. In other words, the sum of the marginal benefits received from each unit must equal total benefit. But the total

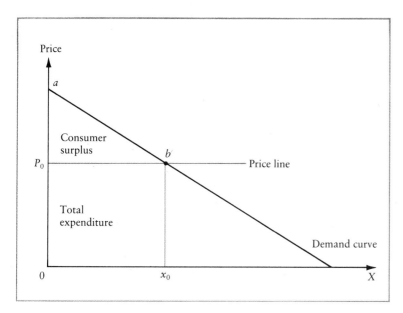

Figure 15.6
Measurement of Consumer Surplus
When the price is positive, consumer surplus is the area below the demand curve and above the price line.

benefit does not equal consumer surplus when the commodity price is positive. At price P_0, consumers must pay an amount equal to $0P_0bx_0$ in order to purchase x_0 units of X. Thus consumer surplus equals the triangle P_0ab, the difference between the amount that consumers are willing to pay ($0abx_0$) and the amount actually paid ($0P_0bx_0$). Consumer surplus is the area below the demand curve and above the price line. Stated differently: Consumer surplus is that portion of total benefit accruing to the consumer (P_0ab), the remainder ($0P_0bx_0$) being that accruing to the producer. Only when the price is zero is consumer surplus equivalent to total benefit and equal to the full area below the demand curve.

A P P L I C A T I O N

15.3

Consumer Surplus and the Traffic Engineer

How can demand theory and consumer surplus be applied to measure the benefits of highway construction? It is a common practice for local authorities to decide on the location of new highway construction on the basis of traffic counts, the logic being that the most heavily traveled roadways must yield the greatest benefit to drivers. Let's examine this assertion by studying the adjacent figure, which contains three demand curves for travel: $\overline{P_1A}$, $\overline{P_2B}$, and $\overline{P_3A}$. For ease, we'll ignore curve $\overline{P_2B}$ for now.

Consider point A, which represents traffic counts along the two routes exhibiting demand curves $\overline{P_1A}$ and $\overline{P_3A}$. The traffic count itself is a poor estimate of the total consumer benefit of travel, because the traffic count A is simply the quantity of travel demanded at zero price. Should we infer that both routes confer equal total

benefit on consumers simply because their traffic counts are the same?

The analysis of consumer surplus teaches us the folly of such a conclusion. The route characterized by demand curve $\overline{P_3A}$ confers greater total benefit on its riders than route $\overline{P_1A}$ does, because the area beneath demand curve $\overline{P_3A}$ is greater than the area beneath demand curve $\overline{P_1A}$. Presumably there are more available substitutes for route $\overline{P_1A}$ than for route $\overline{P_3A}$. In short, traffic

Continued on page 404

counts alone cannot be used to estimate the consumer benefits of alternative travel routes.

But the problem gets worse. Suppose that traffic counts along two alternative arteries yield points A and B. The area beneath demand curve $\overline{P_2B}$ is visibly larger than the area beneath demand curve $\overline{P_1A}$; in this example, the consumer surplus is greater for the road with the lower traffic count because of the difference in the demand for the two roads.

Life is replete with similar examples. Television networks generally air those programs that score highest in the Nielsen ratings in order to attract advertiser financing. But these ratings are just a measure of quantity demanded at zero price. The area beneath the demand curve for educational programming may be much greater than the area beneath the demand curve for the routine situation comedy, even though the audience for the former is smaller than for the latter. Although educational programming may bestow more consumer surplus than alternative network offerings, the audience for the former may not amass the minimum share of the market needed to get the programs aired.

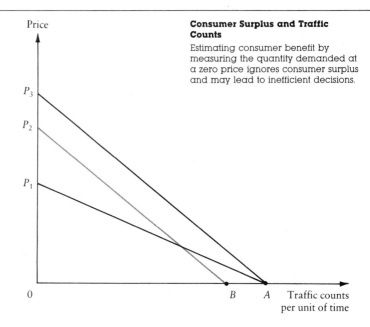

Consumer Surplus and Traffic Counts

Estimating consumer benefit by measuring the quantity demanded at a zero price ignores consumer surplus and may lead to inefficient decisions.

University enrollment funding works the same way. When university administrators decide which programs to finance based solely on enrollment figures, they ignore the possibility that the programs with smaller total enrollments may possess the larger consumer surplus (because of their demand curves). A small dental program may serve a smaller demand (but larger con-

sumer surplus) than a large English doctoral program.

Demand theory alone cannot solve these complex problems, but it certainly helps organize discussion about them and may help policy makers avoid costly errors in decision making. Once the curves are in front of you, they force your mind to go through the right hoops.

APPLICATION

15.4

Value of Scarce but Free Parking Spaces

In the accompanying figure, the line $\overline{DE}$ represents the demand for parking spaces. Drivers are depicted along the horizontal axis in declining order of their marginal benefits from parking, the first driver deriving $\overline{0D}$ benefit and the last driver, at point E, being indifferent between parking and not parking. Thus the demand curve $\overline{DE}$ is a marginal benefit curve for parking.

Say there are $\overline{0E}$ drivers but only $\overline{0A}$ parking spaces. When there is no charge for parking, it is tempting to measure the total benefit as the entire area be-

neath the demand curve, $0DE$. However, the size of this area overstates benefits, because not all drivers will find parking, and those who do look all have an equal chance, regardless of the benefit derived.

Assume that all drivers have an equal chance to find a space. When parking is free, $\overline{0E}$ drivers will search but only $\overline{0A}$ drivers will find spaces. The chance of

finding parking is therefore $\overline{0A}/\overline{0E}$ and equal for all drivers. And each driver's marginal benefit is suppressed by the probability $\overline{0A}/\overline{0E}$ of finding a space.

To construct the probable marginal benefit curve, first draw line $\overline{AF}$ parallel to demand curve $\overline{DE}$. Construct the straight line $\overline{FE}$. At any point along the horizontal axis, the vertical distance to line $\overline{FE}$ is $\overline{0A}/\overline{0E}$ times the distance to the demand curve $\overline{DE}$. For example, $\overline{AG} = (\overline{0A}/\overline{0E}) \cdot \overline{AB}$. Driver A's benefit of parking is $\overline{AB}$ if assured a space. This benefit is reduced to $\overline{AG}$ if the driver is uncertain about finding a space.

The area $\overline{OFGA}$ beneath the probable marginal benefit curve measures the total benefit derived by the $\overline{OE}$ drivers when there is no charge for parking. If a price $\overline{OC}$ is charged, all drivers desiring a space at that price will find one. The total benefit of $\overline{OA}$ parking spaces is the area $\overline{ODBA}$, which can be broken down as expenditures ($\overline{OCBA}$) and consumer surplus ($\overline{CDB}$). Note that $\overline{ODBA} > \overline{OFGA}$: The parking spaces have a greater value to consumers when a price is charged.[*]

[*]William Holahan is grateful to William Vickrey for drawing this diagram on a napkin in a sandwich shop in 1974.

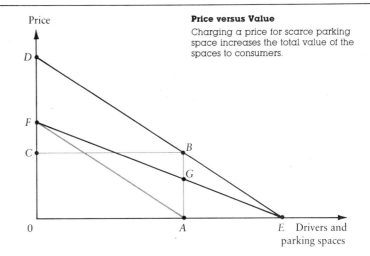

Price versus Value

Charging a price for scarce parking space increases the total value of the spaces to consumers.

15.5

Evaluating Highway Projects

Highway projects provide a particularly interesting application of cost-benefit analysis. They are an extreme departure from market forces and as a good, highways are extremely valuable to consumers.[*] Although typically no price is charged for the use of this good, highways are usually paid for—at least in part—by a gasoline tax.

The questions that arise in highway project evaluation involve the number of highways to be built, their width, and the timing of the highway project. None of these questions is efficiently answered by referring to the funds available from gasoline taxes. Instead, project planners must evaluate the benefits to be derived from a highway project.

The primary benefit of a new highway project is the reduction in travel time. This benefit swamps any other benefit, such as safety, that might be ad-

Continued on page 406

[*]A standard reference on project evaluation is A. Harberger, *Project Evaluation* (Chicago: Markham, 1965).

Consumer Benefits of Highway Projects

The chief benefit of a highway project is the time saved, which can be measured as the consumer surplus associated with the change in time expenditure.

vanced in favor of a project. Hence planners should seek to estimate the value of the time that can be saved by users of the highway and compare that value to the costs of the project.

The figure on page 405 shows a hypothetical demand curve for the daily volume of traffic between a given origin and destination; the time cost is the price variable. The chief value of the highway is to reduce the time costs. The figure shows an initial time cost per trip of $\overline{OA}$ (and resulting traffic volume of V_A) and a time cost per trip after completion of the highway of $\overline{OB}$ (and resulting traffic volume of V_B).

To measure the benefits of saving travel time, we must measure the difference in consumer surplus generated by the two time prices. But we have a problem: We know V_A, the existing traffic volume, but we must estimate traffic volume V_B. Once we have estimated V_B, we can measure the benefit of the project as the area ABED. To estimate V_B, we must know the elasticity of demand for traffic volume with respect to time costs. We may be able to estimate this elasticity by looking at the statistical experience of comparable highways elsewhere.

An inability to estimate V_B precisely need not lead to paralysis. Certainly, we can be confident that area ABED, which we can measure, is smaller than area ABCD, which we must estimate. If area ABCD is greater than costs, the actual net benefits are undoubtedly even greater.

Aside from measuring the elasticity of demand for travel with respect to travel time, mea-

surement problems also include the money value of time saved. Extensive research on this question shows that people generally evaluate the value of travel time saved at between one-half and two-thirds the average wage rate.[†] But their opinions vary considerably, depending on the size of the chunks of time they save and the method by which they save time. For instance, time saved by avoiding stop-and-go traffic is valued more than the same amount of time saved by increasing the speed of a steady flow of traffic.

The central issue of selecting projects according to their maximum net benefit is complicated by the choice of the width, or capacity, of the highway. For example, a large part of the total cost of building a highway is acquiring a long, winding strip of land; this sort of real estate is very costly to obtain except in the most rural areas. But once the land is acquired, should sufficient capacity be built to handle demand well into the future? Or should a smaller highway be built to handle near-term needs, with the intention of adding capacity when traffic volume becomes greater? This problem arises when the economies of scale in one stage of construction are insufficient to outweigh the present value of delaying the addition well into the future.

Suppose the costs of the alternatives are as follows:

C_W = cost of wider road

C_N = cost of narrower road

C_A = cost of delayed addition to narrow road

[†]See Thomas C. Thomas and Gordon I. Thompson, "Value of Time Saved by Trip Purpose," in *Transportation Research Record* (Washington D.C.: National Academy of Sciences, 1976), p. 587.

The question is resolved by comparing the present value of building a wider road at the start to the present value of building the highway in two stages:

$$C_W \gtreqqless C_N + \frac{C_A}{(1 + i)^T}$$

where

i = cost of capital to government

T = time at which addition is built

A little algebra permits the equation to be rearranged:

$$C_W = C_N \gtreqqless \frac{C_A}{(1 + i)^T}$$

or

$$\frac{C_A}{C_W - C_N} \gtreqqless (1 + i)^T$$

or

$$\frac{ln\left(\frac{C_A}{C_W - C_N}\right)}{ln(1 + i)} \gtreqqless \hat{T}$$

If the narrower road will be adequate for $\hat{T}$ years or more, it is cheaper to build the narrower road now and to build the addition later. $\hat{T}$ need not be far into the future. Consider the following numerical example:

C_W = $500,000 per lane mile

C_N = $400,000 per lane mile

C_A = $200,000 per lane mile

i = 10 percent

Using the third variant of the equation, $\hat{T} = ln(2)/ln(1.1) = 7.8$ years. Thus the narrower road should be built if it will handle the traffic volume estimated for the next 7.8 years.

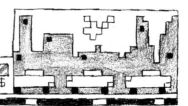

External Costs: Pollution as a Factor of Production

Externalities have been defined as the costs or benefits of a decision that do not enter into decision makers' private comparison of costs and benefits. We have seen the central roles of jointness, nonrivalry, exclusion, and public goods in the generation of external benefits. On the cost side, pollution may be the by-product of the production of an otherwise useful good. Firms often have access to the waste-assimilating properties of the environment (air, water, land) at zero or very low cost. Such firms produce output at profit-maximizing rates that allow for the firms' private costs and revenues but largely ignore the environmental costs imposed on others. As we will soon see, there is a strong incentive to ignore these cost spillovers.

We can address this problem of external costs analytically by considering pollution a factor of production in the sense that the firm's ability to emit one unit of pollution into the environment allows the firm to avoid some cleanup costs. As a result, more capital and labor can be devoted to the production of the useful good out of a fixed cost outlay than would be possible if the pollution unit were not permitted at zero cost. Treating pollution as an input to be combined with labor and capital to produce output leads to the natural construction of the **marginal product of pollution** curve, MP_p, and the **value of marginal product of pollution** curve, VMP_p. These pollution curves correspond to the analogous curves for capital and labor, derived in Chapters 3 and 14. Thus $MP_p = \Delta Q/\Delta Y$ and $VMP_p = (\Delta Q/\Delta Y) \cdot P = MP_p \cdot P$, where Q = units of output of a useful good, P = price of the useful good, and Y = units of pollution emitted.

The efficient level of pollution is determined by balancing the benefits of pollution to firms, as one component of society, and the costs of the pollution to other members of society. For convenience, let's assume that the firm is competitive in output and input markets. The private benefits to firms of additional pollution are measured by the VMP_p curve. Figure 15.7 shows a downward-sloping VMP_p curve, reflecting the diminishing marginal product of the pollution input. The positively sloped curve, $\Sigma_v MD$, is the marginal cost curve. We may assume that each additional unit of pollution causes more additional cost in pollution damages than the preceding unit does. Small doses of pollution are assimilated into the environment at low marginal cost, because of the cleansing effect of winds and running streams. But when the air and water are overloaded, additional units of pollution create rising marginal costs (damages) to health and esthetics. Thus the **marginal damage** curve ($\Sigma_v MD$) measures the costs imposed on members of society; it is the vertical summation of all individual marginal cost curves. Like the external benefits discussed earlier in this chapter, the external costs of pollution are consumed collectively. A meaningful societal marginal damage curve must therefore add vertically the marginal

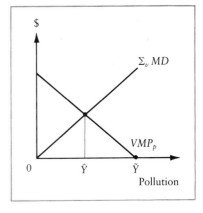

Figure 15.7
Efficient Pollution

Efficient pollution is generally neither zero nor where $VMP_p = 0$. Efficiency requires $VMP_p = \Sigma_v MD$.

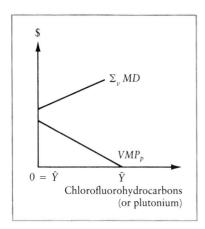

Figure 15.8
The Corner Solution for Pollutants

Some pollutants generate $MD > MB$ at any level.

costs incurred by all damaged parties for each additional unit of pollution.

The optimum "employment" of pollution is $\hat{Y}$, at which VMP_p = $\Sigma_v MD$. But the marginal costs of pollution are external to firms if they are under no obligation to pay for pollution rights or to pay for the damages caused by their pollution. If there is no way to charge firms for their pollution, the price of pollution units is zero; firms will increase pollution as long as VMP_p is positive. Thus actual pollution ($\tilde{Y}$) exceeds the efficient level ($\hat{Y}$).

Note that the efficient pollution level, $\hat{Y}$, is an internal as opposed to a "corner" solution (that is, one on the vertical or horizontal axis): We do not generally wish to set Y equal to zero. The bumper sticker slogan Help Stamp Out Pollution reflects an ignorance of the need to balance benefits and costs at the margin. (But a bumper sticker Help Equate $MB = MD$ would not be likely to motivate the public.)

Of course, there are pollutants that we want virtually none of. For example, there is some evidence that the chlorofluorohydrocarbons, once commonly used in spray-can propellants, rise to the ionosphere and reduce the amount of protective ozone in the atmosphere. (Satellite experiments now being conducted by the National Aeronautics and Space Administration are trying to discover whether the amount of ozone is actually diminishing.) If too many infrared rays make their way to earth, the basic elements of the food chain would be reduced, thereby starving higher organisms. Also, infrared rays can cause skin cancer in light-complected people. Light-complected people dying of cancer and dark-complected people starving to death—these costs, which are external to the production of such cosmetic products as spray deodorants and hairsprays, are clearly undesirable. Thus the "correct" equilibrium of chlorofluorohydrocarbon pollution is virtually zero. In this case, the MD curve for pollution is too high to allow any use of the pollutant; Figure 15.8 illustrates such a corner solution. The damages are so great that an internal solution is ruled out.

Plutonium is another by-product that we cannot tolerate in the environment. Thus plutonium also provides a corner solution at zero levels of pollution. Note that in both examples the corner solution arises not because the by-products are pollutants but because $\Sigma_v MD > VMP_p$ for all units of pollution, including the first unit. Note too that $\tilde{Y}$ rather than 0 will be generated if private firm decisions alone determine the allocation of resources; firms tend to push the VMP_p to zero in an effort to maximize profits.

Internalization of External Costs

When firms have free or nearly free access to the environment, external pollution costs are imposed on damaged parties and a socially excessive level of pollution results. These are inefficient outcomes, because the pollution costs are not borne by polluting firms but instead by third parties with no say in pollution levels. In effect, polluting firms are free riders that enjoy the benefits of pollution without payment. Thus the external costs do not influence firms' decisions appropriately, and pollution levels are too high.

Internalization of externalities is the process of getting the external costs back into decision making. Several policy options exist that are capable of internalizing externalities and promoting "correct" pollution levels.

Assignment of Property Rights: Coase Bargaining Solution

One difficulty in the economics of pollution is that neither the polluting firm nor the members of society damaged by pollution have well-defined property rights to the air and water. Specifically, firms have not been given the right to pollute the air, and consumers have not been given the right to clean air. In a classic article, Ronald Coase pointed out that, if property rights are well defined, the emitters and receptors of pollution would bargain and move to the efficient level of pollution.[4]

For example, suppose a paper mill and a laundry are in a conflict over air pollution. The paper mill emits air pollutants that settle into the clothes at the adjacent laundry, thereby imposing an external cost on the laundry. If the value of the air pollution to the paper mill and the resulting damages to the laundry are measurable and if the environmental pollution rights are well defined, the firms will negotiate the sale of pollution rights until the efficient amount of pollution is established, as Coase has demonstrated. It is essential that one party or the other be assigned pollution rights: Either the paper mill is given the right to pollute or the laundry is given the right to clean air. And surprisingly, Coase showed that if income effects can be ignored, the equilibrium level of pollution will be the same regardless of which firm is assigned the initial pollution rights. Either way, bargaining between the emitter (paper mill) and receptor (laundry) will result ultimately in the same level of pollution. To summarize, the **Coase theorem** asserts that the amount of pollution will be both efficient and independent of the initial assignment of pollution rights. (Strictly speaking, this result requires that transaction costs between the parties be zero and that the bargaining between parties give rise to no net income effects.)

Figure 15.9 illustrates the logic of the Coase theorem in the short run. Begin by assuming that the emitter—the paper mill—is given the right to pollute. The VMP_p curve measures the value of additional pollution to the emitter, and the MD curve measures the damages to the receptor—the laundry.

4. Ronald Coase, "The Problem of Social Cost," *Journal of Law and Economics* 3 (1960): 1–44.

Figure 15.9
Coasian Bargaining

Bargaining produces an efficient use
of pollution regardless of the initial
assignment of pollution rights.

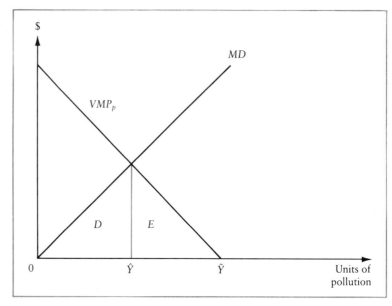

The first step is to show that the equilibrium amount of pollution is $\hat{Y}$, the efficient level, as long as pollution rights are marketable. If the emitter is allowed to pollute at zero private cost, it would
achieve pollution level $\tilde{Y}$, where $VMP_p = 0$. But the receptor has an
incentive to pay the emitter to reduce pollution from $\tilde{Y}$ to $\hat{Y}$, because
for each unit of pollution between $\tilde{Y}$ and $\hat{Y}$, $MD > VMP_p$. In other
words, the receptor is willing to pay the emitter a sum of money
greater than the VMP_p to induce the emitter to stop using those
marginal units of pollution, even though the emitter is legally enti-
tled to them. Thus the emitter receives a larger gain in the payments
to stop polluting than it receives in revenue from the polluting
activity itself for each marginal unit of pollution from $\tilde{Y}$ to $\hat{Y}$. Both
parties enjoy a mutual gain from such bargaining. For marginal
pollution units less than $\hat{Y}$, $VMP_p > MD$; for these pollution units,
the receptor cannot offer the emitter a payment that is at least as
great as the VMP_p. Thus bargaining among parties produces the
efficient pollution level, $\hat{Y}$, when the polluter owns pollution rights.

Now assume that the receptor is given the pollution rights—
that is, the right to clean air. The receptor would no doubt choose
a pollution level of zero, prohibiting the paper mill from producing
any pollution. However, for all marginal units of pollution between
0 and $\hat{Y}$, $VMP_p > MD$. Now the emitting paper mill can offer the
receptor money payments for all its pollution rights in an amount
greater than the receptor's MD but smaller than the emitter's
VMP_p. In other words, the emitter now has an incentive to buy
pollution rights from the receptor, which in turn has an incentive to
sell those rights. As before, the bargaining stops when the emitter
buys $\hat{Y}$ units of pollution rights.

To summarize: Bargaining between parties for pollution rights internalizes the external pollution costs and produces efficient levels of pollution, regardless of the ownership of pollution rights. The Coase theorem is a restatement of market efficiency when property rights are well defined. It also points up the misallocation of resources that can be caused by the failure to establish property rights.[5]

5. The payments that receptors make to emitters to reduce pollution are sometimes called bribes. But the symmetry of the payments reveals that the direction of payment has no moral significance. Thus the pejorative term *bribe* is inappropriate.

15.6

Negotiated Land Development

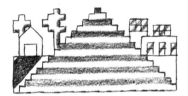

The Whiteflint shopping mall in Montgomery County, Maryland, consists of fine shops and department stores, including the famous Bloomingdale's and Lord and Taylor. The mall was completed in 1978 after being blocked for years by local residents. The negotiated settlement between the developer and the residents that led to the required zoning permits serves as a good example of the process of **negotiated development,** a modern alternative to expensive confrontation.*

The Whiteflint mall was first proposed in 1970 to be built on what was then a golf course. Owners of nearby and abutting property opposed construction for fear of such external costs as lowered property values and uninhabitability due to night lights, car traffic, inadequate storm drainage, tall buildings inconsistent with their bucolic setting, and the detritus accompanying fast-food restaurants.

The outcome of negotiations between the property owners and the developers included several guarantees:

*See the following references for more on this and many other examples of negotiated settlement: Malcolm D. Rivkin, *Negotiated Development: A Breakthrough in Environmental Controversies* (Washington DC: Conservation Foundation, 1977); and L. Susskind and A. Weinstein, "Towards a Theory of Environmental Dispute Resolution," *Boston College Environmental Affairs Law Review* 9, no. 2 (1980/1981).

1. A building height limit of 60 feet
2. Structures set back from the property line
3. Traffic routes around the neighborhood
4. A large 14-foot-high hill, or berm, constructed out of surplus dirt from the excavation and sodded and landscaped to provide a pleasant vista for owners of abutting property (because of the hill and the shopping center setback, homeowners cannot see the development)
5. Indemnification of the homeowners against lost property value, provided by the developer

This package led to approval of the zoning changes and thereby demonstrated the efficiency of negotiation versus confrontation. A valuable development was put into place, and homeowners also benefited.

Several basic economic principles are illustrated in this example:

1. Negotiations will fail unless a package is derived that compensates the residents. The aim is a mutually advantageous trade.
2. The negotiated package should include low-cost methods of compensation, which increase the likelihood that a settlement can be found. For example, the berm was built at practically no cost, because surplus dirt had to be gotten rid of in any case. Also, property values do not generally fall when Bloomingdale's locates nearby; in fact, they usually rise. Thus the developer could indemnify the property owners with little risk.
3. Compensation should address the residents' complaints. Unrelated compensations are inefficient, because marginal damage rises as the degree of the offense increases. For example, if unsightly night lights are the issue, it is cheaper to reduce the unsightliness than to pay people to accept it. (In addition to the inefficiency of unrelated compensations, people react negatively to bribes unless jaded by a course in managerial economics.)
4. The compensation package should usually include a mixture of compensations, aiming for an efficient combination of development and amenities and guarantees. In other words, the marginal benefits and costs of all activities should be equated.

Effluent Charges

The **effluent charge** is another policy option in pollution control. The polluting firm pays the government a price per unit of pollution emitted into the environment and is thereby encouraged to reduce its waste emissions. Figure 15.10 illustrates how effluent charges can establish the efficient level of pollution. Panel a shows the value of marginal product of pollution (VMP_p) curve of the polluting firm, and panel b contains the marginal damage (MD) curve of such pollution to other members of society. The following steps show how the optimum charge can be established by trial and error:

1. Impose effluent charge f_1 and note the level of pollution that the firm produces. The charge f_1 is the marginal cost the firm must pay per unit of pollution. The firm will pollute up to the profit-maximizing level, where $f_1 = VMP_p$. When the fee is f_1, the firm emits Y_1 units of pollution.

2. Measure the marginal damage at pollution level Y_1, or $\overline{Y_1B}$.

3. If marginal damages at Y_1 exceed the charge f_1, we know that $MD(Y_1) > VMP_p(Y_1)$. Thus the effluent charge should be raised to f_2.

4. Measure the pollution level when the fee is f_2 and measure the MD of the pollution level. In Figure 15.10, $f_2 = VMP_p(Y_2) \equiv \overline{Y_2C} > \overline{Y_2D} \equiv MD(Y_2)$.

5. Because $f_2 > MD(Y_2)$, lower the effluent fee to f_3, where $f_2 > f_3 > f_1$ (not shown). Repeat the first four steps until a fee is found that equates the VMP_p and MD. For fee $\hat{f}$, $VMP_p(\hat{Y})$

Figure 15.10
Effluent Charges as a Means of Internalizing Pollution Externalities

(a) The firm will respond to an effluent charge by setting $VMP_p = f_1$.
(b) The fee should be compared to MD and adjusted until $\hat{f} = MD$. This results in $VMP_p = \hat{f} = MD$.

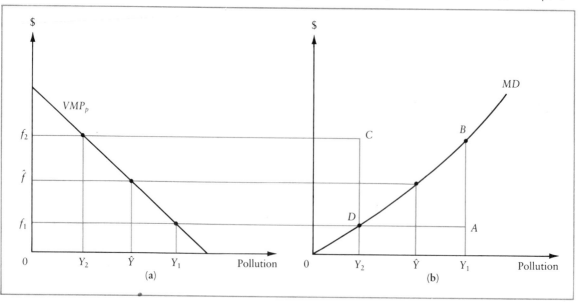

(a)   (b)

$= MD(\hat{Y})$. Fee $\hat{f}$ is therefore the optimum charge, because it produces the efficient level of pollution, $\hat{Y}$.

An important advantage of imposing effluent charges is that the regulatory agency responsible for setting fees need not have knowledge of the polluting firm's VMP_p curve but only society's marginal damages. The firm will reveal points along its VMP_p curve, because at each fee there is a profit-maximizing level of pollution that equates the VMP_p with the established effluent fee.

Effluent Quotas

The Coasian bargaining method and the effluent charge approach are ways of using the price system to allocate pollution resources. In contrast, the **effluent quota** system is a method by which the regulating agency estimates the proper level of pollution and gives a pollution quota to the firm; the firm can pollute up to the quota and no more.

If the regulatory authority happens to pick the correct quota—that is, the pollution level that equates the firm's VMP_p and society's MD curves—the quota system may be a useful control device. But a major weakness of quotas is their inability to approach systematically the efficient pollution levels. For example, the efficient pollution level in Figure 15.11 is $\hat{Y}$, where $VMP_p = MD$. The regulatory authority thus wants to set the quota at $\hat{Y}$. Even if the authority knows MD with certainty, it typically will not know enough about the internal affairs of the firm to know the firm's VMP_p curve. In sharp contrast to the effluent charge strategy, which

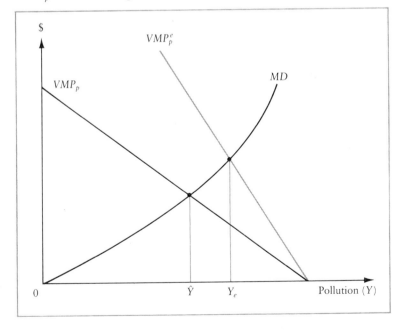

Figure 15.11
Pollution Quotas

Quotas induce firms to exaggerate (or not discover) their VMP_p curves in order to receive higher quotas.

forces the firm through profit incentives to reveal true pollution benefits, the regulatory authority must now seek other ways to estimate the firm's VMP_p curve, starting no doubt with assertions made by the firm itself. But under quotas it is in the profit-maximizing interest of the firm to exaggerate the benefits of pollution as an input and to claim an exaggerated VMP_p, such as VMP_p^e in Figure 15.11. If the true VMP_p curve is VMP_p and the exaggerated curve is VMP_p^e, the firm can increase its profit by convincing the authority that Y_e instead of $\hat{Y}$ is the optimum quota. Without the discipline of the price system, the firm loses its incentive to provide truthful information about pollution benefits. Also, a quota system gives the firm an incentive to hire lawyers to defend its VMP_p^e before the regulatory authority; under the effluent charge system, it has an incentive to hire engineers to clean up its production processes—that is, to find the efficient VMP_p.

APPLICATION

15.7

Effluent Charges versus Quotas: Multiple Firms

We have seen that effluent charges force firms to reveal the true internal benefits of pollution and that quotas encourage them to exaggerate benefits. Effluent charges have another advantage over quotas when, as is typical, there is more than one firm to regulate.

To illustrate, the adjacent figure shows the VMP_p curves of two firms and the horizontal summation of these curves (in the right-hand panel). The optimum effluent charge is $\hat{f}$, which equates $\Sigma_h VMP_p$ and MD at $\hat{Y}$. Each firm chooses a pollution level for which the fee equals VMP_p. And although the firms' amounts of pollution differ, their VMP_p are the same in equilibrium. Thus

$$\hat{f} = VMP_p^1 = VMP_p^2 = MD$$

This equation is the **multifirm efficiency** condition.

When firms have unequal production functions and hence unequal VMP_p curves, a quota system would equalize their VMP_p only by accident. Barring such an accident, a quota system cannot achieve multifirm efficiency.

When a reduction of pollution is called for, the regulatory au-

thority should seek to achieve the efficient level of pollution, $\hat{Y}$, and to achieve $\hat{Y}$ pollution at the lowest cost. Effluent charges have two main advantages over quotas in achieving these goals: (1) true revelation of the firm's VMP_p, allowing the efficient pollution level $\hat{Y}$ to be approached, and (2) equalization of the VMP_p among firms, permitting the efficient pollution level $\hat{Y}$ to be achieved at least cost.

Multifirm Efficiency

Effluent charges achieve multifirm efficiency: $\hat{f} = VMP_p^1 = VMP_p^2 = MD$. The two panels on the left show the VMP_p for two firms. The right-hand panel shows equality of the horizontal sum of the firm's VMP_p and society's marginal damages, MD.

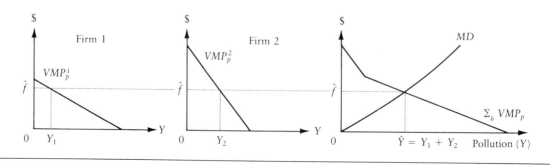

Problems in Economic Policy

All three approaches to solving externalities—Coasian bargaining, effluent charges, and quotas—present many practical difficulties, including the following:

The measurement of pollution at its source.

The measurement of the resulting damages (MD). In measuring both the pollution and the damages, there are engineering and information problems. We need incentive systems that induce the production and revelation of information.

The free-rider problem. All three policy approaches require full participation to achieve efficiency.

Transaction costs. All policies are cumbersome and expensive to implement. If it costs more to set up the regulatory agency, collect information, and organize the participants than is returned in benefits, the transaction costs will prohibit the achievement of efficiency.

A P P L I C A T I O N

15.8

Control of Externalities through Purchased Injunctions

A famous court case illustrates how laws that preserve pollution rights can allocate resources efficiently by recognizing the role of prices in generating information, the very essence of the Coase theorem. The case involved Del Webb, a residential housing developer, and a cattle feedlot owned by Spur Industries.*

Webb developed Sun City, Arizona, a retirement community offering fine homes, clean air, spectacular vistas, community recreation facilities, and an ample number of college and professional sports exhibitions, including the Arizona State University teams and the Milwaukee Brewers' spring training camp. The feedlot was a profitable business that allowed cattle to finish growing under professional inspection before being sent to market.

Initially, Sun City was some distance from the feedlot, but as the

*Spur Industries v. Del Webb, 108 Ariz. 178, 494 P. 2d 700 (1972).

retirement community expanded, it grew toward the feedlot. Soon the feedlot began to impose external costs on the retirees in the form of pungent odors, a large fly population, and the increased potential for disease. Complaints grew, and new homes became harder to sell. Del Webb finally sought a court injunction to force Spur to cease feedlot operations.

The stage was set for the court's ingenious application of economic theory. Although Webb's development of Sun City responded to a real need for housing and was a very profitable business, the feedlot was also very profitable and, after all, had been there first. Webb wanted to be rid of the feedlot at no cost.

The court's solution was to issue a **purchased injunction.**

In effect, the court-issued injunction against operation of the feedlot would become effective only if Webb made a payment to Spur large enough to pay for its exit. Webb would have to pay Spur a price equal to a reasonable estimate of Spur's lost profit due to exit plus moving costs. In other words, if the benefit to Webb of halting the feedlot externalities exceeded the benefit to Spur of continuing operation, Webb could pay Spur to exit— and both parties would come out ahead. Such Coasian bargaining mimics the price system's mechanism for facilitating value-increasing exchange and guiding resources to their most valuable uses.

The purchased injunction order forced Webb to reveal, by money payment, that the value to him of Spur's exit was greater than the value to Spur of remaining.

Continued on page 416

Therefore, it eliminated the possibility of Webb's overstating the value of Spur's moving in order to obtain a profitable but inefficient injunction. It also prevented Spur from overstating its expected lost profit in order to hold out for an inefficient combination of housing and feedlots.

A purchased injunction like this one solves an important information problem by creating a forum in which parties are forced to reveal benefits and, in the process, to establish the optimum combination of activities. If these activities could be made compatible—perhaps through waste treatment, electronic fly control, the breeding of odorless cows, or the maintenance of an efficient distance between homes and feedlots—the incentives would be in place for both parties to discover these mutually profitable techniques. The alternative is for a judge to rule whether the activities are mutually exclusive. Since the primary parties are in a better position to discover these techniques than the judge is, placing the burden on the two parties is an important element of efficiency in the decision.

In the end, the feedlot departed the area with a payment from Webb. The purchased injunction internalized the feedlot externalities and allowed an efficient result to be achieved via private market bargaining.[†]

[†]For an extensive discussion of the legal and economic issues touched on here, see Guido Calabresi and A. Douglas Melamed, "Property Rules, Liability Rules, and Inalienability: One View of the Cathedral," *Harvard Law Review* 85 (April 1972): 1091–1128.

External Costs and Interindustry Equilibrium

The presence of external costs in one industry misdirects productive resources and output in that industry as well as in other industries whose products are substitutes. The essential problem is that, when one component of the supply side of an industry imposes external costs on members of society without charge, incorrect information regarding substitutes is communicated to consumers.

Let's consider two industries producing substitute outputs: Naugahyde coats and cowhide coats. Suppose the tanning of cowhides is a highly polluting activity (which it is) but the production of Naugahyde is a clean activity. Assume also that the hide-tanning firms do not pay the full opportunity cost of their pollution through effluent charges or Coasian bargaining because of some or all of the weaknesses inherent in these schemes. Then the private costs of the firms producing cowhide coats are below the full societal costs of production. What will be the interindustry equilibrium?

Figure 15.12a illustrates the cowhide coat industry's supply and demand curves. The supply curve S_c is the industry supply when all

Figure 15.12
Interindustry Equilibrium

Inefficiencies in one industry spill over into other industries whose products are substitutes. **(a)** Excess pollution in cowhide coat production is translated into the inefficiently low price P_c. **(b)** The price of cowhide coats is a shift parameter in the demand for Naugahyde coats. Thus demand is depressed in the Naugahyde coat market because of excess pollution in the cowhide coat market.

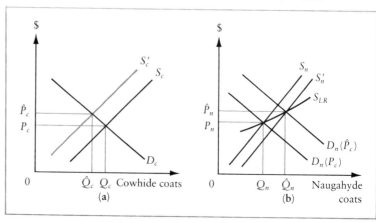

firms ignore environmental costs in their private calculations. Thus all firm's marginal cost curves are too low, and the horizontal sum of firms' marginal costs—the industry supply curve—is overstated. If firms were forced to pay all costs of production, including environmental damages, as they must under an effluent charge or Coasian bargaining arrangement, their costs would increase and the industry supply curve would shift to S_c'. Thus the presence of external costs understates costs and overstates industry supply, which in turn leads to excessive output (Q_c) and too low a price (P_c). By allowing firms to ignore the environmental costs of their activities, the price system allocates too many resources to cowhide coat production at too low a price.

If a way could be found to charge firms for the cost of their environmental pollution, thereby making them take environmental costs into account in their decision making, firms initially breaking even would be pushed to negative economic profits, and long-run exit would ensue. The industry supply curve would shift to the left, putting upward pressure on commodity prices Long-run equilibrium would be reestablished when all firm that earned negative economic profit when forced to pay environmental costs had exited the industry. Some previously inframarginal firms would become marginal firms under the full-cost arrangement. The optimum industry price and output would be $\hat{P}_c$ and $\hat{Q}_c$. Thus the environmental externality allows some firms to produce cowhide coats that could not do so if required to pay for their pollution damage. The presence of such firms keeps industry output above the efficient rates and industry price too low.

But the inefficiencies in the industry experiencing external costs do not remain wholly within the industry. Instead, they spill out into substitute industries as well—to the Naugahyde coat industry in this example. Figure 15.12b shows the Naugahyde coat industry's supply and demand curves. The two industries are tied together because their products are substitutes in consumption. Thus the price of cowhide coats is a shift parameter in the demand curve for Naugahyde coats. For cowhide coat price P_c (the inefficient price), the demand curve for Naugahyde coats is $D_n(P_c)$, and industry price and output are P_n and Q_n. But if an optimum pollution policy raised the price of cowhide coats to $\hat{P}_c$, the demand curve for Naugahyde coats would increase to $D_n(\hat{P}_c)$, in turn raising the price of Naugahyde coats, attracting into the industry additional entrants whose costs were too high at the previous prices, and expanding industry output. Recall from Chapter 7 that the entry of higher-cost firms produces an upward-sloping long-run supply curve (S_{LR}) even for constant-cost industries. The optimum price and quantity of Naugahyde coats are $\hat{P}_n$ and $\hat{Q}_n$. But as long as external costs are not internalized in the cowhide coat industry, Naugahyde coat prices and output will be held at the inefficient levels P_n and Q_n.

Thus the inefficiencies of the cowhide coat industry cause inefficiencies in the Naugahyde coat industry as well. The price and quantity of Naugahyde coats are too low because of the external costs in another industry. The lesson to be learned is that industries become interdependent by virtue of the substitutability of their products in consumption. If external costs disturb efficiency in one market, the inefficiencies will spread into related industries via the inefficient pricing of substitutes.[6]

6. For convenience, the feedback effect of the price of Naugahyde coats on the demand curve for cowhide coats has been ignored. Final general equilibrium between the two markets would be the result of repeated adjustments.

A P P L I C A T I O N

15.9

Interindustry Equilibrium: Effluent Charges versus Quotas

Let's examine the effect of effluent charges and quotas on the costs of a polluting industry and, indirectly, on the equilibrium of related industries. To continue the coat example, assume that the Naugas are successful in convincing the regulatory authority that their competitors—firms selling cowhide coats—should be regulated because of the environmental costs of their production. Figure A illustrates the effects of a quota system on the costs of the firm, Figure B the effects of effluent charges.

Under a perfectly calibrated quota system, the optimum quantity of pollution, $\hat{Y}$, must equate the horizontal sum of firms' VMP_p curves, $\Sigma_h VMP_p$, and the vertical sum of individuals' marginal damages, $\Sigma_v MD$. In Figure A, such a perfect quota means that the firms' marginal cost per unit of pollution is the discontinuous line $0\hat{Y}MC$. The total cost to firms of a $\hat{Y}$ level of pollution is the area beneath the marginal cost curve, which is zero. Firms do not pay anything for the units of environment used up; they merely face a limit on such use. It is like having a limit on the number of workers that a firm can hire for a zero wage. Naturally, such a subsidy results in an oversupply of final output, too low a product price, and too much quantity demanded. These results affect the industry equilibrium of related in-

Figure A
Quota System

The economic rent on the allowed units of pollution is too large. Excessive entry results.

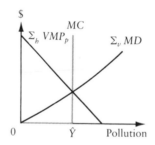

Figure B
Effluent-Charge System

The economic rent is eliminated by the fee $\hat{f}$.

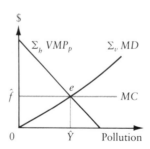

dustries, as we have seen.

Also, because pollution is priced at zero until the quota is reached and afterward priced at infinity, economic rent is incorrectly assigned under quotas. Firms are employing pollution units at zero private cost, which results in excess profits for the polluting firms. Thus regulating pollution via quota allocation entails the additional regulatory responsibility of licensing entry in order to restrict the entry the pollution quotas elicit. One regulation—pollution quotas—gives birth to a new one—the licensing of entry.

Thus a perfect quota system can regulate the use of the environment optimally only if the licensing of new entrants is also undertaken. And even so, quotas typically will not bring the price and output of the regulated industry and its competitors to efficient levels. A pricing mechanism is needed.

Such a pricing mechanism is available in the effluent charge. By trial and error, the optimum effluent charge $\hat{f}$ may be determined. As shown in Figure B, $\hat{f}$ equates the horizontal sum of firms' VMP_p curves, $\Sigma_h VMP_p$, and the vertical sum of individuals' marginal damages, $\Sigma_v MD$. The effluent charge is the marginal cost to firms of additional units of pollution. The total cost to firms of $\hat{Y}$ pollution is the area beneath the marginal cost curve up to $\hat{Y}$, or area $0\hat{i}e\hat{Y}$. Comparing the total cost to firms of polluting at the $\hat{Y}$ level under quotas (TC_q) and effluent charges (TC_{ec}), note that

$$TC_{ec} = 0\hat{i}e\hat{Y} > 0 = TC_q$$

The effluent charge passes the cost of environmental pollution to the public through higher prices, lower output, and less quantity demanded. Also, the substitute industries, such as the Naugahyde coat industry, are allowed to achieve an effluent equilibrium. The pricing mechanism inherent in the effluent charge (as well as Coasian bargaining) can be a useful means of bolstering the market when the pricing signals are otherwise blurred by external costs.

A P P L I C A T I O N

The Environmental Protection Agency has adopted a **bubble policy** to make its effluent quota system more efficient. Under this policy, each polluter is placed under an imaginary bubble that limits its total pollution to a quota. The polluter's VMP_p from its various emission points (vents, stacks, chimneys, and so forth) can then be equated. This system is more efficient than the old system of controlling pollution at each source point.

15. 10

Quotas in a Bubble

Firms are also allowed to apply for a **bubble merger**—two or more firms placed under one bubble. Firms have the incentive to apply for a bubble merger when there is a difference in their

VMP_p for their separate bubbles. Mutually advantageous trades of money for pollution rights can take place within the merger bubble; the firm with a low VMP_p sells pollution rights to the firm with a high VMP_p. When the VMP_p are equated, the total cost of their pollution abatement falls.[*]

[*]For an extensive discussion of the "bubble" policy, see Richard A. Liroff, *Air Pollution Offsets: Trading, Selling, and Banking* (Washington DC: Conservation Foundation, 1980).

Common-Pool Resources

The problem of **common-pool resources** is another intriguing aspect of externality theory. The common-pool problem arises whenever independent economic agents draw a productive resource from a common source. Indeed, it is another manifestation of the absence of property rights. The problem applies to multiple oil wells drawing from large pools of oil; fisheries; woodlands; populations of any species, such as bison or beaver, killed for fun or profit; and even milkshakes shared through many straws out of one glass. In all such cases, firms or individuals are motivated to draw out the resource at an inefficiently high rate, because whatever they do not draw out will be extracted by competitors. There is no incentive to store for the future of the common pool. Instead, oil companies draw out the resources and store them in private tanks. Kids sharing milkshakes just get sick trying to outdo their pals. But give them separate glasses, and they will drink at a more enjoyable (efficient) rate. The same principle applies to firms like oil companies, although it is difficult (if not impossible) to give them separate pools to draw from.

15. 11

Common-Pool Problem: Fisheries

In the fishing industry, the common-pool problem is unrelenting. Under certain circumstances, competitive market forces lead to the extinction of a biological species. Vernon Smith has provided an excellent example of the power of an interdisciplinary approach to such a problem.*

Let's begin with the biological part of the problem. Curve G in Figure A is a biological replenishment curve for fish. The vertical axis measures the change in the fish population per unit of time, ΔF, and the horizontal axis measures the stock of fish at a moment in time, S. Thus the G curve is a rate-of-fish-replenishment curve.

Movements along G measure the changes in the fish population as a function of the stock of fish already in place. When the stock of fish is less than A, the fish stock is too small to form schools large enough to ward off or survive attack by natural enemies. Thus $\Delta F < 0$. Natural extinction will result if restocking is not undertaken. When the fish stock is between A and B, the stock of fish is of sufficient size for natural maintenance and growth. Here $\Delta F > 0$. The fish stock will grow until the stock reaches B. When the fish stock exceeds B, it is too large. Insufficient food causes the weak fish to die, and $\Delta F < 0$. As fish die off, B is approached. Thus, barring total extinction, stock size B is a stable natural equilibrium.

Now let's introduce a predator of fish: people in fishing fleets. We need a graphic depiction of the reality that a larger stock of fish can sustain more competitive fishing firms, the marginal firms of which break even. Line K in Fig-

Figure A
Replenishment Rate

The biological replenishment rate for fish is shown by curve G.

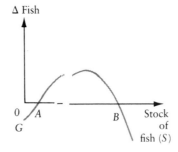

Figure B
Kill Rate

The zero-profit kill rate is shown by curve K.

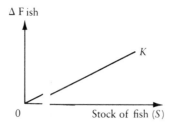

ure B is a fish kill curve; the K line depicts fish kill rates achieved in a competitive market as a function of S, the size of the stock of fish. All along line K, the firms are breaking even; above it there will be entry, below it exit. The K line slopes upward because a larger stock of fish will support a larger fleet of boats, which in turn produces a larger zero-profit kill rate.[†]

The G curve in Figure A is used to depict the biological replenishment process. The K curve in Figure B describes the economic relationship between the size of the fish stock and the quantity of competitive fishing. Now we can put biology and economics together by combining the G and K curves in one diagram. How does the addition of the human predator change the biological equilibrium?

Let technology and costs in the fishing industry result in the kill curve K_1 in Figure C. The addition of the fishing industry changes the steady-state equilibrium stock of fish from B to C. The fishing fleets extract an amount of fish equal to $\overline{BE}$ per time period. At B the natural fish population is stable [$\Delta F(B) = 0$], but the fish kill is positive [$\Delta F(B = \overline{BE} > 0$]. Thus the stock of fish will shrink and the number of competitive fishing firms will fall. The stock of fish will continue to fall as long as the additional kill exceeds the additional natural replenishment.

When the kill rate equals the natural replenishment rate, the stock of fish will remain in equilibrium. This condition is achieved at point C, where $K_1(S_1) = G = \overline{S_1C}$. The stock of fish S_1 determines the number of competitive fishing firms that can be supported, given present fishing technology and costs.

So far it appears that competition is compatible with the coexistence of people and fish and with an orderly extraction of fish within the limits of natural replacement. But suppose a change in fishing technology makes it possible for previously extramarginal fleets to enter the industry. The kill-rate curve shifts upward. If the kill-rate curve shifts up wholly above the replenishment curve, as K_2 does, there will be no stable equilibrium that satisfies both the profit motives of the fishing fleets and the natural

*Vernon Smith, "Economics of Production from Natural Resources," *American Economic Review* 68 (1968): 409–431.

[†]The kill curve, K, need not emanate from the origin, as the K curve does in Figure B. If there is a minimum stock of fish required for any commercial fishing, the K curve would start from a point on the horizontal axis.

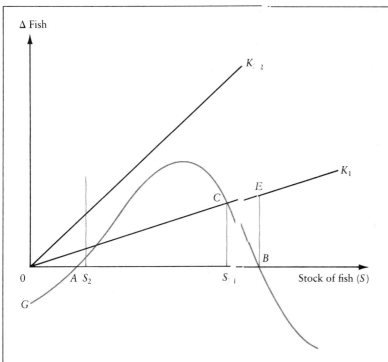

Figure C
**Competitive Rates of Fish Kill and
Natural Reproduction**

If zero-profit kill rates are represented by K_1, equilibrium is achieved at C. If they are represented by K_2, competition results in no fish, no industry.

reproduction rates of the fish. For each stock of fish, there is more extraction due to the number of firms in the industry than normal reproduction rates can replace. The end result of such disequilibrium is the complete extinction of the fish species and therefore of the fishing industry. Surely, such a result is not efficient; yet it represents long-run equilibrium in the absence of intervention when the kill-rate curve is K_2.

Note the central role of the common-pool problem here. Faced with the threat of complete extinction of the species, the individual competitive firm is too small to do anything but participate in the extinction. One firm's reduced drain on the common pool cannot save the species, because it is too small to affect the total kill rate. Hence the firm must also hurry its extraction rate in order to profit from the fish while they last. The profit-maximizing decisions of competitive firms operating from a common pool eventually eliminate the biological species and hence the industry.

In addition, the competitive industry is powerless, without collusion, to counteract the effect of disease or natural disaster on a fish population. Suppose an economic/biological equilibrium is established at point C when the kill-rate curve is K_1 in Figure C. Now suppose the lamprey eel is introduced to the lake and reduces the fish population to S_2. Even if the eel is conquered before the fish species is killed off, the competitive fishing industry would finish the job that the eel started, because at S_2 the kill rate exceeds reproduction.

Clearly, there is a role for government in the restocking of fisheries, the licensing of fishing firms, and the regulation of their technologies. Duck hunters are licensed and limited to shotguns (plenty would use machine guns if allowed to) as a control on the number of ducks taken from the common pool. Thoughtful duck hunters must welcome this regulation as a means of duck preservation. The externalities implicit in a common pool inhibit the ability of unregulated competitive markets to establish efficient rates of extraction.

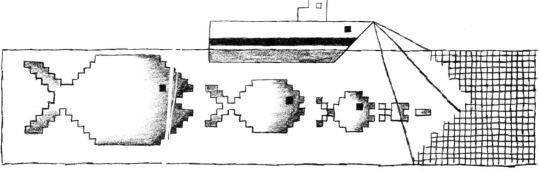

Summary

Bringing the loose ends of this chapter together poses a formidable challenge. Merely to list the concepts shows how vast and interrelated they are: jointness in production and consumption, private versus public goods, externalities, free riders, cost-benefit analysis, the common pool, congestion and pollution, congestion and pollution control policies.

The unifying theme of the theory of externalities and public goods is jointness. Externalities, public goods, and all the associated problems and implications arise from jointness in consumption or production. Jointness in consumption is ultimately more relevant. Jointness in production does not by itself generate externalities and public goods. For example, beef and hides are jointly produced by steers but are not public goods, because they are not jointly consumed.

Education produces both private and public goods. But the public-goods aspect of educational benefits results from the joint consumption of these benefits rather than the joint nature of their production. The same is true of the public good associated with bus ridership. Even the joint production that gives rise to public "bads," such as congestion and pollution, results in externalities only by virtue of the joint consumption of congestion and pollution.

Thus joint consumption is a chief force underlying the public nature of goods. When a good is nonrivalrous, consumption of the good by one person does not use up the good for others. For some public goods, such as national defense, exclusion is not possible. The inability to charge a price to users of such goods is another aspect of the public good. For such public goods as bridges and public parks, exclusion is possible but inefficient, because marginal cost is less than average cost. Clearly, exclusion or nonexclusion is not the central distinguishing feature of public goods. Instead, jointness of consumption is the key aspect.

Another central theme of the chapter is the appropriateness of the price system in devising control systems in industries with important externalities. Free-market Coasian bargaining internalizes pollution externalities and leads to efficient levels of pollution when pollution rights are assigned. In the absence of pollution rights, surrogates for market prices in the form of effluent charges have several advantages over regulation by quotas. Similarly, congestion tolls act as surrogates for market prices in allocating highway congestion and therefore have an advantage over the engineering device of expanding highways. Correctly applied, user charges and tolls generate information that leads to the same efficient resource allocations that would be provided by a free market in the absence of externalities. In short, control devices that place "prices" on public goods mimic the market forces that generate information and efficient resource allocation.

Problems

1. Many production processes impose danger on workers.
   a. Using graphic analysis, show how management and labor would negotiate "the optimum level of danger."

b. Would you expect the "optimum level of danger" to change with the rate of unemployment?

2. A common winter accident is to slip on the sidewalk and hurt one's back. The probability of such an accident is a function of caution by walkers and snow shoveling by the homeowners. What rules might a municipality develop for the optimum shoveling of sidewalks?

3. Suppose that a rancher and a farmer have adjacent property and that the rancher's cattle eat some of the farmer's corn.
   a. Draw a diagram indicating that the optimum number of cattle is 15.
   b. Suppose the state entitles the rancher to 10 cattle. Discuss the bargaining that will ensue.
   c. Calculate the farmer's and the rancher's economic rent inherent in such an entitlement.
   d. Compare this result to an entitlement of 11 cattle; 20 cattle.

4. Until about 40 years ago, buffalo were in danger of extinction; but cattle never were, even though both roamed the range. Use the principle of property rights to explain this observation.

5. Presently in most states, there is no law preventing the construction of buildings that cast shadows on existing buildings and/or property.
   a. What must a property owner do to prevent such construction?
   b. What are the difficulties in determining the optimum height of a new building if there is a potential that it will cast shadows on many surrounding properties?

6. "The preconditions for efficiency in trades of pollution rights are the same as in trades of any other set of goods. Hence the Coase theorem merely restates the results of traditional economic theory." Comment.

7. "Coase trivializes the problem of pollution by assuming away its most nettlesome aspects: the public-good (public-bad) nature of the problem, the high transaction costs, the free-rider problem." Comment.

8. Would a monopolist ever deplete a biological species? If so, under what conditions?

9. Does determination of the most efficient use of a parcel of land depend on who got it first? Assume costless entry and exit.

10. Does the distribution of income depend on the assignment of property rights? (Be careful to consider the distribution of income among people, not occupations.)

11. Consider a fishery. Suppose that the competitive fishing rate threatens to extinguish the fish. Comment on the efficiency of each of the following policies:
   a. Bargaining among boat owners to determine the efficient outcome.
   b. Annual fees sufficient to deter enough entry of boats to bring the catch rate down to the biological replenishment rate.
   c. First-come, first-served licenses sold for a fee just high enough to pay the costs of administering the system. The number of

      licenses should be adjusted until the catch rate equals the replenishment rate.

    d. A fee per fish caught. The fee should be large enough to reduce the catch rate to the replenishment rate.

12. There is at present no agreed-on system for determining the ownership of undersea mining rights. At the same time, overly hasty undersea mining threatens important biological processes. What difference does it make—to mining and to the species—whether the rights are assigned (by, say, the United Nations)?

13. a. Explain the incentives that face polluters contemplating a bubble merger.

    b. What role does the Environmental Protection Agency play in setting up those incentives?

14. a. In what sense is a bubble policy efficient?

    b. In what sense is a bubble policy inferior to an effluent-tax policy?

15. Suppose a firm emits a gas that is not harmful to human health but that turns the sunset green.

    a. What policy would you propose for controlling this pollution? Why?

    b. Why should the firm be permitted to pollute the sunset at all?

16. Suppose that football fans driving to a game cause congestion for themselves and for those who are not going to the game.

    a. What policy would foster efficiency in attendance and traffic?

    b. Suppose that the problem arises because too many fans come just before game time. Would they act more efficiently if they began to miss the first several minutes of the game? Explain your answer.

17. Would the Coase theorem hold in the market for car mufflers? Why or why not?

18. a. Why must pollution damage be measurable for bargaining to lead to efficiency?

    b. If pollution damage is not measurable until long after the damage is done, as is the damage to health from asbestos fibers, what policies would be most likely to bring about the efficient result?

19. a. If accidents are considered the undesirable by-product of producing some useful good, how are they like pollution?

    b. Do the pollution policies we have studied have their analogue in policy making about accidents? Explain your answer.

20. One way to control pollution is to subsidize the purchase of equipment to clean up the effluent. Analyze the efficiency of this approach.

21. Show that a quota entails a vertical marginal cost of pollution curve at the level of the quota.

22. Suppose that a developer wants to buy out a feedlot operator but that the feedlot operator wants a price far in excess of the present value of future profits. Analyze the efficiency of the probable outcome.

23. a. Explain why an ill-maintained home will drive down the value of nearby properties.

b. How can neighborhood groups profit by buying the ill-kept home, fixing it up, and selling it?

24. a. Use the theory of externalities to explain why stores locate near one another.

   b. Why do zoning ordinances restrict the building of homes on land near shopping centers?

25. Airport noise is a problem for nearby homeowners. Often the airport came first. Should the airport compensate the home-owners? Or should the homeowners pay the airport to control its noise? Explain your choice.

26. Oil prorationing is a regulatory device to prevent oil companies from drilling too fast out of common pools. The rationale is that, if the oil is drilled too fast, the capillary action in the pool will be disturbed, leading to a reduction in the pool's economic value.

   a. Using what you have learned about common-pool resources, explain why prorationing is necessary.

   b. Why would the owner of an oil company not come to this realization independently?

   c. How would the efficient rate of output be determined by oil-industry regulators?

Suggested Readings

Buchanan, J. *The Demand and Supply of Public Goods*. Chicago: Rand-McNally, 1969.

Coase, R. "The Problems of Social Cost." *Journal of Law and Economics* 3 (1960): 1–44.

Head, J. G. "Public Goods and Public Policy." *Public Finance* 17 (1962): 197–219.

Samuelson, P. "The Pure Theory of Public Expenditure." *Review of Economics and Statistics* 36 (1954): 387–389.

Smith, Vernon. "Economics of Production from Natural Resources." *American Economic Review* 58 (1968): 409–431.

Appendix

ANTITRUST STATUTES IN BRIEF

Reprinted here are selections from the three main antitrust statutes with economic content. The omitted passages are devoted to jurisdiction and legal procedure. For a complete version of these statutes, see any modern antitrust casebook, such as those in the Suggested Readings at the end of Chapter 13.

Sherman Act[1]

1. Every contract, combination in the form of trust or otherwise, or conspiracy, in restraint of trade or commerce among the several States, or with foreign nations, is declared to be illegal. Every person who shall make any contract or engage in any combination or conspiracy hereby declared to be illegal shall be deemed guilty of a felony, and, on conviction thereof, shall be punished by fine not exceeding one million dollars if a corporation, or, if any other person, one hundred thousand dollars or by imprisonment not exceeding three years, or by both said punishments, in the discretion of the court.

2. Every person who shall monopolize, or attempt to monopolize, or combine or conspire with any other person or persons, to monopolize any part of the trade or commerce among the several States, or with foreign nations, shall be deemed guilty of a felony, and, on conviction thereof, shall be punished by fine not exceeding one million dollars if a corporation, or, if any other person, one hundred thousand dollars or by imprisonment not exceeding three years, or by both said punishments, in the discretion of the court.

---

1. 26 Stat. 209, 15 U.S.C.A. sections 1–7.

Clayton Act[2]

2a. It shall be unlawful for any person engaged in commerce, in the course of such commerce, either directly or indirectly, to discriminate in price between different purchasers of commodities of like grade and quality, where either or any of the purchases involved in such discrimination are in commerce, where such commodities are sold for use, consumption, or resale within the United States or any Territory thereof or the District of Columbia or any insular possession or other place under the jurisdiction of the United States, and where the effect of such discrimination may be substantially to lessen competition or tend to create a monopoly in any line of commerce, or to injure, destroy, or prevent competition with any person who either grants or knowingly receives the benefit of such discrimination, or with customers of either of them: *Provided,* That nothing herein contained shall prevent differentials which make only due allowance for differences in the cost of manufacture, sale, or delivery resulting from the differing methods or quantities in which such commodities are to such purchasers sold or delivered.

b. Upon proof being made, at any hearing on a complaint under this section, that there has been discrimination in price or services or facilities furnished, the burden of rebutting the prima facie case thus made by showing justification shall be upon the person charged with a violation of this section, and unless justification shall be affirmatively shown, the Commission is authorized to issue an order terminating the discrimination: *Provided, however,* That nothing herein contained shall prevent a seller rebutting the prima facie case thus made by showing that his lower price or the furnishing of services or facilities to any purchaser or purchasers was made in good faith to meet an equally low price of a competitor, or the services of facilities furnished by a competitor.

c. It shall be unlawful for any person engaged in commerce, in the course of such commerce, to pay or grant, or to receive or accept, anything of value as a commission, brokerage, or other compensation, or any allowance or discount in lieu thereof, except for services rendered in connection with the sale or purchase of goods, wares, or merchandise, either to the other party to such transaction or to an agent, representative, or other intermediary therein where such intermediary is acting in fact for or in behalf, or is subject to the direct or indirect control, of any party to such transaction other than the person by whom such compensation is so granted or paid.

d. It shall be unlawful for any person engaged in commerce to pay or contract for the payment of anything of value to or for the benefit of a customer of such person in the course of such commerce as compensation or in consideration for any services or facilities furnished by or through such customer in connection with the pro-

2. 38 Stat. 730, 15 U.S.C.A. sections 12–27.

cessing, handling, sale, or offering for sale of any products or commodities manufactured, sold, or offered for sale by such person, unless such payment or consideration is available on proportionally equal terms to all other customers competing in the distribution of such products or commodities.

e. It shall be unlawful for any person to discriminate in favor of one purchaser against another purchaser or purchasers of a commodity bought for resale, with or without processing, by contracting to furnish or furnishing, or by contributing to the furnishing of, any services or facilities connected with the processing, handling, sale, or offering for sale of such commodity so purchased upon terms not accorded to all purchasers on proportionally equal terms.

f. It shall be unlawful for any person engaged in commerce, in the course of such commerce, knowingly to induce or receive a discrimination in price which is prohibited by this section.

3. It shall be unlawful for any person engaged in commerce, in the course of such commerce, to lease or make a sale or contract for sale of goods, wares, merchandise, machinery, supplies, or other commodities, whether patented or unpatented, for use, consumption, or resale within the United States or any Territory thereof or the District of Columbia or any insular possession or other place under the jurisdiction of the United States, or fix a price charged therefor, or discount from, or rebate upon, such price, on the condition, agreement, or understanding that the lessee or purchaser thereof shall not use or deal in the goods, wares, merchandise, machinery, supplies, or other commodities of a competitor or competitors of the lessor or seller, where the effect of such lease, sale, or contract for sale or such condition, agreement, or understanding may be to substantially lessen competition or tend to create a monopoly in any line of commerce.

6. The labor of a human being is not a commodity or article of commerce. Nothing contained in the antitrust laws shall be construed to forbid the existence and operation of labor, agricultural, or horticultural organizations, instituted for the purposes of mutual help, and not having capital stock or conducted for profit, or to forbid or restrain individual members of such organizations from lawfully carrying out the legitimate objects thereof; nor shall such organizations, or the members thereof, be held or construed to be illegal combinations or conspiracies in restraint of trade, under the antitrust laws.

7. No corporation engaged in commerce shall acquire, directly or indirectly, the whole or any part of the stock or other share capital and no corporation subject to the jurisdiction of the Federal Trade Commission shall acquire the whole or any part of the assets of another corporation engaged also in commerce, where in any line of commerce in any section of the country, the effect of such acquisi-

tion may be substantially to lessen competition, or to tend to create a monopoly.

This section shall not apply to corporations purchasing such stock solely for investment and not using the same by voting or otherwise to bring about, or in attempting to bring about, the substantial lessening of competition. Nor shall anything contained in this section prevent a corporation engaged in commerce from causing the formation of subsidiary corporations for the actual carrying on of their immediate lawful business, or the natural and legitimate branches or extensions thereof, or from owning and holding all or a part of the stock of such subsidiary corporations, when the effect of such formation is not to substantially lessen competition.

Federal Trade Commission Act[3]

1. A commission is created and established, to be known as the Federal Trade Commission (hereinafter referred to as the Commission), which shall be composed of five Commissioners, who shall be appointed by the President, by and with the advice and consent of the Senate. Not more than three of the Commissioners shall be members of the same political party.

5a. (1) Unfair methods of competition in or affecting commerce, and unfair or deceptive acts or practices in or affecting commerce, are declared unlawful.

(2) The Commission is empowered and directed to prevent persons, partnerships, or corporations, except banks, common carriers subject to the Acts to regulate commerce, air carriers and foreign air carriers subject to the Federal Aviation Act of 1958, and persons, partnerships, or corporations insofar as they are subject to the Packers and Stockyards Act, 1921, as amended, except as provided in section 406 (b) of said Act, from using unfair methods of competition in or affecting commerce and unfair or deceptive acts or practices in or affecting commerce.

b. Whenever the Commission shall have reason to believe that any such person, partnership, or corporation has been or is using any unfair method of competition or unfair or deceptive act or practice in or affecting commerce, and if it shall appear to the Commission that a proceeding by it in respect thereof would be to the interest of the public, it shall issue and serve upon such person, partnership, or corporation a complaint stating its charges in that respect and containing a notice of a hearing upon a day and at a place therein fixed at least thirty days after the service of said complaint. The person, partnership, or corporation so complained of shall have the right to appear at the place and time so fixed and show cause why an order should not be entered by the Commission requiring such person,

3. 38 Stat. 717, 15 U.S.C.A. sections 41–51.

partnership, or corporation to cease and desist from the violation of the law so charged in said complaint.

(1) Any person, partnership, or corporation who violates an order of the Commission after it has become final, and while such order is in effect, shall forfeit and pay to the United States a civil penalty of not more than $10,000 for each violation, which shall accrue to the United States and may be recovered in a civil action brought by the Attorney General of the United States.

GLOSSARY

The number following each term indicates the chapter in which the term is explained.

A

absolute producer liability, 8 The legal rule under which an injurer is liable for loss due to injury regardless of the negligence of the victim.

accounting costs, 6 Explicit costs incurred by the firm.

accounting profit, 7 The difference between revenue and the accounting cost.

aggregate, 9 The net result of individual behavior, as in the aggregate supply curve.

alternative production, 11 The production of goods that must compete for time on a common factor of production.

ancillary restraints, 13 Restraints of trade that are actually pro-competitive.

arbitrage, 3 Buying at a low price and selling at a higher price. Arbitrage is assumed in the theory of the simple monopolist.

arc elasticity, 4 The calculation of elasticity along a small segment, or arc, of the demand curve.

average cost, 6 Total cost divided by output.

average cost pricing, 9 Setting the price of a public utility equal to the total cost divided by output sold.

average fixed cost, 6 The short-run average (per-unit) cost of obtaining the fixed factor of production: TFC/Q.

average product of labor, 5 The average number of units of output that each worker produces: $AP_L = Q/L|_K$

average revenue, 7 The total revenue divided by the output: TR/Q.

average tax rate, 6 The percentage of total taxable income that a taxpayer pays in taxes.

average total costs, 7 The short-run average (per-unit) cost of obtaining all variable and fixed factors: TC/Q.

average variable cost, 7 The short-run average (per-unit) cost of obtaining the variable factors of production: TVC/Q.

Averch-Johnson effect, 6 When rate-of-return regulation sets a maximum allowable profit on public utility firms in terms of a percentage return on invested capital, firms are induced to select an inefficient input mix by employing too much capital.

B

barometric price leadership, 10 Price experimentation by one firm in an oligopoly. The term *barometric* signifies that the price experimentation reflects industry cost conditions.

barriers to entry, 10 The costs of entry that are not included in required costs. Examples include taxi medallions, licensing restriction, and trade barriers.

basing-point pricing, 10 Cartel pricing of products as if shipped from one location (the basing point).

benefit/cost ratio, 14 The ratio of benefits to costs, used to compare the economic worth of projects.

block pricing, 9 The practice of charging different prices for successive blocks of services, such as electricity.

break-even point, 7 The minimum point on the firm's LAC curve. Breaking even means earning zero economic profit, or exactly covering opportunity costs.

bubble merger, 15 The merging of the pollution rights of multiple sources or firms as if they were one source of pollution with one emissions quota.

bubble policy, 15 The policy of considering multiple pollution sources as if they were under an imaginary bubble. The policy is directed at total emissions within the bubble, not emissions from each source within the bubble.

C

capital, 3 Economic assets that can be invested in one period with the expectation of benefits in many future periods. An education, a machine, a tree, or a building are examples.

capital budgeting, 14 The determination of the best way to spend scarce dollars on capital goods.

cartel, 10 A group of firms in an industry that collude to set output below competitive levels and prices above competitive levels.

ceteris paribus, **2** A Latin phrase meaning "other things constant."

change in demand, 2 A shift in the demand curve resulting from a change in the value of one or more shift parameters.

change in quantity demanded, 2 Any change in the quantity of a good that consumers are willing to buy in a specified period of time. The prime example is a movement along a stationary demand curve due to a change in price.

change in quantity supplied, 2 Any change in the quantity of a good that suppliers are willing to provide in a specified period of time. The prime example is a movement along a stationary supply curve due to a change in price.

change in supply, 2 A shift in the supply curve resulting from a change in the value of one or more shift parameters.

Coase theorem, 15 With well-defined property rights in externalities, bargaining will lead to efficiency.

coinsurance, 8 The fraction of a loss, such as a hospital bill or car crash repair, that the insured party must pay.

collusion, 10 The direct attempt among firms to jointly determine or affect the price, output, or other characteristics of the products that they sell or buy.

common-factor demand curve, 11 The demand curve that represents the demand within a multiproduct firm for the common factor of production required to produce the multiple products.

Thus in a paper firm producing hundreds of kinds of paper using one huge paper machine, the demand for the machine is the aggregate of the individual demands.

common factors of production, 11 The factors that are a common requirement for producing multiple products in a multiproduct firm.

common-pool resources, 15 Resources that people can draw on without efficient restriction, such as boats in a fishery.

comparative statics, 2 A methodology for comparing two market equilibria, before and after a market disturbance.

compensatory damages, 14 The money paid to injured parties after damages to their person or property.

competition, 3 A process of drawing resources and expertise to their highest-valued use in the production of goods and services. Each producer is so small with respect to the aggregate output that each takes input and output prices as parameters.

complement, 2 A good or service used with another, such as cameras and film.

compounding, 14 The continuous accrual of interest.

conglomerate merger, 13 The merger of firms that do not produce output in the same markets, usually to gain access to financial or managerial advantages.

conjectural variation in output, 10 The oligopolist's choice of an output level, and thus a price, without knowing what its rivals will do.

conjectural variation in price, 10 A change in price by one firm assuming a specific response by its rivals.

constant returns to scale, 5 When all inputs are increased (or decreased) by a certain pro-

portion, output increases (or decreases) by the same proportion.

consumer surplus, 15 The difference between the maximum amount that consumers would be willing to pay for goods and the amount that they actually do pay.

contribution margin, 12 In the simple one-output firm, the difference between price and average variable cost. This is the amount contributed to the fixed costs.

cost, 2 The economic value of opportunities forgone when a resource is used.

cost allocation, 11 The attribution of production costs to specific products in a multiproduct firm.

cost-benefit analysis, 15 The comparison of the economic costs and benefits for the purpose of choosing among alternative projects.

cost curves, 6 The geometric diagrams used to illustrate the relationship between costs and output due to the underlying conditions of diminishing marginal product and returns to scale.

cost-plus pricing, 12 A pricing formula in which the prices of products are determined by passing costs plus a fixed fraction on to the consumer. In practice, the fraction is raised and lowered with respect to economic conditions.

cross-price elasticity, 4 The percentage change in the quantity demanded of a good or service with respect to changes in the prices of that good's substitutes or complements.

cross-section studies, 4 Studies of data compiled in the same time period from different data comparison groups—for example, the study of demand elasticity of denture adhesives among fifty-year-old men and fifty-year-old women in 1980.

D

decreasing-cost firms, 9 Firms that experience declines in long-run costs as output is expanded.

decreasing returns to scale, 5 Costs increasing as all outputs are expanded in proportion.

deductible, 8 In an insurance policy, the deductible is the amount of loss that the insured must cover before the insurance policy makes any contribution.

demand, 2 The multidimensional relationship between the quantity consumed and the factors that determine how much is consumed.

demand curve, 2 The relationship between the quantities of a good that consumers are willing to buy and all possible prices, in a specified period of time. *ceteris paribus.*

depreciation, 14 The loss in market value of a capital asset. In accounting, there are rules for depreciating the value of capital assets in the firm's books that often differ from the loss in market values. These rules are used largely as approximations for goods that are not traded enough to provide a direct observation of market value.

depreciation rate, 14 The rate at which a capital asset loses market value.

deviation, 8 A statistical term used to describe the difference between the value of a random variable and its mean average.

diminishing marginal benefit, 15 The decline in the marginal benefit of a good, such as the right to pollute, as more such rights are owned.

diminishing marginal product of labor, 5 The decline in the marginal product of labor as more labor is hired.

diminishing marginal rate of technical substitution, 5 Isoquant curves are convex from the origin when inputs are imperfect substitutes.

diminishing marginal utility, 15 Each unit of a good consumed adds less to total utility than the previous unit did.

discounted value, 14 The result of discounting.

discounting, 14 The calculation of the present value of future amounts.

diseconomies of scale, 6 Increasing costs as larger plants are put into place and used with efficient input combinations.

division of labor, 3 The allocation of tasks among workers so that each is specializing rather than duplicating the efforts of others.

dominant-firm price leadership, 10 The setting of price by the dominant firm in an industry. Competing firms take the price as a parameter.

E

economic cost, 6 The value of the opportunities forgone.

economic efficiency, 8 The allocation of resources so that no activity can be increased without decreasing some other activity.

economic profit, 7 The difference between revenue and all opportunity costs.

economic rent, 7 Payments in excess of what is needed to generate an economic activity.

economies of scale, 6 Decreasing average cost as the output of a plant is increased due to efficient expansion of all input usage.

economies of scope, 11 Decreasing average cost due to the expansion of the plant and the number of products produced within that plant.

effluent charge, 15 A tax on the pollution of a firm imposed to induce an efficient cutback in the pollution.

effluent quota, 15 A limit on the amount of pollution a firm can emit.

elasticity, 4 The percentage change in a dependent variable resulting from a percentage change in an independent variable, *ceteris paribus.* Elasticity is a measure of responsiveness.

Engel curve, 4 The relationship between the units of a good that consumers will buy and all income levels, per unit of time, *ceteris paribus.*

entrepreneurial opportunity cost, 6 The economic value of the entrepreneur's time if applied to the next-best alternative.

entry/exit decision, 7 The long-run decision of which industry to produce in. Economic theory predicts that the entrepreneur will choose the industry where the economic profit is positive.

envelope curve, 6 The long-run average cost curve envelops the efficient points along the short-run average cost curves.

equal marginal benefit principle, 7 To maximize benefits among a group of economic activities, equate their marginal benefits.

equal marginal cost principle, 3 To minimize the costs of producing in a number of plants, equate the marginal cost in the plants.

equal marginal revenue principle, 3 To maximize the revenue from a number of sources, equate their marginal revenue.

equilibrium, 2 An economic condition that provides no incentive to shift resources.

equilibrium price, 2 The price that results in equilibrium.

exclusion, 15 The practice of preventing nonowners from using a resource.

expansion path, 6 In a diagram with axes measuring capital and labor, the locus of efficient combinations of capital and labor as output is increased.

expected lost earnings, 14 In a risky environment, the probability of losing earnings times the amount of lost earnings.

expected value, 8   The sum of all possible values weighted by their probabilities of occurrence.

external benefit, 15   The benefit of a decision realized by a person who is not a voluntary party to the decision.

external cost, 15   The cost of a decision realized by a person who is not a voluntary party to the decision.

externalities, 15   The effects of a decision on a person who is not a voluntary party to the decision.

extramarginal firm, 7   A firm that is earning positive economic profits at the equilibrium price.

extramarginal units, 3   The units that consumers do not purchase because the price exceeds marginal benefit.

F

failure rate, 8   The probability that a product or factor input will fail to perform.

fair rate of return, 7   The market rate of return on an investment of a given risk.

fallacy of composition, 2   The false assumption that what is true of the part must also be true of the whole.

fixed costs, 6   The costs that do not vary with the level of output in the short run.

fixed inputs, 3   Those factors of production that are not varied when the output is varied.

FOB pricing, 10   A fixed charge "at the factory gate" plus the transportation costs required to get the product to the customer.

focal-point pricing, 10   Pricing around or at an identifiable price.

free rider, 13   One who receives the benefit of public goods without paying for it.

free-rider problem, 15   Inefficient financing of public goods when people who refuse to pay cannot be excluded from using the goods.

G

general training, 14   Training that can be transferred from one firm to another.

Giffen goods, 4   Theoretically possible goods that have an upward-sloping demand curve.

H

Herfindahl index, 13   The sum of squared market shares; used to evaluate the consequences of mergers on competition.

hoarding, 2   The accumulation of inventories during shortages to lower the risk of not finding future supplies.

homogeneous production functions, 5   A production function is homogeneous to degree j if when all inputs increase in the proportion λ, outputs increase by the jth power of λ.

horizontal merger, 13   A merger of firms producing products in the same market.

horizontal price fixing, 13   Collusion on price and output by firms selling in the same market.

horizontal summation, 3   The process of aggregating individual demand curves into a market demand curve. For example, to derive the market demand curve, the quantities demanded of all consumers are summed horizontally at each price level.

Hotelling principle, 14   The price of storable nonrenewable resources rises at the rate of interest.

human capital, 14   The skills and training invested in people, which can be used in many future periods.

I

imperfect competition, 10   Competition among firms that do not all face parametric prices.

income effect of a price change, 4   The change in quantity demanded due solely to the change in purchasing power caused by a price change, holding prices fixed.

income elasticity, 4   The percentage change in the quantity of a good demanded because of a percentage change in consumer income, *ceteris paribus*.

increasing returns to scale, 5   When all inputs are increased (or decreased) by a certain proportion, output increases (or decreases) by a larger proportion.

incremental cost, 3   A term often used by business decision makers for what economists call marginal cost.

industry concentration, 10   The tendency of an industry to depart from competition. A measure of concentration is the Herfindahl index.

industry demand curve, 4   The demand facing the entire industry, as opposed to that facing any firm within the industry.

inferior goods, 4   When income rises, *ceteris paribus*, purchases of these goods fall.

inflection point, 5   The point at which the total product curve (or any other curve) stops rising at an increasing rate and begins to rise at a decreasing rate. For example, the marginal product of labor reaches a maximum at the inflection point.

information disclosure, 8   A disclosure by a manufacturer that its product has certain imperfections.

inframarginal firm, 7   A firm that earns positive economic profit at the prevailing price of its product.

inframarginal units, 3   Units of consumption that bestow consumer surplus. At a given price, the marginal benefit of these units exceeds price.

insurance ceiling, 8   In an insurance policy, the maximum loss that an insurance company will cover.

insurance premium, 8   The payment made by the insured party.

internalization, 15   The process by which external effects are reduced to their efficient levels—for example, through taxes or negotiation.

internal rate of return, 14   The rate of interest that renders the time stream of benefits of a project equal to its time stream of costs.

intertemporal analysis, 14   Analysis of economic phenomena over time.

inventory profit, 10   Profits earned on stored resources by virtue of an increase in the market price.

isocost line, 6   Graph showing the different combinations of factors that can be purchased for any given cost with given factor prices.

isoquant curve, 5   A curve showing all labor and capital combinations capable of producing the same quantity of final output.

isoquant map, 5   A family of isoquant curves, each pertaining to a unique rate of output; expresses the firm's long-run production function.

J

jointness, 15   When goods or services are produced together, as beef and hides are produced from steers.

joint production, 11   The production of two or more products from the same resource.

joint profits, 10   The profits earned jointly in an industry; generally, but not necessarily, profits earned collusively.

K

kinked demand curve, 10   A theoretical description of the reluctance of oligopolists to change prices. The key element is the matching of price reductions—but not the matching of price increases.

L

labor, 3   Workers' services to the firm.

law of demand, 2   Consumers buy less at high prices than at low prices, *ceteris paribus*.

law of diminishing returns, 3   When the intensity of use of a fixed input is increased by adding more and more units of a variable input to the production process, the resulting increases in output must eventually get smaller and smaller.

law of variable proportions, 5   See *law of diminishing returns*.

leader-follower model, 10   The dominant firm sets prices; the competitive fringe are price takers.

limit pricing, 12   The practice of holding the price low in order to prevent or retard entry by new firms.

linear homogeneous, 5   The mathematical term used to describe the proportional increases in output resulting from increases of inputs.

long run, 5   A time period long enough to allow the variation of all inputs.

long-run average total cost, 6   The average cost of producing a given output when inputs are combined to achieve production at least cost: LTC/Q.

long-run competitive equilibrium, 7 $P = LAC$ for all firms; the zero-profit theorem of competitive markets.

long-run firm supply curve, 7   The long-run marginal cost curve of the firm.

long-run industry supply curve, 7   The two-dimensional relationship between price and quantity supplied by the industry. Because of entry by new firms, this curve is not the horizontal summation of the marginal cost curves of the firms.

long-run marginal cost, 6   The change in total long-run costs resulting from a small change in output when all cost-minimizing

adjustments in all inputs have been achieved.

long-run total cost, 6   The total cost of producing a given output when inputs are combined to achieve production at the least cost.

loss minimization, 7   In the short run, losses are minimized by producing where marginal cost equals price and by shutting down when average variable costs are less than price.

lump sum, 9   A fixed charge for services independent of the amount of the services consumed.

lumpy entry, 10   Entry by firms that have a large fraction of the capital capacity in the industry.

M

marginal benefit, 3   The extra benefit associated with an extra unit of consumption.

marginal common factor cost curve, 11   The geometric curve used to represent the marginal cost of the common factor of production in a firm producing alternative products.

marginal cost, 3   The extra cost associated with an additional unit of output.

marginal cost of plant openings and closings, 9   The extra cost of opening a plant or closing one down.

marginal-cost pricing, 9   Public-utility pricing that requires the firm to set the price of the marginal unit of production equal to the marginal cost of production.

marginal damage, 15   The extra damage done by an extra unit of pollution.

marginal firm, 7   The firm that is just breaking even at the equilibrium price.

marginalist reasoning, 3   The discipline of considering economic decisions as a comparison of marginal costs and marginal benefits; also the study of the aggregate effects of such decisions.

marginal product of labor, 3 The extra output associated with an extra unit of labor services hired.

marginal product of pollution, 15 The extra output produced because of the right to produce an additional unit of pollution.

marginal rate of technical substitution, 5 The rate at which labor can be substituted for capital in the production process without changing the rate of output; the slope of the isoquant curve.

marginal revenue, 3 The extra revenue derived from the sale of an additional unit of output.

marginal revenue product of capital, 14 The extra revenue derived from the production and sale of extra output due to the use of an additional unit of capital input.

marginal revenue product of labor, 14 The extra revenue derived from the production and sale of extra output due to the use of an additional unit of labor input.

marginal special-factor cost curve, 11 The extra cost associated with factors specific to the production of a product in a multiproduct firm.

marginal tax rate, 6 The change in total tax with respect to changes in total income.

marginal unit, 3 At a given price, the break-even unit.

market-clearing price, 7 The price that produces a quantity demanded equal to the quantity supplied.

market separation, 12 A requirement for price discrimination between two markets; arbitrage cannot take place to thwart the price differences.

markup, 12 The amount by which price exceeds average variable cost.

mergers, 13 The combination of the productive capacities of two or more firms to form a new large firm.

midpoint base, 4 When measuring arc elasticities, the output midpoint base is the average of the two comparison outputs and the price midpoint base is the average of the two comparison prices.

mill pricing, 12 See *FOB pricing*.

minimum efficient size, 13 The smallest output of a firm that will minimize costs.

minimum markup, 11 A law requiring firms to charge prices that are at least a specified fraction above their costs.

models, 1 Devices used to simplify and summarize relationships and to organize thoughts.

monopolist, 3 A firm that faces a downward-sloping demand curve; in the extreme, the sole firm in an industry.

monopolistic competition, 10 Nonprice competition in an industry with low entry costs but differentiated products.

movement parameter, 2 In a two-dimensional diagram, the movement parameter appears on one axis and the independent variable appears on the other axis. A change in the value of the movement parameter causes a movement along the stationary curve. Price is the movement parameter for supply and demand curves.

multifirm efficiency, 15 Each firm must set its marginal cost equal to that in all other firms. In the pollution context, each firm should pay the same price on the margin for the right to pollute in order to minimize the cost of pollution and pollution reduction.

multiperiod analysis, 14 An analysis of economic phenomena over time.

multiplant monopoly, 9 A firm with market power that has more than one plant.

mutatis mutandis, **10** A Latin phrase meaning "all necessary changes having been made."

N

naked restraints, 13 Restraints on trade that have no procompetitive effect, such as price fixing.

natural monopolies, 9 Firms with decreasing long-run average costs up to the point of intersection with the demand curve.

negligence, 8 For purposes of economic modeling, the failure to exercise efficient precautions in the design of products or attempts to prevent accidents.

negotiated development, 15 The agreement to internalize externalities of a property development in exchange for a combination of money payments and esthetic concessions from the developer.

net marginal revenue, 11 The marginal revenue of an alternative product net of its marginal special-factor costs.

net present value, 14 The present value of the revenue of a project minus the present value of its costs.

*n***-firm concentration ratio, 13** The fraction of total industry output produced by the largest (n) firms in the industry.

nonexclusion, 15 The inability to prevent people from enjoying certain goods, such as national defense, once they are produced.

nonprice rationing, 2 The rationing of a good or service by means other than price.

nonrivalry, 15 The condition permitting collective use of a good or service.

normal goods, 4 Goods that are purchased in greater quantities when income rises, *ceteris paribus.*

normal probability density function, 8 The mathematical expression for the "bell curve" of probability values that a random variable can take on.

O

oligopoly, 10 An industry composed of a small number of firms.

opportunity cost, 1 The cost of a resource measured as its most valuable forgone use.

output contracts, 8 Contracts under which a buyer must buy all of the output of a firm.

P

parametric pricing, 3 Setting price according to the industry price. Firms that are too small to affect the price are considered price takers.

payback period, 14 The period in which a project generates sufficient revenue to repay its cost.

peak-load pricing, 9 Charging a higher price when demand is high than when it is low; encourages more efficient use of fixed capacity.

perfect competition, 7 A competitive model that assumes firms are identical.

perfect price discrimination, 12 Charging a price equal to the marginal willingness to pay for all units of a good.

per se violation, 13 In antitrust law, a business act or practice that has so little possibility of redeeming economic benefit that it is unlawful without economic defense.

planning curve, 6 The long-run average cost curve.

point elasticity, 4 The elasticity at a single point on the demand curve.

portfolio effect, 8 The reduction in the ratio of variance to mean due to the accumulation of unrelated risky assets, such as the accumulation of insurance policies by an insurance company.

predatory pricing, 12 The attempt to drive a rival out of business by lowering one's own price.

present value, 14 The amount invested today that will grow at compound interest to a given future value.

price, 2 The economic value paid in exchange for receipt of a good or service; the sum of the money price plus the value of whatever else must be given up, such as time.

price ceiling, 2 The maximum allowable money price for a good or service.

price-determined cost, 7 A cost that changes with changes in the product price. Economic rent is a price-determined cost.

price-determining costs, 7 Costs that, together with demand factors, determine equilibrium prices. Factor costs and the entrepreneur's opportunity costs are price-determining costs.

price discrimination, 12 Charging different prices for different units of a good in a ratio different from the ratio of marginal costs.

price elastic, 4 The condition in which a price change causes total revenue to change in the opposite direction. The coefficient of elasticity is less than -1.

price elasticity, 4 The percentage change in the quantity demanded of a good due to a percentage change in the price.

price inelastic, 4 The condition in which a price change causes total revenue to change in the same direction; the elasticity coefficient is between -1 and 0.

price leader, 10 The price setter in a leader-follower industry or a barometric price leader.

price rationing, 2 Allocating goods and services by price adjustments.

price taker, 3 See *parametric pricing.*

private benefits, 15 Benefits that accrue to the decision maker.

private goods, 15 Goods that can be held for one's exclusive use.

probability, 8 The frequency of occurrence of a particular un-

certain event in a large number of trials.

probability distribution, 8 The mathematical formula describing the probabilities associated with possible events.

producer optimization, 6 Producing a given rate of output at least cost; requires $MP_L/MP_K = w/r$, or $MP_L/w = MP_K/r$.

product differentiation, 10 Efforts to attract customers to a product by emphasizing differences in quality or performance as compared to another producer's version of the product.

product group, 10 A collection of monopolistically competitive firms producing similar, although not identical, products.

production-cost analysis, 6 The study of the relationship between production and costs.

production-cost duality, 6 The one-to-one relationship between the shape of the firm's production curves and the cost curves.

production function, 3 The amounts of final output that can be produced from various combinations of inputs.

production theory, 5 The study of generally recognized relationships between the combination of inputs and the resulting output.

profit, 7 The difference between total revenue and total cost.

profitability index, 14 The ratio of revenue to cost, often unreliable in the ranking of business projects.

profit centers, 12 The individual units of a multidivision firm that are supposed to maximize their own profits.

profit maximization, 3 The effort to maximize the difference between total cost and total revenue.

profit maximizing rule, 7 The equation of marginal revenue and marginal cost.

public benefits, 15 Benefits realized by the public at large due to the nonexclusive nature of certain goods and services.

public goods, 15 Goods that, once produced, are by nature or design not available for exclusive use.

purchased injunction, 15 An injunction that is enforced if the person who will benefit is willing to compensate the person who loses under the injunction.

pure competition, 7 Competition in an industry of price-taking but nonidentical firms.

Q

quantity demanded, 2 The quantity of a good that consumers are willing to buy at a specified price, in a specified time period, *ceteris paribus*.

quantity supplied, 2 The quantity of a good that suppliers are willing to supply at a specified price, in a specified time period, *ceteris paribus*.

R

random variable, 8 A variable that can take any of many different values.

rate-of-return regulation, 6 Controlling the profits of public utility firms by tying the maximum allowable profits to a percentage of invested capital.

reciprocity agreement, 9 An agreement between two firms to purchase each other's output.

regional monopoly, 10 Market power arising from proximity to customers, the distance of competing sellers, and the cost of transportation.

regional pricing, 12 Pricing that splits transportation costs between buyer and seller.

rental rate of capital, 6 The opportunity cost of capital as measured by its market value if rented out.

rent-inclusive long-run average cost curve, 7 The average cost curve that includes all opportunity costs of the firm, including the opportunity to sell the firm.

requirements contracts, 8 Contracts under which the seller agrees to produce all of the buyer's requirements for a particular output.

resale price maintenance, 10 The practice of forcing dealers to keep their resale price at or above a certain minimum in an effort to reduce price competition among dealers.

return on investment, 6 The increase in purchasing power that results from an investment.

return to scale, 5 The change in the average costs of production as all inputs are increased in proportion.

ridge lines, 5 The loci of points on production isoquants that separate stage I and stage III from stage II of production.

risk, 8 The cost associated with the uncertainty of outcomes.

risk aversion, 8 The willingness to pay for risk reduction.

risk spreading, 8 The reduction of the riskiness of outcomes by selling the risk to people or firms who can reduce it or by the accumulation of risky assets. See *portfolio effect*.

rivalry, 15 The condition preventing collective use of a private good.

rule of reason, 13 Determination of the legality of business acts and practices using economic theory and evidence.

S

scales of plant, 6 The array of possible capital investments that a firm may make in a plant.

scarcity, 1 A societal condition caused by limited resources and relatively unlimited wants.

seasonal rates, 9 Utility rates that vary from season to season

in order to approximate the cost of production in each season.

secret bidding, 10 Forcing sellers to bid for orders without knowledge of competing bids in order to discourage bid rigging.

shift parameters, 2 Factors that influence the dependent variable but are not measured on either axis of a two-dimensional diagram. Shift parameters fix the position of a curve; changes in shift parameters shift the curve to a new position.

shortage, 2 The amount by which the quantity demanded exceeds the quantity supplied, at a given price.

short run, 5 An analytic time period in which at least one of the firm's inputs is fixed.

short-run average total cost, 6 The average cost curve in the short run, which includes the opportunity cost of all inputs.

short-run firm supply curve, 7 The marginal cost curve above the minimum of the average variable cost curve.

short-run industry supply curve, 7 The horizontal summation of the *SMC* curves above the minimum average variable cost points but corrected for increases in factor prices caused by industrywide short-run expansion.

short-run marginal cost, 6 The change in total cost resulting from a small increase in output, holding capital fixed.

shutdown analysis, 7 The study of the incentives firms have to minimize losses by shutting down operations rather than operate at a greater loss.

shutdown point, 7 The minimum point of the average variable cost curve.

shutdown price, 7 The price equal in height to the minimum point on the average variable cost curve.

shutdown rule, 7 Production should be shut down if price lies below the minimum average variable cost.

simple compounding, 14 Compounding sums using a constant interest rate.

simple monopoly, 3 A monopolist charging the same price for all units of output.

societal welfare, 7 A measure of the efficiency of the economy in achieving its goals.

spatial price discrimination, 12 A pricing pattern in which the firm shares transportation costs with the customer to maximize profits.

special factors of production, 11 In a multiproduct firm, the factors of production that are not common to all products but specific to particular products.

specific training, 14 Training that is relevant to a particular firm and cannot be marketed to other firms.

stages of production, 5 Stage I exhibits an increasing AP_L and is inefficient. Stage II exhibits a diminishing but positive MP_L and AP_L and is efficient. Stage III exhibits a negative MP_L and is inefficient.

standard deviation, 8 A measure of the spread around the mean of the outcomes of a random variable.

strict liability, 8 The legal rule under which an injurer is liable for the victim's injuries or loss whenever the victim is non-negligent.

subsidy, 2 The difference between the prices that buyers pay and the marginal cost of production.

substitute, 2 A good used in place of another, such as pizza and fried chicken being substitute "finger" foods.

substitution effect of a price change, 4 The change in quantity demanded due solely to a change in relative prices, holding real income constant.

sunk cost, 6 A cost that has already been incurred and does

not vary with decisions in the current period; should not influence decisions.

supply, 2 The multidimensional relationship between quantity supplied and all of its determinants.

supply curve, 2 The two-dimensional relationship between price and quantity supplied, *ceteris paribus*.

surplus, 2 The amount by which the quantity supplied exceeds the quantity demanded, at a given price.

T

technological monopolies, 9 Firms that are monopolies because of decreasing long-run average costs up to the level of demand in the market.

territorial division, 13 The practice of dividing the market for purposes of propping up a cartel is called horizontal territorial division. Vertical territorial division entails dividing the market among dealers in order to reduce price competition among them.

theories, 1 Systematic statements of principles used to explain and predict phenomena.

tied product, 13 A good that is sold along with another.

tie-in sale, 9 The practice of selling one good on the condition that another also be purchased.

time-of-day rates, 9 Rates that change over the course of the day to reflect the marginal cost of production compared to fluctuating demand.

time-series studies, 4 Studies that use data from comparable data sources over time.

total benefit, 15 The sum of all marginal benefits of consuming successive units of a product.

total cost, 6 The sum of all opportunity costs of production.

total expenditures, 4 See *total revenue*.

total fixed cost, 6 Short-run costs that do not vary as output changes.

total product curve, 5 The relationship between labor inputs and final output for a constant quantity of fixed capital.

total profit curve, 7 A curve that measures total revenue less total cost at each output rate.

total revenue, 4 Price times quantity.

total variable cost, 6 The cost of the variable resources needed to produce a given output.

transfer of power, 13 The theory that a firm with a monopoly in one good can add to that monopoly through tie-in sales.

transfer prices, 12 Prices on the sale of goods and services between divisions of a multi-division firm.

transfer pricing, 12 Determination of the profit-maximizing transfer prices.

two-part pricing, 9 A pricing strategy entailing a fixed charge and a per-unit fee.

tying product, 13 A good sold with the condition that the tied product also be bought.

U

uniform delivered pricing, 12 A geographic pricing strategy under which all customers pay the same price regardless of transportation costs. Therefore, the nearby customers subsidize the more distant ones.

unit elastic, 4 The condition in which a change in price leaves price times quantity demanded unchanged.

usury law, 2 A law imposing interest-rate ceilings.

V

value of marginal product of pollution, 15 The theoretical device used to illustrate the economic value, due to costs savings, of a firm's right to pollute.

variable costs, 6 Costs that vary with output in the short run.

variable inputs, 3 Factors that the firm can vary in the short run.

vertical integration, 2 The substitution of permanent ownership for market exchange.

vertical merger, 13 The merger of firms that have a buyer-seller relationship prior to the merger.

vertical restraint, 13 A restraint imposed on a buyer by a seller, as in resale price maintenance, or on a seller by a buyer, as in a contract forbidding the seller to sell to a competitor.

vertical subtraction, 11 The geometric device used to derive the common factor demand curve by subtracting special factor costs from the price of the output.

vertical summation, 3 The geometric addition of curves for each level of output.

Viner-Wong envelope curve, 6 Another term for the long-run average cost curve.

W

wage rate, 6 Compensation for work in terms of money and fringe benefits.

welfare-loss triangle, 9 The measure of economic loss due to underproduction by a monopoly.

Z

zero economic profit, 7 The profit earned by a firm doing no better than it would in its next-best alternative.

INDEX